The Lyre of Orpheus

The Lyre of Orpheus

Popular Music, the Sacred, and the Profane

CHRISTOPHER PARTRIDGE

OXFORD
UNIVERSITY PRESS

OXFORD
UNIVERSITY PRESS

Oxford University Press is a department of the University of Oxford.
It furthers the University's objective of excellence in research, scholarship,
and education by publishing worldwide.

Oxford   New York
Auckland   Cape Town   Dar es Salaam   Hong Kong   Karachi
Kuala Lumpur   Madrid   Melbourne   Mexico City   Nairobi
New Delhi   Shanghai   Taipei   Toronto

With offices in
Argentina   Austria   Brazil   Chile   Czech Republic   France   Greece
Guatemala   Hungary   Italy   Japan   Poland   Portugal   Singapore
South Korea   Switzerland   Thailand   Turkey   Ukraine   Vietnam

Oxford is a registered trade mark of Oxford University Press
in the UK and certain other countries.

Published in the United States of America by
Oxford University Press
198 Madison Avenue, New York, NY 10016

Library of Congress Cataloging-in-Publication Data
Partridge, Christopher H. (Christopher Hugh), 1961–
The lyre of Orpheus : popular music, the sacred, and the profane / Christopher Partridge.
p. cm.
Includes bibliographical references and index.
ISBN 978–0–19–975140–2 (pbk. : alk. paper) — ISBN 978–0–19–975139–6 (hardcover : alk. paper)
1. Popular music—History and criticism. 2. Music—Religious aspects—Christianity. I. Title.
ML3470.P37 2013
201'.678164—dc23
2013015064

9780199751396
9780199751402 (pbk.)

1   3   5   7   9   8   6   4   2

Printed in the United States of America on acid-free paper

For Marcia
Bless the weather that brought you to me
—John Martyn

CONTENTS

ACKNOWLEDGMENTS

The engrossing process of writing a book inevitably erodes the time spent with the important people in one's life. I am particularly conscious of the time I have not spent with my partner, Marcia. Her much valued support and her broad knowledge of popular music have contributed more than she realizes to the development of the ideas in the following pages. This book is for her, with love. Likewise, my sons, Tom, Sam and Jordan, all of whom are enthusiastic music lovers, provide a continual source of inspiration and education. To them I am, as always, lovingly grateful. My thanks also to Cynthia Read at Oxford University Press for her enthusiasm for the project and also to the anonymous readers she invited to read my initial proposal and the final manuscript. Their comments have been helpful. I also want to thank Brett and Rennie Sparks (The Handsome Family) and Drew Nelson for their kindness in allowing me to quote their lyrics. There are some genuinely lovely people in the music business. Finally, this book could not have been written without the generous financial assistance awarded to me by the British Academy.

The Lyre of Orpheus

Introduction

The lyre of Orpheus opens the door of the underworld
—E.T.A. Hoffmann[1]

Music, Hoffmann believed, "reveals to man an unknown realm, a world quite separate from the outer sensual world surrounding him, a world in which he leaves behind all precise feelings in order to embrace an inexpressible longing."[2] This is the power invested in the lyre of Orpheus. Almost uniquely, music has the capacity to move, to guide the imagination, to create spaces within which meaning is constructed. But Orpheus has another equally important significance. As Salomon Reinach put it in his overview of religious history, he represents "the theologian *par excellence* . . . " Orpheus is, he says, quoting Horace, "the interpreter of the gods . . . *Sacer interpresque deorum*. He it was who revealed first to the Thracians and afterward to the other Greeks the necessary knowledge of things divine."[3] Hence, Orpheus represents the confluence of music, emotion, and the sacred with which this book is centrally concerned.[4]

The particular significance of the lyre of Orpheus emerges most clearly in the tragic narrative surrounding his love for Eurydice, who, on their wedding day, was bitten by a snake and died. In grief and despair Orpheus descended to the underworld to retrieve his bride. Carrying only his lyre, with the gentle power of his music he opened the gates of the underworld and bewitched the gods. Moved and enchanted, they agreed to release his bride to him. However, a condition was attached to the release: Orpheus must refrain from looking at his lover until they have emerged from the underworld. Unfortunately, nearing the end of their journey, anxious to know she was still following him, Orpheus turned to look at Eurydice. As he gazed upon her, she slipped away from him into the realm of the shades. He had lost her to death. On returning alone to his home in Thrace, bereft, he retreated from human society into the natural world to play his lyre for trees, rocks, rivers, and wild beasts.[5]

Few of us are not vulnerable to the enchanting strains of the lyre of Orpheus. Indeed, had we any control over that vulnerability, we would not want it to be

1

otherwise. As it is, however, our propensity to music, as Oliver Sacks says, "shows itself in infancy, is manifest and central in every culture, and probably goes back to the very beginnings of our species."[6] Its universal ability to reach into the soul, to open the doors of the underworld, is what makes it so important within human culture. As Scott Wilson has observed, music becomes "an integral part of people's lives, it becomes a way of life, a way of reacting and relating, determining sets of tastes, attitudes and opinions."[7] That this is so is because the lyre of Orpheus is able to evoke meaning through its peculiar appeal to human emotion. This brings us to one of the principal foci of this study. While, for example, analyses of lyrics can be insightful in the study of popular music, this book is more concerned with the significance of music's relationship to emotion and the significance of that relationship to a range of phenomenological and existential features of social life relating to constructions of the sacred and the profane. That is to say, while we will, of course, be referring to lyrics, we will be particularly interested in the sociological analysis of musical experience, in music's role as an active ingredient of social formation and subjectivity. Such an appreciation of the noncognitive dimensions of agency is, we will see, enormously helpful for understanding the complex relationship between popular music and the values and norms, texts and discourses, rituals and symbols, codes and narratives of modern Western cultures.

In her careful account of pre-Romantic music—viewed through the writings of Captain James Cook, Johann Georg Adam Forster, and the British music historian Charles Burney—Vanessa Agnew shows how Orpheus came to constitute "a foundational, self-reflexive gesture for music scholarship in the late eighteenth century. This was articulated," she says, "at the moment when music scholars were beginning to carve out their intellectual turf and to insist on their own specialist knowledge, as well as their prerogative to interpret music on behalf of the nonprofessional listener." Hence "with Orpheus as their emblem, scholars attempted to mediate a new place for serious music in relation to society as a whole."[8] More significantly, however, the myth of Orpheus operated as a discourse of alterity, in which music mediated relations with those of other religions and cultures. This reading of the myth is based on the observation that Orpheus's listeners—the creatures, the rocks, the trees, the rivers, and even the deities of the underworld—exist beyond the bounds of human society and, as such, "his playing represents an effort to draw these listeners into the realm of the social."[9] Through music, relationships can be established with the Other. Hence we might also think of Orpheus in terms of the managing of " . . . the boundaries of the societies in which we live. . . . The mere act of listening – manifest as interest rather than pleasure – is what qualifies the listener for membership."[10] This is important for, as Agnew says, "in prioritizing the socially constitutive role of culture, Orpheus prompts us to ask how music can be used to manage this line between sociopolitical inclusion and exclusion."[11] Orpheus provides, she argues, "a mechanism whereby others can be proximated to hegemonic society through the medium of culture. This model, it should be emphasized, describes more than just chains of cultural influence and appropriation, and it obviates the need to choose between the authentic and the hybrid, the pure and the mixed. It offers instead a rigorous model of social inclusion, a model for the creation of a social group founded upon difference." Moreover, "because Orpheus acts on the margins of society, what is to be known about music – indeed what is to be known about society itself – must be investigated at that liminal edge."[12] It is this Orphic, liminal, boundary-crossing power of music, the power to draw in the Other, to engender *communitas*, to create affective spaces within which new meanings are constructed, that lies at the heart of the relationship between popular music, personal experience, social life, and the sacred. Music's universal power to move, to agitate, and to control listeners, to shape their identities, to structure their everyday lives, to define and to demarcate, and to challenge and to construct hegemonic discourses is central to its relationship with the sacred and the profane.[13]

Again, this is why *The Lyre of Orpheus* seemed a peculiarly appropriate title for this study. It is not only that Orpheus relates something of music's unique power to structure "affective space,"[14] nor is it only because music can be understood to function as *sacer interpresque deorum*, but because within the Orphic myth they are woven together. As such, Orpheus represents the confluence of two of the principal dynamic forces shaping contemporary human life, popular music and the sacred. Moreover, the backward gaze of Orpheus, his inability to stay within the boundaries set by the deities of the underworld, is also significant, in that it brings us to the central theme of the book: transgression. There is something about popular music that matters *because* it is "edgework,"[15] operating at the boundary of the sacred and the profane, at the liminal edge, in the rejected periphery.

It is perhaps odd, therefore, that analyses of the sacred and the profane have been something of a blind spot in popular music studies. To some extent this is simply a reflection of certain blinkered discourses within academia,[16] including the dominant ideological positions informing much critical theory. Having said that, the work done by theorists of popular music, from the Frankfurt School to Birmingham University's Centre for Contemporary Cultural Studies, has always impinged very directly on "the sacred." Some readers may be a little surprised by this comment, largely, I suspect, because they understand "the sacred" to be essentially synonymous with "religion." However, we need not understand the sacred in such terms. Indeed, it is more helpful if we do not. Hence, this is not a book about "popular music and religion" per se. While religious discourses are, of course, centrally concerned with articulations of the sacred, the latter are not limited to the former. Rather, the sacred, as it is discussed here, is closely related to the sociological thesis articulated by Émile Durkheim. As discussed in Chapter 3, the sacred relates to the articulation of what people perceive to be absolute or noncontingent. More specifically, the sacred, whether embedded within religious discourses or not, concerns those ideas which are understood to be set apart from the rest of social life and which exert a profound moral claim over people's lives.

Religion, on the other hand, constitutes a particular way of articulating the sacred, usually within a discourse of the supernatural. Deities, demons, heaven and hell, all become part of the rationale for submitting to and enforcing the claims of the sacred. Hence, following Durkheim, we might think of religion as "a unified system of beliefs and practices relative to sacred things, that is to say, things set apart and surrounded by prohibitions – beliefs and practices which unite its adherents into a single moral community . . . "[17] But the important point to note is that communities unified around a system of beliefs and practices relative to sacred things *need not be* "religious." All human communities tend to be organized around notions of the sacred, around core values considered absolute and binding. In other words, the sacred doesn't simply refer to those things normally defined as "religious," to supernatural beings and symbols, but rather it is understood primarily in terms of the ways people relate to and experience certain things which are considered to be "set apart" from everyday life in some absolute sense. Whether we think of human rights, the protection of children, or the freedom of speech, there is a sense of that within society which is set apart and noncontingent. These can be understood as "forms of the sacred." There are particular moral assumptions that are believed to be so fundamentally self-evident, so essential to civilized social life, that they are beyond question and the violation of them elicits a sense of revulsion and a demand for some form of restitution. In other words, the sacred is organized by cultures into specific, historically contingent manifestations. These manifestations or "sacred forms" comprise, as Gordon Lynch puts it, "constellations of specific symbols, thought/discourse, emotions and actions grounded in the body. These constellations of embodied thought, feeling and action recursively reproduce the sacrality of the sacred form and constitute groups who share these discourses, sentiments and practices."[18] Hence, sacred forms are historically contingent expressions of particular cultures, the products of particular histories and contexts, rather than being ontologically fixed. They change over time according to the shifting contours of the cultures in which they are constructed.[19]

As indicated above, sacred forms need to be understood in a relational or oppositional sense, in that, to quote Mary Douglas's influential study, *Purity and Danger*, "sacred things and places are to be protected from defilement. Holiness and impurity are at opposite poles."[20] Concern with purity and pollution arises in societies focused on constraining their members to conform to social norms. Hence, social and cultural constructions of the sacred are tied to constructions of the profane, in that the latter is constituted as a threat to the former, a threat that needs to be removed. Moreover, the profane accrues a transgressive charge relative to the strength of the sacred: the stronger the sense of the sacred, the greater the revulsion evoked by that which threatens to profane it. Indeed, the revulsion—the sense of profane threat—occasioned by the transgression of a sacred form, such as the abuse of children or the violation of a human right, can be so powerful that it can lead to moral panic and, for some members of society, sanction extreme levels of violence.

The threat of profanation must be expunged in order to limit the pollution of society and to restore the authority and integrity of the sacred. In short, sacred forms communicate those collective moral certainties that must be protected from profanation at all costs if civilized society is to continue.

Popular music is fundamentally transgressive. It may articulate faith, hope, and love in largely innocuous and mundane ways,[21] but it often, though not always, tends to do this from within the contested spaces of the modern world. Even the gentle northern English humor informing Mr. Scruff's "Fish" (*Keep It Unreal*, 1999); "Stockport Carnival," "Donkey Ride" (*Ninja Tuna*, 2008), "Chicken in a Box," "Crisps," and "Large Pies" (*Mr. Scruff*, 1997), or the reflections of The Bonzo Dog Doo-Dah Band on the "Trouser Press" and "My Pink Half of the Drainpipe" (*The Doughnut in Granny's Greenhouse*, 1968) engage, in their surreal celebration of the quotidian, in mild subversion. However, much popular music is conspicuous edgework: "Sex and drugs and rock and roll/ Is all my brain and body need" (Ian Dury, "Sex and Drugs and Rock and Roll," 1977). It is, we will see, largely for this reason that popular music is so closely tied to constructions of the sacred and the profane. Often composed at the liminal edges of hegemonic culture, on the rejected periphery, its very existence, from folk to jazz to dubstep, has always constituted a threat to the sacred center. Not only does it play with rejected discourses, but, again, it does so with a peculiarly effective ability to engage the emotions. As the myth of Orpheus tells us, music *matters*, and it does so because it appears to act, as it were, directly on the soul. This, of course, is why conservative religion is often deeply suspicious of music. Because it is both emotionally compelling and also subversive, it has a very particular social significance. Hence, while moralists may banish it to the rejected periphery of society, denigrate it, and attempt to trivialize it, when Orpheus picks up his lyre, they worry.

From the names of bands such as Christian Death, The Damned, Fuck, Fuck Buttons, Holy Fuck, Public Enemy, The Sex Pistols, and Willing Sinners to album titles such as System of a Down's *Steal This Album!* (2002), Venetian Snares' *Filth* (2009), Slayer's *God Hates Us All* (2001) and Marilyn Manson's *Antichrist Superstar* (1996), as well as singles such as James Brown's "Sex Machine" (1975), Linval Thompson's "I Love Marijuana" (1978), and The Dead Kennedys' "Too Drunk To Fuck" (1981), popular music has embraced its rejection and celebrated profanation. Of course, this is not to say that all popular music can be identified as explicitly profane or as conspicuously transgressive—although some self-appointed moral gatekeepers would beg to differ. It might be argued, for example, that some popular music tends to support dominant constructions of the sacred, such as those relating to gender and relationships.[22] However, while this is true, nevertheless, whether we think of The New York Dolls, Patti Smith, Wayne County, Boy George, Tori Amos, The Spice Girls, Pink, Rihanna, Antony Hegarty, or Lady Gaga, such discourses tend to be contested and negotiated within popular music cultures. Although this is not always articulated particularly cogently, the point is that, within the cultures of popular music, the power of the hegemonic sacred is weakened, interrogated and challenged. Understanding this transgressive bias helps us to grasp its appeal to the liminal imaginary.[23] Again, it also helps us to understand its close and socially significant relationship to the sacred. "The story which precedes the commission or acknowledgement of a transgressive act," notes Chris Jenks, "is the constitution of a center, a center that provides for a social structure, and a structure of meaning that is delimited or marked out by boundaries."[24] Popular music typically tests those boundaries. "There are no rules, there are no limits," insisted Jim Morrison of The Doors.[25] "I've always been attracted to ideas that were about revolt against authority . . . I like ideas about the breaking away or overthrowing of established order. It seems to be the road toward freedom."[26] Similarly, "the idea of the 'freak,'" reflects Marc Almond, "was a preoccupation —and in many ways still is."[27] Indeed, Lady Gaga even opines that "in pop you know you have succeeded when there is an element of crime."[28]

This testing of boundaries has, we will see, frequently been done with references to the resources of occulture. Rejected knowledge and behaviors have been very important within the history of popular music. Whether we think of Rob Zombie's playful fascination with the occult and gore, or Björk's Pagan romanticism, or the extraterrestrial fantasies of Hawkwind, or the psychedelic shamanism of much contemporary psytrance, popular music has had a close and productive relationship with occulture. But what is "occulture"?

Some years ago, I began reflecting on a "spiritual" environment in the West, within which there seemed to be a socially significant confluence of competing discourses, many of which appeared to be related to everyday life through popular culture and the media.[29] On the one hand, it was difficult to ignore the force of the arguments and the evidence marshaled in support of widespread secularization driven by the currents of modernization. It is, for example, irrefutably the case that traditional forms of institutional Christianity in Western liberal democracies (particularly Europe) are experiencing a significant decline in power, popularity, and prestige. Institutional religion may be flourishing beyond the West and it may still occupy a place of significance in the public life of the United States, but, generally speaking, the evidence seems to support a narrative of secularization. On the other hand, within this progressively secular environment, where modernization appeared to be highly corrosive of religion, I was very aware of a widespread and vibrant interest in the paranormal, the pursuit of experiences of transcendence, a fascination with the acquisition of rejected knowledge, and the development of some form of inner-life spirituality. The ostensibly secular Western mind seemed to be haunted by the possibility of an enchanted world.

While some of these ideas and pursuits operated in rarefied worlds of the bizarre and the exotic, it seemed significant that many had become quotidian and ordinary, again, thanks largely to the media and popular culture. From the advertising of everyday products that claim to promote well-being to the ubiquity of sonic and visual cultures fascinated with rejected knowledge and experiences of the paranormal, discourses antagonistic to secularization were being circulated within everyday life. Moreover, there seemed to be a continuity between the esoteric and the everyday, a basic connection between, on the one hand, cultures of the paranormal, of fantastic experience and of rejected knowledge, and what Colin Campbell has identified as the "cultic milieu,"[30] and, on the other hand, the popular growth of interest in mind-body-spirit, the ubiquitous spiritual content of the Internet, the discourses of popular music, and, indeed, much of the day-to-day content of popular culture and the media. In short, it seemed clear that there was an influential culture of enchantment, which encompassed the marginal and the mainstream, the deviant and the conventional, and which circulated ideas, created synergies, and formed new trajectories, all of which were driven by wider cultural forces. Indeed, it became increasingly obvious that, although hegemonic culture considered many of these ideas trivial and peripheral, in actual fact they were contributing to socially significant constructions of the sacred and the profane.

It appeared evident, moreover, that, although technology has progressed significantly in recent decades, and although late-modern societies are different in many ways from their premodern antecedents, it would be unwise to claim an absolute distinction. Hence, although I originally focused on the construction and dissemination of contemporary Western alternative beliefs and their antecedents in the nineteenth century—in order to understand their appeal in late-modern societies[31]—I was confident that the social and cultural processes involved were not exclusively modern or, indeed, exclusively Western. As such, my analysis could quite easily be applied to earlier periods and other cultural contexts. For example, while Christianity shaped medieval society and culture, its ideas were always part of a rich mixture of discourses more widely available in society. The Christian imagination had been filtered through a mesh of overlapping narratives. There may have been a Christian "sacred canopy,"[32] so to speak, a common culture shared by the majority of the people in society, but under it there flourished numerous indigenous practices, rejected discourses, and local folkloric beliefs which formed the contours of everyday life and, as such, contributed to constructions of the sacred.[33] Hence, everyday religious discourse was never purely "Christian," never wholly determined by a society's dominant faith tradition. For example, Karen Jolly's study of elf charms and popular religion in England notes that "invisible powers associated with the Devil afflicted people with physical as well as spiritual ailments; hence Christian words of power made herbal medicine handed down through classical and Germanic lore efficacious against these forces. . . . All of the remedies show the conjunction of good forces against evil forces without a necessary distinction between physical and spiritual, natural and supernatural . . . "[34] Likewise, Keith Thomas has provided evidence for the widespread popular supernaturalism of the medieval period. "By the twelfth and thirteenth centuries the *Lives* of the Saints had assumed a stereotyped pattern. They related the miraculous achievements of holy men, and stressed how they could prophesy the future, control the weather, provide protection against fire and flood, magically transport heavy objects, and bring relief to the sick."[35] Within such environments, interdisciplinary polymaths and protean figures such as John Dee flourished. During the English Renaissance, Dee drew widely on a broad range of ideas in order to interrogate almost every known field of knowledge—including law, mathematics, astrology, cartography, cryptography angelology, alchemy, theology, and mysticism.[36] Indeed, not only did the esoteric and the folkloric play a significant role in the evolution of the modern period,[37] but during the nineteenth century there emerged a common trade in stock occult and paranormal elements, which, primarily through the arts, shaped the Western imagination: " . . . the mist-shrouded castle, the villain sworn to the Devil, ghosts, spectres, sorcerers and witches, a flirting with the weird, the uncanny, the bizarre, with sadomasochistic sexuality – and, underpinning all, the Burkeian obsession with dread and the infinite unknown. Supernatural elements like spectralization triggered new sexual frissons; the old demonological themes of possession, incubi and succubi were eroticized . . . Such disciplines as alchemy, astrology and animal magnetism, and the fringes of physiognomy and phrenology evidently enjoyed a certain vogue."[38] Although these elements have been rebranded and transformed as a result of their confluence with other discourses, they continue to retain their power to enchant the everyday. As Dorothy Scarborough remarked in one of the first twentieth-century analyses of the ghost story, the paranormal "is absolutely in-destructible. . . . " The ghost, she says, "is as unapologetically at home in twentieth-century fiction as in classical mythology, Christian hagiology, medieval legend, or Gothic romance." The phantom "changes with the styles in fiction, but . . . never goes out of fashion."[39] Likewise, darkly charismatic figures such as John Dee and Aleister Crowley, whose contemporary reputations have been organized around occultural constructions of them as profane celebrities, the magi of rejected knowl-edge, have continually fascinated Western imaginations—not least because of their open transgression of sacred forms. It should not surprise us therefore that, as we will see, such figures and ideas have intrigued liminal minds within popular music, from Ozzy Osbourne's "Mr Crowley" (*Blizzard of Ozz*, 1980) and Current 93's *Crowleymass* (1987) to Grant Lee Buffalo's "Goodnight John Dee" (*Storm Hymnal*, 2001) and Damon Albarn's *Dr. Dee* (2012), as well as the numerous sonic genu-flections within black metal, industrial, darkwave, gothic, and so on.

The point is that such discourses, while "officially" rejected as profane and mar-ginalized by society's religious and intellectual gatekeepers, are actually deceptively significant. Indeed, for some people, they may even become more important than official discourses in the construction of "lifeworlds"—those latent, taken-for-granted core values, beliefs, and understandings about who we are, how we relate to others, what the world is like, and how we fit into it.[40] Moreover, it would seem to be the case that, as the forces of modernization ostensibly push the West toward the secular, so they also create spaces for rejected ideas and behaviors to flourish and indeed, eventually to become mainstream. These are important processes in everyday life, central to which have been the liminal cultures of popular music.

Finally, those readers who are as obsessed with music as I am will inevitably ask why I have discussed *this* album and not that, *this* song and not that, *this* artist and not that. While I have, of course, inevitably been influenced by the music I listen to and have some knowledge of, in the final analysis, I can only respond likewise: why discuss *that* album and not this, *that* song and not this, *that* artist and not this? Ideally, of course, such essentially pointless, but nonetheless enjoyable debates should be conducted not in the sober texts and spaces of academia, but late at night following several bottles of wine. And for those readers unfamiliar with the music discussed, I suggest reading the book alongside YouTube.

PART ONE

1

Society and Culture

For years, popular music studies was doubly marginalized. Not only was its subject a form of *popular* culture, and therefore despised by many in the academy for whom culture was synonymous with elite art, it was also *music*, and as a result it was treated with distrust by positivists in the social sciences and humanities. Music, this objection went, referred to nothing, it had no meaning.[1]

Happily, while there are still those within the academy who are bemused, even offended by the existence of popular music studies, generally speaking, the objections to its significance have been laid to rest. The turning of this particular intellectual tide has been largely due to the progress of cultural studies, inspired and influenced by the pioneering work of the Centre for Contemporary Cultural Studies at Birmingham University (1964–2002). Having said that, it was only in the 1990s that the study of popular music can be said to have matured. While, of course, prior to the 1990s, scholars such as Simon Frith, Lawrence Grossberg, Dave Laing, Angela McRobbie, Richard Middleton, and John Shepherd ensured that it didn't escape scholarly scrutiny completely, up until relatively recently cultural research tended to focus on visual media, particularly the analysis of television. Indeed, it is somewhat surprising that, despite the popularity of music shows on television during the 1970s, such as *Top of the Pops* (UK), *Countdown* (Australia), and *Midnight Special* (US), as well as artist-oriented variety shows, such as *The Jacksons* and *Donny and Marie*, the analysis of television excluded any serious discussion of popular music. For example, Raymond Williams' important 1975 discussion, *Television: Technology and Cultural Form*, hardly touched on popular music broadcasting at all.[2] This is odd, bearing in mind that, on the one hand, the raison d'être for cultural studies is the analysis of the media and cultures of everyday life and, on the other hand, popular music is "without doubt . . . a primary leisure resource in late modern society."[3] Since the 1990s, however, the star of popular music studies has been very much in the ascendant. Not only is music per se now understood to convey meaning, but the social and cultural significance of popular music has been recognized and, consequently, the analysis of it has emerged as an established field of research, informed by a range of disciplines, including, in recent years, both theology and the study of religion.[4]

We will begin our journey, however, not in the heartlands of theology and religious studies, but in territory occupied by cultural studies and sociology. This is necessary because a range of ideas and debates central to the study of music, culture, and society need to be discussed. Moreover, it is, of course, important to begin a project by defining the terms one is using. This is particularly important with a project such as this, since "popular," "culture" and "popular music"—not to mention "religion" and "spirituality"—have no universally agreed-upon definitions. That said, it could be argued that an overview of the various ways these terms have been defined is a little redundant in a book such as this, since there are already several good introductions to cultural theory and popular music studies, as well as several worthwhile introductions to the study of religion and popular culture.[5] However, what I intend to do in this chapter is explore some of the ways these terms have been understood, and, in the process, indicate the social and cultural significance of popular music. This will prepare the ground for the following chapter, which provides a more focused analysis of music, religion and emotion. Together, both chapters aim to provide a substantial foundation on which the analyses in the rest of the book are constructed.

Culture, commerce and popularity

"Culture," Raymond Williams concluded, is "one of the two or three most complicated words . . . in the English language."[6] In an attempt to understand how it was being used, he identified "three broad active categories of usage" (1) "the independent and abstract noun which describes a general process of intellectual, spiritual and aesthetic development"; (2) "the independent noun, which indicates a particular way of life, whether of a people, a period or a group"; (3) "the independent and abstract noun which describes the works and practices of intellectual and especially artistic activity."[7] The last of these categories is arguably the most widespread nowadays, in that, outside academia, "culture" tends to refer primarily to signifying practices. As Williams put it, "culture is music, literature, painting and sculpture, theatre and film."[8] When we come to the analysis of *popular* culture, however, we need to broaden this definition, in that we are not simply dealing with cultural products, but also with the ways in which we consume those products. Indeed, John Fiske has argued that this is exactly what the analysis of popular culture should be attending to: how people actually engage, in their everyday lives, with cultural products. To this end, he has sought to distinguish "mass culture"—that which is produced by an industrialized, capitalist society— from "popular culture"—the ways in which people use and subvert the products of mass culture.[9]

While Fiske's definition is helpful, a little more needs to be said about the meaning of "popular." The term was originally derived from *popularis*, a legal term meaning "belonging to the people," the "public." Hence, linked to this word, "popular" has come to mean that which is "well-liked by *many* people."[10] In other words, we are here thinking in terms of a straightforward quantitative definition of "popular" as that which is accessible to, and appeals to a large number of people. "As its very name implies, popular culture is marked by its larger audience."[11] Popular music, therefore, is music that is widely endorsed. Unfortunately, this definition is more problematic than it might first appear. If we gauge popularity by the employment of a quantitative index, we will discover that Bob Dylan, The Beatles, The Rolling Stones, Madonna, Coldplay, Beyonce, and Lady Gaga are identifiably *popular*, in that *many* people enjoy them, purchase their music and attend their concerts. So far, so good! However, although it should be fairly straightforward to decide what is and what is not popular on this basis—by consulting, for example, sales and download figures—problems emerge when determining the level of sales or downloads required in order to establish "popularity." How many listeners are required to enjoy a piece of music for it to be considered popular? Moreover, using a quantitative index as the sole criterion for determining "popular" music raises further issues. For example, if a classical/art composition—a category of music typically distinguished from "popular music"—becomes "popular" because of its ubiquitous airplay as the result of its use in advertising, does that make it "*popular music*"? Take, for example, the music of the Italian operatic tenor Luciano Pavarotti. As a result of his performance of Puccini's "Nessun Dorma" for the 1990 World Cup in Italy, his music became enormously "popular" around the world—many people enjoyed it and purchased it. He could be heard regularly on popular music radio shows and his albums *Essential Pavarotti 1* and *Essential Pavarotti 2*, which were marketed in the same way as popular music albums, topped the British album charts. Does this mean that Pavarotti's work is popular music? Again, if we rely solely on a quantitative index, what are we to make of those forms of music that are so idiosyncratic that they are appreciated only by a small number of devoted enthusiasts, yet are stylistically related to music that is widely endorsed (i.e., "popular" according to this definition)? Much rock and dance music is "popular," according to this definition, but much more is not. For example, using any quantitative index, glitch, neofolk, dark ambient, or postindustrial drone can hardly be considered *popular* music. While Pavarotti, Mozart, Beethoven and Vaughan Williams could be considered *popular* music, in the sense that many people enjoy them and one may hear them as background music while shopping in the local supermarket, "popular musicians" such as Wicked Messenger, Nurse With Wound, Current 93 or Pendle Coven are far more niche, idiosyncratic, obscure, difficult, and *un*-popular. There's certainly little chance that you would be introduced to their work while perusing the vegetables at your local grocery store. Hence while some theorists argue that any definition of popular music requires that the figures for sales, downloads and attendance at concerts should be taken into account, to rely solely on such criteria is problematic.

This highlights, of course, the related problem of understanding popular music as a product that is commercially profitable. Much music is not commercially profitable and, moreover, does not seek to be. That is to say, to define popular music solely in terms of music that circulates commercially as mass entertainment ignores the fact that, while some classical music realizes commercial success, many bands resist commercial pressure and seek marginality. While it is certainly true that much popular music is produced from within an industry seeking commercial success and, therefore, striving to market a product that is "well-liked by *many* people," this definition cannot account for all "popular" music. Nevertheless, whether we consider the relationship with an industrialized, capitalist economy to be positive or negative, there *is* a relationship, and it is difficult to avoid the fact that this must be part of our understanding of popular music. As we will see, religious and political discourse in popular music often has to negotiate this relationship very carefully.

Popular music as folk music

Perhaps rather than being made *for* the people, in the sense of being made commercially available, *popular* music should be understood as that which is, in some sense, *of* "the people," music "actually *made by* the people *for* themselves."[12] In other words, perhaps popular music is simply "folk music," an expression of *cultura popularis* (that which "belongs to the people"). However, unfortunately, as with the term "popular music," the meaning of "folk music" is also not as obvious as it might first appear. While a large body of work has accumulated over the past couple of centuries, there is still debate as to what "folk" might mean when applied to lore, culture, or music. Having said that, some consensus can be discerned. Despite differences of emphasis, central to an understanding of "folk culture" since the Romantics has been the notion of "authenticity." Folk music, for example, is understood to be an authentic expression of a traditional, communal way of life, which may now be in the past or only accessible through the memories of a disappearing older generation. This type of thinking is conspicuous in the work of the principal collectors of folk music in the twentieth century, most notably Cecil Sharp (to whom we'll return below) and the American folklorist and ethnomusicologist Alan Lomax. The latter, for example, argued that "the chief function of song is to express the shared feelings and mold joint activities of some human community."[13] Developing what was, in many ways, a Durkheimian sociology of music, Lomax understood the folk song style to symbolically represent the core elements of a culture, including its sacred forms. This is important because, if correct, it means that music is not of peripheral significance to societies, but rather primary, in that it functions as a way in which communities share values, communicate the sacred, and evoke a sense of belonging. While we will be returning to this argument later in the book, at this point it is the connection with the core elements of a culture that needs to be noted, for it is here where authenticity is located. Folk music functions as a symbolic representation of the true culture of "the folk," who, by the time of Lomax, had become identified with the lower classes, the country workers, the "peasantry." This particular understanding of "the folk" or "the people" is rooted in ideas developed between the late eighteenth century and the early part of the twentieth century. Particularly during the nineteenth century, as John Storey comments, "intellectuals, working under the different banners of nationalism, Romanticism, folklore, and, finally, folk song, 'invented' the first concept of popular culture," for some of whom it was understood in terms of "a quasi-mythical rural 'folk culture.' "[14] This, in turn, was mythologized as the true culture of the nation, which had been obscured by the dark clouds of a modern industrial society. For many this was (and still is) understood in terms of the profanation of the sacred. (These points will be explored more fully in Chapter 4.)

This understanding of the culture of "the people," ideologically informed by the Romantic notion of an authentic culture of the nation, became very influential. It was, for example, notoriously persuasive in Germany during the nineteenth and early twentieth centuries, informing a popular nationalism, a sacred system which eventually shaped an emerging Nazi ideology. As the late Nicholas Goodrick-Clarke discussed, the word *"Volk"* signified "much more than its straightforward translation 'people' to contemporary Germans; it denoted rather the national collectivity inspired by a common creative energy. . . . These metaphysical qualities were supposed to define the unique cultural essence of the German people."[15] This ideological preoccupation with *Volk*, he argues, "arose for two reasons: firstly, this cultural orientation was the result of the delayed political unification of Germany; secondly, it was closely related to a widespread Romantic reaction to modernity."[16] Hence propaganda films, such as *Ich für dich, du für mich* (1934), directed by Carl Froelich, developed a discourse of "racial purity" along two key lines, *"Blut und Boden"* ("blood and soil") and *"Volk und Heimat"* ("people and a homeland"). Together these themes inextricably related ideas of a "master race" to the sacredness of the German soil. Filmed in idyllic pastoral settings, its narrative rejected urban and industrial life in favor of a utopian rural vision.[17] Again, the point here is that the significance of the notion of an authentic *cultura popularis*, variously interpreted, is that it was a central feature of emerging European nationalism and a particular set of sacred forms. Authentic folk culture embodied the nature and character of a nation. Indeed, this was one of the principal reasons why scholars were persuaded that it should be collected and preserved. For example, Johann Gottfried Herder, one of the first intellectuals bewitched by this notion of a distant folk culture that might be retrieved, argued that the folk song had a sacred or civilizing function in that it "suggested the possibility of a return to a more 'grounded' or 'rooted' culture; a return to culture before the Fall into the corrupting conditions of industrialization and urbanization."[18] As such "it carried with it the possibility of purification; the soul of the nation could be made to rise above the contamination and corruption of a mechanical and material civilization."[19] Folk music's close relationship to sacred forms means that it acts as a sanctifying agent against the pollution of profane culture.

Clearly the gaze of the Romantics was focused very much on the past. The urban poor of the present were not the peasants of the middle-class imagination. Hence, for some scholars, a distinction needed to be made between the culture of contemporary working people—what became identified as "popular culture"— and "authentic" folk culture. For example, in the early nineteenth century William Motherwell distinguished between the contemporary culture of the "rabble" and the "vernacular poetry" of "the patriotick children of an ancient and heroick race."[20] Contemporary working people, it was argued, had neglected the nation's folk heritage; they could not be trusted with it. Nevertheless, middle-class intellectuals convinced themselves that, although neglected, "survivals"[21] of an uncorrupted/sacred peasant past could be salvaged from contemporary rural culture. They had a duty, therefore, on behalf of the nation, to be the saviors of its authentic folk culture.

We will return to discuss folk songs in the middle-class imaginary in Chapter 4, but the point to note here is the distinction that emerged between debased popular culture and authentic folk culture. Indeed, this idealized vision of folk culture led to the emergence of a folk elitism. Popular culture and popular music were not only understood as *other than* folk culture and folk music, but the former was demonized as a profane threat to the latter. In the twentieth century, this can be seen in the work of such ideologically different theorists as Frank Raymond Leavis and Richard Hoggart. Both articulated a pessimistic view of the development of mass culture. Hoggart, for example, bemoaned the threat posed to traditional working-class culture by contemporary mass culture, such as the films of Hollywood and popular music. With reference to the "massification of culture," he suggested that a popular culture produced by the techniques of mass production for a mass market was squeezing out a traditional folk culture, which was not motivated by the need to make money. We are, he argued, "moving towards the creation of a mass culture" and "the remnants of what was at least in parts an urban culture 'of the people' are being destroyed."[22] Again, the sacred culture of the people is being threatened by the advance of the profane forces of capitalism and commerce.

Leavis (to whom we'll return below), although distinct from Hoggart in his assessment of working-class culture as anarchic and corrosive, nevertheless argued that, prior to the Industrial Revolution, there was "a rich traditional culture," a "folk culture" of "the people" which should be respected.[23] For example, he was enormously appreciative of the work of one of the most significant middle-class collectors of folk songs and dances, Cecil Sharp, whose work between the years of 1903 and 1924 helped to lay the foundations of the modern folk revival. Between August, 1903, when he began to collect, until his death on Midsummer Eve 1924,

Sharp gathered together 4,977 tunes in England and North America, many of which were published in order to revive what was perceived to be a fading part of traditional culture.[24] Like Motherwell and Herder, Sharp idealized folk music—it was a sacred form, reflecting a longing for an authentic indigenous cultural life. It was, he insisted,

> genuine and true; for instinct is their only guide and the desire of self-expression their only motive. . . . We should, therefore, expect to find, as, indeed, we do find, that the unconscious music of the folk has all the marks of fine art: that it is wholly free from the taint of manufacture, the canker of artificiality; that it is transparently pure and truthful, simple and direct in its utterance. And these are the invariable attributes of the people's music.[25]

It is not surprising, therefore, that he understood folk song to have "value as an educational force."[26] Consequently, he argued for the inclusion of folk songs in "general education," for, he insisted, "good music purifies, just as bad music vulgarises."[27] Folk music would promote the sacred, guard against the profanation of youth, and lead to a revival of the national character and spirit.[28] Leavis wholly agreed:

> Hearing that the English folk-song still persisted in the remoter valleys of those mountains Sharp, during the war of 1914, went over to investigate, and brought back a fabulous haul. More than that, he discovered that the tradition of song and dance . . . had persisted so vigorously because the whole context to which folk-song and folk-dance belong was there too: he discovered, in fact, a civilisation or 'way of life' (in our democratic parlance) that was truly an art of social living. The mountaineers were descended from settlers who had left this country in the eighteenth century.[29]

Folk songs such as those collected by Sharp were, he insisted, very different from the popular music that had emerged since the Industrial Revolution and "the cultural fall" of the Victorian period. Reflecting the Romanticism of Herder, he understood them as an expression of the imagination and industry of an authentic, communally oriented peasantry uncorrupted by profane commercial interests, but which was now being threatened by a profit-oriented mass culture manufactured *for* the people.

This understanding of folk as "sacred" has been extraordinarily resilient. Inspired by Arcadian visions of a simple, rural culture, cloaked in the mists of mythology, it can be traced from Herder into twentieth-century elitist thinking and even to the hippie Romanticism of acid and psychedelic folk groups such as The Incredible String Band and Dr. Strangely Strange,[30] as well as, more recently, to the Pagan imaginaries of such different musicians as Julian Cope, Andy Partridge, and Björk.[31] However, while its significance as a cultural tradition is profound, its cogency as a cultural theory is extremely weak. Apart from the fact that any idea of a cultural fall seems naive nowadays, it is difficult to see how one can credibly distinguish between "popular" and "folk."

The overarching problem, of course, is that there are no stable definitions of the key terms "popular culture" and "folk culture," and, by extension, of "popular music" and "folk music." We have seen that they change over time, being informed by shifting social contexts and ideological agendas. As Derek Scott has commented in his essay on "Music and Social Class in Victorian Society":

> In tandem with the growth of a commercial music industry, the term 'popular' changed its meaning during the course of a century, moving from well known to well received to successful in terms of sheet music sales. A related development was the reluctance to accept as a folk song anything with an identifiable composer, an effective means of excluding commercial popular song. Folk music came to mean national music, an ideological shift aligning it with bourgeois aspirations and identity rather than the lower class. . . . The concept of a national music brought with it the notion that it was to be found in the country rather than the town.[32]

Since the nineteenth century, growing social mobility, increasingly diverse audiences, and the conspicuous effects of the mass media have all made it very difficult to define "folk music" and "popular music" in terms of a particular mode of production, form of transmission, or type of distribution and storage. Likewise, it is difficult to locate the terms convincingly within a particular class or type of society without being unhelpfully specific. Added to this is the issue of musical hybridity. All conceptual membranes between styles of music are permeable. Hence nowadays, those who seek to distinguish between folk music and popular music run into a web of problems. Take, for example, Philip Tagg's discussion of the axiomatic triangle of art, folk, and popular music. He identifies folk music as follows: it is produced by amateurs; mass distribution is unusual; its main mode of transmission is oral; it primarily occurs in nomadic and agrarian societies; and its composers are anonymous. Popular music, on the other hand, is produced by professionals; "conceived for mass distribution to large and often socioculturally heterogeneous groups of listeners"; only possible in an industrial monetary economy where it becomes a commodity; and not anonymous.[33] The question is, of course, on the basis of this typology, what are we to make of musicians such as Ewan McColl, widely recognized to be, in Donald Clarke's words, "one of the most important British 'folkies,'" who was encouraged by no less than Alan Lomax?[34] It is difficult to see how Tagg would have brought us to Clarke's conclusion, with which few would disagree.[35] In other words, circumscribing folk music in this way makes the term practically useless for the analysis of contemporary music and culture.

Part of the problem with contemporary definitions such as Tagg's is that they are, wittingly or unwittingly, too closely tied to the assumptions of Sharp and Leavis, who, we have seen, restrict the folk song to a culture of rural workers, isolated, uneducated, uncontaminated by commerce, and literature.[36] Apart from the problem that this understanding excludes much of the music that would be expected in discussions of the British folk revival or more recent acid folk,[37] it is based on largely idealized notions of a bucolic past. Moreover, in early modern societies, because the folk song represented the culture of a whole society, it was a form of *cultura popularis*. Popular music and folk music were one and the same. The distinction between the two, as we have seen, emerged during the nineteenth century and was informed by a particular ideological agenda, central to which was an understanding of some halcyon rural past as sacred and over against which modern, industrialized society was constructed as its profanation. With the progress of modernity and social differentiation, "folk culture" came to represent only the lower (usually rural) class, rather than the whole of society, with the concept of "popular culture" being reserved for what was perceived to be the degraded mass culture of the new, profane urban-industrial working class. However, as is now widely recognized, there was in actual fact no pure folk culture that could be distinguished from popular culture. Likewise, folk music and popular music could not be so neatly distinguished. As Richard Middleton argues, "most folklorists now would agree on the importance of *interaction* between what they take to be folk music and other musics; and they would agree that folk music itself is rarely homogenous but is subject to social and geographical specification, historical change and cultural layering."[38] Hence, contemporary arguments for distinguishing between the "folk" and the "popular" are problematic on several levels. "In reality," as Middleton concludes, "it is surely unprofitable to attempt to draw a single, categorical line at all."[39] Rather, a more helpful understanding of folk music might be informed by a recognition of its hybridity as a subgenre of popular music, a musically distinct subgenre that tends to articulate ideas and evoke feelings inspired by Romantic, quasi-mythical concepts of "the people" and "the land."

Popular music as other than music-as-art

An arguably more significant distinction, because of its implications, is that between popular music and classical music or "art music," which has been identified with the culture of the social elite. According to this distinction, popular music is often defined as *other than* music-as-art. The question is, of course, can such a dividing line be drawn? Moreover, what purpose does it serve? Some would argue that not only can such a line be drawn, but it *must* be drawn if we are avoid the corrosive discourses of relativism. Julian Johnson, for example, in his provocative book *Who Needs Classical Music?* is very clear that any erosion of such categories should be resisted, along with the contemporary trend towards a relativism of cultural judgments. While some music is art, some is entertainment, and some is little more than aural wallpaper, the choice of which of these types of music we listen to cannot simply be viewed as a matter of personal preference. There are substantial differences that must be recognized between popular music and "music-as-art"/classical music. Attacking the work of Pierre Bourdieu in particular, Johnson insists that such cultural judgments are more than just "a matter of taste."[40] Classical music is, like all true art, distinctive because it works in quite different ways than that *other* music that surrounds us. Indeed, again, the distinction is often articulated in terms of the profanation of the sacred, popular music being the impure other.

> We understand ourselves as particular, physical beings, but we also value the ways we exceed the physical, the ways our capacity for thought, feeling, and imagination seem to transcend our bodily existence. Music-as-art performs a similar alchemy: in projecting a content beyond its acoustic materials, it does not deny its physical aspect but redeems it as the vehicle of something that exceeds the physical. In doing so, it offers us not only a symbol of our transcendent nature but also a means for its repeated enactment.[41]

Moreover, he insists, the value of classical music is "both personal and social: it mirrors within itself the constituent processes of a complex subjectivity and also projects the ideals on which modern democracy is founded."[42] This significance of music-as-art is, however, not immediately discernible. It requires education. Its value is realized through contemplation and intellectual effort. Going beyond the simple, immediate, affective pleasures of that *other* music, popular music, classical music requires work: "art's specific and distinctive claim rests on something beyond its immediate potency and . . . a richer understanding of it involves a sensitivity to its formal properties that goes beyond its immediate emotional effect."[43] Hence, he claims, because classical music is both good for society and also requires education for its full value to be realized—unlike popular music, which can be appreciated without any effort and has minimal social value—it should receive public funding and it should be taught in schools.

While there are several conspicuous problems with this thesis, the principal objection, as far as the present discussion is concerned, is that Johnson's argument for classical music is equally true of much popular music, from jazz to contemporary electronica. As Richard Shusterman has argued, with particular reference to rap music, "works of popular art do in fact display the aesthetic values its critics reserve exclusively for high art."[44] The point is simply that Johnson's rather dated elitism lacks cogency, in that it simply will not do to argue that classical music is peculiarly distinctive and worthwhile because it functions differently from other forms of music (with which he seems to have little familiarity). Indeed, while he dismisses

Bourdieu's analysis of "cultural capital," in which Bourdieu argues that taste is based on an aversion to the "facile," ironically it is very difficult not to read his own essay as a prime example of what Bourdieu is objecting to: "when they have to be justified, [tastes] are asserted purely negatively, by the refusal of other tastes."[45] In other words, Johnson's arguments, while erudite, are little more than an elitist defense of his preferred music genre, rooted in a false dichotomy between classical music and popular music. The dichotomy is false because it relies on arbitrary criteria and caricatures of "popular music" as the debased, depthless *other*: art music is complex, requiring effort to understand it; popular music, is facile, accessible, and immediate. Popular music is almost everything that classical music is not. It acts, he tells us, "like a kind of aural tranquilizer . . . "[46] It is "music that expunges any unfamiliar element, any hint of complexity or self development. . . . This music is inane, stupid, and empty . . . "[47] Again, the obvious objection is that many composers of what he would identify as "art music," such as Schubert or Erik Satie, have conspicuous tranquility-inducing qualities, displaying simplicity and accessibility, whereas it is by no means obvious that the complete oeuvres of, say, Captain Beefheart, Frank Zappa, Miles Davis, or Sun Ra are accessible and facile. It would certainly be misleading to describe their music as "a kind of aural tranquilizer." Moreover, much popular music can credibly claim to equal classical music in both aesthetic ambition and formal complexity. Having said that, Theodore Gracyk is surely correct to warn that "we must be wary of the trap of supposing that only complex, challenging music has real aesthetic value."[48] We need only think of the history of "ambient" music from Satie through *musique concrète* to Brian Eno and contemporary electronica to grasp the force of his point. Hence, the crudely elitist insistence that classical music satisfies a unique artistic function and that popular music does not, because of some arbitrary attribute such as complexity, is deeply flawed.

Perhaps unsurprisingly, Johnson is particularly critical of "classical music functioning as popular music."[49] One gets the impression that it's a corruption of the sacred almost as grievous as urinating in the holy of holies. Making classical music accessible, as the British radio station Classic FM has done, contaminates its aura, and removes its particular value as music-as-art. Well-known, accessible pieces of classical music are played in preference to more lengthy, complex works. This is a problem for Johnson, because, if it is not difficult to process, if it does not require effort to listen to, its intellectual and aesthetic value is compromised. Again, apart from the arbitrary assumption that art should be difficult, the problem with this argument is that it raises the question as to when music-as-art becomes *other than* music-as-art. On the one hand, to repeat the point, one could compile a long list of popular music compositions that are both difficult and require effort, and, on the other hand, it is not easy to see what nonarbitrary criteria might be used to discern when a composition is "music-as-art." For example, when we listen to the German classical violinist David Garrett performing Metallica's "Nothing Else Matters" on his Stradivarius, immediately after listening to his interpretation of Georges Bizet's

"Carmen Fantasie" on his album *Free* (2007), are we witnessing a cultural shift and the profanation of music-as-art? It is hard to imagine how one might construct a scale to determine when his music passes from one category to another. Again, to return to Pavarotti, at what point does his music become profane? That is to say, on the one hand, he was an exceptional tenor, with an instantly recognizable vocal timbre, who had studied under Arrigo Pola and Ettore Campogalliani, and, as Edgardo in *Lucia di Lammermoor*, had performed with Joan Sutherland. However, on the other hand, he had great commercial success, which included the release in 2003 of what was described at the time as his "first pop album,"[50] *Ti Adoro*, which included a remix of "Caruso" featuring the British blues guitarist Jeff Beck. He also worked with a number of other popular music artists, such as U2 and Brian Eno on the single "Miss Sarajevo" (1995),[51] Vanessa Williams on *Saturday Night Live* (1998), and the Argentinian folk musician Mercedes Sosa (1999). The question is, at what point, between, say, *Lucia di Lammermoor* and U2 does his work cease to be "art"? Reading Johnson's book doesn't help. Indeed, it is difficult to see how one might get a straightforward, objective answer to such a question. Any answer, it would appear, is bound to be subjective.

Thinking about the same issue from another angle, in 1969 the rock band Deep Purple released their *Concerto for Group and Orchestra*, composed by Jon Lord (the group's Hammond organist) and performed with The Royal Philharmonic Orchestra, conducted by Malcolm Arnold. Is this music-as-art? If not, why not? If so, why, when, presumably, *Deep Purple in Rock* (1970) is not? Again, it is difficult to avoid the conclusion that such judgments are informed by individual experience. Even Kant conceded that "the judgment of taste is . . . not a judgment of cognition, and is consequently not logical but aesthetical, by which we understand that whose determining ground can be *no other than subjective*."[52]

Beauty and the politics of taste

It may seem a little odd to conclude our brief questioning of elitism with Kant, since some of the elitist ideas we have been discussing can be traced back to a particular interpretation of his aesthetics. Indeed, it may seem doubly odd mentioning Kant in a discussion of music, since, as Herman Parret comments, "within the immense Kantian cathedral," music "is a rarely visited chapel."[53] Kant's student, Reinhold Bernhard Jachmann, records that "he had no particular taste for music and played no instrument . . . He believed that music was incapable of expressing any idea, only sentiments."[54] He remembers that, while "Kant considered music to be an inoffensive pleasure of the senses . . . when I was sixteen he discouraged me, and many others among his students, from devoting myself to its study . . . "[55] Nevertheless, Kant is significant. As the principal architect of traditional philosophical aesthetics, he has provided theories that have aided the construction of cultural canons. In particular, "since Kant," writes Johnson, "art's value has been linked to its autonomy, its separation from the functional demands of everyday life. Popular culture, on the other hand, is bound up with everyday uses that high art seems to shun in preference for the 'functionless' activity of aesthetic contemplation. Popular culture not only deals with materials from daily life far more directly; its use is also far more directly tied into everyday life. High culture is generally removed from the everyday."[56] This conviction concerning art's abstraction from the everyday is rooted in the Kantian assertion of "the *absolute primacy of form over function*, of the mode of representation over the object represented . . . "[57] More fundamentally, it is rooted in Western Christian thought. The spatial language is particularly revealing. *High* culture is identified with that which is *"removed from* the everyday" and is, therefore, sacred. This is because the bodily and the everyday is desacralized and profaned.[58] Hence, for music to be of value, it has to be removed from the everyday. If it is not, as in the case of popular music, it is *low* culture.

While Kant conceded that judgments of taste are subjective, he insisted that this is not the case with judgments of beauty, which are both universal and necessary. Whereas *"everyone has his own taste,"* he argued that "the case is quite different with the beautiful. It would (on the contrary) be laughable if a man who imagined anything to his own taste thought to justify himself by saying: 'This object (the house we see, the coat that person wears, the concert we hear, the poem submitted to our judgment) is beautiful *for me.*' For he must not call it beautiful if it merely pleases him."[59] We speak of beauty "as if it were a property of things"[60] and, therefore, we demand agreement from others. It is not a matter of personal opinion; the pleasure gained from beauty is "disinterested"; it does not depend on the observer's desire. In this sense, Kant understands the observation of beauty in terms of "pure" contemplation and the judgment of beauty as universally valid. Of course, many contemporary readers will find such statements rather odd, to say the least, in that most of us are fully aware that judgments of beauty are not disinterested or universally valid, but rather determined by society, culture, and individual experience. Indeed, they are, in fact, linked to taste and, therefore, subjective. Beauty is in the eye of the beholder.

For those nervous about cultural relativism and the progress of what is sometimes referred to as "anti-foundationalism," for those wanting to return to what Paul Crowther has called a "normative aesthetics,"[61] the questions raised by Bourdieu and others, particularly within cultural studies, have been unwelcome. For their part, the critics of traditional aesthetics insist that cultural products labeled "art" do not possess a timeless quality in the way that Johnson and others contend.[62] Indeed, as Storey has argued, it is now difficult to return to the standard terms of axiology, such as "intrinsic," "objective," "absolute," "universal," and "transcendent"; "cultural studies is not impressed with demands to pay homage to a timeless text of fixed value. A cultural text or practice survives its moment of production – becomes canonical – because," he insists, "it is able to meet the needs and desires of people with cultural power. Surviving its moment of production makes it available to meet the (usually different) desires and needs of other generations of people with cultural power."[63]

This is precisely why Bourdieu was concerned with the implications of Kantian aesthetics. There can be no pure, disinterested contemplation of a cultural text or practice. As confirmation of his thesis that there are fundamental links between one's socioeconomic position and one's "habitus," he argues that taste is a marker of class, reflecting educational attainment, social origin and economic power: "Taste classifies, and it classifies the classifier. Social subjects, classified by their classifications, distinguish themselves by the distinctions they make, between the beautiful and the ugly, the distinguished and the vulgar, in which their position in the objective classifications is expressed or betrayed."[64] The value of classical music has less to do with listening and more to do with the construction of a platform from which to evaluate the tastes and social standing of other listeners.

Based on the results of 1200 questionnaires about lifestyle preferences, from music to cooking, collected from a cross-section of French society in the 1960s, Bourdieu's research concluded that, through taste, people distinguish themselves from the Other, from those whose tastes they consider vulgar or otherwise of less value. There are, of course, problems with Bourdieu's thesis, in that not only does it map specific tastes too rigidly onto class divisions in 1960s French society, which make it difficult to apply to, say, contemporary North America, but it also does not fully account for the plurality of tastes within and between classes. However, the overall argument is an important challenge to traditional aesthetics and to the construction of cultural hierarchies. In particular, he demonstrated how arbitrary tastes and arbitrary lifestyles are transmuted into legitimate tastes and lifestyles. Cultural consumption is a means to produce and legitimize social difference. Learned patterns of cultural consumption are internalized as "natural" cultural preferences and interpreted as evidence of "natural" cultural competences. These are then used to discriminate and justify forms of cultural domination. The ideological sleight of hand is subtle and powerful: the dominant group's cultural tastes, such as classical music, are institutionalized; institutionalized culture is then interpreted as "high culture" by the dominant class; because the taste of the dominant class is for "high culture," it is presented as proof of their cultural and, by implication, social superiority; hegemonic culture is sacralized. In this way, culture becomes a means of establishing and reinforcing social difference. It is a "weapon in strategies of [social] distinction."[65] It is a way of excluding the Other.

Once this ideological process is understood, it is difficult to see how one can insist on an absolute, objective difference between "high" culture and popular culture, between Beethoven and The Beatles. It is, again, largely a matter of taste. Of course, this is not to say that everything is of equal value and that we cannot argue that one album by The Rolling Stones is better than another (we will return to this issue later in the chapter), but rather the argument is simply that the same fundamental processes are taking place when I choose to read a graphic novel and listen to The Stooges as when I "value" a symphony by Edward Elgar or a painting by Mark Rothko. Cultural texts are not the source of value, as Johnson would maintain of classical compositions, but rather sites where value is constructed.

Culture and civilization

The privileging of classical music and the identification of popular music as *other than* "music-as-art" continues a tradition in which "popular culture" is understood less as that which is "widely favored" or "well liked" by the people,[66] and more as that which is *other than* that which edifies (i.e., "culture"). In other words, they are closely related to constructions of the sacred and the profane. As Raymond Williams demonstrated in *Culture and Society, 1780–1950*,[67] the value-laden idea of culture as intellectually and morally improving arose from a dominant English literary tradition, which emerged in reaction to and in consonance with middle-class interests occasioned by the new industrialized economy and the new social order.[68] Particularly during the nineteenth century we see a shift in perspective (largely due to industrialization), the emergence of democracy, and new issues concerning social class. Prior to this period, Williams tells us, culture had meant, primarily,

> the 'tending of natural growth,' and then, by analogy, a process of human training. But this latter use, which had usually been a culture *of* something, was changed, in the nineteenth century, to *culture* as such, a thing in itself. It came to mean, first, 'a general state or habit of the mind,' having close relations with the idea of human perfection. Second, it came to mean 'the general state of intellectual development, in a society as a whole.' Third, it came to mean 'the general body of the arts.' Fourth, later in the century, it came to mean 'a whole way of life, material, intellectual and spiritual.'[69]

The first of these modern usages became particularly significant in the nineteenth century, during which a tradition of discourse about culture emerged that was regulative and disciplinary, its goal being the ideal of human perfection realized through intellectual, aesthetic and spiritual edification. There was a confluence of "culture" and the "sacred." Hence, it was argued by some that everyone should be exposed to the civilizing power of "culture." Through familiarity with culture, the threat of the profane in society could be mitigated. This is particularly evident in the writings of perhaps the first modern theorist of popular culture (although he didn't use the term), the influential poet and literary critic Matthew Arnold, who inaugurated what has become known as "the culture and civilization tradition." For Arnold— the son of Thomas Arnold, the Headmaster of Rugby School and the principal architect of the public school system in England[70]—culture, religion and politics are inextricably related. Although he abandoned the substance of his father's faith,[71] he nevertheless inherited a deep sense of Christian morality and a commitment to education as a force for social improvement. In his book *Culture and Anarchy* (1869), he identified "culture" as that which enables "all men to live in an atmosphere of sweetness and light" by making "the best that has been thought and known in the world current everywhere."[72] Indeed, he even argued that culture enables "reason and the will of God to prevail."[73] Hence, there is a sense in which, for Arnold, the process of becoming cultured is similar to the process of sanctification within Christian theology. Culture enables us to become more Christlike. It protects the sacred and resists the profane. Culture lifts humanity out of the squalor of a profane world. Becoming "cultured" is part of an individual's progress towards "perfection." The very process of becoming cultured manifests in an individual the "moral, social, and beneficent character" of "culture" itself.[74] Consequently, when Arnold spoke of those who were "cultivated" and "cultured," he referred not just to those who were educated and well versed in the arts, but also to those who were morally superior. Hence, again, following in his father's footsteps, he understood the progress of culture as central to civilization. The masses should be encouraged to engage with culture, for it is here that we discover that which is able "to minister to the diseased spirit of our time."[75] This is an important point as far as the study of popular culture and the sacred is concerned. For while Arnold never actually uses the term, it is clear that what we would now understand to be "popular culture" is directly opposed to all that he invested in the term "culture." It is profane, a representation of evil constructed over against the sacred (i.e., "culture"). Popular culture is "anarchy" and has its origins in the basest of human instincts.

While Arnold's understanding of culture and anarchy is, of course, profoundly political rather than primarily theological, it is, nevertheless, an excellent example of the ways in which sacred forms shape social life, creating polarities between those associated with the sacred and those who are associated with its profanation, the latter being excluded and demonized as those who live beyond the boundaries of the civilized, moral community. Of course, for Arnold, "culture" was largely the preserve of the educated and the wealthy, a core characteristic of good breeding. Anarchy, on the other hand, was manifested in the working-class masses and constituted a destabilizing threat to the sacred—to decent society and to the progress of civilization. The social function of culture is, therefore, to resist anarchy, to challenge that which is "raw and uncultivated," hedonistic, banal, and vulgar (i.e., profane), and to transform the uncultured—to familiarize them with the sacred and, thereby, protect society. As far as the aristocracy and the cultured middle classes were concerned, he understood culture to inoculate them against "the diseased spirit of our time."[76]

As always, the social contexts for particular articulations of the sacred are significant. Arnold's understanding of culture was shaped by his concern over the threat of anarchy generated by certain changes that were taking place in nineteenth-century Britain. In general, the Industrial Revolution had witnessed the creation of a new industrial urban civilization. In particular, Victorian industrialization and urbanization had created a space within which popular culture was able to flourish. As well as clear lines of class segregation forming in the cities, with whole areas being populated solely by the working class, there were new work relations in industry; together these led to a cultural shift, in that the working class began developing an independent culture uninfluenced by the culture of the dominant classes. In other words, they were losing control of "culture." New cultural entrepreneurs were emerging and a culture of radicals, forged in dire social circumstances and intended to inspire political agitation, increasingly appealed to many. Consequently, this new working-class culture threatened the social cohesion and stability of the past (from which the dominant classes benefited) and challenged political and cultural authority. It is little surprise, therefore, that Arnold, as a member of the privileged classes, concluded that Britain was in peril and that the profanation of society was a serious possibility. Along with the decline of the aristocracy, the growing political organization of the working classes had led to an erosion of attitudes of subordination and deference. Moreover, as far as Arnold was concerned, working-class people, whom he began to refer to as the "unsound majority,"[77] were uneducated and, therefore, wholly unfit for the power they were beginning to assume. Consequently, becoming increasingly authoritarian during the last decade of his life, he concluded that there was a clear role for the power of the state. Through education and coercion, the state would introduce the masses to the culture of the elite. This culture would, in turn, have the effect of suppressing the appetite of the masses for the profane entertainment that inspired much of their anarchic thinking. However, while he argued that culture would always be good for society, in that it inhibited the tendency towards anarchy, he could not free himself from a fundamental elitism that insisted on bourgeois superiority. The sacred would always be located in the culture of the bourgeoisie. The masses would always be uneducated, rude and vulgar, and therefore always constitute the threat of the profane. Again, for this reason, he insisted that the privileged in society must be protected by the state from the proletariat; "high culture" must be promoted, "popular culture" must be suppressed.

The Arnoldian perspective is important, not only because religion, politics, and culture are so closely related, but also because of Arnold's influence on the elitist core of modernism and, in turn, on subsequent understandings of "popular culture" as profane culture (which have, until recently, inhibited its study in academia). This is evident in early twentieth-century discussions of popular culture right through to contemporary elitist analyses.[78] Beginning in the 1930s, there was a hostility to any cultural manifestation beyond what was considered to be "high culture." In 1930, for example, the journalist and critic, Isaac Goldberg, in his analysis of Tin Pan Alley compositions, argued that the aim of the popular song industry was to "establish formulas, to turn out a product of robots, by robots and for robots . . . formulized, and only pseudo-emotional."[79] Again, although more theoretically sophisticated, the influential art critic Clement Greenberg was no less scathing in his analyses of popular culture or what he referred to as "kitsch" produced "without effort."[80] For Greenberg, Tin Pan Alley compositions represented a "predigested," easily accessible, insipid alternative to genuine music-as-art. This opinion, however, was perhaps most influentially articulated by one of the twentieth century's most important literary critics, the British scholar F.R. Leavis (whom we've already met in relation to folk culture). For Leavis and his wife, Queenie Dorothy Leavis, the cultural crisis Arnold had identified was continuing apace. "Mass culture," particularly evident in the rise of Hollywood, was not only a poor imitation of elitist culture, but it was designed to appeal to the uneducated tastes of the working class. It taught nothing, it conveyed no worthwhile messages, and it communicated no laudable values. Instead, mass culture had the effect of lulling its audience into a false perception of reality, deadening them to the true difficulties of life. Hollywood films, for example, "involve surrender, under conditions of hypnotic receptivity, to the cheapest emotional appeals, appeals the more insidious because they are associated with a compellingly vivid illusion of actual life."[81] Similarly, popular fiction "is the very reverse of recreation, in that it tends, not to strengthen and refresh the addict for living, but to increase his unfitness by habituating him to weak evasions, to the refusal to face reality at all."[82] As with Arnold, Leavis understood culture to belong to the privileged minority. The problem in the twentieth century, however, was that "high culture" was being systematically challenged. The threat of the profane had become increasingly evident. For Arnold, he argued, "it was in some ways less difficult. I am thinking of the so much more desperate plight of culture today."[83] Since Arnold's time, since the Industrial Revolution, there had been a "collapse of authority," an erosion of deference, and a serious questioning of the standards previously set by the privileged minority. The masses were comprehensively revolting against their cultural masters and destroying all that was culturally positive.

While the culture and civilization tradition is conspicuously problematic, based on an elitist, bourgeois, top-down view of society and the masses, it has been enormously influential and, as Storey has argued, "still forms a kind of repressed 'common sense' in certain areas of British and American academic and nonacademic life."[84] Although it is responsible for identifying popular culture as a significant area of everyday life requiring analysis, it has actually impeded serious discussion because of an ideological bent that, from the outset, has interpreted it as "anarchy" and, therefore, profane—detrimental to social life. From Arnold onwards, the tradition has found in popular culture only what it expected to find: namely, drivers of cultural decline and political disorder that, therefore, needed to be controlled and regulated.

As we will argue later in the book, this approach to popular culture, which has become "a kind of repressed common sense,"[85] is important for understanding the power of the perception of popular music as a medium for the transgressive other, an unregulated challenge to the mainstream, an agent of cultural pollution. As we'll see in Chapter 3, when examining popular music's articulation of wild indifference to accepted social mores, or its celebration of sexual freedom, or its declaration of the Dark Lord's challenge to the Christian mainstream, or its happy immersion in alcohol and hallucinogens, it is important to begin by understanding the significance of its identification as profane culture. That is to say, the social and cultural histories within which popular music evolved as the rejected other is key to understanding its contemporary significance.

The power of the banal

The Frankfurt Institute for Social Research, founded in 1923 by a group of left-wing German Jewish intellectuals, has also been particularly significant for the development of the serious analysis of popular culture and popular music. When Hitler rose to power in the 1930s, the Institute relocated from Frankfurt to Columbia University, New York, with some members moving to Los Angeles. In 1949 the "Frankfurt School" moved back to Germany, although some members remained in the United States. These geographical, political and cultural contexts are important in that they shaped the School's analysis of popular culture. On the one hand, the School was greatly occupied by the significance of the influence of Hollywood and, particularly in the case of Theodor Adorno, the cultural prominence of Tin Pan Alley compositions and the emergence of jazz. On the other hand, directly affected by the rise of Fascist and Stalinist totalitarianism and a virulent anti-Semitism, their Marxist analysis was shaped by a deep concern for human freedom. Acutely sensitive to totalitarian social control and attempts to monopolize the production of culture and the construction of social and personal identities, they interpreted the prevalence of popular culture in the United States in terms of the totalitarianism they had witnessed in Europe. Hence Adorno argued that, while they may have escaped fascism, freedom was nevertheless being threatened by a more subtle form of totalitarianism, a system over which people had no control and which shaped their understanding of the world: "the culture industry"—a term he coined to refer to the products and processes of "mass culture."[86] He was particularly sensitive to the increasingly ubiquitous influence of popular music in this respect: "The power of the street ballad, the catchy tune and all the swarming forms of the banal" had, he argued, "made itself felt since the beginning of the bourgeois era" and now "the power of the banal extends over the entire society."[87] In a response to Aldous Huxley's question about who, in a place of amusement, is really being amused, Adorno asks, "whom music for entertainment still entertains. Rather it seems to complement the reduction of people to silence, the dying out of speech as expression, the inability to communicate at all. It inhabits the pockets of silence that develop between people moulded by anxiety, work and undemanding docility. . . . It is perceived purely as background."[88]

Central to Adorno's thinking about "the power of the banal," of course, was the idea that the masses were operating with what Marx had identified as a "false consciousness" imposed on them by the ruling class.[89] That is to say, not only are the dominant ideas and values in a society those of the ruling class, reflecting and maintaining their interests, but they shape the way all the members of that society think about the world and their place in it, including the subordinate classes, who simply accept these ideas as an accurate reflection of reality. This "false consciousness," this false view of reality, is circulated through the culture industry, which convinces the masses that not only is this the way things *are* but this is the way they *should be*. Again, this suggests a deceptive totalitarian tendency, in that, rather than simply stating this explicitly, the culture industry insinuates its ideology into people's minds, suppressing individual autonomy and creativity. Hence the unthinking, mechanistic use of the standardized song in commercial popular music is central to the maintenance of a false consciousness, in that it epitomizes the conformism, commodification, and decline of critical faculties and human agency in the emerging political and economic environment.

It has to be said, of course, that Adorno's interest in what he clearly understood to be a debased and inferior form of music cannot be divorced from his own circumstances, just as Arnold's analysis of "culture and anarchy" was shaped by his privileged position in society and just as Johnson's criticisms of popular music are informed by his particular cultural presuppositions. Not only was Adorno, like Johnson, an accomplished composer, musician and musicologist, but he was a highly educated, upper-middle-class intellectual. Hence if Bourdieu is correct in thinking that "nothing more clearly affirms one's class, nothing more infallibly classifies, than tastes in music,"[90] then Adorno's distaste for popular music is hardly surprising. Having said that, while it is often assumed that Adorno's critique is rooted in a familiar elitism which distinguishes between serious "art" music and commercial "pop" music,[91] his concerns were actually more subtle than that and, indeed, have subverted this distinction to some extent. While, on the one hand, he understood the division between "popular music" and "serious music" to be relatively superficial, on the other hand, he identified a more worrying distinction that roughly mapped onto this division, namely that between tendencies in music which support the social, political and cultural status quo and those which subvert it. Subversive tendencies he discerned, not within popular music, but within the music of the avant garde, particularly that of Arnold Schoenberg. Much music, however, whether popular or classical, pacifies listeners rather than disorientating and disturbing their thinking. While this is based on a caricatured and naive understanding of popular music—much of which is, by Adorno's own criteria, subversively healthy—the point is an enormously important one.

Adorno's understanding of popular music is, of course, rooted in a Marxist analysis of the modern history of bourgeois society, central to which was his critique of mass culture. As Richard Middleton comments:

The decreasing significance of patronage in the nineteenth century and the permeation of musical life by market relations has two dialectically related effects: commodification of musical works and rationalization of the production system are accompanied by a new level of musical autonomy associated with market freedom and a decline of social function. Music is caught between these two tendencies, and good music embodies both in a satisfying unity, at once affirming the objective movement of bourgeois society and also negating this through subjective critique. In a sense the struggle is between developing compositional technique (for Adorno, the most important force of production) and prevailing relations of musical production, which represent contemporary technological, musical and social norms.[92]

Unfortunately, Adorno argued that, particularly since Beethoven, commodity musical production had waxed, while compositional autonomy had waned. Both popular and serious forms of music had become standardized, "coupling formula and fetishized effect."[93] However, because we are bewitched by the idea that art is "self-expression," a unique creative event, standardization is obscured by a patina of faux artisanship or "pseudo-individualization." This deceit is particularly evident, argued Adorno, in the evolution of jazz. He was keen to argue this point, not least because significant claims were being made about jazz in relation to modern art music. His theory of popular music, which he often inaccurately referred to simply as "jazz," was determined by the identification of the two processes of "standardization" and "pseudo-individualization." Popular music is standardized in that the songs, including improvised jazz compositions, are actually structured in much the same way. This, he argued, is typical of the ways in which the profanation of the culture industry undermines originality and authenticity with "patterned and predigested" products that erode any intellectual stimulation which might lead people to question the mechanisms of oppression that underpin the capitalist mode of production. However, because listeners seek and identify individual expression, there is a continual need for novelty. This is why, says Adorno, "the necessary correlate of musical standardization is pseudo-individualization."[94] Pseudo-individualization, through various superficial and stylistic changes, makes each piece of music appear unique and different. The listener is beguiled by "the veneer of individual 'effects'"[95] that make the "patterned and pre-digested" product look interesting and novel. Jazz, for example, constitutes, "in its distinctive sound, an amalgam of deviation and excess on the one hand and utter rigidity on the other. One of its vital components . . . is the vibrato which causes a tone that is rigid and objective to tremble as if standing alone."[96] This, as Robert Witkin points out, "ascribes subjective emotions to the note without this being allowed to interrupt the fixedness of the basic sound pattern, just as the syncopation is not allowed to interrupt the basic metre."[97] The point is that, for Adorno, jazz is a commodity in the strict sense. Its marketability permeates its production. It is always the laws of the market and the distribution of competitors and consumers which condition the production of jazz. Those elements in which immediacy appears to be present – the improvisatory moments, the varieties of syncopation, etc. – are added to the rigid commodity form in order to mask it but without ever gaining power over it. Jazz . . . seeks to improve its marketability while masking its commodity character.[98]

Again, the significance of all this for Adorno is that, along with other forms of mass-produced entertainment, "the banal" distracts the workers and ensures their passivity. While the pseudo-individualized effects are enchanting, in actual fact the culture industry creates and manipulates the desire for music, thereby producing a "circle of manipulation and retroactive need in which the unity of the system grows ever stronger."[99] Any notion of individual expression is illusory, popular music simply being "social cement."[100] Again, popular music tunes "lull the listener to inattention. They tell him not to worry for he will not miss anything."[101] They offer relief "from both boredom and effort simultaneously" and can be produced on demand in a way that guarantees the relaxation of the workforce. Such tunes calm the workers' minds, pacify them, and erode any desire to transform their conditions.

In this way, the culture industry can be said to have a narcotic effect on the masses, dulling the senses to the iniquities of modern society and, thereby, preserving conformity to the basic structures of capitalism: "the power of the culture industry's ideology is such that conformity has replaced consciousness."[102] As Marx said of religion, so, in effect, Adorno concluded of popular culture, it is "the opium of the masses." Indeed, for Adorno, the culture industry had effectively replaced religion's role in this respect—the latter now functioning as a commodity within capitalist society.[103] Those who submit to its soporific influence are induced into accepting a false consciousness. "The culture industry deals in falsehoods not truths, in false needs and false solutions, rather than real needs and real solutions. It solves problems 'only in appearance,' not as they should be resolved in the real world. It offers the semblance not the substance of resolving problems, the false satisfaction of false needs as a substitution for the real solution of real problems. In doing this, it takes over the consciousness of the masses."[104] Its narcotic effects ensure that the workers are cultural dopes by providing superficial and temporary pleasure, rather than genuine well-being and fulfillment: "the substitute gratification which it prepares for human beings, cheats them out of the same happiness which it deceitfully projects."[105]

Viewed in this way, popular culture can be considered profane, in that it stands over and against certain sacred forms, notably freedom. It undermines genuine agency and, thereby, well-being. If societies are to have any chance of protecting freedom and resisting totalitarianism, they require art that disturbs, art that awakens and sharpens critical faculties, rather than art that drugs, art that produces sanguine distortion. To this end, Adorno appreciated the negative and affirmative characteristics of the atonal and twelve-tone music of Schoenberg,[106] as well as the writing of, among others, Samuel Beckett and Georges Bataille. Their work, he argued, has an unsettling effect on the human mind, forcing it to question and subvert oppressive "grand narrative" schemes. Indeed, as with many European intellectuals, Schoenberg himself was likewise convinced that mass culture was detrimental to civilization. As Timothy Day has commented, "the whole point of Schoenberg's Society for the Private Performance of Music, which operated in Vienna between 1918 and 1922, was to remove new music from the public's gaze, from commercialization, from the dictates of fashion, and from the corrupting influence of market forces."[107] For Adorno, it was only such avant-garde art, which resisted the market forces of mass culture and mass media by means of social isolation and deliberate incomprehensibility, which could challenge the profane energy of totalitarianism. Whereas popular music, because it is lacking the vital aesthetic principle of individuation and thus is shaped by the very forces that it needs to resist, is simply unable to subvert the status quo, the avant garde "aids enlightenment."[108] Again, the music of Schoenberg, he argues,

> demands from the very beginning active and concentrated participation, the most acute attention to simultaneous multiplicity, the renunciation of the customary crutches of a listening which always knows what to expect ... it requires the listener to spontaneously compose its inner movement and demands of him, not mere contemplation, but praxis.[109]

Adorno was convinced of music's capacity to foster critical consciousness, largely because its materials are organized in such a way that it countered convention and habit. The avoidance of musical cliché and the preservation of dissonance, rather than simply offering musical resolution and gratification, encourages the mind "to challenge cognitive, perceptual and emotional habits associated with the rise of 'total sociation,' habits that reinforced, as a matter of reflex, relations of power and administration in ways that made those relations seem natural, inevitable, and real." [110]

While there are conspicuous problems with Adorno's thesis, there is also much that is exciting, cogent and powerful. Clearly, it cannot simply be dismissed as the ill-informed and prejudiced musings of a mid-twentieth-century ivory tower intellectual, whose introduction to the everyday world of working people was brief and biased.[111] We are all aware of the ubiquity of popular music and its ability to manipulate mood;[112] we can all think of instances of how it has been used to sell everything from ice cream to ideas; many have been disappointed by icons of popular music whom they have learned to admire as subversive and transgressive—such as Iggy Pop, Ozzy Osbourne, and John Lydon—because they seem to have had their strings so easily pulled by large corporations wanting to sell their products; few interested in music have not whined over wine into the early hours about the conservative, inoffensive, formulaic, lowest- common-denominator music that seems to flood the airwaves. The culture industry is conspicuously more concerned about money than about art and subversion. As Simon Frith puts it, "the music industry question is straightforward: how to make money out of music?"[113] Hence whether we think of *The Eurovision Song Contest, The X-Factor*, or the seemingly endless conveyor belt of manufactured pop acts, it is difficult not to sympathise with Adorno. However, recognizing this is a long way from uncritically accepting all he had to say.

While we will return to Adorno and learn from him, it's important to remember that his thought, as indicated above, was shaped by a particular context, a particular moment in history: Germany in the 1930s. This is important to remember because the totalitarian tendencies he identified, the tendencies which dominated his thinking, became a distorting lens through which he viewed the whole of modern history. In particular, he missed the fact that, as Middleton comments, "alongside an increase in centralized control has been persistent dissent; domination – social, economic and ideological – has been maintained only through *struggle*."[114] This, of course, is equally true of the culture industries. Consequently, whereas Adorno was right to expose the trend towards monopoly and control, account also needs to be taken of "the elements of lack of 'fit' – between institutions (record companies, broadcasters, publishers, and so on), and between functionally differentiated individuals and groups within each institution."[115] Whether we think of the rise of independent labels or the arguments between record companies and musicians— such as that between The Sex Pistols and EMI—or the efforts of some musicians to subvert the music industry—such as Bill Drummond and Jimmy Cauty of The KLF—the history of the popular music industry has not been one of unalloyed monopoly. Moreover, as we'll see in Chapter 3, there is much contemporary popular music that is explicitly disturbing in much the same way that the music of Schoenberg was and the philosophy of Bataille was (and, indeed, still is). Empirical studies of both the industry and consumption cannot support Adorno's Marxist-Hegelian interpretation of the history of popular music. That said, on the one hand, one wonders whether, if he had been around today, his views about popular music might have been far less pessimistic as to its social significance. Yet, on the other hand, as Middleton observes, "who could deny that the tendential strategies of the entertainment conglomerates and their 'gatekeepers' often approximate to the Adornian nightmare? Any cultural theory of pop's meanings must work with fully open eyes within this horizon . . . "[116]

2

Emotion and Meaning

There are a series of important issues which have over the years come to the fore in the study of popular music, some of which are directly relevant to understanding its relationship with the sacred: the relationship of popular music to society; its problematic relationship to class identity; its determining of friendship groups; its ideological significance; its relationship to emotion and the reflexive self. Although much work has tended to focus on music production and semiotic readings of musical forms, in more recent years there has been an appreciation of music as a dynamic medium in the construction of personal and social identities. This is important for an understanding of the extent to which popular music might contribute to an awareness of the self and to the social and religious networks in which it is embedded. While it is of course important to understand how music evolves, and how it is enabled and inhabited by its cultures and worlds of production,[1] it is equally important to understand the extent to which it meshes with emotion, with thought, with action, with the phenomenological and existential features of social life. As Tia DeNora has commented of the sociological analysis of music more generally, "even when sociologists considered music consumption, the focus was directed less to the matter of musical experience than to the ways in which tastes, musical values, and listening practices served as symbolic boundaries for status groups and status differences."[2] (We have noted Pierre Bourdieu's articulation of this type of analysis.) However, in the last decade or so, "music's role as an active ingredient of social formation and subjectivity has been restored. Within this 'new' music sociology of emotions, it is possible to conceptualize music as a device for the constitution of emotive action in and across a range of social settings."[3] An appreciation of such noncognitive dimensions of agency is enormously important for understanding the relationship between popular music and religion.

Later in this chapter we will be focusing on the continuities between religion, popular music and emotion. However, before we begin that analysis, we need to lay a little more groundwork. In particular, we need to explore the relationship between popular music and "affective space." This term is important in that it is used here to refer to the internal and social worlds of individuals. Indeed, to some extent, it is close to what Anthony Giddens refers to as "the reflexivity of the self."[4] If we think of reflexivity as a process of self-construction, then, as will be argued, the use of popular music to create affective space is, for many people, an important part of that process. This is because, firstly, music has a fundamental relationship with emotion and, secondly, human emotionality is central to meaning making and what Jürgen Habermas has referred to as the individual's "lifeworld"—the latent, taken-for-granted core values, beliefs, and understandings about who we are, how we relate to others, what the world is like, and how we fit into it.[5] This, in turn, is important for understanding the religious and moral life. Hence, treatments of popular music and religion that focus on the details of performers' biographies, performances and lyrics (as many do), but do not attend to the "affective spaces" created, risk failing to see the wood for the trees.

The social meaning of popular music: some initial comments

Central to the work of Theodor Adorno, we have seen, was his contention that music, determined by its composition, manipulates consciousness and contributes to social management: "Music is largely social cement. And the meaning listeners attribute to a material, the inherent logic of which is inaccessible to them, is above all a means by which they achieve some psychical adjustment to the mechanisms of present-day life."[6] That is to say, Adorno explores, as DeNora puts it, "the idea that music interiorizes and is able to instigate forms of social organization in and through the ways that it works on and configures its subject-recipient. Put bluntly, Adorno conceived of music as active, indeed formative, in relation to consciousness. In this regard, his work makes some of the strongest claims on behalf of music's power in any discipline."[7] Music has everyday significance. However, as we have suggested, there are problems with his work, one of the principal ones being that it always remained at the level of theory, lacking significant empirical analysis of the ways in which it might have everyday significance or might be a means by which people "achieve some psychical adjustment to the mechanisms of present-day life." In other words, its abstraction was problematic. As Simon Frith has pointed out, "the actual use of music by pop fans is scarcely examined – passivity is assumed. The supposed effects of pop are, rather, deduced from the nature of the music itself."[8] Indeed, reacting to this approach, Frith has been one of a number of scholars whose work has encouraged a quite different view of popular music than Adorno had presented. As the discipline of popular music studies was beginning to coalesce, a new appreciation of the social significance of music evolved. Drawing on the work of cultural theorists such as Raymond Williams, Richard Hoggart and Stuart Hall, as well as the renewed interest in the writings of political theorists such as Antonio Gramsci in particular, scholars such as Paul Willis, Simon Jones, and Dick Hebdige reversed the sociological gaze.[9] In an attempt to demonstrate that popular music functions as a resource in and through which agency and identity are produced, they examined its social presence and the subcultures it generated and supported.

The development of these methodologies and foci were, of course, inevitable since the early study of popular music was, for the most part, undertaken by sociologists, anthropologists and cultural theorists, rather than musicologists. That said, in more recent years these developments have begun to inform musicology. Influenced by popular music studies and shaped by the thinking of musicologists such as Derek Scott, Allan Moore, Richard Middleton, Lawrence Kramer and Susan McClary, the discipline of critical musicology (often referred to as "new musicology" in the United States) has emerged since the mid-1990s out of a conviction that the production and reception of music can only properly be understood with reference to its social and cultural contexts. To this end, critical musicology is not only necessarily multidisciplinary, but it has been enormously important in bringing musicology into conversation with popular music studies.

It is perhaps important to reiterate at this point that, while much recent analysis of the significance of popular music has, for good reasons, been highly critical of Adorno's assessment, in actual fact the theoretical trajectories of popular music studies and critical musicology generally support his central thesis, namely that music is fundamentally connected to habits of mind, to social organization, and to modes of subjectivity. "Dedicated to exploring the hypothesis that musical organization is a simulacrum for social organization, Adorno's work conceives of music as formative of social consciousness." It is in this regard, says DeNora, that Adorno's work "represents the most significant development in the twentieth century of the idea that music is a 'force' in social life, a building material of consciousness and social structure."[10] Popular music, ubiquitous in the everyday lives of most modern people—from their radio-accompanied showers in the morning, to the companionship of their iPods on the train, to the recreational spaces they inhabit—needs to be taken seriously as formative of social situations and of an individual's sense of identity and agency.[11] As such, it would be very odd if it were not also related to the construction and articulation of the sacred in the modern world.

Adorno's focus on the relationship of music and social being is evident in much recent analysis of popular music that explores homologies between social situations, subjectivities, and music. What Stuart Hall referred to as "articulations"[12] are clearly evident between subcultures, social worlds, and popular music. For example, based on the empirical analysis of the production and reception of music, Paul Willis's work on the social meaning of popular music, *Profane Culture*, provided an essentially class-based discussion of the uses of music by middle-class hippies and working-class bikers. The latter, seeking an "antidote to boredom,"[13] preferred rock 'n' roll with its simple musical arrangements, because it stimulated the production of adrenaline and, therefore, the dynamism associated with their social world: "if you hear a fast record you've got to get up and do something."[14] Hippies, on the other hand, preferred the more complex and intricate compositions of progressive rock. These articulated a more contemplative attitude of "serious listening," as well as a desire to restructure "normal time," to expand it into a reflective, affective space. Unlike a biker's preference for singles—which articulated their desire to be on the move at speed—the hippie preferred the LP format, which provided extended musical worlds to inhabit, sonic environments populated by sound effects, reverb and feedback, all of which engendered an impression of "space and lateral extension,"[15] particularly if accompanied by induced altered states. This, in turn, made its confluence with "spirituality" and metaphysical reflection natural and easy. Whereas Chris Spedding's "Motor Bikin" (1975)[16] communicated, perhaps better than any other single, the principal features of the adrenalin-fuelled affective space sought by bikers,[17] the 1973 album by Yes, *Tales From Topographic Oceans* and Hawkwind's *Warrior on the Edge of Time* (1975) are good examples of music for beanbag culture, produced for contemplation, imagination and altered states. We might think of the former in terms of "body music" and the latter in terms of "head music."

The fact that music has the ability to restructure our perception of time, which in turn influences the way we respond to it, is an important one. A helpful way of understanding this is provided by Rupert Till. In his short discussion of music and time, he distinguishes between the Greek words *chronos* and *kairos*: *chronos* refers to the measured time of everyday life, the minutes and hours that tick by, while *kairos* refers to a particular quality of time, a moment of significance. Hence, in the New Testament and subsequent Christian theology, *kairos* is used of moments of particular importance, such as the advent of Christ (e.g., Mark 1:15). Indeed, in the ancient world it carried a number of strategic rhetorical meanings.[18] However, Till's point is essentially that music relocates listeners, moving them from *chronos* to *kairos*. It acts as "a bridge" between the two:

> When one experiences music and/or dance, one is no longer synchronized to the pulse of the second, the hour, the day . . . one's internal clock is linked to the musical time that is passing, whether bars, beats or phrases. It thus helps one to become unlocked from *chronos*, from a normal perception of time, and for one's state of mind or consciousness to change. It also allows a number of people to synchronize their sense of time, and their bodies, together, which is a powerful communal experience.[19]

Although he doesn't develop the point, music's peculiar ability to shift a person between *chronos* and *kairos* is enormously important for understanding its spiritual and psychological significance. As we'll see below, temporal manipulation is central to music's function as an affective technology.

This function, moreover, can be enhanced by the inclusion of culturally specific sounds. For example, typically conducive to the engendering of affective spaces informed by countercultural spiritual concerns in the late 1960s and early 1970s was the use of mantras and instruments associated with India. As Sheila Whiteley notes of the period, "raga motifs . . . tambouras, dilruba, tabla and sitar resonate both with the beads, bells and joss sticks of the underground and with the India of the *Bhagavad Gita*."[20] Mantras and the sitar, with their easy orientalist musical references to India and "the East," accompanied by music aimed at producing *kairos* moments conducive to relaxation and contemplation, introduced conspicuous spiritual content into the affective space of the hippie.[21] As Susan Fast comments of fans' responses to Led Zeppelin's "Kashmir," "they make . . . a general association between the East and spirituality, including mysticism."[22] This is explicit in the music of Quintessence (*In Blissful Company*, 1969; *Quintessence*, 1970), John McLaughlin (*My Goal's Beyond*, 1971), the Mahavishnu Orchestra (*The Inner Mounting Flame*, 1971), and Carlos Santana (with Alice Coltrane, *Illuminations*, 1974), and, perhaps most famously, several tracks by The Beatles on which George Harrison plays sitar, such as "Tomorrow Never Knows" (*Revolver*, 1966) and "Within You Without You" (*Sgt. Pepper's Lonely Hearts Club Band*, 1967).[23] The point is that the early ethnography of popular music began to reveal music as dynamic, "a kind of aesthetic technology, or an instrument of social ordering"[24] capable of informing values, shaping habits, controlling the perception of time and, as we will see, structuring experiences of the sacred.

Listeners, texts and contexts

Popular music, like all technologies, "is often linked, through convention, to social scenarios, often according to the social uses for which it was initially produced – waltz music for dancing, march music for marching and so on."[25] In other words, music often contextualizes and gives meaning to situations because of what might be thought of as its intertextual relationship to compositional conventions.[26]

It is important to note at this point that in referring to intertextuality, the process which Julia Kristeva is generally understood to have initially theorized, we are thinking, in general terms, of the way in which a text, "as a signifying practice, presupposes the existence of other discourses . . . This is to say that every text is from the outset under the jurisdiction of other discourses which impose a universe on it."[27] Kristeva's notion of other discourses imposing a universe upon a text is an evocative and important one to which we'll return. At a more mundane level, however, an implication of this observation is that, as Roland Barthes famously argued, "we know that a text is not a line of words releasing a single 'theological' meaning (the 'message' of the Author-God) but a multi-dimensional space in which a variety of writings, none of them original, blend and clash. The text is a tissue of quotations drawn from the innumerable centers of culture."[28] (The "sampleology" of remix culture can be understood as an explicit articulation of this, in that a musical text is selectively or wholly constructed from gobbets of music, found sounds and speech, using a cut and paste method.[29]) Again, we might also learn from Stanley Fish's social reader-response thesis. For Fish, one cannot speak of texts without also speaking of readers and contexts. "In the procedures I would urge, the reader's activities are at the center of attention, where they are regarded not as leading to meaning but as *having* meaning."[30] That said, the range of available meanings is limited by the "interpretive communities" to which one belongs. In other words, readers' subjective responses to texts are, in the final analysis, not particularly subjective, in that "interpretive communities, rather than either the text or the reader . . . produce meanings"[31] An interpretive community is, he argues, made up of those who share "the interpretive strategies" which are always, wittingly or unwittingly, brought to texts. Whereas some people will be fully cognizant of the interpretive strategies they employ, such as those following a Marxist intellectual and political trajectory, others will be unaware that they belong to any interpretive community at all. Nevertheless, we all belong to interpretative communities, the strategies of which are shaped by various presuppositions that influence our expectations as to what meanings we might discover in a text. Readers come to texts already predisposed to read them in particular ways. Hence, for example, whereas the interpretive communities of most listeners predispose them to a reading of The Beatles' 1968 album *The Beatles* (known as "The White Album") in terms of an anti-establishment, largely ironic, eclectic and experimental hippie text, its meaning was very different when viewed through the millenarian gaze of Charles Manson. The Beatles and the Bible were merged and John, Paul, George and Ringo became the four angels described in Revelation 9: 14–15. "The White Album" was read as an apocalyptic text, prophesying "Helter Skelter," a racial uprising in which African Americans would seek the armed overthrow of the white establishment.[32] Viewed through the lens of Kristeva's thesis, "The White Album" came under the jurisdiction of a particular reading of biblical apocalyptic discourse that imposed a terrifying universe upon it, the tragic result of which was murder and mayhem. The point to note here is that a text should not be thought of as having a fixed meaning independent of the reader, but rather, in a significant sense, its meaning comes into being as the text is being read (i.e., listened to). Constructions of the sacred (and the profane), those sacred forms around which people's everyday lives are oriented, are organically woven into the process of reading.

Bearing the above in mind, we might also mention how the meaning of a musical text can shift significantly as the result of interpretation by another artist, particularly if that artist has a conspicuously distinct ideology. Take, for example, "Personal Jesus" by Depeche Mode (*Violator*, 1990). The song is about personal relationships and the way in which one partner can be significantly dependent on the other. In this sense, one partner becomes "the savior," "the confessor," "the Jesus," of the other partner. However, the meaning of the text shifted radically when it was covered in 2002 by Johnny Cash (*American IV*), a convert to evangelical Christianity, and then again in 2004 by Marilyn Manson (*Lest We Forget*), whose misanthropic rhetoric and membership of the Church of Satan is well known. Sung by the Christian Cash in old age, "Personal Jesus" becomes a touching devotional song. Sung by Marilyn Manson, it drips with irony and profane meaning—made explicit in the video, which is conspicuously transgressive in its careful mixing of sacred and profane imagery. Both are equally as powerful, but quite distinct from the original text, evoking very different affective states and, therefore, distinct meanings.

Thinking of music in this way, as text, we are also helped toward understanding why sounds have particular meanings. For example, the sitar is able to evoke associations with Indian spirituality, which, because of an intertextual relationship with a relatively recent history of Orientalist discourse in the West, suggests the ethereal and the mystical.[33] Sound can also, of course, have a conspicuous intertextual relationship to sonic structures evident in the natural and social worlds. For example, echo can give the impression of space, just as lightly playing the keys of a glockenspiel or brushing crotales can communicate the impression of a stream or a gentle breeze. This is conspicuous in the work of Grouper (Liz Harris), which seeks to create affective spaces in which the natural world is prominent. She explains how her recordings "often sound as though they've been made against a vast mountainscape: voice and instruments – muted piano, spider-strummed guitar or growling drone – are steeped in reverb and delay. 'When you have reverb and smeared-out sounds there's an implied expansiveness. My music is partly about making a sound that reflects an actual physical space that's wide and empty.' "[34] Again, music frequently has historical social and cultural associations. For example, Eric Coates' "Dam Busters March" from the 1955 film *The Dam Busters* signifies, for some people, a nostalgic form of postwar British patriotism. Consequently, it is now played at military parades in the UK. Also powerfully evocative are the dramatic stabbing jabs of strings in their upper registers, which, because they were used in Bernard Herrmann's score for Alfred Hitchcock's 1960 film *Psycho*, now consistently signify menace.[35] The point is that, because of this intertextuality, whether we think of the use of strings in *Psycho*, the "Dam Busters March" or, indeed, the theme from *The Twilight Zone*, or Bob Dylan's "Mr Tambourine Man" (*Bringing It All Back Home*, 1965), popular music is invested with meaning by the listener. Our encounter with music, therefore, elicits particular values and attitudes: aggression, calm, patriotism, subversion, mysticism, devotion, sobriety, eroticism, trance, fear, unease. It creates an affective space within which meaning making occurs. While we may read particular meanings into specific pieces of popular music because of their associations with moments within our own histories, the same pieces may also convey meanings as a result of their associations with ideas in wider culture, ideas that have formed within the interpretive communities to which we belong. In this sense, Frith is correct to insist that "we are not free to read anything we want into a song." Rather, "the experience of pop music is an experience of placing: in responding to a song, we are drawn, haphazardly, into affective and emotional alliances with the performers and with the performers' other fans,"[36] as well as with wider interpretive strategies. It is in this sense that we can speak of music communicating meaning and emotion in much the same way that language does.[37]

To approach this point from a slightly different angle, we might think of inter-textuality and interpretive strategies in terms of what the perceptual psychologist James Gibson referred to as "affordances."[38] That is to say, certain environments and stimuli "afford" certain responses and preclude others. Hence, for example, generally speaking, Gregorian chant possesses particular affordances, fundamental to which is Christian worship, rather than, say, electronic dance culture. Because Gregorian chant, the central tradition of Western plainchant,[39] is culturally associated with a particular form of devotion and a particular ecclesiastical setting, it is difficult to detach it from that context when we hear it. Hence, we respond accordingly, in that, because, it is a gentle form of music associated with the sacred, the affective space it creates is, for many people, calming and "spiritual." But there is of course usually more than this. Our reading of Gregorian chant will typically include feelings of reverence, informed by, perhaps, Romantic, possibly Gothic notions of medieval ecclesiastical life and processions of chanting cowled monks. This, of course, is why some contemporary esoteric groups make liberal use of cowls and liturgical chant in seeking to construct affective spaces conducive to the perception of sacred gravitas. For example, the soundtrack to a video of a ceremony of the esoteric Order of the Solar Temple, seized by police in Quebec following a mass suicide, included Gregorian chant and showed members performing their rituals in cowls.[40] Similarly, in popular culture the gravity of occult ritual is often conveyed visually with cowls and candles and aurally with liturgical chant. Indeed, it is because of these affordances that it is used to great effect in films such as Roman Polanski's *The Ninth Gate* (1999) and Stanley Kubrick's *Eyes Wide Shut* (1999); the soundtrack to the latter includes Jocelyn Pook's haunting "Masked Ball" (*Flood*, 1999), for which Romanian liturgical chant was sampled and played backwards. Again, just as cowls and candles are used in music videos by bands wanting to evoke a sense of Gothic gravity,[41] so Gregorian chant is employed for similar reasons. Of course, as we will see, occultural intertextuality is key here. That cowls and chant are used in film, that they articulate a Gothic aesthetic, and that they are linked to esoteric ritual is highly significant, in that musicians are now able to use them in the knowledge that their meanings are relatively stable. These meanings are explicit in the use of chant on "The Song of the Sibyl" by Dead Can Dance (*Aion*, 1990) and "Sign of the Cross" by Iron Maiden (*The X Factor*, 1995), both of which focus on biblical apocalyptic themes and seek to evoke a sense of the medieval sacred. However, the point here is simply that chant is used by musicians, esoteric organizations and film directors, because it possesses certain common affordances. That this is the case hardly needs arguing, since it will be obvious to most Western readers. For example, the following comment, entitled "Ominous Latin Chanting," was posted by a contributor to the "TV Tropes" wiki:

Somewhere over the past few centuries, Latin became the 'ominous' language. Maybe it's the fact that it's the language of a once mighty civilization from well over a thousand years ago. Maybe it's because it's also the traditional language of the Church, and thus associated with spirituality, mystery, and death. And from there it's only a hop, skip and a jump to the idea of magic — often *bad* magic. And then there's the music with which Latin is often associated — for example, the unique sounds of the Gregorian chant — which can sound decidedly sombre, even spooky to a modern ear. . . . So whenever you hear a choir singing in Latin, it means that something epic is going on (even when it's not). This association is so strong that this trope is extremely common in movie trailers; Hollywood will tell you that nothing says 'watch this movie' more than choir chants in a language most viewers don't know, and that *this* is the way to give a scene that extra bit of ominous importance. The actual meaning of the words is unimportant. They could be singing Latin nursery rhymes (or reading from a Roman phone book) for all we know; it's the *sound* that matters. Bonus points if the lyrics and/or tune are reminiscent of or outright stolen from Carl Orff's *Carmina Burana*, especially 'O Fortuna.' Most of the lyrics of *Carmina Burana* are secular poems from the Middle Ages about life, death, drinking, and sex that were often sung by the medieval equivalent of frat boys — but they're in Latin, so that makes them awesome. The lyrics in 'O Fortuna,' however, are *genuinely* ominous.[42]

Chant—particularly if, according to the above, it is sung in Latin—can create a sense of ominousness. Many would agree. Certainly this is the affective response Iron Maiden sought to elicit in "Sign of the Cross."

Because music affords certain responses, it can be used creatively with other music to create particular affective spaces. The chanted cover versions of pop and rock songs by the German band Gregorian are a good example this. More interesting, however, because of their elision of the sacred and the profane,[43] is the incorporation of chant into electronic dance music in Shaggy's evocatively entitled "Church Heathen" (*Intoxication*, 2007) and particularly Enigma's "Sadeness" (*MCMXC a.D.*, 1990), the latter being one of the most internationally successful records of 1991.[44] Although "Sadeness" is a piece of music conspicuously linked with the Marquis de Sade, including sexually suggestive female vocals, the affordances Gregorian chant possesses are still powerfully present. Hence when juxtaposed with that which would typically, in a Christian culture, be considered profane, the effect is powerful, creating a particularly evocative dissonance, which, in turn, creates a sense of the impure sacred—the "church heathen."

If we now return to Fish's reader-response approach, we can gain some understanding of how a particular affective space might be created by "Sadeness." The track begins by introducing the listener to a strong, repetitive dance beat and heavy bass. This is significant because, generally speaking, we have learned to think of this sound in terms of the profane, largely because the music is motoric: wittingly or unwittingly, we keep time to rhythm. Music is corporeal and immediately related to the body: "We listen to music," observed Nietzsche, "with our muscles."[45] This, in a Christian culture, has tended to be treated with suspicion. As John De Gruchy has argued of Nietzsche's critique of Christianity, it has remained "one of the sharpest of all because it touches a raw nerve in exposing the way in which Christianity – the religion of the incarnation – has too often been guilty of denying the body, the senses and human creativity."[46]

The bias against the body in Christian culture, as De Gruchy suggests, can be traced back to Augustine, "who, knowing so well the desires and delights of the body, came to fear the power of the senses after his conversion."[47] Indeed, the Western priority of the rational soul over the sensual body can be traced back to the New Testament and to Paul who, while arguing for the significance of the body in the religious life, clearly privileged celibacy. It is hardly surprising then that central to much subsequent spirituality in the West has been a concern with the body and, in particular, the control of the mind, the will, and "the Spirit" over the flesh.[48] Allied to this, of course, has been a rejection of those forms of culture, those beliefs and practices "in the world" that appear to have a bodily focus, such as music. For example, George Fox, whose preaching led to the formation of the Society of Friends (Quakers) in mid-seventeenth century North-West England, is typical in being "moved . . . to cry against all sorts of music," because it "burdened the pure life, and stirred up peoples minds to vanity."[49] More than that, music, particularly that of "fiddlers," inevitably leads to dancing, which, he insisted, was to be involved "in the flesh, not in the Lord."[50] Hence although Christian approaches to the body and the world have tended to swing between the Apollonian and the Dionysian, between what De Gruchy, following Paul Tillich, refers to as "bourgeois righteousness and stability" and a "spirit-filled ecstatic dynamism," there has been a conspicuous bias toward the former: "an inbred Christian sensing of the risk of releasing uncontrollable, even demonic, energies has generally preferred the values of Apollo to those of Dionysus."[51] This understanding of the body as a site of potential profanation has bled into wider Western culture. For example, Susan McClary's thoughtful analysis of the opera *Carmen* demonstrates that "Bizet grounds Carmen's music in the physical impulses of exotic, pseudogypsy dance," linking it to rhythms that indicate "she is very much aware of her body" and, as such, she is portrayed musically as the profane "dissonant Other."[52] Whether one considers that "it is by now a deeply rooted commonsense assumption that a funk beat necessarily *means* sex,"[53] or that much rock music is essentially "cock rock,"[54] or that "Presley's breakthrough was that he was the first male white singer to propose that fucking was a desirable activity,"[55] or that disco can be described in terms of "'whole body' eroticism,"[56] the articulations between popular music, dance and sexuality have been widely discussed.[57] The point here is that this association with the bodily and the sexual has contributed significantly to an understanding of popular music as profane—a challenge to certain sacred forms.

Returning to our discussion of Enigma's "Sadeness," the point is that, because of the affordances dance music possesses, on beginning to listen to Enigma's "Sadeness" we arrive at particular meanings which engender a feeling of confidence as to how to respond to the sound and (whether we are conscious of it or not) anticipate a number of possible ways in which the piece might progress—all of which include ideas associated with the affective spaces normally encouraged by contemporary dance music. These expectations circumscribe the possible meanings of the next layer of music, Gregorian chant, which arrives unexpectedly. The problem is that (to paraphrase Fish's evocative description of the reader's shift from certainty to uncertainty), rather than following the music along a well-lighted path—determined by the conventions of electronic dance music—the inclusion of chant leaves the listener to look for a way forward.[58] While this is dance music, body music, the profane other, alien affordances are now being added to it. Next, while seeking resolution for the conceptual dissonance between the sacred and the profane, the ancient and the modern, the dissonance is actually increased by the explicit inclusion of breathy female vocals and explicitly erotic signification (made conspicuous in the video). The spiritual and the sexual are elided within the same affective space. This transgressive impact, produced by the confluence of sacred chant and corporeal profanity, was, I suggest, an important factor in the appeal of "Sadeness."

Analyzing popular music using "reader-response" criticism, we can map the pattern by which the music structures the listener's response while listening. As such a piece of music becomes an event that acts on a person, *does something* to a listener, stimulating the creation of an affective space within which meaning occurs. The concepts of intertextuality and affordances help us to understand that, while we may have some agency in our use of music, for the most part, this agency is limited by our cultures, our backgrounds, our social contexts and the affordances the music itself possesses. Gregorian chant, Christian hymns, Buddhist mantras, dance music, and heavy metal possess certain affordances and, therefore, carry certain meanings that are difficult to dispense with—although those meanings are shaped by our own reception and understanding of particular affordances. Understanding the implications of this will assist analysis of some of the issues surrounding religion and popular music.

Transactional theory

In order to clarify and develop the ideas so far discussed, we ought to note a couple of points relating to what might be called the ethnographic imperative in the understanding of society and culture.[59] DeNora's work has been particularly helpful in warning against "theoretical short cuts" that avoid analyzing the reception of music by everyday listeners. This is important. Those seeking to understand the social meanings and significance of music cannot learn from textual analysis alone. Observation and participation are necessary. This is part of the problem with Adorno's theorizing of popular music. As an armchair theorist, he did not consider it necessary to observe in any meaningful ethnographic sense or, perish the thought, participate in popular music culture. Hence his work is based on minimal empirical knowledge of that which drew his vitriol. Few scholars nowadays, especially those working in sociology, but also increasingly in musicology and cultural theory, would approve of Adorno's methods of detached analysis. At the very least, there needs to be some engagement with popular music, some observation of the lives of those who listen to popular music and some conversation with those involved. As DeNora insists, "a sociology of musical affect cannot *presume* to know what music causes, or what semiotic force it will convey, at the level of reception, action, experience."[60] Because persons are shaped by social forces, informed by interpretive communities, subject to the jurisdiction of discourses and particular lifeworlds, their individual responses to music will necessarily have a unique quality. Meaning emerges as a particular listener *listens* to a particular piece of music. Hence analysis of what listeners say and write about the music is important. How do actors represent themselves, the music, and their relationship to the music?

Having stressed the importance of the listener, we are brought back again to the importance of the music itself in the process of meaning making. In other words, the tendency toward a subjective reader-response theory, in which the reader's response *is* itself the text, is not helpful. Rather, we might learn from Louise Rosenblatt, whose transactional reader-response theory emphasizes the importance of the reader-text *relationship* for the production of meaning. Of course, it is, as she says of poetry, "hard to liberate ourselves from the notion that the poem is something either entirely mental or entirely external to readers. 'The poem' cannot be equated solely with *either* the text *or* the experience of a reader."[61] However, she continues, "something encapsulated in the reader's mind without relevance to the text may be a wonderful fantasy, but the term 'poem' ... would not be applicable to such a mental experience any more than to an entity apart from a reader."[62] For Rosenblatt, the poem is less an object and more an event, in the sense that it can be described as an experience shaped by the reader, but under the guidance of the text. This dynamic understanding of the relationship between text and reader is enormously helpful in our analysis of meaning in music. On the one hand, we cannot deny, of course, that, as Rosenblatt says of poetry, "what each reader makes of the text is, indeed, *for him* the poem, in the sense that this is his only direct perception of it. No one else can read it for him."[63] Similarly, as I sit at my desk typing this paragraph, while listening to Eivind Aarset's *Sonic Codex*, the experience is mine alone, in that nobody else can hear it for me. The event is unique. No other person can respond to it with my feelings, memories, and personal associations. The resulting affective space that I inhabit during the listening event is unique to me. However, on the other hand, while this is all true, to paraphrase Frith, I am not free to read anything I want into *Sonic Codex*. I may be a person shaped by particular discourses, which will necessarily inform my encounter with the music, but the music itself is no tabula rasa; it also brings something to the encounter and contributes to the process of meaning making; it encourages certain affective responses and discourages others. As we have seen with Gregorian chant, even when relocated to electronic dance music or heavy metal, it is difficult to reinterpret completely the sounds we hear, in the sense that we cannot read from them entirely novel ideas and feelings. Hence, while the meaning carried by Gregorian chant can be used and manipulated, we cannot absolutely impose our will upon it and change it completely. We do have some agency in the production of meaning, *but* we are guided by the music. Again, it is in the event of the transaction between the listener and the sound that meaning is constructed.

Jimi Hendrix's interpretation of "The Star-Spangled Banner," for example, typically elicited two very different general responses from those who witnessed it live for the first time. On the one hand, when played at the Woodstock festival in 1969,[64] it tended to be understood in terms of a powerful response to the Vietnam War, not only because of the signification associated with the person playing it and the context in which it was played, but also because the original song carried very particular patriotic meanings for most Americans. Hence, subverting the traditional meanings attaching to the song, many at Woodstock constructed a countercultural, antiwar interpretation of Hendrix's rendition.[65] On the other hand, when "The Star-Spangled Banner" was encountered by more conservative listeners at the Dallas Memorial Auditorium, most of whom operated with interpretative strategies distinct from those dominant at Woodstock, the transaction elicited a quite different response: "The audience rioted, breaking chairs, rushing the stage and engaging in hand-to-hand combat with uniformed police."[66]

Similarly, to return to Gregorian chant, a particular type of person, in a particularly quiet setting, in perhaps a contemplative frame of mind, will find it soothing and calming. This isn't *solely* because of the music or *solely* because of the listener. It is because of the nature of the transaction: a particular type of person, with a particular history, in a particular setting, in a particular frame of mind has an encounter with the music that elicits particular meanings. Another person, in another setting, in another frame of mind will have a different encounter, which may elicit a set of quite different meanings. Gregorian chant can be quite different for two different people. For example, one person I spoke to, who did not consider herself to be particularly "religious," related to me an uneasy relationship with Gregorian chant. She had travelled to an old theological seminary to run an art and craft workshop. She arrived the previous evening. Although it was getting dark, prior to settling down for the evening, she decided to wander around the cloisters and admire the architecture and the stonework. As she did so, through the silence, she faintly heard chanting, which she described as both beautiful and "eerie." When I asked why she thought it was "eerie," she immediately replied that it had made her think of the film *The*

Name of the Rose, which, based on the book by Umberto Eco,[67] is set in a shadowy Benedictine monastery in Northern Italy in 1327 and relates the story of an investigation by a Franciscan friar into a series of mysterious deaths. This memory, it appears, as well as, no doubt, other affordances encouraged by popular culture, gave the singing a "haunted" feel. Indeed, not only did the setting remind her of the film, but the soundtrack included Gregorian chant. Hence, while the sound was "beautiful," it elicited an emotional response of unease. It was, she recalled, "creepy"; it "made my heart race." My point is that, rather than locating the eeriness in the music alone, or in the listener alone, it needs to be located in the transaction between the music and the listener. This event leads to the construction of an affective space in which a set of meanings emerges. For this listener walking around the cloisters, the combination of old, ecclesiastical architecture, the dimming light, the lengthening shadows, the unfamiliarity of the immediate environment, the vulnerability of being a woman alone in a male institution, and her memories of a particular film— the soundtrack and set of which had obvious continuities with the context in which she now found herself—were all gathered together in the event of encountering ostensibly "beautiful music," the result of which was an affective space defined by the eerie and the creepy. Hence in the case of this particular female, the affective space created by Gregorian chant was not one of relaxation, but rather one of mild panic and fear. Indeed, she related that her fear was increased when a shadow of a monk appeared, followed shortly afterward by its owner, who turned out to be "a lovely, gentle man" who calmed her and spoke to her about plainchant. From then on she enjoyed the music as simply "beautiful music," because her relationship to it changed. Because of the kindly monk, she had shifted into a different affective space.

Bearing this focus on transaction in mind, DeNora's criticism of Richard Middleton's institutional theory of meaning *in* music is worth noting. Middleton argues that certain pieces of music become invested with long-standing, widely accepted connotations, which are then perceived as part of the music. This is certainly true. For example, whether we think of Gregorian chant or "The Star-Spangled Banner," music can carry meanings that become all but inseparable from the sound. Hence, however arbitrary musical meanings and conventions are, argues Middleton, "rather than being 'natural,' or determined by some human essence or by the needs of class expression—once particular musical elements are put together in particular ways, and acquire particular connotations, these can be hard to shift. It would be difficult, for instance, to move the 'Marseillaise' out of the set of meanings sedimented around it . . . which derive from the history of the revolutionary French bourgeoisie."[68] DeNora, however, suggests that there is, nevertheless, "still a short cut here."[69] Although I'm not convinced Middleton is as culpable as she suggests, her point is an important one. We cannot simply grant that there are stable meanings in music, because "we cannot make assumptions about social responses to music without also offering a description of how those responses are actually produced."[70] This, we have argued, requires analysis of the transaction. While, on the one hand, music might be embedded in a set of broadly stable meanings, such as the "Marseillaise" or "The Star Spangled Banner," and, therefore, have significant semiotic force, on the other hand, understanding the relationship particular listeners have with the music requires ethnography.

Music as a prosthetic technology

Music matters. For many of us, it eases the passage from the cradle to the grave. That's why the nodding heads of twenty-first century humans are typically accompanied by two thin wires. Of course, while iPods may be a relatively recent provider of sound to the human brain, the psychosomatic impact of music has long been recognised. Tatian, for instance, in one of the earliest examples of Christian polemics against music, observing the behavior of his contemporaries, makes the following disapproving remark in his late-second-century work *Discourse to the Greeks*: "I do not wish to gape at many singers, nor do I care to look benignly upon a man who is nodding and motioning in an unnatural way."[71] From a more considered perspective, we might note the observations of Plato and Aristotle, both of whom reflected on the social, psychological, and "spiritual," significance of music.[72] It is clear, asserts Aristotle, that "music possesses the power of producing an effect on the character of the soul."[73] The point is simply that whether we walk the streets of the ancient Mediterranean world or stand at a bus stop in Lancaster tomorrow morning, at some point we will be accompanied by people physically moved by music. Music engages humans. It is because of this capacity to manipulate, to enable and to constrain people, that it can be understood in terms of a prosthetic technology. In other words, it has the power to extend the natural abilities of the body and the mind.[74]

It is, of course, not difficult to find examples of the ways in which music has been used to organize subjects, increase the flow of adrenalin, slow the body, manipulate the perception of time, provide rhythm, aid relaxation, control feeling, and manage thought. For example, Willis's ethnographic work with "hippies" demonstrated this prosthetic potential, in that it showed music to be clearly "capable of influencing feeling and emotion. People who were depressed or in a period of personal crisis often turned their attention massively to music."[75] Indeed, where people couldn't help a person, he notes, "sounds" often could. "They seemed to take over and express disorganized feeling in a way that was impossible in words. The music itself partly shaped the form of emotion, so that in accounts afterwards of 'strange' or 'depressed' episodes, music would figure prominently, and would be used as a way of explaining what happened. Occasionally people would say that a certain track has 'made them understand,' had 'changed them.' "[76] Again, DeNora's research into the use of music for aerobic exercise[77] and her discussion of the use of music by airlines to calm passengers, to demand their attention, and to inculcate their faith in "expert systems," indicates just how powerful it is as a prosthetic technology.[78] Similarly, marketers and social planners have not been slow to exploit music's power, whether in the manipulation of consumer behavior in stores or in the reduction of vandalism in social spaces.[79] Adrian North, David Hargreaves and Jennifer McKendrick, for example, have demonstrated that stereotypically French and German music influences the choice of French and German wines by supermarket customers. "Over a two-week period, French and German music was played on alternate days from an in-store display of French and German wines. French music led to French wines outselling German ones, whereas German music led to the opposite effect on sales of French wine. Responses to a questionnaire suggested that customers were unaware of these effects of music on their product choices."[80] In a similar way, as we'll see below, music has been shown to be enormously powerful in the manipulation of mood and in the creation of spiritually significant affective spaces, from the use of ambient electronic music at emerging church gatherings to hymns and choruses in more traditional worship settings.[81]

Perhaps needless to say, the affective power of music can also have negative effects. For example, Joseph Lanza has noted just how inappropriately titled Brian Eno's *Music for Airports* (1978) is, in that, when played at "the Greater Pittsburgh International Airport for a nine-day period from noon until 10 p.m. . . . many patrons reportedly complained to airport personnel about this *un*easy listening and asked that the regular background music be restored."[82] Indeed, it is interesting to read Eno's own account of his thinking behind the composition. Having conceived the work at Cologne Bonn Airport, he wanted to make "music that prepares you for dying – that doesn't get all bright and cheerful and pretend you're not a little apprehensive, but which makes you say to yourself, 'Actually, it's not a big deal if I die.' "[83] While ambitious and laudable as a project to create affective spaces that will be comforting to people facing possible death, it clearly failed in its objective—largely, I suggest, because Eno had not considered the possibility that, generally speaking, humans would prefer not to dwell on the likelihood of their imminent demise at all, let alone immediately prior to boarding a plane. However, again, fail though *Music for Airports* did in creating a calming affective space, it was powerful in manipulating the emotional states of travelers.[84]

Studies have also shown that, because music is effective in the manipulation of mood,[85] it can have a significant positive impact on performance at work. Teresa Lesiuk's study, for example, measured the effect of music listening on the creativity of computer information systems developers. Bearing in mind that creativity—defined in this context as "the ability to produce work that is both novel and appropriate"—tends to be adversely influenced by stress and negative affective states, it was found that because "mild positive feelings" were a constructive influence on the way cognitive material was organized, this led to an improvement in creativity.[86] Hence, carefully chosen music was shown to have a beneficial effect on the performance of certain tasks because of the "increases in state positive affect" stimulated by the music. In other words, "when music evokes a pleasant mood and an increased arousal state, participants perform better on non-musical tasks," including "an increase in creative problem solving."[87] Comments received from workers "revealed the value of music listening for positive mood change and enhanced perception on design while working." Moreover, results also indicated that "state positive affect and quality-of-work were lowest with no music, while time-on-task was longest when music was removed."[88] Overall, the study suggests "the presence of a learning curve in the use of music for positive mood alteration."[89]

Similar results can be found in studies of the relationship between music and health.[90] For example, there is evidence that music is an effective anxiolytic treatment. Oliver Sacks, in his work with post-encephalitic Parkinsonism sufferers, describes the treatment he used for a particular patient's recurrent "crises":

> By far the best treatment of her crises was music, the effects of which were almost uncanny. One minute would see Miss D. compressed, clenched and blocked, or jerking, ticking and jabbering – like a sort of human bomb; the next, with the sound of music . . . the complete disappearance of all these obstructive-explosive phenomena and their replacement by a blissful ease and flow of movement as Miss D., suddenly freed of her automatisms, smilingly 'conducted' the music, or rose and danced to it.[91]

More recently, in their overview of the literature on physiological responses to music and sound stimuli, Wendy Knight and Nikki Rickard have shown that, in clinical populations, "music appears to quite consistently reduce sympathetic nervous system-related indices of stress." For example, they note that "coronary patients exposed to music showed lower heart and respiratory rates than patients who were not exposed to music." Likewise, when surgical patients listened to music, they "showed a decrease in blood pressure and heart rate . . . and a reduction of cortisol levels . . . when compared to patients not exposed to music." Finally, they note that "immune responses were found to be enhanced in patients exposed to music when compared to patients not exposed to music . . . "[92] Indeed, I can testify myself to the psychosomatic significance of music. As a migraine sufferer, before my introduction to the drug sumatriptan, like many long-term sufferers, I found my own way of dealing with the peculiar pain, nausea and photophobia I experienced. As well as the usual medication and confinement to a dark room, I managed to control my pain and nausea by listening to dub reggae and certain types of ambient music—including *Music for Airports*. Eno's *The Shutov Assembly* (1992) was particularly helpful. This may seem rather odd to many readers, but this music had a peculiar ability to create an affective space within which I was able to move into a different, more relaxed relationship with my pain. The result was that I no longer felt controlled by it, but, thinking of my response to dub reggae, through focusing on the steady beat, the gentle pulse of the bass, the reverb and the echo, I seemed to be able to manage it.

At times, it was as if I could perceive the pain as an object, something alien to myself that I could mentally handle and place into the sound. It was as though I'd immersed the pain in a river of sound, which, flowing from me, relieved me of it. This process, even in the midst of excruciating nausea, became so relaxing and comforting I would drift into sleep. Other forms of music, of course, such as, to my mind, the cruelly inappropriately titled *Onze Danses Pour Combattre la Migraine* (1977) by the Belgian avant-rock band Aksak Maboul, had quite the opposite effect!

I suspect that, for most people, such research does little more than demonstrate the blindingly obvious. That music creates mood and manipulates affective states is hardly a groundbreaking revelation. At some level, most of us will instinctively recognise a psychosomatic relationship to music and understand exactly what John Lee Hooker meant when he sang "the blues healed me" ("The Healer," *The Healer*, 1989). It is common knowledge that, as DeNora puts it, music has the power to influence "how people compose their bodies, how they conduct themselves, how they experience the passage of time, how they feel – in terms of energy and emotion – about themselves, about others, about situations."[93] The point, however, is that this is why it has such significant prosthetic potential. John Sloboda's psychological research (which directly supports Willis's ethnographic work with hippies) is worth noting here:

> . . . when 67 regular listeners of music were asked to describe the nature of their most valued responses to music, two common themes emerged. The first theme was of music as a change agent, in which it helped the individual to move from a less desirable to a more desirable psychological state. This was evident in statements such as 'music relaxes me when I am tense and anxious,' 'music motivates and inspires me to be a better person (e.g., more agreeable and loving).' The second theme was of music as promoting the intensifications or release of existing emotions. This was indicated by statements such as 'Music helps me discover what I am actually feeling,' and 'Music reconnects me to be myself when my emotions are ignored or suppressed through sheer busyness.'[94]

This type of response to music is movingly expressed by the musician Mike Oldfield. As a sufferer of recurring panic attacks, he recalls that, at times, he was "sick . . . couldn't eat . . . was really upset . . . completely freaked out" and "just couldn't go on . . . " Indeed, he remembers that "when I was going through my worst times I felt I was possessed." However, "when it all became too much," he says, "I could retreat into my musical world. It was like a cocoon around me, everything inside was just beautiful and safe. I could imagine every single instrument saying something – the bass wouldn't just be a bass guitar, it would be a big, deep personality. Music was as familiar to me as the human voice and human language, with proper words and sentences. It all made sense, in its own musical way." He continues, "the wonderful musical world was . . . a kind of nirvana in music, a place of safety that I lived in and that stopped the panic attacks from coming."[95]

It is unsurprising, therefore, that music, an invisible force that structures affective space, has been formally theologized. For example, in Hinduism, the notion of *Nāda-Brahman* refers to the divine as "sound consciousness" or what Guy Beck has translated as "sonic theology"—the experience of the universe as sound. There is understood to be an integral relationship between music and *Nāda*, which, in turn, is "essential to Indian views of the soteriological significance of music, for music, as a manifestation of *Nāda*, is seen as a mode of access to the highest reality."[96] Similar sonic theologies can be found in cultures around the world, all of which understand music to be, at some level, a source of spiritual growth and social cohesion, a method of communicating the sacred and achieving mental states conducive to enlightenment.[97] The point is made explicit by the popular qawwali singer, Nusrat Fateh Ali Khan: "When I sing for God, I feel myself in accord with God. . . . I feel like I am in another world when I sing, the spiritual world. I am not in the material world. . . . I'm totally in another world. I am withdrawn from my materialistic senses, I am totally in my spiritual senses . . . "[98] (It is, then, perhaps no accident of history that the term "music" is derived from Greek word *mousikē*, the sacred realm of the Muses.[99])

Some thoughts on absolute expressionism

There has been much discussion concerning those intrinsic qualities of sound that elicit profound emotions, what Leonard Bernstein referred to as the affective theory of musical expression—"why is the minor 'sad' and the major 'glad'?"[100] Attempts to answer this question have raised a number of important considerations, particularly in the psychology of music. Leonard Meyer, for example, sought a mediating position between two classic theories in Western philosophical aesthetics, the absolutist and the referentialist. The former locates musical meaning exclusively within the context of the work itself and the latter locates it in "the extramusical world of concepts, actions, emotional states, and character."[101] Similarly, Meyer also sought a *via media* between formalism and expressionism. While both, he commented, "may see the meaning of music as being essentially intramusical (non-referential)," the formalist argues that "the meaning of music lies in the perception and understanding of the musical relationships set forth in the work of art and that meaning in music is primarily intellectual," whereas the expressionist contends that "these same relationships are in some sense capable of exciting feelings and emotions in the listener."[102] However, while it is clear that he sought to eliminate the weaknesses and accentuate the strengths of both positions, in actual fact his own approach betrayed a bias toward absolute expressionism. This is evident from the outset in his principal work, *Emotion and Meaning in Music*: "music . . . operates as a closed system," in that "it employs no signs or symbols referring to the non-musical world of objects, concepts, and human desires."[103]

While the psychological and philosophical analysis of meaning in music[104] would take us too far beyond the parameters of the present study, Meyer's thought-provoking book does raise a number of important issues relating to music's affective significance, the principal of which, for our purposes, is its articulation of the absolute expressionist approach, central to which, we have seen, is the guiding notion that intramusical meaning is fundamentally emotional.[105] Essentially, the musical relationships within a piece of music arouse emotion within the listener and the value of a piece of music is dependent on its ability to elicit that emotion. This is an idea that perhaps few people would disagree with, in that it seems to be conspicuously and universally the case that music is able to elicit emotion and, moreover, that emotion informs judgment. When we hear a series of sounds—typically, a melodic or harmonic sequence, or a harmonic or melodic acceleration to cadence, or a melodic appoggiatura—we do get a lump in the throat and moist eyes without any apparent reference to a particular narrative.[106] Again, as Sloboda has shown, an enharmonic change, or a delay of a final cadence, or new and unprepared harmonies, or a descending circle of fifths in harmony typically elicit emotion that produces goose pimples and sends shivers down the spine. Likewise, a musician is able to produce in listeners a racing heart rate and "pit of the stomach" sensations simply by the use of harmonic or melodic acceleration, or a sudden dynamic or textual change, or, as in much jazz and rock, repeated syncopation. While we are not particularly concerned here with the details of affective science, the point is that there appears to be good empirical evidence to support the suggestion that music per se, in some sense, does have the power, through engagement with psychological mechanisms, to induce emotional states. Moreover, it is also true that, for many people, the more music is able to do this, the greater it is valued as significant. For example, the songs that most move people tend to mean most to them and, as such, become their treasured "desert island discs."

The question is, of course, how does the sound of music itself convey meaning and emotion? Interestingly, while there has been a good amount of psychological, not to say philosophical work done in recent years to answer this question,[107] there is, as yet, no consensus as to why humans perceive the minor as sad and the major as glad. Although many would probably agree that a principal feature of emotions is that they involve intentional objects,[108] in that they have a focus (e.g., we are happy or sad because of an event, such as a party or a family bereavement), there is some uncertainty as to what musical emotions are about. In other words, the problem is that the conditions for eliciting musical emotions appear to be different from those in everyday life in that they are not related to events, goals, or processes which affect us: "most emotional reactions to music do not involve implications for goals in life, which explains why they are regarded as mysterious: 'The listener's sad response appears to lack the beliefs that typically go with sadness.'"[109] Hence, again, we come up against a basic question, which absolute expressionism struggles to answer convincingly. "How do sounds, which are, after all, just sounds, have the power to so deeply move those involved with them?"[110] It is very difficult to see how a sequence of sounds can elicit an emotional response in the human brain. The fundamental problem for the absolute expressionist, it seems to me, is that adequate answers to questions of musical meaning can only be given by those who attend to the social and cultural contexts of music. Music's meanings are inseparable from the social and cultural situations and circumstances in which they arise. As we have seen in the discussion of texts and contexts, the reception of music is not neutral and its interpretation cannot be disinterested. Following Fish, we have argued that the range of available meanings is limited by the "interpretive communities" to which one belongs. That is to say, "interpretive communities, rather than either the text or the reader . . . produce meanings . . . "[111]

Transactional reader-response theory in particular emphasizes the importance of the reader-text *relationship* for the production of meaning. To a large extent, this approach concurs with Peter Martin's sociological thesis that "the constraints on the interpretation of cultural objects are to be found neither within the objects nor 'hard-wired' into the individual's psyche. Rather, they are *social* processes in which . . . individuals come to share definitions of what constitutes the cultural object, to 'take for granted' the conventions and rules of the game, to accept or challenge interpretative strategies, and so on."[112] Similarly, from the perspective of musicology, Lawrence Kramer has been particularly forthright in his insistence that "musical immediacy, however distinctive and significant we may acknowledge it to be, cannot ground the putative unworldliness of music, either in the strong form that treats music as a numinous presence or in the weak form that acknowledges music to be contextually situated but still affirms a 'relative autonomy' that allows some works or styles to transcend the limits of their contexts. *Neither music not anything else can be other than worldly through and through.*"[113] It simply will not do to argue that music constitutes an autonomous and primarily aesthetic domain.

Concluding comments

Why is one piece of music perceived as mystical, another as eerie, another as celebratory, another as erotic, and yet another as demonic? What is it about music *per se* that is peculiarly evocative and moving? In working our way toward an answer to this question, we approach an understanding of the significance of music and sound, of sonic environments, in manifesting a sense of the sacred. Regardless of lyrical content, we have seen that music is able to contribute to the construction of affective space and to meaning making. More specifically, central to understanding music's relationship to the sacred is understanding its relationship to emotion, for both the sacred (particularly articulated within religion) and music are peculiarly powerful affective agents. As Douglas Davies puts it, "the processes that combine . . . emotions with ultimate values"—or what we might call "the sacred"— "to produce self-identity underlie all aspects of life, though they often become most explicit in what we call religion. . . . One way of thinking about these emotions and values is to see them as being appropriated by individuals in nuanced ways that help to develop the identity of those individuals."[114] The point for us to note is that music is a peculiarly effective agent in the process of appropriating and communicating emotions and values. Through the construction of affective space it contributes to the development of identity, by which we mean, broadly speaking, our sense of self and who we are in relation to others and to what we collectively experience as "the sacred." (We will explore this more fully in the following chapter.)

We might understand our relationship to music and the sacred in terms of "objectification" and "subjectification." In their sociological analysis of religious emotion, Ole Riis and Linda Woodhead interpret objectification as the production of symbols "aimed at expressing and evoking certain emotions."[115] We can include here, of course, the composition of music, as well as sacred art, architecture, rituals, drama and so on. However, their point is that, "through acts of objectification, emotional expressions become fixed and communicable."[116] In terms of the discussion in this chapter, we might describe them as portable texts, in that other individuals in other contexts are able to "read" them and perceive something of the emotional force they were created to evoke or have evoked in others. That said, the idea that the emotional expressions become "fixed" perhaps needs a little qualification (not that I suspect Riis and Woodhead would disagree, in that they are also careful to refer to them as "relatively fixed"). My point is simply that, as we have seen, central to understanding this process are particular affordances possessed by texts, which are then modified in relation to other affordances. Indeed, we have seen that precisely because music does possess certain affordances, its meaning can be played with. For example, if we think of a common sacred symbol such as the crucifix, it is solely because its meaning is stable within Western culture that inverting it is so powerful in communicating dark occultural content. Its meaning is stable, but not fixed. Affordances within music are no different. We have discussed this regarding Gregorian chant, the meanings of which are stable and correspond to a certain emotional scale. They are not, however, "fixed", which is why intertextual relationships can subvert dominant meanings, as in the use of Gregorian chant on "Sadeness" by Enigma. That is to say, "Sadeness" is able to both evoke certain emotions, because of the stability of certain meanings relating to the sacred, and simultaneously to subvert them through a fusion with dance music and references to the erotic, both of which carry equally stable meanings relating to the profane. The intertextual relationship between Gregorian chant, dance, and sexual references create an explicitly transgressive text.[117]

The overall point is that the reception and interpretation of texts cannot be disinterested, in that, as we have seen, the range of available meanings is limited by the "interpretive communities" to which one belongs. This brings us in a roundabout way to what Riis and Woodhead refer to as "subjectification." Their articulation of this comes close to what has been referred to here as the construction of affective space, which is related to identity formation. "In religious subjectification, an object provokes an emotional reaction that is considered religious."[118] The reception and interpretation of a text, such as a piece of music, provokes such a powerful emotional response that the presence of the sacred is felt. Of course, we have seen that music is particularly evocative in this respect. As the British theologian Peter Taylor Forsyth commented in his lectures on art in 1911, "there is a vaster power in music . . . than in any other art of entering sympathetically into the shades and varieties of emotion; and this sets up a very close bond between the musician and his varied audience, and enables him, as it were, to pour his soul directly into theirs, duly dividing the word of power in flame that flickers on every head. And in worship it gives a facility for the common spiritual expression of unutterable things."[119] His reference to the descent of the Holy Spirit at Pentecost (Acts 2:1-3) is an attempt to articulate the theological significance of the affective impact of music, which can, depending on "set and setting,"[120] be so profound that individuals feel that they are standing on sacred ground, that they have encountered the holy in some sense. As we'll see in the final chapter, the theologian Herbert Henry Farmer understood the theological force of this experience in terms of a shift from adjectival to substantival religion. This is enormously important for understanding the peculiar force of popular music in the creation of affective spaces within which sacred meaning is constructed. Having said that, this engagement with the sacred needs to be carefully understood, in that, as we'll see in the next chapter, much of Western popular music's energy is drawn from the left. It needs to be understood in terms of transgression and the articulation of the impure sacred.

PART TWO

3

Transgression

Seamus Heaney reminds us of "the world-marking power of a dividing line, such as the first furrow ploughed in a field."[1] The symbolic power of the line can, as a boundary, protect, constrain, and when traversed, transform a simple act of the will into an ontologically significant transgressive event, whether one drives across road surface markings into oncoming traffic or passes into sacred space from the profane. As indicated in the previous chapter, the sacred–profane polarity and the emotional power of the transgressive lie at the heart of popular music culture. However, before we turn our attention to popular music, we need to unpack just what we mean when we use the terms "transgression," "sacred," and "profane."

Sympathy for the Devil

The temptation to "cross the line," which few in popular music resist and many embrace, lies at the heart of the human condition. Indeed, one of the primary functions of religion has been the managing of this temptation. Consequently, while, strictly speaking, the meaning of the term "transgression" simply refers to the act of "stepping across" a boundary, its core meaning in the West has always been nuanced along Augustinian lines. That is to say, it has tended to suggest trespass, the breaking of some law or code of behavior, an offense against the sacred. In other words, it has been shaped by the Christian understanding of sin, which, Augustine tells us, is to "wilfully transgress the commandment of the Lord."[2] It is this that gives it its "world-marking power", as Heaney puts it. In the West the will to transgress has been understood to be a fundamental bias within the human condition, interpreted theologically in terms of a "fallen" nature: "For all have sinned, and come short of the glory of God." (Romans 3:23); "I do not understand my own actions. For I do not do what I want, but I do the very thing I hate." (Romans 7.15). From the outset, Christian theology has taught us that the human desire to transgress boundaries consistently overrides respect for them. As Walter Brueggemann remarks of Genesis 3:1–7, "the prohibition which seemed a *given* is now scrutinized as though it were not a given but an *option*. The serpent engages in a bit of sociology of law in order to relativize even the rule of God. Theological-ethical talk here is not to serve, but to avoid the claims of God. . . . The givenness of God's rule is no longer the boundary of a safe place. God is now a barrier to be circumvented. . . . The *prohibition* of 2:17 is violated . . . "[3] It is, however, more than this, in that it is not simply that the prohibition becomes optional, but that it too, in the act of identifying something as taboo, thereby invests it with enormous magnetic power. Hence, the cultural force of the story of the Fall and the narrative of sin and redemption, which has shaped Western lifeworlds,[4] is its identification of the charged relationship between taboo and transgression that lies at the heart of human experience.

It is the power of this narrative which provides the backdrop to the Dionysian spirit of popular music: Jim Morrison's hypnotically primal and sensual presence on stage with The Doors; Jimi Hendrix's shamanic moments of brilliance, a "Voodoo Child" knelt over his burning guitar at the 1967 Monterey Pop Festival as if invoking the dark forces of "Wild Thing" (*Jimi Plays Monterey*, 1986); Johnny Rotten's spitting and barking out the declaration that he is "an anti-Christ" ("Anarchy in the UK," *Never Mind the Bollocks, Here's The Sex Pistols*, 1977); Glen Benton's guttural growl, with characteristic satanic venom, "Damned to hell, end my life. . . . Sin, my soul is blessed with fire." ("Sacrifical Suicide," *Deicide*, 1990); Peter Hammill's unnerving articulation of the sinister and the apocalyptic in "Gog Magog (In Bromine Chambers)" (*In Camera*, 1974); the brooding melancholia of This Mortal Coil's *It'll End in Tears* (1984); and the confident eroticism of Madonna or Lady Gaga's performances. Again, the point is that, because the boundary lines inscribed into Western culture were not drawn by secular hands, the will to transgress has sacred weight: sin, hell, the demonic, the Antichrist, the eschatological.

Looking a little closer at the nature of transgression, it is clear that, while it requires the wilful violation or infringement of "the limits set by a commandment or law or convention," it is also, as Chris Jenks notes, "to announce and even laudate the commandment, law or the convention. Transgression is a deeply reflexive act of denial and affirmation."[5] As Michael Taussig has put it, "the barrier crossed by transgression does not so much exist in its own right as erupt into being on account of its being transgressed."[6] In wilfully crossing a line, the line itself is manifested. Again, there is a fundamental relationship between taboo and transgression.

The boundary lines protected by religions and by the cultures they have shaped (and, again, I am thinking here particularly of Christianity and Western culture, although the net could be cast far more widely) serve, not only to structure life, but to dichotomize it, to dissect it into binary oppositions: sacred–profane; pollution–cleanliness; good–evil; sanity–madness; high–low; normal–deviant; saved–damned. Such boundary marking leaves few gray areas. This, in turn, has informed the progress of modernity in the West, which has always involved strategies of exclusion. Much of the dynamism of modernity, as John Jervis has argued, "has derived from the ability to image and denigrate what is set up as contrast, even as this contrast is thereby constituted as *internal* to modernity itself, as an image of its own unacceptable face. In this sense, an understanding of modernity is inseparable from an understanding of its 'other side,' what is expelled as unacceptable or unthinkable, or reduced to inferior status."[7] It is in terms of this perspective, the perspective of the "other side," that we can begin to see the significance of popular music.

Michel Foucault has argued that "at the root of this discourse on God which Western culture has maintained for so long . . . a singular experience is shaped: that of transgression. Perhaps one day it will seem as decisive for our culture, as much a part of its soil, as the experience of contradiction was at an earlier time for dialectical thought."[8] That day has almost certainly arrived. Because the boundaries and constraints within late-modern societies are increasingly fluid and difficult to determine, the analysis of transgression has become an important contemporary preoccupation. Not only does the search for limits, conspicuous in popular music cultures, seem to require a constant trespassing beyond them, but the religious concerns of previous generations regarding "sin" and its post-mortem consequences have all but evaporated. That said, while the doctrines of sin and hell, along with their attendant demonologies, are now little more than interesting texts for popular music's occultural collagists, and while Christianity's laws and codes of behavior are creatively flouted, nevertheless, it is "this discourse on God" which still haunts Western culture, which provides the dynamism and strength driving transgressive creativity. More than that, as we will see, there is a sense in which The Rolling Stones' song "Sympathy for the Devil" (*Beggars Banquet*, 1968) is perceptive in its articulation of the importance of the demonic other for the identification of the good: "the sacred is incomplete without the profane."[9]

Boundaries and social facts

"The story which precedes the commission or acknowledgement of a transgressive act is the constitution of a center, a center that provides for a social structure, and a structure of meaning that is delimited or marked out by boundaries."[10] To help us toward an understanding of the significance of these boundaries and the power of taboo, we begin by considering Émile Durkheim's discussion of "social facts" (*faits sociaux*). While there is much within Durkheim's social thought that is unhelpful, such as the essentialist and evolutionary framework within which he interpreted the "religious life"—typical of late nineteenth and early twentieth century anthropology[11]—judiciously read, his ideas are still enormously helpful for those of us seeking to understand the significance of the sacred in the modern world.[12]

For Durkheim, the discipline of sociology is concerned with the analysis of social facts, by which, broadly speaking, he meant social phenomena and forces. Describing such "facts" as "things,"[13] he argued that they are realities external to the individual, existing independently of an individual's thought about them and predating the individual. That is to say, one is born into a world of social facts, just as much as one is born into a world of physical facts. In this sense, he insisted, sociology is no less a science than psychology or biology. It is the scientific study of "a category of facts with very distinctive characteristics: it consists of ways of acting, thinking, and feeling external to the individual, and endowed with a power of coercion, by reason of which they control him."[14] Hence, while, on the one hand, such facts should not be confused with biological phenomena, on the other hand, neither are they the concern of psychology, in that they are external to the individual consciousness. In summary, "a social fact is every way of acting, fixed or not, capable of exercising on the individual an external constraint; or, again, every way of acting which is general throughout a given society, while at the same time existing in its own right independent of its individual manifestations."[15]

Produced collectively throughout human history, social facts are effectively representations of moral consensus arising from a society's "collective consciousness." They are givens, providing the conditions for thought and action within a community, constraining individuals to perform in established and predictable ways. Indeed, in many cases we may not understand or even be aware of these social forces acting upon us. The laws of a society, the conventions that govern behavior, the systems of signs we use to convey our ideas, the notions that shape our relationships with family and friends, the monetary systems with which we are involved when we purchase a CD or a bottle of wine, all function independently of us. In this sense, whether we like it or not, social facts exert considerable coercive power over our beliefs and behavior.[16] That said, in freely conforming to these forces, we barely feel their power. Like a stick floating in a stream we simply go with the flow. However, to stand still in a stream or to begin to move upstream immediately subjects us to the full force of the current and the weight of the water. What was all but invisible, has, because of our action, become tangible and dangerous. To commit a transgressive act is, effectively, a stand against the current and weight of social facts. This is why, of course, the taboo contains such energy and charge. In the attempt to violate social currents, the pressure can become almost unbearable in the pain that it can cause and the effort that can be required on the part of the transgressor. As Zygmunt Bauman comments, "bitter and painful awakening awaits all those who by ignorance or ill will behave as if 'social facts' were but figments of imagination. We cannot go unpunished through the space they fill, just like we cannot try to pass through a locked door without bruising our heads or knees."[17]

Numerous musicians, in pursuing a path of transgression, some bravely, some recklessly, have felt the full weight of social facts against them. This, we will see, has been central to their construction as icons within a youth culture that feels alienated and disenfranchised. In standing against the flow of social facts, they have resisted the alienating, disenfranchising, and othering hegemonies of modernity. For transgressive subcultures, the popular music icon is an Athanasius *contra mundum,* one who stands against the world and against social forces in the service of what might be perceived as "the sacred"—in this case freedom, autonomy, self-determination. Jim Morrison is an obvious example. From the outset, he made his position conspicuous: "There are no rules, there are no limits," he consistently declared.[18] "I've always been attracted to ideas that were about revolt against authority. When you make your peace with authority, you become an authority. I like ideas about the breaking away or overthrowing of established order. It seems to be the road toward freedom."[19] Unfortunately, he discovered less a road to freedom and more a path of oppression, a path that eventually led to his demise. Society can be ruthless in its protection of social facts, which are, of course, perceived as sacred. Their profanation must, therefore, be resisted. For the protection of society—articulated within religious discourses as obedience to God and the resistance of the demonic—the transgressor must be punished, imprisoned, burned at the stake. Morrison was quickly marked as a troublemaker, hounded by the police, frequently arrested, and demonized in the media.[20] He became a figurehead, recalls Ray Manzarek (co-founder and keyboardist of The Doors): "They were going to stop all of rock 'n' roll by stopping The Doors. As far as Americans were concerned, he was the most dangerous . . . . They called us the Kings of Acid Rock, so there was plenty of hounding. It's always hardest for the groundbreakers. You come against the morality of a country for the first time and the shit's gonna hit the fan, man."[21] This is precisely Durkheim's point. As Morrison bemoaned to *Rolling Stone*, "you can do anything as long as it's in tune with the forces of the universe, nature, society. . . . If, for some reason, you're on a different track from other people, it's going to jangle everybody's sensibilities . . . "[22]

Hence the immediate problem that popular music faces is that social facts are not only norms, in that they are general throughout a human society, but, as such, they are perceived as "good." Consequently, popular music culture is quickly identified as that which is *other than* "good." For Durkheim, because morality needs to be understood in terms of social cohesion, social facts are perceived as good and sacred because they support the collective life, they reflect the collective consciousness, they represent the shared beliefs and moral attitudes of a particular society. To live according to their guidance is to support society and thereby to act morally; to violate them is to act against society and thereby to act immorally. The former represents the sacred, the latter represents the profane. For reasons we will discuss below, as a predominantly transgressive culture, popular music consistently stands over against "the mainstream," thereby attracting accusations of immorality and profanity. Moreover, because, in advanced societies, systems of law formally reflect and support social facts, to act "immorally" can lead to the imposition of legal sanctions, as Jim Morrison discovered. Consequently, again, transgression is not only risky, but serves to separate the transgressor from wider society—there is a formal removal of the profane from the sacred sphere.

From this perspective, an understanding of the nature of the sacred is enormously important to the analysis of popular music and society. For Durkheim, "the sacred is collective, supple forces that can bring anything – any object, person, or gesture – into the category of the sacred. Society as a whole (as opposed to an assortment of disparate individuals) is 'a moral being' that transcends its members even as it resides within them and fashions them."[23] Hence, the articulation of "society" in his work is essentially theological, in that, as indicated above, "society," the source of morality, is the real object to which the word "God" points.[24] This is most clearly developed in his discussion of totemism in "simple societies," for which the totem—understood as a divinity—is in fact the symbolic conception of society: "If the totem is both the symbol of god and of society, are these not one and the same?"[25] More than that, however, as protector of order, "the sacred" can be understood as a conservative force, the Apollonian heart of human social life. This, however, is not the only perspective. Jim Morrison probably would not have shared it. His understanding of the sacred was decidedly more Dionysian and it is this more ecstatic, transgressive understanding that we will need to explore below. However, at this point we are simply excavating the hegemonic notion of the sacred in order to grasp why popular music is periodically othered as profane, as a reckless threat to social order.

As to organized religion, which is so often at the forefront of attacks on popular music, this can only "adequately and inclusively be characterized as ideas and rites oriented toward the setting aside and protection of *sacred* things."[26] Central to the religious perspective is a fundamental sacred–profane polarity. For Durkheim, the sacred is absolutely and qualitatively other than the profane and, to a large extent, religion constitutes those beliefs and actions designed to maintain the boundary between the two.

The impure sacred and liminal antistructure

Now, while this might seem relatively straightforward in terms of the distinct spheres of the sacred and the profane,[27] in actual fact the very term "sacred" introduces a further fascinating complexity—a complexity which opens it up to the Dionysian interpretation we have just noted. The English word "sacred" (like the French *sacré* in Durkheim's work) is derived from the Latin *sacer*, which has a more complex meaning than simply "holy" or "consecrated." Unpicking these strands of meaning, which informed Durkheim's thinking, William Pickering identifies three: firstly, "holy, consecrated, as in a holy place, sacred art"; secondly, "inviolable – that which cannot be broken – as in '*mon devoir sacré*' (my bounden duty)"; thirdly, and importantly for this chapter, "damned, cursed, profane, bloody: '*Votre sacré chien*' (your damned dog)." This, of course, is because *sacer*, as well as meaning holy and consecrated, also suggests "accursed or horrible, as something devoted to a divinity for destruction, and hence criminal, impious, wicked, infamous."[28] This complexity, which Durkheim articulates, has led to the development of two distinct traditions in the interpretation of his ideas, one of which is concerned with the "pure sacred" and another which is concerned with the "impure sacred." As Gordon Lynch comments, "the focus on the 'pure' sacred addresses sacred forms *as* cultural structures, exploring not only the content of specific sacred forms, but also the circulation, reproduction, and contestation of these structures through social life. By contrast, the focus on the 'impure' sacred conceives of the sacred in terms of experiences and states that arise precisely through the *suspension* or *transgression* of cultural structures."[29]

The relationship between the right/pure sacred and the left/impure sacred is a complex one for Durkheim, not least because, simply by a change in exterior circumstances, a pure sacred object can become impure without, thereby, becoming profane. For example,

> the victim immolated in expiatory sacrifices is laden with impurity, since it has been heaped with sins that must be redeemed. Yet once it has been slaughtered, its flesh and blood are put to the most pious uses. . . . Therefore, the pure and the impure are not two separate genera but two varieties of the same genus that includes all sacred things. . . . And not only is there no discontinuity between the two forms, but the same object can pass from one to the other without changing its nature. The pure can be made impure, and vice versa . . . [The] pure can contaminate just as the impure sometimes serves to sanctify.[30]

This then is the intriguingly ambiguous nature of the sacred—the pure can contaminate and the impure can sanctify. That the impure can communicate the sacred is enormously interesting and socially significant. Again, it is this insight that opens up the Dionysian world of popular music to the study of the sacred.

Apollonian prohibition, which separates the domains of the sacred and the profane, is actively, even aggressively, transgressed in the Dionysian cultures of popular music. There is an overthrowing of convention, a challenging of taboo, and a disruption of order in creative acts of transgression. The Stooges' *Raw Power* (1973), The Sex Pistols' *Never Mind the Bollocks, Here's The Sex Pistols* (1977), The Dead Kennedys' *Fresh Fruit for Rotting Vegetables* (1980), The Cramps' *Songs the Lord Taught Us* (1980), Venom's *Welcome to Hell* (1981), Death's *Scream Bloody Gore* (1987), Cannibal Corpse's *Butchered at Birth* (1991), Madonna's *Erotica* (1992), Slayer's *God Hates Us All* (2001), Demdike Stare's *Forest of Evil* (2010) and so on all play with alternative discourses to those provided by hegemonic culture. Moreover, concerning the use of sound, as Paul Hegarty has discussed in his history of noise, the uses of which provide a potent medium for transgressive discourses, "noise is a negativity (it can never be positively, definitively and timelessly located), a resistance, but also defined by what society resists."[31] Indeed, I write this following an evening's reflection immersed in the continuous, bass-heavy, floor-shaking, surround sound, black metal thunder of a Sunn O))) concert. Following the dark ritual, I walked onto the streets of Manchester, my hearing impaired, with a sense of what I think was awe. In the Dionysian subversion of the Apollonian and the violent resistance to quotidian order, I experienced something profound. To be drawn out of everyday life and immersed in continuous, bone-shatteringly loud, dense, sonic dissonance for two hours evokes a sense of both unease and "mystical" detachment from the conditioning rationality of modernity. As we will see, the ability of popular music to do this has significance in terms of our experience of the sacred/profane.

From gentle pop to noise music, from the implicit rejection of received Christian morality to the explicit fascination with the satanic, and from a flirtation with sex and violence to pornography and explicit misanthropy, popular music has, perhaps more than any other art form, challenged taboos.[32] While that is to state little more than the obvious, the key question is, how are we able to understand the exceeding of constraint and the transgression of taboo as sacred? Studies of transgression in recent years, from Foucault's work to the more recent analyses of Peter Stallybrass, Allon White and Chris Jenks, have found Georges Bataille's insights concerning the impure sacred provocative and inspiring. As well as being a follower of Durkheim's nephew and protégé, Marcel Mauss, Bataille became interested in the avant-garde and surrealism.[33] These interests, along with a brief early flirtation with Roman Catholicism, stimulated a fascination with the nature of the sacred. Early in 1937, with Roger Caillois, he formed the short-lived neo-Durkheimian group, the *Collège de Sociologie*, "a transgressive, subversive group of marginal adepts who attempted to recreate and reinvoke the power of the sacred and of the mythic as effervescent, quasi-religious elements outside the official political arena."[34] Needless to say, like the periodic demonization of popular music culture, Bataille's group "attracted a wild and sometimes dark reputation for its interest in the extreme faces of such collective effervescence and experience of the sacred. There was even a rumor circulating among some of those close to the group that they intended at one point to carry out a human sacrifice."[35] This interest in extremity was the result of a deconstruction of the older structuralist binaries of the sacred and the profane. Rethinking the meaning of *sacer* as not simply holy and consecrated, but also as "accursed or horrible . . . criminal, impious, wicked, infamous,"[36] Bataille pursued an investigation into what he referred to as "the accursed share."[37] He was interested in the analysis of extreme states associated with the profane, such as experiences of nausea, sickness, pain, and anguish. They concerned him, as Fred Botting and Scott Wilson comment, "precisely to the degree that they are uncontrollable, in so far as they shatter the composed rationality of the isolated individual." It is these that constitute "the sacred" for Bataille. "That which is revolting, shocking, that which disarms predictable patterns of thinking and feeling, that which lies at the unhallowed extremes and unavowed interstices of social, philosophical or theoretical frameworks, are the objects of Bataille's fascination. Encounters with horror, violent disgust, that miraculously transform into experiences of laughter, intoxication, ecstasy, constitute, for Bataille, inner experiences that overwhelm any sense of the distinction between interiority and exteriority."[38] Hence, these "inner experiences" might be understood as powerfully mystical—experiences in which there is a going beyond or outside of oneself: "states of ecstasy, of rapture, at least of mediated emotion . . . an experience laid bare, free of ties . . ."[39]

But if the sacred is located in the realm of the excessive and the destructive, where is the site of the profane? As with Durkheim, the profane, for Bataille, is *other* than the sacred. That is to say, the realm of the profane is the everyday world of work, of regulation, of constraint: "the profane world is the world of taboos" and the "sacred world depends on limited acts of transgression."[40] The sacred breaks into the profane and disturbs it. It can lift an individual out of the sphere of the profane in an experience of mystical intensity. Clearly, as Bataille was aware, this approach to the sacred is a difficult one, in that the concept simultaneously has two contradictory meanings. For Bataille, this meant that "whatever is the subject of a prohibition is basically sacred." He continues:

> The taboo gives a negative definition of the sacred object and inspires us with awe on the religious plane. Carried to extremes that feeling becomes one of devotion and adoration. The gods who incarnate this sacred essence put fear into the hearts of those who reverence them, but men do reverence them nonetheless. Men are swayed by two simultaneous emotions: they are driven away by terror and drawn by an awed fascination. Taboo and transgression reflect these two contradictory urges. The taboo would forbid the transgression, but the fascination compels it. Taboos and the divine are opposed to each other in one sense only, for the sacred aspect of the taboo is what draws men towards it and transfigures the original interdiction. The often intertwined themes of mythology spring from these factors.[41]

Again, the sacred is experienced in transgressing that which is prohibited. Taboo is, therefore, charged with sacred energy. God, moreover, perhaps counterintuitively, can be understood as both sacred and profane. On the one hand, deity is the profane manifestation of the rational, the ordered, and the self-disciplined aspects of society, the protector of the boundaries of the workaday world; on the other hand, deity, as the lawgiver, is invested with the all the power of taboo and as such is the incarnation of the pure sacred. The profane is the sphere of those homological virtues of the workaday world that enable societies to function at all—justice, decency, respect, stability—all of which are threatened by the Dionysian excess and power of the impure sacred. As Bataille says, this is not easy to hold in our heads, particularly when we are used to thinking in terms of the pure sacred, for which such eruptions of the impure sacred are understood as profane.

The point for us to note, however, is that, viewed from this angle, the significance of popular music begins to come into focus. Arresting moments of transgression and excess, such as those in industrial music and extreme metal, begin to glow with the aura of the sacred. In these all too human acts of creativity, amateur and crass though some may be, something rather important is taking place. A good example of this is the work of Genesis P-Orridge, whose performance art collective, COUM Transmissions, aroused the ire of the Conservative government and the right wing press in the 1970s. Typical were the comments of the British Conservative politician Nicholas Fairbairn, who, in 1976, declared in the *Daily Mail* that "these people are the wreckers of civilization."[42] One would have to search diligently for a more explicit declaration of the profane threat to the sacred than that! In public performances involving blood, excrement, sex, nudity and the treatment of subjects such as prostitution, COUM transgressed core taboos. But, in the very act of transgressing a taboo, in their threats to civilization, the sacred was illuminated. Hence, there is a sense in which the response of the pioneering DJ John Peel was (not untypically) perceptive in this respect: "with their performances designed to perplex and involve the audience in something other than traditional responses, some might say that Genesis and COUM were madmen, but constant exposure to mankind forces me to believe that we need more madmen like them."[43] Bataille would have agreed. This is the point. "My entire life," P-Orridge tells us, "has been about goading, prodding, and exposing the pus-filled underbelly of the established social status quo."[44] If, as Bataille and Foucault have argued, the interest in transgression emerged as a response to forces associated with modernity and the apparent loss of the sacred in modern industrial societies, then, counterintuitive though it may seem, P-Orridge is a good example of a conspicuously explicit attempt to rediscover the sacred. Indeed, there are some artists, such as Soft Cell's Marc Almond, who have explicitly drawn inspiration from Bataille in their quest to excavate the sacred through an exploration and celebration of excess (*Violent Silence*, 1986).[45]

This highlights the importance of the theoretical trajectory we have been outlining. While attention to sacred forms as normative and to the profane as a threat to those forms can be helpful in the study of popular music, the analysis of its significance in terms of the "impure sacred" and the fierce logic of transgression and taboo is particularly promising. Nevertheless, whether we follow the tradition of the pure sacred or the impure sacred, the binary of the sacred and the profane cannot but be central to the analysis of popular music and society. As Jeffrey Alexander comments:

> In semiotic terms, evil is the necessary contrast for 'good.' In moral terms, exploring heinous evil is the only way to understand and experience the pure and the upright. In terms of narrative dynamics, only by creating antiheroes can we implot the dramatic tension between the protagonist and the antagonist that is transformed by *Bildung* or resolved catharsis. In ritual terms, it is only the crystallization of evil, with all its stigmatization and polluting potential, that makes rites of purification culturally necessary and sociologically possible. Religiously, the sacred is incomplete without

the profane, the promise of salvation meaningless without the threat of damnation . . . [For] every value there is an equal and opposite antivalue, for every norm an antinorm. For every effort to institutionalize comforting and inspiring images of the socially good and right, there is an interlinked and equally determined effort to construct social evil in a horrendous, frightening, and equally realistic way.[46]

Similarly, in a particularly evocative passage, Bataille points out that, while "Evil seems to be understandable," it is only so "to the extent to which Good is the key to it. If the luminous intensity of Good did not give the night of Evil its blackness, Evil would lose its appeal. This is a difficult point to understand. Something flinches in him who faces up to it. And yet we know that the strongest effects on the senses are caused by contrasts."[47] Again, popular music proves to be a particularly important site for such analysis.

Also helpful to understanding the significance of the impure sacred in popular music is Victor Turner's theorising of liminality and *communitas*. Following Henri Junod and particularly Arnold van Gennep, Turner developed a theory of the ritual process as a movement from structure to antistructure and then back again to structure. Central to this process are the existentially meaningful moments of antistructure, which he described in terms of liminality, at the core of which is transgression—the traversing of boundaries, the crossing of "thresholds" (*limen*).[48] It shouldn't take a great leap of the imagination to see how this might relate to our study of popular music and the sacred.

"The attributes of liminality or of liminal *personae* ('threshold people') are necessarily ambiguous," notes Turner, in that

> this condition and these persons elude or slip through the network of classifications that normally locate states and positions in cultural space. Liminal entities are neither here nor there; they are betwixt and between the positions assigned and arrayed by law, custom, convention, and ceremonial. As such, their ambiguous and indeterminate attributes are expressed by a rich variety of symbols in many societies that ritualize social and cultural transitions. Thus, liminality is frequently likened to death, to being in the womb, to invisibility, to darkness, to bisexuality, to the wilderness, and to an eclipse of the sun or moon.[49]

Liminality identifies a temporary disorienting period of reflection during which a community experiences a form of "acceptable disorder" when conventional structures are suspended and questioned; everyday values and behaviors are challenged; transgression is not merely tolerated, but celebrated. Consequently, while, on the one hand, this is an opportunity for a community to reevaluate itself, to reflect upon its structure, to define what is and what is not sacred to it, on the other hand, it constitutes a transient but discombobulating threat to social order. Whether one examines the tribal rituals of the Ndembu in northwestern Zambia or Jack Kerouac's largely autobiographical Dionysian text, *On the Road*,[50] Turner argued that the *limen* is a universally significant period during which, so to speak, one slips through the looking glass into a "realm of pure possibility": "in this gap between ordered worlds almost anything may happen. In this interim of 'liminality,' the possibility exists of standing aside not only from one's own social position, but from all social positions and of formulating a potentially unlimited series of alternative social arrangements."[51] As John Peel said of P-Orridge, his exploration of "other than traditional responses" provided a space for important reflection about how we want to live and who we want to be. Indeed, John Peel's programme itself was an important disseminator of "other than traditional responses." It was on his show, on November 19, 1976, that Johnny Rotten first snarled out "Anarchy in the UK." As Peel's wife commented, "the BBC were refusing to accommodate it in its daytime schedules, a situation that was repeated the following May when John played 'God Save the Queen,' which had been disparaged by the BBC for displaying 'gross bad taste.' "[52] Over the many years he broadcasted, right up to his untimely death in 2004, many eager young minds were introduced to "other than traditional responses." The point, however, is that through disorder and the inhabiting of subjunctive worlds, the very possibility of openness and change emerges. Moments of ecstasy, transgression and creativity ignite passion and stimulate vitality through a temporary release from social and cultural structures that might otherwise become dry and oppressive.

While the threat of collapse into destructive individualism, which is so unsettling for societies, is always present, in actual fact quite the opposite is usually the case. That is to say, an important byproduct of liminality is the erosion of everyday differences between liminal *personae*—differences such as social class. That is to say, there is a subversion of hierarchy that leads to a sense of equality and common humanity. This Turner refers to as *communitas*. Furthermore, liminality has a wider significance. Because all societies are in process, open-ended, rather than fixed and stable, their development is dependent upon their reflexive potential, which is, in turn, stimulated by moments of transgression. In other words, boundary crossing encourages self-reflection on values, on what a society considers important, on what it identifies as sacred and profane. Hence, certain moments, such as those witnessed during the 1960s, have led to important and decisive change.[53] (We will unpack these ideas in more detail below.)

Diabolus in musica and the return to chaos

Thinking about popular music a little more closely in relation to what Bataille referred to as the "heterological,"[54] that which is "other"[55] or "impure," while this is abundantly evident in the lyrics, videos, and cover art in popular music, as well as the reported lifestyles and recreational interests of many popular musicians, there is also an important sense in which the sonic environment itself can produce transgressive and subversive affective space. From the use of distortion and dissonance in genres such as gabber, noise, and black metal, to sampled vocal sounds produced by pain or sexual arousal,[56] sonic environments are created which communicate transgression. Drawing the listener into a particular affective space, nonverbal sounds encourage critical reflection about, as Turner puts it, "a potentially unlimited series of alternative social arrangements."[57] For example, at its most obvious, Serge Gainsbourg's 1969 single, recorded with his lover Jane Birkin, "Je t'aime . . . moi non plus" (available on *Jane Birkin, Serge Gainsbourg*, 1968), included simulated sounds of female orgasm. At a more abstract level, the use of noise and dissonance by a musician such as Merzbow (e.g., *Merzbient*, 2010),[58] or the violent musical segues from the traditionally melodic to the brutally frenetic by artists such as Venetian Snares (e.g., *Rossz Csillag Alatt Született*, 2005; *Detrimentalist*, 2008), and the various projects of Richard James (e.g., *Caustic Window*, 1995), provide what Caillois referred to as a "paroxysmic eruption of excess," a sonic invasion of dissonance into the listeners' everyday ordered world. Viewed mythically, this transgression, this shift into distortion amounts to a Dionysian regression into chaos. It represents an inversion of the mythic rationale informing creation narratives and, as such, Christian theological teleology: "in the ancient Near East, as to a certain extent today, the ordered world was constantly threatened by images of chaos. In ancient times, this chaos was the primordial soup out of which order emerged and to which life was under constant threat of returning."[59] It is this threat of a return to chaos that some popular music articulates particularly well. As such it can be understood as having a sacred function, in that, on the one hand, it engenders a yearning for order and, on the other hand, in taking us back to chaos, noise opens up the possibility for recreation. Again, this understanding of the significance of chaos has been cogently developed by Caillois in his analysis of the festival, which he understood to be central to society's capacity to withstand and integrate transgression, disorder, the unconscious, the fantastic, the demonic and the monstrous. As I will argue of popular music, the festival constitutes a cathartic, paroxysmic eruption of collective excess.[60] Read as myth, it is "chaos rediscovered and newly created." It recalls "the time of creative license, preceding and engendering order, form, and taboo (the three notions are related and, together, are the opposite of chaos)."[61]

A good example of the sacred force of sonic chaos is the use of "the Devil's interval," a musical interval that spans three whole tones, such as the diminished fifth, which was anathematized by the medieval Church as the *diabolus in musica*. Consequently, it has since contributed significantly to the liminal discourses of extreme metal, some believing that it was banned because it was used to invoke Satan or, relatedly, to arouse sexual feelings in those who heard it. Again, the power of the sacred invested in the taboo is conspicuous, illuminated in its transgression. That is to say, for those who recognize the force of the taboo, the playing of the Devil's interval is not simply discordant, but rather a deeply profane/sacred moment. This, of course, accounts for the vital relationship between a simple musical interval and the demonic. As Derek Scott comments, "the tritone has long represented the Devil in music by negating a sense of modal or tonal stability. Originally, it acquired the name of *diabolus in musica* because of its disruptive effect on the concordant fourths and fifths of Western European medieval music: the interval B to F needed to be 'corrected' by flattening the B or sharpening the F."[62] In theological terms, because in medieval musicology dissonance was a manifestation of the disruption of order, it was thereby a subversion of the will of the Creator and, as such, evidence of the demonic. Hence, the treatises and sets of rules that forbade the use of the interval on musical grounds also provided a theological rationale for the ban. Since then, the *diabolus in musica* has enjoyed great popularity, particularly among composers during the nineteenth century who built Romantic notions of the demonic around the interval.[63] Wagner used it to great effect in *Götterdämmerung* and it has since been used in popular music from Robert Johnson through contemporary heavy metal to reference the satanic (e.g., Slayer, *Diabolus in Musica*, 1998). However, it is no coincidence, of course, that, in tracing the roots of modern Western popular music, we find ourselves surrounded by concepts drawn from Christian demonology.[64] In the liminal cultures of popular music, in the chaotic upside-down worlds of the rejected other, in these spheres of transgression, there is an embracing of the profane. This is particularly conspicuous in the mythologies of jazz and blues, the apotheosis of which is arguably the spectral figure of Robert Johnson, who, as well as being transgressive in almost every area of his life, is said to have met the Devil at the crossroads of highways 61 and 49 outside Clarksdale, Mississippi, entered into a Faustian pact, and duly received his prodigious musical abilities. A mythology originally related by fellow bluesman Son House and then spread by Alan Lomax, informed by Afro-Christian folk occulture, it created a blues super-antihero—which, in continuing to retain significant mythic power, is still woven into the transgressive discourses of rock.[65] It was not simply that, as Jon Michael Spencer has commented, "the black blues singer was traditionally viewed by the constituency of the 'overculture' (the culture of white dominance) as a 'bad nigger,' "[66] but that this othering was embraced and mythologised by an oppressed black community. It had a sacred significance. *Communitas* coalesced around the elusive, Romantic-demonic figure of the bluesman. As such he accrued enormous mythic power. Stackolee, for example, "probably the most notorious of the black badmen (because of his womanizing, gambling, and homicide), was said to have been born with supernatural powers that were enhanced when he later sold his soul."[67] The closer his relationship with the profane, the greater his sacred significance.

It was not unusual, of course, for bluesmen to contribute to their own mythic status. As one of Johnson's songs claims, he was constantly aware of the close presence of a "hellhound" ("Hellhound on my Trail," *The Complete Recordings*,

1990). Likewise, Peetie Wheatstraw referred to himself as "the Devil's Son-in-law" and the "High Sheriff of Hell."[68] Such mythic appellations, however, need to be understood carefully, in that we are not quite in the dualistic realm of popular Christian demonology, but more likely in the presence of one of the Yoruba *orisha*, Esu-Elegbara/Esu, or Legba, a similar deity of the neighbouring Fon in Benin. It is this deity, "Papa Legba," which probably best personified the blues and who has since, like the bluesmen, become something of a celebrity in popular music culture—e.g., The Talking Heads, "Papa Legba" (*True Stories*, 1986); Elton John, "Hey, Papa Legba" (released as the B-side of "Blue Eyes," 1982); Malcolm McLaren, "Legba" (*Duck Rock*, 1990); Sun God, "Legba" (*Sun God*, 1995). Hence, rather than the biblical Satan, it is almost certainly he whom Robert Johnson imagined at the crossroads, since Legba—the god of communication, the interpreter of the gods, responsible for patrolling the boundary between deity and humanity—is known as "the god of the crossroads," the gateway god. That bluesmen often referred to him as "the Devil" is not difficult to understand. As Spencer says, "just as early Christian missionaries to the Fon taught their converts that Legba was Satan, so did the semi-dualism of Christianity, imposed upon the holistic cosmology of the Africans brought to America as captives, force Legba . . . into a satanic role."[69] The interesting point, however, is that Legba—who embodies many characteristics typical of the trickster—such as deceit, lawlessness, sexual promiscuity, and frivolity—was introduced specifically because he manifests the bipolar nature of the sacred: pure and impure. Not only is he "an emulative model of heroic action that the blues person embodied," but he is "both malevolent and benevolent, disruptive and reconciliatory, profane and sacred."[70] He is, in other words, a threshold deity, a metaphysical manifestation of liminality. Likewise, bluesmen manifested these liminal, trickster qualities. They too were threshold people, Promethean beings, tricksters who played with divine fire, standing between Legba and the listener, creating music that was suspected of being not entirely human, "devil songs," as the Church would call them.[71] As such they represented a direct challenge to the taboos of the dominant social order. This, in turn, meant that they were simultaneously sinful and salvific, "prophets and visionaries of the black poor."[72] In addressing tangible social evils that were the everyday experience of many African-Americans, they contributed to the construction of a *communitas* of the oppressed. From a similar perspective, the black theologian James Cone made much of this sacred/profane function in the blues in his 1972 book *The Spirituals and the Blues*. The blues, he argues, represents "a stubborn refusal to go beyond the existential problem and substitute otherworldly answers." He continues, "it is not that the blues reject God; rather they *ignore* God by embracing the joys and sorrows of life."[73] This is what might be understood as a sacred secular response to existence. Again, in a discussion suggesting very clearly the construction of blues *communitas* and the significance of "the sacred," he argues that while the blues reject an 'objective transcendence', they do not reject 'historical transcendence.' In so far as the blues affirm the somebodiness of black people, they are transcendent reflections on black humanity. Through the sheer power of melody and rhythm of song, black people transcended historical restrictions and affirmed a meaning for their lives not made with hands. They refused to accept white rules and regulations as the definition of their community. To be sure, they cried, 'I got the blues an' can't keep from cryin.'' They were hurt, and they were bruised. But through the sharing of their troubles with each other, black people were able to move to another level of human existence and be, in spite of the nonbeing of the white community.[74]

The blues affirmed black humanity in the teeth of a brutal racism that denied their humanity. The preacher and former bluesman Rubin Lacy touches on this prophetic function of the blues: "Sometimes I preach now and I get up and tell the people now that . . . I used to be a famous blues singer and I told more truth in my blues that the average person tells in his church songs. . . . The blues is just more truer than a whole lot of church songs that people sing."[75] Hence, although it has been argued by some theorists that "for the most part the blues is strictly secular in content,"[76] and that it constitutes "a secular [response] to the conditions of slavery in the USA,"[77] this is to misunderstand the nature of the sacred and the early black communities in which the blues emerged. "Devil music" provided a sacred lens through which a community could assess its place in the world, unite and resist oppression.

Interestingly, of course, because the power of the blues was rooted in transgression, the narrow moralism of institutional religion, the denunciations of some preachers on Sunday morning against the bluesmen, highlighting their demonic taint,[78] were, because of the logic of taboo and transgression, central to that power. The blues would not have had the mythic energy to move and unite that it did have had it not been for its profanation. It was this that shaped the blues as a center of sacred gravity around which *communitas* formed. Vivid descriptions of love, sex, and violence in the blues revealed the sacred in their redemptive capacity to bind the oppressed together through the articulation of truth, through the sharing of experience, through reflection on a common existence. In this sense, blues compositions were, as Cone argued, secular spirituals.

Prohibition and profanation

The Edwardian folk elitist Cecil Sharp, we have seen, distinguished between music that purified and music that vulgarized.[79] This concurred with the principal contours of the culture and civilization tradition. As Matthew Arnold had argued, the preoccupations of the masses could only lead to anarchy, whereas what he understood to be "culture" ("high culture") lifted humanity out of the squalor of a sinful world. This type of thinking can be viewed through a Durkheimian lens, in that "anarchy," as Arnold defined it, runs counter to the "moral, social, and beneficent character" of society itself.[80] It profanes the sacred. Consequently, when Arnold spoke of those who were "cultivated" and "cultured," he referred not just to those who were educated and well versed in the arts, but also to those he considered to be morally superior. The cultured, in other words, support social cohesion and manifest the sacred. Popular culture, on the other hand, is a profane threat to social cohesion and key sacred forms. Consequently, it needed to be regulated, if not prohibited. Censorship is a popular weapon in the armory of those who would protect sacred forms.[81]

A good example of this type of concern and the attempt to censor popular music is the Parents' Music Resource Center (PMRC).[82] Founded in 1985 by Tipper Gore, following her outrage at the discovery of her daughter listening to Prince's sexually explicit song "Darling Nikki" (*Purple Rain*, 1984), the PMRC successfully campaigned for the use of the Parental Advisory Label—what became known as the "Tipper Sticker."[83] However, while, on the one hand, this is a good example of an attempt to resist profanation, on the other hand, it also serves to highlight the significance of transgression. That is to say, if we think of the sacred in terms of that which individuals collectively experience as absolute, as a non-contingent reality, as that which is normative, oganizing the meanings and conduct of social life, then Gore and the PMRC are protecting a specific instance of the sacred—a "sacred form." In this case, the sacred form is childhood innocence. As Lynch comments, understood as absolute, normative realities, "sacred forms are so obvious as to become an often assumed part of people's social worlds. They operate as more fundamental assumptions than what we might explicitly describe as 'good.'"[84] This describes well the workaday world of regulation and taboo, the carefully managed everyday life, which resists change, disturbance, transgression. This is evident in Eric Nuzum's overview of music censorship:

> Throughout the history of rock, censors haven't really cared about Chuck Berry, Ozzy Osbourne or 2 Live Crew. What they *have* cared about is what these artists represent: change. The struggles associated with music censorship are battles between . . . truth and assumptions. Passion overrides logic. In their ardent beliefs in concepts like patriotism, the innocence of childhood, the sanctity of church and family, people will jettison truth to satisfy their need to feel that everything will remain the same. . . . To them, rock music threatens what they hold dearest. It expresses feelings they either don't understand or forgot about long ago; it serves as a stimulus for their children to act differently than they do . . . [85]

This passage identifies a number of sacred forms, central to which, in the case of popular music, is (as we'll discuss in the final chapter) the protection of children from harm, from moral pollution, from profanity. The notion of the innocence of childhood establishes a normative claim over social life. Consequently, the deliberate harming or corruption of children, as Jenks says, "strikes at the most vulnerable part of our collective affects."[86] In the case of Gore, it was Prince's profane text and her daughter's consumption of that text that led to the identification of the threat posed by popular music to the sacred. The founding of the PMRC and the introduction of the Parental Advisory Label highlights the Durkheimian point that the profane provides a lens through which to clearly see the sacred.

Unfortunately for the PMRC, the identification of sites of the profane had the opposite effect to what they intended, largely because they failed to understand the significance of transgression within the liminal cultures of popular music. The Parental Advisory Label actually increased the threat of transgression. Indeed, within liminal *communitas*, the greater the taboo, the stronger the drive to transgress and the more significant the transgression is felt to be. It functions as an indicator of authenticity, in that it highlights what has been explicitly rejected by mainstream society. As Scott Wilson comments, "faced with the choice of a marked or unmarked CD, most children interested in rap or metal will unquestionably opt for the 'harder' record authenticated by Tipper's sticker."[87] Indeed, not only were some fans rather disappointed if a favorite artist's album was not considered worthy of a Parental Advisory Label, but it wasn't long before the design of the label was appearing on T-shirts and posters. Because it was an indicator of taboo and, therefore, a conductor of a transgressive charge, it accrued subcultural capital—it was "cool"! Again, the PMRC failed to grasp that, the act of prohibition functions as "an imperative that directs consumer choice."[88] And, of course (as we'll discuss in Chapter 5), there are few more effective such imperatives than the attacks of those who consider themselves to be society's moral guardians—protectors of the sacred. Hence, for example, when fundamentalist Christian campaigners such as Bob Larson insist that "it is possible that any person who has danced for substantial lengths of time to rock music may have come under the influence of demons,"[89] or that "Satan is attempting to capture the souls of our youth through rock and roll music,"[90] the response is almost always one of valuing the music more. When the weight of religious denunciation is attached to taboo, when the full force of the sacred is explicitly invested in a prohibition, the desire to transgress is increased significantly. The transgression becomes more meaningful. This is one of the reasons why musicians are keen to sample hostile denunciations of popular music or other examples of right-wing Christian rhetoric in their compositions. Like the Tipper sticker, it invests the music with transgressive charge. Indeed, Front 242's "Angst" (*Official Version*, 1987) is simply a recording of a fundamentalist preacher without any music accompanying it. Without a grasp of the significance of transgression in liminal *communitas* this makes little sense. Again, one of the most important and influential records of the post-punk period, *My Life in the Bush of Ghosts* (1981) by Brian Eno and David Byrne, included, on the track "Help Me Somebody," sampled rhetoric from a recorded sermon by the fundamentalist preacher Rev. Paul Morton. The affective force of the track, like "The Jezebel Spirit" from the same album, which includes a recording of an exorcism, is almost tangible. Because popular music culture is fundamentally transgressive, that which is damned is cherished and that which is sacred is profaned.

Industrial transgression

Since the late-1970s, the liminal beings of the industrial scene have transformed their sense of alienation into, as David Keenan puts it, "powerful interrogations of systems of control, be they aesthetic, cultural or political."[91] British bands such as Cabaret Voltaire, Clock DVA, Cassandra Complex, Coil, Nurse With Wound, Test Department, Throbbing Gristle, Psychic TV, and Whitehouse; US bands such as Nine Inch Nails, Swans, and Velvet Acid Christ; Canadian bands such as Skinny Puppy and Front Line Assembly; and Australia bands, such as SPK, as well as a number of bands from continental Europe, notably Einstürzende Neubauten and :Wumpscut: (Germany), Front 242 (Belgium), and Laibach (Slovenia), have consistently focused on the shadow side of modernity. As Hegarty points out, like punk, industrial was "suspicious of musicality, but its hatred of contemporary art and society went deeper, its critique harsher as a result. Like Dada, it offers an anti-aesthetic, using the tools of art to undo art. Unlike punk, the answer was not change, but awareness of the fetid state of capitalist society. . . . Like Derrida, industrial music knows there is no outside to escape to that is not already consumed by the inside."[92] Hence, perhaps unsurprisingly, as Keenan comments, their questioning "led them down some decidedly bizarre roads, and one of the most useful side products of industrial culture is the vast archives of esoterica and arcane knowledge its participants amassed over the years."[93] They embraced their role as the damned in society and enthusiastically excavated what the modern world had rejected—including occult thought, far right political discourse and sadistic criminality.

Musically, their work was equally transgressive. Einstürzende Neubauten and Test Department, for example, along with the use of samples, they created crude instruments out of scrap metal and industrial machinery. They also made much use of what were to become known as samples. Indeed, to some extent, there are similarities between industrial music and *musique concrète*, in that the latter had, as Hegarty comments, developed Futurist ideas of synthetic sonic architecture and sampled found sounds. However, the politeness of *musique concrète* meant, as Hegarty says, "academization, a newly professionalized subgenre of official programme music made by composers."[94] Industrial music, on the other hand, brought together elements from many avant-gardes, many noise moments, to structure and de-structure a new noise. This noise would be made of non-musicianship, non-musicality, a refusal of all norms (in theory) in the interest of pushing experience as far as possible. In this, it shows its connection to art practice, art schools, performance art. This music would not 'change your ideas through art,' but threaten you, expose your limits, so that even if as a listener you did not agree with the new vision, it will still have been inflicted on you.[95]

Arguably the cardinal pioneer within the industrial scene, and certainly one of its most interesting and transgressive figures, is Genesis P-Orridge. Not only has he spent much of his career excavating the mechanisms of social control, but he has been conspicuous in the exploration of esoteric thought. Drawing inspiration from Paganism, which he considers "a form of anti-establishment activity . . . ,"[96] he has conspicuously followed in the footsteps of two icons of Western transgression, Aleister Crowley and William S. Burroughs. Just as Crowley found in sexual magic "the most intense experience of transgression, the overstepping of conventional taboos, as a means to unleash an ecstatic, liberating power,"[97] so P-Orridge found in the confluence of sex, the occult, drugs, and popular music a transformative transgressive energy. His various projects, notably the performance art project COUM Transmissions, the bands Throbbing Gristle, Psychic TV and Splinter Test, the spoken word project Thee Majesty, and the occult network Thee Temple ov Psychick Youth, constitute particular articulations of an idiosyncratic form of experimental sonic and visual transgressive art. A confluence of pornography, violence, death, degradation, noise, and esotericism, his work is rarely less than confrontational. Again, as Hegarty comments of Throbbing Gristle's music, it offered "a thoroughgoing critique or even attack on conventional, modern, Christian, artistic, moral, capitalist thought and living," much of which could be understood in terms of "transgression and perversion."[98] While, of course, many have understood such work in terms of the delight gained from extreme behavior and the offence caused by the provocative challenging of taboos—which, of course, it is—P-Orridge has always claimed to articulate "a deeply rooted desire to expose and challenge the hidden mechanisms of social control."[99] Again, as John Peel commented, it represented an attempt to elicit "other than traditional responses" from listeners.

Bearing in mind Bauman's comment that "bitter and painful awakening awaits all those who by ignorance or ill will behave as if 'social facts' were but figments of imagination,"[100] it is hardly surprising that P-Orridge has suffered for his art. Threats to the sacred rarely go unpunished by society. In his writing and interviews he regularly expresses concern, even weariness, regarding the social forces pressing in upon him: "People think we're worse than irresponsible, they think we're downright subversive and immoral."[101] Indeed, on several occasions he has faced legal sanction, having found himself at the center of moral panics. According to

Fairbairn, whose vitriol we have already noted, COUM's exhibition at the Institute of Contemporary Arts (ICA) in 1976, entitled *Prostitution*, celebrated "every kind of social evil."[102] Similarly, the right-wing newspapers, *The Sun* and *The Daily Mail*, declared COUM's work to be "antisocial and unhealthy," an attack on British values, and "part of the sickness of an already ailing nation."[103] Identification as profane, a threat to the sacred can lead to—as those suspected of witchcraft in premodern societies discovered[104]—gratuitous othering and, as such, association with almost any degree of evil.[105] Consequently, as has often been the case in the history of popular music—from Elvis to Frankie Goes to Hollywood and from the blues to contemporary extreme metal[106]—P-Orridge has been subject to systematic demonization. The most salient example of this was an episode of *Dispatches*, a television current affairs documentary series broadcast in Britain on Channel 4. Entitled "Beyond Belief" and aired on February 19, 1992, it claimed to expose devil worship and that most profane of acts, the ritual sacrifice of an infant. The accusations were, perhaps needless to say, entirely false. However, the point is that, having identified a threat to the sacred, the media encouraged the public anathematization of P-Orridge by associating him with the manifestation of heinous evil.[107] The result was a classic moral panic,[108] which exerted such pressure on P-Orridge that he felt constrained to leave the UK and settle in the United States. British society had exorcized one of itds demons. It had protected a number of sacred forms by expelling a notorious source of profanation. As Jeffrey Alexander put it, "in ritual terms, it is only the crystallization of evil, with all its stigmatization and polluting potential, that makes rites of purification culturally necessary and sociologically possible. . . . For every effort to institutionalize comforting and inspiring images of the socially good and right, there is an interlinked and equally determined effort to construct social evil in a horrendous, frightening, and equally realistic way."[109]

So profound is such evil felt to be at times, that its pollution extends beyond the immediate agents of transgression to individuals, institutions and forms of culture with which they have been involved. Demons have been loosed and circles of corruption have been formed. For example, as a result of P-Orridge's performance of *Prostitution*, the venue itself was considered profane. Consequently, Arts Council funding to the ICA was significantly reduced and the senior management had to be reorganised following the forced resignation of two of its members, including the Chairman, Robert Loder. Again, when a sense of threat to the sacred becomes significantly heightened, as it does during a moral panic, there is an imperative, as Bernhard Giesen has argued, to "overcome disorder and evil by banning, expelling, or defeating it."[110]

As well as his transgressive performances with COUM Transmissions, P-Orridge's development of what I have called "industrial Paganism"[111] has also been central to the cultural construction of him as a threat to the sacred. Explicitly resisting the sacralized bucolic Paganism of 1960s and 1970s hippie culture (to which we'll return in the next chapter), the ideas articulated in the work of Throbbing Gristle and Psychic TV are urban and decadent. His entrance into the sacred is explicitly profane, being what might be described as Crowleyesque "therapeutic blasphemy."[112] It is confrontational, subversive, experimental, and, to a large extent, dystopian. It is industrial. A good example of this is the album *Heathen Earth* (1980), recorded live before an invited audience,[113] the music of which is challenging, disorienting, and melancholic. Again, while the words on the cover are taken from 1960s California counterculture, they speak not of "flower power," but are rather lifted from a particularly profane moment within that culture. They reflect melancholy, menace and murder. Above a violent image of a dog's skull are the words of Charles Manson: " . . . can the world be as sad as it seems?" The evocation of a dark affective space continues as one opens up the album or flicks through the booklet accompanying the CD. There are unsettling photographs of Peter Christopherson with blood soaked hands leaning over a body, P-Orridge wearing combat paraphernalia standing alone in an inner city setting, and a mound of human skulls being picked at by ravens. This is Throbbing Gristle's heathen earth—dark, violent, decadent, dystopian.

The term "industrial" is important here. The industrial genre, which took its name from the record label P-Orridge founded, "Industrial Records," frequently referenced the industrial use of humans as a resource and particularly the mechanized, rational, impersonal, and sustained mass destruction of human beings, which requires state-administered organization and which is often sanctioned by science and law.[114] Industrial music thus bends our sight toward some of the darkest corners of modernity. This brings us back to the observations of Alexander and Bataille that evil is understandable only to the extent to which good is the key to it. "If the luminous intensity of Good did not give the night of Evil its blackness, Evil would lose its appeal. . . . Something flinches in him who faces up to it. And yet we know that the strongest effects on the senses are caused by contrasts."[115] It is unsurprising, therefore, that the use of contrasts to accentuate the profane is conspicuous in industrial culture. A good example of this is Throbbing Gristle's third album, the inoccuously entitled *20 Jazz Funk Greats* (1979). Firstly, there is very little music on this album than can be described as "jazz funk." Accessible though it is for Throbbing Gristle, it is nevertheless dark, industrial music. Secondly, and more strikingly, the cover is a photograph of the group standing in a rural setting, dressed as respectable, middle-class young adults, smiling, as if about to sit down on the grass and enjoy a picnic of lemonade and sandwiches. In the background a Range Rover is parked, signifying material success. In other words, this is an aspirational photograph signifying a good, wholesome middle-class life in the 1970s. However, there is another text operating here, which fans are alerted to by the title of the second track on the album, "Beachy Head." This is one of England's most notorious suicide spots. "There we were smiling in flowers", recalls P-Orridge, "and everyone says 'how nice' and actually we're smiling where people who are totally in despair commit suicide."[116] The contrast is shocking, forcing us face the angst, brutality, and death which many in our societies experience. "To us, Beachy Head encompassed all our fascinations with double meanings, ambiguity and the melancholy of sprawling suburban angst. . . . Exploring the metaphors of Beachy Head was a logical progression after using the ovens at Auschwitz as a record label logo."[117]

Less ambiguously, the album *Leng Tch'e* (1992) by John Zorn's free jazz, grindcore, broadly industrial Naked City project is explicitly influenced by Battaille's discussions of violence and the sacred in *Tears of Eros* (see also Naked City's *Torture Garden*, 1990; *Grand Guignol*, 1992; *Heretic: Jeux Des Dames Cruelles*, 1992). Analysing society from its underbelly, it subverts the hegemonies of Christianity and neoliberalism. At its most engaging, industrial explores the dark side of what we have learned to think of as the progress of modernity. To illuminate this point, it's worth quoting Omer Bartov's disturbing study of the Holocaust:

> War, slaughter, and genocide, are, of course, as old as human civilization itself. Industrial killing, however, is a much newer phenomenon, not only in that its main precondition was the industrialization of human society, but also in the sense that this process of industrialization came to be associated with progress and improvement, hope and optimism, liberty and democracy, science and the rule of law. Industrial killing was not the dark side of modernity, some aberration of a generally salutary process; rather it was, and is inherent to it, a perpetual of precisely the same energies and ideas, technologies and ideologies that have brought about the 'great transformation' of humanity. But precisely because modernity means to many of us progress and improvement, we cannot easily come to terms with the idea that it also means mass annihilation. We see genocide as a throwback to another, premodern, barbarous past, a perversion, an error, an accident. All the evidence to the contrary, we repeatedly believe that *this* time, in *this* war, it will finally be stamped out and eradicated, never to reappear again. *Yet even this well-meant urge reveals our complicity in modernity's destructive, unrelenting, intolerant nature. We wish to annihilate destruction, to kill war, to eradicate genocide, by the most effective and deadly means at our disposal. And we want to marginalize evil, repress it, push it out of our own time and context, attribute it to everything that we are not, to anything that is foreign to our civilization.*[118]

Whereas Jean Baudrillard had observed that "society as a whole takes on the appearance of a factory,"[119] Throbbing Gristle, far more viscerally, spoke of "death factory society," naming their recording studio "The Death Factory" and producing audiovisual collages about serial killers and genocide. Likewise, those who saw Cabaret Voltaire in the 1980s will recall the film footage of war, acts of violence, industrial societies, and urban deprivation. Crawling through the carnage and dirt of modernity, industrial musicians refuse to ignore the evil in our midst. Hence, industrial art can be read as a brutal reflection of the modern world. It pushes through the sacred fences erected by hegemonic culture, embraces that which has been declared profane, and drinks from wells condemned as polluted. The thin veneer of respectability and order covering Western societies, which is disturbed periodically by incidents of extreme violence and degradation, is deliberately peeled back by industrial musicians. As such, through exposure to explicitly transgressive discourses and sonic environments, the listener is exposed both to the profane and, concurrently, to the sacred. That is to say, having been exposed to the profane by industrial music, it is difficult not to reflect on the sacred, on that which one wants to protect as noncontingent and absolute—although, importantly, one's understanding of that which is noncontingent and absolute may have been significantly refocused.

Finally, as with other transgressive scenes, such as that of extreme metal,[120] industrial music opened Pandora's box, from which a host of artists emerged for whom the freedom to transgress was all but absolute—the greater the extent to which that freedom was exercised the more authentic it was felt to be. Hence, industrial culture came to represent a particularly anarchic and nihilistic interpretation of Crowley's Law of Thelema—"Do what thou wilt shall be the whole of the Law"—the connection with which is made explicit on Psychic TV's debut album, Force the Hand of Chance (1982).[121] It is interesting, therefore, to learn that P-Orridge was concerned about the level of transgression that industrial culture had encouraged: "we'd left a rather unhealthy residue of people and ideas, albeit because these people had chosen to misunderstand what we were saying. It got into this thing of who could shock each other the most, SPK doing videos of dead bodies . . . "[122] Indeed, he recalls that he "instantly totally despised" bands such as Whitehouse, in that they seemed to wallow in degradation. The material of Whitehouse, in particular, focused uncritically and luridly on sexual violence and serial killers (e.g., Psychopathia Sexualis,[123] 1982). "Making a hole for those kind of people to crawl through was quite scary."[124] He wasn't alone. Richard H. Kirk of Cabaret Voltaire had similar concerns.[125] This raises some important questions about the nature of transgression.

There are, again, some obvious parallels here with Bataille's work, in that industrial music was designed to shock, to break listeners out of the conditioning rationality of modernity. Indeed, it can be understood in terms of Bataille's notion of "sovereignty," the predisposition to unconstrained action, which respects no boundaries or codes of behavior. The purpose and significance of this concept is that it functions as "a replacement for and corruption of 'reason.' That sovereignty makes us look at violence, aggression and eroticism in human thought and action enables us to think outside of that all-persuasive human canon of the mild-mannered but wholly calculating rationality that has forged modernity."[126] Consequently, it "ensures a breakdown of hierarchies and a scrambling of the proper, worthy, replicable, true with the dirty, untidy, obscene and peculiar."[127] This has been central to the declared rationale of much early industrial music. However, perhaps inevitably, problems emerged as a result of an uncritical embracing of the profane. In effect, it represented an attempt to reify liminality. As perhaps P-Orridge began to recognise, profanation became *de rigueur*, expected, normalized. All boundaries were removed and, as such, the moment of transgression was made impotent. That is to say, transgression can only ever be a transitory experience, during which a boundary is exposed and a taboo challenged. A *state* of transgression is a contradiction in terms. Transgression requires taboo. To remove taboos through the creation of norms dissolves the possibility of transgression. Hence the problem for 1980s industrial music is that it appeared to want to make the brutal discourses of transgression the norm. In so doing, it became mired in profane banality. Again, this, I suspect, is why P-Orridge became concerned at the "rather unhealthy residue of people and ideas" who, he felt, had "chosen to misunderstand" what industrial music was trying to do. As with Bataille, he wanted to keep taboos in focus, in order to transgress them, rather than removing them altogether—"we are interested in taboos . . . boundaries . . . "[128] It is in the act of violating taboo, says Bataille, that "we feel the anguish of mind without which taboo could not exist: that is the experience of sin. The experience leads to the completed transgression, the successful transgression which, in maintaining the prohibition, maintains it in order to benefit by it."[129]

Nevertheless, regardless of the tensions within industrial culture, its relationship with wider society as the profane other can still be considered significant. Its conception of the sacred in terms of experiences and states that arise precisely through transgression, through the alienation of noise, distortion and explicitly profane discourse, provided a brutal critique of the modern world. It held a mirror up to a society that had rationalized production to the point where humans are resources and death is industrialized.

Death, decay and the grotesque body

What Roland Boer says of Nick Cave's work is true of a number of artists across a range of genres from industrial and punk through goth and extreme metal: "unlike the tendency to compartmentalize death in our (post)modern world, to sequester the elderly into compounds known as 'retirement villages,' to block death through the frenzy of consuming commodified trash, to separate death from life, and for rock singers to favor lust and love, in all its triumphs, frustrations and disappointments, Cave is refreshingly, if at times scandalously, direct."[130] Few liminal beings are anything less than scandalously direct. Like Bataille, they do not evade the pain of our limited existence.[131] One need only acquaint oneself cursorily with the obsessions of grindcore and death metal to realize just how direct they can be.[132] Carcass's *Reek of Putrefaction* (1988) is a particularly salient and ludic example, its track titles providing an indication of the lascivious nature of its devotion to gore: "Genital Grinder," "Regurgitation of Giblets," "Maggot Colony," "Vomited Anal

Tract," "Fermenting Innards," "Excreted Alive," "Foeticide," "Feast on Dismembered Carnage," "Splattered Cavities," "Psychopathologist," "Burnt to a Crisp," "Pungent Excruciation," and so on. The carnivalesque nature of their transgressive discourse, typical of the scene, is evident in the lyrics of their evocatively entitled celebration of body-snatching and cannibalism, "Exhume to Consume" (*Symphonies of Sickness*, 1989): "Ulcerated flesh I munch/ Rotting corpses are my lunch." Such lyricism is typical of liminal discourse, in that, albeit a vivid example, it is simply an embracing of the impure. Hence, at one level, death metal can be understood as the simple working out of liminal identity. As disenfranchised youth, situated beyond "their mundane structural context," they are, to quote Turner's anthropological work, "in a sense 'dead' to the world." This is why, separated from normative cultural structures, liminal culture "has many symbols of death – novices may be classed with spirits or painted black. . . . They are also 'polluting' . . . because they transgress classificatory boundaries. Sometimes they are identified with feces; usually they are allowed to revert to nature by letting their hair and nails grow and their bodies get covered with dust."[133] Because certain physical substances and objects—notably those linked with blood, excrement, and death—signify impurity, and are therefore associated with taboos, liminality explicitly inverts this signification. In this way, liminal cultures are inherently disturbing, contesting hierarchies and challenging social order. Moreover, as we have seen in our discussion of industrial culture, their transgressive discourses cannot but negatively reflect dominant constructions of the sacred and related tabooed behaviors.

At another level, of course, there is something significant in the act of transgression itself. This takes on a very particular form in death metal, in that the affective impact is key. The lyrics, which may or may not make sense, are, arguably, of less importance than the names of the bands and the titles of the records and tracks, since they are deliberately obscured by a particular guttural vocal style known as "death growling." That is to say, the use of this form of bestial vocalization, along with the aggressive power communicated sonically through distorted and downtuned guitars, subverts reflexivity. There is little space for discursive thought and there is not meant to be. The song titles and band names—Autopsy, Cannibal Corpse, Carcass, Death, Defecation Menstruation, Dismember, Dying Fetus, Entombed, Exhumed, Immolation, Massacre, Napalm Death, Obituary, Pestilence, Post Mortem, Suffocation, and so on—are central to the construction of the profane affective spaces created by the brutality of the music and the guttural screams amplified through the microphone. Hearing the lyrics is almost superfluous to the experience. Michelle Phillipov concurs in her recent thoughtful analysis of the genre:

> the pleasures of death metal lyrics center around the aesthetic and affective experiences offered by transgressive forms of representation. As a result, death metal may offer its fans experiences of intensity more like those of graphic horror film viewers than those of politically committed punk or

hip hop fans that are so idealized by progressive critics ... Approaching the
pleasures of death metal as akin to the pleasures of horror highlights the
way that transgressive material can be enjoyed at an emotional remove, not
to be taken too seriously, and not necessarily absorbed as part of the listeners' own politics.[134]

In other words, she argues that "a reflexive anti-reflexive engagement with transgressive imagery may instead be one of the ways in which the music is deliberately
and ideally experienced."[135] This is surely correct. Indeed, bearing this in mind, it is
significant that death metal is essentially a live music genre, in that it needs to be an
extremely loud and immersive experience. The effect, I would argue, is to generate
what Bataille referred to as "inner experiences," atheological moments of mystical
ecstasy. Hence, the end result is not simply one of pleasure, but rather a level of *communitas* which enables identification with the transgression of taboos relating death,
decay and extreme violence. In this way, the experience disarms predictable patterns
of thinking and feeling. (Below, we will explore more fully the relationship between
communitas and violence.)

This brings us back to Nick Cave's work in that in popular music a number of
transgressive perspectives concerned with the provoking of horror and unease—
particularly through reflection on death, decay and the grotesque—have been discussed in terms of contemporary Gothic with which he has been associated. That
said, because contemporary Gothic has been so ubiquitously hybridized, it is somewhat artificial to restrict it to a particular movement, subculture, or genre of music.[136]
It is perhaps better understood as a way of reading culture, rather than as a subcultural phenomenon to be studied—although, of course, it is that as well. Whether
we think of extreme metal, electronica, industrial, Americana, folk, or indeed, early
'80s post-punk, "Gothic" in popular music indicates the construction of particular
affective spaces informed by reflection on a world of sadness, pain, death, and the
dis-ease at the heart of modern life. It is a way of prising open the fissures that run
through the modern world by refusing to respect the boundaries that distinguish
darkness and light, death and life, sickness and health, past and present. As such, it
is a useful way of reading the transgressive and excessive in popular music.

Nevertheless, as a discussion of popular music, we cannot ignore the fact that con-
temporary Gothic has become a particular subcultural focus. Indeed, goth subculture first coalesced around music. Emerging in the early 1980s, it can be traced back
to bands such as Bauhaus, The Birthday Party, Christian Death, The Cure, Danse
Society, Flesh for Lulu, Gene Loves Jezebel, The March Violets, Play Dead, Sex
Gang Children, Sisters of Mercy, Siouxsie and the Banshees, Southern Death Cult,
Theatre of Hate, The Virgin Prunes, and 45 Grave, and to clubs such as particularly
London's Batcave. From the outset, central to much "goth" discourse has been what
can be understood as a neo-Romantic expression of industrial concerns, informed
by ideas drawn from earlier artists and movements, such as the glam-androgyny

of Marc Bolan and David Bowie.[137] Musically, it was a development of post-punk affective spaces evoked by bands such as Joy Division and Crispy Ambulance. (The ludic juxtaposition of two such unlikely words as "crispy" and "ambulance" is, I think, a good example of the carnivalesque subversion of normative discourses.) As Michael Bibby has noted, "through distorted guitars and foregrounded basslines, Joy Division articulated an aural melancholia that has since become central to goth style."[138] This is particularly evident on Bauhaus's genre-defining "Bela Lugosi's Dead" (1979), which, while darkly ethereal, drew heavily on the atmospheric, bass heavy dub techniques developed within reggae and adopted by many post-punk pioneers. Indeed, although a seminal piece of music in the emergence of goth culture, with its playful references to Lugosi and vampirism, musically it was not doing very much more than other singles released in the same year, such as Killing Joke's "Turn to Red" (1979) or Public Image Ltd's "Death Disco" (1979).[139] However, its haunting repetition of "dead, undead," its eerie cover art—the original of which was a still lifted from Robert Wiene's landmark German Expressionist film *Das Cabinet des Dr. Caligari* (1920)—its stripped down, spidery, delicate sound, conspired to shape what was to become a distinctively Gothic affective space. Although evolving during the same period as grindcore and death metal, goth culture was far more thoughtful about its treatment of death, decay and the grotesque, providing "a language and a lexicon through which anxieties both personal and collective can be discussed."[140] As it began to take shape during the 1980s, it increasingly turned its neo-Romantic gaze to industrial's boundary-crossing fascination with the dark recesses of modernity, with ruin, with atrocity, with taboo, and, as such, with constructions of the sacred/profane. While a funereal corner of the foppish "new romantic" dressing-up box was regularly raided in an effort to embody these ideas sartorially,[141] as it progressed into the 1990s, and as its discourse became increasingly influenced by industrial themes, there was a heightened sense that goths had become, as Nick Cave put it, "entwined together in this culture of death" ("Abattoir Blues," *Abattoir Blues/ The Lyre Of Orpheus*, 2004).[142]

Pulling away from the mainstream, hiding from its light, creating a culture that is other, a culture that feeds on the forbidden, goths focussed on death, sacrifice, eroticism, and excess. As such, this culture of the shadows challenged the hegemonic fetishization of health and happiness in Western societies. The Cure's *Pornography* (1982), a claustrophobic study in self-loathing, is a good example of this, as is Nick Cave's collection of songs on *Murder Ballads* (1996), which recounts 66 murders in all, more than a few of which take place in "O'Malley's Bar"—"one of the best instances of a song in which death is inflicted," according to Boer; "... self-absorption, clinical attention to detail, sexual climax, and religion all weave together."[143] Moreover, this perspective is typically, if often unwittingly, informed by recognition of the Christian sin–redemption binary, in that, salvation, if we are to achieve it at all, depends on humanity facing its own depravity. It is here, in the dirt and corruption of the underside of modernity that truth is to be found. Hence again, it is by attending to the profane that the sacred comes into focus. Indeed, in its own way, contemporary Gothic makes much of the disconcerting contrast between the sacred and the profane that Bataille and Alexander have drawn our attention to. "We find beauty in the macabre,"[144] says Rebecca Schraffenberger. This helps to explain the sinister aesthetic of goth, the desire to remove society's thin veneer of respectability, its persistent preoccupation with transgression, the darkened lens through which it views the world. "There are birds in the darkness that nest in wooden crutches," sings Brett Sparks of The Handsome Family, whose music perfectly exemplifies what might be described as Appalachian Gothic "Eyepatches and bandages, broken spinal columns/ Pots of withered plants/ Birds you cannot see, filling every tree, falling out of closets and perched on the hands of dying men . . . " ("Birds You Can Not See," *Twilight*, 2001). "Death looms large," says Nick Cave, "because it should."[145] And as it does, so theological moments manifest.

It is little surprise, therefore, that contemporary Gothic's exploration of a "culture of death" has consistently been drawn to the detritus of institutional religion left scattered throughout the modern world. Taking a far more nuanced approach, though no less confrontational, than that taken by death metal—which also articulated a virulent opposition to Christian hegemony (e.g., Deicide, *Deicide*, 1990; *Once Upon the Cross*, 1995)—goth's fascination with religion has been typically transgressive, in its "aureolizing[146] of the profane and its profanation of the sacred: the sexualised nun, the degenerate priest, the inverted crucifix, the redemptive sin, the sordid salvation, the dark sacrament, the healing wound, the welcome death, the beautiful corpse, and the embrace of the undead. In so doing, although, again, there is a critique of the oppressive hegemony of organised religion, there is also a gesture toward the discourse of religion to signify that which lies beyond the explicatory powers of empirical science. Religion may have been abandoned, but the supernatural world it helped to construct has not. That is to say, in encouraging reflection on the unhallowed supernatural, the Gothic subverts both rational codes of understanding and orthodox theologies. The sacred and the profane are reimagined.

This is, of course, all very modern, in that it is only in a modern culture that death, the undead and the demonic can be exhumed from profane ground and cannibalized in order to draw energy into the construction of affective spaces with little risk of genuine angst. In premodern cultures, ideas that now furnish the Gothic imagination were too real, too close. The consequences of sin and the progress of the unsanctified soul were too awful to contemplate. Gothic can only really be a modern discourse. Hence, while, on the one hand, it can be interpreted as a reaction to the erosion of the supernatural in modern societies, on the other hand, it is a product of that erosion. In its subversion of the rationalism of modernity, the Gothic imagination can venture into the shadowlands of enchanted worlds to summon the spirits, demons, revenants, and forces of darkness, precisely because it is not itself vulnerable to the menace and angst such boundary crossing would have occasioned in premodern cultures. Had Schraffenberger, for example—who produced an emic chapter for the book *Goth: Undead Subculture*—been living in the twelfth century, she would not have found "beauty" in "what is dreadful and forbidding," she would not have embraced the "sinister" as a way of dealing with the "brutality" of life, she would not have had "a deep-rooted attraction to anything mysterious and super- natural."[147] It is only because she is a modern person shaped by disenchantment that she can seek enchantment in the shadows. She can, as can we all, delight in the frisson of fear evoked by imagining oneself into dark, unknown, unhallowed spaces.

Along with this sinister turn, however, there has been a far more medieval devel- opment, in the form of a sophisticated discourse of the macabre and the embodied self. Contemporary Gothic is, as Catherine Spooner has observed, "more obsessed with bodies than in any of its previous phases: bodies become spectacle, provoking disgust, modified, reconstructed and artificially augmented."[148] This brings us to a formative current within Gothic the fascination with the grotesque. While some- times deliberately disturbing, the discourse often betrays explicitly sacred over- tones, not only in the symbolism used—much of which is informed by ideas and behaviours related to rites of passage—but in its exploration of the human condi- tion. To step outside popular music culture for a moment, take, for example, the photography of Joel-Peter Witkin. Composed and distressed to encourage a sense of ageing, it appears to provide a window into another time and place, where the pro- fane is sacred and the abnormal is normal. Exploring eroticism, death, and the gro- tesque, he draws explicitly on religious and classical symbolism, forcing the viewer to question fundamental taboos, to reassess the profane, to look beneath the façade of the modern world. In so doing, he examines the self and what people experience as absolute: "the camera is a sacred vessel through which pass, on rays of light, clues to the ultimate mysteries of existence."[149] It is perhaps not surprising, therefore, that his work has been influential within both industrial and Gothic cultures—evidence of which can be found in Mark Romanek's video for "Closer" by Nine Inch Nails (from the album *Downward Spiral*, 1994) and the cover art of Pungent Stench's *Been Caught Buttering* (1991), which uses his photograph of an amorous encounter be- tween two severed heads ("The Kiss," 1982). (Of course, such grotesque cover art is not new. For example, in 1966 The Beatles caused controversy with the "butcher cover" produced for their compilation *Yesterday And Today*, featuring the band in white butcher's coats, covered with decapitated baby dolls and pieces of fresh meat, suggesting the carnage of infanticide.) This fascination with the grotesque is fun- damentally linked to performative notions of identity, in that the body becomes a physical manifestation of the affective spaces created.

This interest, which lies at the heart of Gothic can be understood in terms of Mikhail Bakhtin's theory of the grotesque body, which he developed as a result of his observation of "the compelling difference between the human body as repre- sented in popular festivity and the body as represented in classical statuary in the Renaissance."[150] Usually elevated on a pedestal, viewed from below, closed, "with no openings or orifices," affectively detached from its viewer, static and disengaged, the classical body can be understood as distant and, in this sense, "disembodied."[151] In particular, in closing bodily orifices, it attempts to restrict the engagement of the body with the external world, hide all signs of inner life processes and bodily functions (hence, for example, the cultural taboos surrounding farting, urination, defecation, menstruation, and even breast feeding in public), ignore all evidence of fecundation and pregnancy, eliminate bodily protrusions, and obscure evidence of death and decay. The aim is to present an image of a completed, rational, individual body. It is this approach to the human form which became reified in the West as a "bodily canon," shaped and maintained by a culture determined by particular ideas of politeness, taste, manners, and rational, institutional values.

Consequently, the modern bodily canon obscured an earlier, premodern—arguably "Pagan"[152]—fascination with the "grotesque body." However, argues Bakhtin, this earlier embrace of the "earthy" still persists in the modern world, particularly in the folkloric imagination and in humour—and, we might argue, in film, contemporary art and, popular music. Images of the grotesque body, he notes,

> predominate in extra-official life of the people. For example, the theme of mockery and abuse is almost entirely bodily and grotesque. The body that figures in all the expressions of the unofficial speech of the people is the body that fecundates and is fecundated, that gives birth and is born, devours and is devoured, drinks, defecates, is sick and dying. In all languages there is a great number of expressions related to genital organs, the anus and buttocks, the belly, the mouth and nose.[153]

Gothic, industrial, grindcore, death metal, and punk offer just such an extra-official critique of the bodily canon through their transgression of taboos, their carnivalesque disregard of the politics of politeness and respectability, and their creative and enthusiastic celebration of the bodily, the sexual, and the earthy. They embrace depravity and, in so doing, challenge Christian hegemony. This is particularly evident in P-Orridge's "Stations Ov Thee Cross." Not only is this an inversion of the Christian "Stations of the Cross" (i.e., images representing key moments in the passion of Christ), but, hooded and in darkness, P-Orridge provides a reinterpretation in terms of birth, death and resurrection—thereby explicitly subverting Christian discourse: "Within the ritual circumstances of Stations ov Thee Cross the hood translates into the hood of the condemned, the darkness before execution, the veil of darkness before birth. . . . P-Orridge uses ritual in order to access deeper states of altered consciousness and to gain access to the fundamental workings of the mind. He is generally initiated into these states by . . . the process of cutting and 'blood-letting' . . . The cut is also viewed as a Yoni, a slit in the skin which has significant feminine overtones, used to induce a periodic flow of blood which marks the decay of the old body in order to facilitate renewal."[154] More disturbingly and viscerally, Kevin Michael "GG" Allin embraced the grotesque during his notorious live performances, including defecation, coprophagia, and self-mutilation. A troubled man, he even planned to commit suicide on stage, the execution of which was preempted by an accidental heroin overdose on June 28, 1993. Typically, the requests regarding his funeral had been outlined in his song, "When I Die" (available on the "The Troubled Troubadour EP," 1990).

This returns us to the conclusion of the previous section, in that it addresses the profound contradiction at the heart of Western attitudes to death. On the one hand, it represents an experience of *mysterium tremendum et fascinans*,[155] that experience of the sacred which both frightens and fascinates, and, on the other hand, it is simply a termination, which can be dealt with industrially and mechanically, as witnessed in the genocides and abattoirs of modernity. In a world addicted to surface, to consumption, to all that distances the reality of death and decay, Gothic will not let us pretend. In a culture that trades in a desire for the body beautiful, that insists on white-toothed happiness as normative, that promotes the received bodily canon, Gothic's transgressive embrace of the profane, its reflection upon human corporeality *in extremis* forces us to engage with truth about our selves and the world. That which is othered as impure, which is required to be hidden, we carry around inside us. Gothic transports us to a de-sanitized, premodern affective space in which the ecstasy of sex and the horror of death are never far apart—sex finds its *telos*, not in life and the body enhanced, but in defilement, decrepitude, and destruction.

Hardcore violence

Similar misanthropic and transgressive themes to those developed within industrial, goth and extreme metal cultures were articulated within the influential American hardcore scene by bands such as Agent Orange, Bad Brains, Black Flag, The Dead Kennedys, Minor Threat, The Misfits, and State of Alert. Although there are significant differences musically and culturally between the two scenes, both were influenced by British punk and responded to urban decay and a perception of systemic disenfranchisement, depleted agency, and a stolen future: "living in darkness, living in a world of my own" (Agent Orange, "Living in Darkness," *Living in Darkness*, 1981). Typically, hardcore youths bristled with anger and embraced the aesthetics of violence and excess. "Society is burning me up," sing the Circle Jerks, so as far as its rules and conventions are concerned, "Rip 'em up, tear 'em down" ("World Up my Ass," *Group Sex*, 1980).[156] The music, which was brutal, fast and loud, reflected this sense of alienation and anger. As Michael Azerrad comments of Black Flag's 1982 album, *Damaged*, "perhaps *the* key hardcore document . . . it boiled over with rage on several fronts: police harassment, materialism, alcohol abuse, the stultifying effects of consumer culture, and, on just about every track on the album, a particularly virulent strain of self-lacerating angst – all against a savage, brutal backdrop that welded apoplectic punk rock to the anomie of dark seventies metal like Black

Sabbath."[157] The violence of the music and visceral anger articulated in the lyrics often reflected a troubled upbringing, abuse, and alienation: "street punks and runaways found their home in the hardcore scene," recalls Steven Blush. "At shows, you'd see plenty of damaged and abused kids with anger, rage, and pain. For them the scene offered hope."[158] On "Broken Home, Broken Heart" by Hüsker Dü, Bob Mould speaks for these young people: "Now you know just how it feels/ To have to cry yourself to sleep at night" (*Zen Arcade*, 1984).[159] Indeed, as a gay man, Mould himself has written movingly of his own anger, sexual frustration, and self-loathing during this period.[160] For example, in the song "Whatever" (*Zen Arcade*), he explores the struggle he had with his parents: "I'm not the son you wanted, but what did you expect?/ I've made my world of happiness to combat your neglect."[161] Of course, not all those involved in hardcore had a troubled background. Many did not. However, the point is that it was and, to some extent, still is a subculture defined by anger and angst. Consequently, the affective spaces created during the early 1980s manifested at gigs in the form of ritualized violence—"moshing."[162]

For Durkheim, the social significance of the sacred derives, in part, from its role as the focus for intense, effervescent emotion, which is generated through particular kinds of group activity, such as moshing. The ritualized violence of hardcore serves to arouse a passionate intensity—"collective effervescence"[163]—through which individuals experience something greater than themselves. Such emotion, stimulated by, as Lynch puts it, "the experience of being caught up in the power of the social group, found itself channeled through sacred symbols in the same way that a lightning rod conducts a lightning strike." As he says, "this meeting of the cognitive symbol and the power of group emotion enlivened the sacred, reinforcing the symbolic distinctiveness of the sacred with an experience of encountering a power greater than the individual self."[164] Again, my point is that we can think of the relationship between the individual, the music, the band, the violence, and *communitas* in terms of this process.

It's important to understand the particular significance of violence here. I am not simply speaking about the generation of a particular quality of emotion. The individual's transition to an affective space shaped by the power of the social group is effected through a process of transgression. This is occasioned by "collective effervescence." Rina Arya, quoting Durkheim, makes this point in her analysis of football violence in the UK: "What happens is that the individuals within the group experience a heightening of sensations, 'they experience themselves as grander than at ordinary times; they do things they would not do at other times; they feel, and at that moment really are, joined with each other and with the totemic being. They come to experience themselves as sharing one and the same essence – with the totemic animal, with representation, and with each other.'"[165] The heightening of sensations, "which occurs throughout the ritual and transforms the group from being individuated and apart from one another to partaking of a fervor which binds them communally, conveys the switch from the profane to the sacred."[166] Helpfully comparing this process to the shift from *Gesellschaft* to *Gemeinschaft*, as developed by Ferdinand Tönnies, she notes that there emerges a collective sense of identity, "which imparts a feeling of totality, where the whole is greater than the sum of its parts."[167] It is this sense of being part of that which is more powerful than both one-self and the gathered *communitas* that touches on the sacred. Within this affective space the individual experiences a profound moment of belonging and meaning in a way not dissimilar to the individuals within the context of religious worship. However, the difference here is that the transition to this feeling of totality, the shift to the group emotion that enlivens the sacred, draws its power from communal violence. As it became more frenzied, more transgressive, so individuals enter into that "inner experience" that Bataille understands in terms of a mystical state. It is hardly surprising, therefore, that moshing quickly escalated to become definitive of hardcore culture. As Azerrad notes of Black Flag concerts, they "became more and more a focal point for violence.... All the media hype was now attracting a crowd that was actually *looking* for violence."[168] This impure sacred space, this space within which cultural norms are temporarily suspended, the mosh pit, was attracting pilgrims.

Rene Girard's widely read work on violence and the sacred sheds a little more light on the significance of this experience. Central to his analysis is the premise that violence is a universal feature of human life. Because of this, when the object of violence is not available, a surrogate needs to be found in order to release the buildup of aggression. Hence, for Girard, sacrificial rituals have a key social function, in that the sacrificial victim is the necessary surrogate: "society is seeking to deflect upon a relatively indifferent victim, a 'sacrificable' victim, the violence that would otherwise be vented on its own members, the people it most desires to protect."[169] The key point is that "violence is not to be denied."[170] These words of Girard might one day be painted above the doors of hardcore clubs. Although key figures such as Ian MacKaye (Minor Threat, Fugazi) and Bob Mould (Hüsker Dü, Sugar) became weary of the excessive violence,[171] 1980s hardcore was bursting with aggression and malevolence. This was not the semi-intellectualized transgression of industrial culture; it was raw anger – summed up in the inch-high letters still etched across Henry Rollins' back: "SEARCH AND DESTROY."[172] Moments of ritualized aggression, during which numerous small secular sacrifices were made, acted as an important release, which, again, served to bind the community. In this sense, it served a sacred purpose. "Maleficence," argues Girard,[173] provides an important social function in restoring harmony and reinforcing social bonds within the community. As we have seen, *communitas* is what one would expect of trangressive behaviors within liminal cultures.

There needs to be a mosh pit. Listening to Black Flag on an iPod, worshipping as a solitary hardcore hermit, is not enough. There has to be a crossing of the threshold between mimetic violence and what Arya has referred to as the "real presence" of violence. Launching into the mosh pit, physically engaging with others, and drawing blood in small sacrifices is significant; the shift from the mimetic to the transgressive is an important one. "From the first stage of mimetic violence to the second phase of the 'real presence' of violence we experience something which is different not simply in degree but also in kind."[174] There is a shift, in other words, from the individual to the collective, from the mundane to the sacred. This shift has, insists Girard, a cathartic effect that benefits both the individual and the community: "If the sacrificial catharsis actually succeeds in preventing the unlimited propagation of violence, a sort of *infection* is in fact being checked."[175]

While this section has discussed ritualized violence within hardcore culture, the scene has evolved significantly since the early 1980s and, moreover, moshing has spilled over into other popular music scenes. The aggression at the heart of punk philosophy, stimulated by a lack of hope and agency, has been theorized and developed in several interesting ideological directions, including anarchism, veganism/vegetarianism, and animal rights.[176] These ideological foci have been developed within perhaps the most distinctive hardcore subculture to emerge in the 1980s, namely "straight edge."

Transgressive abstinence

During the early years of hardcore a counterintuitive trajectory formed around the music and ideas of Ian MacKaye and Al Barile (SS Decontrol) as well as those of, a little later, Henry Rollins.[177] Within the hardcore culture of excess, an angry abstinence movement coalesced as a reaction to the drink-, drug-, and sex-oriented cultures of rock and punk.[178] Naming their identity after MacKaye's Minor Threat song "Straight Edge" (*Minor Threat*), they adopted an ascetic stance, eschewing drugs, alcohol and, for some, even sex: "I choose not to drink or smoke or get fucked up and diminish my capacities."[179] Electing to construct an identity around abstinence *as transgression* in a culture of excess introduced an abrasive dynamic into hardcore.[180] Indeed, interestingly, there was an emic perception that straight edge had crossed a line, that it had transgressed in some fundamental sense. "The reaction we got for being straight was so contemptuous," recalls MacKaye, "we couldn't believe it. We thought being straight was just like being another type of deviant in the community, just like junkies. I didn't realise it was going to upset the applecart so much."[181] This was, I suggest, because he hadn't realised how important drugs, alcohol and sex were to hardcore identity. Hence it wasn't simply a case of some within the community deciding not to drink, take drugs, or have sex, but rather that straight edge seemed to represent a remarkable volte-face on key hardcore values. It was perceived as a significant act of transgression within the hardcore liminal *communitas*.

Some combination of sex, drink, and drugs has, of course, always been central to the liminal identities of most countercultures.[182] Illicit drugs are particularly appealing in that, as illegal, they belong to rejected culture, inducing affective states that belong to liminal life. They thereby bind the *communitas* of the damned – the rejected in society. In this sense, they are sacramental. Invested with "subcultural capital,"[183] they introduce the reader to a world of "subterranean values." As Jock Young has noted of drugs, they enable individuals "to step out into a world free of the norms of workaday life; not . . . to an asocial world. For there are norms of appropriate behavior when drunk or 'stoned,' just as there are norms of appropriate behavior when sober. For . . . the effects of drugs, although physiologically induced, are socially shared."[184] While there are, of course, numerous social, psychological and physiological factors involved in alcohol and drug use,[185] that they are often shared is particularly significant. They are part of everyday liminal social life, regulated by certain "soft" codes of behavior. The point is that, central to the development of hardcore *communitas* and the bonding that takes place in the mosh pit is the use of alcohol and drugs: "You got the beer, we got the time/ You got the coke, gimme a line" (Gang Green, "Alcohol," *Another Wasted Night*, 1986).[186] This is the first step in the process of the deconstruction of subjectivity, prior to the acceleration of aggression, the release of adrenalin, the moshing, and the shift into a collective sense of identity. That everyone shares the induced experience and respects the same soft boundaries, the same codes of behavior, is important to the sense of oneness/*communitas* produced.

"These constellations of embodied thought, feeling and action recursively reproduce the sacrality of the sacred form and constitute groups who share these discourses, sentiments and practices."[187] Hence, for straight edge musicians to sing "get all your drugs away from me" (SS Decontrol, "Get it Away," *Get It Away*, 1982)[188] constitutes a direct threat to hardcore *communitas*. It is to introduce the profane – the workaday world of order, regulation, and boundaries, which they are seeking, collectively, to resist and to transcend. This is why MacKaye and his straight-edge ideology received such a hostile reaction. Of course, then, to verbally ridicule and physically assault those who are drunk or high and to differentiate oneself from the inebriated hardcore *communitas* by, for example, tattooing a large "X" on one's forearm[189] increased the sense of threat.[190] The result of this othering was escalating aggression.

Straight edgers, of course, as liminal beings, do not consider themselves aligned to mainstream society or to hegemonic constructions of the sacred. Indeed, their position is that drug use detracts from the ideologically informed music, which should be the principal focus of the *communitas*. Hardcore, MacKaye repeatedly states in interviews, is all about the music, in that it was the music and its antiestablishment discourse that bound them together against the hegemonic values of the modern world. More than this, however, straight edge, following MacKaye, was keen to distance itself from the temperance morality of the Christian right: "we got our heads shaved and we're totally punk rockers and we're totally going against what [society] wants."[191] Indeed, the discourse around abstinence is interesting. Because of police harassment, they experienced the laws regulating alcohol and drug use as a way for the state to entrap teenagers. Consequently, abstinence was interpreted as subversion, a way to thwart the control of the state. As Nathan Strejcek of Teen Idols and Youth Brigade comments, "Since we weren't allowed to legally drink . . . we said, 'Fine, we don't want to,' just to piss the lawmakers off. This is where we established a new place in modern society for ourselves . . . clear-minded thinking against the most evil of all, the adults!"[192] Hence, the twin foci that emerged in straight edge were music and control: hardcore culture should be about music; straight-edge culture was about control. They freed themselves from the control of the state by avoiding drugs and increased their agency over everyday life through a concentration on physical and mental health. "In this life, I strive for control at all times."[193] Consequently, inebriation was a profane state because it was a distraction from the music, a magnet for the forces of authority, and, most significantly, it undermined control: "I don't make any stupid decisions," insisted one straight edger. "I like to have complete control of my mind, my body, my soul. I like to be the driver of my body, not some foreign substance . . . "[194] However, particularly in the early years, straight edge dealt with this evil in their midst through the escalation of little sacrifices – increased controlled violence.

Focussing on the body and personal discipline, *communitas* was organised around the core values of health, strength, and control. Consequently, emerging as a predominantly masculine culture, fueled by testosterone, for some, such as Rollins, the body became the primary site of representation. As a discursive text, it communicated an opposition to recreational drugs and uncontrolled behaviour, as well as representing a physical and moral superiority over those who did not abstain: "OK, fine, you take drugs, drink, whatever," stated MacKaye. "But obviously I have the edge on you because I'm sober, I'm in control of what I'm doing."[195] Within this ideological context, the violence at straight edge gigs became peculiarly significant as straightedgers in the mosh pit bonded around the idea that they were purer, stronger and better equipped to fight. It is through acts of violence that transgressive transcendence is achieved and *communitas* is established.

As indicated above, however, straight edge has since developed several significant ideological directions shaped by its politics of health, purity and control. For example, emerging particularly in the 1990s, bands such as Raid, Vegan Reich and Earth Crisis, not only developed a sound more influenced by heavy metal than by earlier hardcore, but they were more conspicuously political, focusing on particularly environmentalism and animal rights. This led to new discourses of violence and purity around veganism. As Robert Wood comments of Earth Crisis, their lyrics are "notorious for their frequent depiction of brutal violence committed against drug users, meat eaters, and straight edge backstabbers."[196] However, the point is that there are very clear constructions of the sacred and the profane articulated within the uncompromising militancy of straight edge discourse.

A world turned upside down

When the Beastie Boys urged their contemporaries to "fight for the right to party" (*Licensed to Ill*, 1986), although they were actually parodying party songs (of the type they unwittingly released), they nevertheless made some important points regarding transgression. The song's video provides a particularly good scenario in this respect. It begins with a finger-wagging mother setting boundaries for her two naïve, bespectacled sons prior to going out for the evening. As soon as the boys' parents disappear through the door, the desire for transgression surfaces with a question: "Do you like parties?" This is followed shortly after by the nervousness typical of one approaching a significant boundary for the first time, a nervousness revealed by the concerned statement, "I hope no bad people show up." They do! The rest of the video depicts an urbane, sedate party rapidly escalating into decadent transgression. When the "bad people" show up the boys are quickly transported across several boundaries: sex, drugs and rock 'n' roll. The message is one of liberation, ecstasy and carnival.

As well as the work of Roger Caillois on chaos and festivals, which we have already noted, a particularly helpful way into understanding the significance of the carnivalesque within popular music is, again, through the work of Mikhail Bakhtin, whose *Rabelais and His World* carefully explores the social significance of transgression, with particular reference to the medieval carnival as a potent, populist, hierarchy inversion. In other words, the carnival articulates a "world turned upside down" methodology. Exploring the significance of the binary oppositions that structure life (good–bad, pure–impure, clean–unclean, body–soul) —the deliberate confusion of which, we have seen, was central to industrial culture—he shows how boundaries are transgressed and authority is subverted for a limited period of time.[197] While this may be understood in terms of challenging the moral guardianship of the parent, as in the Beastie Boys video, typically the aim is to subvert the authority of the institutional guardians of "the sacred," from the Church and the education system to the police and the judiciary. Because the carnivalesque in the modern world is often created within liminal spaces, it has always been central to the rejected cultures of popular music. From Elvis, Little Richard and Bob Dylan to Marilyn Manson, Madonna, and Lady Gaga, systematic challenges are regularly being made to hegemonic discourses.

It is hardly surprising, therefore, that, since early Christianity, "popular music" has always been perceived as an unnecessary and spiritually perilous frivolity. We have mentioned Tatian's distaste for singers and for those "nodding and motioning in an unnatural way." Likewise, Tertullian, Cyprian and John Chrysostom felt that certain elements within folk culture were more a gift from Satan, than from God.[198] It was a debauched challenge to divine order, distracting people from the straight, narrow, carefully regulated path to heaven. There was, as Calvin Stapert comments in his analysis of attitudes to music in the early Church, a uniformity of hostility to what was considered Pagan entertainment.[199] "Only permanent seriousness, remorse, and sorrow for his sins befit the Christian."[200] Likewise, in his study of laughter in the Middle Ages, Bakhtin discusses its systematic exclusion from the official spheres of ideology and from all "strict forms of social relations." Laughter, he observes, "was eliminated from religious cult, from feudal and state ceremonials, etiquette, and from all genres of high speculation. An intolerant, one-sided tone of seriousness is characteristic of official medieval culture."[201] In medieval society, of course, this was important, for a serious disposition expressed one's humility, religious awe, and fear. This, in turn, demonstrated one's commitment to "the sacred"— to truth and goodness, and "all that was essential and meaningful."[202]

Persistent seriousness, however, is not easy to police. Hence to avoid a revolt and to maintain control, fun needed to be regulated, rather than prohibited: "this intolerant seriousness of the official church ideology made it necessary to legalize the gaiety, laughter, and jests which had been eliminated from the canonized ritual and etiquette."[203] Indeed, not only was fun legalized, but transgressive elements of local Pagan fertility rites, within which joviality and laughter were celebrated, were gradually allowed into the liturgies and rites of the Church, albeit "sublimated and toned down."[204] Although some of the more transgressive elements were subsequently banned from the liturgy, they were, nevertheless, allowed to continue beyond the church walls.[205] For example, the "feasts of fools," which were celebrated on the feast of St Stephen, New Year's Day, and the feasts of the Holy Innocents, the Epiphany, and St. John, "were originally held in the churches and bore a fully legitimate character. Later they became only semilegal, and at the end of the Middle Ages were completely banned from the churches but continued to exist in the streets and the taverns, where they were absorbed into carnival merriment and amusements."[206]

This historical development of licensed transgression lends support to the "safety-valve" thesis suggested in the work of Caillois. That is to say, carnivals/festivities of misrule, understood as managed, bounded eruptions of popular energies, have the effect of reducing the likelihood of more serious, unregulated outbreaks of transgression, thereby limiting the threat of the profane.[207] Hence, in allowing a little steam out of the social pressure cooker, so to speak, an explosive revolt is averted. Consequently, carnival, with all its irreverence and celebration of profanity, can actually be interpreted as a largely conservative social force in the service of the hegemonic sacred forms. As one Parisian apologist put it in 1444,

> foolishness, which is our second nature and seems to be inherent in man, might spend itself at least once a year. Wine barrels burst if from time to time we do not open them and let in some air. All of us men are barrels poorly put together, which should burst from the wine of wisdom, if this wine remains in a state of constant fermentation of piousness and fear of God. We must give it air in order not to let it spoil. This is why we permit folly on certain days so that we may later return with greater zeal to the service of God.[208]

Again, Claire Sponsler's study of morris dancing concludes that "festivities of misrule were . . . rarely genuinely subversive and were in fact most often deeply conservative."[209] For example, at Christmas, a Lord of Misrule or an Abbot of Unreason might be appointed (Henry VII paid for the services of both),[210] their role being one of overseeing a period of inversion, parody, and organized chaos. Again, the effect was that society was protected from an eruption of unregulated transgression. The hegemonic sacred was protected by the containment and control of profane forces. Similarly, we might understand the Dionysian "world turned upside down" environment of the mosh pit, or the disco, or the club, or the music festival as a bounded sphere within which the build up of excessive profane energy and trangressive desire can be expended. Consequently, from the perspective of social policy, they should be encouraged as confined liminal spaces within which revolutionary bubbles of discontent are allowed to burst and expend their energy. Hence, properly understood, within these bounded, carnivalesque contexts, transgression cannot be interpreted as disorder per se, in that, following Caillois, it exposes chaos and reminds us of the necessity of order. Although, of course, this doesn't necessarily mean a return to the old order, it does mean that hegemonic sacred forms are more or less preserved. Put crudely, there are two effects: firstly, transgressive spaces, such as music festivals, can be understood as fulfilling a conservative role in society, rather than as being an expression of sustained transgression;[211] secondly, they are, nevertheless, important transgressive spaces in which news ways of being are imagined and experienced. Consequently, their effects can never be wholly contained. They will always lead to change, no matter how apparently insignificant and personal.

That these spaces are bounded temporally and spatially within a wider profane/ sacred context is important, in that, as we have discussed, transgression cannot be sustained for long periods of time. Misrule is *mis*rule because it is a temporary transgression of regulated life; disorder is *dis*order because it is a momentary disruption of order. Transgression must have boundaries to cross and sacred forms to profane.

Having said that, to develop the countercultural point noted above, the long-term subversive potential of transgression should not be underestimated. While transgressive acts and events, such as the carnival, are bounded, temporary moments, they can have profound political significance. To turn the world upside down, even for a short time, leaves that world reconfigured. The party in the Beastie Boys video may only have lasted for a few hours, but it became a transgressive space within which, for the hosts, a lifeworld-changing process had begun. They were introduced to formative new ideas and perspectives. Hence, I think we must question Lynch's conclusion that there is no convincing basis for assuming that such "moments of ecstasy, transgression, creativity and *communitas*, which give life by temporarily releasing people from cultural structures" might stand behind the "specific sacred forms that animate contemporary social life."[212] As Bakhtin says, an ephemeral truth acted out during the carnival may become adopted as "unofficial truth."[213] This unofficial truth may, then, have a long-term effect through subverting the power of dominant discourses. As he says of laughter,

> it was the victory of laughter that most impressed medieval man. It was not only a victory over the mystic terror of God, but also a victory over the awe inspired by the forces of nature, and most of all over the oppression and guilt related to all that was consecrated and forbidden ('mana' and 'taboo'). It was the defeat of divine and human power, of authoritarian commandments and prohibitions, of death and punishment after death, hell and all that is more terrifying than the earth itself. Through this victory laughter clarified man's consciousness and gave him a new outlook on life. This truth was ephemeral; it was followed by the fears and oppressions of everyday life, but from these brief moments another unofficial truth emerged . . .[214]

This bring us back to Lynch's cultural sociological analysis: "Sacred forms are . . . cultural expressions not determined by some form of universal ontology, but socially and culturally constructed through particular historical trajectories. They are 'shifting cultural constructions' subject to means of symbolic production, which are 'fatefully affected by the power and identity of the agents in charge, by the competition of symbolic control, and the structures of power and distribution of resources.'" As he says, "even cherished forms of the sacred . . . can be understood, not as timeless truths, but as the products of particular cultural histories whose preservation and extension demand ongoing cultural labor."[215] Transgression has been central to this cultural labor. Bearing in mind the discussion thus far, how could it not be? To ignore this impure sacred perspective, as Lynch seems to, misses much that is of value.

Within popular music culture taboos are playfully transgressed and, to quote Bakhtin again, "the diableries [are] legalized and the devils [are] allowed to run about freely in the streets and in the suburbs . . . and to create a demonic and unbridled atmosphere."[216] The religious strictures on everyday life and the fear of the profane encouraged by sacred forms are parodied and subverted, the carnivalesque thereby becoming a catalyst for a process of reorientation. Once individuals have been introduced to a new way of looking at the world, previous hegemonic perspectives become problematic. To cross a boundary is to weaken it. To a large extent, this sums up the cultural force of popular music. Understood in this way, it is hardly surprising that Matthew Arnold was concerned about the anarchic potential of popular culture. Hence again, the point is that carnivalesque spaces, while they can be understood as socially conservative safety valves, also have the potential to create the conditions for lasting subversion, which may eventually weaken the power of hegemonies and allow the emergence of new perspectives.[217] Boundaries are crossed, hierarchies are challenged and new relationships are formed at both personal and institutional levels.

It could be argued, of course, that the power of the carnival has been diminished somewhat since the medieval period. Certainly, there is an obvious sense in which it can no longer "belong to the whole of the people" in late modern societies in the way that it used to in medieval societies.[218] However, that said, there is another sense in which its influence, disseminated through contemporary media, has increased. Indeed, there is a very real sense in which we can talk about a carnivalized media. In the medieval period, the principal location for the carnival was, as Bhaktin points out, the square and the streets adjoining it.

> To be sure, carnival also invaded the home; in essence it was limited in time only; carnival knows neither stage nor footlights. But the central arena could only be the square, for by its very idea carnival *belongs to the whole people*, it is *universal, everyone* must participate in its familiar contact. The public square was the symbol of communal performance. The carnival square – the square of carnival acts – acquired an additional symbolic overtone that broadened and deepened it. In carnivalized literature the square . . . becomes two-leveled and ambivalent: it is as if there glimmered through the actual square the carnival square of free familiar contact and communal performances of crowning and decrowning. Other places of action as well . . . can, if they become meeting- and contact-points for heterogeneous people – streets, taverns, roads, bathhouses, decks of ships, and so on – take on this additional carnival-square significance . . . [219]

Today, however, popular music, film, television, and the advent of electronic media, particularly digital technologies, such as the iPod, have ubiquitized carnival. Clubs, gigs and festivals, of course, become carnivalesque meeting-points for heterogenous people, but in the modern world carnivalesque affective spaces can be constructed anywhere through earphones and on small screens. We are witnessing, through the development of mobile technologies, a mobilization of the social and with it the subversive potential of the carnival.[220]

Concerning the relationship between institutional religion and carnival, at least since the medieval period, it has been a close one, in that, as we have noted, the Church has maintained a place of honour as a cardinal focus of ridicule. In the medieval world, of course, this was largely because ecclesiastical authorities dominated the lives of ordinary people through a politics of fear. As Bakhtin observes, nearly all the revelries of the feast of fools were "a grotesque degradation of various church rituals and symbols and their transfer to the material bodily level: gluttony and drunken orgies on the altar table, indecent gestures, disrobing."[221] While religion in the West no longer enjoys the position it used to in society, nevertheless, because of a vestigial Christian hegemony, which informs the dominant moral value system enshrined in state legislation, and because of conservative Christianity's periodic vitriolic resistance to what it considers profane, the Church has managed to hang on to its place of honor in popular music culture as a focus for ridicule and parody.

Consider David Byrne's work. He has, from relatively early in his career, consistently articulated thoughtful carnivalesque rhetoric against Christian culture. While with The Talking Heads he commissioned the folk artist and idiosyncratic fundamentalist minister Howard Finister to produce the album cover for *Little Creatures* (1985), which depicted the band in a bizarre sacred universe. Again, entitling the band's fifth studio album *Speaking in Tongues* (1983), he referenced the glossolalia believed to be divine communication within Pentecostal and charismatic Christianity, thereby introducing the sacred into profane space in a spirit of playful subversion. More directly, the cover of his solo album *Uh-Oh* (1992) depicts angels around a heavenly throne worshipping a foolish-looking "dog" (i.e., the word "God" reversed). Likewise many of his lyrics and pieces of art are particularly transgressive in this respect, acerbic examples of which are "U.B. Jesus" (*Look Into the Eyeball*, 2001) and "Something Ain't Right" (*Uh-Oh*, 1992). He is particularly critical of lazy theodicies that seek to defend the omnipotence and omnibenevolence of God in the face of ubiquitous and grinding suffering. In "Something Ain't Right," he rails against a deity that "can turn the world around," yet pushes it "in the dirt," while demanding obedience. Such an "old fart," as he puts it, clearly has no concern for those innocent millions throughout history who have been damaged in the process. Moreover, to claim that "We are the flowers growin' in God's garden/ And that is why he spreads the shit around" ("The Cowboy Mambo (Hey Lookit Me Now)," *Uh-Oh*) – which is essentially the position of second century theologian Irenaeus and the late John Hick – does little to alleviate the problem. What sort of demonic deity are theists organizing their lives around? Again, in 2001, he produced a book, the aim of which was to directly question a number of sacred forms in the modern world. Published in both Spanish and English, entitled *The New Sins* and parodying texts such as particularly the Gideon's Bible, it was specifically created to be placed anonymously in hotel rooms during the first Valencia Biennial[222] in 2001: "I had been asked to do a project for this art Biennial they have in Valencia, in Spain. They liked my proposal to do a Bible-esque book that they would put in the hotel rooms where people would be staying . . . just like the Bibles they put in hotel drawers."[223] Claiming to be "conceived by the Better-emancipated Strivers for Heaven, in loose conjunction with the Second Congregation of Trustees of Tomorrow," it describes as "new sins" what Christian hegemony considers to be virtues. In other words, it is an exercise in carnivalesque inversion: "the levels of hell are filled with the virtuous"; "cleanliness is not next to godliness"; "hope . . . encourages the most ridiculous, vile and treacherous acts"; "Hope is . . . a way of keeping people blinded, ignorant and servile, ignorant of the true and mystical beauty of the universe, a universe which is meaningless and amoral"; "love is a lie, a beautiful lie, told by God to all His creatures"; "chaos is beautiful"; "no one will help us. Not God, not scientists, academics, DJs, pop stars or Saints"; "In The True Heaven we are equal to God. We are just like Him. We sit around and crack jokes and He laughs."[224]

The parodying of religion, often with the transgressive political intent to subvert dominant sacred forms, is, again, not uncommon in popular music. The British group Alabama 3 (known as A3 in the United States) became well-known for their song "Woke Up this Morning" (*Coldharbour Lane*, 1997), a remix of which was adopted as the opening theme tune for the HBO series, *The Sopranos* (*La Peste*, 2000). Formed by Rob Spragg and Jake Black, who adopted the pseudonyms Larry Love and the Very Reverend Dr. D. Wayne Love, Alabama 3 have consistently parodied the argot and performance of "Bible Belt" fundamentalism in their live shows and on albums such as *Power in the Blood* (2002), *There Will Be Peace in the Valley . . . When We Get the Keys to the Mansion on the Hill* (2011), and *Shoplifting for Jesus* (2011). Brought up as a Mormon in the Welsh town of Merthyr Tydfil and familiar with the evangelical preaching of the Welsh valleys, Spragg's carnivalesque critique of Christian culture is informed and thoughtful. When they are singing choruses that parody the worship of fundamentalist revival meetings, such as "Let's go back to church" ("Conversion," *Coldharbour Lane*), their audience, familiar with carnivalesque discourse, is fully aware of the message: "Why would anyone want to go back to church?" Brandishing Bibles, calling their audience to repentance, accompanied by backing singers dressed as nuns wearing stockings and suspenders, Alabama 3's transgressive performance is explicitly subversive. The audience is drawn into the transgressive mockery and inversion. Again, as Bakhtin put it, the carnival is a spectacle without a stage,[225] in the sense that it "does not acknowledge any distinction between actors and spectators . . . Carnival is not a spectacle seen by the people; they live in it and everyone participates because its very idea embraces all the people."[226] The transgression and subversion of Christianity is embodied in and owned by the *communitas*.

Women who run with wolves

The subject of this section should be addressed in a large volume, for while the relationship between gender and popular music has become an important site of analysis over the last couple of decades and the study of gender and religion has a longer and wider history, very little has been done at the interface of these areas of enquiry. This is a significant omission, particularly as a number of female artists have not been shy of addressing many of the complex issues surrounding transgression, religion, gender, and sex.

It is largely the product of Western Christian culture and its sacred forms that the enactment of male sexuality is still viewed differently than the enactment of female sexuality. As Susan McClary comments, "throughout Western history, women musicians have usually been assumed to be publically available, have had to fight hard against pressures to yield, or have accepted the granting of sexual favors as one of the prices of having a career . . . Women on stage are viewed as sexual commodities regardless of their appearance or seriousness."[227] However, little attention has been given to the religio-cultural context within which popular music's patriarchy emerged. Yet, it is precisely because of this context that female transgression has been viewed as more profane and socially threatening than male transgression. Of course, this is hardly a new phenomenon.[228] For example, McClary also points out that "a kind of desire-dread-purge mechanism prevails in operas in which . . . a passive male encounters a strong, sexually aggressive female character. In operas such as *Carmen*, *Lulu*, and *Salome*, the 'victimized male' who has been aroused by the temptress finally must kill her in order to reinstate social order."[229] But, of course, even McClary's use of the term "temptress" is, in itself, loaded with religious baggage. Eve sinned and Adam lost control! Hence, the point here is that the female artist, by being sexually independent and "tempting," transgresses and threatens the hegemonic sacred. Consequently, there needs to be repentance or exorcism.

Having said that, much popular music, particularly in the 1950s and 1960s, did perpetuate patriarchal hegemony by sublimating female sexuality through its interpretation in terms of romance. That is to say, songs such as Tammy Wynette's "Stand By Your Man" (*Stand By Your Man*, 1969) were conservative, in that they protected sacred forms, such as female loyalty, submission, and domesticity. Hence Wynette's song is, as Holly Kruse comments, "often used as an example of how female artists have helped to perpetuate traditional notions of gender roles and thus their own oppression. Lines like 'Give him two arms to cling to/ And something warm to come to' have been widely interpreted as a reactionary espousal of a prefeminist point of view."[230] Although it has also been argued that lines such as "Sometimes its hard to be a woman/ Giving all your love to just one man" constitute "an expression of dissatisfaction with women's traditional roles within monogamous relationships,"[231] such lines should perhaps be read in a more obvious and traditionally Christian sense. That is to say, while Wynette recognizes that it might be hard being a faithful woman and giving all your love to just one man, nevertheless, this is the right thing to do. Indeed, other songs on the album reinforce such conservative values: "Everything I need is everything I see in you" ("I Stayed Long Enough"); "What you do is wrong but my love stays strong for you/ I don't think I'll change a thing at all" ("My Arms Stay Open Late").

This reinforcement of traditional gender roles and the patriarchal angst regarding the profanity of ungovernable female energy and uncontrolled female sexuality (i.e., ungovernable and uncontrolled by masculine power) has, particularly since the emergence of punk in the mid-1970s, been addressed by many female artists.[232] Although punk was riddled with misogyny and sexism, it, nevertheless, provided a space for the development of aggressive female sexuality. As Liz Naylor, co-editor of the Manchester punk fanzine *City Fun*, comments, during the 1970s, "women were destroying the established image of femininity, aggressively tearing it down."[233] From that point on, deconstruction has continued apace. For example, transgressive assaults on traditional sacred forms are powerfully evident in the work of X-Ray Spex, Siouxsie and the Banshees, The Raincoats, The Slits, Patti Smith, Lydia Lunch, Cosey Fanni Tutti, Diamanda Galás, Kim Gordon, Ut, PJ Harvey, Alanis Morissette, Sinéad O'Connor, Tori Amos, Ani DiFranco, Hole, Babes in Toyland, Fiona Apple, and Me'Shell Ndegéocello, not to mention the much discussed riot grrrl movement.[234]

As well as this significant flowering of aggressive female sexuality, the names of artists such as Mother Superia and Madonna; the articulations of Paganism by such as Kate Bush, Tori Amos, and Björk; and the rejection of Christian patriarchal discourse in the work of Ani DiFranco, Sinéad O'Connor and Patti Smith, witness to a focus on the relationship between religion, sex and patriarchy. For example, Siouxsie and the Banshees, for their first gig under that name, at the 100 Club punk festival in 1976, played a rambling fifteen minute interpretation of "The Lord's Prayer" (released on their second album, *Join Hands*, 1979), into which were interjected references to sex, fury, chastity, guilt, sacrifice, revenge, as well as an attack on the whole notion of Heaven and eschatological reward. Indeed, the very reference to the Celtic mythology of the banshee is a significant challenge to patriarchal and Christian sacred forms. A wild feminine spirit, a messenger from the Otherworld, associated with animals, whose wail is an omen of death, represents an explicit mythic profane threat to patriarchy. As Clarissa Pinkola Estés has explored in her widely read book, *Women Who Run With Wolves*, the notion of the "wild woman" is a powerful one: "We are filled with a longing for the wild. There are few culturally sanctioned antidotes for this yearning. We were taught to feel shame for such desire. We grew our hair long and used it to hide our feelings. But the shadow of the Wild Woman still lurks behind us during our days and in our nights. No matter where we are, the shadow that trots behind us is definitely four-footed."[235] This sense of the feral feminine is, in many ways, at the heart of transgression in popular music and is distilled in the image of the banshee. Whether we think of—along with Siouxsie Sioux—Janis Joplin, Patti Smith, Tori Amos, or Madonna, their presence is an inauspicious sign to patriarchy that the female human animal is loose and, through their banshee wail, their sonic power, the end of patriarchy is signaled.

A particularly creative transgressive reading of a biblical text is provided by Me'Shell Ndegéocello in her "Mary Magdelene" (*Peace Beyond Passion*, 1996), which subverts traditionally oppressive readings. A black, bisexual musician, Ndegéocello writes herself into a text, the interpretation of which has been used to legitimize sexism and misogyny. In the song, Mary becomes the object of her desire, perhaps even scopophilia. She is desired, not judged. She is loved, longed for, and valued without having to "wash the feet of unworthy men," as Ndegéocello puts it. She does not need to repent for the life she has lived in a patriarchal society – treated by males as an object. Again, this is an important rereading of a figure who has been, as Jane Schaberg notes, a "liminal and strange woman, silent, dominated by the great image of Jesus crucified, resurrected. She symbolizes the belief that women are made only deficiently in the image of God, and are ultimately a symbol of evil and of dependent, sinful humanity."[236] Indeed, at the heart of this dominant patriarchal reading of Mary Magdelene is the message that "women can be forgiven; Eros can be controlled."[237] Ndegéocello's song subverts this harlotization completely, embracing her, allowing the listener to understand her story as, says Mélisse Lafrance, "a tale of same-sex love, interracial harmony, and female empowerment, rather than one of fallen women, mighty men, and racially coded slavery."[238]

Similarly, Patti Smith's work confrontationally addresses religion and sex. For example, on her seminal 1975 album *Horses*, she reworks Van Morrison's song (recorded with his band Them) about masculine lust and sexual conquest, "Gloria," inverting its original meaning and embedding it in a critique of Christian discourse. The track, the first on the album, opens with the arrestingly transgressive line, "Jesus died for somebody's sins, but not mine." Moreover, as Richard Middleton says of the song, "Smith's vocal extremes – the switching of registers, which confuses gender norms, the vast range of vocal effects, the barely coherent climaxes – seem both to parody the conventions of cock-rock and appropriate them, thereby inverting the traditional structure of sexual positioning."[239] Again, this is feminist critique, but it has to be understood within the context of Christian constructions of the sacred, which begin to come more clearly into focus on her second album *Radio Ethiopia* (1976). Her liner notes to that album are littered with religious references and revealing biographical comments: "as a child I got stoned on the Bible . . . A celestial baby . . . it made my heart beat harder . . . but a few things disturbed me. The relentless preoccupation for predestined order." She then turns to the figure of Satan: "the artist in me was already aroused . . . and Satan . . . the first absolute artist . . . was the first to have a vision of existence beyond what was imposed on him."[240] Like Satan, she questioned the order imposed upon her, the sacred forms she had inherited from a devout mother, the sexual submission expected of her. Indeed, the scrambling of religion and sex is explicit. As she once said of "Ain't It Strange" (*Radio Ethiopia*) – in which she sings "Turn, God, make a move/ Turn, Lord" – "It's a challenge to God . . . I wanna be God's daughter. No . . . I wanna be God's mistress. I'm not willing to witness one miracle and believe. I wanna be fucked by God. Not just once, a thousand times." She continues, "If Jesus was around, if I was a groupie, I'd really get behind that guy . . . That's why I think Mary Magdalene was so cool, she was the first groupie. . . . All this stuff about Jesus, how wonderful he was, and how he was gonna save us. All I'd like to know is if he was a good lay. That interests me."[241] Similar transgressive sentiments are expressed in the tracks "Hymn" (*Wave*, 1979) and "Privilege (Set Me Free)" (*Easter*, 1978), the latter including a reworking of Psalm 23. While, there is, of course, transgressive hyperbole in Smith's work,[242] nevertheless, she is making an important point about the relationship between gender, sex, and religion in Western culture. Firstly, informed to some extent by the concerns of second-wave feminism, she is clearly conscious that, as Gerda Lerner has argued, Western culture has been made toxic by the fundamental conceptual error of androcentricity.[243] Secondly, she seems aware that, as some feminist theologians have insisted, this toxic culture is rooted in masculine gendered language about God: if God is male, the male is god. This, of course, is why thinkers such as Naomi Goldenberg have insisted that the Judaeo-Christian God, as the architect of patriarchal society, must go.[244] Hence, in Patti Smith's treatment of sex and religion, she is inverting the phallic authority evident in religion, society, and, of course, rock music –"cock rock" – and directing her gaze, her scopophilic control, toward the author of masculine patriarchal power, God.

An admirer of Patti Smith, Madonna,[245] having been brought up within Catholicism, has built her transgressive persona and stage performances around an ambivalence toward the faith of her childhood. In particular, the titles, artwork, and much of the content of her early albums prior to *Erotica* in 1992 – *Madonna* (1983), *Like a Virgin* (1984), *Like a Prayer* (1989) and *The Immaculate Collection* (1990) – play with traditional theological signification relating to virginity, juxtaposing it with signification relating to sexual promiscuity (e.g., the wearing of a large belt buckle declaring "Boy Toy" below a conspicuous crucifix). In other words, the religious texts are, from the outset, under the jurisdiction of sexually promiscuous discourses[246] that impose a profane universe upon them. This is important for an understanding of the incredible popularity of Madonna and the longevity of her career. As Laurie Schultze, Anne Barton White and Jane Brown have argued, much of her significance as a performer can be located in "her ability to tap into and disturb established hierarchies of gender and sexuality."[247] More specifically, there is a sense in which Madonna's work is particularly sophisticated in that it follows the contours of much Western Christian patriarchal thought regarding women. That is to say, there is an implicit (and often explicit) understanding of the female as both fallen and redeemed: the Madonna represents life, motherhood, and sublimated spiritual femininity; Eve represents sin, death and the introduction of sex[248] (which, to some extent, maps on to Freud's patriarchal Madonna-whore complex). This subversion of traditional Catholic sexual ethics – the embodying of the Madonna and Eve – through a transgressive reinterpretation of popular Catholic Marian theology, including the doctrine of Mary's perpetual virginity, was conspicuously subversive.[249] Religious and erotic ecstasies are scrambled. The intertextual relationship between virginity, purity, and Christian symbolism, on the one hand, and simulated sex at concerts, appearances in *Playboy* and *Penthouse*, and a collection of erotic photographs[250] on the other, is a complex one. The image she has carefully cultivated as an artist, both in music and film, has been one of the impure Madonna. Significantly, according to Tori Amos, "the joining of the themes 'Madonna' and 'Virgin' and sex . . . represented a major sexual awakening for Christian girls . . . The significance of a female called Madonna singing the words 'Like a Virgin' could not be downplayed, nor could the effect on little girls around the world singing along with her."[251] In this way, a contemporary Abbess of Unreason, she presides over the inversion of traditional sacred categories, playfully crossing boundaries, taking her listeners with her as participants in a carnival. Ideas are challenged, perspectives are changed and discourses of liberation are suggested.[252]

Tori Amos herself, the daughter of a Christian minister, has likewise explored similar ideas in her music. Indeed, she has explicitly stated that her "mission" is "to expose the dark side of Christianity."[253] Consequently, as Lafrance has argued, her work is a "disruptive" presence, in that her "complicated and often obscure symbolic incursions into the regulatory technologies of Christianity and male supremacy tend to make her music disconcerting."[254] However, unlike Madonna, there is a sense in which her work directly confronts the self-perception of impotent otherness, which, as a woman, she has been constrained to accept in a patriarchal society. As Judith Butler comments, "as Other, women are not devoid of choice; rather they are constrained to choose against their own sense of agency, and so to distort and undermine the very meaning of choice."[255] With particular reference to Christian patriarchy, Amos inverts the hierarchy, portraying God as the impotent Other, the one who lacks agency and choice, the one who loves, but cannot protect, the one who needs feminine assistance: "God, sometimes you just don't come through/ Do you need a woman to look after you?" ("God," *Under the Pink*, 1994).

It is very clear that Amos feels the violence and oppression of patriarchy very keenly. As Lafrance argues, "it is in patriarchal society's best interest to ensure that women are constantly aware of the threat of violence against them. It is these persistent social sanctions, real and imagined, that persuade women to self-survey and to discipline their thoughts, actions, and life choices."[256] Indeed, it is of particular significance that, as referenced in her song "Me and a Gun" (*Little Earthquakes*, 1992), Amos was the victim of rape at knifepoint (although, in the song, she substitutes a knife for a gun): "I sang 'holy holy' as he buttoned down his pants." Where was God? Sometimes he just doesn't come through! As she related in an interview, "you feel like your boundaries have been crossed to such an extent that there's no law anymore . . . that there is no God."[257] More than that, she was aware that the judiciary in a patriarchal society would not come through either. Hence she refused to go to the police because the likelihood was that, because of the way rape is currently investigated, she would be subjected to yet more pain and further violation: "with American law as it is and the fact that I'm an entertainer and the kind of performer I was . . . I knew I was going to be set up . . . And I was not going to be the victim of another experience." The result was, she recalls, "I became a victim of myself."[258] She experienced the nightmares, she felt the guilt and the shame, she bore the pain and the self-destructive hatred. To be a transgressive female, to threaten the profanation of sacred forms, to challenge hegemonic patriarchal discourses is dangerous. When it comes to questioning social facts and transgressing sacred forms, "we cannot try to pass through a locked door without bruising our heads or knees."[259]

Concluding comments

Popular music can be "edgework"[260] —a risky, excessive, transgressive activity located at the boundaries of chaos. It disturbs and challenges the ordered, sanitized worlds of modernity. Destructive, dangerous and irrational though it can be, transgression is socially important. Hierarchies and "common sense" organized around sacred forms need to be challenged. This is, of course, because sacred forms are not themselves stable and fixed. They are socially and culturally constructed. Consequently, transgressive discourses represent a necessary search for boundaries, an important challenge to hegemonic constructions of the sacred.

Slavoj Žižek's analysis of the nature of transgression in "societies of consumption" is helpful here: "late capitalism . . . is no longer Order sustained by some founding Prohibition which calls to be transgressed in a heroic act – in the generalized perversion of later capitalism, transgression itself is solicited, we are daily bombarded by . . . social forms, which not only enable us to live with our perversions, but even directly conjure new perversions."[261] Drawing attention to what he believes to be an omission in much political philosophy, Žižek argues that more thought needs to be given to the cultural practices of communities that involve what he calls "inherent transgression." However, unlike Bakhtin, who examined "idealized" versions of transgression in the form of temporally and spatially limited carnivals, Žižek argues that, in actual fact, "periodic transgressions are inherent in the social order; they function as a condition of the latter's stability."[262] There is, in other words, more of the everyday about Žižek's understanding of transgression. He identifies a shared and often denied complicity in what we have discussed in terms of othering and the exorcising of the profane in society. For example, he comments on the prevalence of lynchings in the American South in the 1920s:

> the rule of the official public Law was accompanied by its shadowy double, the nightly terror of the Ku Klux Klan, with its lynchings of helpless blacks: a (white) man could be forgiven minor infractions of the Law, especially when they could be justified by a 'code of honour' – the community still recognizes him as 'one of us.' But he would be effectively excommunicated, perceived as 'not one of us,' the moment that he disavowed the specific form of *transgression* that pertains to this community – say, the moment he refused to partake in ritual lynchings by the Klan, or even reported them to the Law (which, of course, did not want to hear about them since they represented its own hidden underside).[263]

To extend his point, we can think of Lilian Smith's 1944 novel *Strange Fruit*,[264] in which she confronts, as Anne Loveland put it, "the paradox of a culture that teaches hospitality, democracy, and Christian charity at the same time that it violently denies the humanity of blacks."[265] This paradox is explained, to some extent, by Žižek's point that there is a solidarity-in-guilt shaped by participation in a common transgression. This is evident, for example, in the banning of *Strange Fruit* in the United States, the Massachusetts Supreme Court declaring it to be "obscene, indecent and impure."[266] Indeed, the title of the book proved to be particularly controversial because of its association with Lewis Allen's song of the same name sung by Billie Holiday, which exposed the horrors of lynching and racism, becoming one of the earliest protest songs to receive national attention in the United States. The point, however, is that the heroic transgressive moments of Smith and Holiday exposed society's "inherent transgression": violent and sadistic racism. In other words, genuinely subversive gestures, such as those of Smith and Holiday, "undermine the fundamental identification with the 'transgressive' mode of enjoyment [*jouissance*] that holds a community together . . . "[267]

This helps us to understand the transgressive significance of popular music in society in relation to the sacred. Although one cannot, of course, generalize – since much popular music itself conforms to the generalized perversion of late capitalism – certain moments in popular music history can be understood as exposing inherent transgression, speaking truth to power, identifying the sacred. Hence, to return to the profane significance of racism, that dominant sacred form within American white society that sanctioned ritualized murder. Such was its significance, that many white church members became willingly involved in lynchings. As the political theologian Reinhold Niebuhr memorably bemoaned in 1923, "if there were a drunken orgy somewhere, I would bet ten to one a church member was not in it . . . But if there were a lynching, I would be ten to one a church member was in it."[268] In other words, the sanctity of life, historically central to Christian teaching, became a subjugated sacred form under the dominant sacred form of white supremacy and solidarity with white society. Hence "Strange Fruit" was transgressive in its subversion of the inherent transgression that held a white "Christian" community together. In so doing, it threw into sharp relief key sacred forms, which had become subjugated.

There is much that is self-indulgent, hedonistic, juvenile and destructive in popular music, as one would expect within liminal cultures, but its role as a site of transgression is an important one. Far from being "wreckers of civilization," there is much to suggest that such transgressors have contributed to its construction. After all, a "civilization" that produced Zyklon B, that has been complicit in the industrial slaughter of humans, in the factory farming of animals, in the alienating systems of modernity, in the abuses and injustices of patriarchal religion and society, in the exploitation and degradation of sexual commodification, in global injustice, and in the rape of the planet, can hardly be considered socially and morally advanced. As such, the transgressive discourses of the liminal cultures of popular music fulfil an important role in the contestation of the sacred in the modern world. John Peel makes the point pretty well in a short discussion of death metal: "people . . . warn me, as they have warned me about so many other things, from Little Richard to Run-DMC ('You shouldn't play that. That's the music of black criminals,' a colleague told me), stuff like that can be damaging to impressionable young minds. What, more damaging than a diet of war, rape, pestilence and unearned celebrity they're fed daily by the media? I don't think so. 'Swarming Vulgar Mass of Infected Virulancy' anyone? Come on in. The blood's fine . . . "[269]

4

Romanticism

I went to the Garden of Love,
And saw what I never had seen:
A Chapel was built in the midst,
Where I used to play on the green.

And the gates of this Chapel were shut,
And Thou shalt not. writ over the door;
So I turn'd to the Garden of Love,
That so many sweet flowers bore.

And I saw it was filled with graves,
And tomb-stones where flowers should be:
And Priests in black gowns, were walking their rounds,
And binding with briars my joys and desires.[1]

     —William Blake, 'The Garden of Love'

One could turn to almost any words from the pen of William Blake to begin a chapter on the Romantic in popular music. However, there is something about this poem's indignant and piercing criticism of the severe, unnatural profanity of institutional religion alongside its gentle celebration of the sacred in nature, in love, in sexual experience that makes it a beautifully appropriate note on which to begin. It is from this perspective of questioning the "Thou shalt nots," of cutting away the briars of guilt, of turning from the strictures of black-gowned, institutional religion and toward the "Garden of Love," of "getting back to the garden" as Joni Mitchell put it ("Woodstock," *Ladies of the Canyon*, 1970), that I want us to think about popular music's intense Romantic yearning. Indeed, in turning to the Romantic we have not left the ecstatic and the transgressive, in that, as Kierkegaard put it, "Romantic means precisely that [which] oversteps all bounds."[2] We are simply continuing the discussion in the previous chapter.

 There have been, of course—in the tradition of anti-Romantic developments since the Enlightenment—what might be described as periodic attempts at a modernist aesthetic, a rationalist resistance in the form of cool, detached, urban electronica. This loathing of randomness, typical of "International Style" architecture, of Le Corbusier's "white world" rather than the human world of clutter and compromise, is most conspicuously articulated in Kraftwerk's celebration of the "Autobahn" (*Autobahn*, 1974), the "Geiger Counter" (*Radioactivity*, 1975), the "Trans-Europe Express" (*Trans-Europe Express*, 1977), "The Robots" (*The Man Machine*, 1978), and computing (*Computer Word*, 1981).[3] However, for much of its history, popular music has cultivated a more sensual, more metaphysical, more Romantic aesthetic. Indeed, we will see that, as electronic music evolved, many musicians, some influenced by Kraftwerk, used contemporary technology to create affective spaces conducive to the evocation of altered states with a spiritual significance.

A sense of something still more deeply interfused

"Nineteenth century Romanticism lives on in the mass culture of the twentieth century and The Sex Pistols come to fulfill the prophecies of Shelley."[4] So claims Robert Pattison in an idiosyncratic analysis of rock music and Romanticism, which seeks to provide an explanation for many of the central ideas that constitute the mythology of rock. One of his main theses is that rock music is a form of cultural "vulgarity" that derives from nineteenth-century Romantic attempts to deal with the discrepancy between popular culture and "elite" cultural forms by reworking pantheistic beliefs and celebrating myths of anticultural primitivism. "Rock is the quintessence of vulgarity. It's loud, crude and tasteless. Rock is vulgarity militant, and modern vulgarity is one incarnation of Romantic pantheism."[5] With his sights firmly fixed on Walt Whitman, he simply asserts, with all the sophistication of fundamentalist anti-rock discourse, that pantheism is "a garbage-pail philosophy, indiscriminately mixing scraps of everything," being particularly corrupted by ideas of relativism and the impossibility of transcendent values: "fine distinctions between right and wrong, high and low, true and false, the worthy and the unworthy, disappear in pantheism's tolerant and eclectic one that refuses to scorn any particular of the many."[6] It is in this sense that pantheism (as Pattison understands it) can be said to be vulgar. That is to say, in the classical sense of *volgos*, the vulgar is that which concerns the ordinary and the profane in the sense that Matthew Arnold understood the uncultured life. "Vulgarity is common. The great mass of men who lack refinement are vulgar."[7] Like the pantheist, the vulgar do not discriminate or lift themselves above or transcend material existence and the basic functions of embodied existence. Consequently, popular music is, claims Pattison, "pantheistic" in its "untranscendent" vulgarization: it "screws or fucks" rather than "makes love"; it "cannot discriminate between sensations"; it "has no taste." Moreover, rock's vulgarization, he contends, "lies not only in the mass audience rock reaches with its Romantic conventions, nor in the loud presentation it gives to the sublime concerns of Romantic art." In rock, he says, the grand questions which refined taste has made the object of conscious and painful deliberation are handled with instinctive and cheerful abandon. What Wordsworth treated with studied craftsmanship, rock manhandles with reckless spontaneity. By its nature, rock cannot achieve the poetic finish, the historical awareness, or the rational depths of the great Romantic poetry, because these all require the imposition of transcendent order on the materials of feeling. Rock's vulgarity subordinates reason to emotion, denies transcendence, and exalts perpetual youth. . . . Western society now supports two brands of Romanticism. The refined, transcendent variety believes with Wordsworth and Ruskin in an emotional universe redeemed by the spiritual powers of "the philosophic mind." The bastard, pantheist variety accepts the emotional universe as pure feeling. It denies transcendence, equates "the philosophic mind" with the death of the spirit, and looks for apotheosis of the self in the purity of youthful instinct. We stand between two worlds, one dead, the other unwilling to grow up.[8]

I mention this study, not simply because it introduces an interesting perspective, but also because, in attempting to compare the "two brands of Romanticism," his analysis becomes typically Procrustean. That is to say, through the selective quotation of lyrics (which, of course, like all selection, can be used to make any point one wishes to make), he attempts to fit rock music into a particular interpretation of nineteenth-century Romanticism and then criticises it for being a childish and unsophisticated manifestation of it. In other words, to put the point rather crudely, to compare Shelley with Jim Morrison, and then to attack Morrison for being a facile imitation of Shelley, misunderstands the nature of popular music and what some mean when they refer to manifestations of the Dionysian and the Romantic within popular music.[9] Again, similarly problematic, but writing from a different perspective and with different concerns in mind, Theodore Gracyk, in his criticism of those who understand popular music as Romantic, seems to fail to understand how and why the term is used. Hence, he argues at length a rather sweeping and ultimately redundant point that musicians cannot be seen as the "modern counterparts of Wordsworth, Coleridge, Shelley, Keats, and Byron" because they "have always had crass commercial motives."[10] That's not the point. If it was, we might list many more dissimilarities than simply their involvement in the music industry and a desire for wealth—which, of course, not all share. Relatedly, he also worries that "musicians manipulate Romanticism for their own commercial gain."[11] Not only is this too cynical, but even if it is true of every individual who stepped up to a microphone or picked up a guitar, the important questions concern *why* they are attracted by Romanticism in the first place. Indeed, what is it about the Romantic spirit that is so attractive to a particular *communitas* that musicians are likely to profit from a relationship to it? Hence, the premise of this chapter is that there is a sense in which, in the transgressive liminality of popular music culture, in the ability of music to present feeling and emotion directly, and in the nature of the affective spaces it seeks to evoke, there is that which can usefully be discussed in terms of Romanticism. We have no interest at all in the identification of Romantic benchmarks, based on nineteenth-century paradigms, against which contemporary manifestations might be judged.

With that in mind, we begin by briefly commenting on the sense in which music itself is commonly interpreted as creating its own world, shaping an affective space within which the pressures of everyday life recede. This retreat from the everyday, this immersion in that which is in some sense other than the everyday, is a key component of the Romantic impulse, frequently described in terms Wordsworth would have recognized as "the spontaneous overflow of powerful feelings."[12] For the Romantics, creativity required a "temporary escape from the conscious ego and a liberation of instinct and emotion . . . " There was a belief that "creativity required a regression to a state of consciousness characterized by emotion and instinct, a fusion between self and world, and freedom from rationality and convention."[13] It is this sense of "fusion," of course, which moves us toward experiences that can be described as mystical. As Paul Marshall points out in his thoughtful discussion of mystical encounters with the natural world, "Romantic philosophy and literature disseminated ideas about nature and perception that shaded into the mystical. Unity was a key word: the unity of the subject and the object, of self and world, in the creative act of perception, and the organic unity of nature in which humankind is a part. Reintegration with the spiritual whole – the *All-Einheit* ('All-Unity') or *hen kai pan* ('One and All') – was a goal to which the alienated self of the Romantic poet aspired."[14]

Interpretations of the affective impact of music in terms of transcendence, as discussed in Chapter 2, are inspired by just this sense of unity, this mystical fusion. In these moments there is a frequently reported feeling of being drawn out of oneself, of being "lost in music," as Sister Sledge put it: "We're lost in music/Feel so alive." As such, popular music is often articulated as liberation, even "salvation" ("Lost in Music," 1979). Moreover, within communal settings, this sense of being transported by, or "lost in" the music translates into deep feelings of unity with other selves. There is, in other words, a significant sense of *communitas* about which religious terminology—particularly relating to spirituality, mysticism and esotericism— seems peculiarly appropriate. This esoteric experience of oneness has been communicated to me a number times by participants and musicians at dub sound system events and has, likewise, been the subject of much research into the reception of electronic dance music in clubs and raves. For example, Joshua Schmidt's work on Israeli "psytrance" (i.e., psychedelic trance) and "*transistim*" (attendees at all-night psytrance events) refers to a "magical sense of temporary communion experienced at psytrance gatherings." There is, he continues, "an extraordinary, almost mystical bond to be formed between the *transistim*. This union may be understood as an imaginative form of dance therapy and one which provides *transistim* with a unique remedy for coping with the pressure cooker of Israeli society and politics."[15] Again, individuals are lifted out of their everyday lives by a "spontaneous overflow of powerful feelings" which evokes a sense of shared love.

Reflecting on his experiences as a member of the audience—and, by extension, how his own audiences might receive him—Iggy Pop suggested that it is "obvious that rock 'n' roll is a religion; it's formatted exactly as a religion. You're out there in the audience, and you see a person or a group of people take the stage, and those first moments of music are really powerful. The music cascades off you like crystals, like little crystals of energy, and those people on stage are transformed. They're living gods at that moment – you're looking at humans made gods. That fascinates people because their day-to-day existence, which is so tawdry, doesn't measure up to it . . . I've had spiritual experiences at rock concerts."[16] This is put very well. The power and shape of the experience, the collective effervescence, is such that it can only be articulated in ecstatic religious terms. The sacred is glimpsed in significant, immersive, atheological moments of "inner experience," as Bataille referred to them, during which we are brought face to face with the insignificance of our personal, everyday mundanity *and also*—within an episode of spontaneous *communitas* driven by the affective impact of the music—transcend that profane existence.

Likewise, from the supply side, so to speak, "the Romantic aesthetics to which our music practices are heir," says Allan Moore, "are founded . . . on the assumption of the autonomy – the separation from the outside world – of the musical experience."[17] As Rupert Till puts it, the experience of producing music is akin to a "transcendental experience . . . an altered state of consciousness . . . an enhanced level of connection with [one's] emotions . . . fellow musicians and . . . audience in comparison to when not playing music."[18] As if agreeing with Sister Sledge, Mick Jagger confirms that "you do lose yourself" in music. He continues, "When that transcendental moment happens, it can be quite scary. Because sometimes you lose yourself onstage and there are a lot of people out there. You can just get lost for whole moments, and I get scared when those moments happen. You wonder if you've been in that reverie too long. In jazz parlance, they used to call it being gone. They'd say, 'He's gone.'"[19] Again, Iggy Pop is convinced that it's about "the vibe and the quality of the thing; it's about totally losing yourself and understanding that what you're doing right here, right now, is the most important thing in the world."[20] It's a sacred moment.

Thinking more closely about the sacred significance of this moment, the prolific avant-garde jazz musician John Zorn has concluded that, "in addition to the nuts and bolts involved in the craft of sculpting a piece of music, there is the divine spark of inspiration that gives it birth, which often is just as much of a mystery to the artists who experience it as it is to the uninitiated who have not."[21] Such statements are explicitly Romantic in their desire to describe the creation of music as a sacred process, an encounter with the ineffable. He continues:

This unfathomable element of the creative equation is rarely spoken by musicians, perhaps out of the belief (or fear) that to speak of it would cause it to vanish, never to return. But it is there, equally veiled as it is vital – at time overwhelming. Described alternately as being in the zone or the flow, channeling the muse, self-hypnosis or the piece of writing itself, the feeling is a universal yet ineffable one of being in touch with something outside or larger than oneself. The manifestations of this can include an unusually intense concentration on one's work resulting in a lost sense of self, a merging of action and awareness to the extent that that successes and failures become immediately apparent, a perfect balance between ability level and challenge, a powerful sense of personal control rendering the process effortless, and often an altered or lost sense of time. Goals become so clear as to be almost absent – one exists inside the hot crucible of creativity itself, connected with a spirit, energy or historical lineage that is overpowering, exhilarating, frightening. One is one's goal, and the creative act is existence – rewarding in and of itself. At these times, freedom (so normally equated with artists) becomes obeisance. One does what one is compelled to do, inevitably resulting in something beyond your known abilities. . . . Unless you have actually experienced this remarkable phenomenon, it sounds suspiciously like Romantic fantasy. But it is real. There are places beyond thought, beyond thinking; places where intuition merges with destiny – places of transcendence – and in our newly formed, hi-speed, digitized world of the multitask, it may be that the only way to retain our innate inner-born humanity is in taking on and tapping into the challenge of the unknowable stream of the eternal.[22]

It is unsurprising, therefore, that, for Zorn, "mysticism, magic and alchemy all come into play in the creative process."[23] Indeed, Zorn's volume from which this quotation is taken, *Arcana V*, is an intriguing and, at points, beautifully enigmatic collection of esoteric reflections on the creation and reception of music by musicians themselves.[24]

Bearing in mind this Romantic bias toward enchantment, it is, as noted in the Introduction, rather odd that, until relatively recently, the sacred has been something of a blind spot in popular music studies. Indeed, this is particularly odd in that some of the dominant discourses in popular music have had explicitly religious/spiritual/occult content. Apart from music associated with particular religious traditions, such as gospel, reggae, and qawwali, there have been very clear articulations of an interest in the sacred and the supernatural. Whether we think of the much-mythologized Crowleyesque preoccupations of Jimmy Page and the speculation surrounding the occult signification within the music and cover art of *Led Zeppelin IV*;[25] or the bewitching influence of Crowley's *Diary of a Drug Fiend* on Peter Perrett of The Only

Ones;[26] or the occult mist hanging over the Blue Öyster Cult; or the understated traces of M.R. James haunting the work of the cantankerous Mancunian Mark E. Smith of The Fall;[27] or the idiosyncratic and often quaint musings on the bucolic and the Pagan in the songs of The Watersons, The Incredible String Band, Andy Partridge, The Waterboys, Julian Cope, and Björk; or the penchant for the Gothic in the music of Siouxsie and the Banshees, Nick Cave, Bauhaus, and The Sisters of Mercy; or black metal's litanies to the Southern Lord and the affective spaces shaped by its meditations on the dark solitude of Northern wildernesses, there is a pronounced Romantic preoccupation with the sacred woven through popular music culture.

In using the polysemous term "Romanticism" we are not, of course, thinking primarily of the "new romantic" genre in popular music that flourished between 1979 and 1981. While there was that which was affectively Romantic about new romantic music, such as that of early Duran Duran and particularly Visage, the focus tended to be primarily foppish and sartorial rather than, so to speak, ideologically Romantic—not that being a fop necessarily lacked Romantic significance. Rather, as the poem at the beginning of the chapter indicates, the term, as it is used in this discussion, refers to a broad stream of ideas, aesthetic and ideological, that have some continuity with those associated with early nineteenth-century Romanticism and, to a lesser extent, the related Gothic tradition.[28] There were, of course, various national Romanticisms, each of which were philosophically distinct, just as each had their strengths and weaknesses in the ways they expressed themselves through the arts.[29] In using the term here, however, while having an eye on English Romanticism, I am generalizing.

In our examination of the sacred, there are several key Romantic themes that can be traced through into contemporary popular music. These can be delineated as follows. Firstly, although the Romantics radically modified or abandoned the cardinal forms of Christian orthodoxy, they generally favored what might be described as a "spiritual" view of life.[30] Hence, for example, the word "God" could be used symbolically for "the Absolute, or the World Soul, or the Power of Nature, or Providence, or perhaps," says Bernard Reardon, recalling Wordsworth's "Lines Written a Few Miles Above Tintern Abbey," "only a scarcely articulate 'sense of something still more deeply interfused.' "[31] Likewise, in much popular music there is a rejection of "religion," particularly patriarchal thou-shalt-not-Christianity, in favor of a sense of depth.

Secondly, there was a critique of the skeptical and rationalist teaching that emerged out of the eighteenth-century Enlightenment, which, in philosophy, was developed in terms of the idealist metaphysical systems of Fichte, Schelling, and Hegel and the religious philosophy of Schleiermacher, all of whom "opposed the abstractions of Newtonian 'reason' with a new appeal to experience – the apprehension and appreciation of life in all its range and variety, its accomplishment and promise."[32] At the heart of this experience was the feeling human being.

There was—as particularly articulated in music—a resistance to the hegemony of rationalism. Opposed to the idea that reality can be known simply by the application of human reason, Romanticism argued that there needs to be a complementary emphasis on human emotion, intuition and imagination. Reason may be a useful tool, but it is limited in its abilities. Hence, for example, Wordsworth and Coleridge appealed to the imagination as a faculty capable of transcending the limitations of human reason. Again, the construction of affective spaces which subvert rationalism and within which the meaning-making imagination is stimulated is key to the power of music. Individuals can, argued the Romantics, by the use of imagination see the infinite within the finite, feel the metaphysical animating the physical, observe the spiritual flowing through the material. Enlarging reason, the universe is viewed, not simply as a collection of rationally quantifiable matter, but rather as a living, creative entity permeated with a spiritual "presence" that cannot be discerned by the simple application of logic and reason. Again, the very nature of music communicates the Romantic impulse particularly well, which is why it has always been so central to cultures for which immediate experience is key. For example, Timothy Miller expresses this point very well in his discussion of American hippie culture in the sixties and seventies: "Insofar as this chapter is rational, it will, the hippies would have said, miss dealing with the real power of rock, since the music was preeminently something to be experienced and could not be explained entirely rationally. To the hippies, rock was not just sound; it was part and parcel of a way of life."[33]

Thirdly, this, however, did not mean that the empirical perspectives of science were to be dismissed: "Newton might be hated but he could not be ignored."[34] Consequently, while, on the one hand, science needed to be broadened to encompass the range of human experience, on the other hand, religion could not be expected to escape rational scrutiny. Indeed, there was great confidence in the individual's ability to know the truth about the nature of reality without recourse to divinely revealed propositions or to religious authorities. So whereas rationalism emphasized the abilities of unaided human reason in this respect, Romanticism, still focusing on the autonomy of the individual, stressed feeling, intuition and imagination. It is very likely that God will be more evident in the "Garden of Love" than in the "chapel." The point is, however, that the spiritual life, as "a vital mode of human experience," falls within "the scope of a philosophy which recognized that the life of humanity, emotional as well as rational, affords the only possible approach for a comprehensive intelligence of the world."[35]

Finally, as we have seen is the case with Zorn, there is a conspicuous Romantic concern with artistic authenticity, which tends to be understood in terms of spontaneity, originality and "inner truth."[36] We should stop here for a moment to remind ourselves that authenticity is a problematic concept, which some, for very sound reasons, would like to consign to "the intellectual dustheap,"[37] since it is primarily a subjective, ideological construction. Nonetheless, because we are concerned in this discussion with articulations of the sacred—understood variously as personal and cultural expressions not determined by a universal ontology or dependent on a foundationalist discourse but rather socially and culturally constructed—the concept of authenticity is an important one in helping us toward identifying perceptions of the sacred at particular moments in a culture's history. Hence, if it is not already obvious, I have no interest in what may or what may not be "authentic," but rather in *why* particular cultural practices *are perceived as* authentic. So, to return to the previous discussion—when Zorn speaks of that which is authentic, he is consciously walking on sacred ground, communicating depth, identifying what is "real" and "true" to him and to those who that share that discourse.[38] Again, as Nicola Dibben comments in her discussion of Björk's music, "authenticity . . . is manifested as the expression of true emotions in artistic output through qualities associated with intimacy and immediacy; it is a sincere commitment to one's creativity, evidenced through a lack of artifice, connection to the primal, artistic motivations rather than those of fame or money, and by the refusal to court the mainstream."[39] Such ideas, conspicuous in discussions of folk music, reflect the concerns expressed in Wordsworth's Preface to the 1800 edition of *Lyrical Ballads*:

> The principal object then which I proposed to myself in these Poems was to make the incidents of common life interesting by tracing in them, truly though not ostentatiously, the primary laws of our nature: chiefly as far as regards the manner in which we associate ideas in a state of excitement. Low and rustic life was generally chosen because in that situation the essential passions of the heart find better soil in which they can attain their maturity, are less under restraint, and speak a plainer and more emphatic language; because in that situation our elementary feelings exist in a state of greater simplicity and consequently may be more accurately contemplated and more forcibly communicated; because the manners of rural life germinate from those elementary feelings; and from the necessary character of rural occupations are more easily comprehended; and are more durable; and lastly, because in that situation the passions of men are incorporated with the beautiful and permanent forms of nature. The language too of these men is adopted . . . because such men hourly communicate with the best objects from which the best part of language is originally derived; and because, from their rank in society and the sameness and narrow circle of their intercourse, being less under the action of social vanity they convey their feelings and notions in simple and unelaborated expressions.[40]

This focus on the "low and rustic life," on the communication of "feelings and notions in simple and unelaborated expressions," is typical within folk ideology. The point is made very precisely by the folklorist and musician Bob Pegg of the band Mr. Fox: "We were very influenced by Wordsworth and Coleridge – the plain speech that informs *Lyrical Ballads* is behind a lot of the songs. In fact, I was pursuing an illusion, and I did come to realise this eventually, but that was part of the attraction of the [Yorkshire] Dales, this kind of innocence, this rawness, this unslickness in the music, and the fact that this music is also rooted in place."[41] Again, it is for this reason that Richard Thompson celebrates Appalachian music, for in it, he says, "you hear the old stuff. In some cases the ballads have survived more intact in Appalachia than they have in England. In purer form with less change."[42] Subjectivity is channelled with an uncluttered, uncontrived directness. As such, the music is thought to communicate, as closely as possible, the affects and meanings that originally gave birth to it. The aim was to retreat as far as possible from the artifice of the modern world to that "better soil" in which "the essential passions of the heart . . . can attain their maturity, are less under restraint, and speak a plainer and more emphatic language." To compromise this was to compromise more than taste. Indeed, to a large extent, this explains the reaction to Bob Dylan's use of electric guitar on *Bringing It All Back Home* (1965), in that it upset folk purists such as Ewan MacColl and led to the now famous outburst, "Judas," from a member of the audience at Manchester's Free Trade Hall in 1966. There was a sense that something sacred had been profaned, a sense that authenticity had been compromised and that, because the sin had been committed by a musician with his influence, an axe had been laid at the root of a tree that had taken years to grow and that many had spent their lives nurturing. Again, for those who felt betrayed, it signified more than a difference in taste. Like Judas's kissing of Jesus in Gethsemane, Dylan's picking up of an electric guitar was a deeply profound event, a profane moment.

In summary, to return to my earlier comments, at the heart of what I understand to be the Romantic gaze within popular music is, again, what Wordsworth referred to as the "sense sublime, of something far more deeply interfused."[43] This may take the form of nostalgia for a vanished past when, it is imagined, the world was a simpler, more enchanted place; it may manifest in a desire for an organic unity between people, culture, and nature; it may be that cast of mind, so beautifully articulated in the songs of Nick Drake, that is able to see, as William Blake put it, "a world in a grain of sand, and a heaven in a wild flower";[44] it may, as in Gothic, seek enchantment in the shadows, peering through the cracks of the everyday into the dark recesses of human experience. All such tributaries feed into the occultural reservoir from which much popular music has, over the years, refreshed itself. Whether we think of the fascination with the human relationship to nature, or the acquisition of arcane knowledge, or the interest in premodern imagery and mythologies, or the concern to retrieve folk cultures and retreat to rural living, or the penchant for all things Germanic, gloomy, morbid, and darkly ethereal, popular music has consistently sought to evoke Romantic affective space.

Nature, technology, and the sacred

Much countercultural discourse about nature, technology and the sacred, wittingly or unwittingly, follows "the White thesis," as it has come to be known after the influential 1967 essay by the historian Lynn White.[45] This thesis describes Paganism's retreat before Christianity in Europe in terms of a psychic revolution, which laid the foundations for the technological despoliation of nature and the contemporary environmental crisis. Essentially, because the Creator is understood to be transcendent—*other than* the created order—nature and the sacred are divorced. As such, however it is interpreted, the long arc of institutional monotheism holds the key to the progressive disenchantment of the natural world. As Max Weber had argued, instead of worrying about a host of competing, capricious deities, spirits and entities in nature, because the monotheist is concerned to obey only one transcendent God, understood as wholly other than the mundane, the ethical is rationalized and the scope of the sacred shrinks as the mysterious, the miraculous, and the magical are expunged from the world. For example, the Greek deity Pan " . . . was identified with nature, or indeed with matter itself. Pictured as a hybrid of goat and man, he captured the tension between the *kosmos* and the *theos* of Greek pantheism, and as bringer of panic discouraged the misuse of wilderness."[46] With his death at the hands of Christians, again, the divine was situated outside nature and the taboos associated with the natural world evaporated. Nature became vulnerable. It became merely the physical arena in which one obeyed God and exploited the divine provision. Hence, while, as Keith Thomas's work suggests, popular religion and magic continued to thrive during the medieval period, as the logic of Christian theology took hold of the European mind their influence waned.[47] By the time of the industrial revolution the forces of disenchantment were conspicuous. Nature became mastered by science, its value was measured by economics, and its potentiality was determined by technology.

While White's thesis has not, of course, gone unchallenged, and certainly needs to be understood within a larger frame, nevertheless the general point is fairly robust: it is difficult to deny that what Friedrich Schiller referred to as *die Entgötterung der Natur*—the "dis-godding" of nature—changed the perception of the natural world.[48] That said, robust or not, the point here is that it is this type of thinking that we find informing much countercultural discourse since the 1960s. Indeed, even if the relationship with monotheism was not fully understood, nevertheless, it did tend to be the case that the turn to nature was, more often than not, accompanied by a turn away from traditional Christianity. Consequently, most early hippie writings on the environment tended to be, as Miller notes, "philosophically based on Eastern metaphysics and pieces of the Native American tradition"[49]— i.e., nature-oriented traditions not implicated in scientific, industrial modernity.

Such concerns around the progress of what was referred to as a "technocratic totalitarianism" were clearly articulated by Theodore Roszak in his influential study at the close of the 1960s, *The Making of a Counter Culture*:

> ... from my own point view, the counter culture, far more than merely 'meriting' attention, desperately requires it, since I am at a loss to know where, besides among these dissenting young people and their heirs of the next generations, the radical discontent and innovation can be found that might transform this disoriented civilization of ours into something a human being can identify as home. They are the matrix in which an alternative, but still excessively fragile future is taking shape. Granted that alternative comes dressed in a garish motley, its costume borrowed from many and exotic sources – from depth psychiatry, from the mellowed remnants of left-wing ideology, from the oriental religions, from Romantic *Weltschmertz*, from anarchist social theory, from Dada and American Indian lore, and, I suppose, the perennial wisdom. Still it looks to me like all we have to hold against the final consolidation of a technocratic totalitarianism in which we shall find ourselves ingeniously adapted to an existence wholly estranged from everything that has made the life of man an interesting adventure.[50]

We will return to some of these issues, but the point here is that, while artists such as Nick Drake, John Martyn and Joni Mitchell refrained from singing old folk songs about rural life, nevertheless their music resonated with, as Rob Young puts it, "Romantic yearning for an intense communion with nature and the desire to reclaim a stolen innocence."[51] Like many artists of the period, they were, in part, responding to what they understood to be the technological profanation of the modern world, a profanation, moreover, that seemed to follow in the wake of an aggressive capitalistic, Christian culture. Joni Mitchell is typical in calling for farmers to abandon DDT and the pursuit of perfect fruit in order to protect wildlife and the wilderness. Unfortunately, "They paved paradise/And put up a parking lot" (Joni Mitchell, "Big Yellow Taxi," *Ladies of the Canyon*, 1970). Indeed, there was a sense that, on the one hand, the stolen innocence was both premodern and pre-Christian, and, on the other hand, nature, rural living, folk culture, and indigenous spiritualities represented the principal contours of a sacred lifeworld they wanted to recover. Likewise, more recent artists, such as Drew Nelson, who draws inspiration from Native American culture, carefully articulate a similarly Romantic critique of the profanation of nature, as well as a sense of a stolen innocence: "Wal-Mart came and the Orchard's gone/ You can buy tires there pretty cheap/ Just can't climb no apple tree ... There's a cell phone tower where the barn used to be ... Old McDonald had a cow when they tore that sucker down ... " ("Wal-Mart V2.0," *Immigrant Son*, 2005).

The ideal of returning to a preindustrial, rural idyll was particularly evident in the growth of music festivals, especially the free festivals of the late sixties and seventies. Hence many of these events were far more significant than simply gatherings of people wanting to listen to music in fields. Idealistic, romanticized notions of love, community, spirituality, and a relationship to nature were expressed by many who sought to retreat from the modern world. Indeed, it is significant that Timothy Miller describes such festivals in explicitly religious terms: "They were as important to the hip world as any pilgrimages, crusades, or revivals have ever been to their own constituencies. They . . . provided the best opportunities for massive indulgence in the sacraments: dope, nudity, sex, rock, community."[52] Likewise, one need only flick through Ron Reid's photographs from the period in his and Jeremy Sandford's *Tomorrow's People* to get a sense of the sacred that permeated festival idealism. As Miller suggests, the periodic nudity at the early festivals, the open displays of emotion and sexuality, were an important expression of a yearning for a holistic relationship with nature through which something good, wholesome, and enlightening might be perceived. In other words, festivals became spaces within which the sacred alternative to everyday urban existence could be experienced in a spirit of *communitas* and freedom. From the flower painted on a person's chest to the grass, the mud, the trees, and the open sky, it all signified separation from a profane, technocratic, industrial society: "Young people hate the cities of today," explained one festivalgoer to Sandford at Glastonbury Fayre. "They know that the schools they go to are a swindle. They are often emotionally deprived, perhaps because they have no prenatal intelligence of their worth. They have an unclean feeling of feeling. So, they want to get out into the country, where they can return to a more real form of living. The festivals enable them to do this."[53] As Sandford himself says of what he calls "the Glastonbury ethic," it concerned "caring for ourselves in conjunction with the environment; a consciousness of your effect on the environment while you're living in it, and the effect of the environment on you . . . I think that most people who were at Glastonbury were changed by it; changed by the knowledge that all of this was free and the result of people working for it because they believed in giving. We learned a sort of proximity in spiritual terms from Glastonbury; one lesson we learned was we are the earth, the earth is in us."[54] This type of yearning is conspicuous in the songs of the period, such as Joni Mitchell's longing to "get back to the garden" in "Woodstock" (*Ladies of the Canyon*, 1970), or John Martyn's ethereal "One World" (*One World*, 1977), or Spirit's poignant "Nature's Way" (*Twelve Dreams of Dr. Sardonicus*, 1970). The vision was, as far as possible, to live together in harmony with nature.[55]

The turn to nature and the suspicion of technology usually entailed the romanticization of a rural past. Hence, for example, the pseudoarchaic spelling of "fayre," used of the first Glastonbury festival, is significant. As one of those involved in the organization of the festival put it, "we had in mind a 'fayre' like the old fayres of Mediaeval Britain."[56] More than that, however, specific occultural connections to sacred space were frequently made: "the fayre was held at Glastonbury because it is a very holy place. Glastonbury is impregnated with the life of the spirit down the ages. It is the very heart centre of this body of England. And the wonderful things that are going to be, are going to start here, exactly here. What drew these people to Glastonbury was a feeling that from this ancient sacred place a new spirit is to spread among men. They were here to bear witness to the birth of the new era, the Age of Aquarius."[57] An imagined premodern past provided the key to the future return of the sacred. The Christian/Piscean age of industry and militarism was coming to a close and, as the 1967 musical *Hair* triumphantly declared, humanity was witnessing the "dawning of the age of Aquarius." This utopian confluence of nature, heritage, myth, and elements of contemporary occulture was made explicit in Glastonbury's manifesto: "It will be in the medieval tradition, embodying the legends of the area, with music, dance, poetry, theatre, lights and the opportunity for spontaneous entertainment. There will be no monetary profit – it will be free." It continues, "Man is fast ruining his environment. He is suffering from the effects of pollution; from the neurosis brought about by a basically urban industrial society; from the lack of spirituality in his life. The aims of Glastonbury Fayre are, therefore: the conservation of our natural resources; a respect for nature and life; and a spiritual awakening."[58] "The last hours of darkness are the longest," says Reid in a concluding statement to the festivalgoers he had photographed, "and you are the first light that creases the dawn of Aquarius."[59] In other words, there was a sense in which the festival represented a microcosm of a new, utopian community on the edges of an old, decadent, profane society, divorced from nature by patriarchal religion and the "dark Satanic mills" of greed, consumerism, and technology.[60] As someone commented on one of the recent websites devoted to the Woodstock festival, "Woodstock is no longer a place, but let this place be sacred, for it is where it all came together for so many people . . . It has nothing to do with drugs, or the music, or even Bethel, N.Y. It has to do with the people and their way of thinking, their way of loving and believing." As John Street says, "for this person, Woodstock exists as a symbolic resource, a way of thinking about the 'good life.'" He continues, "this use of Woodstock is not exclusive to its place of origin. According to Greil Marcus, the demonstrators in Tiananmen Square justified themselves 'with images of Woodstock.'"[61] As with all such constructions of utopia, they tell us much about contemporary perceptions of the sacred and the profane. As such, they are, of course, politically significant, in that they indicate how nonutopian societies might be redeemed and how profane threats to the realization of that vision might be resisted.

To some extent, the countercultural utopianism of the sixties and seventies had continuities with the Romantic vision central to Blake's 1804 poem, "And did those feet in ancient time." Explicitly linking England to the apocalyptic Jerusalem of Revelation 21—which describes the consummation of all things, the renewal of creation, and the establishment of peace and love—it is contrasted with the "dark Satanic mills" of the Industrial Revolution. Indeed, some popular musicians have transposed Blake's vision into the harsh realities of life in Britain at the beginning of the 1970s. Genesis, for example, in "Supper's Ready" (*Foxtrot*, 1972) provided Blakean reflection on contemporary society—but with a far more traditionally Christian reading of the book of Revelation. The song looks beyond the hardships, the power cuts, the unemployment, and the faded dreams of the postwar generation to a time of peace and well-being. With direct reference to the Christ of 1 Timothy 6:15—"the King of kings and Lord of lords"—the song declares that he "Has returned to lead his children home/To take them to the New Jerusalem." Significantly more Blakean was *Blake's New Jerusalem* (1978) by Tim Blake, which drew together a number of occultural strands relating Glastonbury legends to the idea of an Aquarian New Jerusalem.[62] Other artists who have been similarly drawn to these utopian sacred forms have simply adapted Hubert Parry's 1916 composition "Jerusalem" –which sets Blake's poem to music—notable examples being Emerson, Lake and Palmer ("Jerusalem," *Brain Salad Surgery*, 1973) and The Fall ("Jerusalem," *I am Kurious Orange*, 1988). The point is, however, that following the contours of Blake's thought, there are morally and emotionally layered constructions of the sacred and the profane operating here. The ideal of an inclusive civil society, supporting the happiness and well-being of all, is distilled, albeit nebulously, in the concept of the New Jerusalem, which has been constructed over against ideas of the profane nature of contemporary industrial society.

Modernity's "dark Satanic mills," on the other hand, were increasingly viewed, as the profane often is, through an apocalyptic lens. Lyrics were littered with references to "the imminent demise of the dominant culture, the urgency of cultural revolution, the dead end of modern technological culture."[63] This discourse had particular poignancy following the Cuban missile crisis of October, 1962, which had the effect of bringing Armageddon to the forefront of Western minds. The corrupting profanity of technology unbound was nowhere more conspicuous than in the development of the atom bomb, the mushroom cloud being its most potent symbol: "mushroom clouds are forming . . . Little children dying" (Love, "Mushroom Clouds," *Love*, 1966). (Note the juxtaposition with the innocence of childhood, the effect of which is to accentuate the profanity of nuclear weapons.) The Romantic sense of a lost innocence finds its dark nadir in a secular apocalypse. "This is where the summer ends/In a flash of pure destruction no one wins" (Ryan Adams, "Nuclear," *Demolition*, 2002). Consequently, since the mid-sixties, particularly during the Cold War years, apocalyptic discourse became prominent in popular music, from hardcore to reggae: e.g., Earth Crisis, *Destroy All Machines* (1995), *Gomorah's Season Ends* (1996);[64] Peter Tosh, *No Nuclear War* (1987); Mikey Dread, *World War III* (1980); Mighty Maytones, *Madness* (1976); and Michael Jackson, "Earth Song" (1995).[65] In other words, as thoughtfully articulated in Black Sabbath's "War Pigs" (*Paranoid*, 1970), the Satanic profanation of society is identified, as in Blake's poem, not as supernatural evil, but as the irresponsible use of technology. Likening conclaves of generals to covens and black masses, there is a very clear identification of the real threat to humanity, namely, the politicians and military strategists, whose "Evil minds . . . plot destruction." It is they who are the "Sorcerers of death's construction." The most potent of dark forces are not demonic, but technological. That said, it is, of course, important to understand that it is "war pig" politics, not technology per se, that Black Sabbath identifies as a profane threat to life. This is an important point, in that, for many musicians, it was increasingly the misuse of technology that was problematic, not the technology itself—after all they were happy to use amplifiers and take LSD. As Steve Levine, an editor of the *San Francisco Oracle*, responded when asked by Leonard and Deborah Wolf how the counterculture could reconcile its objections to technology with the necessity of technology for rock, "the objection was never so much to technology itself as to its uses."[66] While technology could take hippies to Woodstock, enable them to listen to Hendrix, get them stoned, and prevent unplanned pregnancies, it needed to be used wisely in the service of the sacred—love and peace.

It would, of course, be naïve to suggest that there was a consensus about nature, technology and the sacred in popular music culture. There wasn't. Indeed, by the close of the sixties, increasing numbers were beginning to implicitly align themselves with Francis Bacon's thesis that science should seek to understand and change the world through technological intervention. Although there may be limits to what humanity could and should do, nevertheless technology should be embraced and nature should by subdued and brought under control. The human empire should be extended into the natural world. Kraftwerk's blend of art, mass culture, and technology is a conspicuous example of this anti-Romantic trajectory. For example, the cover art for the German release of *Autobahn* (1974) and the title track both articulate a Baconian interventionist attitude to the natural world. Celebrating the first autobahn, the Bundesautobahn 555 between Cologne and Bonn, the steady machine regularity of the music communicates a sleek, modern, freedom-enhancing passage through the German landscape, subduing the wild unpredictability of nature. It represents a sanitized, mechanized, computerized paean to the machine. Pop rationalism. Evoking a very different affective space to much previous rock music, Kraftwerk encouraged the listener to view the rise of modern technology as not simply a side effect of nature's desacralization, as if its deliberate disenchantment subsequently allowed the expansion into nature of technological operations that had been restricted by the threat of supernatural reprisal. Rather, technology is the desacralization of nature. It performs a *necessary* disenchantment. As technology's powers advance, as the autobahn subdues nature and carves a path through the landscape, so the natural world is sanitized, brought under control and managed. It's wild unpredictability is reined in, made safe: "Here in my car/I feel safest of all," sang a relieved Gary Numan five years later ("Cars," 1979).

The liminal Romantic spirit, however, is adaptable. It need not retreat before the advance of technology. Just as many folk musicians followed Bob Dylan to the amplifier store, so many found ways to express the Romantic spirit electronically through oscillators, including combining synthesizer technology with sounds sampled from the natural world (e.g., Wendy Carlos, *Sonic Seasonings*, 1972). While such musicians may have agreed with Kraftwerk that the purpose of technology is to serve humanity (e.g., "The Robots," *The Man-Machine*, 1978), they felt that listeners might be best served through the creation of affective spaces that drew them back to nature. For example, on their fourth album, *Atem* (1973), Tangerine Dream moved away from the guitar-oriented psychedelic sound they had been developing since *Electronic Meditation* (1967) to experiment more fully with the new technology. Making particular use of the Moog synthesizer (Chris Franke) and an early type of sampler, the mellotron (Edgar Froese), they sought to create atmospheric spaces within which the listener might be drawn away from the workaday world into imaginary landscapes. A good example of this is the track "Fauni Gena," which opens with the gentle hum of jungle sounds. There is, as Paul Stump comments, a "departure into rapt nature-worship." The "forest-murmuring 'Fauni Gena'" immediately transports the listener into the wild: "a miraculous, pellucid piece of mellotron virtuosity from Froese, all fake sul pont strings and chirruping wood-flutes in hauntingly beautiful minor keys with snatches of elusive phrases peeping out of the undergrowth here and there."[67] This is sonic reenchantment. Likewise, the haunting and menacing synthesizer soundscapes produced on the track "Circulation of Events" takes us a long way from the shiny, industrial future imagined by Kraftwerk to darker, wilder places in which ancient spirits still reside. The point is that their use of technology sought not to subdue nature with its machine regularity, to push forward the process of secularization, but to evoke its majesty and mystery, and affectively to immerse the listener in it. Developing this aesthetic, their next album, *Phaedra* (1974), introduced the sequencer in order to weave trancelike rhythms through atmospheric soundscapes, thereby slowing down time and creating affective spaces ideal for the hippie psychonauts of beanbag culture. Of course, such meditative evocations of nature have become a prominent feature of contemporary electronica, from the gentle atmospheres of Brian Eno's *On Land* (1982), inspired by rural locations around the British Isles, to the sonic textures mimetic of the Icelandic environment in the work of Björk and Sigur Rós. The music of Björk, for example, includes sampled sounds from nature, such as beats constructed from cracking ice on "Frosti" and footsteps in the snow on "Aurora" (*Vespertine*, 2001). Again, as we will see below, technology is creating affective spaces within which nature is evoked and Pan is resurrected.

Getting back to the garden

As we have seen, nostalgia for a vanished past and rhetoric regarding authenticity and the close relationship between humanity and nature is common in articulations of folk culture. Such cultures are described as authentic expressions of a traditional, communal way of life, which is now past or only accessible through the memories of a disappearing older generation. This discourse, the roots of which lie in the Enlightenment, Romanticism, and the bourgeois appropriation of folk culture, is constructed around an understanding of, on the one hand, nature as intrinsically good and, on the other hand, civilization building as a process of estrangement from nature. As Richard Middleton comments, "conscience 'speaks to us in the language of nature,' but few hear it. Rousseau's dramatization of the depths and struggles of authentic identity, whose 'inner voice,' if only uncovered beneath the babble of social conditioning, is what we should be true to, strikes a recognizably modern note: 'I long for the time,' he wrote, 'when, freed from the fetters of the body, I shall be myself, no longer torn in two, when I myself shall suffice for my own happiness.' "[68] As Middleton reminds us, for Rousseau, the original locus of this voice was projected in the figure of "noble savage"—a manifestation of authentic humanity, uncorrupted by civilization, open to innate, natural guidance, and free. The point is that it is this discourse which has informed concepts of truth and authenticity in much contemporary, Romantic countercultural thought and alternative spirituality.[69] To some extent, folk culture has been constructed as the culture of the noble savage over and against the profane culture of commerce and artifice, which is exemplified in popular music. For example, we have seen that this type of thinking is evident in the work of the principal collectors of folk music, Cecil Sharp and Alan Lomax, both of whom understood the folk song style to represent symbolically the core elements of a nation's culture—Rousseau's "voice of nature." Hence they believed that there was a significant sense in which the traditional folk song was able to connect, affectively, listeners to key sacred forms which were closely tied to that which was authentic—to that which was "real."

Bearing this in mind, in the tradition of Romantic conceptions of art and creativity, the folk musician came to be understood as a prophet of that which lies within, a priestly figure manifesting that "inexpugnable feeling that the finite is not self-explanatory and self-justifying, but that behind it and within it – shining, as it were, through it – there is always an infinite 'beyond.' "[70] This is important, because "he who has once glimpsed the infinity that permeates as well as transcends all finitude can never again rest content with the paltry this-and-that, the rationalized simplicities, of everyday life."[71] Hence, again, there is that which is prophetic, sacred, about the agent of transformative revelation.

The discourse around a quasi-mythical rural "folk culture," reified and sacralized as the authentic culture of a nation, can be traced through into more recent popular music. At a relatively superficial level, it is manifested in the names of bands and titles of songs and albums across a range of genres, from the experimental and psychedelic outlands of The Red Krayola's 1967 debut *The Parable of Arable Land* (1967) to Jethro Tull's more mainstream folk-rock albums *Living in the Past* (1972), *Minstrel in the Gallery* (1975), and *Songs from the Wood* (1977). Again, we might think of The Watersons' *Frost and Fire: A Calendar of Ritual and Magical Songs* (1965), The

Incredible String Band's *The Hangman's Beautiful Daughter* (1968), Traffic's *John Barleycorn Must Die* (1970), Neil Young's *After the Gold Rush* (1970) and *Harvest* (1972), John Martyn's *Bless the Weather* (1971), Mellow Candle's *Swaddling Songs* (1972), XTC's *English Settlement* (1982), and *Seeds on the Ground* (2008) by the Shanghai band, Cold Fairyland. References to the myth of an American promised land in the music of Bruce Springsteen,[72] or to Albion in English music,[73] or to pre-Christian indigenous religion and culture, or simply to agrarian societies litter popular music, bearing witness to a longing for lost authenticity and a yearning to hear the "voice of nature." Such cultural work constructs and supports sacred forms. For example, Björk's reflections on her family and ancestry consistently articulate a continuity with rural peasant life, which lies at the heart of Icelandic national identity.[74] Similarly, Julian Cope has, for the last couple of decades, been on something of a campaign to reclaim the ancient heritage of Europe through his music (e.g., *Peggy Suicide*, 1991; *Jehovahkill*, 1992), his Head Heritage project,[75] and two large, idiosyncratic guidebooks to prehistoric sites, *The Modern Antiquarian* and *The Megalithic European*—"ignorance of your culture is not considered cool."[76] Indeed, following a number of disagreements with Island Records, the label eventually terminated his contract in 1992, partly, so it was claimed, because *Jehovahkill* was considered too critical of Christianity. Whether this is entirely true or not, certainly the album foregrounded his celebration of an ancient, pre-Christian Paganism and his opposition to the more recent Christian religion: "Jesus and Mary—huh/That was only yesterday" ('Megalithomania,' *Jehovahkill*). "5000 years ago," he writes in the liner notes to *Jehovahkill*, "Ancient Man built a huge Serpent Temple, or Dracontium, at Avebury, 80 miles west of London. . . . Yet by the middle of the last century, the temple had been almost obliterated by deconstructive sin-obsessed, small-minded, do-gooders in the name of the Christian God. . . . Visit Avebury and see how we worshipped before denial and sin was our obsession."[77]

Articulations of the authentic in the music of Björk and Julian Cope leave us in little doubt as to the location of the sacred and the profane. In other words, notions of the authentic/sacred are established through a set of binaries that enable the identification of an inauthentic other: Paganism and monotheism; modernity and premodernity; rural and urban; nature and technology. It is this discourse of difference that identifies modernity in terms of cultural regression rather than progression and insists that the key to vibrant, authentic contemporary well-being is the resurgence of the premodern. If we dig deep enough we will discover the bedrock of reality—authenticity, the sacred. There is an emotional continuity with the imagined values of an idealized past when our ancestors, those "noble savages," used to live in a harmonious, symbiotic relationship with the land.[78]

The conviction that values from these Neverlands of the past might have survived in folk songs, protected within isolated "primitive" rural communities living away from the corrosive effects of modernity, owes much to the work of Oxford University's first Professor of Anthropology, Edward Burnett Tylor. Published in

1871, his influential *Primitive Culture* argued that cultures contain "survivals" of earlier, more "primitive" cultures—"fragments of a dead lower culture embedded in a higher one."[79] While human progress had taken us from "savagery" through "barbarous hordes" to "civilized nations," there is evidence of sporadic cultural stalling scattered throughout advanced societies:

> Look at the modern European peasant using his hatchet and hoe, see his food boiling or roasting over the log-fire, observe the exact place which beer holds in his calculation of happiness, hear his tale of the ghost in the nearest haunted house, and of the farmer's niece who was bewitched with knots in her inside till she fell into fits and died. If we choose out in this way things which have altered little in a long course of centuries, we may draw a picture where there shall be scarce a hand's breadth difference between an English ploughman and a negro of Central Africa.[80]

These survivals, he argued, remind modern people of the "primitive cultures" from which their own societies emerged. However, unlike the champions of folk culture, for Tylor, "Pagan survivals" in both the colonies and the new industrial towns and cities of Europe and the United States indicated a profane threat to civilized ways of life.

Tylor's influence is seen very clearly in the writings of Sharp and Ralph Vaughan Williams: "I am a psychical researcher," declared Vaughan Williams, "who has actually seen a ghost, for I have been among the more primitive people of England and have noted down their songs."[81] As the folk musician Bob Pegg commented in his own study of European folklore, "one of the tales we like to believe is that popular folk or folk customs are survivals from a time when the members of a poor but contented peasantry, whose lives were rooted in the land they worked, celebrated the turning of the seasons and the accompanying vegetative cycle with simple jollity and innocent sexual licence."[82] Having said that, generally speaking, the assessment of such folk survivals was far more indebted to Rousseau than to Tylor. There was something pure and fundamentally good about folk culture. Indeed, it possessed a simplicity that could be used to resist the profane savagery of Britain's contemporary working-class culture. This type of elitism is, of course, as we saw in Chapter 1, very close to that of F.R. Leavis. As John Storey comments,

> The rural worker – the peasant – was mythologized as a figure of nature, a 'noble savage' walking the country lanes and working without complaint the fields of his or her betters – the living evidence of, and a link to, a purer and more stable past. The urban-industrial worker, however, was fixed firmly in the present, completely detached from any salvation the past may have been able to offer. Proof of a fall from grace was there for all to see in the urban-industrial worker's unquenchable taste for the corrupt and corrupting songs of the music hall.[83]

Hence, whereas the bourgeoisie might be encouraged to embrace a more organic past through an appreciation of folk songs, there was a feeling that the working class would have to be "forcefully schooled in folk song in the hope of softening their urban and industrial barbarism, especially as it was made manifest in their enjoyment of the songs of the music hall."[84] Sir Hubert Parry, for example, in his "Inaugural Address to the Folk Song Society" in 1899, worried that "there is an enemy at the door of folk music which is driving it out, namely, the common popular [music hall] songs of the day; and this enemy is one of the most repulsive and most insidious." He continues,

> If one thinks of the . . . terribly overgrown towns . . . where one sees all around the tawdriness of sham jewellery and shoddy clothes . . . [and] people who, for the most part, have the most false ideals, or none at all . . . who think that the commonest rowdyism is the highest expression of human emotion; it is for them that the modern popular music is made, and it is made with commercial intention out of snippets of musical slang.[85]

There could hardly be a more robust othering of popular music as inauthentic and profane. The sacrality of folk music, on the other hand, is obvious, it being "among the purest products of the human mind."[86] To state the point bluntly, just as there is a very clear sense of the sacred attached to folk music, so there is also a very clear sense of the profane attached to that which threatens it—commercial popular music.

Within a century, however, it would become very difficult to distinguish between the two. Popular musicians became the prophets and priests of a counterculture, which had adopted earlier Romantic sacred forms that demonized the urban and idealized the rural. Although they drew on earlier Romantic notions of folk culture, it was now commercially successful popular musicians who sought to reveal what lay beyond the senses, to transfigure reality, to create affective spaces within which the sacred could be experienced. It was these new Romantic heroes, these Orphic, liminal beings who were able, hypnotically, to provide a new vision for people mired in the mundane reality of everyday life. Within the affective spaces their music evoked, individuals could cross the conceptual threshold between the urban profane and the rural sacred: "We all live in the city/And imagine country scenes," sang Sandy Denny (Fotheringay, "The Pond and the Stream," *Fotheringay*, 1970). As Philip Abrams and Andrew McCulloch comment in their study of communes in Britain in the 1970s, not only did "craft work and agricultural labour" function as "images of an unalienated life," but they did so because "the smith and the ploughman were life-asserting figures in our folklore long before they were taken up in fantasies of escape from industrialism."[87] Jethro Tull, The Woods Band, Magna Carta, Trees, Forest, Mr. Fox—the very names of the bands seemed to embody the ideals of nature-oriented peasantry, as did the pastoral references in their songs, their sartorial taste, and, of course, their album covers: *The Hangman's Beautiful Daughter* (1968) by The Incredible String Band depicts the musicians as rural peasantry; Heron's *Twice as Nice For Half the Price* (1971) is a photograph of the band's rural cottage, suggesting simplicity and unworried, organic purity; *The North Star Grassman and the Ravens* (1971) by Sandy Denny, has her seated at a table in an old cottage kitchen pondering herbs, evocative of a premodern wise woman; Crosby, Stills, Nash and Young's *Déjà Vu* (1970) makes use of a pseudoarchaic typeface and a grainy photograph of the band with a gun and a dog to summon up the idealized values of the old West. Again, lyrically, Donovan's second album, *Fairytale* (1965), is typical of the period, in that, as Young describes it, its "benignly stoned odes fondly and naively imagined a long-lost, bucolic Avalon where like minds of a forever young flower generation might sit in peace, singing, dancing, smoking, making love and contemplating the universe in a guilt-free environment."[88]

While it may seem faintly naïve and quaint nowadays, again, it is important to understand that such contours in popular music culture reflect contemporary sacred forms, rather than simply being a manifestation of style—although they were that as well. While this was certainly not the case for all musicians, some practiced what they preached—and they did preach! Donovan, for example, having become wealthy, bourgeois and conspicuously un-peasant-like, purchased three remote Scottish islands—Islay, Mingay, and Clett—in order to realize his Romantic vision of rural bliss. Claiming to be "the last of the English minstrels," he sought to create a geographic sacred space, "a place where the twentieth century had never existed":[89] "Felt like a tide/left me here" ("Isle of Islay," *A Gift From A Flower To A Garden*, 1967). Similarly, in 1968, Vashti Bunyan—whose work has been a significant influence on more recent alternative folk musicians such as Adem, Devendra Banhart, Joanna Newsom, and Greg Weeks—began an idealistic, Luddite journey from Kent, by horse and cart, to the Outer Hebrides where she sought, with her partner Robert Lewis, to live a simple, premodern life.[90] The couple's song "Hebridean Sun," released on her previously overlooked, but now celebrated album *Just Another Diamond Day* (1970), reflects the desire to realize this utopian ideal: "Travelling towards a Hebridean sun/To build a white tower in our heads begun." Indeed, the whole album, particularly the title track, which includes members of The Incredible String Band and Fairport Convention, conveys an underlying yearning for premodern simplicity. As she says, "screening out modernity is exactly what we were doing . . . I got quite obsessive about rejecting the modern world in the end . . . So yes, we got completely fixated on old versus new."[91]

L.P. Hartley's memorable opening sentence in *The Go-Between* comes to mind: "The past is a foreign country: they do things differently there."[92] The past is important precisely because *they do things differently there* and it's foreign precisely because it's *nonmodern*. It is this *nonmodern* status that invests it with authenticity and sacred weight. In other words, it's important to make a distinction between *the past* and the *pre/nonmodern*, in that the difference is between the sacred and the profane, not past and present. The underlying motivation is to retreat from the hegemony of the contemporary profane and to recover the lost sacred. Hence, for many, there was no need to abandon drugs, electricity, and motor vehicles, but there was a need (perhaps through them) to recover that which was authentic, sacred, and foreign to the culture in which they lived.

Traffic are an excellent example of this flight from the modern in search of *pre/nonmodern* authenticity. In 1967 they retreated to a remote cottage in Berkshire near Aston Tirrold with their electric guitars and an ample sufficiency of psychedelics and cannabis. In this rural setting, away from everyday modernity, they believed they could search for reality and create music to express to their fans what they had found. What they produced was an aptly entitled album, *Mr Fantasy* (1967), the photograph on the gatefold cover of which gives some indication of the warm, hazy, languid, psychedelic cocoon they had created for themselves far from the madding crowd of the modern world.[93] As David Dalton commented in his article for *Rolling Stone*, following a visit to the band's rural idyll in 1969, "the cottage is an hour and a half from London, but it's a thousand light years from Soho Square"—a premodern foreign country, a thousand light years from the brightly lit consumerism and decadence of the modern world. Hence, the journey he describes is less about traveling across land and more an ideological account of the passage he takes between the urban profane and the rural sacred.

> Henley is like driving through a postcard, and then you pass through dozens of little English hamlets with names as heavy as a slice of farmhouse bread: Nettlebed, Wallingford, Uffington, Didcot. When we get to Aston Tirrold, we stop in at the pub to ask directions to the cottage. The owners are a friendly, florid old couple, who invite us in while the husband phones the cottage to see if we are permitted to go up. We cross the main road just outside tiny Aston Tirrold and dip down into the dirt track that leads to the cottage. There are really deep ruts in the road, and when it rains, it is impossible to take the upper road at all. Everyone who drives up for the first time stops here. Can this really be the road? Jim Capaldi had mentioned the white farm gate, giving us directions to get up here. You are reassured when you see it, it's the right road, everything is cool. Bristling hedges, moldy wooden fences; behind a clump of bushes there are some white wooden beehives, and, on the other side, vast fields recede endlessly into space. Weird, impossible perspectives curl around the horizon; covered hills interrupt infinity.[94]

Reading through his wonderfully evocative account, the sense of Romantic premodernity is palpable. This is not simply a rural location, it is sacred space: "the land in Berkshire is," he says, "especially numinous, filled with spirits; in these valleys between Oxford and London, the Thames basin, tribes of Stone Age and Bronze Age settled, farmed and built their monuments, mainly giant earthworks like Silbury and Uffington, which is five minutes from the cottage by Land Rover . . . " An occultural mist hangs over the landscape. Ancient cultures "have left their tracks, their scent on the land and everywhere it seeps through."[95]

Unsurprisingly, so culturally significant was this attempt to orientate life around a particular Romantic sacred form that it became part of the marketing strategy for a number of record companies. Island Records, for example, photographed Traffic in rural settings, nonchalantly walking through fields, strolling down country lanes, holding wildflowers, chopping wood, or relaxing next to Uffington's famous prehistoric White Horse carved into the side of an Oxfordshire hill. Again, to return to Dalton's narrative, he communicates the cultural and occultural significance of such marketing very well.

> Traffic were photographed for the centerfold of their second album [*Traffic*, 1968] at Uffington, sitting in the middle of the giant Neolithic chalk drawing which overlooks a dragon mound. It was in these valleys that Arthur, the spiritual and physical embodiment of the Celtic mysteries, fought off the invading hordes of Saxons and Vikings between 516 and 537 AD. Roman Hill is the highest point in Berkshire, and you can easily walk to it from the cottage. Stevie likes to take you up there as soon as you arrive, rattling across fields and lanes in Dave Mason's Land Rover climbing its steep sides to reach the small round platform. Sitting on top of the world, have a smoke, lie down in the long grass, exhausted with wonder, looking out on the soft green downs that stretch out forever into the misty blue distance. A low mound rising almost imperceptibly all around you like a green circular wave is all that is left on the surface of a Roman Temple, and of Celtic and Stone Age sanctuaries before it. In the center of the ring is a cement ordnance survey marker covered with symbols and numbers, indicating the elevation in feet above sea level . . . A dozen cultures overlapping in celebration of a sacred place, and a reminder of our own, looking ill at ease as the earth around gently devours it . . . The idyllic Berkshire cottage was part of Traffic's image. Island Records didn't neglect to tell you about it; it was a stock part of their publicity. What could have been more ideal? Four funky cats in this idyllic scene deep in the English countryside, where there is nothing really to do except get stoned, groove and make music.[96]

The key point, however, is that for Dalton, Traffic, and their fans, these photographs describe "a grove of sanity outside London's trendy mod world . . . " Again, this is not so much about the past per se, for, as he says, "looking out into the country around the cottage, you can imagine you are at any time in history." Rather the key point is that "there are no traces of the twentieth century to be seen anywhere – no houses or pylons, nothing to indicate time or place except the group's van standing in front of the cottage with the names of groupies scrawled on its dusty sides." It is the affective space created and the repertoires of meaning that are important. This comes across very clearly in the conclusion to his *Rolling Stone* article: "Chris [Wood] puts on some sounds, a group called the Watersons, who sing really ancient-sounding English folk songs, unaccompanied voices, weird harmonies . . . They are just a young group, just three kids, I think, but they have their sound down beautifully. Why do you think kids are getting so hung up on old things right now, like the Watersons, old clothes and stuff? 'It's because they don't want to live through this time, they don't want to be a part of it . . . ' says Chris."[97] That's the point! And, moreover, it's a point that has been central to the internal logic of eschatological discourse throughout history: "we don't want to live through this time, we don't want to be a part of it!" Such sentiments were, for example, distilled in the eschatology of the spirituals. As Lawrence Levine comments, "the slaves sang of 'rollin' thro' an unfriendly world,' of being 'a-trouble in de mind,' of living in a world which was a 'howling wilderness,' 'a hell to me,' of feeling like 'a motherless child,' 'a po' little orphan chile in de worl',' a 'home-e-less child,' of fearing that 'Trouble will bury me down.' "[98] Hence, they looked beyond the profane contemporary world—"This world is not my home"—to a sacred, idealised "home in heaven"—"They'll be joy on tomorrow . . . When my work on earth is through."[99] It is, I suggest, a form of the same utopian longing that motivates the Romantic idealization of rural life.

As indicated above, the desire to cross the threshold between the urban-profane and the rural-sacred was not uncommon. For example, in 1967, John Lennon purchased Dorinish, an uninhabited island in Clew Bay, County Mayo, Ireland, which he intended to develop into a retreat—but never did. He did, however, in 1970, invite the activist Sid Rawle, whom the press had dubbed "King of the Hippies," to establish a commune there, which he managed to do with twenty-five other hippies until 1972. Across the Irish Sea in Wales, Jimmy Page and Robert Plant of Led Zeppelin took up residence at Bron-Yr-Aur, a remote eighteenth-century cottage without running water and electricity in Snowdonia: "I think I'm basically a Romantic," said Page. "I can't relate to this age . . . "[100] Likewise, the Incredible String Band purchased a rural cottage at Glen Row, near Innerleithen in the Scottish Borders. In 1969, Fairport Convention moved into a Queen Anne mansion at Farley Chamberlayne near Winchester. Accompanied by birdsong, Roger Waters describes a warm, bucolic, pastoral scene at "Grantchester Meadows" in Cambridgeshire (Pink Floyd, *Ummagumma*, 1969), where guitarist Syd Barrett lived. And, perhaps most famously, in 1966 Paul McCartney purchased High Park Farm, a remote estate in Scotland, which became, said his wife Linda, a place for "getting back to natural life – we have horses and sheep and we plant our own vegetables, and it's the only place we can go that is very natural, in this unnatural world."[101] This *natural* tranquility is transfigured for their fans living everyday *unnatural* lives in the cities and the suburbs on albums such as *Ram* (1971) and songs such as "Mull of Kintyre" (1977), the latter of which drips with bucolic sentimentality. Through listening to their music, imagining ourselves into the narratives they share with us, we bask in their enlightenment, their Romantic beatification, their purification in nature. They fulfill (and perhaps create) our longing to be somewhere *other than* here.

As suggested in Led Zeppelin's song "Going to California," the "children of the sun" in the United States, with "love in [their] eyes and flowers in [their] hair," were inspired by a parallel vision, orienting their lives around very similar ideas of the sacred. James Perone, for example, has noted that the Back to the Land movements in the United States "featured a return to rural living, farming, and a resurgence of interest in traditional folk and country music . . . Even apart from the communes, there were close ties between the interest in returning to the land and renewed interest in American roots music."[102] These ties became conspicuous at Woodstock. As Alistair Cooke, the well-known British journalist, referred to the festivalgoers he witnessed making their way to Max Yasgur's farmland in Bethel, New York, they were "beautiful people who assumed that nature would provide . . . "[103] And their Romantic idealism was perhaps nowhere more beautifully articulated than in Joni Mitchell's song "Woodstock" (*Ladies of the Canyon*, 1970). Although written as the festival was taking place, she never actually made it there herself. Indeed, she recalls, "I don't know if I would have written the song . . . if I had gone. I was the fan that couldn't go . . . So it afforded me a different perspective."[104] She imagines traveling to the festival and, on the way, meeting "a child of God" walking down the road to "Yasgur's Farm" to "camp out on the land," to "lose the smog," to "free" his "soul"; she imagines bombers turning into butterflies; she asks us to think of ourselves as part of the cosmos—"We are stardust"—and, if there is to be any meaningful future at all, "we've got to get ourselves back to the garden." A sense of the redemptive power of nature, a yearning for a return to the sacred earth, and the need to leave the pollution and militarism of modernity is voiced almost achingly. Covered in the same year by both Matthews Southern Comfort (*Later That Same Year*, 1970) and Crosby, Still, Nash, and Young (*Déjà Vu*, 1970), the song immediately became an important hippie text, a lens that seemed to bring an inchoate sense of the sacred into focus. Of course, there were other similarly important texts, such as Canned Heat's celebration of leaving the city ("We might even leave the USA") for a rural promised land "where the water tastes like wine" ("Going Up the Country," *Living the Blues*, 1969). The religious imagery was frequently explicit. Indeed, even the name of the place where the festival was eventually held seemed significant to the organizers when they were looking for land: "About a quarter mile up, we broached the top of the hill and there it was. 'STOP THE CAR!' I shouted, barely able to believe my eyes. It was the field of my dreams – what I had hoped for from the first. It was not lost on me that we had . . . arrive[d] in *Bethel* – 'the House of God.' I left the car and walked into this perfect green bowl."[105] Again, the almost eschatological sense of arriving in sacred space is conspicuous. Moreover, because the festival was implicitly organized around sacred forms that had a compelling emotional force, which was subsequently mythologized in popular music culture, even today websites devoted to Woodstock[106] are, as Street discovered, "less concerned with the minute details of the performances in 1969, but rather with preserving the spirit of those days. The sites want to retain the mystique and aura of those distant days, to evoke the bucolic pleasures of communing with nature and with each other . . . Juan Morales says of Woodstock that it epitomized the 'social changes in human freedom and expression . . . we learned not to be ashamed of our bodies in the nude, we smoked grass to expand our horizons with the music, we spent time with our kids . . . it was LIFE!!' "[107] Although it has, of course, been sentimentalized and, as such, lost some of its original moral force, nevertheless, at the time, it was a significant catalytic and transgressive moment to which subsequent personal life changes, perhaps even social changes, can be traced back. Reflecting on the festival for a *Rolling Stone* article in 1969, Greil Marcus considered it to be "a confused, chaotic founding of something new, something our world must now find a way to deal with. The limits have changed now, they've been pushed out, the priorities have been rearranged, and new, 'impractical' ideas must be taken seriously. The mind boggles."[108] Although vibrant with the affective impact of the festival, these words still make good sense.

Pagan poetry

"A triple combination of drugs, sex, and Pagan spirituality . . . would give the Woodstock nation a mother Church,"[109] or so it was claimed by the short-lived hippie community, the Psychedelic Venus Church, founded in 1969. While this particular organization dissolved in 1973, its broadly Pagan focus was not unusual in the liminal cultures of the 1960s. Although we will see that many turned East, others, like the Psychedelic Venus Church, were occulturally more eclectic, mixing Eastern ideas with Romantic notions of Paganism. Nick Drake, for example, was not untypical, if the description of him as "a mystical concoction of Blake, Yeats and Buddhism"[110] is an accurate one. Indeed, many did follow in the footsteps of nineteenth-century Romantics and Transcendentalists. "Getting back to the garden" was often accompanied by an appreciation of pantheistic perspectives and the perceived authenticity of Pagan and indigenous spiritualities. Sometimes this influence was ambient and subtle; at other times it was conspicuous and explicitly transgressive. Hence, whereas, on the one hand, such sentiments are gently, almost imperceptibly, woven into an album such as Mike Oldfield's *Hergest Ridge* (1974), which communicates a sense of pantheistic oneness with the Herefordshire countryside around his home, just as folklore and Tolkienesque fantasy are innocently communicated in *Water Bearer* (1978) by his sister, Sally Oldfield, on the other hand, sixties and seventies popular music witnessed the emergence of an explicit fascination with occult ceremony and ritual, as evident in the live performances of bands such as Coven and Black Widow.

Concerning the gentler, ambient Pagan sympathies that color much popular music, some musicians, like their fans, are fascinated by liminal/threshhold ideas: the supernatural, the paranormal, and an interest in fantasy that created sacred texts out of books such as Tolkien's *Lord of the Rings*—which was, noted Warren Hinckle in 1967, "absolutely the favorite book of every hippy"[111]—Robert Heinlein's *Stranger in a Strange Land*—a foundational document for the Pagan group, The Church of All Worlds—and Robert Graves' *The White Goddess*, an influential text for many Pagans. As Graham Harvey comments in his study of the construction of contemporary Paganism, while studies of folklore have been important, "Tolkien's *Lord of the Rings* and other fantasy writings are more frequently mentioned by Pagans. Fantasy reenchants the world for many people, allowing them to talk of elves, goblins, dragons, talking-trees, and magic. It also encourages contemplation of different ways of relating to the world . . . "[112] Certainly fantasy-inspired discourse, particularly around *Lord of the Rings*,[113] was encouraged within popular music culture in the late-1960s and early 1970s. As Mike Oldfield says of Jon Anderson (of the band Yes), he "told me he believes totally in fairies and little beings. That's his reality, and it's fine by me, and who's to say there aren't little forces around everywhere . . . "[114] He wasn't alone. Tolkienesque occulture and stories of other worlds enchanted youth culture and meshed easily with hippie idealism. As Young points out,

> . . . it's easy to understand the appeal of Tolkien's Middle-earth to the British generation of Hobbit heads. Britain *was* Middle-earth: a conflicted cluster of kingdoms and languages, with a very aged ancient history that was written in scattered fragments and dialects across its map. The Shire, homeland of the Hobbits, is a caricature of the Anglo-Saxon ideal of Merrie England, all rolling downs, village greens and easeful plenty. The weed that is smoked in Hobbits' clay pipes, it's even hinted, is a mild narcotic that triggers their love of spinning epic yarns of distant yore. In Middle-earth, the counterforce is the dark land of Mordor to the southeast. With its engines of war and the fiery, white heat of technology of Mount Doom, Mordor is a military-industrial complex gearing up to wage a battle of evermore, forever disrupting the stability of the rest of Middle-earth. As a rough, fantastical mapping of the previous twenty years of world history, Tolkien wove a convincing enough analogy, and it certainly spoke to the children born in the middle of the real-life conflict who now just wanted to retreat to the Shires to do their own thing in peace.[115]

Again, the Romantic constructions of the sacred and the profane are conspicuous. For those seeking to get back to the garden, yet trapped in the disenchanted world of everyday life, fantasy provided an appealing utopian vision. This is why, for example, underground newspapers had titles such as *Middle Earth* (Iowa) and *Jabberwock* (New York),[116] and why, in 1967, "the young Marc Bolan handed copies of *The Hobbit* and *Lord of the Rings* to producer Tony Visconti with the words, 'If you're gonna record me, you gotta read these.'"[117]

Similarly, the early songs of Genesis, which were typical of prog-rock Paganism, seek to draw the listener into an imaginary otherworld. Their 1970 song "Shepherd" (now available on *Genesis Archive 1967–75*, 1998) begins with, as Hegarty and Halliwell remind us, "a dramatic bardic opening, 'Rise Up! Take your Lyre and sing/ Listen! To the news I bring,' and then transports the listener to a fairytale world of dreams and imagination."[118] As well as band names such as Elf, Goblin, and Pan, album titles indicative of this reenchanted discourse were The Hobbits' *Down to Middle Earth* (1967), Tyrannosaurus Rex's *Prophets Seers and Sages: The Angels of the Ages* (1968) and *Unicorn* (1969), Bo Hansson's *Music Inspired by Lord of the Rings* (1970) and *Magician's Hat* (1972), Uriah Heep's *Demons and Wizards* (1972) and *The Magician's Birthday* (1972), Peter Bellamy's *Merlin's Isle of Gramarye* (1972), Hawkwind's *Warrior on the Edge of Time* (1975), Tom Newman's *Faerie Symphony* (1977), and Bob Johnson and Peter Knight's *The King of Elfland's Daughter* (1977). Nick Drake, the quintessential Romantic troubadour—remembered by his close friend, Ross Grainger, as a "modern Pagan"—was typical of many liminal/ threshhold *personae* fascinated by the dominant themes of contemporary occulture. "Bored by conventional life," he had a keen interest in "the supernatural."[119] Recalling the times he spent with Drake, Grainger remembers that they "often discussed spirits, Stonehenge, ley lines and the little people. We used to discuss these kinds of things for hours."[120] "I was made to love magic/All its wonder to know" (Nick Drake, "I Was Made to Love Magic," *Time of No Reply*, 1986). As with many young people, something within Drake longed to retreat from the disenchanted spaces of the modern world. There was a sense in which, to quote a line from Kenneth Grahame's *Pagan Papers*, the "blood" of liminal *personae* was yearning to "dance to imagined pipings of Pan from happy fields far distant"[121]—as indicated by Syd Barrett when he chose to lift a beautifully evocative chapter title from Grahame's *Wind in the Willows* for the title of Pink Floyd's debut album, *Piper at the Gates of Dawn* (1967).

Again, we have noted that this turn to Pan was driven by a liminal questioning of received orthodoxies about the nature of reality, a growing concern about humanity's dislocation from the natural world, and the emergence of a culture of burgeoning speculation about the occult, spirituality, and the cosmos, fostered by a suspicion that what society had relegated to childhood fancy might actually be repressed knowledge waiting to be discovered by minds attuned to new horizons. Hence, whether relaxing with a cup of herbal tea, a piece of carob cake and a joint in the incense haze of Gandalf's Garden on the King's Road in London, or listening to John Peel play records at the Middle Earth club in a basement in Covent Garden, or purchasing a kaftan from Granny Takes a Trip, or crouching by a babbling brook patiently awaiting an elven advent, or, more likely, slumped in a beanbag pondering Jimmy Cauty's ubiquitous poster of Gandalf, romanticized affective spaces shaped by imagined cosmologies were *de rigueur* in the late sixties and early seventies. As Erik Davis remembers of his own Californian hippie past, "I wrote Lovecraftian poetry and decorated my walls with Roger Dean posters, maps of Middle-earth, and hermetic diagrams ripped from *Man, Myth & Magic* books I lifted from the library."[122] Again, writing of a slightly earlier period in London, Jane Ormsby-Gore remembers that "we were very influenced by Byron . . . Spenser's *Faerie Queene* . . . that sort of mood, rather Romantic."[123] Hence while comparatively few actually joined covens or organized Pagan groups during this early period, there was a wide-spread fascination with associated ideas, which were used in the construction of enchanted affective spaces that were able to transcend quotidian routine.[124] Lyrics such as those of the Incredible String Band didn't need to make immediate sense, in that what was required was that they contribute to a state of mind: "The bent twig of darkness/Grows the petals of the morning" ("Chinese White," *5000 Spirits or the Layers of the Onion*, 1967). As the former Archbishop of Canterbury, Rowan Williams, has commented, "for those of us who fell in love with the Incredible String Band, there was a feeling of breathing the air of a very expansive imagination indeed. It was alright to be enchanted . . . I'd also have to say that it was a discovery of the holy; not the solemn, not the saintly, but the holy, which makes you silent and sometimes makes you laugh and which above all makes the landscape different once and for all."[125] That is precisely the point. Through an engagement with the Other, new perspectives are formed and nothing is quite the same again: "Strangely Strange, But Oddly Normal" (Dr. Strangely Strange, *Kip of the Serenes*, 1969). Moreover, as Williams indicates, we are here on quite different sacred ground to that mapped out by traditional Christian theology. As the Incredible String Band opined, the cogency of traditional religious discourse had been eroded: " . . . Jesus will stretch out his hand no more." However, there is hope: "In the warm south winds the lost flowers move again." ("The Mad Hatter's Song," *5000 Spirits or the Layers of the Onion*, 1967).[126] Here, in the spaces shaped by popular music, reenchanted minds could make out "imagined pipings of Pan from happy fields far distant." There was a feeling that the time has come for monotheisms to retreat as the ancient gods of Pagan premodernity pushed their way back through the undergrowth. As Björk has put it, "God isn't a big part of our lives . . . We go out into nature instead . . . Nature is our chapel."[127]

As we have seen, festivals have been particularly important spaces for breathing the air of expansive imaginations and for charting enchanted landscapes.[128] In 1972, the first Windsor Free Festival was held in the UK, and, a few years later the first Stonehenge festival, the latter becoming the longest-lasting annual free countercultural event. As with the Glastonbury Festival, its location was significant, in that it was not chosen because of its archaeological interest as an historic monument. Festivalgoers were not tourists interested in walking around ancient monuments taking photographs of the stonework, they were pilgrims interested in both music and sacred space, Stonehenge being understood to have links with pre-Christian Druidry. Held between 1974 and 1984, it became the most important of the free festivals in the UK. Initiated by Phil Russell, "a kind of charismatic hippie mystic,"[129] and known to his friends as Wally Hope, he and a group of his followers, the "Wallies," squatted the site in 1974 and held a small summer solstice gathering, declaring that "our generation is the best mass movement in history."[130] The poster advertising the 1975 festival, drawn by the late Roger Hutchinson in consultation with Russell, carefully articulates a countercultural, Romantic Pagan discourse.[131] Describing it as a "Summer Solstice Celebration," the key words are "harmony," "music," "freedom," and "sunrises and sunsets." The illustration comprises Stonehenge, an all-seeing eye surrounded by petals, psilocybin mushrooms and, watching paternally over the proceedings, a Druid with a sickle in one hand and a sprig of oak in the other. What this poster communicates very clearly is that, at these early festivals, as at later raves, the music functioned less as entertainment—although, of course, it was that—and more as a prosthetic technology for creating spaces and atmospheres conducive to experiencing the occultural and the countercultural. The music was, as Michael Clarke notes, "only one of a variety of activities which . . . may include . . . various manifestations of commitment to ecological awareness and to the occult."[132] As Nik Turner of Hawkwind recalls of a "fertility ritual" at the 1984 solstice at Stonehenge, "it was an all-night thing, the death of the sun-king in the evening and the rebirth of the new with the solstice sunrise."[133] Again, for Russell, the festival was about "experimenting with anything in our search for love and peace." He continues, "our temple is sound, we fight our battles with music, drums like thunder, cymbals like lightening, banks of electronic equipment like nuclear missiles of sound."[134] Indeed, the utopian, almost eschatological vision informing these early festivals was frequently conspicuous: "We are not squatters," argued Russell, "we are men of God. We want to plant a garden of Eden with apricots and cherries, where there will be guitars instead of guns and the sun will be our nuclear bomb."[135]

While the Romantic, *Faerie Queene*-Pagan discourse of the early 1970s remained influential, it increasingly gave way to a more knowing, committed articulation of ideas informed by the growth of confidence in Paganism as a spiritual path and by a conspicuous rejection of Christian hegemony: "Ancient rituals of spring/ No church ever killed" (Inquisicion, "Pagan Rites," *Steel Vengeance*, 1996). More recently, Björk has described her album *Medúlla* (2004) as music expressive of a "Pagan element," by which she is referring to a premodern, utopian nature religion "going back to the roots – before time, or civilization, or patriotism."[136] She imagines a simple world in which divisions between humans, nations, and religions do not yet exist—humanity living at one with nature, its forces and spirits. Indeed, she articulates a form of deep ecological biocentric egalitarianism, in that she extends the circle of moral concern beyond the human species and beyond even sentient life. There is a very clear sense of the earth as sacred, and that, as the Norwegian philosopher Arne Naess put it, "landscapes are living beings and so are rivers."[137] Hence, in the final analysis, biocentric egalitarianism insists that "there is no firm ontological divide in the field of existence." There is, in other words, no "bifurcation in reality between the human and the nonhuman realms."[138] It is this expanded view of "the self," what Naess has referred to as "self-realization," that is explicit in Björk's work. She encourages a gradual expansion of self-perception to include other humans, other sentient beings, and finally the whole ecological web: "the other is none other than yourself."[139] "I'm a tree that grows hearts" ("Bachelorette," *Homogenic*, 1997); "one breath away from mother oceania/your nimble feet make prints in my sands" ("Oceania," *Medúlla*, 2004). Such statements expressing identification with nature echo those found in the work of philosophers such as J. Baird Callicott, who, re-calling his feelings as he contemplated the Mississippi River, wrote the following memorable passage:

> As I gazed at the brown silt-choked waters absorbing a black plume of industrial and municipal sewage from Memphis, and as my eye tracked bits of some unknown beige froth floating continually down from Cincin-nati, Louisville, or St. Louis, I experienced a palpable pain. It was not dis-tinctly locable in any of my extremities, nor was it like a headache or nausea. Still, it was very real. I had no plans to swim in the river, no need to drink from it, no intention of buying real estate on its shores. My narrowly personal interests were not affected, and yet somehow I was personally injured. It occurred to me then, in a flash of self-discovery, that *the river was a part of me.*[140]

Similarly, John Seed, arguing that a proper understanding of one's place within the ecological web can only be truly grasped by a process of internalisation, whereby "alienation subsides," suggests that statements such as "I am protecting the rainfor-est" need to develop into "I am part of the rainforest protecting myself. I am that part of the rainforest recently emerged into thinking."[141] This same biocentric ideology was also important within the 1990s rave counterculture. For example, the cover of *Knees Up Mother Earth* (1993) by the Knights of the Occasional Table includes the following Vedantic statement: "The bright eternal Self that is the earth, the bright eternal self that lives in the body are one and the same." Again, central to the rave scene in Britain in the 1990s was Spiral Tribe, who articulated an influential techno-Pagan biocentrism. As Simon Reynolds recalls, "dancing with the stars overhead," it was "hard not to succumb to the back-to-Nature romanticism. It's all part of Spiral Tribe's eco-mystical creed, which [was] crystallized in the buzzword 'terra-technic': using technology to unlock the primal energy of Mother Earth."[142]

As noted above, however, while many have developed a sense of the sacred in nature, which they are happy to refer to as "Pagan," since the mid-sixties there has been a gradual increase in musicians interested in explicitly Pagan faith and practice. This interest emerged quite naturally out of an interest in folk culture, which, as we have seen, itself relied heavily on the resources of Romantic occulture. Several of the more experimental bands were particularly significant in this respect. For example, drawing on folkloric myth and magic, Comus (e.g., "Song to Comus," *First Utterance*, 1971) and The Watersons (e.g., *Frost and Fire: A Calendar of Ritual and Magical Songs*, 1965) both sought to articulate a more visceral affective space: "that the cycles of nature are those with which humanity should commune, even to the point of human sacrifice as a means of ensuring fertility. Encompassing every type of activity and emotion in a celebration of rural life, the song-cycle is also about work as a means of engaging with the land."[143] Musically, bands such as the Incredible String Band and Comus began to plough what was to become a distinct furrow within folk culture, a furrow that would lead them to progressive acid folk and folk-rock that had, to some extent, sloughed off traditional folk. As Hegarty and Halliwell say of Comus, "the band twisted traditional instrumentation into an ecstatic, mounting discordance where a lost, sexual and often deadly nature could be summoned. The pastoral is about an unleashing of energy that taps into a host of Pagan gods and stories . . . "[144] Even some artists who were, musically, more traditional, were attracted to folk occulture, explicitly articulating a Romantic embrace of Pagan traditions. For example, the folk duo Dave and Toni Arthur began exploring Wicca, following a meeting with Britain's occult celebrity, Alex Sanders—who rejoiced in the title "King of the Witches."

> We'd talk about magic, as we'd got into witchcraft and studying it, to find out how witchcraft was reflected in the traditional song – if magical ballads were anything to do with what was perceived then as Wicca, the witch covens that were going round in England, and whether they were actually related or whether it was a separate thing. And so we started going to meetings of witches and going through their ritual books and things, and we were invited as guests to all sorts of coven meetings, and then we were stuck in 'Tam Lin' and all these magical ballads and somehow trying to relate them to what was going on in the occult world and find out what the connections were.[145]

The point is that finding such connections was not difficult in the occulture of the late-1960s and 1970s, in that, as Richard Thompson put it, "you find a lot of magic in traditional music. . . . A lot of songs about Faery Queens and people cavorting with the elemental beasties."[146] This made traditional music peculiarly appropriate for those seeking to construct Pagan affective space. For example, the title of Dave and Toni Arthurs' album, *Hearken to the Witches Rune* (1970), is taken from Alex Sanders' "Witches' Chant"—based on a chant composed by the famous British Wiccan, Doreen Valiente: "Darksome night and shining moon . . . Hearken to the witches' rune. . . . " The fact that it's not actually sung on the album, but only printed on the back cover and used in the title indicates its significance for the couple and its perceived appropriateness for a folk album. Indeed, the text printed on the cover serves to transform the record into a sacred artifact, the implication being that the album's true significance lies beyond mere entertainment.

Such discourses, while largely restricted to a vibrant and burgeoning occult underground, surfaced spectacularly in popular culture in Robin Hardy's 1973 film, *The Wicker Man*. Based on David Pinner's 1967 novel *Ritual*, which related the occult murder of a child in a remote Cornish village,[147] *The Wicker Man* depicted the survival of an isolated Pagan community on a small island off the Scottish coast. Leaning heavily on the ideas developed by Tylor and particularly by James Frazer in *The Golden Bough*,[148] through its gentle evocation of sacred awe, of *mysterium tremendum et fascinans*, the film gives us a sense of the emotional power of Pagan occultural discourse at the time. Watching the film nowadays is like stumbling through a hidden door into the secret garden of late sixties and early seventies occulture. In a society still shaped by Christian hegemony, it depicts an ancient elemental power and a level of commitment to natural forces that are both fascinating and frightening, both attractive and repelling. The viewer is drawn, not just into the narrative arc, but also into a Romantic affective space, a Pagan place. Certainly, as a reflection of the changes taking place in sixties and early seventies religion and society, the film is particularly interesting. It is imagined that there is a place, Summerisle, where there survives a pre-Christian religion, in tune with nature, unfettered by the mean morality of conservative Christianity, but savage at its core. The screenwriter, Anthony Shaffer, was drawn to the swelling tide of popular occultural interest in folklore and magic, as well as to the rural Romanticism of, for example, the Incredible String Band's album *The Hangman's Beautiful Daughter* (1968).[149] Central to the affective space evoked by the film is the soundtrack composed by Paul Giovanni and played by his band, Magnet (formed specifically for the purpose).[150] Throughout the film, folk music is explicitly identified with the survival of pre-Christian indigenous religion. Indeed, it is used to create a boundary between the sacred and the profane, between the Christianity of the staunchly Presbyterian Sergeant Howie (Edward Woodward) investigating the disappearance of a child and the Pagan space inhabited by the islanders and overseen by Lord Summerisle (Christopher Lee). The use of music and dance evokes the vibrancy of nature religion over against the dry formalism of mainland Calvinist theology. However, it does so in a way that problematizes the boundary, in the sense that it is not always clear whether the music identifies the profane—the demonic, as the protagonist would understand it—or the sacred—the pure, the innocent, and the natural as the Summerisle community would understand it. Although Christopher Lee's role as Lord Summerisle—following his many other portrayals of icons of the profane for Hammer Film Productions—tended to bias the interpretation a little, nevertheless, the location of the sacred in *The Wicker Man* is ambiguous.

This ambiguity and the core themes within the film, which reflect the religious and cultural shifts that had begun to gain ground during the 1960s, have ensured its continuing presence within popular music culture. Indeed, numerous musicians still directly reference the film: Iron Maiden, "The Wicker Man" (*Brave New World*, 2000); Momus and Anne Laplantine, *Summerisle* (2004); Plague Lounge, *The Wicker Image* (1996); Us and Them, *Summerisle* (2011); Agalloch, "Summerisle: Reprise" (*Whitedivisiongrey*, 2012)—the last of which concludes with a sample of dialogue from the film. More directly, many have registered their interest in the occultural content of the film by covering songs from the soundtrack. For example, the Italian neofolk band, The Green Man, produced a version of "The Maypole Song" ("Summerisle," *From Irem to Summerisle*, 2009) and "Willow's Song," the most popular from the soundtrack, has been covered by artists as disparate as Doves (*Lost Sides*, 2003), The Sneaker Pimps ("How Do," *Becoming X*, 1996), The Go! Team (as a bonus track on the Japanese release of *Proof of Youth*, 2007), Nature and Organization ("The Wicker Man Song," *Beauty Reaps The Blood Of Solitude*, 1994), Faith and the Muse (*The Burning Season*, 2003) and Us and Them (*Summerisle*, 2011). As the Pagan writer Jason Pitzl-Waters comments, "It is hard to overstate the influence *The Wicker Man* soundtrack has had on Pagan and occult-themed music. It not only became a reference point for Pagan artists, but a touchstone for a wide variety of musicians from seemingly disparate genres, entranced by the atmospherics and authenticity of the music."[151] However, it is within the neofolk and postindustrial scenes that the film has had its most conspicuous impact, largely because of its cementing of the relationship between folk music and Pagan survivals. For example, not only is the online magazine *Compulsion*, which discusses postindustrial culture, committed to documenting the continuing significance of *The Wicker Man*,[152] but the compilation *Looking for Europe: A Neofolk Compendium* (2005) includes Magnet's version of "Willow's Song" taken from the film. Again, "The Unbroken Circle" website, which discusses contemporary "wyrd folk," insists that the film is "the point where . . . the perceived realization of folk music as important in the social and magical context was made. It does not matter whether this realization was factual or just a perception, what matters is the transformation it created in the minds of many."[153] This point is an important one.

> Of course, similar folk music was made before this film and afterwards without any link to the film. However, it has become a kind of fulcrum from which many complementary areas have grown. It acts as the perfect achievement in wyrd-folk as the numerous cover versions and samples attest. In this it has become the reference point and comparison for much other music. By exploring without genre cliche or condemnation we have a relatively objective framework or template that facilitates intelligent consideration and a genuine evocation of the past.[154]

It is, of course, naïve to claim objectivity here, but the point is nevertheless a significant one, in that the "genuine evocation of the past" has been central to the music we have been discussing, including the film's articulation of the sacred and the profane and the music's relationship to that discourse.

The sacred–profane ambiguity at the heart of *The Wicker Man* is evident in the music of the neofolk pioneer David Tibet. Emerging out of the transgressive culture that gave shape to industrial music, his work in the early 1980s is essentially an occultural reading of Christian apocalyptic thought through a Crowleyan lens.[155] *Nature Unveiled* (1984), for example, the first album with his band Current 93, comprises two tracks, "Ach Golgotha (Maldoror Is Dead)" and "The Mystical Body Of Christ In Chorazaim (The Great In The Small)," both of which are dark, intertextually complex, atmospherically liturgical compositions. Bearing in mind that "every text is from the outset under the jurisdiction of other discourses which impose a universe on it,"[156] the primary discourse on this album is, broadly speaking, Thelemic (i.e., based on Aleister Crowley's religious system of "Thelema"—a term taken from the ancient Greek for "will").[157] Although it is clearly an exploration at the interface of the discursive worlds of Lord Summerisle and Sergeant Howie, that of Summerisle is dominant: chanting, bells, gongs, prayers, weeping and screaming contribute to a disturbing cacophonic and primal energy, which, on "Ach Golgotha (Maldoror Is Dead)," is haunted by a loop of Crowley chanting "Om." "I was trying to make a truly majestic and apocalyptic album," recalls Tibet, the aim being to construct a genuinely disturbing affective space. "To me it's like a long song that builds up in power . . . It's not a Black Mass, but it is literally a diabolical record in some ways." Crowley once said "I fought all night with God and the Devil. Finally God won, but I'm not sure which God it was." Current 93's *Nature Unveiled*, he suggests, "has that tension."[158] However, this boundary work, so central to transgressive discourse, takes a very different musical and, to some extent, ideological direction in the late-1980s, beginning with *Swastikas for Noddy* (1988), an album inspired by a catalytic, LSD-induced vision of Noddy crucified in the sky above London.[159] The vision, although interpreted by Tibet within a Gnostic frame, which elided puppets with crucified deities in what he termed a "puppet theology,"[160] also led to a backward gaze into childhood: "I needed to return to what moved me, which was nursery rhymes and folk music. Not folk rock, just really simple unadorned melodies, maybe no choruses, just direct, a minute or two long. So, *Swastikas for Noddy* marked my decision to rethink the way that I expressed the emotions that I felt about the things that were moving me."[161] Again, there is that which is fundamentally Romantic in this conversion experience. Although not explicitly seeking a return to the premodern, implicitly he is doing just that in his longing to return to a state of innocence located in childhood, "the last time I was ever happy."[162] This, I think, is important, in that premodernity is understood in terms of childhood innocence, wonder, and delight in nature. Rousseau's noble savage is childlike. Hence, childhood innocence becomes sacred form over against the profanity of the modern world which he is forced to inhabit as an adult: "as we get older and we become more and more unhappy, as we see more and more the terrible state of the world and the terrible things it does to us, and that *we* also do back to *it*, [so] childhood becomes more and more perfect." He continues, "this life is not as it should be and we know that's the case and so we desperately try to find a time when the world was as we pictured it as a child, full of marvels, mysteries, full of wonder, full of joy and immanence." Hence, he argues, it is because of this enchanted interior that we have hope, that "we can redeem ourselves somehow"—"harking back to the innocence of childhood... [is] one way that we start to do that ... We paint the past in a way that appeals to our sense of recovering the paradise that we've lost."[163]

Consequently, not only did Noddy become, for Tibet, "the total epitome of innocent childhood,"[164] but folk music became the ideal sonic expression of this yearning. Hence, there was from the outset an umbilical connection with the folk of the sixties and, through that movement, with earlier traditions. The significance of this connection is evident in the list of releases on his own Durtro label, which includes a compilation of songs by Shirley Collins (*Fountain of Snow*, 1992) and Bill Fay's, *Tomorrow, Tomorrow and Tomorrow* (2005). He has also collaborated with several artists from the period, including Clodagh Simonds from Mellow Candle and, interestingly, produced his own interpretation of the cover of The Incredible String Band's seminal *The Hangman's Beautiful Daughter* (1968) for Current 93's *Earth Covers Earth* (1988). However, again, the point is that, in looking back to folk music, he is attempting to connect with a certain innocence, an innocence he identifies with childhood. That said, for Tibet and much subsequent neofolk, this is, to some extent, the innocence of Summerisle. That is to say, it is a sacred innocence lived in the shadow of the profane. On the one hand, it is an innocence that carries within it a Summerisle-esque Pagan darkness and, on the other hand, an innocence constantly threatened by the profane Other of modernity—mainland Christian morality/Noddy crucified. This is indicated in the title of the album, *Swastikas for Noddy*, in that the innocence represented by Noddy is juxtaposed with the extreme profanity of modernity and the "grown-up" world associated with the swastika: "what would be the most unsuitable thing you could give Noddy as a present? I felt that it was probably swastikas."[165] Understood, through the lens of this seminal album, and with the sacred-profane ambiguity of *The Wicker Man* in mind, we come close to the primary contours of neofolk.

In turning to U.S. free folk and to what has become known as the "New Weird America," we can, perhaps, move almost seamlessly back from Tibet, through industrial culture, *The Wicker Man*, and late-1960s occultism to another important channel of music and occulture, the proto-psychedelic occultist, folklorist, filmmaker and music collector, Harry Smith. His three-volume *Anthology of American Folk Music*, released in 1952, became the primary document of the American folk revival. However, not only did it introduce a host of musicians—including Pete Seeger, Bob Dylan, Joan Baez, John Fahey, and Jerry Garcia—to the music of the 1920s and 1930s, but the liner notes also introduced them to the seventeenth century English Paracelsian philosopher and physician Robert Fludd, the esotericist and founder of Anthroposophy, Rudolf Steiner, the occultist, Aleister Crowley, and the anthropologist who succeeded Tylor at Oxford University, R.R. Marett. At the conclusion of his notes, he claimed that the following quotations had been useful in compiling the *Anthology*: "In elementary music the relation of Earth to the sphere of water is 4 to 3, as there are in the Earth four quarters of frigidity to three of water" (Fludd); "Civilized man thinks out his difficulties, at least he thinks he does, primitive man dances out his difficulties" (Marrett); "Do as thy wilt shall be the whole of the law" (Crowley); "The in-breathing becomes thought, and the out-breathing becomes the will manifestation of thought" (Steiner).[166] While even the most imaginative esoteric mind would have difficulty applying this collection of eclectic gobbets to the process of compiling an anthology of folk music, nevertheless the confluence itself is an interesting one, in that a stream of "Pagan poetry" has continued to flow underground, occasionally bubbling to the surface in springs of fresh countercultural and liminal enthusiasm. Even Smith's surreal occult film, *Heaven and Earth Magic* (originally released in 1957 and then again in 1962), has attracted the attention of musicians such as John Zorn, who has performed a live soundtrack during screenings of it, as have Deerhoof ("Look Away," *Friend Opportunity*, 2007) and Flying Lotus. Indeed, the liner notes for the album *Heretic: Jeux Des Dames Cruelles* (1992) by Zorn's improvisational project Naked City declare that "this record is dedicated to Harry Smith. Mystical Animator, Pioneer Ethnomusicologist, Hermetic Scholar, Creator of 'Heaven + Earth Magic', one of the greatest films of all time." And the Brattleboro Free Folk Festival, the principal gathering of the New Weird America movement, constitutes, says David Keenan, "an attempt to muster the same recurrent and archetypal forms that archivist and mystic Harry Smith saw manifest in the American folk music of the early twentieth century." Here liminal *personae* merge in a new weird *communitas* to listen to "outsider voices from an earlier generation"; here gather "lone visionaries, hermetic isolationists, young marginalized artists, hippy revolutionaries, country punks, ex-cons, project kids, avant experimentalists, luddite refuseniks, psychedelic rockers and assorted misfits in an attempt to make space for an alternative American narrative, irreconcilable with the prevailing neoconservative vision of the 'New American Century.'" And, as Keenan comments, "like Smith before them, many of the main players regard their music as a potential catalyst for change."[167] This is a force for good, a sacred challenge to a profane order. "Either you can have your spirit smashed over and over again by the current state of the world," says guitarist Ben Chasny (who has also worked with Current 93), "or you can create something for your friends and loved ones." The New Weird America, like the old weird world of the sixties, is "a political stance. If only to say 'fuck you' . . . to corporations who suck the magic out of life and . . . to our grotesque leaders who probably listen to The White Stripes behind the doors of their offices as they engage in orgies of blood, whores and money."[168] Indeed, rooted in albums such as, again, The Incredible String Band's *The Hangman's Beautiful Daughter* (1968), "one of the scene's founding documents,"[169] there is a clear sense that the New Weird America is creating, as Chasny puts it, alternative affective spaces within which one might "summon up ancient forces that once only took shape in drawings in hermetic books."[170] Moreover, again, he seems to feel that, in going back to traditional folk instruments, there is an authenticity that connects the sound with the beyond: "not that music that uses electricity cannot be transcendental. It's just a matter of studying the forms of sounds that are closer to human existence in order to understand the correspondence with higher forms, with the heavens."[171] The lines of continuity between traditional folk, influential figures such as Smith, and the psychedelic-pantheistic musings of sixties experimentalists such as Comus and The Incredible String Band—particularly, again, *The Hangman's Beautiful Daughter*, an album that connects much of what we have been discussing, from *The Wicker Man* to neofolk to New Weird America—have remained important in the search for authenticity and transcendence.

Lucifer rising

If *The Wicker Man* contributed to contemporary discourse about premodern Pagan communal life and its close relationship with the natural world, the films of Kenneth Anger can be read as reflecting the contours of contemporary Romantic individualism, which has been a central feature of much popular music culture.

Popular music culture's relationship with Anger is a close one, not least because he used musicians in his films, notably Bobby Beausoleil and The Rolling Stones entourage, whom he viewed as the "provocative heralds of his new aeon."[172] Indeed, both Beausoleil and Jimmy Page produced soundtracks for *Lucifer Rising*[173] and albums reflecting the occult chic of the late-sixties, such as particularly *Their Satanic Majesties Request* (1967) by The Rolling Stones, betray his influence. More significantly, however, there are two interrelated themes in Anger's work that are worth following through into popular music, both of which were conspicuous within the occulture of the period. The first, and most obvious, is that of Lucifer as an icon of individualism, whose name Anger had tattooed across his chest, and the second is that of art as a conduit for occult energy. We will deal with the former in this section and the latter in the following section.

In accordance with the Romantic conception of Satan, Anger's Lucifer is not solely profane, but as "Venus, the Morning Star," is a more ambiguous figure. *Lucifer Rising*, he explained, was "a film about the love generation – the birthday party of the Aquarian Age. Showing actual ceremonies to make Lucifer rise. Lucifer is the Light God, not the Devil – the Rebel Angel behind what's happening in the world today. His message is that the key of joy is disobedience."[174] This disobedience, moreover, is interpreted Romantically in terms of a sacred individualistic act, arrogant in its transgressive assertion of personal rights and self-determination, and single-minded in its intention to subvert oppressive hegemonies informed by

Western morality and religion. Hence Lucifer is understood quite literally as "the bringer of light," "the morning star," "the son of dawn" (Isaiah 14:12), who is related to the dawning of a new age of enlightenment and liberty. As fundamentally Dionysian and Promethean, Anger's Lucifer is reflective of key features of the Romantic hero and an exemplar of qualities identified as "good" in the liminal cultures of popular music. As Jeffrey Burton Russell discusses with regard to the nineteenth-century Romantics, their "distaste for the Church was reciprocated, and clerical attacks on the Romantics only intensified their view that Christianity was evil and its opponents good. It followed that if the greatest enemy of traditional Christianity was Satan, then Satan must be good." Of course, this was "a philosophically incoherent statement contradicting the core meaning of the Devil, and indeed the Romantics intended such a statement, not as a theological proposition, but rather as an imaginative challenge and as a political program."[175] Their point was that, as symbolic of the challenge to unjust and repressive authority, Satan is the archetypal Romantic idea of the hero, which, "derived from the concept of the sublime, stands in contradiction to the classic epic notion of the hero as one devoted to the welfare of his family and people. The Romantic hero is individual, alone in the world, self-assertive, ambitious, powerful, and a liberator in rebellion against the society that blocks the way to progress toward liberty, beauty, and love; the Romantics read these qualities in Milton's Satan."[176] Hence, just as the figure of Satan merged with that of "the rock star" in the minds of those fearful of a threat to the sacred in society, particularly within right-wing religion,[177] so in liminal minds, for very different reasons, Satan and the rock star were elided in the figure of the Romantic hero—both are champions of truth and liberty.

Byron's poetic drama *Cain: A Mystery* (1821) is strikingly contemporary in this sense. Both Cain, representing humanity in general, and Lucifer are reconstructed with Promethean qualities and morally ambiguous. Cain, in the final analysis, is misguided in his revolt against divine tyranny, in that, consumed by zeal and blind to familial love, he kills his brother in whom he can see the reflection of Jehovah. Lucifer, on the other hand, while unloving and unmoved by human suffering, is nevertheless supportive of Cain's heroic rebellion against Jehovah's tyranny. He is a champion of liberty and of excess in pursuit of that liberty, whatever the consequences. Hence, fences that restrict excess and, therefore, liberty (such as drug laws) are themselves understood to be profane and, as such, need to be challenged. Consequently, in *Cain*, because it is suggested that Jehovah rules the world with unjustly repressive laws, the reader is asked who the real Devil is: "Lucifer, who wanted Adam and Eve to have knowledge and prompted the serpent to tell them the truth about the tree, or Jehovah who drove them out of the garden into exile and death?"[178] For the Romantic, yesterday and today, the answer is obvious. Hence while the figure of Satan in popular music culture has to be understood as a symbol of transgression, a personification of evil to be exalted, he also needs to be understood contextually as a Romantic hero engaged in countercultural direct action.

Where is the real evil? Is it with those who want people to be free, to live their lives as they want to, to gain knowledge of good and evil by whatever means they judge appropriate, or with oppressive religious and political hegemonies, which seek to regulate personal life, take people to war, and construct discriminatory hierarchies of power? (Again, such concerns are eloquently expressed by Blake in "The Garden of Love," with which we began this chapter.) Of course, as in the case of Byron's *Cain*, there is danger here, in that individualism, unfettered excess, and an insistence of self-determination risks the constraints of love and the eventual tearing apart of the social fabric that enabled the individualism to flourish in the first place. Hence, as we have seen, transgressive, individualistic trajectories of excess and experiences of the impure sacred can only ever be fleeting—although in challenging oppressive hegemonies and illuminating the sacred, their effects may be lasting and beneficial.

With this last point in mind, it's also worth noting that there is a sense in which The Rolling Stones' song "Sympathy for the Devil" (*Beggars Banquet*, 1968) provides a reading of Lucifer as the demonic Other who is necessary for the identification of the good: "the sacred is incomplete without the profane."[179] That is to say, Jagger, who was closely involved with Anger for a short period, constructs an essentially Romantic Devil. Rather than being a transgressive exaltation of evil personified, as in the ad hoc Satanist discourse of much black metal, his "man of wealth and taste" is a far more ambiguous figure. Indeed, it is unsurprising that in an interview with Jann Wenner for *Rolling Stone*, he recalls that his inspiration probably came from French literature: "I think that was taken from an old idea of Baudelaire's, I think, but I could be wrong. Sometimes when I look at my Baudelaire books, I can't see it in there. But it was an idea I got from French writing."[180] Certainly, Lucifer in "Sympathy for the Devil" can be compared to the "Prince of the exile" who has been "wronged" in Baudelaire's "Litanies to Satan." That said, there are also significant parallels with Mikhail Bulgakov's *The Master and Margarita*, which, apparently, Jagger has also claimed as an inspiration, having received the book as a gift from Marianne Faithfull.[181] Bearing in mind that Bulgakov's Satan is essentially "a man of wealth and taste" who visits Moscow and attempts to argue the case for his existence, the core themes of the song, and its Russian references suggest that this was indeed Jagger's primary source of inspiration. However, whether it was or not, the point is that, as we saw in the previous chapter, in facing the profane, we are also forced to embrace the sacred. As Satan declares in Bulgakov's novel, "Kindly consider the question: what would your good do and what would earth look like if shadows disappeared from it? Shadows are cast by objects and people. Here is the shadow of my sword. Trees and living beings also have shadows. Do you want to skin the whole earth, tearing all the trees and living things off it, because of your fantasy of enjoying bare light? You're a fool."[182] The profane serves to bring the sacred into focus. Hence there needs to be some sympathy for the Devil. We need to give evil its due. "A rigorous morality," argued Bataille, "results from complicity in the knowledge of Evil."[183]

Finally, thinking more generally of the Romantic tendency to "transpose the Christian God into a symbol of evil, the Christian idea of humanity into God (in the sense that humanity became the ultimate concern), and the Christian Satan into a hero,"[184] this is explicitly evident in Satanist discourse, which understands "socialization as repression" and Satan as a "force, model, symbol or expression of the self."[185] Satanism, in other words, was developed as a form of "self-religion,"[186] a project devoted to the excavation and empowerment of the authentic inner self, which has been corrupted by the profane forces of socialization. As Anton LaVey—founder of the Church of Satan in San Francisco, in 1966—describes his philosophy, it is "the ultimate conscious alternative to herd mentality and institutionalized thought." Its aim is "to liberate individuals from a contagion of mindlessness that destroys innovation." Consequently, he says, "Satanism means 'the opposition' and epitomizes all symbols of nonconformity."[187] Satan, the Romantic hero, is "the spirit of progress, the inspirer of all great movements that contribute to the development of civilization and the advancement of mankind. He is the spirit of revolt that leads to freedom, the embodiment of all heresies that liberate."[188] It is perhaps hardly surprising, therefore, that there are conspicuous lines of continuity linking popular music, the Romantic hero, Satan, Satanism, and transgression. Having said that, they do need to be untangled a little, not least because there is a question as to whether, in the final analysis, the very idea of a Satanist Romantic hero is a contradiction in terms. In short, would Satan be a Satanist? While there are a few popular musicians, such as Boyd Rice, Marilyn Manson, and King Diamond of Mercyful Fate, who have found LaVeyan Satanism appealing as a philosophy, others have clearly interpreted it in terms of a hindrance to individualism, unfettered excess, and self-determination. Indeed, LaVey was, as Jean LaFontaine notes, "a firm believer in order and observing the rule of law"[189] and, as with some other Satanist organizations, opposed to the use of drugs.[190] This is because, for all its discourse around individualism and however loosely defined, Satanism is a system, a régime, a set of principles and techniques for the realization of "self-godhood." As Asbjørn Dyrendal notes (quoting Don Webb of the Temple of Set),

> Rulership of the inner world involves controlling the body, mind, emotions and will, and means that the initiate achieves 'a sense of reality and purpose in what one does.' To reach this goal, one should find factors that hinder development at all levels, and remove them. Forces opposing the *body* are 'those things which shorten life, remove energy, or dull the senses' and range from drugs to the wrong kind of food to cultural and environmental factors. Forces opposing the *mind* are all 'habits of non-thinking' involved in herd conformity.[191]

This type of thinking, as LaFontaine puts it, "appears somewhat inconsistent with rebellion against authority."[192] There is, in other words, an Apollonian-Dionysian tension. Organizational Satanism has routinized and reified Dionysian individualism. As such, it has profaned that which the Romantic hero holds sacred—an embrace of excess in the pursuit of liberty and enlightenment. This goes some way to explaining the negative attitudes toward Satanic organizations evident within extreme metal. For example, the black metal label Deathlike Silence Productions, as Dyrendal comments, "sometimes featured a picture of LaVey in a circle with a line drawn through it – similar to conventional 'no smoking' signs." Understood in terms of the above discussion, this rejection is directly related to the fact that, "whereas LaVey's Church of Satan espouses 'nine parts respectability to one part outrageousness,' the discourse and ethos of transgression in the early black metal scene inverts the proportions." That is to say, "while the Church of Satan . . . values transgression as well as control, only a few individual Satanists, many of which are marginal, would value transgression to the extent implied in black metal discourse."[193] The individualistic creed of the Romantic hero resists control, order, and regulation, embracing excess in the pursuit of liberty.

There was also the issue for the liminal ad hoc Satanists of early black metal culture that, not only had the individualistic creed been routinized, but, in some Satanist discourse, Satan himself had been detraditionalized, becoming little more than a principle of self-development, rather than the literal infernal being of traditional Christian demonology.[194] This humanist intellectualization and, in effect, sanitization, reduced his transgressive potency.

Musick and esoterrorism

Turning to the Romantic idea that art might be a conduit for occult energy, at the center of Anger's work is an almost devout commitment to occult ritual, which draws heavily on the work of Crowley. For Anger, films are, as Carel Rowe commented in an early analysis of his work, "a search for light and enlightenment."[195] "Making a movie is casting a spell," claims Anger, and "the cinematograph" is a "magick weapon."[196] Hence his films, which are densely symbolic, are understood in terms of "evocations or invocations, attempting to conjure primal forces which, once visually released, are designed to have the effect of 'casting a spell' on the audience. The magick in the film is related to the magickal effect of the film on the audience."[197] It is this conviction that most clearly represents a particular fascination with the occult in popular music and also perhaps the most conspicuously Orphic use of music as an affective prosthetic technology. While some have observed that Anger's "concise body of films stretching over five decades has provided a mother lode of ideas mined to this day by rock video directors,"[198] and while others have produced homages to his life and work as representative of the transgressive discourses of late-sixties psychedelic occultism, such as Death in Vegas's, *Scorpio Rising* (2002), there are yet others—who do not necessarily look back to Anger—for whom the notion that music might be able to summon primal forces and manipulate energies is an attractive one. That is to say, Anger is representative of a particular Orphic understanding of the relationship between popular music and the occult—music is powerful magic in an affective universe. However, the point here is that some have understood it very literally in terms of alchemy and "magick." Music becomes "musick," "a conjuration of Pagan forces," "a surge of spiritual and mystical power."[199]

Such understandings are, of course, not new. The history of music is not unused to shadowy magi fascinated by notions of the esoteric potential of Orpheus' lyre. For example, Alexander Scriabin's Piano Sonata No. 9, Op. 68 (1913) was dubbed by his friend, Alexi Podgaetsky, "The Black Mass"—a title the composer approved, in that, through it, he was seeking to express an inexpressible darkness. Hovering around the interval of the diminished fifth, which, we have seen, is popularly understood as "the Devil's interval," Scriabin's notation reads as follows: "a sweetness gradually becoming more and more caressing and poisonous."[200] As Faubian Bowers comments, "its ritual is perverse. The rite is spitting at all that is holy or sacred ... Corruption, perversity, diabolism recurs."[201] Scriabin was reaching into a particularly dark corner of contemporary Russian occulture.[202] However, the point is that, like the work of Psychic TV, Coil, and Current 93, the performance of the "Black Mass" wasn't simply understood as entertainment, but rather as a more dynamically metaphysical happening.[203] Indeed, the Russian concert pianist Yevgeny Sudbin notes that Scriabin even believed that "he was 'practicing sorcery' whenever playing this sonata."[204]

Fifty-six years later, a similar, but cruder fascination with the occult potential of music surfaced in the United States in the work of Coven, who performed what they considered to be an authentic black mass, a recording of which is released on their debut album, *Witchcraft Destroys Minds and Reaps Souls* (1969). "To the best of our knowledge, this is the first Black Mass to be recorded in written words or in audio. It is as authentic," they claimed, "as hundreds of hours of research in every known source can make it ... " In actual fact, it was composed by their producer, Bill Traut, an ardent fan of H.P. Lovecraft, and much of it seems to have been lifted from the accounts of rituals in Dennis Wheatley novels—which is unsurprising, bearing in mind Traut's literary interests and the popularity in 1968 of Terence Fisher's film, *The Devil Rides Out*, based on Wheatley's novel. Nevertheless, whatever the source material, they provided a Wheatleyesque warning in their sleeve notes (and with this warning, increased the record's transgressive, occult aura): "we do not recommend its use by anyone who has not thoroughly studied Black Magic and is aware of the risks and dangers involved." This was immediately appealing to liminal minds, the implication being, of course, that the record was able to infuse the affective space created by the music with occult energy. Again, as with Dave and Toni Arthur's *Hearken to the Witches Rune* (1970), it was far more meaningful than merely entertainment, far more significant than simply a record. Thus fetishized, it was an occult artifact with an energy waiting to be released by a stylus. To remove this record from its protective sleeve and to place it on the turntable was to begin an occult ritual, to enter an affective sacred space within which one might encounter primal, elemental forces.

Likewise, in the UK, Black Widow's progressive rock single "Come to the Sabbat" (*Sacrifice*, 1970) sought to evoke a similar affective space. The transgressive sense of occult energy was enhanced during their early performances by the inclusion of a mock sacrifice of a nude woman, choreographed by members of Leicester's Phoenix Theatre Company. Moreover, again, like Dave and Toni Arthur, they made it known that they had been tutored in ritual magic by the "King of the Witches," Alex Sanders. However, unlike the Arthurs, Black Widow produced a performance with Sanders' wife, Maxine, as the naked Lady Astaroth.[205] "Discard your clothes and come on foot.... Come to the Sabbat, Satan's there!"

Another musician fascinated with the confluence of music and the occult was Graham Bond, a gifted but troubled man, who believed himself to be Crowley's son. A central figure in the British blues movement, he had, by the close of the sixties, formed Magick, a group intended to channel his interests in the occult in much the same way that Anger had sought to do through film—although far more chaotically. The band released two albums, *Holy Magick* (1970) and *We Put Our Magick on You* (1971), both of which were occulturally eclectic, infused with obscure esoteric meaning and folklore—as indicated by the track titles: "Meditation Aumgu"; "The Word of Aeon"; "The Qabalistic Cross"; "Invocation to the Light"; "The Pentagram Ritual"; "The Holy Words Iao Sabao"; "Aquarius Mantra"; "Enochian (Atlantean) Call"; "Return of Arthur"; "The Magician"; "My Archangel Mikael"; "Druid"; "I Put My Magick on You"; "Hail Ra Harakhite"; "Time to Die." Sadly, the last of these titles was rather prescient in that, in April, 1974, following a nervous breakdown, significant personal problems, and the failure of his next band, Magus—which included Carole Pegg of Mr. Fox—he died under the wheels of a train at Finsbury Park station, London.

Since this period, the notion that music might be used as a conduit for occult energy has been developed across an increasingly broad spectrum, both by the musicians themselves and by fans hoping that this might be the case: from mythologies surrounding the occult symbolism and Crowleyan energies of Led Zeppelin's fourth album (1971) to the creation of music designed to evoke contemplative affective spaces, such Steve Hillage's *Rainbow Dome Musick* (1979)—composed to be played at the 1979 Mind, Body, Spirit Festival in London—and from contemporary electronic dance music embedded in psychedelic, shamanic discourse to Killing Joke's live spoken word project, *The Courtauld Talks* (1989), which has Jaz Coleman, with minimal musical accompaniment, explaining the occult significance of their work.[206] However, some of the most distinctive and carefully theorized occult trajectories have their roots in industrial culture. Of particular note in this respect are Genesis P-Orridge's ideas concerning "esoterrorism" and Paganism as "a form of anti-establishment activity."[207]

A founder of the experimental ritual magick network, Thee Temple ov Psychick Youth (TOPY), P-Orridge began his musical career as a naïve occultist. Although his friend Carl Abrahamsson notes that he "read and studied . . . occultism all through his youth,"[208] in actual fact, at least initially, this was an area in which he tended to follow rather than to lead. While he may have had an early fascination with the occult and the supernatural, as many young people do, as the work of COUM Transmissions evolved into Throbbing Gristle and eventually into Psychic TV, several friends began to shape his thinking more formatively, notably his fellow musicians, the late John Balance[209] and particularly David Tibet.[210] For example, concerning the important influence of the occultist and artist Austin Osman Spare on P-Orridge's thought, especially the use of sigils, "it was Balance, alongside Hilmer Örn Hilmarsson, who together thoroughly infused . . . Spare into the Psychic TV melting pot."[211] Balance had become obsessed with the ideas of Spare: "I'd go to the Atlantic bookshop . . . looking for books and paintings by him. . . . But the thing is, I genuinely felt this instant connection. . . . It wasn't joking around. Our thing was that we were going to try and follow in this guy's footsteps."[212] He even claimed to have developed a form of what he has referred to as "ancestor worship," during which he communicated with the deceased artist through a Sparean method of meditating on his drawings.[213] Again, acknowledging the significant influence of Tibet,[214] P-Orridge notes that, not only was Tibet "obsessed with Aleister Crowley," but he "wrongly assumed I was well read and researched in the museum of magick. *I am not*."[215] Nevertheless, Paganism and the occult became important sites of exploration, which alongside a fascination with notorious cult leaders, such as Charles Manson and Jim Jones, provided a transgressive lens through which to analyse the sacred and profane in society.

As with Anger, P-Orridge came to believe that occult ideas and methods, communicated through music, could be used to change minds, subvert accepted social mores, and *convert* people to new perceptions of the sacred. This is "esoterrorism." As Abrahamsson notes, his interest was always less in the "the lure and romance of mediaeval magicians, cloaked in robes and waving wands," and more in "the apparent changing ability the human mind and activities actually have."[216] Hence, during the late-1970s, P-Orridge became interested in "how a small number of fanatical individuals could have a disproportionate impact on culture."[217] He reasoned that occult ideas articulated and developed by film directors, authors, artists and musicians are, through synergies and networks, able to have a disproportionate influence on large numbers of people and, consequently, on institutions and societies.[218] However, to understand where this type of thinking is being drawn from, we need to return to the ideas of Spare, who is, arguably, a more important influence on P-Orridge's occultism than Crowley.

Working from within a tradition of Romantic occultism, Spare demonstrated an aversion to moralism and taboos, as well as a fascination with the sexual and the bodily (particularly the significance of combining orgasm with the will and the sigil-focused imagination), and a keen interest in the potential of occult power to manifest desire. A talented artist and draughtsman, at an early age Spare became fascinated with the occult, a fascination that quickly found an outlet in his drawings. Following an early exhibition at London's Bruton Gallery in October 1907, at which the public were introduced to his highly sexualized drawings, which included much occult symbolism, he was contacted by Crowley. By 1910, after contributing four small drawings to Crowley's publication *The Equinox*, Spare had become a probationer of his Argenteum Astrum order, which he had formed following his estrangement from the Hermetic Order of the Golden Dawn. Although the two parted company, with Crowley referring to Spare as his "black brother," the latter's esoteric explorations continued. Developing a system of magical sigils, he became "probably the first modern occultist to evolve a self-contained working hypothesis about the nature of psychic energy which could be applied without all the paraphernalia of traditional rituals, grimoires, and magical incantations."[219] Without unpacking Spare's rather convoluted esoteric thought in detail,[220] the terms "Kia" and "Zos" do need to be introduced, the former being a primal and universal source of being, and the latter being the human body, a channel through which to communicate the occult energies of the psyche. The technique used to summon these primal energies he referred to as "atavistic resurgence," a method that involved "focusing the will on magical sigils, or individualized symbols, which, in effect, represented instructions to the subconscious."[221] It was these ideas that stimulated imaginations within industrial culture. P-Orridge even encouraged John Gosling to name his music project Zos Kia. The advice was accepted and several recordings were released under that name in the mid-1980s (e.g., *Transparent*, 1984). Since then, although still relatively obscure, Sparean esotericism and the terms "Zos" and "Kia" have entered popular music occulture (e.g., Behemoth, *Zos Kia Cultus*, 2002; Zero Kama, "Prayer of Zos,"[222] *The Goatherd And The Beast*, 2001; Limbo, *Zos Kia Kaos*, 1994). And, as Davis notes, back in 1971, Jimmy Page, who had become interested in Spare, designed a personal symbol for the fourth Led Zeppelin album—"Zoso"—which was probably intended to be a sigil for Zos. As Page himself commented enigmatically, "it wasn't supposed to be a word at all, but something entirely different."[223]

P-Orridge has been far less secretive about Spare's influence. Inspired by Kenneth Grant's *Images and Oracles of Austin Osman Spare* (to which he was almost certainly introduced by Tibet[224]), he developed a Sparean understanding of his own visual and musical creations as sigils. Spare's work also encouraged him to theorize and intellectualize the sexual, so that his fascination with the body (which, we have seen, is conspicuous throughout much of his work) was channeled into the formulation of an esoteric philosophy. Just as Spare had employed a technique of ecstasy, central to which was the orgasm, so P-Orridge states (using deliberately idiosyncratic spelling), "thee moment ov orgasm is central to thee process. It is special and all should be done to make it so . . . Sex is thee medium for thee magickal act, enacted physically and with direct control ov thee Individual. It generates thee greatest power which, when released, is diverted from its ordinary object and thrust with thee intense force ov will towards thee fulfillment of desire."[225] This is pure Spare. The key here is deeply felt desire, the Romantic emphasis on powerfully felt emotion (which, of course, can be evoked by the lyre of Orpheus), on feeling that moves and inspires, on the construction of a highly charged affective space for the purpose of meaning making. This, of course, is central to modern occult thought, in the belief that any desire deeply felt at the core of the human consciousness is believed to be capable of fulfillment. A carefully planned orgasm adds depth to the feeling, thereby increasing the chances of success in manifesting the desire. However, as we have noted, Spare's system also included an added extra—the use of sigils.

Spare's sigilization involved, for example, the writing down of a sentence as concisely as possible, which expresses one's desire; letters are then crossed out so that no letter is repeated; the remaining letters are then combined to produce a sigil. Indeed, sometimes the letters are merged to produce an abstract design. The sigil is then focused on and mentally absorbed, before being destroyed and, as far as possible, completely forgotten—unlike, it has to be said, Page's "Zoso" sigil (if that's what it is). The theory is that, at the depths of the subconscious, occulted from the conscious mind, it begins to work. Innate psychic energies manifest the sigilized desire. It is not too difficult to understand how P-Orridge believed this occult practice of sigilization might be developed in relation to his own work.[226] Indeed, statements such as popular music is "a platform for propaganda"[227] need to be understood in this Sparean sense, as the manifestation of sigilized desire. Of course, as we have seen, at a relatively mundane level, a musician is able to have a significant affective impact on the thinking of fans and, through that influence, acquires the potential to subvert mainstream thinking and challenge established authorities. However, if one imagines that such activities can be coupled with the energies made available by sigilization, then the potential for esoterrorism is significantly increased. Music becomes a "magick weapon" and performances become the "casting of spells."[228] Music as magick.

Returning to P-Orridge's spelling and grammar, it's worth noting here that this is understood to be a subversive technique, rather than simply a quaint idiosyncrasy. The spelling of "magick" is, of course, simply taken from Crowley's usage to signify high or ritual magic. Hence, the addition of a "k" to other words signifies esoteric meaning (e.g., Steve Hillage's *Rainbow Dome Musick* (1979) and Coil's *Musick to Play in the Dark* (1999)). However, the other idiosyncratic spellings and grammatical constructions are intended to constitute a challenge to thought and ways of reading; a challenge to the ways in which we have learned to think; our angle of vision is bent during the process of reading; we are drawn into closer examination; words are given "added levels of meaning."[229] In short, sigils, neologisms, idiosyncratic spelling, and dissonant sound subverts learned behaviors and challenges received worldviews. Again, as Davis says of Led Zeppelin's fourth album, the official title of which is spelled out with four well-known symbols/sigils, it seems "to communicate something without saying anything at all." He continues, "when confronted with such inscrutable signs, our natural impulse is to *decode* them, to 'know what they mean.'" However, when it comes to the four sigils identifying this album, "strict meanings are neither their nature nor their function. These sigils, and the musical sounds they announce, don't *mean* stuff so much as *make stuff happen*. And they make stuff happen by frustrating the conventional process of meaning."[230]

In the case of P-Orridge, in accordance with the contours of Romanticism, he has an explicitly Promethean agenda in mind:

> We live in limbo and thirst for freedom. . . . Vested interests of every kind want us lazy and atrophied. . . . Man's fall from grace is his fall from inner security. His defeat is his surrender to conditioned boundaries imposed by the strict regime of acceptability instead of the natural honesty of his individual instinct that recognizes all things to be in a state of flux. . . . We are trained to not even *want* to think. Decondition the condition. Conditioning is control. Control is stability. Stability is safety for those with a vested interest in control. Let's go out of control. What breaks this cycle is a psychic jolt. *Music is magick*, a religious phenomena that short circuits control through human response. The moment we forget ourselves and end the limbo-dance we enter a world of struggle, joy and clarity. A tragic, but magickal world where it is possible to accept mortality and thereby deny death. Experience without dogma, anguish without shame or sham. A morality of anti-cult. Occult culture. Its rituals are collective, yet private, performed in public, but invisible. . . . The rites of youth.[231]

William S. Burroughs had been articulating similar ideas for some years. Indeed, in an interview with Jimmy Page in 1975, not only did he argue that "Western man has been stifled in a nonmagical universe known as 'the way things are,'" but he insisted that "rock music can be seen as one attempt to break out of this dead soulless universe and reassert the universe of magic."[232]

Again, it's important to understand here that, as with the ad hoc Satanism of particularly "first wave" and "second wave" black metal, such ideas are quite distinct from ritualized systems of magick, which introduce elements of control and reflect the conventions of hierarchical "profane" society. Unlike Page, P-Orridge was not interested in "the magick of the Golden Dawn, designed for the stately Victorian manor." Rather, his was a magick intended "for the blank-eyed, TV-flattened, prematurely abyss-dwelling youth of the late twentieth century – like the punk kids in Derek Jarman's *Jubilee*, who have never ventured out of the council flats they were born in."[233] Hence, "rather than high ceremony, drawing-room intrigue and exalted initiatory ritual, the focus more often than not became simple survival and defense of individual vision from a malevolently dehumanizing culture that the Victorians and Modernists . . . could never have foreseen."[234] Similarly, in *Thee Grey Book*—a compendium of techniques written for TOPY and significantly influenced by Tibet and Balance—he states that, "recognizing thee implicit powers ov thee human brain (neuromancy) linked with guiltless sexuality focused through Will Structure (sigils) . . . magick empowers thee individual to embrace and realize their dreams and maximize their natural potential."[235]

As well as P-Orridge's work, Balance's own music, particularly with Peter Christopherson as Coil, was an explicit attempt to experiment with occult power. Drawing on the subversive methodologies of Burroughs (to whom we'll return below) and, he claimed, the divinatory theories of John Dee, Crowley, and Spare, he believed he was able to create "a lunar consciousness musick for the foreseeable future."[236] As John Everall comments, Coil "warped, twisted and transmitted sound in a manner pertinent to their immersion in the world of esoteric ideas."[237] For example, the album *Scatology* (1985) "contained numerous references to the alchemical process," says Balance. "I'm obsessed with the idea of turning base matter into gold, transmuting base materials, i.e., raw sound, into something else—the gold in the process. We recorded some rather peculiar practices which we then transformed and manipulated in accordance with our specific aims."[238] Indeed, rather enigmatically, Christopherson insisted that Coil was "a code. A hidden universal. A key . . . a spell, a spiral . . . A whirlwind in a double helix. Electricity and elementals, atonal noise and brutal poetry. A vehicle for obsessions. Kabbalah and Khaus [*sic*]. Thanatos and Thelema. Archangels and Antichrists. Truth and deliberation. Traps and disorientation."[239] Balance notes that "Certain tracks on certain Coil records are designed to trigger altered states. . . . Without wishing to sound pompous, we want to make sacred music."[240] Indeed, following Sparean thought, through the manipulation of sound they claimed to have developed "sidereal sound": "obviously the term sidereal relates to stars," says Balance, "but also through wordplay to looking at reality sideways, from a new angle or perspective. So as Spare twisted images in space, we adopt a similar process with sound. We've always been into sonic deviation and experimentation."[241]

Central to industrial "musick" is, we have seen, the attempt to subvert control. The ideas informing this discourse are fundamentally indebted to the work of Burroughs, who became, effectively, an unwitting guru for industrial culture. At a fairly basic level, they drew a transgressive energy from his countercultural persona, from his notoriety, from his status as a Dionysian celebrity. They asked him, for example, to "recite certain key words and phrases." This, they claimed, invested the music with "a shamanic quality," his speech lending it the force of "a magickal spell"; "he describes the invisible world, he documents the hidden mechanisms. This is what we also seek out; the secret mechanisms, the occult, if you like . . . "[242] More important, however, was Burroughs' cut-up technique, which has been a significant influence on numerous artists as diverse as Gus Van Sant, Bill Laswell, Kurt Cobain, David Bowie, Patti Smith, and Thom Yorke. Bowie, for example, in the 1974 BBC documentary *Cracked Actor*, is filmed by Alan Yentob tearing up sheets of lyrics, repositioning the pieces, and, with this jigsaw method, creating new lines. This is the cut-up technique. However, it is P-Orridge who has been most enthusiastic in making use of the method. Having known Burroughs since 1971, P-Orridge had, for several years, requested an introduction to his friend Brion Gysin, the principal architect of the cut-up method. (Having experimented with it in 1959, it was then developed and popularised by Burroughs.) Eventually, Burroughs wrote him a letter of introduction and P-Orridge met Gysin in Paris, probably in 1980,[243] and quickly established a close relationship.[244] While P-Orridge was enormously influenced by a number of Gysin's ideas (such as his theories regarding the "Dream Machine"[245]), it was the cut-up method, as discussed in *The Third Mind* (a book-length collage manifesto on the method and its uses), which became central to his thought. "Whatever you do in your head," insisted Gysin, "bears the prerecorded pattern of your head. Cut through that pattern and all patterns if you want something new . . . Cut through the word lines to hear a new voice off the page."[246] This method of subverting current patterns of thought and belief was, for artists such as Bowie, Smith, and P-Orridge, revolutionary. Gysin, P-Orridge argued, "understood more than anyone else at that point in culture that, just as we can take apart particles until there's a mystery, so we can do the same with culture, with words, language and image. Everything can be sliced and diced and reassembled, with no limit to the possible combinations."[247] He continues:

> If one didn't look at the very nature of how we build and describe our world, [Gysin] thought, we get into very dangerous places. Once you believe things are permanent, you're trapped in a world without doors. Gysin constructed a room with infinite doors for us to walk through. What amazed me about Gysin's work was how it could be applied to behaviour: there were techniques to free oneself through the equivalent of cutting up and reassembling words. If we confound and break up the proposed unfolding the world impresses upon us, we can give ourselves the space to consider what we want to be as a species. . . . He would take words, break them down into hieroglyphics, then turn the paper and do it again and again until the magical square was filled with words. Gysin worked with the idea of painting as magic, to change the perception of people and to reprogramme the human nervous system. . . . I made an agreement with Gysin before his death that I would try to champion and vindicate his work and legacy.[248]

What is consistently articulated, however, is the sense of sacred endeavor in the subversion of control, in the striving for liberty, which is understood in terms of a resistance to the profane. This is evident in much discourse surrounding the Dionysian in popular music, but it is explicit in the rationale for cut-up, as is conspicuous in P-Orridge's work. "It can be said, for me at least, that sampling, looping

and reassembling both found materials and site-specific sounds selected for preci-
sion ov relevance to thee message implications ov a piece ov music or a Transmedia
exploration, is an All-Chemical, even a Magickal phenomenon."[249]

Not only did he use the cut-up method to produce new subversive ideas and
sounds, but he applied it, quite literally, to his own body in an attempt to recreate
himself. He and his late partner, Jacqueline Breyer ("Lady Jaye"), following their
marriage in 1993, embarked on what he termed the "Pandrogeny Project,"[250] which,
informed by the cut-up technique, embraced the aesthetics of body modification
as the first step toward becoming a single "pandrogenous" being. Indeed, it's important to understand that, speaking in terms of a "genderless state," for P-Orridge,
who now has breast implants and looks feminine, the surgery was not motivated by
transsexual concerns. That is to say, he is not struggling to be female while trapped
in a male body. The surgery was not even, primarily, about the construction of a
posthuman, postgendered self, such as Marilyn Manson attempted to explore on
Mechanical Animals (1998).[251] Rather, this was far more of an occult project, in that
it was an expression of his belief that the self is pure consciousness trapped in flesh
and controlled by DNA. Humans are, he believes, at an early stage in their psychic
evolution toward fleshless consciousness; the Pandrogeny Project is a step toward
that evolutionary goal, a step away from the "control" of the DNA. He and "Lady
Jaye," therefore, sought to become one, in the sense of becoming a "third being"[252]—
they referred to themselves *together*, in the *singular*, as Breyer P-Orridge. However,
as with much of P-Orridge's thought, it is typically occultural, in that pandrogeny is
a synergy of ideas, the principal thesis drawing on a common stock of esoteric and
transpersonal theories of consciousness and "Mind."[253] In other words, in a typically
occultural manner, P-Orridge, wittingly or unwittingly, remixes a range of ideas with
theories learned from Gysin and Burroughs, as well as his own longstanding interest
in body modification.

For the esoterrorist, therefore, cut-up and the cultivation of occult culture are
central to the subversion of social control, just as pandrogeny is an act of resistance
to the control of the DNA.

> Control needs Time (like a junkie needs junk). Time appears linear.
> Cut-ups make time arbitrary, nonlinear. They reveal, locate and negate
> Control. Control hides in social structures like Politics, Religion, Educa-
> tion, Mass Media. Control exists like a virus for its own sake. Cut-ups
> loosen rational order, break preconceptions and expected response. They
> retrain our perception and acceptance of what we are told is thee nature of
> reality. They confound and short-circuit Control. All Control ultimately
> relies upon manipulation of behavior. . . . Magick as a method is a Cut-up
> Process that goes further than description. It is infused with emotion, in-
> tuition, instinct and impulse, and includes emotions and feelings. . . . Thee
> method is a contemporary, non-mystical interpretation of 'Magick.' Thee

aim is reclamation of self-determination, conscious and unconscious, to the Individual. Thee result is to neutralize and challenge thee essence of social control.[254]

A key conduit for this esoterrorist resistance to control was the band Psychic TV (formed by P-Orridge, with Peter Christopherson and Alex Fergusson, following the break up of Throbbing Gristle)[255] and the related occult organization TOPY, which he established in 1981 with, amongst others, Balance and Tibet[256] and also, significantly, members of The Process Church of the Final Judgment,[257] the latter having had an influence (via his early interest in Charles Manson) on the development of his occult thought.[258] While TOPY was founded at the same time as Psychic TV as a parallel occult think tank, it became both a fan community and an occult network in its own right, which has continued beyond P-Orridge's departure in 1991.[259]

The idea of "psychic TV" is significant. Although highly critical of television *per se*, in that he understands it to be a tool of mind control and mass indoctrination,[260] he argues that, like popular music, it might also be used by an esoterrorist as a form of magick to combat "control"—"a modern alchemical weapon":

> [Psychic TV] are attempting to knit together thee fine lines ov shamanic initiation and voodoo invokation allegorically coded into western X-tian myth. TV itself becoums thee ceremony, thee language ov thee tribe. It becoums apparent that, cloaked in spurious messianic trivia, are ancient tantric rituals involving small death, limbo and resurrection that have now been literalised and usurped by a base language system named religion. Just as religion cloaks ancient knowledge and techniques, so Television cloaks its power to invoke thee lowest coumon denominator ov revelation ... We intend to reinstate thee ability ov TV to empower and entrance thee viewer. To remove thee window and passivity, and re-enter thee world ov dreams beyond. We believe TV is a Modern alchemical weapon that can have a positive and cumulative effect upon Intuition.[261]

This, of course, is, again, very close to Anger's understanding of film as an occult weapon, a channel of Luciferian energy. Indeed, concerning what P-Orridge refers to as "thee fine lines ov shamanic initiation and voodoo invokation," not only did Psychic TV's performances include much disturbing imagery and occult sigilization, but there was an attempt, in much the same vein as the early occult bands, such as Coven and Black Widow, to perform transgression in a staged ritual. For example, this was done using the Tibetan thighbone trumpet, the *kangling*.[262] Although it was only used on their first album, *Force the Hand of Chance* (1982) and on the track "23 Tibetan Human Thigh Bones" released on *First Transmission* (1982), it attracted the attention they sought and, to some extent, served to shape the band's dark occultural image. It was, again, Tibet who introduced the instrument to P-Orridge during discussions about the formation of Psychic TV as a conduit for occult power. "If you talk to people who don't know much about it, they'll say it's a black magical rite for raising demons, which it is in a sense." Again, this is not dissimilar to attempts in the late sixties and early seventies to manifest occult power and create dark affective space through the performance of ritual magick. Tibet continues:

> There's a rite where you sit in a graveyard. You're meant to sit on a corpse cross-legged and blow this thighbone and this summons up the demons. So what it basically means is that you're sitting in a graveyard, you're shit scared and you're blowing something that is made out of a thighbone. It's a way of bringing all your fears to the surface. You're stealing terror that they had and becoming stronger and cleansing yourself. They always had to be made from either the thighbone of a very young virgin who'd been. . . . killed, or the murderer. The idea is that you're trying to summon out the worst parts of you. The instrument that you're actually using had to be the closest you could possibly get to evil, which is the little virgin girl, the purity destroyed, or the murderer. . . . I first used the instrument when I met [Genesis] and we were formulating the ideas of [Psychic TV]. They were almost impossible to get hold of and we liked the sound and the whole image of it, the mystique and the atmosphere behind them.[263]

Needless to say, the evocation of experiences of the impure sacred through such transgressive discourse and disorienting sonic atmospheres meant that the affective spaces created during early Psychic TV performances could be intense and challenging. The intention, however, it was consistently claimed, was to recalibrate received ways of thinking. As Balance put it, "we see no difference between our philosophy, our lifestyle and our art. We are what we do. What Spare did in art, we try to do through music. . . . . We try to do with sound what he did with pictures."[264]

Blood and soil

While resurgent atavism has often been accompanied by the search for a premodern and pre-Christian sense of the sacred in nature, we have seen that it has also been a feature of far right political discourse. It is not surprising, therefore, that the far right has sought to nurture nostalgia through a celebration of national folk culture. Ashley Hutchings, for example, recalls that The Albion Band, which he formed in 1971, "were, if you like, flying the flag for the history of England."[265] Unfortunately, however, this idealistic turn toward Britain's mythical past, its rural community life and its relationship to the land unwittingly attracted the mean imagination of the far right. Hence, as Hutchings recalls, "it became a very difficult position, our wish to celebrate this country's past, because we'd been hijacked to a certain extent by the British National Party."[266] Likewise, the current leader of the British National Party (BNP), Nick Griffin, has recently championed English folk music as one element within a wider cultural strategy to establish a relationship between the deeply felt sense of socioeconomic marginalization prevalent within some communities and his far right nationalist agenda. This, of course, has outraged many within the folk community, such as Billy Bragg,[267] who make a very clear distinction between patriotism—"progressive patriotism"—and far right nationalism. The point was stridently made by Eliza Carthy in an article for *The Guardian*, on learning that Griffin had mentioned her own music in this respect:

> People have said to me in the last few days that everyone who knows me and my work in traditional English song knows I am not far right. I collaborate with musicians from all over the world and have performed concerts for the promotion and recognition of migrant musicians in this country. I also come, albeit distantly, from a Gypsy family, and I believe in free movement, liberty and social justice for everyone. But music that stirs is political, be it a 100-year-old narrative about a murder, or an older song about a young girl struggling with unwanted pregnancy within a prurient society. And I have always made a point of performing English music almost exclusively, engaging in media discussions about what this means, and how to celebrate the ancient culture of where you are from without pushing anyone away; in fact treating a strong cultural history and music as an invitation, essentially 'you show me yours and I'll show you mine' – pride in oneself engendering mutual respect without hostility. I have been lucky enough to perform all over the world and I have held my head up among the most stunning, proud people because I know who I am and where I come from. My country has its ugliness. But I feel part of the positive side of us.[268]

Unfortunately, there is, of course, little consensus within the world of popular music regarding the relationship between folk culture and far right concerns. There is a history of the "atavistic endeavour" (to use Hunter S. Thompson's evocative term), "the dream-trip into the past,"[269] being informed by right wing political discourse. The problem is that, regardless of one's politics, celebrating a nation's past always runs the risk of attracting extreme right-wing political ugliness, largely because it can be read as constructing Romantic notions of national identity based on homogeneous ethnicity—blood and soil. This identity is, in the far-right imagination, interpreted as having been profaned by immigration and multiculturalism. Consequently, woven into the atavistic endeavor is a desire for cultural cleansing, a purging of the profane through a recovery of the past. The purity of the blood and its relationship to the soil in the past highlights the profanity of the present, and vice versa. Hence, again, regardless of the politics of the musicians themselves, the Romanticism of folk narratives depicting ethnically homogeneous and racially distinctive cultures, along with, at times, a conspicuous resurgent atavism that seeks to recover an imagined halcyon period in the history of a nation—a golden age—steers meaning toward the right.

Such narratives are significant, of course, because they have rhetorical power. They are able to insinuate themselves into personal histories and accrue emotional commitment. This is an important issue, and one that returns us to our earlier discussions of texts, affect, and values. However, at this point it's worth mentioning Lawrence Grossberg's discussion of "affective investments." Emotional responses are, he argues, a result of the articulation of two planes, signification and affect. The point to note here is that affect is a plane of human experience that does not concern meaning, but is rather about levels of intensity, sites of significance, which direct energy. In other words, some things matter to us more or in different ways than other things and thus become foci for energy investment. "The same experience will change drastically as its affective investment or state changes."[270] Because "affect operates across all of our senses and experiences, across all of the domains of effects which construct daily life," because it is what gives "color," "tone," or "texture" to everyday life, our experience of the world is "organized" through an affective field.[271] This field is, in turn, "organized according to maps which direct people's investments in and into the world." These, he refers to as "mattering maps," which "tell people where, how and with what intensities they can become absorbed – into the world and their lives. This 'absorption' constructs the places and events, which are, or can become, significant. These are the places at which people can anchor themselves into the world, the locations of the things that matter."[272] Our values are those things that "matter" to us, those points on our personal maps where there is an affective intensity, those areas in which we make affective investment. It is around these points that our beliefs and emotional energies cluster. Consequently, "it is the affective investment in particular ideological sites . . . that explains the power of the articulation which bonds particular representations and realities. It is the affective investment which enables ideological relations to be internalized and, consequently, naturalized."[273] This increases our understanding of the Orphic significance of popular music—how particular compositions matter to people. "By making certain things matter, people 'authorize' them to speak for them, not only as a spokesperson, but also as a surrogate voice (e.g., when we sing along to popular songs). People give authority to that which they invest in; they let the objects of such investments speak for and in their stead. They let them organize their emotional and narrative life and identity."[274] Hence, for example, as Bob Dylan's friend Paul Nelson commented, people looked to him for meaning: "Hungry for a sign, the world used to follow him around, just waiting for him to drop a cigarette butt. When he did, they'd sift through the remains, looking for significance. The scary part is, they'd find it."[275]

Indeed, as Hugh McLeod notes of German Romanticism in the nineteenth century, "there was a belief in salvation through art, literature, and music. . . . Beethoven, Wagner, and, above all, Goethe and Schiller, acquired the status of prophets. Their writings provided the basis for a religion of freedom, self-fulfillment, creativity, and belief in humanity." However, his point is that their equivalents in the 1960s "were popular singers, such as Bob Dylan, whose songs were treated with a reverence similar to that accorded by nineteenth-century Germans to the poems of Goethe and Schiller."[276] Popular musicians became shapers of opinion, prophets for a new, liminal generation. Popular music provided ways of experiencing and making sense of the world, marking out the sacred and the profane: the East was sacred, the West profane; peace was sacred, war profane; nature was sacred, industry profane; the counterculture was sacred, the establishment profane, and so on. That is to say, and this is Grossberg's key point, "the investment in rock," for example, "may make an investment in certain ideological positions more likely . . . " As he argues, "affect is the plane or mechanism of belonging and identification. . . . Affect defines a structure and economy of belonging."[277] The lyre of Orpheus is able to wield significant ideological power.

Returning to the discussion in this section, because popular music is of enormous affective significance in liminal cultures, its discourses tend to organize emotional and narrative life and identity of individuals. Discourses become woven into their lives and the ideas presented can shape ideological positions, influence perceptions of reality, determine understandings of "the way things are" and what constitutes "common sense." Hence when the contours on mattering maps are guided by contemporary social problems, or Romantic constructions of the past, or folklore, or national identity, or the idealization of rural life, or cultural heritage, these concerns can be organized and augmented in such a way that they reinforce each other and become focused into an ideological commitment. Again, affect is key here, in that it determines the way individuals emotionally invest in particular discourses.

With this in mind and following the contours of transactional reader-response theory (discussed in Chapter 2), we can think of the music as less an object and more an event, in the sense that it is an experience shaped by the reader, but under the guidance of the text. Firstly, what each listener makes of the music is shaped by particular mattering maps and cannot be entirely determined by music itself. Secondly, as we have argued, while this is true, people are *not free* to read *anything* they want into musical texts, in that, while their investments may be shaped by such maps, the music itself also brings something to the encounter and contributes to the process of meaning making; it encourages certain affective investments and discourages others. Hence, when a particular piece of music engages with the ideas and feelings of an individual, it can have an organizing effect, making certain things matter and suggesting certain ideological trajectories. The process is, of course, a complex and subtle intertextual one, including a range of variables.

Take, for example, a band such as Wardruna, formed in Norway by Einar Selvik (Kvitrafn) and including Kristian Eivind Espedal (Gaahl), both of whom played in—and therefore carry some of the semiotic baggage from—the Norwegian black metal band Gorgoroth, who have become notorious for their articulation of the Satanic and the macabre. Wardruna, however, explicitly promotes Norse religion and culture, using traditional instruments and drawing on the themes and compositional conventions of local folk music (e.g., *Runaljod—Gap Var Ginnunga*, 2009). For example, Selvik informs us that the principal foci of Wardruna are "the cultic musical language found in the near-forgotten arts of *galder, seidr* and the daily acts of the cultic life"; "each album will feature eight runes . . . " and will be recorded "partly . . . outdoors at locations relevant to the different runes"; "the instruments we use are mainly old and historical instruments, such as deer-hide frame drums and ceremonial drums, mouth harp, clove/hoof rattles from deer and goat, bone flute, goat and cow horns, Hardanger fiddle and bowed lyres"; "more unconventional inputs like trees, stones, water, fire etc. are also employed to enhance the nature of the rune being 'portrayed.'"[278] Innocent though this appears and, indeed, may very well be, the point here is simply that, regardless of the politics of Kvitrafn and Gaahl, along with the anti-Christian signification which attaches to them as a result of their association with Gorgoroth, their articulation of Norse religion, of cultural heritage, and of the premodern, constitute a number of nodal points around which certain far right affective centers of gravity cluster.

The same is obviously true of black metal per se, in that it makes certain far right concerns matter to liminal minds, which then *authorize* bands to speak for them "as a surrogate voice." Affective investment in black metal bands gives them authority to speak for fans, to let them "organize their emotional and narrative life and identity." This increases the likelihood of a fan's emotional investment in certain ideological positions, which, of course, shapes their understanding of the sacred and the profane, which, in turn, can legitimate acts of extreme violence. In black metal culture a confluence of discourses around an ancient Norse culture usurped by Christianization, a sense of continuity with a premodern warrior culture, and Satanism understood in terms of opposition to the profane hegemony of Christianity, as well as the collective effervescence stimulated by transgressive violence, led to church burning understood as a sacred commitment. Gry Mørk's comments are worth noting here, The "use of concepts and metaphors related to kinship (e.g., 'ancestors,' 'forefathers,' 'son of Odin') and botany (e.g., 'roots'), as well as possessive pronouns such as 'our' or 'ours' when referring to the heathen ancestors and the Norse cultural heritage," is, she says, connected "to private memories, to intimate and important experiences from one's own life." This, she argues, invests black metal discourse with emotional weight and "contributes to the development of a heathen self-perception and sense of belonging together by activating a feeling of commitment and loyalty."[279] In Scandinavia, this is particularly evident with the subgenre of Viking metal. However, this bias toward far right discourse is conspicuous throughout black metal culture, being vituperatively focused within National Socialist Black Metal, where the protection of the perceived purity of blood and soil is understood in terms of a sacred commitment. For example, the cover of *The Fate Worse Than Death* (2002) by the Polish band Thor's Hammer depicts a black male embracing a white female against an apocalyptic background, the less than subtle message being that nuclear apocalypse is preferable to miscegenation.

This also helps us to understand the wilderness aesthetic in black metal, evoked beautifully on the homepage of the "Black Metal Theory" website:[280] a black and white photograph of a pristine northern landscape; water, ice, and rock under a clear sky, completely devoid of flora and fauna, except for a small, solitary, black figure in the distance; although dwarfed by the majesty of the towering shards of rock and ice, the figure becomes the most significant point to which the eye is drawn; there is something both heroic and inhuman about an individual existing in such a hostile environment; here in the frigid, northern lands is a thinking being. This is where recent black metal theory begins: northern lands; wild, unforgiving nature; solitary heroism; misanthropy; intelligence. This discourse is made explicit in the "black metal film" made by Ted Skjellum (Nocturno Culto of Darkthrone), *The Misanthrope*, which foregrounds the northern wilderness. Indeed, it does little more than film the wilderness and introduce viewers to a simple Norwegian rural life—fishing through ice, walking through forests, and retreating to remote wooden cabins.[281] However, regardless of the fact that the cover of Darkthrone's *Transilvanian Hunger* (1994) identifies his music as "Norsk Arisk Black Metal" ("Norwegian Aryan Black Metal"), it is still difficult not to read the film in terms of propaganda around the archetypes of nature, purity and race as articulated in films produced for the Reich Propaganda Directorate of the Nazi Party, such as Carl Froelich's *Ich für dich, du für mich* (1934). There is little sense in *The Misanthrope* that Norway is a multicultural society with a Christian heritage. Through Romantic representation, cultural identity is essentialized and nature is idealized—blood and soil. In other words, this is a film intended to organize affective investments.

That the film is not simply a film about Norwegian life is indicated in the title. Although the film doesn't actually portray a misanthrope as such, the title suggests a racial disillusionment, a concern about a society that seems to frustrate the atavistic endeavor. Hence, there is a turning within, a turning away from a culture that has betrayed its heritage, a turning back to the wilderness. Only in this misanthropic space is the purity of the sacred relationship between blood and soil assured. This is certainly true of the black metal film, *Journey of a Misanthrope* (2008) by Russell Menzies (Sin Nanna of Striborg), which is a far more explicit portrayal of misanthropy and the turn away from society to solitude and the wilderness. This turn within and away from society and the ideology informing it leads to the development of a Romantic nature mysticism—a dense, darkened, uncanny, eerie, transgressive mysticism, a *Diabolical Fullmoon Mysticism* (Immortal, 2007): "we're now directed as much to the astral plane above us as to the soil and rocks below."[282] This

Romantic turn from society as profane to the wilderness as sacred[283] is, again, most conspicuously represented visually. The cover art for the following albums is typical of this aesthetic: Burzum, *Hvis Lyset Tar Oss* (1994), *Filosofem* (1996), *Hliðskjálf* (1999), *Belus* (2010); Dornenreich, *Hexenwind* (2005), *Durch Den Traum* (2006); Altorių Šešėliai, *Margi Sakalai* (2008); Belenos, *Spicilège* (2002); Woods of Infinity, *F&L* (2004); Primordial, *The Gathering Wilderness* (2005); Ulver, *Bergtatt* (1994); In the Woods, *Heart of the Ages* (1995); Mysticum, *In the Streams of Inferno* (1996); Nadja, *Radiance of Shadows* (2007). However, it is also represented in the evolution of the genre toward dense, ambient soundscapes and sampled natural sounds. For example, San Francisco's Lurker of Chalice (Jef Whitehead), begins his mesmerizing "Piercing Where They Might" by gently drawing the listener into the wilderness, signified by samples of crows cawing, prior to the descent of brooding, ambient black metal (*Lurker of Chalice*, 2005). Likewise, his "Spectre as Valkerie Is" begins with the sound of wind and concludes in a sonic miasma of dark despair. The point is, however, that from within the intertextual relationships among the various themes in black metal, the wilderness emerges, not only as a signifier of solitude, but also representing a turn within, away from a profane society to the soil, to a lifeworld shaped by a particular view of folk culture, of traditional beliefs and practices. Blood and soil constitute sacred forms, drawing their power from Romantic constructions of the past, which, when transposed into the present, reveal significant cultural dislocation: "Christian churches and other buildings of non-Nordic cultures disgrace our land, our heritage";[284] "They want to make us all believe that Judeo-Christianity is older than our Pagan religion. . . . I will not tolerate this attempt to continue the rape of our race and our culture, our religion and everything that is ours. . . . We will speak the truth to the people, we will revive our religion . . . and we will bring back Baldr after this thousand year long spiritual *Ragnarök*. We have found the gold of the past in the green grass, we have found the trails our forefathers walked and the spirit they lived for . . . The Kingdom of the Sun has returned, to crush the Judeo-Christian Empire of Darkness! Hail the Return of Baldr! *Heil og Sael.*"[285]

The Romantic articulation of pride in national identity, of course, need not be imbricated within the blood and soil discourse of the far right. As we have seen Eliza Carthy insist, musicians can "celebrate the ancient culture of where [they] are from without pushing anyone away." Likewise, while Björk focuses on very similar Nordic historic and cultural themes to those articulated in black metal, her work, like Carthy's, resists far right interpretation. Hence, for example, her turn to nature, to the Pagan, and to Icelandic religious and cultural heritage is often articulated in relation to the sea, understood as maternal: "my home was by the sea. If I walked down to the sea and sat down by the shore, I was home. That's my mother, the ocean. Nothing can go wrong."[286] This is important, for in articulating the idea of sea as mother, the source of all life, which surrounds the globe, embracing all lands, she both draws on Iceland's religious and cultural heritage, while at the same time explicitly subverting far right nationalist discourse. "Oceania" (*Medúlla*, 2004), for example, which was, significantly, performed at the opening ceremony of the Athens Olympics in 2004, was written, she says "from the point of view of the ocean that surrounds all land and watches over all humans to see how they are doing after millions of years of evolution. It sees no borders, different races or religion . . . "[287] The affective investment in this cluster of ideas, therefore, shapes Björk's interpretation of national pride. For example, she celebrates Icelandic Viking ancestry within a discourse of migration. Hence, instead of misanthropically turning inwards or, indeed, focusing on Viking warrior culture, the key ideas are those of being carried by the sea beyond national shores to other cultures: "I feel at home whenever/the unknown surrounds me" ("Wanderlust," *Volta*, 2007). Hence her music—the musicians she works with, the instruments she uses, the styles she employs—while rooted in her native land, articulates an enthusiasm to engage with other cultures. This is particularly noticeable on *Volta*. As Nicola Dibben comments, "the idea of global travel and encounters with other cultures is signified by the presence of music from a wide variety of cultures, and the sounds of water and ships act as the acoustic 'glue' between individual tracks. The sea, then, is used as a utopian symbol of humankind understood as a single entity and emphasizes commonalities between people from different cultures."[288] Hence, Björk's mattering map includes both national pride and what might be thought of as an egalitarian cosmopolitanism, in that her primary allegiance is to the global community of human beings, which is, in turn, informed by indigenous Icelandic religious and cultural ideas. Indeed, because both are areas in which she makes affective investment and around which her beliefs and emotional energies cluster, her atavistic endeavor to retrieve an indigenous religious identity takes her back through Icelandic history to, she says, "the roots – before time, or civilization, or religion, or patriotism."[289] In interviews about *Medúlla*, says Dibben, "Björk used the notion of Paganism to articulate a utopian idea of a world in which humans are not divided by religion or nationality."[290] Hence, both the sea and the conception of a primal Pagan culture become key tropes in her work, expressing a core egalitarian ethic. Consequently, if a fan's investment in her music has the effect of making a commitment to an ideological position more likely, it is almost certain to be a very different one than that encouraged by Darkthrone or Thor's Hammer.

Finally, we return to folk music and Eliza Carthy's concerns. In 2007 she became involved in a project the aim of which was to rescue discussions of British identity from profanation by the far right. The Imagined Village,[291] organized by Simon Emmerson, included, as well as Eliza Carthy, a number of other musicians interested in folk music and culture, such as Martin Carthy (her father), Billy Bragg, and Chris Wood.[292]

> We are not trying to reinvent the wheel or, for that matter, reinvent the English folk tradition. What we are interested in is building an inclusive, creative community where we can engage in the debate passed down to us by the late Victorian collectors of English song, dance and stories,

spearheaded by Cecil Sharp and his contemporaries and brought into contemporary resonance by Georgina Boyes, in her book *The Imagined Village*, Billy Bragg's recent work *The Progressive Patriot*. . . . Paul Gilroy's . . . *After Empire: Melancholia or Convivial Culture?* and the commentaries of musicians such as Chris Wood, Eliza and Martin Carthy amongst others . . . We all walk in the footsteps of our Victorian song collecting ancestors, but feel it is more relevant now than ever to question who decides what it is to be authentic and English and more importantly what it is that makes us proud to be English musicians.[293]

A good example of this is "Tam Lyn Retold" (*The Imagined Village*, 2007), a reworking of "Tam Lin," a Scottish ballad that carries forward a wealth of ancient folklore with roots stretching back at least into the sixteenth century and which has, since the 1960s, been covered by numerous artists, including Ewan MacColl and Peggy Seeger (*Cold Snap*, 1978), Steeleye Span (*Time*, 1996), Fairport Convention (*Liege and Lief*, 1969), Pyewackett (*The Man in the Moon Drinks Claret*, 1982), and The Mediaeval Baebes (*Mirabilis*, 2005). Although there are several surviving versions of the original ballad, essentially it tells the story of the relationship between Tam Lin and Janet. Trespassing into the realm of faery at Carterhaugh, Janet plucks a rose, sacred to faeries and elves, the result of which is an encounter with the elven Tam Lin who, in some versions, seduces her and takes her virginity as payment. On discovering that the encounter has left her pregnant, she goes in search of the child's enchanted father. Returning to Carterhaugh, she plucks another rose, her not unreasonable expectation being that her lover will return to her. Instead, she learns that he was once mortal, that the faeries stole him, and that he is now anxious to return to the human world, but cannot. Faery politics are rarely less than complicated:

> Every seventh year fairies must pay a tithe to hell. They usually pass off an abducted mortal in order to save one of their own. Tam Lin, being 'so fair and full of flesh,' fears he is the next victim. To disenchant her lover, Janet must pull him from his horse while he rides in the fairy troop on Halloween at midnight (verses 25-26), holding him fast as he passes through a series of repulsive or dangerous shapes (verses 31-33). A bath in well water, his nakedness then covered with Janet's cloak, will complete Tam Lin's transformation from elf back to human being (verses 34-35). Janet follows instructions, redeeming him (verses 36-39).[294]

The Imagined Village's version, however, does not take the listener back to an enchanted rural past. The sacred and the profane are identified elsewhere. Retold by the Rastafarian dub poet Benjamin Zephaniah, it is accompanied, not only by traditional folk instruments and singing, but primarily by bass-heavy, electronic dub reggae. While retaining some traditional folk elements, the composition nevertheless introduces a very different slice of British culture—one that challenges far right interpretations of British identity and attitudes toward immigration. Against the backdrop of a confluence of British and Jamaican musical styles, the location is reimagined in twenty-first century urban clubland and retold as the story of a young woman who, on the first day of May—the traditional day for celebrating springtime fertility—acquires, not a rose, but some "holy herb," which she smokes in an "organic chillum." She is then approached by Tam Lyn, an asylum seeker (an alien, like the elven Tam Lin), who, having observed her smoking the chillum, is concerned for her well-being and safety. The magic of the first day of May weaves its spell—she seduces him and subsequently finds herself "heavy with child." Hence, on the advice of her father, she goes in search of her alien lover, only to learn that, while he is anxious to stay with her and help raise their child, he cannot. As with faery politics, those of asylum and immigration are rarely less than complicated. He is a "war refugee" about to be sent back to his troubled homeland where his life is threatened. But love "ignores traditions and conventions" and nor is it "bound by human constructs, jurisprudence, and the laws of men . . . " At court, she takes him in her arms and, with the force of her love, exorcises the demons of right wing rhetoric that have oppressed him: he turns into a "victim," a "loser," a "criminal" and, finally, into "himself, just a cool human being." The judiciary see him for what he is and accept his application for asylum. The two settle down and contribute to British society in much the same way as any other British family. Hence, drawing on traditional folklore, Zephaniah and The Imagined Village identify some of the nation's core egalitarian values and subvert casual, and not so casual, right wing bigotry. "Make love not war/This is how we do it."

The music of Björk and The Imagined Village subverts what some of those proud of their cultural heritage have sought to do. They do not retreat from the modern world. Theirs is a discourse informed by a concern for contemporary political relevance. Indeed, The Imagined Village project in particular can be understood as a critique of overly Romantic, otherworldly, politically disengaged music and lifestyles. Such Romantic yearning for the premodern easily becomes detached from the everyday and, therefore, from the concerns and contexts of folk music itself. More specifically, it becomes detached from particular sacred forms, such as the right of asylum seekers to be treated as human beings and the need for children to be loved and protected by their parents, regardless of their ethnicity or political status. The past is important principally as a way of improving the present.

Turning on and turning within

We have seen that, during the 1960s and 1970s, not only were large numbers of musicians and countercultural bricoleurs going gently feral in the countryside, but many were also, like their Romantic predecessors, turning within.[295] Indeed, the turn away from the West and the modern and the turn toward nature and the premodern were driven by the same Romantic impulse, central to which was a turn from the transcendent to the immanent, from the God above to the life-force within, from creeds and external authority to epistemological individualism. Typically, during the sixties, this turn within involved the assistance of what can be understood as technologies of transformation, substances which were able to induce altered states conducive to self-realization and the creation of affective spaces within which the distance between the self and the divine was shortened or removed altogether. As Paul McCartney, who might be considered typical of many in popular music culture during the sixties, stated: "God is in everything. God is in the space between us. God is in that table in front of you. God is everything and everywhere and everyone. It just happens that I realised all this through acid, but it could have been through anything. It really doesn't matter how I made it. . . . The final result is all that counts."[296] Hence, unsurprisingly, like the nineteenth-century Romantics and Transcendentalists, the immanentist philosophy of "the East" became enormously appealing. As the "Christian West" was increasingly perceived as profaned—a technologically advanced, but spiritually arid place, which frustrated the individual's necessary quest for self-realization—so the East glowed brighter with sacred promise. And, of course, as the new prophets within popular music "turned on," they became lenses through which this psychedelic, "Eastern" turn within was magnified.[297] As Arthur Marwick has argued of the sixties, youth culture's newly acquired spending power (particularly within the working class), its sense of freedom and its desire to challenge dominant values, such as those of institutional religion, were primarily informed by popular music.[298] Perhaps the most salient example of this eastward gaze and turn within was The Beatles' relationship with the Maharishi Mahesh Yogi and their eight-month public espousal of Transcendental Meditation, which, it has been argued, "turned an interest shared by only a few in the West in 1965 into a subject of discussion right across Western society."[299] However, in seeking to understand the context within which such discourses flourished, something needs to be said about what Max Weber referred to as "rationalization" and "the disenchantment of the world."[300]

Rationalization, which drives disenchantment, concerns modernity's preoccupation with routines, procedures, predictability, order, and increased efficiency. It leads both to the expansion of bureaucracy and also to an emphasis on process and organization. Everything can and should be done better, faster, cheaper, and more efficiently. Hence, the first point to note is that traditional religious belief is inevitably going to be at odds with key currents within modernity, in that a reliance on the efficacy of, for example, petitionary prayer, divine providence, meditation, or the casting of spells is increasingly challenged by a culture that values predictability, order, routine, and immediate quantifiable returns. The default position for many westerners, including those with religious convictions, is an acceptance that there are more practically effective ways of getting through life than traditionally "religious" ways—although a "spiritual life" may be a psychologically useful complementary discourse. Allied to this assumption is, of course, the further assumption that science and technology have left relatively little space in the world for traditional belief in the supernatural to occupy. Not only are there decreasingly small gaps in scientific knowledge for the "god of the gaps" to[301] work in, but such a deity may already be facing redundancy, in that what cannot be wholly explained by science cannot credibly be accounted for by the supernatural. Hence whereas, in premodern societies, immediate religious and moral connections would be made with physical events, such as crop success or failure, and prayers of thanksgiving or contrition would be offered and rituals performed, in the modern, urban, industrialized world, the individual instinctively acknowledges the connection between physical causes and physical effects, and, in cases of adversity, seeks physical remedies. Christians may pray for relief from pain, but few will not first avail themselves of the appropriate medication. Just as few will accept that schizophrenia is the result of demonic possession, so few will insist that the death of a neighbor's cow is the result of witchcraft. Screamin' Jay Hawkins may have sung "I Put a Spell on You" (1957), but would he have considered it a genuine possibility? Perhaps. But even if he did believe that casting spells to elicit love was an intelligent course of action, his understanding of the process would have been very different from that of our premodern ancestors.

Another key process of the modern period has been pluralization. Communities in which people operated with a shared sense of the sacred, a shared morality, and a shared identity, and within which an individual's material, intellectual, and spiritual sustenance was provided for, are rapidly fragmenting and disappearing. The sixties was an important decade in this respect, in that it witnessed an acceleration of pluralization. Peter Berger in particular has drawn attention to the fact that, unlike premodern societies in which a single, unifying concept of the sacred was dominant, permeating all areas of community life, in modern societies there are few shared values to which one can appeal and the beliefs an individual does hold cannot be taken for granted. "The pluralistic situation multiplies the number of plausibility structures competing with each other. *Ipso facto*, it relativizes their religious contents. More specifically, the religious contents are 'de-objectivated,' that is, deprived of their status as taken-for-granted, objective reality in consciousness."[302] Consequently, they become "subjectivized." Indeed, they become subjectivized in a double sense: "Their 'reality' becomes a 'private' affair of individuals, that is, loses the quality of self-evident intersubjective plausibility – this one 'cannot really talk' about religion anymore. And their 'reality,' insofar as it is still maintained by the individual, is apprehended as being rooted within the consciousness of the individual rather than in any facticities of the external world – religion no longer refers to the cosmos or to history, but to individual *Existenz* or psychology."[303] This, of course, presents a problem for religious institutions, in that they now exist in societies in which their definitions of reality no longer operate as foundational presuppositions. Moreover, not only does this create space for an easy and happy rejection of the supernatural altogether, but, for many young people in the sixties, it also created space for experimentation with fresh expressions of the sacred. Hence, as Robert Wuthnow notes, the decade "began with Christian theologians declaring that God was dead; it ended with millions of Americans finding that God could be approached and made relevant to their lives in more ways than they had ever imagined. . . . New religious movements of Asian origin, such as Zen and Hare Krishna, spread in metropolitan areas, as did the humanistic spirituality of such groups as . . . Scientology."[304]

In the final analysis, it became clear to the sixties generation that beliefs which had been handed down to them were not only lacking in cogency, but were also not the only ones on offer. This situation led to a crisis of credibility in dogmatism and, as such, a widespread collapse of the plausibility of traditional religious definitions of reality.[305] In other words, there is a relationship between the *subjective* secularization of an individual's consciousness and *objective* secularization at the social-structural level. "Subjectively, the man in the street tends to be uncertain about religious matters. Objectively, the man in the street is confronted with a wide variety of religious and other reality-defining agencies that compete for his allegiance or at least attention, and none of which is in a position to coerce him into allegiance."[306] In other words, as Berger argues, "pluralism" is a social-structural correlate of the secularization of consciousness. Similarly, Steve Bruce makes the point that "by forcing people to do religion as a matter of personal choice rather than as fate, pluralism universalizes 'heresy.' A chosen religion is weaker than a religion of fate because we are aware that we chose the gods rather than the gods choosing us."[307]

The acceleration of the democratization of subjectivization since the 1960s has meant thinking in the register of freedom, autonomy from power, and equality in difference. More specifically, it has meant a shift away from "life lived in terms of external or 'objective' roles, duties and obligations," and "towards life lived by reference to one's own subjective experiences. . . ."[308] There has been a sacralization of subjectivities, an increasing focus on states of consciousness, emotions, passions, sensations, bodily experiences, dreams, visions, and feelings. There has been a turn within. The Beatles' "Within You, Without You" (*Sgt. Pepper's Lonely Hearts Club Band*, 1967) and "All You Need is Love" (1967)[309] reflected this shift in the 1960s,[310] this "expressive revolution" as Talcott Parsons memorably referred to it,[311] just as black metal misanthropy,[312] global psytrance,[313] and even Lady Gaga's "Born This Way" (2011) are representative of the changes brought about by that revolution. The key question is still that posed by Jimi Hendrix, *Are You Experienced*? (1967).

As the primary locus of the expressive revolution, the 1960s is of particular importance in that, as we have noted, it witnessed an accelerated decline in the social significance of Christianity, a disillusionment with Western modernity, and a turn toward discourses focused on the self, particularly those from the East.[314] Hence, it is no coincidence that, while Andrew Rawlinson's work identifies 1963 as the year in which the "full bloom" of Eastern religions in the West began,[315] in an entirely separate discussion, Callum Brown considers that year to be the crucial year for the decline of Christianity in Britain and the rise of the secular condition. Why 1963? The rationale is closely tied to the emerging significance of the "swinging sixties." For a thousand years, says Brown,

> Christianity penetrated deeply into the lives of the people, enduring Reformation, Enlightenment and industrial revolution by adapting to each new social and cultural context that arose. Then, really quite suddenly in 1963, something very profound ruptured the character of the nation and its people, sending organised Christianity on a downward spiral to the margins of social significance. In unprecedented numbers, the British people since the 1960s have stopped going to church, have allowed their church membership to lapse, have stopped marrying in church and have neglected to baptise their children. . . . The cycle of inter-generational renewal of Christian affiliation, a cycle which had for so many centuries tied the people however closely or loosely to the churches and to Christian moral benchmarks, was permanently disrupted by the 'swinging sixties.' Since then, a formerly religious people have entirely forsaken organised Christianity in a sudden plunge into a truly secular condition.[316]

Driven in part by popular music and youth culture, attitudes and worldviews shifted significantly away from traditional Christianity and conservative politics:

> In the 1960s, the institutional structures of cultural traditionalism started to crumble in Britain: the ending of the worst excesses of moral censorship (notably after the 1960 trial of *Lady Chatterley's Lover* and the ending in 1968 of the Lord Chamberlain's control over the British theatre); the legalisation of abortion (1967) and homosexuality (1967) and the granting of easier divorce (1969); the emergence of the women's liberation movement, especially from 1968; the flourishing of youth culture centred on popular music (especially after the emergence of The Beatles in late 1962) and incorporating a range of cultural pursuits and identities (ranging from the widespread use of drugs to the fashion revolution); and the appearance of student rebellion (notably between 1968 and the early 1970s).[317]

While we might want to question Brown's claim that Western societies have taken "a sudden plunge into a truly *secular* condition," his point regarding the significance of the 1960s as a decade in which, for a variety of reasons, steps were taken away from institutional Christianity and toward countercultural alternatives is important, not least because the Orphic power of popular music was central to the process: "pop music – buying it, listening to it, dancing to it, and making it – released the generation of fifties' and sixties' children from conventional forms of popular culture and conventional discourses."[318] Nevertheless, as I have argued elsewhere, Brown's understanding of religion in the 1960s is incomplete in that he fails to analyze adequately emergent alternative religious vitality. While he notes that, in the final three years of their existence as a band, The Beatles wrote songs in which "romance had been displaced by complex and varied lyrical themes influenced by, amongst other things, the anti-war movement, nihilism, existentialism, nostalgia, and eastern mysticism,"[319] this deserves more than a mention. The shift in lyrical content reflects enormously significant social and cultural changes. As Colin Campbell argues, "the cultural upheaval of the 1960s and the associated growth of new religious and spiritual movements has presented the sociologist of religion with particularly acute problems of analysis and interpretation." He continues:

> Prior to this decade, the image of modern society that was most widely accepted was one in which secularization, variously conceived, was considered to be the prevailing feature, although it was recognized that this process did not proceed unevenly and could be interrupted by periods of religious revival such as occurred in the United States in the mid-fifties. The various phenomena, such as the rise of Eastern religion, the occult revival, the astrology craze and the new Pentecostalism, which can collectively be called the 'new religiosity', did not, on the face of it, fit into this picture. For they did not resemble the standard pattern of religious revivals, as they were all too often in stark opposition to the churches and denominations, while at the same time, it required a fairly convoluted form of argument to maintain that such movements were evidence of continuing secularization.[320]

Rather it appeared to be less a case of secularization and more a case of relocation, in that individuals seemed not to be abandoning "the spiritual," but simply looking elsewhere for it, guided primarily by the needs/desires of the subjective life, rather than by the claims and demands of external religious authorities. That said, few would have been able to say with Van Morrison, *No Guru, No Method, No Teacher* (1986)—not even Morrison—in that most were, of course, following in others footsteps and rejoicing in the guidance offered by the new prophets of popular culture, not to mention the burgeoning milieu of New Age gurus, methods, and teachers. The result was a widespread embracing of ideas which had previously only been available to a minority. Within just a few years, texts on Vedantic thought and books such as Huxley's *Doors of Perception* became *de rigueur*.[321] Since then, as Wuthnow has argued, the West has witnessed the "decline of a spirituality of dwelling" and "the rise of a spirituality of seeking,"[322] or what Wade Clark Roof has identified as an emerging "quest culture."[323]

It is this democratization of spiritual choice, this culture of seeking that can be attributed in large measure to the growing cultural significance of popular music during the 1960s. As we have seen, musicians and key figures of the counterculture, such as The Beatles, Bob Dylan, and Allen Ginsberg, not only articulated and authorized vaguely formed doubts about traditional religious belief within the minds of many Westerners, but they liberated the subjective life, introducing new spiritual trajectories, new experiences of Eastern and indigenous traditions. For example, from the mid-sixties on the music of The Beatles celebrated aspects of Hindu philosophy and culture, George Harrison eventually embracing the Hare Krishna Movement (e.g., *All Things Must Pass*, 1970; *Living in a Material World*, 1973; *Dark Horse*, 1974);[324] the work of both John McLaughlin (e.g., *Inner Mounting Flame*, 1971; *Between Nothingness and Eternity*, 1973) and Carlos Santana (e.g., *Lotus*, 1975) reflected the ideas of their guru, Sri Chimnoy; The Incredible String Band's 1969 album, *Changing Horses*, gently articulated their growing interest in Scientology;[325] Van Morrison took his Romantic Celtic mysticism on a nomadic quest through Theosophy and Scientology;[326] Pete Townshend of The Who, in 1968, announced himself a follower of Meher Baba, introducing his teachings into the narratives of both *Tommy* (1969) and *Quadrophenia* (1973); The Moody Blues' *In Search of the Lost Chord* (1968) sought to evoke the mystical in their exploration of psychedelics and Indian spirituality;[327] and, of course, numerous less well-known bands such as Quintessence or record labels such as Kama Sutra Records reflected the turn away from the West and the turn within.

In a fairly short period of time, the West witnessed the growth of a wide range of beliefs and practices aimed at facilitating the turn within, many of which flowed out of the increasingly varied occultural resources of the psychedelic revolution. Central to this "revolution," of course, and emerging out of Beat culture, was the combination of drugs, free love, sacralized subjectivities, and, usually, Eastern thought.[328] The physicist Fritjof Capra, for example, in his influential book, *The Tao of Physics: An Exploration of Parallels Between Modern Physics and Eastern Mysticism*, recalls the significance of one of his own psychedelic experiences in the sixties. Having taken a hallucinogen, he recalls "sitting by the ocean one late summer afternoon, watching the waves rolling in and feeling the rhythm of my breathing." He then suddenly became aware of his "whole environment" and experienced a sense of "being engaged in a gigantic cosmic dance."

> Being a physicist, I knew that the sand, rocks, water and air around me were made of vibrating molecules and atoms, and that these consisted of particles which interacted with one another by creating and destroying other particles. I knew also that the Earth's atmosphere was continually bombarded by showers of 'cosmic rays', particles of high energy undergoing multiple collisions as they penetrated the air. All this was familiar to me from my research in high-energy physics, but until that moment I had only experienced it through graphs, diagrams and mathematical theories. As I sat on that beach my former experiences came to life; I 'saw' cascades

coming down from outer space, in which particles of energy were created and destroyed in rhythmic pulses; I 'saw' the atoms of the elements and those of my body participating in this cosmic dance of energy; I felt its rhythm and I 'heard' its sound, and at that moment I *knew* that this was the Dance of Shiva, the Lord of the Dancers worshipped by the Hindus.[329]

It was this experience that led to his thesis in *The Tao of Physics*: "Eastern mysticism provides a consistent and beautiful philosophical framework which can accommodate our most advanced theories of the physical world";[330] "the central aim of Eastern mysticism," which is "to experience all phenomena in the world as manifestations of the same ultimate reality," concurs with contemporary physics; this reality "is seen as the essence of the universe, underlying and unifying the multitude of things and events we observe.... This ultimate essence ... cannot be separated from its multiple manifestations. It is central to its very nature to manifest itself in myriad forms which come into being and disintegrate, transforming themselves into one another without end. In its phenomenal aspect, the cosmic One is thus intrinsically dynamic, and apprehension of its dynamic nature is basic to all schools of Eastern mysticism."[331] Expresing fundamentally the same convictions to those of Paul McCartney quoted at the beginning of this section, Capra's insistence on the ontological priority of the One over the many is typical of the psychedelic turn within articulated by many in the 1960s counterculture. Indeed, the bibliography in *The Tao of Physics* is interesting in that, along with a selection of books of a scientific nature, there are far more titles which are explicitly "spiritual," including D. T. Suzuki's and Alan Watts' volumes on Buddhism, the enormously popular books by Carlos Castaneda claiming to provide emic accounts of shamanism, Maharishi Mahesh Yogi's translation of the *Bhagavad Gita*, Vivekananda's *Jnana Yoga*, Fung Yu-Lan's *A Short History if Chinese Philosophy*, Lama Anagarika Govinda's *Foundations of Tibetan Buddhism*, the *Tao Te Ching* and the *I Ching*, and William Blake's *Complete Writings*. Again, whereas, prior to the sixties, the distribution of such ideas and of psychedelics was confined to "a hand-picked coterie of the gifted and influential," such as Aldous Huxley and Gerald Heard,[332] the expressive revolution democratized them and, as such, changed thinking in the West. As Nick Bromell comments in his excellent discussion of the significance of music and psychedelics in the sixties:

In the '60s, the self-willed breakthrough to alternative states of consciousness (what Emerson . . . calls 'flash-of-lightening faith') was much more widely publicized and consequently much more commonly experienced. When Ralph Waldo Emerson or William James or even Allen Ginsberg wrote about the private experience of breakthrough, their work was available to a relatively small circle of cognoscenti. When Virginia Woolf developed a prose style that conveyed these other states of consciousness with breathtaking force, she found an audience (small, cosmopolitan, educated) that understood and appreciated her achievement. But when Bob Dylan proclaimed with mocking good humor that '*Everybody* must get stoned' and proceeded to unfold songs that constructed a play-space for the altered consciousness, he reached an audience of tens of millions, and the vast majority of these were kids – teenagers, adolescents. The audience that gathered around The Beatles was even larger. In turn, this extraordinary publication of the breakthrough experience briefly created a wild paradox: it created a culture that defined itself as a 'counter' culture, as a 'benign climate' where the 'flash-of-lightening' experiences of transcendence, flux, and radical self-redefinition were honored and sustained.[333]

Without getting embroiled in a contentious chicken-and egg-discussion (i.e., which came first?), the point here is simply that, during the sixties, turning on and turning East informed the turn within—indeed, the whole notion of 'turning on' was interpreted as a fundamentally spiritual pursuit. Timothy Leary, in his programmatic psychedelic text *High Priest*, makes this explicit by rewriting the initial verses of the Gospel of John:

> In the beginning was the turn on. The flash, the illumination. The electric trip. The sudden bolt of energy that starts the new system. The turn on was God. . . . In this turn on was life; and the life was the light of men. It has always been the same. . . . It is the brilliant neurological glare that illuminates the shadows of man's mind. The God-intoxicated revelation. The Divine Union. The vision of harmony, satori, ecstasy which we now call psychedelic. What happens when you turn on? Where do you go when you take a trip? You go within. . . . The external world doesn't change, but your experience of it becomes drastically altered.[334]

He could hardly have articulated the turn from Christianity to the East and the psychedelic turn from God above to the divine within more explicitly. Hailed by Ginsberg "a hero of American consciousness . . . faced with the task of a messiah,"[335] Leary wanted to change society by transforming individuals. As "*high* priest," he would begin with the formation of a religious community organized around the sacramental use of hallucinogens. "They would undertake the spiritual search in a communal setting and report back to the rest of the world. They would keep records, compile statistics, and compile articles in their own journal, *The Psychedelic Review*. Above all, they would become an active, educative, and regenerative force, an example for others to follow."[336]

The term "psychedelic," originally coined by Humphrey Osmond in a letter to Huxley, became common currency and rapidly expanded to include all forms of culture which were thought to be inspired by the use of hallucinogens.[337] A great deal of time and creative energy was invested in the production of particularly music and visual art which would encourage constructive altered states. Indeed, the psychedelic and the spiritual collapsed into each other as subjectivities were sacralized. A powerful experience at a concert, making love, looking at a piece of art, smoking marijuana with friends, was "spiritual." When Hendrix spoke of being "experienced," this is what he was thinking of: spiritual/experience. The goal was always the "experience" and the drugs were simply a way of achieving it—"not necessarily stoned, but beautiful," as Hendrix put it ("Are You Experienced?", *Are You Experienced?* 1967). And as one Grateful Dead fan commented of the band, "they really seemed to open up some kind of interior space that was very refreshing and satisfying to have access to. Listening to their music I was able to lose myself to a greater extent than with any other kind of music or any other experience. . . . The Grateful Dead symbolized some sort of nexus of expanded experiences of consciousness." Consequently, he concluded, "it more closely approaches the sacred than anything else I've ever experienced."[338] Nevertheless, again, while drugs weren't absolutely necessary, they were considered sacramentally important, in that they could remove minds from profane society and place them in sacred space, thereby creating the conditions for an "experience." As Paul McCartney commented, being high meant "really thinking for the first time."[339] Likewise, for George Harrison, "up until LSD. . . . I never realized that there was anything beyond this normal waking consciousness."[340] Hence, as David Farber has argued, "to make drug consciousness . . . a major force in the youth movement of the 1960s is not something that comes easily to an academic, but those academicians who have written about the 1960s without any attempt to seriously or analytically relate drug consciousness to the events of the 1960s have done so at the cost of warping and misconstructing much of what went on."[341]

Central to the making sense of "drug consciousness" were the classic texts of the period: Kerouac's *Dharma Bums*;[342] Watts' widely read volumes *Beat Zen, Square Zen, and Zen* and *The Joyous Cosmology*;[343] Huxley's *The Doors of Perception* (the text that inspired the band name The Doors);[344] and particularly *The Psychedelic Experience: A Manual Based on the Tibetan Book of the Dead* by Leary, Ralph Metzner and Richard Alpert (later to be renamed Ram Dass by his guru Neem Karoli Baba). Such writings helped people toward new ways of experiencing and interpreting the world. More important still were musical texts, such as The Beatles' *Sergeant Pepper's Lonely Hearts Club Band* (1967), the cover of which, as well as including images of key cultural figures, such as Huxley and Crowley, and religious icons, such as the Buddha and Lakshmi, also had the faces of Mahatma Gandhi and four Indian gurus looking out at inquisitive fans: Sri Yukteswar Giri, Paramahansa Yogananda, Swami Vivekananda, and Mahavatar Babaji.

Musically, having introduced the sitar into "Norwegian Wood (This Bird has Flown)" in 1965 (*Rubber Soul*)—"an unprecedented event" in the history of Western popular music—following which Harrison's "Love to You" (*Revolver*, 1966) became "the first song in the Euro-American pop music canon . . . scored predominantly for

Asian musical instruments," the ideas on *Sergeant Pepper's* consolidated this turn to the East—"Within You, Without You" being an almost entirely Indian composition.[345] Central to this musical turn to the East was the Indian sitarist Ravi Shankar, who, by the mid-1960s, had established himself as the principal representative of Indian music in the West. Indeed, his influence was already being felt within popular music culture prior to the release of "Norwegian Wood." For example, Ray Davies of The Kinks had introduced pseudo-Indian drones into "See My Friends" (1965), Jimmy Page had bought a sitar from an Indian musician hired to play on The Yardbirds' "Heart Full of Soul" (1965)—eventually replaced by Jeff Beck on the guitar—and The Byrds had also become interested in Shankar.[346] According to David Crosby of The Byrds, it was he who introduced Harrison and Lennon to Shankar's music. Whether this is true of Harrison or not, it does seem to be the case that Lennon's interest in the sitar dates from August 24, 1965, a heady day of LSD and music that he and Harrison spent with Roger McGuinn and Crosby at a house on Mulholland Drive, Los Angeles. It was this session, it appears, during which they discussed Indian classical music, that led to the sitar on "Norwegian Wood." However, novel though it may have been, by the time it was released, interest in the Indian sound had become almost *de rigueur*. As Steve Marriott of the Small Faces put it in 1966, "we'll be able to get plastic sitars in our cornflakes soon."[347]

Nevertheless, while The Beatles were part of a wider musical and "spiritual" turn East, MacDonald isn't entirely wide of the mark when he states that "the popular (and generally sincere) fascination with oriental wisdom, which ensued in the late sixties and thereafter, owes almost everything to The Beatles in their role as the cultural antennae of the mainstream. It was their absorption in Indian religion which started the spiritual revival of the late sixties . . . "[348] Again, while this overstates their significance somewhat, in that it is almost always a mistake to attribute such enormous and widespread sociocultural changes to any particular band or artist, nevertheless, the point is an important one. It is difficult to avoid the nodal significance of The Beatles. Certainly for Leary and other cultural engineers, they were key: "I declare that The Beatles are mutants. Prototypes of evolutionary agents sent by God with a mysterious power to create a new species – a young race of laughing free men. . . . They are the wisest, holiest, most effective avatars the human race has ever produced."[349] Again, "the message from Liverpool is the Newest Testament, chanted by four Evangelists – saints, John, Paul, George, and Ringo. Pure Vedanta, divine revelation . . . "[350] Charles Manson's deranged and LSD-addled mind also received a revelation from John, Paul, George, and Ringo indicating that America was standing on the brink of an African American uprising against the white "little piggies," a revelation which would inaugurate a short, violent period of manipulation, abuse, and murder.[351]

Initially, the psychedelic revolution was concerned with little more than the turn within. There was a belief that social change could be inspired by altered perceptions of reality and the cultivation of vague ideas such as "All You Need is Love."

Indeed, during this period, Leary himself was explicitly apolitical: "Quit school. Quit your job. Don't vote. Avoid all politics. . . . Political choices are meaningless. . . . Dismiss the Judaic-Christian-Marxist-puritan-literary-existentialist suggestion that the drop-out is escape and that the conformist cop-out is reality. Dropping out is the hardest yoga of all."[352] The only way to transform society was via the spiritual/psychedelic transformation of individuals. Consequently, the ideals of the psychedelic movement and those of the New Left were at odds. The hippies had, as Warren Hinckle reported in 1967, "resolved their goals, but not their means." Hence, he continues, "the crisis of the hippie ethic is precisely this: it is all right to turn on, but it is not enough to drop out,"[353] which, of course, is precisely what Leary had encouraged: "turn on, tune in, drop out."[354] In the final analysis, many felt that, regardless of its intentions and the undoubted positive effects of a withdrawal from a profaned society, psychedelia's underlying philosophy seemed only to create a movement primarily consisting of people not unlike those portrayed by Gilbert Shelton in his seminal underground comic strip, *The Fabulous Furry Freak Brothers*, driven by little more than the experience of getting high: "dope will get you through times of no money better than money will get you through times of no dope" was the sage wisdom of one of the brothers, Freewheelin' Franklin.[355] Hence New Left activists of the period, such as the leader of "the yippies," Jerry Rubin, found the psychedelic turn within frustrating. The world could only be changed by political activism, not by the sacralization of subjectivities and disengagement from society.

Having said that, eventually the growing sense of threat posed by what was considered to be a profane establishment led to a commitment to protect and promote the sacred. That is to say, there was a dawning realization that the sacred could not simply be chemically detached from the profane culture within which it existed. Hence Leary's views, although remaining utopian about the spiritual and educational potential of psychedelics, began to change. This became evident when he announced that he had decided to challenge the incumbent Governor of California, Ronald Reagan, who was particularly despised within the counterculture because of his deployment of the National Guard at a student protest in Berkeley: "if it takes a blood bath," he declared, "let's get it over with."[356] Hence, in 1969 Leary announced that, as the representative of a new party, FERVOR (Free Enterprise, Reward, Virtue and Order), he would be running for Governor of California against Reagan.[357] "The High Priest had suddenly become political!"[358] Many welcomed this engagement with the establishment as a sacred act of resistance. John Lennon, who quickly joined the cause, took Leary's campaigning slogan, "come together,"[359] and produced the campaign song ("Come Together," *Abbey Road*, 1969). Although, again, MacDonald enthusiastically overstates its significance, he nevertheless highlights the importance of this Learyesque anthem and the message it bore: "Enthusiastically received in campus and underground circles, 'Come Together' is *the* key song at the turn of the decade, isolating a pivotal moment when the free world's coming generation rejected established wisdom, knowledge, ethics, and be-havior for a drug-inspired relativism which has since undermined the intellectual foundations of Western culture."[360] Unfortunately for the campaign, however, its leader was arrested for drug offenses in February 1970 and given a ten-year prison sentence by a Texas court. Leary quickly lodged an appeal, but was refused bail. Although he escaped in September, 1970 and fled the country, he was eventually recaptured and finally released in 1976, by which time the culture he had sought to nurture had changed significantly, much of it going underground or simply evaporating.

Having said that, while the psychedelic revolution of the 1960s was short-lived, it did not die out completely. As such, the relationship between turning within and turning on has also continued. Certainly, since the early 1980s, there has been a growing appreciation of sixties psychedelia, not only musically in the work of in-fluential bands such as Spacemen 3—who covered early psychedelic tracks such as The Red Krayola's "Transparent Radiation" (*The Perfect Prescription*, 1987) and declared that they were *Taking Drugs to Make Music to Take Drugs To* (1994)—but, ideologically, the confluence of turning on, turning within, and turning East sur-faced in post-disco electronic dance music culture (EDMC).[361] Indeed, I suspect that few popular music cultures will be able to resist the lure of psychedelia and, as such, will always look back fondly to the sixties, just as some imagine folk cul-tures, with a sense of longing for authenticity and the utopian sacred—the period's Romantic confluence of hedonism, transgression, ideology, and spirituality, and its organic relationship with visual and musical creativity, simply make far too much sense to liminal imaginations to be ignored. Hence, it was not surprising to wit-ness early rave culture explicitly paying homage to Leary and 1960s psychedelia—although, by that time, the drug of choice had become ecstasy/E (MDMA).[362] For example, as Stuart Metcalfe writes:

> There was a rash of individuals and groups releasing their own Ecstasy-inspired records, and the loved-up vibe continued through 1989 and into 1990. One typical example of an ecstasy-inspired record from the period is the white-label 12 inch produced by the Liverpudlian group Mind, Body and Soul. Whilst the band's name referred to a brand of LSD particularly popular in Liverpool in the late-1980s, the song, a version of Jefferson Airplane's psychedelic anthem 'White Rabbit', sampled the acid guru Tim-othy Leary's call to arms, 'Turn On, Tune In, and Drop Out,' prefacing it with a sampled voice saying simply 'ecstasy'. The track also included a spoken reading of the rhyme sent by the English psychiatrist Humphrey Osmond to Aldous Huxley in 1955 that suggested a name for the group of drugs that both had been experimenting with: 'to fathom hell or soar an-gelic, just take a pinch of psychedelic.[363]

Indeed, as he notes, with reference to a single by the Manchester band Northside, "Shall We Take a Trip" (1990), "direct connections were made with the song lyrics of the 1960s psychedelic revolution."[364] Again, Sheila Whiteley observes that there was

> a strong sense of shared identity between the sixties hippy philosophy and that of nineties alternative culture. Similarities are present in the music, the influence of the drug experience, an awareness of the destruction and ruination of the Earth and the poisoning of the seas. New Age Travellers share the hippy philosophy of alternative family groupings and the freedom to opt out of mainstream society, whilst free festivals and raves provide the space both to trip out and experience a range of house and ambient bands. Publications such as the *Freak Emporium* provide guidance to a range of psychedelic music, magazines and books, whilst *Bush Telegraph* provides features on cannabis and the dream mechanism, homeopathy and growing hemp in the UK. Collective experience, music and drugs appear, once again, to provide the means whereby young people can explore the politics of consciousness, to set up an alternative lifestyle.[365]

Moreover, as well as ecstasy-inspired Romantic utopianism, manifested in, for example, the desire to create "a greed-free culture,"[366] there was also the articulation of explicitly spiritual trajectories. Many found in the confluence of the new technologies of transformation (especially MDMA) and electronic dance music what some hippies had discovered through LSD at a Grateful Dead concert: "the realm of the mystical and spiritual."[367] As Mary Anna Wright comments, the E experience often involved "intense insights into the depth of the human psyche that touched on a spiritual revelation or metanoia."[368] Similarly, while Simon Reynolds drew attention to the simple desire to go "mental at the weekend," he also noted that many thought of "the music-drugs-technology nexus" as "fused with spirituality . . . "[369]

This is particularly evident in what became known as psytrance. Emerging in the mid-1990s and directly continuous with hippie culture,[370] it has its roots in the "full moon parties" at Anjuna beach, Goa, the Christian state in India to which many hippies traveled in the 1960s and 1970s. During the early 1970s, as Anthony D'Andrea says, a community of hippies "colonized the northern Goa beach areas of Anjuna and Vagator. Paradoxically, although fleeing from the West, they benefited from the Goans' Christian-Westernized legacy of relative tolerance for leisure practices and individualism." As such, this small Christian state became "a signifier for a party-cum-drug paradise during winter seasons" and eventually, in the late-1980s "the scene turned digital and tribal, with post-hippie, post-punk freaks developing a new style of electronic music in rituals of psychedelic intensity."[371] Indeed, it is interesting that several "hippies" from the sixties and seventies have carried their occultural baggage and their commitment to the creation of sonic environments conducive to self-exploration through into rave/trance culture. One of the most obvious examples is the flautist Ron Rothfield, who had played in the archetypal hippie band Quintessence (e.g., *In Blissful Company*, 1969). Having transformed into Raja Ram, he founded the leading proto-psytrance label TIP Records and inspired some key developments in electronic dance music as part of several projects, notably The Infinity Project with Graham Wood and particularly Shpongle with Simon Posford. Likewise, Steve Hillage, formerly a member of another archetypal hippie band, Gong, produced the experimental ambient album *Rainbow Dome Musick* (1979), worked with The Orb on their important psychedelia-influenced, dub-oriented techno albums *The Orb's Adventures Beyond the Ultraworld* (1991) and *U.F.Orb* (1992) and finally, with his partner, Miquette Giraudy (who had also played with Gong), formed the influential techno/trance outfit System 7—"the hedonistic element is important, but it's about more than that. It's about how you use new technological gifts in a positive and life-enhancing way."[372] While the music changed, the core occultural elements of the counterculture have remained—turn on and turn within. It is this continuity that contributed significantly to Goa becoming, as Jane Bussmann observed at the time, "an appropriate destination for the mystical raver."[373] The DJ James Munro describes the scene and the affective spaces evoked: "the Goa party . . . starts about 1 a.m. and the majority of people have taken acid and they're treating it as a journey. You're surrendering to a drug and to a musical stimulation . . . In the context of Indian mythology, we are dancing the dance of Shiva. This is the symbolic dance of creation, destruction and rebirth. Shiva's dance is the synthesis of all life experience and an image of all-pervading energy."[374] He continues: "it opened me up to religion, seeing how you can be happy without materialism. The ambitions I had when I was earning shitloads of money just went."[375] Indeed, he states that his music is "not just inspired by Goa, but by the whole Indian spirituality. The peak of my last trip was the [Kumbh] Mela [sic], a congregation of Holy Men on the banks of the Ganges. It was almost like stepping off the planet, into another existence – meeting yogis and sadhus, naked apart from ash and holy fires."[376]

As psytrance culture evolved, becoming increasingly cosmopolitan and plural, so the occultural pool of ideas expanded away to include a rich mix of Pagan, indigenous, occult and paranormal ideas.[377] Just as we have seen the memes of occultural discourse spread through folk and rock cultures, replicating and changing as they encountered other occultural memes, so similar Romantic occultural ideas emerged within rave and later psytrance. As Reynolds notes of the early British rave music, "instigated by anarcho-mystic outfits like Spiral Tribe and by neo-hippy travelers on the 'free festival' circuit . . . the techno-Pagan spirit" evolved. Spiral Tribe, the most influential of the early sound systems, "preached a creed they called Terra-Technic, arguing that ravers' non-stop ritual dancing reconnected mankind with the primordial energy of the Earth."[378] Again, Pagan, shamanic and indigenous themes emerged in the "doofs" of Australian rave culture. For example, Des Tramacchi found that "Neo-Pagan spiritualities have . . . exerted an influence on *doof* ideologies, Chaos Magick and symbolism being particularly prominent."[379] Again, the liner notes of the influential early Return to the Source compilation, *Deep Trance and Ritual Beats* (1995) claims that the Return to the Source project seeks "to trace a line from the strobes and drum machines of the 20th century to the Pagan fire and lost rituals of our ancestors." The idea of returning to "Pagan fire and lost rituals" is, as we have seen in much Romantic discourse, explicitly linked to notions of the recovery of the premodern sacred and the rejection of authoritarian, creedal religion as a profane threat to *inner* spirituality and natural/sacred "energy": "they smashed our temples and burnt our healers. They put the fire goddess in chains and burnt her at the stake. They worked hard to eradicate the memory of the dance ritual but it remained as a seed deep within us all, to emerge one day in a new age of technology. . . . Gradually the spirit of the people would return as they recognised the sacred power of trance, once again opening up the channels to the Great Spirit. They would join together as one tribe, 'the rainbow tribe': all colors, all races, all as one. The temples may have changed, but the sacred earth to dance upon is still the same."[380] Indeed, the Return to the Source club in London, just prior to opening its doors to devotees, invited "shamanic friends" to sprinkle "Chalice Well water" from Glastonbury, "through the venue and burnt sage which the American Indians use to cleanse energy. These ancient and sacred acts give us positive energy, empower our intention and open the dance floor up to the possibilities of the dance as ritual."[381] As a resident DJ at Return to the Source, DJ Chrisbo, commented, "Return to the Source represents a new Paganism, a New Age revival."[382] And indicating the occultural nature of the discourse within trance culture, one of the musicians at Return to the Source, Jules, makes the following point: "people at Return to the Source have the kind of consciousness where they're trying to connect things into a bigger picture, things like UFOs, ancient civilizations, the shamanistic thing, dancing, music. It's all being pulled together."[383]

Since the mid-1990s, psytrance has become a global phenomenon, occulturally progressive and culturally plural, yet, nevertheless, still maintaining strong continuities with the principal contours of the 1960s psychedelic counterculture in its exploration of new ways to both turn on and turn within.[384] In the Romantic culture of psytrance, a space is provided in which the Dionysian spirit is celebrated, the "affect-expressive" components of modern cultures are sacralized, induced revelations and spiritually varied journeys to inner space are sought, and the profane everyday world is distanced. Indeed, although it would be unhelpfully Procrustean to make any sweeping claims about global psytrance culture, as if it constitutes a homogenous "subculture" or "scene"—both of which terms are notoriously problematic—nevertheless, one can identify a common articulation of the sacred, in as much as subjectivities are sacralized and a distinction is made between the values articulated within the culture and those that are dominant beyond it in wider society. Hence, the individual's psytrance experience tends to be less about going to a disco or "having a night out," and more about being part of a countercultural happening in which the "unique" or "authentic" self is catered for. In the words of the DJ Goa Gil, "It is not a disco under coconut trees; it is spiritual initiation."[385] Likewise, the late Nicholas Saunders—a veteran campaigner for holistic well-being, a founding father of Neal's Yard in Covent Garden, London, and author, in 1970, of the groundbreaking guide, *Alternative London*—argued that raves contain the "important elements of mystical experience" and are "very much part of contemporary spirituality."[386] Again, this thesis has been unpacked in some detail by Robin Sylvan in his book *Trance Formation*, which argues that rave culture is a "legitimate source of spirituality and a new form of religion."[387] Whether it is or not, the point here is that rave culture exposes very clearly the subjective turn in Western societies and demonstrates the continuity of Romantic sacred forms that were developed and democratized in the counterculture of the 1960s, and that have been developed and disseminated within popular music cultures since then.

Concluding comment

In thinking through some of the points made thus far, Charles Taylor provides some helpful clarification in positing a distinction between the bounded or buffered self of modernity and the porous self of the premodern world. "For the modern, buffered self, the possibility exists of taking a distance from, disengaging from everything outside the mind. My ultimate purposes are those which rise within me, the crucial meanings of things are those defined in my responses to them. . . . As a bounded self I can see the boundary as a buffer, such that things beyond don't need to 'get to me'. . . . This self can see itself as invulnerable, as master of the meanings of things for it."[388] The porous self, on the other hand, cannot stand back from its environment, because that which is external to the self continually presses in upon it, haunting it, tempting it, frightening it. There is no reasoning one's way back to contentment because the source of the porous self's most powerful and important emotions are outside the "self." As Taylor puts it, "the very notion that there is a clear boundary, allowing us to define an inner base area, grounded in which we can disengage from the rest, has no sense." Hence, he continues, the two important facets of the contrast are as follows: "First, the porous self is vulnerable, to spirits, demons, cosmic forces. And along with this go certain fears which can grip it in certain circumstances. The buffered self has been taken out of the world of this kind of fear." The interesting point for us to note and, according to Taylor, a clear indication of the shift that has taken place in the modern world, is that today "many people look back to the world of the porous self with nostalgia. As though the creation of a thick emotional boundary between us and the cosmos were now lived as a loss. The aim is to try to recover some measure of this lost feeling."[389] Drugs and music can facilitate this recovery. The Romantic buffered selves of modernity seek depth and authenticity, as well as the frisson experienced by the porous self of premodernity. Of course, it makes a significant difference that the liminal self is buffered. Unlike its premodern ancestors, hell will never be quite as real to us as the world outside our front doors and goblins will never meet us in the way our neighbors do. As modern people, we can embrace enchantment because we can control it. We can look back to the premodern world nostalgically and sentimentally, because we don't have to live in it. We can lift the beauty of the natural world out from the hardship and squalor of premodern rural living only because we view it from afar. We can embrace folklore without worrying about the dark and dangerous social contexts in which it was embedded and yearn for the solitude of the forests, because we no longer have porous selves. We can turn within and find our own paths to spiritual well-being because external authorities no longer command the same degree of deference that they once did. Romanticism in popular music only works in the way that it does because the buffered selves of modernity are able to control and regulate our exposure to an enchanted world of unfettered supernaturalism. Popular music, through its Orphic power to create affective spaces, reenchants the past through a process of translation and colonization. "The past is a foreign country" colonized by modern minds eager for a new place to live. Its indigenous cultures are pressed into the service of the colonizer's imagination.

5

Religion

Music as an affective technology and a source of social cohesion has played a significant role in religious ritual. As Guy Beck's work has shown, group performances of sacred songs or hymns consolidate human communities into religious worlds of their own, "reinforcing identities and boundaries as if by some mysterious thread. In each case, music was the 'glue' in the ritual that bound together word and action and also reinforced static social and religious hierarchies."[1] There is something peculiarly potent about the lyre of Orpheus as *sacer interpresque deorum*. Indeed, for Plato, "the authentic interlocutor of music is the soul," in that it has a peculiar ability to "touch and condition the *psychē*."[2] It is this invisible power of music to stir that which is deep within us, to manipulate emotion, which has made it both peculiarly conducive to the cultivation of a sense of the otherworldly and also, as we will see, peculiarly suspect as a force of profanation.

Music as a prosthetic technology in religion

In Chapter 2, we explored music's Orphic power as a prosthetic technology and, as such, came very close to the results of empirical research in the psychology of religion.[3] That is to say, while not wanting to dismiss emic assessments regarding the significance of the divine-human encounter and pastoral care, our comments about music largely repeated those about the perceived benefits of spiritual practice for many believers. Through its peculiar ability to create affective space as a site of meaning making, the lyre of Orpheus encourages psychosomatic states that much spiritual practice seeks to cultivate. For example, as with studies into the effects of music, so studies into the effects of prayer show that it tends to "reduce negative emotional expressions under stress," that it induces relaxation, and thereby contributes to "decreased metabolism, heart rate, rate of breathing and distinctive slower brain waves."[4] It is for this reason, of course, that it has found a home within religious cultures as *sacer interpresque deorum*. In other words, it is used as a prosthetic technology to manipulate mood and thereby contribute to the construction of sacred affective space. This, in turn, makes music peculiarly potent within the contexts of, not only worship, but also healing and pastoral care. Hence, healing rituals often include both music and prayer. This is particularly conspicuous in indigenous communities. As Benjamin Koen comments, "most, if not all, traditional healing contexts consider religion or the supernatural critical to the success of any intervention, which virtually always includes some form of music, specialized sound, and prayer. . . . In some cases, prayer and its sound or musical form are one. Notably, the relationship between music/sound and prayer is such that one component might make an intervention (that includes music or prayer) efficacious or powerless . . . "[5]

As to the spiritual life generally, many believers would concur with the conviction of the Russian Orthodox composer, Igor Stravinsky, that "the profound meaning of music and its essential aim . . . is to promote a communion, a union of man with his fellow man and with the Supreme Being."[6] This was certainly how the popular qawwali singer Nusrat Fateh Ali Khan interpreted his own work: "whenever I sing about God, or the Prophet Muhammad, I feel like I am in front of him . . . I feel like I am in another world when I sing, the spiritual world. I am not in the material world . . . I am totally in another world. I am withdrawn from my materialistic senses, I am totally in my spiritual senses, and I am intoxicated by the Holy Prophet, God, and other Sufi saints."[7] However, at its most basic, this Orphic relationship between music and religion is not particularly difficult to understand: because music can be the source of strong emotion and because emotion is central to religious behaviors,[8] there is an easy elision of the musical and the spiritual. Consequently, music functions very effectively as a prosthetic technology in religious contexts—heightening emotion, creating contemplative states, providing succor. This is evident from work done in both ethnomusicology and the ethnographic study of religion. Graham Hughes' research, for example, suggests that it is the music, rather than the words within Christian worship, that provides perhaps the most powerful medium of meaning. Whereas Protestantism has typically insisted that the words of hymns carry their meaning, Hughes asks why, if this is the case, do we bother singing. "What does the actual musicality of the music do in terms of generating, or bearing, the meaning of the song? Why are sung responses almost always experienced as more meaningful than the same words spoken? Is music conceivably a deep and ancient instinctive response to moments of high elation and terrifying solemnity?"[9] While the details of Hughes' thesis might be debated, his central point is irrefutable. As discussed in Part One, music conveys meaning.

Throughout the history of religions, from Caribbean religions in New York City to mainstream global Christianity, from Shamanism to Judaism, and from alternative spiritualities to Islam, music has been ubiquitous and central.[10] As Beck comments of his own research into the sacred uses of music,

I spent many years observing a wide variety of religious traditions and noting the use of chant and music in each as part of public and private religious practice. Throughout America and Europe, I attended services of the Christian churches and cathedrals, Jewish temples and synagogues, Islamic Mosques, Sufi centres, meeting places of new religious movements, and many different kinds of retreat centres. In all cases there were tonal recitations, chants, hymns, sacred songs, or other musical numbers that seemed to generate spiritual elation, social cohesion, and empowerment within identifiable communities. Extended excursions to India and Nepal provided similar evidence of how music and chant pervade myriad types of religious worship in the East. Besides visiting traditional Hindu, Buddhist, Jain, and Sikh gatherings, my itinerary included many modern religious organizations. At the end of the day, I determined that there were almost no communities or groups within the major world religions in which chant and music did not play a *vital role*.[11]

Again, the ubiquity of music within religion relates directly to its Orphic significance as a prosthetic technology.

For some, of course, this raises important issues regarding the role and significance of music in worship. The psychiatrist Anthony Storr puts the point bluntly: "music's power to fan the flame of piety may be more apparent than real."[12] Should the frequent interpretation of music as spiritually significant perhaps be understood in terms of the nature and effect of manipulated emotion, the enhancing of group feeling, and the construction of affective space? In stating that, I am, again, not seeking to dismiss emic interpretations of trance and transcendence evoked by music, or, indeed, the spiritual significance of emotion in worship. That is not the purpose of this discussion, in that we are not here engaged in theological analysis per se. Having said that, I first started thinking seriously about the relationship between music, emotion, and religion almost two decades ago when reading the work of the English theologian Herbert Henry Farmer, who, in his own way, was peculiarly alive to the significance of these issues, particularly the prosthetic potential of music as an affective technology (although he wouldn't have expressed it in such terms). For example, in his Gifford Lectures, delivered in 1950 at the University of Glasgow, he identified continuities between the altered states sought through the use of alcohol and opium and an "aesthetic intoxication" induced by listening to the choir in King's College Chapel at Cambridge, where he was Norris-Hulse Professor of Divinity. The experience of being "lifted right out of the world" by choral music induced "a refreshing withdrawal and escape from the everyday pressures of things."[13] Relatedly, in an earlier lecture, he had noted the quite different affect created at the "Nazi rallies at Nuremberg, with their carefully planned stimulation of mass emotion . . . throbbing music, hypnotic chanting . . . a kind of corporate self-stimulation."[14] While, again, this is not the place discuss Farmer's theological analysis,[15] it is interesting to note that he identified in his reception of music what he referred to as "adjectival religion." By this he meant that which affectively engages us in much the same way as "substantival religion" does, but *without being substantival*. This latter form of religion was understood in terms of an *actual* divine-human encounter. Substantival religion is a response to the pressure of the divine on the human will: a willed engagement with "the dimension of the eternal."[16] It would be foolish, of course, for the theologian to attempt to categorize the nature and veracity of another's religious experience—although the history of religion is, in part, an unedifying catalogue of such attempts. Nevertheless, there is, Farmer contended, a fundamental difference between the two types of religion. While we might, of course, want to take issue with his particular distinction between genuine sacred depth (substantival religion) and its aesthetic simulacrum (adjectival religion), the point here is that he identified in his encounter with music something of the texture of a genuine experience of the divine.[17] Surrounded by music, he was, even if only adjectivally, experiencing a sense of transcendence. For Farmer, music was able to create or, perhaps, recover states of mind that could be identified in spiritual ecstasy and, as such, produce the release normally associated with that experience. This is important. For the reasons we have noted, affective spaces, which are at least analogous to religious experience, can be produced by music. Having said that, he was also convinced that, if the conditions were right, the adjectival might stimulate, rather than merely simulate, the substantival. In other words, he did not rule out the possibility that an affective space created by music might become a site for a divine-human encounter. Through our search for relaxation or entertainment, the lyre of Orpheus might be heard—we are drawn into the sacred, moved and enchanted. Again, music becomes, like Orpheus, *sacer interpresque deorum*.

Others, however, within religion have understood this power to move to be equally open to profane influence. Hence, drawing on discussions in the previous chapters, this final chapter brings our analysis to a close by exploring the various ways in which religion has engaged popular music and interpreted its prosthetic power. In order to assist our thinking about the various ways in which this relationship has been understood, we will make use of H. Richard Niebuhr's helpful typology in *Christ and Culture*. Although Niebuhr—a Christian theologian writing in the U.S. in 1951—had different concerns in mind to those that occupy us in this volume, and although the typology itself has been criticized, nevertheless, it provides a useful place to begin analysing the issues facing religion.

Niebuhr's typology and popular music

One of the core problems Niebuhr seeks to address is what he refers to as the "double wrestle" of the Church (i.e., the Christian's struggle with what the Bible teaches and the culture "with which it lives in symbiosis"[18]). He concludes that there has never been a consensus concerning the relationship between "Christ" (i.e., Christian faith and experience) and "culture" (i.e., "the world"/secular society). Consequently, there have always been a number of often overlapping theological models: antithetical (Christ *against* culture); correlational (the Christ *of* culture); hierarchical (Christ *above* culture); paradoxical (Christ *and* culture); and transformative (Christ *the transformer of* culture). Of course, all of these models assume the basic binary of "Christ" *and* "culture," which is inherently problematic, in that the Christ event *is itself* a cultural event. Christ and Christianity are already inextricably enmeshed in culture. The one does not stand apart from the other except in the imaginations of some Christians—which are, of course, themselves encultured. However, I am not concerned here to critique the typology. Although I am interested in cultural constructions of the sacred and the profane, I am simply using the typology as a jumping off point to explore religious approaches to popular music cultures.

The first approach, "Christ against culture," imagines an opposition between the two, dismissing engagement with culture as theological disobedience.[19] Typical of the highly dualistic conservative theologies of particularly monotheistic religions, it makes a strong distinction between the sacred and the profane, arguing that the "world," determined by profane forces, is intellectually and spiritually opposed to the sacred as this is articulated within religion. Hence, in Christianity, because the difference between "Christ" and "culture" is presented so starkly, as a binary of the sacred and the profane, the individual is persuaded to understand it as a choice between light and darkness, truth and falsity, good and evil. Extreme examples of this approach include world-rejecting new religions, which seek to separate themselves physically from the surrounding culture. However, even those theologies that do not insist on physical separation do construct formidable social and psychological boundaries between "Christ" and "culture," seeking to limit an individual's exposure to profane culture as much as possible. Of course, for those reasons articulated in the previous chapters, popular music has been a particular focus of concern. Books such as Bob Larson's *Rock & Roll: the Devil's Diversion* and John Blanchard's *Pop Goes the Gospel* articulate these concerns in the starkest terms, reading popular music culture through the lens of Christian demonology.[20]

The second approach identified by Niebuhr, "the Christ of culture," stands at the opposite end of the spectrum to "Christ against culture."[21] This culturally positive approach assumes that religion is manifested within culture. More specifically, Christ is actively revealed through both culture and faith. Hence, for example, human institutions or systems of government, such as democracy, embody sacred forms. Likewise, the arts and popular music are themselves invested with sacred significance. Whereas the first approach operates with a strong doctrine of *special* revelation (which understands the sacred to be revealed through a special individual, text, or icon)—and therefore constructs boundaries to protect from profanation what has been revealed—this approach might be understood to operate with a strong doctrine of *general* revelation (which understands the sacred to be revealed universally through nature, the conscience, or human creativity). In this sense, popular music has religious significance as a manifestation of revelation. Jeff Keuss's theological reflection on popular music, *Your Neighbor's Hymnal*, develops something akin to this approach, encouraging listeners to be "sonic mystics": "many people listen to pop songs, not as a distraction, but with deep hunger for something spiritual and transcendent"—and they find it.[22] To use Farmer's terminology, he suggests that, in listening to popular music, there can be a shift from the adjectival to the substantival, from surface to depth: "even a simple pop song . . . will bring us to joy unbridled, torrents of tears, and into the presence of the transcendent God in ways we often cannot fully grasp."[23] Indeed, he argues that "the movement of sound mirrors the movement of the mystical experience that is deep in the Christian tradition."[24] However, although these understandings are germane to our analysis in this chapter, developing Niebuhr's approach, we are more interested in *religious* popular music. That is to say, we are not here interested in the *instrumental use of* popular music *by* religion (e.g., Christian heavy metal) or, as in Keuss's work, the interpretation of it as a site for theological reflection, but rather we are concerned with popular music which has been specifically developed as a religious discourse (e.g., roots reggae).

The final three approaches provide mediating positions between these two poles and, according to Niebuhr, offer more mature theologies, which can inform a nonrevolutionary faith that seeks the gradual transformation of cultures. The most important and influential of these is his final approach, "Christ the transformer of culture."[25] While it adopts a similarly negative understanding of culture to the first approach, nevertheless it seeks positive engagement, what Niebuhr refers to as "the conversionist answer to the problem of Christ and culture."[26] This approach is based on a threefold thesis: culture is a manifestation of the divine act of creation and an outgrowth of human creativity; sin corrupts creation, including human culture; Christianity can redeem culture, in that it can transform it by identifying and nurturing that which is sacred within it, while also identifying and resisting that which is profane. In other words, this is a broadly missiological approach, in that theological engagement with popular music is motivated by the desire to transform it according to Christian values. It is converted and transformed into a carrier of the sacred. We can identify this approach within much contemporary Christian music (often simply referred to as CCM), in that the music itself is understood to be more or less a sanctified vehicle to carry a particular message. As such it claims to be different from "secular music" in that it is understood to be, like a sermon, a carrier of theological truth, which requires a faith response from listeners: "artists demand that the audience agree with . . . [their] religious beliefs."[27] Perhaps the most obvious example of this approach within Christianity is the Salvation Army: "I rather enjoy robbing the Devil of his choice tunes," declared the organization's founder, William Booth, in 1877.[28] Again, unlike the Christ of culture approach, popular music itself was not understood to be sacred, but rather it was viewed as a vehicle that might be sanctified—stolen from the Devil—and pressed into the service of the Holy Spirit. This could be done simply through the addition of a sacred text—new words were put to popular songs. "Daisy Give Me Your Answer Do," for example, was baptised and raised as "Jesus I Love Thee With All My Heart." As Pamela Walker's study of the Salvation Army in Victorian Britain found, "these adaptations made the Army's music memorable and associated it with what was popular and current in a community."[29] Indeed, the posters advertising Salvation Army services and the lively style of the services themselves "so closely resembled music-hall performances and notices that observers sometimes failed to distinguish them. Thus, they drew large, enthusiastic crowds."[30]

Adapting Niebuhr's typology—and beginning with his second approach—we might think of these broad areas of analysis as follows: (1) religion against popular music; (2) religion as the transformer of popular music; and (3) religious popular music. Finally, some attention needs to be given to the related issue of the fetishization of popular musicians, in which the role of Orpheus as *sacer interpresque deorum* becomes grotesquely exaggerated: (4) the transfiguration of popular musicians.

Religion against popular music

What Niebuhr identified as the "Christ against culture" approach—which views religion and culture in terms of a stark "either-or" binary[31]—constructs popular music as a specific site of profanation, a particularly toxic threat to key sacred forms. Evidence of this, it is argued, is conspicuous in its celebration of openly transgressive ideas and behaviors relating to sex, drugs, violence, and "false" religiosity, most conspicuously evident in its apparent embrace of the occult. Moreover, its profanation is particularly acute because of its perceived influence on the minds of the young. The very fact that it is directly related to the profanation of childhood and adolescence magnifies the perceived threat of pollution and danger. As such, it also explicitly confronts fundamental sacred forms relating to the sacrality of the family unit: good children from good homes are being defiled and parental authority is being undermined. Consequently, "Christian society" itself is threatened by popular music. This becomes particularly apparent in the discourses of fear occasioned by extreme acts of violence by youths thought to have been influenced by popular music, such as the Columbine shootings.[32]

Childhood is a protected period of innocence, central to which is moral socialization, the establishment of a set of ethical norms and principles that sanction certain practices while prohibiting others. Popular music is perceived as dangerous because it is understood to be a direct challenge to this process and, therefore, to the stability of the sacred. That is to say, the socialization of children ensures the future health of society and culture, in that the successfully socialized child will grow into an adult who respects society's dominant sacred forms. Hence, for a number of related reasons, the protection of children from profanation is perceived as a categorical imperative: an absolute, unconditional moral requirement that asserts its authority in all circumstances. Hence, for example, Plato insists in *The Republic*,

> We shall thus prevent our guardians being brought up among representa-
> tions of what is evil, and so day by day and little by little, by grazing widely
> as it were in an unhealthy pasture, insensibly doing themselves a cumula-
> tive psychological damage that is very serious. We must look for artists and
> craftsmen capable of perceiving the real nature of what is beautiful, and
> then our young men, living as it were in a healthy climate, will benefit be-
> cause all the works of art they see and hear influence them for good, like
> the breezes from some healthy country, insensibly leading them from
> earliest childhood into close sympathy and conformity with beauty and
> reason. That would indeed be the best way to bring them up. . . . [33]

Likewise, as Walter Brueggemann has argued, "no dimension of ethical passion is more central in the tradition of the Bible than the protection of orphans. . . . *Nurture* for our own children and *defense* of other vulnerable children are elements of the same agenda. It will not do to invest in the former as a parochial matter to the ne-glect of the latter as a public matter."[34] However this sacred form is understood, throughout all human societies the protection of children is an absolute normative reality, a basic assumption. To abuse children or to otherwise violate their inno-cence is to strike at "the very temple of the sacred," to commit a "transgressive act of almost unimaginable dimensions," to "attack the repository of social sentiment and the very embodiment of 'goodness.' Indeed, such an act epitomizes absolute evil."[35]

It is hardly surprising therefore that, in the imaginations of the religious right—who frequently employ demonologies to explain profanation—popular music, which is focussed principally on the young, is a key component of a wider satanic conspiracy, a demonic device to defile the "good," erode the sacred, and terminate divinely instituted order. Hence there are those within conservative cultures (as we saw in Chapter 3) who fear that some forms of the sonic and visual arts within youth culture constitute a "wrecking of civilization."[36] There is also, of course, a sense in which such moral panic "looks backwards to a golden age of moral certainties from which there has been only moral decline, in which people – especially the young – can no longer tell the difference between right or wrong. The remedy prescribed," says Kenneth Thompson, "is a return to a basic set of rules, in the style of the Ten Commandments, which can be taught in families and schools."[37] However, we have seen that such prescriptions serve only to invite transgression from liminal personae, thereby increasing the concern felt by conservative moral and religious gatekeepers.

Historically, conservative evangelical moral crusaders have, as Jason Bivins com-ments, "maintained vigilance against the possible seductions of leisure time and the 'taint' of fallen cultures. . . . Beginning in the 1970s, peaking in the 1980s, but very much still a part of public culture ... anti-rock preachers saw in the popularity of rock music a series of social dangers and widespread falsehoods – most powerfully expressed in heavy metal and rap – that captured for them the larger process of socio-political decline."[38] Having said that, the claim that anti-popular music discourse began in the 1970s is a little misleading. As we have seen, the Christian moral concern of the 1970s has many substantial precedents. Certainly in the modern period, popular culture—including nineteenth-century music halls, jazz and blues—has been a perpetual cause of anxiety for the religious right who worry about the progress of the profane and the collapse of social order. More recently, Eileen Luhr has shown that, "during much of the post-1945 period, popular music provided conservative Christians with a catchall explanation for everything that was geopolitically threatening, physically perilous, or spiritually sinister." She continues, "their fears intensified in the 1960s. Assertions about rock music differed as to its precise sins, but conservatives generally agreed that the genre was a pernicious force in American society. Held to be synonymous with the counterculture and the 1960s, rock 'n' roll was thought to have conspired with communist and Satanist groups, encouraged miscegenation, altered sexual mores, and incited sustained social unrest."[39]

Constructed within broader Christian conspiracy theories, popular music, as Luhr notes, is often linked to other perceived threats to the sacred. For example, it became central to Christian concerns about the influence on young minds of competing ideologies and religions, concerns that were occasioned by the growth of the counterculture, the emergence of New Left social criticism, and Easternization. As the titles of books such as Bob Larson's *Hippies, Hindus and Rock 'n' Roll* (1972), Lowell Hart's *Satan's Music Exposed* (1981) and David Noebel's *Communism, Hypnotism and The Beatles* (1969) suggest, a number of malevolent ideological and theological influences were imagined. Noebel, for example, was an industrious and influential champion of the anticommunist concerns of the religious and political right. For many years he was a member of the John Birch Society—a right-wing organization with a strong bias toward conspiracist discourse[40]—and, prior to that, a McCarthyite evangelist for Billy James Hargis's fundamentalist Christian Crusade. He was also the Dean of the Christian Crusade Anti-Communist Youth University and founder of Summit Ministries in 1962. During the 1960s and 1970s he consistently argued that popular music had become central to a communist offensive against American Christian values.[41] This line of argument is significant in the history of anti-popular music discourse, in that it goes beyond simply identifying it as profane entertainment. Rather, it understands popular music to be an instrument of profanation controlled by a malevolent will and, as such, part of a wider conspiracy to instigate the demise of the "Christian West."

As is generally the case with conspiracy theories, anti-popular music discourses are driven by an overwhelming conviction that evil forces from beyond the sacred community are controlling history. As Daniel Wojcik comments, "conspiratorial modes of thought view history as controlled by massive, demonic forces engaged in a cosmic struggle with the forces of good." Characterized by a "paranoid style," a "dualistic view of the world, suspiciousness, and feelings of persecution," conspiracy theories "offer explanations for perceived ills and the problem of evil in the world and . . . appear to be related to perceptions of crisis and fear of catastrophe."[42] Moreover, because the instrument of profanation in a conspiracy theory is guided by a malevolent intelligence seeking to disguise its activities, there is a conviction that everything is not as it appears to be. The offensive against the sacred is often covert and deceptive, masquerading as innocence and righteousness. All these elements are conspicuous in Noebel's anti-popular music rhetoric, which suffers from the lack of a close shave with Occam's razor. For example, "some of the fronts for Communist machinations and operations in the United States have been certain record companies,"[43] notably the ostensibly innocent Young People's Records and the Children's Record Guild. Rather than concluding that these organizations were what the empirical evidence suggested they were—companies interested in producing and distributing music for children—Noebel argued that they were in fact cultural facades for communist mind control. Using techniques developed within clinical hypnotism, communists used popular music "to invade the privacy of our children's minds, to render them mentally incompetent and neurotic."[44] However, he says, this is only the tip of the iceberg: "our younger children are not the only ones being tampered with by the communists. Our teenager is also being exploited. Exploited for at least three reasons: (a) his own demoralization; (b) to create in him mental illness through artificial neurosis; and (c) to prepare him to riot and ultimately revolution in order to destroy our American form of government and the basic Christian principles governing our way of life."[45] Again, the argument is that, beginning with small children and progressing to adolescents, popular music is an apparently innocent, but actually potent means of undermining the culture, religion and politics of the United States and the West.

Such rhetoric can be understood as a conspiracist modification of some of the concerns of the "culture and civilization tradition" (as discussed in Chapter 1). Just as Matthew Arnold had argued for a distinction between culture, which enables "reason and the will of God to prevail," and the rude entertainment of the masses, which leads only to low morals and anarchy,[46] so Noebel claimed that "the barrier between classical music and certain types of popular music" had been transgressed by communists who seek to substitute "a perverted form . . . for standardized classical form." Communists, in other words, are seeking to subvert Christian culture with "anarchy." The promotion of popular music, Noebel argues, overturns hierarchies of cultural value, replacing music that ennobles with "jungle noises."[47] Such revealingly offensive comments introduce us to a component of Noebel's anti-popular music rhetoric that betray its far right roots: communists are "inundating the American public with the music of Negro people."[48] Indeed, it is very clear that, in seeking to identify popular music as a communist attempt to introduce anarchy, he wants to characterize it as that which is *other than* Christian, Western, white and civilizing.[49] To some extent, of course, such rhetoric can be found throughout the history of Christianity. As Timothy Fitzgerald has argued of Protestantism, there is a discourse—conspicuously articulated within the history of missions—concerning the rationality and civility of Protestant nations over and against the irrational barbarity of non-Christian "heathens."[50] It is this self-representation of civility and rationality over and against the backwardness of "the heathen" that is threatened by popular music. In other words, popular music, associated with "uncivilized," "heathen" societies, threatens the sacred by reversing the missionary process. Noebel is unapologetically explicit about this: popular music is "a designed reversion to savagery."[51] The argument, such as it is, claims that "the origins of rock 'n' roll" can be traced back to "the heart of Africa," where the rhythms of drums were "used to incite warriors to such a frenzy that by nightfall neighbors were cooked in carnage pots!" Drawing explicitly on racist stereotypes, he insists that the music of Africans, "the true epitome of popular music,"[52] is "sexual, un-Christian, mentally unsettling and riot producing."[53] The communists, he argues, having realised this, banned it in their own societies[54] and introduced it into Western societies in order to create delinquency, "scientifically induced" neuroses, and, in the final analysis, "a generation of young people with sick minds, loose morals and little desire or ability to defend themselves from those who would bury them."[55]

To summarize, his conspiracy theory claims that "communists have a master music plan for all age brackets of American youth. We know from documented proof that such is the case for babies, one- and two-year olds with their rhythmic music; we know such is the case for school children with their rhythmic music and university students with their folk music."[56] Repetitive music, rooted in the heathen savagery of Africa,[57] has been used by communists to "brainwash" the most vulnerable members of American society in order to undermine its values and instigate its collapse: "the frightening – even terrifying – aspect of this mentally conditioned process is the fact that these young people, in this highly excited, hypnotic state, can be told to do practically anything – and they will. One can scarcely conceive of the possibility," he says, "but nevertheless the method exists, wherein the enemies of our Republic could actually use . . . The Beatles (or some other rock 'n' roll or even rock 'n' folk group) to place thousands upon thousands of our teenagers into a frenzied, hypnotic state and send them forth into the streets to riot and revolt."[58]

For the conspiracists of the religious right, however, communism is not the only agent of profanation to use popular music. Indeed, communism is itself part of a cosmic "superconspiracy"—"conspiratorial constructs in which multiple conspiracies are believed to be linked together hierarchically"[59]—at the controlling apex of which is the cardinal source of all profanation, Satan. Within Christianity, the essential role of Satan has always been that of opposition and his relationship to the Church has, therefore, been interpreted primarily in terms of struggle and resistance, articulated as a dualistic combat mythology: good and evil; church and world; angels and demons; true faith and false religion; salvation and damnation. The opposition to popular music, therefore, is constructed as an *imitatio Christi*, an engagement in the perpetual struggle between the sacred and the profane, between the forces of goodness and order and those of evil and chaos.

John Blanchard's anti-popular music rhetoric is typical in this respect, being primarily oriented around three demonological premises: firstly, "Satan and his forces have deeply invaded man's social and cultural structures – and music has not been left out"; secondly, "one of the greatest powers possessed by Satan and his agents is their ability to appear harmless, benign, or even helpful"; thirdly, Satan and his agents "have the power to bring about physical, mental and spiritual disorder, as well as to cause their victims to be gripped by sin of one kind or another."[60] Again, these premises reflect the key principles informing most conspiracy theories: nothing happens by accident; nothing is as it seems; everything is connected.[61] Social unrest, secularization, shifting moral standards, adolescent despair and violence, religious pluralism, popular music and so on are all connected and all betray the design of a demonic intelligence. Similarly, Jeff Godwin, whose books include *The Devil's Disciples: The Truth About Rock* (1985), *Dancing With Demons: The Music's Real Master* (1988), and *Rock & Roll Religion: A War Against God* (1995), contends that popular music is used by Satan to corrupt children, destroy families, subvert "true religion" and profane society. It has, he argues, "smeared smut" throughout American culture and consistently "preached rebellion, hatred, drug abuse, suicide, fornication, and the dark things of Satan."[62] Again, in his study of the dynamics of satanic panics (i.e., moral panics generated by conspiracies relating to a fear of Satanism) Jeffrey Victor discusses Mike Adams' conspiracist rhetoric about popular music in the 1980s and early 1990s, central to which was the conviction that "Satan is attempting to capture the souls of our youth through rock and roll music." Victor attended one of his seminars, during which "he went through a litany of claims about how rock musicians promote drug addiction, sexual orgies, and violence," even making bizarre and naïve statements, such as "70 percent of all rock musicians are homosexuals" and that "many hundreds of teenagers commit suicide each year because of the Satanic influence of rock music."[63]

There have been, of course, similar concerns in other religious communities. In the Islamic world, for example, heavy metal musicians and fans have been vilified as the "high council of Satan Worship" and accused of "holding orgies, skinning cats, and writing their names in rat's blood ... "[64] Indeed, not only have young people been arrested simply because of their association with particular types of popular music, but, in Egypt, the "state-appointed mufti, Sheikh Nasr Farid Wassil, demanded that those arrested either repent or face the death penalty for apostasy."[65] Similarly, in Morocco in 2003, following an investigation by the Mukhabarat, fourteen heavy metal fans and musicians were arrested, tried and convicted for being "Satanists who recruited for an international cult of devil-worship." Being such an extreme source of profanation, they were also convicted of "shaking the foundations of Islam," "infringing upon public morals," "undermining the faith of a Muslim," and "attempting to convert a Muslim to another faith" (i.e., Satanism).[66]

Such is the perceived gravity of popular music's threat to the sacred and the comprehensive nature of the conspiracy imaginary that even musicians with religious convictions who use popular music for the purposes of worship and evangelism risk accusations of covertly insinuating the profane into personal and institutional sacred space. Such popular music, it is imagined, is consistent with the fifth column tactics of the demonic. Indeed, according to Hubert Spence, "the world has come to love gospel music, because gospel music has become worldly in its presentation." As such, he insists, along with Christian popular music generally, it is now a key factor in the "world's full acceptance of the Antichrist." Popular music, he claims, "will be the final instrument to set the world in a mood to bow to the image of the Son of Perdition."[67] That is to say, Christian music, although appearing sacred, is actually a profane threat from within. From musicals such as *Jesus Christ Superstar*, which betray clear evidence of "satanic inspiration," to "so-called gospel music," Christians, argues Larson, are "being deceived" and risking demonic possession.[68] Likewise, Blanchard insists that "the case against the use of pop music in evangelism is overwhelming"—"using it in evangelism is spiritually perilous."[69]

Similarly, within Orthodox Judaism, an approach that might be described as "Torah against culture" has been responsible for debate over the use of non-kosher musical styles. Lipa Schmeltzer, for example, although a devout and popular Haredi singer, who sings in Yiddish and derives his lyrics from sacred texts, is severely criticized by some rabbis for producing music that is indecent and unfit for the Jewish public. According to Rabbi Ephraim Luft of Israel's ultraorthodox Committee for Jewish Music, such musicians "are leading the public astray and are causing a great negative influence on the young generation." Interestingly, while he is, of course, critical of the lyrical content of secular popular music, his concern is more to do with its instrumentation: "The main part of the music should be the melody. Percussion should be secondary. They should not bend notes electronically and should not use instruments like electric guitars, bass guitars or saxophones in Jewish music."[70] To do so is inherently corrupting. For example, in "Rules for Playing Kosher Music" (published by the Committee for Jewish Music) we are told that "the saxophone has replaced the clarinet in [Haredi] rock music because it produces . . . indecent sounds. . . . When the saxophone was adopted for use in jazz bands in the 1920s it received the name 'the Devil's flute' because of its indecent seductive tones."[71] Indeed, the "purpose of modern music," insists Rabbi Luft, "is to distract young people and change good characters into bad." This is why even well-intentioned Jewish popular music, "where the dangerous beat plays more of a part than the melody, has no place in a society where people are trying to keep their moral standards high . . . "[72] Such is the influence of bodies like the Committee for Jewish Music and the Guardians of Sanctity and Education within the Haredi community that their criticisms led to many public concerts by ultraorthodox musicians being banned in Israel. Even Menahem Toker, an award-winning disc jockey, was dismissed from a radio show as a result of pressure from Haredi activists.[73]

More recently, popular music has been identified as a particular source of profanation in the north of the musically rich African country of Mali. As Andy Morgan reported:

> The pickup halted in Kidal, the far-flung Malian desert town that is home to members of the Grammy award-winning band Tinariwen. Seven AK47-toting militiamen got out and marched to the family home of a local musician. He wasn't home, but the message delivered to his sister was chilling: "If you speak to him, tell him that if he ever shows his face in this town again, we'll cut off all the fingers he uses to play his guitar with." The gang then removed guitars, amplifiers, speakers, microphones and a drum kit from the house, doused them with petrol, and set them ablaze. In northern Mali, religious war has been declared on music.[74]

This is one of many incidents that are increasingly occurring as a result of a frightening development of tensions within Mali, as Islamic militants seek to impose Sharia law in the country. The home of the famous "Festival in the Desert" and numerous internationally influential musicians, such as Ali Farka Touré, Vieux Farka Touré, Rokia Traoré, Toumani Diabaté, Afel Bocoum, Amadou and Mariam, Salif Keita and the Grammy award-winning band Tinariwen, Mali has produced music that has been celebrated by numerous Western musicians, such as Bono of U2 and Damon Albarn of Blur (Mali Music, 2002). Now identified as a profane threat, on August 22, 2012, an official decree banning all western music was issued by Islamic militants: "We don't want the music of Satan. Qur'anic verses must take its place. Sharia demands it."[75]

Such responses are the products of cultural work, which simplifies empirical complexity into rigid polarities. Such stark opposition between the sacred and the profane, in which grey areas are distilled into antagonistic black and white forms, is typical of Niebuhr's antithetical, either-or model of the relationship between religion and culture. As he comments, "in the early period of church history, the Jewish rejection of Jesus . . . found its counterpart in Christian antagonism to Jewish culture, while Roman outlawry of the new faith was accompanied by Christian flight from or attack upon Greco-Roman civilization. In medieval times monastic orders and sectarian movements called on believers living in what purported to be a Christian culture to abandon the 'world' and to 'come out from among them and be separate.' "[76] Little has changed.

Religion as the transformer of popular music

Similar but less exclusivist and conspiratorial concerns about popular music as a threat to the sacred inform the rhetoric of those seeking what Niebuhr refers to as "the conversionist answer to the problem of Christ and culture."[77] As we have seen, in Christianity, this approach is based on a threefold theological thesis: culture is a manifestation of the divine act of creation and an outgrowth of human creativity; evil/sin permeates and corrupts creation, including human culture; Christianity (animated by the sanctifying power of the Holy Spirit) can redeem culture, in that it can transform it by nurturing that which is sacred within it and by resisting that which is profane. This perspective has perhaps been developed most systematically within contemporary Christian music.[78] The premise is that popular music can be redeemed and become a servant of the sacred, because the music itself is neutral—a tabula rasa. Lyrics invest music with sacred or profane meaning. For example, the band Christafari, formed in 1989 by Mark Mohr, seeks to redeem reggae music by transforming Rastafarian discourse into *Christ*afarian/evangelical rhetoric. Hence, a track such as "Gwaan Natty" from the album *No Compromise* (2009) reinterprets Rastafarian doctrine concerning the divinity of Haile Selassie/Rastafari: "he was just . . . a man . . . who called himself a sinner . . . " and "denied being Christ": "The dreadlocks, the Orthodox and Niyabinghi too/The baldhead and Bobo Ashanti dread/Love and respect for you/Come make we reason "bout Ras Tafari/ He was a servant of the Most High/ He studied the teachings of Jesus Christ/ And fought for the truth and right . . . Jesus Christ is the way unto wisdom/ Natty dread, natty dread inna Babylon Jesus is salvation." Mohr also points out that Selassie exhorted his followers "to lead . . . sisters and brothers to our savior, Jesus Christ," and "actually sent a missionary to Jamaica to reach the Rastas!"[79] Even Bob Marley, the principal icon of global reggae, is transformed and put to work as an exemplar of evangelical conversion: "A lot of people don't know this," says Mohr, but "seven months before Bob Marley died . . . in a night full of tears and repentance, he gave his life to Jesus . . . denounced the lordship of Selassie."[80] The point is that reggae music is redeemed by reorienting the discourse around new constructions of the sacred and the profane. Within this revised Christafarian discourse, key Rastafarian beliefs and practices can be rejected and new sacred forms affirmed. For example, songs such as "Most High" (*No Compromise*, 2009) articulate conservative fears about the use of marijuana: "I tried to get high, but I really got low/ Tried to escape, but with nowhere to go/ Caught in an illusion, me really want to know/ Just how my life it went up in smoke . . . Yes my life was wasted/ Next was cocaine and then LSD/ opium and nitrous by the age of 16/ Crack then crystal methamphetamine/ Dealing drugs, had me living on the streets."[81] The moral panic narrative is a familiar one. Cannabis leads to hard drug use, depression, and life on the streets. As such, it constitutes a profane threat to "good kids" from "good homes" and is a core agent of pollution within Rastafarianism. The alternative "high," of course, is found through conversion and abstinence. Everything changed the "day that I heard his call/ Accepted Christ as the Lord of all. I got high, high, high on the Most High!" Hence, Mohr claims, his music is able to provide "counter-cult, drug aversion ministry," which uses "the uplifting sounds of reggae to bring the lost into the light."[82]

The use of the "uplifting sounds" of popular music "to bring the lost into the light" is not, we have seen, a novel phenomenon. Not only did William Booth and The Salvation Army adopt the method, but one of the most well-known eighteenth-century preachers in Britain and the American colonies, George Whitefield, drew on his knowledge of the theatre and popular culture to commend his theology to the public. Sometimes using "a sacred tune adapted from one of the tavern folk songs," he made use of popular music in much the same way that it was used in music halls, namely "to mobilize his audience, to transform them from passive viewers to participants."[83] As Harry Stout discusses, "following a period of song," which created an affective space pregnant with sanctified enthusiasm and expectation, "Whitefield would launch into a spontaneous prayer, which would set the context for his extemporaneous sermon."[84] Similarly, early radio evangelists such as Paul Rader, Charles Fuller, and Percy Crawford used popular entertainment, including popular music, as an evangelistic device.[85] It was not, however, until the late 1960s and early 1970s that the relationship between popular music and evangelical Christianity was fully consummated. What became known in 1967 as "the Jesus movement"[86] baptized existing musical styles, using them as vehicles for evangelical discourse. "To save hippies, inspiring music was needed. Even churches intent on reaching out to youthful worshippers were almost hopelessly out of it."[87] Hence contemporary rock music was pressed into service as "a means of evangelistic outreach, with artists stepping in for ministers and singing 'mini-sermons' to spiritually lost youth."[88] Again, central to the thinking informing the evangelistic use of popular music was the understanding of music as neutral, a sonic vehicle, which could be used for sacred or profane purposes. As such, popular music genres were tailored to target particular subcultures. In this sense, the music functioned as a Trojan horse, transporting evangelical rhetoric into enemy territory. As Billy Ray Hearn, founder of Sparrow Records, a Christian record label, commented, "contemporary Christian music has nothing to do with the musical style. It has only to do with the lyrics."[89] Hence, any musical style can become an evangelistic Trojan horse.

The problem, of course, was that, regardless of the music, few non-Christians were interested in explicitly Christian lyrics, which are perceived as promoting— if not directly, then simply by association—hegemonic sacred forms. Put bluntly, Christian songs flatten transgressive appeal. Hence, from the outset, contemporary Christian music has faced the problem of being predominantly an insider discourse—emic entertainment for the converted. Inevitably, therefore, since the early 1970s it has followed its primary market and moved away from the predominantly evangelistic rationale of the "Jesus freaks" and toward a broadly pastoral rationale. That is to say, the music has tended to focus less on the conversion of the unsaved and more on the devotional and moral lives of the saved. Although the evangelistic, centrifugal discourse, which has been so important to evangelical culture, is still evident in much contemporary Christian music—and is still central to its declared raison d'être—the focus has effectively shifted toward the production of music for insiders. As such, it tends to provide sacred interpretations of the "profane music" Christians enjoy in an effort to reinforce commitment to evangelical sacred forms and, as such, also to resist the profane influence of non-Christian music on "the saved." Having said that, other artists have sought to progress beyond the claustrophobic confines of the Christian community, identifying themselves more as artists who happen to be Christians, rather than specifically Christian artists. Hence, a spectrum has emerged, at one end of which is popular music composed for Christians or for specifically missiological reasons and at the other end of which is music composed by Christians who have "crossed over" into the secular music world. Between these two poles there is a wide range of attempts to straddle both worlds.

Concerning contemporary Christian music's ambiguous relationship with the secular music industry, arguably the dominant forces shaping the rapprochement have been less of God and more of Mammon. Initially, of course, the Christian music industry was formed around separatist and evangelistic ideals, which have, as William Romanowski comments, "shaped the way evangelicals thought about, produced, and consumed culture." They emphasized "evangelistic value as the primary evaluative standard."[90] Hence, again, the core problem it has always faced has been that of negotiating a passage between the Scylla of evangelistically ineffective insider music, which appeals only to the converted, and the Charybdis of evangelistically ineffective popular music that has "crossed over" so successfully that it has become indistinguishable from non-Christian popular music. Put differently, on the one hand, for the evangelistic rationale to make sense, many Christians insisted that the message needed to be clear, evangelical, and uncompromising. This, they argue, is the only way for a Christian with integrity to engage with the profane world of popular music. On the other hand, who on earth, apart from the converted and the bewildered, would want to listen to poorly produced music, the aim of which was conversion to conservative religion and morality? That is to say, apart from the inadequate production quality of much Christian popular music in the 1960s and 1970s, it, again, simply failed to address the transgressive requirements of liminal subcultures, many members of which, quite naturally, craved sex, drugs, and experimentation with the profane. Hence, it tended to be viewed as an insipid imitation of secular popular music which, to make matters worse, preached conservative social values. Consequently, again, it quickly became an exercise in singing to the converted. As such, Christian records were not stocked in mainstream record stores. This was, to say the least, not ideal for either business or evangelism.

As some indication of the tensions these problems caused, intense rivalry broke out "between gospel record companies and independent religious distributors battling for slim profit margins in the small evangelical market. Evangelical record labels and distributors sued each other over contract disputes."[91] Hence as the Christian music business evolved and as it became increasingly keen to secure wider recognition—in order, ostensibly, to increase its sphere of ministry—so it required more resources and, as such, moved closer to the secular music industry with its greater financial, marketing, and distribution muscle. That is to say, in order to build a larger fan base and experience a growth in profits, the Christian music industry needed to look beyond the small, increasingly crowded evangelical market.[92]

The point to note is that the uneasy relationship Christian music had with the sacred and the profane highlights the problems conversionist strategies face. For evangelistic credibility and business reasons, it needed to engage with the secular music industry, but as it did, it inevitably drifted further from its original ideals. If contemporary Christian music was to be successful as popular music, it couldn't be too vociferous or direct in its communication of evangelical theology and social concerns. As Romanowski puts it, "ecclesiastical purposes originally supplied the 'sacred' justification evangelicals needed to record and perform 'secular' music and to establish the Christian music industry, but these rules limited acceptable lyrical content to "confessional" themes for worship and evangelism."[93] Such themes were never going to garner sufficient popular support to be attractive to the secular music industry. After all, their profits relied on subcultures that challenged many of the core sacred forms defended by conservative religion. Hence, co-distribution deals, such as that between Myrrh and A&M, which enabled evangelical artists to "cross over" onto mainstream popular music playlists required that those artists reveal little of their evangelical religious and cultural roots. Consequently, songs were written "about life experience *without any hidden spiritual agenda*,"[94] as Amy Grant said of her album, *Heart in Motion* (1991). The strategy was a commercially effective one. Grant, for example, became "Christian music's bestselling female artist."[95] Likewise, other successful Christian artists and bands, such as Sufjan Stevens and P.O.D., while not denying theistic belief, increasingly avoided aligning themselves with socially and theologically conservative evangelical rhetoric. God is there, but he is in the background.[96] For example, in a *Rolling Stone* interview, P.O.D. made the following point: "Just because P.O.D. are a spiritual band doesn't mean we adhere to any one religion, and all kinds of people want to use us as a symbol for their thing. There's a thousand different definitions of what a Christian is, but we don't feel like there are any lines."[97] Similarly, Stevens believes that "there is truth in every corner . . . I don't make any claims about the faith. All I can account for is myself and my own belief. . . . I can't make any claims about other religions. There's no condemnation in Christ, that's one of the fundamentals of Christianity." Indeed, he believes the church to be much the same as any other institution, in that "it's incredibly corrupt . . . it's full of dysfunctional people and people who are hurt and battered and abused. . . . That's unfortunate. I find it very difficult, I find church culture very difficult you know; I think a lot of churches now are just fundamentally flawed."[98] Needless to say, stances such as these have drawn criticism from evangelical apologists who suspect them of profanation. For example, the anti-popular music campaigner Terry Watkins of Dial-the-Truth Ministries states that "P.O.D. has subtly introduced and indoctrinated Christian young people to a false, anti-Jesus, religion." Apparently, they "disobey the clear teachings of the Bible, use filthy profanity in their speech, proudly admit to drinking alcoholic beverages, promote openly wicked, vulgar, and satanic music, corrupt the pure teachings of Jesus Christ with the false religion of Rastafarianism, [and] attack Bible believing Christians and Christianity."[99]

At the other end of the spectrum to Amy Grant and P.O.D., and informed by a more separatist rationale, some conservative religious musicians have been keen to baptize popular music, to transform it into a force for good in the lives of the faithful. This is conspicuously evident within, for example, conservative Islamic and Christian metal, which, while stylistically the same as heavy metal, articulates a particular construction of the sacred, in which the Satanic and the misanthropic are replaced by core religious and moral themes.[100] For example, the Indonesian death metal band from Jakarta, Tengkorak, promotes conservative religious themes, including, explicit anti-Semitic and anti-Western ideas: "Destroy Zionism," "Capitalism Agenda" (*Civil Emergency*, 2005); "Boycott Israel," "Zionist Exaggration" (*Agenda Suram*, 2007). In an attempt to sanctify metal, they have also instituted what has become known as the "one finger movement," which replaces the two-finger "sign of the horns" typically used by heavy metal fans at concerts. Pointing upward, fans of Islamic metal demonstrate their commitment to Allah. This rhetoric against the profanation of metal itself is particularly conspicuous within the Christian metal scene. For example, the Australian band Mortification have established a fan club called the "Infiltration Squad" and refer to their fans as "Priests of the Underground." With its own militaristic coat of arms, fans are encouraged to engage in spiritual warfare against the dark forces that profane heavy metal. "The Infiltration Squad is for Christians who love heavy metal music. . . . To wear the Infiltration Squad coat of arms on our backs we are telling the world," declares guitarist and founding member Steve Rowe, that, as metal fans, "we are united under a banner that says . . . we are good news Christians. Our aim, together, is to infiltrate the devil's territory as. . . . Priests of the Underground. No leader except Jesus Christ our Lord and Savior! We are all simply servants under command." As such, he says, they want their fans to be "committed to praying for one another and for the metal scene, both Christian and non-Christian."[101] As for the music itself, apart from the lyrics, it would be difficult to distinguish it from "non-Christian" metal. As Johannes Jonsson, who runs the website "Metal for Jesus," points out, Christian metal may be "made by Christians" and may include an explicitly "Christian message," but it is "just as brutal and heavy" as secular metal.[102] While this may appear a little incongruous, the rationale is, again, that of many within contemporary Christian music, namely that meaning is located in the lyrics alone. The music is, he says, "like a knife," in that "in itself it's neutral, but depending on the motive behind it, it can be used for good or evil purposes. A doctor can use a knife to save someone's life, but the same knife can also be used . . . to kill someone. The knife in itself is totally neutral." Hence, it is important that "the lyrics in Christian Metal. . . . They tell the good news about Jesus Christ" and "uplift their fans and bring them closer to Christ. . . . So the music is "the same," but the lyrics are very different."[103]

Unfortunately, the logic is flawed. Indeed, this is evident in their approach to composition. For example, all the Christian metal musicians Marcus Moberg interviewed in his study of the scene in Finland admitted that their lyrics were influenced by the style of the music they played. As one artist commented to him, "in principle I have always thought that music is music and, as such . . . neutral." Consequently, "you can splash on it any kind of lyrics you want, but, of course, they will not always work if the contrast is huge." He continues, "in my opinion, you . . . cannot just sing the kind of 'Jesus loves you . . . ' style of thing to death metal." To do so is, he says, "a bit of a style break." Rather, "lyrics should be written according to musical style."[104] This statement unwittingly highlights the core issue. Their evangelical rationale requires that they articulate a "music as neutral" thesis. In order to distance themselves from that which they identify as profane, that which is felt to be a threat to the sacred, that which they have been saved from, *and yet also* incorporate it within a sacred context, they need to argue that it can be redeemed without any loss of genre identity. Hence, they separate the lyrics and the music, arguing that the latter is simply a vehicle. As such, in playing the music, they are not profaning themselves or their listeners. The problem with this thesis is that, as we have seen, music and sonic environments do convey meaning. Music is never simply a vehicle, which is precisely why certain lyrics seem at odds with certain types of music and why music sometimes seems to add unintentional layers of meaning to lyrics. The score from the film *Psycho*, for example, would not naturally accompany the hymn "All Things Bright and Beautiful" in a church service, because the music itself carries meanings that are at odds with the words of the hymn. The dissonance produced would be more disturbing than uplifting. Again, as one Christian metal fan related to me, it's difficult to sing about love and Jesus with a "death growl." Death metal singers, as Ian Christie puts it, "tore out their larynxes to summon images of decaying corpses and giant catastrophic horrors. This created a nearly insurmountable barrier to entry for the casual listener"[105]—and, of course, also encouraged affective spaces not normally associated with Christian worship.

This means that when extreme metal is informed by an evangelistic rationale, the lyrics will need to be chosen carefully to avoid dissonance. As Pekka Taina, from the Finnish Christian death metal band Sotahuuto, concedes, "lyrics should be written in accordance with metal's genre-conventions, that is, written in a way that suits the character of the music."[106] This suggests that, not only is the music not neutral, but the meanings it communicates are primary. In other words, extreme metal music provides the dominant discourse, determining, to some extent, any Christian discourse accompanying it. Fortunately for Christians, "Jesus loves you" isn't the only text they have. Indeed, there is a tradition within evangelicalism of constructing dark, fearful affective spaces around the macabre and the apocalyptic. One only has to think of Jonathon Edwards' sermon on July 8, 1741 in Enfield, Connecticut, "Sinners in the Hands of an Angry God." Edwards famously sought to create, as many preachers and prophets throughout religious history have done, an affective space within which hell is experienced as a reality, the torments thereof almost being felt. His rhetoric of fear sought to persuade listeners of the intimately personal significance of his theology. As George Marsden comments, "through sheer intensity he generated emotion." It was as though those who heard him "suddenly realized they were horribly doomed"[107]—"before the sermon was done . . . there was a great moaning and crying out throughout the whole house."[108] It is this type of apocalyptic rhetoric of fear that Christian metal musicians are naturally drawn to, because the sonic environments created by extreme metal will allow very little else. The religious text is from the outset under the jurisdiction of the discourse of extreme metal music; Christian rhetoric is constrained by the affective spaces created by extreme metal and by the subcultures it has nurtured.[109] There is little room for all things bright and beautiful here. Not to submit to the genre conventions would risk the music losing its transgressive identity as extreme metal. Hence, again, the only way this transformation can be cogently achieved is through the construction of a similarly violent, macabre and demonic discourse, which retains continuity with the primary discourse of extreme metal.

Of course, because, as I have argued elsewhere, Christian demonological and apocalyptic discourses have significantly influenced popular occulture and, as such, have had a formative influence on the evolution of extreme metal culture,[110] Christians have been able to capitalize on the areas of discursive overlap between the worlds of evangelicalism and extreme metal. That is to say, they have been able to execute their conversionist project by retaining the affective spaces created by extreme metal music, while replacing profane, anti-Christian rhetoric with evangelical interpretations of biblical apocalyptic and demonological themes. Again, because Christian theology is oriented around an act of hideous violence, which, as Georges Bataille opined, "carries human dread to a representation of loss and human degradation,"[111] its core sacred imagery is entirely consistent with much extreme metal discourse (as discussed in Chapter 3): "whoever eats my flesh and drinks my blood has eternal life" (Jn 6:54); "my flesh is real food and my blood is real drink" (Jn 6:55); "the law requires that nearly everything be cleansed with blood, and without the shedding of blood there is no forgiveness" (Heb 9:22) "they have washed their robes and made them white in the blood of the Lamb" (Rev 7:14). Consequently, Christian hymnody, which often celebrates bathing in blood and feasting on flesh, provides much material for the redemption of the macabre in Christian extreme metal. Hence, while titles such as Mortification's "Brutal Warfare," "Bathed in Blood" (Mortification, 1991), and "Blood World" (*Blood World*, 1994) reflect the themes of extreme metal, they also articulate the theology of hymns and choruses. Other compositions, while ostensibly exploring the occult themes of extreme metal, such as Mortification's "Necromanicide" (*Scrolls Of The Megilloth*, 1992), are converted into evangelical warnings against the profane: "Communication with the dead/ Contact with those in the grave . . . This foul practice must be stopped/ Before your cadaver starts to rot/ Fall prostrate before the cross/ Bathe in the blood of the sacrifice." However, the overall point is that, because the agenda is set by the music, not the theology, it is difficult for Christian extreme metal musicians to stray too far beyond the themes of violence, death, and the apocalyptic.

As far as evangelism is concerned, as Moberg discovered, there is little evidence to suggest that the transformation of metal does much more than "function as an alternative form of worship and religious expression."[112] As he pointed out to me, "I have found no evidence whatsoever that Christian metal would have any real impact beyond its immediate audience . . . Nor did I ever find any empirical/ethnographic evidence that some people actually become attracted to the faith through the music . . . As I recall, none of my informants had found faith through Christian metal. They were all believers prior to starting listening to the music or becoming involved in the scene. But, the music clearly does provide them with an alternative way of expressing and 'doing' their faith. So, in reality, it's very much music for people who are already Christians."[113] In other words, although an evangelistic rationale is often central to the self-legitimizing discourse of Christian metal, there is actually no significant evidence of evangelistic impact. Hence, even though some bands have been released on secular labels, such as Germany's Nuclear Blast (the world's largest independent heavy metal label), Christian metal tends to be a particular type of *Christian* music.[114] Again, because of its close relationship to conservative constructions of the sacred in society and its resistance to the profane, in the final analysis, it fails to create the transgressive affective spaces sought within extreme metal culture; separatist contemporary Christian discourse will always, to some degree, neutralize the transgressive potential of popular music through its defence of the sacred and its othering of the profane.

Of course, this is not to deny that musicians with religious convictions are unable to negotiate a mediating position between the cogent articulation of their faith and the composition of music that finds its way on to the iPods of the unconverted. Firstly, levels of tolerance for confessional religious discourse depend on social and cultural contexts. We have seen, for example, how Hindu ideas became popular in the Easternized context of the late-1960s, within which young people were turning away from the religious hegemonies of the West. Secondly, some musicians' articulations of the sacred are more nuanced, ambiguous, and embedded in everyday culture than others. P.O.D.'s subtle Christian rhetoric, for example, is imbricated with their use of Rastafarian terminology—"Jah," "Zion," "Babylon" (e.g., "Set Your Eyes to Zion," *Fundamental Elements Of Southtown*, 1999)—and a focus on social justice (e.g., "Ghetto," "Youth of the Nation," *Satellite*, 2001). Again, other Christian bands have tended to focus on the experiential, the expressive and the mystical, rather than the dogmatic and the propositional aspects of their religion. As such, their music is more appealing to liminal minds shaped by the subjective turn in modern Western culture.[115] Sweden's Crimson Moonlight, for example, explores the apophatic theology of the Greek Fathers, along with some of the core themes of "northern culture" typical of Scandinavian black metal (as discussed in the previous chapter): "I prefer to speak of God by negation, through all that which he is not . . . The more we learn about God, the more we understand that we know nothing at all . . . In the end, God's light shines so brightly that it turns into darkness . . . And so we rest. In Divine Darkness."[116] Such discourses are, broadly speaking, more occulturally friendly, and, as such, perceived to be at a conceptual distance from the conservative constructions of the sacred typical within evangelicalism. As such, a band such as Crimson Moonlight is able, to some extent, to redeem black metal discourse, but in a way that allows ambiguity and resists the dogmatism of much evangelical discourse.

Religious popular music

As noted above, this section is not primarily concerned with the instrumental use of popular music by religion or with the interpretation of it as a site for theological reflection. Rather, our concern is with popular music that has been specifically developed as a religio-political discourse, one of the most conspicuous examples of which is "roots reggae," a form of reggae that self-consciously reflects on religion, culture and history. As Derek Walmsley puts it, "for all the talk of bone-shaking bass, what really makes the earth move is its heavy Judeo-Christian metaphysics."[117] Again, Steve Barrow and Peter Dalton make the point that, although "to most Jamaicans a roots record is simply one that concerns itself with the life of the ghetto sufferer . . . with 'reality,'" it is actually shaped by a culture "informed by the millennial cult of Rastafarianism."[118] As such, it is conspicuously oriented around a number of prominent sacred forms that have "roots" in a particular postcolonial discourse. Incorporating a range of music from ska to ragga, the term "roots reggae" was first used in the mid-1970s to describe the work of artists immersed in religious and political postcolonial analysis. Focussed on a number of sacred forms distilled in the phrase "roots and culture," it became central to the work of the most important reggae artists of the 1970s, such as The Abyssinians, Horace Andy, Big Youth, Black Uhuru, Glen Brown, Burning Spear, Johnny Clarke, The Congos, Culture, The Ethiopians, Ijahman Levi, Vivian Jackson, Bob Marley, Jacob Miller, Hugh Mundell, Augustus Pablo, Lee Perry, Max Romeo, Peter Tosh, Bunny Wailer, The Wailing Souls, and Tappa Zukie. Hence, although roots and culture discourse has been a continuous thread running through reggae from its inception in Jamaica in the 1960s to its global presence today, if pressed to identify its golden age, there are few more obvious high points than the early 1970s through to the early 1980s. It was during this period that Island Records and later Virgin Records introduced a number of key roots artists into the international rock industry. Consequently, for most Westerners at the time, reggae meant roots reggae and roots reggae meant Rastafari.

For the Rastafarian, music is, as the dub poet Yasus Afari puts it, "the unspoken language of the soul" and roots reggae articulates "the message and livity of the Rastafarians," thereby functioning as "a tool for liberation, communicating the values and concepts of the faith and movement of Rastafari."[119] In this sense, as we will see, it is "religious," in that it is used both devotionally, to encourage reflection on "livity" and the divine, and ideologically, to disseminate key sacred forms: "a universal message of one love, African redemption, hope, inspiration, justice, equality, peace and goodwill to all humanity."[120] Concerning "livity," this is an important concept, in that, in the argot of Rastafari, it is "the living celebration of life in which every moment, every breath, every thought, every word and every deed is paying eternal homage and service in recognition of the Everloving, Everliving and Everlasting Creator who made everything possible, through the Ivine (divine) powers of the most high, Jah Rastafari."[121] Moreover, politically, the argot itself is both an important facet of livity and a key feature of reggae's postcolonial discourse. "In the Jamaican experience," says Afari, "the languages of the colonialists were imposed on the colonized people in order to control, manipulate and dominate peoples' minds, thoughts, mentality, actions and their entire life." As such, it "served to bridle the natural indigenous tongue of the people, so as to subdue them under the colonial yoke of downpression." Consequently, Afari argues, Rastafarian argot functions "to uplift, liberate and free the mind of the people, by dismantling the colonial mentality that the colonial languages imposed upon it."[122] As we will see, it is this "mental calibration,"[123] as he refers to it, that is so central to the perception of reggae as a sacred force. It "deconstructs the colonial mentality."[124]

The historical context of colonialism is, therefore, key to understanding roots reggae. Concerning this context, we now have, as Simon Jones says, "a good understanding of the mechanisms of retention and adaptation under slavery by which key aspects of those cultures were preserved, blended with European forms and maintained in a whole array of practices and beliefs in the New World."[125] Of particular importance during the period of slavery in Jamaica was the maintenance of Christian hegemony through the granting of concessions in order to secure consensus. That is to say, while the British sought to secure control over the slaves transported from West Africa by the imposition of the English language and Christianity, they allowed the retention of certain African cultural elements in order to encourage compliance. The result was Jamaican Creole and Afro-Christianity. On the one hand, this created some distance between the slaves and the dominant culture, thereby allowing an expression of resistance and the assertion of their dignity in an oppressive context. But, on the other hand, it constituted an incorporation into the dominant culture. In other words, what evolved was not wholly English, Christian or African, but rather a negotiated position in which colonial hegemony remained in place largely because the subordinate groups were allowed to incorporate something of their own culture in the dominant culture, thereby weakening their desire to rebel. Again, reggae and Rastafari need to be understood from this colonial perspective, for, as Leonard Barrett argues, the psyche of Jamaican people is a product of resistance to oppression. "Jamaicans are by nature some of the most fun-loving, hardworking, and gregarious people in the Caribbean. Treated with kindness and respect, they are likely to remain the most confident and dependable friends on earth. But if treated with impunity and disrespect, all the rage of a deep psychic revenge may surface with unpredictable consequences. This calm-and-storm personality of contemporary Jamaicans is," he says, "a direct inheritance of that group of Africans who suffered the most frustrating and oppressive slavery ever experienced in a British colony."[126] Yet, much has been drawn from that hegemonic culture of oppression. For example, Myalism, perhaps the principal formative West African tradition to emerge in Jamaica in the later 18th century, borrowed from observed Christian worship and even included versions of hymns by Moody and Sankey. Likewise, many reggae melodies and harmonies are taken directly from Christian hymnody. As Linton Kwesi Johnson comments concerning Burning Spear's music, "a lot of his songs are like Baptist hymns or Bible songs. All those influences are very strong."[127] Similarly, the Wingless Angels' debut album, *Wingless Angels* (1997), includes Wesleyan hymns.

Consequently, as in Rastafarianism, at the heart of reggae's postcolonial discourse there is a concern to remember life within "Plantation-America"—the societies moulded by the rigidly stratified plantation system that depended on African slave labour.[128] Burning Spear's "Slavery Days" (*Marcus Garvey*, 1975), Culture's "Too Long in Slavery" (*International Herb*, 1977), Bob Marley and the Wailers' "Slave Driver" (*Catch a Fire*, 1973), and Misty in Roots' "Slavery Days" (*Wise and Foolish*, 1981) are typical of songs which confront the listener with the brutality of the slave trade, the effects of which, even today, shape African-Caribbean society and their constructions of the sacred and the profane. As Dick Hebdige notes, "even in present-day Jamaica there are social and economic problems which can be traced back directly to the old plantation system. Jamaica's poverty, unemployment and racial and social inequality are all largely inherited from the past."[129] Consequently, reggae has never simply been "a set of highly danceable rhythms," but rather, rooted in this history, it has always been shaped by a self-reflexive questioning of African-Caribbean "poverty and inequality and black identity."[130] However, while Hebdige is correct, this is still a rather skewed perspective, in that, while he recognizes, as others have done[131]—how could they fail to?—that "the Bible is a central determining force in both reggae music and popular West Indian consciousness in general" and "the supremely ambiguous means through which the black community can most readily make sense of its subordinate position within an alien society,"[132] nevertheless, as with much early analysis, he does not account fully for the significance of religious discourse. As noted in the Introduction, analysis in cultural studies has always been rather blinkered in this respect, focusing on the social and political significance of subcultures, with religion tending to be treated as an aberrant and slightly irritating private concern, which, if it has to be mentioned at all, should be treated separately from what is considered to be the "secular" sphere. Such approaches are always Procrustean and frequently unhelpful. Certainly as far as reggae is concerned, the sacred and the secular, the religious and the political cannot be separated without violence having been done to both.

A particularly distinctive feature of much Rastafarian political thought is its conspicuous millenarian orientation. Hence, during the period within which roots reggae evolved out of ska and rocksteady in the late-1960s and up until the early 1980s most Rastas expressed a strident millenarian ideology, which informed the construction of a number of core sacred forms and allied beliefs, including, as Nathaniel Murrell notes:

> belief in the beauty of black people's African heritage; belief that Ras Tafari Haile Selassie I, Emperor of Ethiopia, is the living God and black Messiah; belief in repatriation to Ethiopia, *qua* Africa, the true home and redemption of black people, as having been foretold and . . . soon to occur; the view that the ways of the white men are evil, especially for the black race; belief in the apocalyptic fall of Jamaica as Babylon, the corrupt world of the white man, and that once the white man's world crumbles, the current master/slave pattern [of existence] will be reversed. Jah Ras Tafari will overthrow or destroy the present order, and Rastafarians and other Blacks will be the benefactors of that destruction; they will reign with Jah in the new kingdom.[133]

In a way not dissimilar to Martin Luther's understanding of "the Babylonian captivity of the Church,"[134] Rastas thought of themselves, their roots and their culture, in terms of captivity within an unrighteous system: U Roy, *Dread in a Babylon* (1975); Martha Velez, *Escape from Babylon* (1976); Merger, *Exiles in Babylon* (1977). Indeed, organizing its various millenarian doctrines was an underlying biblically informed exilic discourse. Like the Israelites, with whom they strongly identified, Africans were forcibly transported from the "Promised Land" to "Babylon." It is this narrative that informs an apocalyptic discourse that looks forward to the end of the current exilic period. The time of mental and physical slavery will be terminated, the current world order will end, and a happier existence for black people will dawn. However, again, such theologies were not lifted wholesale from traditional Christian eschatology. As Ennis Edmonds comments, even when African slaves converted to Christianity, the beliefs "to which they showed the greatest affinity were those that reinforced their Afrocentric worldview, informed their struggle for liberation, and promised them eventual freedom from and redress of the evil perpetrated against them by the colonial system."[135] This confluence of postcolonial ideology and millenarian expectation running through Jamaican history is effectively set to music in roots reggae. Numerous reggae songs urge Africans to set their faces toward "Zion" and await deliverance and the apocalyptic destruction of oppressive bureaucracies and societies (i.e., "Babylon").

In classic Judaic thought, statehood is understood in terms of the fulfilment of God's promises to the Patriarchs, the progenitors of the people. Hence, in the period of exile (135–1948 CE), the longing to return to the homeland occupied a central place in Jewish religio-political discourse. Exile and redemption became dominant theological themes that eventually shaped Zionist thought. Influenced by similar themes, a form of Zionism evolved within Jamaica, for which, as Patrick Taylor comments, "a past African Golden Age [became] a future millennial Zion."[136] This became explicit in Rastafarianism and, as such, is frequently articulated in reggae. For example, "Africa" by The Mighty Diamonds (*Right Time*, 1976) makes an explicit "articulation" (as Stuart Hall might refer to it) between a subversive African Zionist ideology and the New Jerusalem of Christian eschatology. On the one hand, Africa is a land for black people, a sacred symbol of black supremacy, and, on the other hand, reflecting the vision described in Revelation 21, it is the utopian goal of history, a place where "crying," "victimization," and "starvation" will cease. Moreover, as we have seen, just as Africa became a symbol of sacred space, so the rest of the world was identified as profane space, "Babylon." [137] Indeed, reinterpreting the story of the Israelites' journey from Egypt to the Promised Land, as detailed in the Pentateuch, the Atlantic Ocean came to be understood in terms of the River Jordan, a boundary separating the sacred from the profane. A yearning to cross that boundary—a theme common to many gospel choruses and spirituals—is expressed in numerous roots reggae songs, such as Burning Spear's "Jordan River" (*Marcus Garvey*, 1975), Barry Brown's "Moving on to the Promised Land" (*Cool Pon Your Corner*, 1979), Peter Yellow's "How Fe Cross River Jordan" (*Hot*, 1982), Count Ossie and the Rasta Family's "Crossing the River Jordan" (*Man From Higher Heights*, 1983), and Dennis Brown's "Promised Land" (*The Promised Land*, 2002). One happy day in the future, the oppressed will cross the Jordan and set their feet on the shores of a land flowing with milk and honey, the Promised Land of peace and plenty.

The mundane, temporal hope for such a Jordan-crossing event was stimulated by the emergence of an identifiable "back-to-Africa" movement, as initially theorised by Edward Wilmot Blyden.[138] The pioneer of Pan-Africanism,[139] Blyden argued a thesis that is now at the heart of Rastafarian thought, namely that Ethiopia represents the pinnacle of civilization and learning. Again, drawing on biblical references, Ethiopia and the celebration of its supremacy became identified with Africa per se. Passages such as Psalm 68 were commonly cited: "Let God arise, let his enemies be scattered . . . Let Ethiopia hasten to stretch out her hands to God." Hence, for many within the African diaspora, Ethiopia became a synonym for the entire continent: it was the heart of Africa; it was the symbol of a free, sovereign, and sacred Africa;

it was, therefore, as Neil Savishinsky discusses, "a potent source of inspiration for African nationalist leaders, many of whom chose the 'pan-African' colors of the Ethiopian flag as a symbol for their emerging political parties and newly independent states."[140] In short, Ethiopianism, as African Zionism, "espoused a vision of African liberation and a future Ethiopian empire."[141] To some extent, of course, the identification of Ethiopia and Africa was inevitable. As Barrett comments, "by the time of the emergence of the Black churches, Africa (as a geographical entity) was just about obliterated from their minds. Their only vision of a homeland was the biblical Ethiopia. It was the vision of a golden past – and the promise that Ethiopia should once more stretch forth its hands to God – that revitalized the hope of an oppressed people. Ethiopia to the Blacks in America was like Zion or Jerusalem to the Jews."[142]

While Ethiopianism never actually coalesced into the movement for resistance that Blyden hoped it would, he looked forward to the day when a "black Moses" would lead the dispersed peoples of African origin back to their homeland and out of the land of oppression. Again, this vision has become central to the discourse of roots reggae. For example, it is explicitly articulated on the title track of the album declared by *Time Magazine* to have been the most important album of the twentieth century, Bob Marley's *Exodus* (1976).[143] As well as the refrain "movement of Jah people" and references to "leaving Babylon" for "our father's land," there is also a petitionary prayer to Jah to send "another brother Moses," "to break downpression," to "wipe away transgression," and to "set the captives free." Again, the reference to "Moses" is particularly significant, in that, drawing on biblical imagery, it repeats Blyden's hope that there will arise a "Negro leader of the Exodus . . . a Negro of Negroes, like Moses was a Hebrew of the Hebrews – even if brought up in Pharaoh's palace [i.e., at the heart of the land of oppression] he will be found. No half Hebrew and half Egyptian will do the work . . . for this work, heart, soul and faith are needed."[144] If, in Blyden's day, there was little sign of his vision being realized in North America, this was not the case in Jamaica. Largely because of its more militant history of slave rebellion, the embers of radical political Ethiopianism were smouldering and simply needed someone to fan them. That person was Marcus Garvey. As Barrett argues, "the movement that was to embody the Ethiopian ideology par excellence was the Back-to-Africa Movement of Marcus Garvey. It was in Garvey – the prophet of African redemption – that the spirit of Ethiopianism came into full blossom."[145]

Marcus Mosiah Garvey—the significance of whose middle name is not lost on Rastas—was born in St Ann's Bay, Jamaica, and was to become the leader of the first genuine large-scale black movement. Indeed, with reference to Blyden's "prophecy," he was popularly referred to as "Black Moses." Like Blyden before him, central to his teaching and to that of the Universal Negro Improvement Association (UNIA)—which he founded on July 20, 1914 in Kingston, Jamaica—was the return of Africans to Africa, the only place, he believed, where black people would truly be at home and be respected as a race. Very quickly Garveyism became influential and international, being the movement for African repatriation and self-government that many oppressed Africans had, since Blyden, been longing for. As Peter Clarke points out, "the Garvey movement, like the Rastafarian movement, was born perhaps as much from despair of ending injustice and discrimination in America as it was from a vision of Africa as a 'Land without Evil.'"[146] As their efforts to resist the profane were frustrated, so the sacred seemed to shine all the more brightly. In a way that previous movements had failed to do, the UNIA was able to provide a focus for their hope of salvation from a profane world. It was able to do so because, not only did it provide a renewed vision of Africa as Zion, but, more importantly, it provided a physical means of getting there. Hence there was a very real sense of the hour of redemption being close at hand. The Black Star Line, owned solely by blacks, was a project which was intended to encourage trade between black communities around the Atlantic, as well as providing the means for Africans to return to Africa.[147] A source of great pride, reggae artists still reflect on the sacred symbolic significance this endeavour: Fred Locks, "Black Star Liners" (*Black Star Liner*, 1976); Culture, "Black Starliner Must Come" (*Two Sevens Clash*, 1977); Trinity, "Black Starliner" (*Showcase*, 1978); Prince Far I, "Black Starliner Must Come" (*Long Life*, 1978); Earl Sixteen, "The Black Starliner" (*Songs of Love and Hardship*, 1984).

Furthermore, like Blyden, Garvey focused the thinking of the African diaspora on a number of key sacred forms around which they could rally, central to which was the worship a black God "through the spectacles of Ethiopia":

> We, as Negroes, have found a new ideal. Whilst our God has no colour, yet it is human to see everything through one's own spectacles, and since the white people have seen their God through white spectacles, we have only now started out (late though it be) to see our God through our own spectacles. The God of Isaac and the God of Jacob let him exist for the race that believe in the God of Isaac and the God of Jacob. We Negroes believe in the God of Ethiopia, the everlasting God – God to Son, God the Holy Ghost, the one God of all ages. That is the God in whom we believe, but we shall worship him through the spectacles of Ethiopia.[148]

It is perhaps rather surprising, therefore, that Garvey himself never visited Africa. Indeed, as with many early reggae artists, his vision of Africa was based less on actual knowledge of the continent and more on a romantic reading of the Bible. Nevertheless, while his dream of physical repatriation was never realised—which is why Marley was still petitioning Jah to "send another brother Moses" over three decades later—he did succeed in focusing the minds of Africans on issues that were to become central to the millenarian thought of Rastafari. Psychologically, emotionally, culturally, and spiritually Garvey led his people out of Babylon and back to Zion by raising African consciousness and ensuring that Ethiopia would be a focal point for the liberation discourse of succeeding generations. As such, reggae constitutes a manifestation of Garvey's achievements, in that, globally, it continues the work of consciousness raising and the articulation of what is, essentially, a liberation theology—an interpretation of faith from the underside of history, from the particularity of the African-Caribbean experience of oppression.[149] It is out of this experience that, as Afari puts it, "the Rastafarians have assiduously and conscientiously inspired and created music that is relentlessly aimed at enlightenment, upliftment, social awareness and inity (unity) of purpose, that are in harmony with the noble ideals of 'one Love' and good will to all humanity. In this connection, the Rastafarians have played an indispensible role in the birth, development and defining the character of reggae music, as well as in the creation of the collective consciousness and nature of the Jamaican culture, that has imposed itself upon the international community."[150]

Of course, of particular significance to reggae's consciousness raising are Garvey's comments concerning an African redeemer. For example, he interpreted Psalm 68:31 as follows: "We go from the white man to the yellow man, and see the same unenviable characteristics in the Japanese. Therefore, we must believe that the Psalmist had great hopes [for this] race of ours when he prophesied 'Princes shall come out of Egypt and Ethiopia shall stretch forth [their] hands to God.' "[151] Indeed, many Rastas also believe him to have prophesied the following, although there is actually little evidence for the statements:[152] "Look to Africa for the crowning of a Black King; he shall be the Redeemer";[153] "Look to Africa when a black king shall be crowned for the day of deliverance is near."[154] Who would this Ethiopian/African messiah be? The answer, for Garvey and for many Jamaican Garveyites, came on November 2, 1930, when Ras (meaning "Prince") Tafari Makonnen was crowned Negus of Ethiopia and took the name Haile Selassie I. Several days after the coronation, on November 8, 1930, Garvey published an article in his Jamaican newspaper *The Blackman*, which referred back to his earlier comments: "The Psalmist prophesied that Princes would come out of Egypt and Ethiopia would stretch forth her hands unto God. We have no doubt that the time has now come. Ethiopia is now really stretching forth her hands. This great kingdom of the East has been hidden for many centuries, but gradually she is rising to take a leading place in the world and it is for us of the Negro race to assist in every way to hold up the hand of the Emperor Ras Tafari."[155] In Haile Selassie, many saw the fulfilment of biblical prophecy, even God incarnate. Consequently, it was this event that led to "the full flowering of Ethiopianism as a broad-based popular movement" and which "came to a head with the emergence of the Rastafari movement in 1933–34, and the mass-mobilization around the crisis of the Italo-Ethiopian War of 1935–36."[156] Also significant was a series of influential articles by L.F.C. Mantle published in *Plain Talk* between July and November 1935, entitled "In Defense of Abyssinia and its History." Part of Mantle's argument rested on an interpretation of the events in Ethiopia in terms of biblical prophecy, along with an articulation of the divinity of Haile Selassie. For example, on November 2, 1935, he made the following rather garbled interpretation of the events unfolding in Ethiopia: "I beg to inform you hypocrites [i.e., Christian clergy] that what you have taught us about Jesus is fulfilling in the land of Ethiopia right now: with the said same Romans or so-called Italian or Fascist. These are the said people who crucified Jesus 2000 years ago, and, as we read after 2000 years, Satan's kingdom or organization shall fall; and righteousness shall prevail in all the earth, as the waters cover the sea . . . we are now in the time that the 2000 years have expired."[157] Largely because of the millennarian bias in Afro-Christian political discourse, this type of eschatological speculation, which focused on the sacred significance of Selassie and the imminent destruction of the forces of profanation—articulated in terms of Babylon, apocalyptic evil and Satan—has been enormously influential, not least within the Rastafarian discourse of roots reggae.

It was into this climate of millenarian speculation that one of the principal architects of Rastafarianism began preaching.[158] Having lived in North America for some years, Leonard Percival Howell returned to Jamaica in November 1932 and quickly became the "catalytic agent in igniting the radical millenarian consciousness that based itself on the doctrine of divine kingship of Ethiopia's Ras Tafari."[159] Selassie, it was argued, is the figure in Revelation 5:5, "the Lion of the tribe of Judah, the Root of David . . . " In other words, he was understood to occupy the place that Christ would normally occupy in Christian eschatology. Christ and Selassie are conflated, in that, as Ras Bongo Time, the Rastafarian high priest of the Nyabinghi Order, puts it, "His Majesty is the resurrected personality of Christ"[160]—Haile Selassie I is Christ returned. This, not unreasonably, led to a conviction that Rastas are the divinely ordained interpreters of the Book of Revelation because it is their Messiah, the Lion of the tribe of Judah, who is the only one in heaven and on earth "able to open the scroll and its seven seals" (Rev 5.5). Again, not only did this type of thinking encourage millenarian speculation within the movement, but it gave roots reggae, as the international mouthpiece of Rastafari, a particularly significant expository role. Indeed, as well as being articulated in the music, this millenarian understanding of Selassie was frequently communicated in reggae cover art. For example, the cover of the Lee Perry-produced compilation *The Black Ark Presents Rastafari Liveth Itinually* (1996) depicts the royal figure of Selassie travelling in a chariot pulled by a lion (signifying the Lion of the Tribe of Judah) against a background of dark clouds and volcanic fire. Such discourses of apocalyptic catastrophism and of redemption from radical evil by Selassie are expounded on the album in songs such as "Forward With Jah Orthodox" and "Judgment Day." More generally, as Chris Morrow points out in his overview of reggae album cover art, "Haile Selassie is shown on album covers mainly as a powerful deity or . . . king. On illustrated sleeves like *African Museum All Star* and *Rockers Almighty Dub*, he assumes supernatural powers, showering the earth with lightning and using his dreadlocks to destroy the structures of Babylon."[161] Even the musicians themselves are occasionally depicted as prophetic defenders of the sacred, end-time witnesses to truth, and warriors resisting an absolute evil (e.g., Alpha Blondy, *Jerusalem*, 1986).

As indicated above, the stark millenarian sacred-profane dualism Rastas had inherited from Afro-Christianity and Back-to-Africa political thought taught them, not only to view Ethiopia as Zion and Selassie as the divine redeemer, but also to understand that which threatened and oppressed them as Babylon. Hence law enforcement agencies, understood as tools of oppression and, therefore, as manifestations of radical evil, became a special object of hatred as Rastas began to be imprisoned for a range of offences—including the smoking of ganga (marijuana), which many of them considered to be sacramental.[162] However, while some early followers of Howell did engage in violent resistance, as the movement evolved and as Howell's influence began to recede, the use of violence tended to separate mainstream Rastafarian belief from that of the Garveyites. Unlike the Rastas, Garveyites were less inclined to wait for a supernatural solution to racial discrimination and suffering. Rastas, on the other hand, adopted an attitude of passive endurance and patient waiting for a preordained apocalypse. This is partly why reggae is understood to be important, in that it is a non-violent, divinely ordained means of subverting the "Babylon System" (Bob Marley, *Survival*, 1979). In speaking truth to profane power, reggae constitutes a form of direct action that will ultimately contribute to the downfall of Babylon. This is what Bob Marley was referring to when he sang " . . . music you're the key . . . reggae music, chant down Babylon" ("Chant Down Babylon," *Confrontation*, 1983).

This understanding of roots reggae as sacred energy is rooted in the Rastafarian understanding of the supernatural efficacy of the spoken word and sound—understood to be a manifestation of divine presence with the power to create and destroy. As Ziggy Marley comments, "Babylon causes the system . . . It's a devil system . . . who cause so much problems on the face of the earth . . . And by 'chanting down' I mean by putting positive messages out there. That is the way we'll fight a negative with a positive . . . "[163] Again, Caroline Cooper argues that Bob Marley's "chant against Babylon is both medium and message. For Babylon, the oppressive State, the formal social and political institutions of Anglo/American imperialism, is bolstered by the authority of the written word, articulate in English. 'Head-decay-shun,' the punning, *dread* inversion of the English word "education," is antithetical to the cultural practices of Rastafarians, whose chant against Babylon has biblical resonances of the fall of Jericho."[164] Hence, central to the sacred work of reggae is, as we have seen Afari argue, undoing the "head-decay-shun," a subverting of the colonization of the mind. As Peter Tosh put it, "Babylon is where they tell you that everything that is wrong is right, and everything that is right is wrong. Everywhere is Babylon."[165] The point, however, is that the notion of chanting down Babylon is shaped by a confluence of postcolonial and apocalyptic discourses. This is why many roots reggae musicians interpret their music as an explicitly religious activity. As Tony Rebel says, "I see myself as an instrument of the Most High and definitely it's not for me alone to chant down Babylon. I'm a link in a chain. . . . We know that the music is very influential. The word is power. They chant around Jericho wall and it fell down. So, therefore, we can use music to chant down Babylon walls also. That is not a literal wall. Is like emancipating the people from those kind of mentality that is negative."[166] This is why references to the destruction of Babylon and to Judgement Day, when radical, subhuman evil will be eliminated, are ubiquitous within reggae: Junior Byles, *Beat Down Babylon* (1972); Junior Ross, *Babylon Fall* (1976); Yabby You, *Chant Down Babylon Kingdom* (1976); Trinity, "Judgment Day" (Ranking Trevor and Trinity, *Three Piece Chicken and Chips*, 1978); Earl Zero, "None Shall Escape the Judgment" (*Visions of Love*, 1979); The Overnight Players, *Babylon Destruction* (1981); The Memory of Justice Band, *Mash Down Babylon* (1983); Don Carlos, "Judgment Day" (*Plantation*, 1984); Knowledge, "Judgment" (*Straight Outta Trenchtown*, 2002); U Roy, *Babylon Burning* (2002); Fred Locks, "Babylon Falling Down" (*Glorify the Lord*, 2008).

As the 1960s progressed, so the complexity of Rastafarianism increased, its appeal broadening and extending beyond the poor areas of Jamaica. Gradually more privileged social groups, particularly students, joined the movement. This broadening of appeal led to an evolution of thinking. Although many were committed to notions of black power and Pan-Africanism, because they were not particularly poor, they were not overly concerned to return to Africa. Hence, there was a strengthening of theories of *symbolic* repatriation. As in much Pan-Africanism and Rastafarianism today, many began to think in terms simply of a return to an African consciousness. In other words, as indicated above, the rhetoric shifted toward a focus on "mental decolonization, a process of deconversion, of turning away from the ethos, mores, and values of colonial society and a reconversion to the African view and way of life."[167] In short, it was argued that the mind of Babylon needed to be replaced by the mind of Zion. Consequently, there was a focus on the nurturing of an African consciousness and the challenging of the profane social, spiritual and cultural structures of Babylon from within. Of course, reggae is again significant in this respect, in that, just as it is able to chant down Babylon, so it is able to "chant up Zion," to raise African consciousness. Hence, although there were intellectuals—such as particularly the Guyanese historian Walter Rodney[168]—who were challenging the colonial government in Jamaica, it was apparent to many Rastas in the 1960s and 1970s that musicians would become key actors in their salvation history, gradually transforming minds and subverting the Babylon system through music.

A contributing factor to this significance of reggae has been its apparently easy globalization. As I have discussed elsewhere,[169] by the close of the 1960s local Jamaican recordings were receiving an enthusiastic reception, not least by entrepreneurs such as, most notably, Edward Seaga, a Harvard-educated anthropologist, who would eventually become a prominent member of the Jamaican Labour Party and Prime Minister of the country (1980–1989), and Chris Blackwell, an aide-de-camp to the Governor General of Jamaica and the son of a wealthy, white English-born plantation owner and a Costa Rican-born Jewish mother with Jamaican ancestral roots going back to the seventeenth century. The shrewd business acumen of Blackwell in particular would eventually lead, in 1959, to the founding of the enormously successful Island record label. In 1962, after securing licensing agreements with the leading producers, Blackwell moved to London in order to supply Jamaican releases to Britain's growing expatriate community. Other labels followed and, as a result, the reach of Rastafarian millenarian discourse was extended "outernationally" (i.e., beyond the shores of Jamaica).

This is particularly interesting, in that, by the late 1970s, Rastafarian discourse was transposed into punk and postpunk culture. For example, when The Ruts achieved chart success with "Babylon's Burning" (*The Crack*, 1979), some may have been bemused by the reference to Babylon. However, for many disaffected white youths, who had, like The Ruts, become fascinated with roots reggae, the reference was obvious and made sense. By the late-1970s unemployment was soaring; the Conservative government seemed uncaring, greedy, and ruthless; relations with the police had got steadily worse; institutional racism was conspicuous; and the inner cities had become powder kegs. "Babylon's Burning" imagined—prophetically as it transpired—the inner cities being razed in an apocalyptic conflagration. Within two years, as if to reinforce the stark message of "Babylon's Burning," The Ruts released the heavily dub reggae-influenced "Jah War" (*The Crack*, 1979) to coincide with London's Southall race riots of July 1981. Babylon was burning. As Cashmore comments, "the riots of 1980 and 1981 gave some indication of the growing currency of Babylon as a way of interpreting the world."[170] Hence, while there is more than a little truth to Hebdige's thesis that British punk culture itself was a yearning for a "white ethnicity" similar to Rastafarianism,[171] the point here is that the vibrancy and imagery of its religio-political discourse, shaped by a history of violence and oppression, directly informed much countercultural thought in the UK. New understandings of the sacred and the profane were being constructed in Britain's inner cities. Indeed, the use of the term "Babylon" by Jamaicans to refer primarily to the police[172] quickly became the dominant subcultural understanding in the UK in the 1970s and 1980s.

Within roots reggae, however, understandings of the sacred and the profane, and of judgement and the destruction of Babylon were almost always informed by the Book of Revelation: Jah Shaka, "Revelation 18" (*Revelation Songs*, 1983); Mike Brooks, *Book of Revelation* (2001); Revelation, *Book of Revelation* (1979); Dennis Brown, "Revelation Fulfill" (*Dennis Brown in Dub*, 2002). Quotations from Revelation are even printed as prooftexts on album covers (e.g., Fred Locks, *Glorify the Lord*, 2008). However, the point is that, as Cooper says of Bob Marley's rhetoric concerning radical social change, it is consistently "metaphorically expressed in Rastafarian iconography as Babylon, the whore, the fallen woman of St. John's Revelation."[173] Particularly interesting in this respect is the cover of *Confrontation* (1983), painted by the Rasta artist, activist, and close friend of Marley, Neville Garrick, who "even joined the Wailers onstage as a percussionist because Marley felt that the more involved [he] was with [their] music, the better he could visually interpret it."[174] The cover portrays Marley as Saint George slaying a dragon. While most English children will be familiar with George as the patron saint of England who dispatched a dragon, the legend also has a long history in North African Coptic Christianity, being particularly notable in the hagiography of the Ethiopian Orthodox Tewahedo Church. Hence, the cover, which conflates St. George and Marley, intertextually suggests that roots reggae slays the forces of Babylon. It is an image of the sacred subduing the profane, just as the music itself has the sacred energy to "chant down" evil and unrighteousness. More than this, however, it also suggests the final battle between the angelic and the demonic as depicted in Revelation 12: 7–9: "And there was war in heaven. Michael and his angels fought against the dragon, and the dragon and his angels fought back. But he was not strong enough, and they lost their place in heaven. The great dragon was hurled down – that ancient serpent called the devil, or Satan, who leads the whole world astray. He was hurled to the earth, and his angels with him." Speaking of reggae's "sound and powerful lyrics," Garrick says of the work, which he painted after Marley's death, it was "a tribute to Bob Marley, depicting him as the Ethiopian St. Giorgis, or St. George, in the final conflict when good overcomes evil."[175]

It is hardly surprising, therefore, that, as with much Christian premillenarian discourse, reggae, especially during the 1970s and 1980s, focussed on biblical signs of the end, on the prevalence of "wars and rumors of wars" (Matt 24.6; Mk 13.7; Lk 21.9), paying particular attention to nuclear holocaust and Armageddon. Although, bearing in mind the cold war context, antinuclear rhetoric wasn't unusual within the popular music of the period, what is distinctive in roots reggae is the explicit premillenarian association of the superpowers with Babylon and of nuclear war with Armageddon. A good example is Bunny Wailer's "Armagidion" (*Black Heart Man*, 1976), which, not only draws on biblical references to "wars and rumors of war," but links ideas of nuclear catastrophe to eschatological notions of "the gates of doom and hell," spiritual battles between light and darkness, human unrighteousness, radical evil, and Satan. It also articulates a biblical vision of redemption and postapocalyptic utopianism when "night is passed and day is come." Likewise, Steel Pulse's "Earth Crisis" (*Earth Crisis*, 1984) references violence, corruption, environmental catastrophe and the possibility of nuclear holocaust in Babylon's "last days," repeating, in the chorus, references to "doctrines of the fallen angels" and the "eternal flames of hell." It also issues a premillenarian declaration of hope in the form of "Jah kingdom rising." Again, these themes were frequently communicated, not simply through the music, but also through the album cover art of the period: Peter Tosh, *No Nuclear War* (1987); Mikey Dread, *World War III* (1980); Mighty Maytones, *Madness* (1976); Michael Prophet, *Righteous are the Conqueror* (1980); Mutabaruka, *Outcry* (1984); Ranking Joe, *Armageddon* (1982). Indeed, some songs and some of the cover art of the period are explicit in their identification of the unrighteous leaders of Babylon. For example, not only does Ranking Ann's "Something Fishy Going On" (*Something Fishy Going On*, 1984) outline an apocalyptic scenario with reference to contemporary politics and international relations, but the cover art reinforces her thesis, depicting a scene of nuclear Armageddon, at the centre of which Ronald Reagan and Margaret Thatcher are pictured in a nuclear submarine.

While many would agree with Ranking Ann's summary of Cold War politics in the early 1980s, some reggae artists were more imaginative in their understanding of the Babylon system. The millenarian mind is very often populated by elaborate conspiracy theories. Rastafarianism is no exception. As in the Christian fundamentalist imaginary, it is frequently intimated in roots reggae that there are dark forces working against the "people of Jah." The sacred–profane binary is portrayed in stark terms. Their reading of the political, moral, and religious landscape is viewed through a lens of spiritual warfare. Political organisations, social structures, multinational companies, and world systems are all understood to be inherently evil, concrete manifestations of Babylon and demonic activity. For example, a reggae singer and member of the Twelve Tribes of Israel once expressed to me that he would not use credit cards and that he was particularly reluctant to use the Internet, principally because of a conspiracy theory he subscribed to relating to the Antichrist. With reference to Hal Lindsey's enormously popular fundamentalist text, *The Late Great Planet Earth*,[176] and quoting Revelation 13:16–18, he indicated that he wanted to distance himself from electronic media in order to avoid becoming drawn into the activities of the Antichrist. Demonstrating a familiarity with Western conspiracy occulture, this singer was convinced that, through the Illuminati (a staple of conspiracy culture), the Antichrist would ensure that all economic transactions and everyone involved in "the Babylon system" would bear his numerical mark—"666." It was now apparent, he argued, that this would be done by means of microchips. It wouldn't be long, he reasoned, before the population would be required to have chips implanted in their hands or foreheads. This is a surprisingly popular conviction within fundamentalist occulture and, indeed, he is not the only reggae musician, or indeed member of the Twelve Tribes of Israel, to have been persuaded by Lindsey's work. In an interview close to the end of his life, Bob Marley responded to a question about what books he was reading as follows: "I'll tell ya one kind book that I love, the first book is the Bible. Next book I ever read that I love is *The Late Great Planet Earth*. That's the second book I ever read where I really *interested* in reading. Y'know? *The Late Great Planet Earth*. "Cause all dem prophesy is true. Y'know wha I mean? Ya can't want anything nearer to the truth."[177]

Having discussed some of the core apocalyptic discourses informing roots reggae's postcolonial constructions of the sacred and the profane, we now turn to analyse the significance of its mystical and spiritist elements through an examination of its most avant-garde subgenre, "dub."[178] The term "dub," which is now widely used in dance music and electronica, refers to a process of deconstruction developed in Jamaica, whereby the engineer strips the music down to its basic rhythm components and introduces novel elements, particularly echo and reverb. The genesis of dub, in the contemporary sense of a fundamentally deconstructed version of a song, first appeared in 1972 and was largely the creation of a single engineer, "King Tubby" (Osbourne Ruddock).[179] Although his Kingston sound system, Tubby's Home Town Hi Fi, was successful, his skills were always more clearly evident in the recording studio, having become, during the late-1960s, a noted engineer at the Treasure Isle studio. Eventually, he built his own studio at the back of his home, 18 Dromily Avenue, Waterhouse, Kingston, and, with the freedom this afforded, began developing what were by then known as "versions"—instrumentals of reggae songs. Although constrained by poverty and, therefore, using relatively basic equipment, his experiments with the manipulation of sound were pioneering.[180] By 1972, having acquired a cutting machine and a two-track tape machine, and drawing on his background in electrical engineering, he started constructing relatively sophisticated equipment which was able to produce novel sonic environments. As Prince Jammy (Lloyd James)[181] comments, "the reverb unit that we used to use there was a Fisher reverb, an' we change it to become a King Tubby and Fisher! The slides that we used to use, we change them from the original slides, because the mixin' console was so old you couldn't get replacement parts. We use other models to incorporate in that console."[182] He also constructed an echo delay unit "by passing a loop of tape over the heads of an old two-track machine."[183]

The heart of dub reggae is the drum and bass rhythm: "dub means raw riddim," says Prince Jammy. "Dub jus' mean raw music, nuttin' water-down. Version is like your creativeness off the riddim, without voice."[184] Moving away from the upbeat rhythms of ska, dub worked with slower, more reflective, "churchical" riddims. This gave the music a more serious and devotional feel, a foundation upon which Tubby constructed layered soundscapes through the use of echo, equalization effects, and found sounds. Initial exposure to the aural effect of what he produced was so stunning that early descriptions resorted to metaphysical terminology, the nearest equivalent experience being that induced by psychedelics. It was as if the music was psychoactive, able in itself to evoke mystical altered states. For example, in 1976, the British *Melody Maker* journalist Richard Williams, describes the sense of reality-shift that the genre can induce: "One's overriding impression, on initial exposure to dub at the high volume for which it is intended, is that this is the nearest aural equivalent to a drug experience, in the sense that reality (the original material) is being manipulated and distorted."[185] Again, Luke Ehrlich notes that, "with dub, Jamaican music spaced out completely. If reggae is Africa in the New World, then dub must be Africa on the moon; it's the psychedelic music I expected to hear in the '60s and didn't. The bass and the drums conjure up a dark, vast space, a musical portrait of outer space, with sounds suspended like glowing planets or with fragments of instruments careening by, leaving trails like comets and meteors."[186] Likewise, David Toop describes dub as "a long echo delay, looping through time. Regenerating every few years, sometimes so quiet that only a disciple could hear, sometimes shatteringly loud, dub unpicks music in the commercial sphere. Spreading out a song or a groove over a vast landscape of peaks and deep trenches, extending hooks and beats to vanishing point, dub creates new maps of time, intangible sound sculptures, sacred sites, balm and shock for mind, body and spirit."[187] As in much ambient music, there is a sense in which time slows.[188] The listener, as Simon Frith comments of ambient minimalism, is "placed in a virtual time which has no history (no story line), no architecture (no outline), no apparent beginning, middle, or end; there is neither musical resolution nor musical expectation, nothing to help us make narrative sense of what we hear." Quoting the composer Wim Mertens, he describes minimalist music as "a 'field of intensity,' a 'free flow of energy,' less a human statement than a kind of eternal force: the music was there before we started listening and will continue after we stop."[189] This communicates well the affective spaces evoked by dub. Similarly, while the following reflection by Jonathon Kramer describes his experience of listening to the "Vexations" section of Erik Satie's *Pages Mystiques*, he might easily be describing the experience of listening to certain extended dub compositions.

> I found myself moving into a different listening mode. I was entering the vertical time of the piece. My present expanded as I forgot about the music's past and future. I was no longer bored. And I was no longer frustrated because I had given up expecting. I had left behind my habits of teleological listening. I found myself fascinated with what I was hearing. . . . True, my attention did wander and return, but during the periods of attending I found the composition to hold great interest. I became incredibly sensitive to even the smallest performance nuance . . . I never lost touch with myself or surroundings. Although I listened deeply enough to the music to accept its extended present, I never ceased to be aware of my mental and physical environment.[190]

Again, it is perhaps not surprising that dub lends itself to Romantic interpretation, as reggae's mysticism: Winston Riley, *Meditation Dub* (1976); The Disciples and The Rootsman, *Rebirth* (1997); The Hazardous Dub Company, "Mystical Dub," "Spiritual Dub" (*Dangerous Dubs Vol. 2*, 1993); Jah Shaka, "Immortal Dub," "Mystic Dub" (*Dub Symphony*, 1990). What Frith says of minimal and ambient composers is equally applicable to those who have experimented with dub, particularly since the early 1980s and postpunk, namely that they have been attracted by Eastern religions and monistic thought, for "virtual time here describes an experience of bodilessness, an indifference to materiality."[191] There is a sense of the ethereal encouraged by a feeling of space and depth induced by the careful use of echo and the emphasis on the offbeat.

Also significant for the creation of a spiritually oriented sonic environment is the fact that dub culture is almost always, as Linton Kwesi Johnson describes it, "Bass Culture" (*Bass Culture*, 1980). Bass is a central feature of what Simon Frith would call its "genre world."[192] "Our God In a Way is Bass" (*Ryder Style*, 2004) declare the

Bass Lo-Ryders. Typically experienced at high volume, dub sound system events usually include large batteries of speakers fed by powerful amplifiers.[193] For example, in 1981, Lloyd Coxsone commented that while he generally used around twenty bass speakers, "other sounds play around 50."[194] Similarly, over a decade later, in 1991, The Disciples recalled that they had "built up a sound powering some 5000 watts, 4000 of which were used on the bass end alone, running through to twelve 400-watt 18" Fane Colossus speakers."[195] The size of a speaker, of course, is directly correlated to how much bass it can produce. Moreover, the lower the bass gets, the more power is required to make it audible. Hence, sound systems require significant amplification, with "bass extension" down to lower frequencies, such as 20 hertz, requiring enormous power. Because human hearing is far less sensitive in the bass range than in the midrange, to be perceptually as loud as midrange sound, bass actually needs to be substantially louder. Put simply, loud bass requires moving lots of air. This is why, sound systems are preoccupied with the size of speakers and the power of the amplification—large speakers will move more air than small speakers with the same excursion (i.e., the same amount of back and forth motion), but to do so require a high wattage of amplification.

This relationship between bass and power often signifies the sacred–profane relationship between the Rasta and Babylon discussed above. On the one hand, "heavyweight" bass signifies the power required to overthrow the forces of Babylon and, on the other hand, it also signifies the seriousness of the "dread" situation of the righteous in Babylon. In an early essay published in *Race and Class*, Linton Kwesi Johnson reflects on the significance of the bass, referring to reggae and dub as

an essentially experiential music, not merely in the sense that the people *experience* the music, but also in the sense that the music is true to the historical experience of the people, that the music reflects the historical experience. It is the *spiritual expression* of the *historical experience* of the Afro-Jamaican. In making the music, the musicians themselves enter a common stream of consciousness, and what they create is an invitation to the listeners to be entered into that consciousness—which is also the consciousness of their people. The feel of the music is the feel of their common history, the burden of their history; their suffering and their woe; their endurance and their strength; their poverty and their pain. . . . This is precisely what Leroy Sibbles of the Heptones means when he says of 'dub' . . . "well . . . it signifies some kind of African feeling, the beat and the drum and the bass. We are all black and we have Africa deep within us. Yeah we feel it . . . Deep down inside from you hear it, you feel it." You feel it because the 'bad bass bounce' is your "blood a leap an pulse a pounce," you feel it because this "rhythm of a tropical electrical storm . . . rhythm cutting so sharp so," it cuts at your hurt; you feel it for the "bass history is a moving/ is a hurting black story"; you feel it because it is your pain; you feel it because it is your hunger; it is your sprout. "Deep down inside, from you hear it, you feel it," for it is your heart-song and it touches your soul's senses. The youth sufferers who live in the ghettoes and shanty towns of Jamaica describe the music in terms of their own existence, which is basically a rebel existence.... [The] music is expressive of how they 'feel'.[196]

Whereas the echo and reverb evoke a sense of the mystical and the transcendent, it is the weight of the bass that communicates the sacred, rooted in a history of suffering, and the power of the bass that communicates the hope of redemption from a dread situation. Bass will shake the walls of Babylon, shake the profane structures of an unrighteous society, just as the children of Israel chanted down the walls of Jericho with sacred music. Bass is subversive.

Bass, of course, also has a interesting affective impact. Jah Wobble, whose work since the late-1970s with Public Image Ltd has been rooted in dub reggae, has made much of the signification of bass. It is, for example, significant that he named his record label 30 Hertz Records. Although hearing varies from person to person, with numerous factors influencing the range of frequencies that any one individual can detect, generally speaking humans can hear frequencies as low as 20 hertz and as high as 20 kilohertz. However, as we approach these frequency limits our hearing ability gradually fades. Hence, for most people, clear bass sound is limited to around 30 hertz. For example, a piano's bottom note C vibrates at roughly 33 hertz, a frequency very close to the limits of the human hearing range. Beyond this limit lies bass infrasound, which is *felt* rather than heard. This is important, for feeling is very similar to hearing, in that both are ways of detecting sonic vibration. This is why some deaf people, who are more sensitive to changes in vibration frequency, are able to enjoy music. Indeed, research has shown that congenitally deaf people process sound vibrations in the auditory cortex (i.e., the same part of the brain in which hearing people process sound).[197] Moreover, experiments have also shown that exposure to such low frequency infrasonic tones increases the affective impact of the music. Concertgoers report higher emotional states during the times when infrasound was present. This, some have argued, is why pipe organ music, which produces notes as low as 16 hertz, might elicit powerful emotions, which, in affective spaces informed by religious signification, as in a cathedral, are subsequently invested with spiritual significance.[198] In other words, there are good reasons for metaphysical interpretations of bass.[199] It is an invisible force, which has a direct relationship to the embodied self. Fred D'Aguiar, for example, refers to the "head-shaking, spine-twisting" impact of the dub reggae.[200] Likewise, Greg Whitfield speaks of the "primal underpinning" of the bass, a sound which you can "feel in your abdomen, threatening to rearrange and pummel your internal organs."[201] Similarly, Colin McGlashan refers to dub as "music you can *feel*. You feel it in your feet, in the vibrations of a Coke tin . . . you feel it through your partner's body. The first time you hear it, it's unbelievable, unbearable."[202] Again, Lol Bell-Brown of The

Disciples seeks to create bass that "hits your chest. That's where you 'hear' it, rather than with your ears. . . . Your rib cage resonates alarmingly. . . . 'Awesome.'"[203] "The first thing that strikes you in a reggae sound system session," says Julian Henriques, "is the sound itself. The sheer physical force, volume, weight and mass of it. Sonic dominance is hard, extreme and excessive. At the same time the sound is also soft and embracing and it makes for an enveloping, immersive and intense experience. The sound pervades, or even invades the body, like a smell. Sonic dominance is both a near overload of sound and a super saturation of sound. You're lost inside it, submerged under it. . . . Sound at the level cannot but touch you and connect to your body. It's not just heard in the ears, but felt over the entire surface of the skin. The bass line beats on your chest, vibrating the flesh, playing on the bone, and resonating the genitals."[204] When the somatic impact of this unseen energy at dub sound system events is accompanied by layers of echo, a confluence of the familiar with the unfamiliar, religious signifiers, and, usually, the use of marijuana, the experience is not very different from those of a spiritual/mystical nature. Again, this is frequently articulated in the titles of albums and tracks, such as Alpha and Omega's *The Sacred Art of Dub* (1998).

This experience of dub has provided a firm affective foundation on which to build explicitly religious discourses. For example, the work of one of the most important and innovative producers of dub, Lee Perry, is frequently discussed using semimystical or even alchemical or paranormal terminology. Kodwo Eshun is not untypical in this respect: "*Return of the Super Ape* is dub that disturbs the atmosphere until it yields poltergeists. Arriving ahead of cause, sound turns motiveless, premonitional, inexplicable. . . . The wind of Baudelaire's wings of madness sends sound effects careering across living space. . . . The Black Ark studio switches on a technology-magic discontinuum. Operating the mixing desk demand you explore its network of altering spaces. Perry crosses into its ghost dimension, walks through the temporal maze of aural architecture."[205] Perry himself has not discouraged such interpretations. Working at his now famous Black Ark Studio, where he claimed to "lay down the Ten Commandments of reggae,"[206] he constructed a mythology which drew on elements of West African Myalism.[207] Indeed, the Black Ark, now viewed as something of an inner sanctum of dub, has been "symbolically likened by Perry to the Ark of the Covenant."[208] Again, amidst rumours that he was involved in Obeah (popularly understood within Myalism as sorcery), he referred to himself as "the Ghost Captain,"[209] and frequently spoke of dub in terms of an esoteric art, which exposed and infiltrated the spiritual world, all of which has significantly contributed to its mythology as an occult energy. However, this interpretation of dub has been articulated perhaps most conspicuously and enthusiastically by Bill Laswell in a number collaborations with a broad range of musicians from around the globe: *Divination: Ambient Dub, Vol. I* (Subharmonic, 1993); *Divination: Dead Slow—Ambient Dub, Vol. II* (1993); *Divination: Akasha* (1995); *Divination: Distill* (1996); *Divination: Sacrifice* (1998); *Sacred System: Chapter 1—Book of Entrance*

(ROIR, 1996); *Sacred System:Chapter 2* (ROIR, 1997); *Dub Chamber 3* (ROIR, 2000); *Sacred System: Dub Chamber 4—Book of Exit* (ROIR, 2002); *Sacred System: Nagual Site* (Wicklow/BMG, 1998); *Silent Recoil: Dub System One* (1995); *Axiom Dub: Mysteries of Creation* (Axiom, 1996); *Radioaxiom: A Dub Transmission* (Palm Pictures, 2001).[210] Hence, unsurprisingly, dub has itself become an interesting occultural signifier in the countercultural imaginary. For example, William Gibson's classic, genre-defining "cyberpunk" novel *Neuromancer* (1984), in referencing "the bass-heavy rocksteady of Zion dub,"[211] indicates the genre's significance as a symbol of the sacred: "As they worked, Case gradually became aware of the music that pulsed constantly through the cluster. It was called dub, a sensuous mosaic cooked from the vast libraries of digitized pop; it was worship, Molly said, and a sense of community. . . . Zion smelled of cooked vegetables, humanity, and ganga."[212]

Religion and the transfiguration of popular musicians

"We all know who the fans are. They're the ones who wear the colours of their favourite team, the ones who record their soap operas . . . to watch after the work day is over, the ones who tell you every detail about a movie star's life and work, the ones who sit in line for hours for front row tickets to rock concerts. Fans are, in fact, the most visible and identifiable of audiences."[213] Fans are also commonly associated with superficial and irrational responses to popular culture and, as such, can be identified with the least critical and self-reflective of audiences. However, such assessments are, in themselves, guilty of superficiality, in that fandom identifies a significant set of human behaviours relating to what we have seen Grossberg refer to as "maps of mattering." Indeed, at some level, we are all fans of something or someone. To be a fan is to identify with that which matters to us. As the theologian Karl Barth wrote of Mozart, although "I am not a musician or a musicologist . . . I can—indeed I must—testify to my devotion to Mozart . . . [who] has become more and more of a constant in my life."[214] He even opined that "the invention of the phonograph . . . can never be praised enough", for it allowed him to begin "each day with Mozart." He even confesses that "if I ever get to heaven, I would first of all seek out Mozart. . ."[215] Again, such sentiments are far from unusual. As Grossberg points out, "everyone is constantly a fan of various sorts of things, for one cannot exist in a world where nothing matters." In fact, as he goes on to argue (and as Barth's comments confirm), "what we today refer to as a 'fan' is the contemporary articulation of a necessary relationship which has historically constituted the popular, involving relationships to such diverse things as labor, religion, morality and politics. Thus, there is no reason why the fan relationship is located primarily on the terrain of commercial popular culture."[216] Certainly, I would argue that we might think of explicitly religious behaviours in these terms, such as the veneration of particular saints. That said, as Grossberg goes on to argue, for many people in advanced capitalist societies, popular culture "is increasingly the only space where the fan relationship can take shape."[217] More specifically, because it is within consumer culture that many of us construct meaning, it is here that individuals become sanctified and idolized as foci of devotion; it is here that we create affective spaces within which we are touched so profoundly that, in some small or significant sense, the products of popular culture become centers of affective gravity in our lives. They *matter* to us and, because they do, they become fetishized. We can be moved by the Orphic power of their art to such an extent that the encounter becomes invested with a particular significance for which religious language seems peculiarly appropriate. In opening his heart to his fans, "Saint Morrissey," as Mark Simpson reverentially refers to him,[218] engages in an act of redemption, identifying with their private sufferings and disappointments. Consequently, as Eoin Devereux discusses, "Morrissey is variously deified, canonized or cast in the role of preacher."[219] Again, as one not untypical fan of the Grateful Dead commented, their music might easily have been described as "alternate reality rock," or "transcendental rock," in that "it wasn't earth music, but a search for a spiritual/alchemical transfiguration."[220] Likewise, one respondent to a survey on rave culture, who is, again, not untypical, stated the following: rave events "make me feel like being in tune with the eternal cosmic pulsation. For me it is a kind of spiritual experience to be in a rave."[221] Similarly, a psytrance DJ at Goa argued that "the Goa party is a shamanic journey. . . . It starts about 1 a.m. and the majority of people have taken acid and they're treating it as a journey. You're surrendering to a drug and to musical stimulation. . . . In the context of Indian mythology, we are dancing the dance of Shiva. This is the symbolic dance of creation, destruction and rebirth. Shiva's dance is the synthesis of all life experience and an image of all-pervading energy."[222] Likewise, James Munro of Technossomy has spoken of being exposed "to religion" and of having an epiphany about how people "can be happy without materialism. The ambitions I had when I was earning shitloads of money just went."[223] Again, it is hardly surprising, therefore, that some psytrance DJs, such as Goa Gil, have been described in elevated terms traditionally reserved for religious figures.[224] However, the point here is that, while such responses are not unusual, in that popular music, like religion,[225] is centrally concerned with the Orphic manipulation of emotion, for a few people the emotional intensity appears to become so focused that their fandom is transformed into a level of fetishistic devotion and their behaviors begin to resemble those within religious communities. It is not simply that the music provides a context within which profound experiences are encouraged—although it does do that, as in the case of raves or Grateful Dead concerts—but that the medium becomes the message in a very particular sense. Hence, for example, it is not unusual for objects/memorabilia related to the mediated persona to acquire a magical significance.

For some fans there appears to be a confusion of categories that leads to a "transfiguration of the commonplace"—to use the art critic Arthur Danto's evocative phrase.[226] Although, of course, Danto was not interested in culture *as* religion, artist *as* icon, memorabilia *as* fetish in the senses discussed here, nevertheless, his understanding of "art"—informed by a particular cultural context/"artworld"—evoking and embodying meaning, provides a useful starting point. The ostensibly everyday is, within certain contexts, transfigured, invested with particular meaning. A musician, such as Elvis, might move from simply being an entertainer to a very special individual who matters in a significant sense and, finally, to a sacralized icon. As such, that which is related to him acquires a fetishistic significance—"like all pilgrims, visitors to Graceland want to take away a piece of the holy land. It is possible to buy little glass bottles with a coin in 'from Graceland' and grains of soil, encased in glass and reminiscent of the talismans bought by pilgrims at medieval European shrines."[227] Fetishized celebrities become conductors of sacred meaning and anything related to them, anything that has been touched by their presence in some way, is sacralized, in that it is perceived to provide a link to them.[228] Again, metaphorical identification (e.g., "Elvis is king") becomes, through a process of transfiguration, "religious" identification (e.g., Elvis as saint): "he prays for us in heaven."[229] As one Elvis devotee put it, "there is a distance between human beings and God. That is why we are close to Elvis. He is like a bridge between God and us. . . . I believe in Jesus Christ and I believe in God . . . but Elvis was special. Elvis was . . . given to us to remind us to be good . . . "[230] Hence, although, typically, like many of their contemporaries in the late modern Western world, devotees resist the idea that their behavior is "religious"—perhaps because of a sensitivity to the notion of "religion" in what they perceive to be a secular culture or perhaps because of a sensitivity to the notion of "idolatry" within a Christian culture—nevertheless, in their veneration of a particular celebrity, they provide constructions of the sacred not very different from those in religion. The commonplace becomes impregnated with the solemn, the serious, the sublime, and the sacred.[231] Hence, it is not entirely surprising to read accounts such as that of Gregory Reece, who, in the summer of 1991, found himself, in the early hours of the morning, sitting in a hospital emergency room in Memphis, Tennessee. On the chair next to him was a woman who had been crying.

> Her mother had suffered a stroke and she was waiting to hear from the doctors. This was especially difficult, she said, because she had no family in Memphis. A few years before, she had divorced her husband, said goodbye to her children, packed up her mother, and moved from southern California to Memphis, Tennessee. She moved, she said, "just to be with Elvis." It was then that I noticed that the ring on her left hand, as well as her earrings and necklace, were adorned with images of Elvis. Elvis, she told me, was the most important thing in the world to her. He gave her inspiration and hope. The one good thing about the passing away of her mother was that her mother would then get to go to heaven to be with Elvis.[232]

Pilgrimages, shrines, mythologies, conspiracy theories, religious art and iconography testify to the significance of the transfiguration of celebrities, which, like that of saints, orders the lives and shapes the identities of individuals, providing sacred forms around which the everyday is oriented.

Few things guarantee success more effectively in the personality cult business than death. As Chris Rojek notes, "the pilgrims who flock to Graceland . . . do not so much honour a dead god as proclaim the presence of a living secular one . . ."[233] Although, of course, individuals can be transfigured in this life—as in the case of Mao Zedong[234] and, to a lesser extent, the Indian film actor Amitabh Bachchan ("the Big B")—when they eventually ascend from the earthly plane into the neverland of hagiographic immortality, transcending the mundane existences that we everyday mortals inhabit, the process of transfiguration is made complete. Death leads to resurrection and ultimately to deification. Once icons whom are invested with some level of sacred significance die, once they are no longer bound by embodied life, no longer subject to the flaws and limitations of human existence, then their lives can be mythologized. Then they are made perfect. Because they once experienced the vicissitudes of human existence, the joy, the pain, the grief, the blessings, and the temptations, the process of transfiguration transforms them into sympathetic saints who can understand the lives of fans and intercede for them. Again, the transfiguration of Elvis is a good example of this, in that he was transformed from a bloated, paranoid drug addict who died in less than seraphic circumstances into the glorious and blessed "Dead Elvis," the Christian avatar, the American saint, the prophet who walked among us for a while—"then he was not, for God took him" (Genesis 5:24). As Lucinda Ebersole comments, "the postmodern myth of Elvis presents us with a god. He is a misunderstood, but benevolent creature. He attracts disciples who believe he can do no wrong, imitators who replicate his gesture and dress, followers who make pilgrimages to the Mecca that is Graceland." More particularly, "he offers a path to righteousness, a cure for those who are sick, and according to many, a transcendence of death. He exists in the present. His life offers the elements from which the gods of mythology are made."[235]

There is also a sense in which the memorialization of death, as Ian Reader comments, draws individuals "out of their ordinary routines into acts of a religious nature."[236] This is particularly the case during pilgrimage, when an individual makes a journey away from the everyday, initiated by an emotional and focused response to a deceased icon. During the process of leaving the profane and the quotidian, an individual's identity becomes bound up with that of the saint, who is, in turn, increasingly elevated and venerated. Again, during Elvis Presley International Tribute Week, "fans from all over the world . . . travel, like pilgrims everywhere, singly or in groups, in a spirit of devotion."[237] "I am dedicated to the man," said one fan.[238] Here, at Graceland, away from everyday life, away from the mundane and the profane, all that matters is one's affective embrace of Elvis, supported by the collective veneration of a verifying community of believers/pilgrims.

Similarly, "the *espace* Morrison," the area surrounding Jim Morrison's grave in Père Lachaise Cemetery, Paris, has become a *locus sanctus*, a pilgrimage site for devotees, some of whom believe that they can, in some sense, still communicate with him. Although the lead singer of The Doors was, as Danny Sugarman comments, "well on his way to becoming a mythic hero while he was still alive,"[239] it was in death that he was transfigured. As we saw in Chapter 3, in pursuing a path of transgression, musicians such as Morrison became Dionysian and Orphic icons of the counterculture in standing against the dictatorship of "social facts." That is to say, in standing against the flow of social facts, he resisted the alienating, disenfranchising, and othering hegemonies of modern Western culture. He became an Athanasius *contra mundum*, one who stood against the world, against social forces in the service of "the sacred self"—freedom, autonomy, self-determination. From the outset, we have noted, he made his position conspicuous: "There are no rules, there are no limits."[240] "I've always been attracted to ideas that were about revolt against authority. When you make your peace with authority, you become an authority. I like ideas about the breaking away or overthrowing of established order. It seems to be the road toward freedom."[241] Society, however, as many in the counterculture found, can be ruthless in its protection of social facts—sacred forms. Their profanation must be resisted and transgressors must be demonized and punished.[242] Consequently, we have seen that he became a messianic figure for the disenfranchised, liminal beings of the counterculture. Indeed, Sugarman is himself a believer: "Morrison changed my life." He even goes so far as to claim that, in some sense, "Jim Morrison was a god." Of course, he recognizes that, to many people, this "may sound extravagant; to others, at least eccentric." Nevertheless, "I just wanted to say that Jim Morrison was a modern-day god. . . . There will never be another one like him."[243] Such popular veneration surrounding Morrison increased significantly in the 1990s following the release of *The Doors*, a film directed by another of Morrison's devotees, Oliver Stone.[244] Of course, the film is itself effectively a countercultural hagiography in which Morrison is beatified by Stone. As Margry comments, "the film opens significantly with a mystical representation, set to music, of how Morrison took on [shamanic] qualities as a small child by means of 'spiritual transmission' from a dying Native American in the New Mexico desert. With references made in passing to the secularization . . . of American society, the film continues with the words 'the ceremony is now to begin'. . . . His interest in the occult and his shamanistic trances and performances during concerts are shown at length." Margry's point, supported by some interesting ethnographic research, is that the film has contributed to the construction of Morrison as "someone with supernatural or transcendent qualities."[245] Likewise, Joel Brodsky's iconic "Young Lion" series of photographs, the most arresting of which was used for the cover of *The Best of the* Doors (1985),[246] has had a significant impact on Morrison's transfiguration. As Margry found, "not only did fans see him as someone divine, but for many fans these photos functioned as images of the human ideal."[247]

The point is that, in the process of transfiguration, celebrities themselves become the objects of devotion, rather than simply conduits or interpreters of sacred meaning—although, of course, they are that too. They themselves become symbols of the sacred, foci of sacred forms relating to, for example, love or freedom. As such, they become drawn into established discourses about the sacred, into unified systems of belief and behavior relative to the sacred,[248] as formally articulated within "religious" traditions. For example, the Dionysian construction of Jim Morrison becomes imbricated with discourses within Native North American shamanism and the occult, and Elvis fans, some of whom, claim to have had visions of him,[249] locate him within the dominant religious discourses of Christianity. They "mix their Elvis badges with their crucifixes" and "talk of him in religious terms, saying that he is 'safe with Jesus,' 'he prays for us in heaven.'"[250] For some, he functions "as a religious guide leading them to Jesus," helping them "to live their lives as they walk in his steps." For others, he performs "miracles at his shrine."[251]

Finally, this confluence of discourses has not escaped the interest of artists who have, wittingly or unwittingly, often functioned as iconographers, merging the traditionally religious with transfigured celebrities. Paintings such as Alexander Guy's *Crucifixion* (1992), Rena LaCaria's *Elvis the King* (1989), Carol Robinson's *Crying Icons* (1992), Joanne Stephens' *Homage to Elvis* (1991), and Bill Barminski's *Elvis Christ* (1988), are good examples of the visual articulation of celebrity transfiguration.[252]

Concluding comment

Throughout this volume we have explored the relationship between popular music, the sacred, and the profane. While in previous chapters the focus has been on the analysis of popular music's engagement with and construction of the sacred and the profane, in this chapter the focus has been on "religion." That is to say, the discussion has concentrated specifically on the ways in which religious discourses have articulated a relationship with popular music as sacred and profane. Bearing in mind that, on the one hand, religion is, following Durkheim, "a unified system of beliefs and practices relative to sacred things, that is to say, things set apart and surrounded by prohibitions,"[253] and that, on the other hand, much of the vitality of popular music, much of its Romantic power, is rooted in boundary-crossing discourses and the construction of identity around transgression, it is unsurprising that the two have spent a lot of time gazing at each other. There is a mutual fascination and repulsion. Certainly, as far as popular music is concerned, because contemporary sacred forms have a religious past and, as such, are often directly associated with contemporary faith traditions and communities, which play a part in their maintenance, "religion" continues to be a focus for its transgressive cultural work. As far as religion is concerned, because popular music is often explicitly transgressive and iconoclastic, it is perceived as a particularly profane threat to hegemonic sacred forms. This concern, we have seen, is not new. As Sir John Herschel commented in 1839, "music and dancing (more's the pity) have become so closely associated with ideas of riot and debauchery among the less cultivated classes, that a taste for them, for their own sakes, can hardly be said to exist, and before they can be recommended as innocent or safe amusements, a very great change of ideas must take place."[254] Of course, such concerns were also influentially articulated by Matthew Arnold and the culture and civilization tradition. However, the point is that, historically, this demonization has meant that popular music has always tended to be part of a rejected culture, the culture of "the less cultivated classes," of the low and the profane. It is from within that rejected cultural space that it has constructed itself as profane, that it has drawn on the rejected discourses of occulture, that it has risen up as a challenge to hegemonic sacred forms, as an influential counterculture within liminal lifeworlds.

This last point is an important one. The elitist demonization of popular music has led to the carving out of a cultural space, "a profane space," within which the rejected ideas of occulture and counter-hegemonic discourses have flourished. This, for example, helps to explain why, as we have seen, there is a problem for those within hegemonic religion who still enjoy popular music. How can those subscribing to "a unified system of beliefs and practices relative to sacred things,"[255] to a culture sensitive to the profanation of sacred forms, cultivate a relationship with the rejected discourses of popular music? There have been two principal religious responses to this question: (a) the negative demonization of popular music as a profane threat to the sacred and (b) the conversion of popular music from the profane to the sacred. The first, we have seen, is a crude, but straightforward solution. The second is a little less straightforward and a little more problematic. In its attempts to maintain an affective presence in both worlds, it has failed to understand that the sacred–profane polarity cannot easily be subverted. While there are, of course, degrees of success, there is always dissonance. Nevertheless, while contemporary Christian music will always be primarily *Christian* music *for Christians* with little appeal to those beyond the Christian community, in that it is simply unable to establish a credible presence in profane affective space, it has proved pastorally useful, in that it provides subcultural capital for Christians *within* Christianity. It is "cool" music for those adhering to hegemonic sacred discourses. It provides mild transgressive appeal, whilst concurrently supporting core sacred forms. In other words, it creates space for a mediated level of liminality *within* Christian culture. As such, it alleviates the symptoms of withdrawal from profane culture by providing a substitute that sounds the same, but resists the profane. That is to say, without embracing transgression, Christian bands and Christian music festivals seek to replicate as closely as possible the affective spaces created by profane culture. Body piercing, long hair, shaved heads, mohawk/mohican hairstyles, goth dress, tattoos and all the key signifiers of profane subcultures are allowed within the bounded area of the sacred. As such, contemporary Christian music culture nurtures and protects the "saved" from profanation by providing a sacred sweetener for those who crave profane sugar. As such, like religion itself, it supports core sacred forms within society.

For those who still enjoy some sugar, we have seen that, increasingly, religious leaders who share their sweet tooth, encourage a theological reading of popular music. This correlationist methodology encourages listeners to convert popular music texts into questions about the sacred, which can then be answered with reference to the dominant ideas within religion. Popular music is read through a biblical lens, as a "hymnal,"[256] the effect of which is to filter out profane influence: "I pray that as you listen anew to [popular music] . . . that you would find blessing in the songs themselves, the singers and the songwriters, and trust yourself as readers and listeners to find new ways to find faith, hope and love."[257] The blessing, in other words, is realised through the inhibiting of popular music's transgressive impact and the reinforcing of core sacred forms.

The overall point, however, is that by employing the resources of cultural sociology we can better understand the contested relationships between religion and popular music. We can begin to understand why contemporary Christian music, unlike contemporary Rastafarian music, will always fail to appeal to listeners beyond a particular religious community and why popular music will always be a threat to some religious institutions. As to why there is little, if any, dissonance between some forms of religion and popular music, we have seen that this is the case when "religion" is itself transgressive and resistant to hegemonic sacred forms. That is to say, certain religious discourses are able to accrue subcultural capital within the minds of liminal personae because they are, in some respect, transgressive. While this is all but impossible for conservative constructions of Christianity, it is not the case for Rastafarianism, Spiritism, Satanism, and Easternized self-spirituality, which are perceived to be fundamentally counterhegemonic and subversively profane in Western societies. They are also, of course, as rejected discourses, shaped by the self-oriented, deference-resistant occultures of the late-modern West.

NOTES

Introduction

1. E.T.A. Hoffmann, "Kreisleriana," in *E.T.A. Hoffmann's Musical Writings: Kreisleriana, The Poet and the Composer, Music Criticism,* ed. David Charlton (Cambridge: Cambridge University Press, 1989), 96. Note: the actual translation is as follows: "Orpheus's lyre opened the gates of Orcus"—Orcus, like Hades, is the name of both a deity and the underworld.
2. E.T.A. Hoffmann, "Kreisleriana," 96.
3. Salomon Reinach, *Orpheus: A History of Religions,* trans. Florence Simmonds (London: George Routledge & Sons, 1931), v.
4. See D.P. Walker, "Orpheus the Theologian and Renaissance Platonists," *Journal of the Warburg and Courtauld Institutes* 16 (1953): 100–120.
5. See Fritz Graf and Sarah Johnston, *Ritual Texts for the Afterlife: Orpheus and the Bacchic Gold Tablets* (Abingdon: Routledge, 2007), 165–184.
6. Oliver Sacks, *Musicophilia: Tales of Music and the Brain* (London: Picador, 2008), ix–x.
7. Scott Wilson, *Great Satan's Rage: American Negativity and Rap/Metal in the Age of Supercapitalism* (Manchester: Manchester University Press, 2008), 7. See also Tia DeNora, *Music in Everyday Life* (Cambridge: Cambridge University Press, 2000) and Jeanette Bicknell, *Why Music Moves Us* (London: Palgrave Macmillan, 2009).
8. Vanessa Agnew, *Enlightenment Orpheus: The Power of Music in Other Worlds* (New York: Oxford University Press, 2008), 9.
9. Agnew, *Enlightenment Orpheus,* 9.
10. Agnew, *Enlightenment Orpheus,* 9.
11. Agnew, *Enlightenment Orpheus,* 9.
12. Agnew, *Enlightenment Orpheus,* 10.
13. We will see that "despite the theological chasms between different groups' belief systems and practices . . . a person from one culture and religious background can be deeply moved by devotional or ritual music from a vastly different culture and religious system." Jean During, "Therapeutic Dimensions of Music in Islamic Culture," in *The Oxford Handbook of Medical Ethnomusicology,* ed. Benjamin D. Koen (New York: Oxford University Press, 2008), 375. See also, Frank Burch Brown, "Music," in *The Oxford Handbook of Religion and Emotion,* ed. John Corrigan (Oxford: Oxford University Press, 2008), 200.
14. Although I use the term slightly differently, I am indebted to Clive Marsh for introducing me to it in his Fernley-Hartley Lecture, delivered at the University of Leicester: "Adventures in Affective Space: The Reconstruction of Piety in an Age of Entertainment" (May 7, 2010).
15. Chris Jenks, *Transgression* (London: Routledge, 2003), 178–180.

16. See Christian Smith, ed., *The Secular Revolution: Power Interests and Conflict in the Secularization of American Public Life* (Berkeley: University of California Press, 2003).

17. Émile Durkheim, *The Elementary Forms of Religious Life*, trans. Carol Cosman (Oxford: Oxford University Press, 2001), 46.

18. Gordon Lynch, *The Sacred in the Modern World: A Cultural Sociological Approach* (Oxford: Oxford University Press, 2012), 29.

19. See Jeffrey Alexander's discussion of the historical contingency of sacred forms in his analysis of shifting perceptions of the Holocaust: *The Meanings of Social Life: A Cultural Sociology* (New York: Oxford University Press, 2003), 27–84.

20. Mary Douglas, *Purity and Danger: An Analysis of the Concept of Pollution and Taboo* (London: Routledge, 2002 [1966]), 9.

21. On faith, hope and love in popular music, see Jeff Keuss's theological discussion, *Your Neighbor's Hymnal: What Popular Music Teaches Us About Faith, Hope, and Love* (Eugene: Cascade Books, 2011).

22. There have been numerous thoughtful studies of popular music and gender. See, for example, Lori Burns and Mélisse Lafrance, *Disruptive Divas: Feminism, Identity and Popular Music* (New York: Routledge, 2002); Marion Leonard, *Gender in the Music Industry: Rock, Discourse and Girl Power* (Aldershot: Ashgate, 2007); Helen Reddington, *The Lost Women of Rock Music: Female Musicians of the Punk Era* (Sheffield: Equinox, 2012); and Sheila Whiteley, ed., *Sexing the Groove: Popular Music and Gender* (London: Routledge, 1997).

23. See jan jagodzinski, *Music in Youth Culture: A Lacanian Approach* (New York: Palgrave Macmillan, 2005).

24. Chris Jenks, *Transgression* (London: Routledge, 2003), 15.

25. Jim Morrison, quoted in Jerry Hopkins and Danny Sugarman, *No One Here Gets Out Alive* (London: Plexus, 1980), 232.

26. Jim Morrison, quoted in James Riordan and Jerry Prochnicky, *Break on Through: The Life and Death of Jim Morrison* (London: Plexus, 1991), 373.

27. Marc Almond, *Tainted Life: The Autobiography* (London: Sidgwick & Jackson, 1999), 59.

28. Lady Gaga, "Amen Fashion," http://amenfashion.tumblr.com/ (accessed December 02, 2012).

29. Christopher Partridge, *The Re-Enchantment of the West: Alternative Spiritualities, Sacralization, Popular Culture and Occulture*. 2 vols. (London: T&T Clark International, 2004, 2005).

30. Colin Campbell, "The Cult, the Cultic Milieu and Secularization," in *Sociological Yearbook of Religion in Britain 5*, ed. Michael Hill (London: SCM Press, 1972), 119–136.

31. See Christopher Partridge, *The Re-Enchantment of the West: Alternative Spiritualities, Sacralization, Popular Culture and Occulture*, 2 vols. (London: T&T Clark International, 2004, 2005).

32. Peter Berger, *The Sacred Canopy: Elements of a Sociological Theory of Religion* (New York: Anchor Books, 1967).

33. Alan Gilbert, *The Making of Post-Christian Britain: A History of the Secularization of Modern Society* (London: Longman, 1980), 19.

34. Karen Jolly, *Popular Religion in Late Saxon England: Elf Charms in Context* (Chapel Hill: University of North Carolina Press, 1996), 170–171.

35. Keith Thomas, *Religion and the Decline of Magic: Studies in Popular Beliefs in Sixteenth and Seventeenth Century England* (Harmondsworth: Penguin, 1973), 28. See also Ronald Hutton's *The Stations of the Sun: A History of the Ritual Year in Britain* (Oxford: Oxford University Press, 1996), and *The Rise and Fall of Merry England: The Ritual Year, 1400–1700* (Oxford: Oxford University Press, 1994).

36. See Stephen Clucas, ed., *John Dee: Interdisciplinary Studies in English Renaissance Thought*. International Archives of the History of Ideas 193 (Dordrecht: Springer, 2006); Francis Yates, *The Occult Philosophy in the Elizabethan Age* (London: Ark 1983).

37. Brian Gibbons, *Spirituality and the Occult: From the Renaissance to the Modern Age* (London: Routledge, 2001).

38. Roy Porter, "Witchcraft and Magic in Enlightenment, Romantic and Liberal Thought," in *Witchcraft and Magic in Europe: The Eighteenth and Nineteenth Centuries*, eds. Bengt Ankarloo and Stuart Clark (Philadelphia: University of Pennsylvania Press 1999), 249–250.
39. Dorothy Scarborough, quoted in Srdjan Smajić, *Ghost-Seers, Detectives, and Spiritualists: Theories of Vision in Victorian Literature and Science* (New York: Oxford University Press, 2010), 13.
40. Jürgen Habermas, *The Theory of Communicative Action: A Critique of Functionalist Reason*, trans. T. McCarthy, vol. 2 (London: Polity Press, 1987), 113–198.

Chapter 1

1. Andy Bennett, Barry Shank, and Jason Toynbee, "Introduction," in *The Popular Music Studies Reader*, eds. Andy Bennett, Barry Shank, and Jason Toynbee (London: Routledge, 2006), 5.
2. Raymond Williams, *Television: Technology and Cultural Form* (London: Routledge, 1990).
3. Andy Bennett, *Cultures of Popular Music* (Buckingham: Open University Press, 2001), 1. See also Tia DeNora, *Music in Everyday Life* (Cambridge: Cambridge University Press, 2000).
4. See, for example: Andy Bennett and Donna Weston, eds., *Pop Pagans: Paganism and Popular Music* (London: Equinox, 2012); Michael J. Gilmour, ed., *Call Me the Seeker: Listening to Religion in Popular Music* (London: Continuum, 2005); Lydia Guzy, ed., *Religion and Music: Proceedings of the Interdisciplinary Workshop at the Institute for Scientific Studies of Religions, Freie Universität Berlin, May 2006* (Berlin: Weißensee Verlag, 2008); Gavin Hopps, *Morrissey: The Pageant of His Bleeding Heart* (London: Continuum, 2009); Christopher Partridge, *Dub in Babylon: Understanding the Evolution and Significance of Dub Reggae in Jamaica and Britain from King Tubby to Post-punk* (London: Equinox, 2010); Christopher Partridge, ed., *Anthems of Apocalypse: Popular Music and Apocalyptic Thought* (Sheffield: Phoenix Press, 2012); Graham St. John, ed., *Rave Culture and Religion* (London: Routledge, 2004); David W. Stowe, *No Sympathy for the Devil: Christian Pop Music and the Transformation of American Evangelicalism* (Chapel Hill: University of North Carolina Press, 2011); Rupert Till, *Pop Cult: Religion and Popular Music* (London: Continuum, 2010).
5. See, for example, Kelton Cobb, *The Blackwell Guide to Theology and Popular Culture* (Oxford: Blackwell, 2005); Stewart M. Hoover, *Religion in the Media Age* (London: Routledge, 2006); Gordon Lynch, *Understanding Theology and Popular Culture* (Oxford: Blackwell, 2005); Gordon Lynch, ed., *Between Sacred and Profane: Researching Religion and Popular Culture* (London: I.B. Tauris, 2007); Gordon Lynch and Jolyon Mitchell, eds., *Religion, Media and Culture: A Reader* (London: Routledge, 2011).
6. Raymond Williams, *Keywords: A Vocabulary of Culture and Society* (London: Fontana, 1988), 87.
7. Williams, Keywords, 90. See also Raymond Williams, *The Long Revolution* (Harmondsworth: Penguin, 1965), 57–58.
8. Williams, *Keywords*, 90.
9. See John Fiske, *Understanding Popular Culture* (London: Routledge, 1989).
10. Williams, *Keywords*, 236 (emphasis added).
11. Bruce Forbes and Jeffrey Mahan, "Introduction: Finding Religion in Unexpected Places," in *Religion and Popular Culture in America*, eds. Bruce Forbes and Jeffrey Mahan (Berkeley: University of California Press, 2000), 3.
12. Williams, *Keywords*, 237.
13. Alan Lomax, *Folk Song Style and Culture* (Washington, DC: American Association for the Advancement of Science, 1968), 3.
14. John Storey, *Inventing Popular Culture: From Folklore to Globalization* (Oxford: Blackwell, 2003), 1. See also Anahid Kassabian, "Popular," in *Key Terms in Popular Music and Culture*, eds. Bruce Horner and Thomas Swiss (Oxford: Blackwell, 1999), 116.
15. Nicholas Goodrick-Clarke, *The Occult Roots of Nazism* (New York: New York University Press, 1992), 3.

16. Goodrick-Clarke, *Occult Roots of Nazism*, 3.
17. See David Welch, *The Third Reich: Politics and Propaganda*, 2nd ed. (London: Routledge, 2002), 82–107.
18. Storey, *Inventing Popular Culture*, 3.
19. Storey, *Inventing Popular Culture*, 3.
20. William Motherwell, *Minstrelsy, Ancient and Modern*, vol. 1 (Boston: William D. Ticknor & Co., 1846), 12.
21. The term was coined by Edward Burnett Tyler in his influential *Primitive Culture*, vol. 1 (London: John Murray, 1871).
22. See Richard Hoggart, *The Uses of Literacy* (New Brunswick: Transaction Publishers, 1998), 9.
23. See F.R. Leavis, *A Common Pursuit* (New York: New York University Press, 1964), 189–190.
24. See Maud Karpeles, *Cecil Sharp: His Life and Work* (London: Routledge & Kegan Paul, 1967).
25. Cecil Sharp, *English Folk Song: Some Conclusions* (London: Simpkin & Co., 1907), 34.
26. Sharp, *English Folk Song*, 134.
27. Sharp, *English Folk Song*, 134–135.
28. See John Francmanis, "National Music to National Redeemer: The Consolidation of a 'Folk-song' construct in Edwardian England," *Popular Music* 21 (2002): 1–25.
29. Leavis, *Common Pursuit*, 190.
30. See Jeanette Leech, *Seasons They Change: The Story of Acid and Psychedelic Folk* (London: Jawbone Press, 2010).
31. See Julian Cope, *The Modern Antiquarian: A Pre-Millennial Odyssey Through Megalithic Britain* (London: Thorsons, 1998); Adrian Whittaker, ed., *Be Glad: An Incredible String Band Compendium* (London: Helter Skelter Publishing, 2003); Rob Young, *Electric Eden: Unearthing Britain's Visionary Music* (London: Faber & Faber, 2010).
32. Derek B. Scott, *Musical Style and Social Meaning: Selected Essays* (Farnham: Ashgate, 2010), 205–206.
33. Philip Tagg, "Analysing Popular Music: Theory, Method and Practice," *Popular Music* 2 (1982): 4.
34. Donald Clarke, *The Rise and Fall of Popular Music* (Harmondsworth: Penguin, 1995), 451. See also John Szwed, *Alan Lomax: The Man Who Recorded the World* (London: Arrow Books, 2011), 258–280.
35. See Michael Brocken, *The British Folk Revival, 1944–2002* (Aldershot: Ashgate, 2003), 25–42.
36. Sharp, *English Folk Song*, 1–5.
37. See Brocken, *British Folk Revival*; Leech, *Seasons They Change*.
38. Richard Middleton, *Studying Popular Music* (Milton Keynes: Open University Press, 1990), 128.
39. Middleton, *Studying Popular Music*, 128.
40. See Julian Johnson, *Who Needs Classical Music? Cultural Choice and Musical Value* (New York: Oxford University Press, 2002), 5–6, 112–113.
41. Johnson, *Who Needs Classical Music?*, 130.
42. Johnson, *Who Needs Classical Music?*, 130.
43. Johnson, *Who Needs Classical Music?*, 75.
44. Quoted in Theodore Gracyk, *Listening to Popular Music: Or, How I Learned to Stop Worrying and Love Led Zeppelin* (Ann Arbor: University of Michigan Press, 2007), 24–25. See Richard Shusterman, *Pragmatist Aesthetics: Living Beauty, Rethinking Art* (Oxford: Blackwell, 1992), 200.
45. Pierre Bourdieu, *Distinction: A Social Critique of the Judgement of Taste* (Cambridge: Harvard University Press, 1984), 56.
46. Johnson, *Who Needs Classical Music?*, 114.
47. Johnson, *Who Needs Classical Music?*, 114.
48. Gracyk, *Listening to Popular Music*, 27.

49. Johnson, *Who Needs Classical Music?*, 75.

50. Louise Jury, "Pavarotti Makes His First Pop Album After Agonising Year of Bereavements," *The Independent*, October 7, 2003, accessed August 22, 2011, http://www.independent.co.uk/arts-entertainment/music/news/pavarotti-makes-his-first-pop-album-after-agonising-year-of-bereavements-582533.html.

51. "Miss Sarajevo," by U2 and Brian Eno, is taken from the November 1995 album *Original Soundtracks 1* by Passengers (U2 and Brian Eno).

52. Immanuel Kant, *Critique of Judgement*, trans. J.H. Bernard (New York: Hafner Press, 1951), 37.

53. Herman Parett, "Kant on Music and the Hierarchy of the Arts," *Journal of Aesthetics and Art Criticism* 56 (1998): 251.

54. Quoted in Parett, "Kant on Music," 251.

55. Quoted in Parett, "Kant on Music," 251.

56. Johnson, *Who Needs Classical Music?*, 39.

57. Bourdieu, *Distinction*, 30. Cf. 486–487.

58. See Richard Roberts' overview of the depiction of the body in the West: "Body," in *The Blackwell Companion to the Study of Religion*, ed. Robert A. Segal (Oxford: Blackwell, 2006), 216–221.

59. Kant, *Critique of Judgement*, 47.

60. Kant, *Critique of Judgement*, 47.

61. See Paul Crowther, *Defining Art, Creating a Canon: Artistic Value in an Era of Doubt* (Oxford: Oxford University Press, 2007), 2, 79.

62. "Art-works . . . project a content that self-evidently slices through time, transcends its power over the material, and strikes us with a force with a force that vivifies our present experience with a unique intensity. In doing so, art exerts a powerful symbolic force: it redeems what is past by bringing it into a living relationship with the present." Johnson, *Who Needs Classical Music?*, 95.

63. John Storey, *An Introduction to Cultural Theory and Popular Culture*, 2nd ed. (London: Prentice Hall, 1997), 196.

64. Bourdieu, *Distinction*, 6.

65. Bourdieu, *Distinction*, 66.

66. Williams, *Keywords*, 236.

67. Raymond Williams, *Culture and Society, 1780–1950* (New York: Anchor Books, 1960).

68. Williams, *Culture and Society*, xv.

69. Williams, *Culture and Society*, xiv.

70. See Terence Copley, *Black Tom. Arnold of Rugby: The Myth and the Man* (London: Continuum, 2002). It is perhaps also significant that he was the godson of John Keble, one of the leaders of the Tractarian/Oxford Movement.

71. At some point during his adolescence, for apparently ethical reasons, Arnold abandoned Christianity in favor of agnosticism. This led to complex relationships with those closest to him, notably his liberal Christian father and, particularly, the religious conservative John Henry Newman, whom he greatly admired.

72. Matthew Arnold, *Culture and Anarchy* (Cambridge: Cambridge University Press, 1971), 70.

73. Arnold, *Culture and Anarchy*, 34.

74. Arnold, *Culture and Anarchy*, 46.

75. Arnold, *Culture and Anarchy*, 163.

76. Matthew Arnold, *Culture and Anarchy* (Cambridge: Cambridge University Press, 1971), 163–64, 184–185.

77. Matthew Arnold, *Discourses in America* (London: Macmillan & Co., 1912), 21, 65.

78. For a recent defense of such positions, see Johnson's response to the negative use of "elitist": *Who Needs Classical Music?*, 83–90.

79. Isaac Goldberg, quoted in Keir Keightley, "Taking Popular Music (and Tin Pan Alley and Jazz) Seriously," *Journal of Popular Music Studies* 22 (2010): 94.

80. See particularly Greenberg's much-cited early essay, "Avant-Garde and Kitsch," reproduced in *The Collected Essays and Criticism. Volume 1: Perceptions and Judgments 1939–1944*, ed. John O'Brien (Chicago: University of Chicago Press, 1986), 5–22.

81. F.R. Leavis, "Mass Civilization and Minority Culture," in *Cultural Theory and Popular Culture: A Reader*, ed. John Storey (Harlow: Pearson Education, 2006), 14.

82. F.R. Leavis and Denys Thompson, *Culture and Environment* (Westport: Greenwood Press, 1977), 100.

83. F.R. Leavis, "Mass Civilization and Minority Culture," 12.

84. Storey, *Introduction to Cultural Theory*, 42–43.

85. Storey, *Introduction to Cultural Theory*, 42–43.

86. Theodor W. Adorno, *The Culture Industry* (London: Routledge, 1991).

87. Adorno, *The Culture Industry*, 34.

88. Adorno, *The Culture Industry*, 30.

89. For a good discussion of the Marxist analysis of music, with particular reference to the writings of Karl Marx, rather than Adornian/quasi-Adornian criticism, see *Music and Marx: Ideas, Practice, Politics*, ed. Regula B. Qureshi (New York: Routledge, 2002).

90. Bourdieu, *Distinction*, 18.

91. See Andy Bennett, *Popular Music and Youth Culture: Music, Identity and Place* (Houndmills: Macmillan, 2000), 30.

92. Middleton, *Studying Popular Music*, 36.

93. Middleton, *Studying Popular Music*, 36.

94. Theodor W. Adorno, "On Popular Music," in *On Record: Rock, Pop, and the Written Word*, eds. Simon Frith and Andrew Goodwin (New York: Pantheon Books, 1990), 308.

95. Adorno, "On Popular Music," 302.

96. Robert W. Witkin, *Adorno on Music* (London: Routledge, 1998), 163.

97. Witkin, *Adorno on Music*, 163.

98. Witkin, *Adorno on Music*, 163.

99. Theodor W. Adorno and Max Horkheimer, "The Culture Industry: Enlightenment as Mass Deception," in *The Cultural Studies Reader*, ed. Simon During (London: Routledge, 1993), 31.

100. Adorno, "On Popular Music," 311.

101. Adorno, "On Popular Music," 311.

102. Adorno, *The Culture Industry*, 90.

103. See Andrew McKinnon, "Reading 'Opium of the People': Expression, Protest and the Dialectics of Religion," *Critical Sociology* 31 (2005): 25–26.

104. Dominic Strinati, *An Introduction to Theories of Popular Culture*, 2nd ed. (London: Routledge, 2004), 57.

105. Adorno, *The Culture Industry*, 106.

106. See Theodor W. Adorno, *Philosophy of New Music*, trans. Robert Hullot-Kentor (Minneapolis: University of Minnesota Press, 2006).

107. Timothy Day, *A Century of Recorded Music: Listening to Musical History* (New Haven: Yale University Press, 2000), 207.

108. Quoted in DeNora, *Music in Everyday Life*, 1.

109. Quoted in DeNora, *Music in Everyday Life*, 1.

110. DeNora, *Music in Everyday Life*, 1–2.

111. Robert Miklitsch, for example, rather unfairly considers him "absurdly out of touch with the times" like some frozen Madame Tussaud wax figure. See his *Roll Over Adorno: Critical Theory, Popular Culture, Audiovisual Media* (Albany: State University of New York Press, 2006), 44.

112. See Joseph Lanza, *Elevator Music: A Surreal History of Muzak, Easy-Listening, and Other Moodsong* (Ann Arbor: University of Michigan Press, 2004).

113. Simon Frith, "The Popular Music Industry," in *The Cambridge Companion to Pop and Rock*, eds. Simon Frith, Will Straw, and John Street (Cambridge: Cambridge University Press, 2001), 26. See also, Will Straw, "Consumption," in *Cambridge Companion to Pop and Rock*, 53–73.

114. Middleton, *Studying Popular Music*, 37. Cf. Simon Frith, "The Industrialization of Music," in *The Popular Music Reader*, eds. Andy Bennett, Barry Shank, and Jason Toynbee (London: Routledge, 2006), 231–238.

115. Middleton, *Studying Popular Music*, 37.

116. Richard Middleton, "Pop, Rock and Interpretation," in *Popular Music Reader*, 216.

Chapter 2

1. See Peter J. Martin, *Music and the Sociological Gaze: Art Worlds and Cultural Production* (Manchester: Manchester University Press, 2006).

2. Tia DeNora, "Aesthetic Agency and Musical Practice: New Directions in the Sociology of Music," in *Music and Emotion: Theory and Research*, eds. Patrik Juslin and John Sloboda (Oxford: Oxford University Press, 2001), 165.

3. DeNora, "Aesthetic Agency," 165.

4. See Anthony Giddens, *Modernity and Self-Identity: Self and Society in the Late Modern Age* (Stanford: Stanford University Press, 1991), 76.

5. Jürgen Habermas, *The Theory of Communicative Action: A Critique of Functionalist Reason*, trans. T. McCarthy, vol. 2 (London: Polity Press, 1987), 113–198.

6. Theodor W. Adorno, "On Popular Music," in *On Record: Rock, Pop, and the Written Word*, eds. Simon Frith and Andrew Goodwin (New York: Pantheon Books, 1990), 311–312.

7. DeNora, "Aesthetic Agency," 165. Cf. Martin, *Sounds and Society*, 75–125.

8. Simon Frith, *Sound Effects: Youth, Leisure, and the Politics of Rock 'n' Roll* (New York: Pantheon, 1981), 45.

9. See Frith, *Sound Effects*; Dick Hebdige, *Subculture: The Meaning of Style* (London: Methuen & Co., 1979); Simon Jones, *Black Culture, White Youth: The Reggae Tradition from JA to UK* (London: Macmillan Education, 1988); Paul Willis, *Profane Culture* (London: Routledge, 1978).

10. DeNora, *Music in Everyday Life*, 2.

11. See Sara Cohen, "Ethnography and Popular Music Studies," *Popular Music* 12 (1994): 179–190.

12. Stuart Hall, "Recent Developments in Theories of Language and Ideology: A Critical Note," in *Culture, Media, Language: Working Papers in Cultural Studies 1972–1979*, eds. Stuart Hall, Dorothy Hobson, Andrew Lowe, and Paul Willis (London: Hutchinson, 1980), 157–162.

13. Willis, *Profane Culture*, 68.

14. Willis, *Profane Culture*, 73.

15. Willis, *Profane Culture*, 157, 167–168.

16. Available on *Chris Spedding* (1976).

17. Wanting to move away from the darker connotations of biker culture, particularly violence and death, to a more positive life-affirming perception, Spedding's use of tempo and reverb accompanied the lyrics well: "We're doin' about 95. So good to be alive . . . " See Kimberley Bright, *Chris Spedding: Reluctant Guitar Hero* (Lincoln: iUniverse, 2007), 239.

18. See Phillip Sipiora and James S. Baumlin, eds., *Rhetoric and Kairos: Essays in History, Theory and Praxis* (Albany: State University of New York Press, 2002).

19. Till, *Pop Cult*, 9.

20. Sheila Whiteley, *The Space Between the Notes: Rock and the Counter-culture* (London: Routledge, 1992), 50–51.

21. See Christopher Partridge, *The Re-Enchantment of the West: Alternative Spiritualities, Sacralization, Popular Culture and Occulture*, vol. 1 (London: T&T Clark International, 2004), 100–102. See also, Harvey Cox, *Turning East: The Promise and Peril of the New Orientalism* (New York: Simon and Schuster, 1977); John Hutnyk, *Critique of Exotica: Music, Politics, and the Culture Industry* (London: Pluto Press, 2000), 87–113.

22. Susan Fast, *In the Houses of the Holy: Led Zeppelin and the Power of Rock Music* (New York: Oxford University Press, 2001), 91.

23. See Wilfred Mellers, *Twilight of the Gods: The Beatles in Retrospect* (London: Faber & Faber, 1973), 94; Jonathon Bellman, "Indian Resonances in the British Invasion, 1965–1968," in *The Exotic in Western Music*, ed. Jonathon Bellman (Boston: Northeastern University Press, 1998), 293–294.

24. DeNora, *Music in Everyday Life*, 7.

25. DeNora, *Music in Everyday Life*, 11.

26. See David Machin and John Richardson, "Discourses of Unity and Purpose in the Sounds of Fascist Music: A Multimodal Approach," *Critical Discourse Studies* 9 (2012): 329–345; Simon McKerrell, "Hearing Sectarianism: Understanding Scottish Sectarianism as Song," *Critical Discourse Studies* 9 (2012): 363–374.

27. Julia Kristeva, quoted in Jonathan Culler, *The Pursuit of Signs: Semiotics, Literature, Deconstruction* (London: Routledge, 2001), 116. See also Julia Kristeva, *Desire in Language: A Semiotic Approach to Literature and Art* (New York: Columbia University Press, 1980).

28. Roland Barthes, *Image, Music, Text*, trans. Stephen Heath (London: Fontana Press, 1977), 146.

29. See Paul Miller, *Sound Unbound: Sampling, Digital Music and Culture* (Cambridge, MA: MIT Press, 2000).

30. Stanley Fish, *Is There a Text in This Class? The Authority of Interpretive Communities* (Cambridge: Harvard University Press, 1980), 158.

31. Fish, *Is There a Text in This Class?*, 14.

32. See Vincent Bugliosi and Curt Gentry, *Helter Skelter* (London: Arrow Books, 1992 [1974]), 300.

33. See Jonathon Bellman, "Indian Resonances," 292–306. See also: Derek Scott, *Musical Style and Social Meaning: Selected Essays* (Franham: Ashgate, 2010), 137–164; Ralph Locke, "On Music and Orientalism," in *Music, Culture, and Society: A Reader*, ed. Derek B. Scott (Oxford: Oxford University Press, 2000), 103–109; David Beard and Kenneth Gloag, *Musicology: The Key Concepts* (Abingdon: Routledge, 2005), 129.

34. Nick Richardson, "In-between Worlds: Grouper," *The Wire* 334 (December, 2011): 28. Listen particularly to Grouper's albums *Wide* (2006) and *Dragging a Dead Deer Up a Hill* (2008).

35. For useful discussions of Hermann's use of sound to evoke menace, see James Wierzbicki, "Psycho-Analysis: Form and Function in Bernard Hermann's Music for Hitchcock's Masterpiece," in *Terror Tracks: Music, Sound and Horror Cinema*, ed. Philip Hayward (London: Equinox, 2009), 14–46; Ross J. Fenimore, "Voices That Lie Within: The Heard and the Unheard in *Psycho*," in *Music in the Horror Film*, ed. Neil Lerner (New York: Routledge, 2010), 88–89.

36. Simon Frith, *Taking Popular Music Seriously: Selected Essays* (Aldershot: Ashgate, 2007), 263.

37. Anniruddh D. Patel, *Music, Language and the Brain* (New York: Oxford University Press, 2008).

38. See John Sloboda's discussion in *Exploring the Musical Mind: Cognition, Emotion, Ability, Function* (Oxford: Oxford University Press, 2005), 347.

39. For a good introduction to Gregorian chant, see David Hiley, *Gregorian Chant* (Cambridge: Cambridge University Press, 2009).

40. See Susan Palmer, "Purity and Danger in the Solar Temple," in *The Order of the Solar Temple: The Temple of Death*, ed. James R. Lewis (Aldershot: Ashgate, 2006), 48. John R. Hall and Philip Schuyler, "The Mystical Apocalypse of the Solar Temple," in *The Order of the Solar Temple: The Temple of Death*, ed. James R. Lewis (Aldershot: Ashgate, 2006), 67.

41. See, for example, Joseph Stannard's worthwhile interview with Sunn O))): "The Gathering Storm," *The Wire* 302 (April, 2009): 42–47. See also the video for "Eulogy" by LA Vampires and Zola Jesus. The track is available on *LA Vampires Meets Zola Jesus* (Not Not Fun Records, 2010): http://www.youtube.com/watch?v=JCSPki_yz9E (accessed, June 29, 2013).

42. "Ominous Latin Chanting," Comment on *TV Tropes*, Accessed: November 13, 2011. <http://tvtropes.org/pmwiki/pmwiki.php/Main/OminousLatinChanting>

43. We will explore this binary in the following chapter, when we make use of the work of Georges Bataille.

44. Dave Laing, "'Sadeness,' Scorpions and Single Markets: National and Transnational Trends in European Popular Music," *Popular Music* 11(1992): 127.

45. Quoted in Oliver Sacks, *Musicophilia: Tales of Music and the Brain* (London: Picador, 2008), xii. See also DeNora, *Music in Everyday Life*, 75–108.

46. John W. De Gruchy, *Christianity, Art, and Transformation: Theological Aesthetics in the Struggle for Justice* (Cambridge: Cambridge University Press, 2001), 15–16. See also Richard H. Roberts, "Body," in *The Blackwell Companion to the Study of Religion*, ed. Robert A. Segal (Oxford: Blackwell, 2006), 213–228.

47. De Gruchy, *Christianity, Art, and Transformation*, 15–16. See also Roberts, "Body," 213–228.

48. See Peter Brown, *The Body and Society: Men, Women, and Sexual Renunciation in Early Christianity* (New York: Columbia University Press, 1988).

49. George Fox, *Journal of George Fox* (Cambridge: Cambridge University Press, 1952), 38.

50. Fox, *Journal*, 206. See also H. Larry Ingle, *First Among Friends: George Fox and the Creation of Quakerism* (New York: Oxford University Press, 1994), 62.

51. De Gruchy, *Christianity, Art, and Transformation*, 16. See also Friedrich W. Nietzsche, *The Birth of Tragedy and Other Writings*, trans. Ronald Speirs (Cambridge: Cambridge University Press, 1999), 122.

52. Susan McClary, *Feminine Endings: Music, Gender and Sexuality* (Minneapolis: University of Minnesota Press, 1991), 57.

53. Frith, *Performing Rites*, 102. See also Simon Frith and Angela McRobbie, "Rock and Sexuality," in *On Record: Rock, Pop and the Written Word*, eds. Simon Frith and Andrew Goodwin (New York: Pantheon Books, 1990), 371–389.

54. Frith and McRobbie, "Rock and Sexuality," 374.

55. Sue Wise, "Sexing Elvis," in Frith and Goodwin, *On Record*, 392.

56. Richard Dyer, "In Defense of Disco," in Frith and Goodwin, *On Record*, 413.

57. See Frith and Goodwin, *On Record*, 369–424; Sheila Whitely, *Sexing the Groove: Popular Music and Gender* (London: Routledge, 1997).

58. See Fish, *Is There a Text in This Class?*, 24.

59. For a good introduction to the debates and approaches in ethnographic research, see Paul Atkinson, Amanda Coffey, Sara Delamont, John Lofland and Lyn Lofland, eds. *Handbook of Ethnography* (London: Sage, 2001).

60. DeNora, *Music in Everyday Life*, 31 (emphasis added).

61. Louise Rosenblatt, *The Reader, The Text, The Poem: The Transactional Theory of the Literary Work* (Carbondale: Southern Illinois University Press, 1978), 105.

62. Rosenblatt, *The Reader, The Text, The Poem*, 105.

63. Rosenblatt, *The Reader, The Text, The Poem*, 105.

64. Available on *Jimi Hendrix, Live at Woodstock* (1999).

65. See Sheila Whiteley, "'1, 2, 3 What Are We Fighting 4?' Music, Meaning and 'The Star Spangled Banner,'" in *Remembering Woodstock*, ed. Andy Bennett (Aldershot: Ashgate, 2004), 18–28.

66. Jerry Hopkins, *The Jimi Hendrix Experience* (New York: Arcade Publishing, 1996), 195. See also Samuel A. Floyd Jr., *Hendrix, The Power of Black Music: Interpreting its History from Africa to the United States* (New York: Oxford University Press, 1995), 202–203.

67. Umberto Eco, *The Name of the Rose* (Orlando: Harcourt Brace Jovanovich, 1983).

68. Quoted in DeNora, *Music in Everyday Life*, 32. Middleton, *Studying Popular Music*, 10.

69. DeNora, *Music in Everyday Life*, 32.

70. DeNora, *Music in Everyday Life*, 32.

71. James McKinnon, *Music in Early Christian Literature* (Cambridge: Cambridge University Press, 1987), 22.

72. See Francesco Pelosi, *Plato on Music, Soul and Body*, trans. Sophie Henderson (Cambridge: Cambridge University Press, 2010).

73. Quoted in DeNora, *Music in Everyday Life*, 21.
74. DeNora, *Music in Everyday Life*, 102–108.
75. Willis, *Profane Culture*, 164.
76. Willis, *Profane Culture*, 164.
77. DeNora, *Music in Everyday Life*, 89–108.
78. DeNora, *Music in Everyday Life*, 9–14.
79. See DeNora, *Music in Everyday Life*, 18–19, 140–142.
80. Adrian C. North, David J. Hargreaves, and Jennifer McKendrick, "The Influence of In-Store Music on Wine Selections," *Journal of Applied Psychology* 84 (1999): 271.
81. See Mark Evans, *Open Up the Doors: Music in the Modern Church* (London; Equinox, 2006), 136–157; James Abbington, ed., *Readings in African American Church Music and Worship* (Chicago: GIA Publications, 2001), 267–382.
82. Lanza, *Elevator Music*, 212.
83. Brian Eno, "Ambient Music," in *Audio Culture: Readings in Modern Music*, eds. Christopher Cox and Daniel Warner (New York: Continuum, 2004), 96.
84. An interesting discussion of the significance of sonic environments can be found in Anthony Storr, *Music and the Mind* (London: HarperCollins, 1992), 89–107.
85. Eno, "Ambient Music," 95. See also Partridge, *Re-Enchantment of the West*, vol.1, 175–178.
86. Teresa Lesiuk, "The Effect of Music Listening on Work Performance," *Psychology of Music* 33 (2005): 173.
87. Lesiuk, "The Effect of Music Listening," 173–174.
88. Lesiuk, "The Effect of Music Listening," 173.
89. Lesiuk, "The Effect of Music Listening," 173.
90. For a good overview, see Suzanne Hanser, "Music, Health and Well-Being," in *Handbook of Music and Emotion: Theory, Research, Applications*, eds. Patrik N. Juslin and John Sloboda (Oxford: Oxford University Press, 2010), 849–878. See also, Therese West and Gail Ironson, "Effects of Music on Human Health and Wellness: Physiological Measurements and Research Design," in *The Oxford Handbook of Medical Ethnomusicology*, ed. Benjamin D. Koen (New York: Oxford University Press, 2008), 410–443; David Aldridge and Jörg Fachner, eds., *Music and Altered States: Consciousness, Transcendence, Therapy and Addictions* (London: Jessica Kinglsey Publishers, 2006).
91. Quoted in Storr, *Music and the Mind*, 34. See also, Oliver Sacks, *Musicophilia: Tales of Music and the Brain* (London: Picador, 2008), 333–338.
92. Wendy E.J. Knight and Nikki S. Rickard, "Relaxing Music Prevents Stress-Induced Increases in Subjective Anxiety, Systolic Blood Pressure, and Heart rate in Healthy Males and Females," *Journal of Music Therapy* 38: 4 (2001): 256. See also: Nikki S. Rickard and Katrina McFerran, eds., *Lifelong Engagement with Music: Benefits for Mental Health and Well-Being* (New York: Nova Publishers, 2012); Harold Koenig, "Religion, Spirituality, and Healing: Research, Dialogue, and Directions," in *Oxford Handbook of Medical Ethnomusicology*, 46–71.
93. DeNora, *Music in Everyday Life*, 17.
94. Sloboda, *Exploring the Musical Mind*, 215–216. See also Daniel Craig, "Exploring Music Preference: Meaningfulness of Music as a Function of Emotional Reactions," *Nordic Journal of Music Therapy* 18: 1 (2009):57–69.
95. Mike Oldfield, *Changeling* (London: Virgin Books, 2008), 98–99, 160–161.
96. Guy Beck, *Sonic Theology: Hinduism and Sacred Sound* (Delhi: Motilal Banarsidass Publishers, 1995), 108.
97. See Guy Beck, ed., *Sacred Sounds: Experiencing Music in World Religions* (Waterloo: Wilfred Laurier University Press, 2006). On the confluence of spirituality, wellbeing, and music, see the anthology edited by Don Campbell, *Music: Physician for the Times to Come*, 2nd ed. (Wheaton: Quest Books, 2000).
98. Nusrat Fateh Ali Khan, quoted in Dimitri Ehrlich, *Inside the Music: Conversations with Contemporary Musicians About Spirituality, Creativity and Consciousness* (Boston: Shambhala, 1997), 121.

99. See Penelope Murray and Peter Wilson, eds., *Music and the Muses: The Culture of Mousike in the Classical Athenian City* (Oxford: Oxford University Press, 2004).

100. Leonard Bernstein, *The Unanswered Question: Six Talks at Harvard* (Cambridge: Harvard University Press, 1976), 177.

101. Leonard Meyer, *Emotion and Meaning in Music* (Chicago: University of Chicago Press, 1956), 3.

102. Meyer, *Emotion and Meaning in Music*, 3.

103. Meyer, *Emotion and Meaning in Music*, vii.

104. See Ian Cross and Elizabeth Tolbert, "Music and Meaning," in *The Oxford Handbook of Music Psychology*, eds. Susan Hallam, Ian Cross, and Michael Thaut (Oxford: Oxford University Press, 2009), 24–34.

105. A philosophical analysis of music from a broadly expressivist perspective can be found in Roger Scruton, *Understanding Music: Philosophy and Interpretation* (London: Continuum, 2009). See also Begbie's discussion in *Theology, Music, and Time*, 15–19.

106. See Sloboda, *Exploring the Musical Mind*, 260.

107. See Patrik N. Juslin and John Sloboda, eds., *Music and Emotion: Theory and Research* (Oxford: Oxford University Press, 2001); Juslin and Sloboda, *Handbook of Music and Emotion*; Sloboda, *Exploring the Musical Mind*.

108. See Patrik N. Juslin and Daniel Västfjäll, "Emotional Responses to Music: The Need to Consider Underlying Mechanisms," *Behavioral and Brain Sciences* 31 (2008): 560.

109. Juslin and Daniel Västfjäll, "Emotional Responses to Music: The Need to Consider Underlying Mechanisms," 560. The quotation is taken from Stephen Davies "Philosophical Perspectives on Music's Expressiveness," in Juslin and Sloboda, *Music and Emotion*, 37.

110. Quoted in Juslin and Daniel Västfjäll, "Emotional Responses to Music: The Need to Consider Underlying Mechanisms," 559. The quotation is from Bennett Reimar's *A Philosophy of Music Education*, 3rd ed. (Englewood Cliffs: Prentice-Hall, 2003).

111. Fish, *Is There a Text in This Class?*, 14.

112. Martin, *Music and the Sociological Gaze*, 5.

113. Lawrence Kramer, *Classical Music and Postmodern Knowledge* (Berkeley: University of California Press, 1995), 17.

114. Davies, *Emotion, Identity and Religion*, 1.

115. Ole Riis and Linda Woodhead, *A Sociology of Religious Emotion* (Oxford: Oxford University Press, 2010), 96.

116. Riis and Woodhead, *A Sociology of Religious Emotion*, 97.

117. Riis and Woodhead hint at this process when they state that "each symbol may be experienced afresh by individuals in their own emotional experience, as subjective experiences are canalized in terms of objective culture." *A Sociology of Religious Emotion*, 97–98.

118. Riis and Woodhead, *A Sociology of Religious Emotion*, 99.

119. Peter Taylor Forsyth, *Christ on Parnassus: Lectures on Art, Ethic and Theology* (London: Hodder and Stoughton, 1911), 216.

120. The term, coined by Timothy Leary, refers to the context in which a psychedelic drug is taken: "set" is the psychological state a person brings to the experience—their thoughts, their mood and their expectations; "setting" is the physical and social environment within which the experience takes place. The point is that, as with music, set and setting contribute significantly to the construction of affective space and, as such, to meaning making.

Chapter 3

1. Dennis O'Driscoll, *Stepping Stones: Interviews with Seamus Heaney* (London: Faber and Faber, 2008), 309.

2. Augustine, *Nicene and Post-Nicene Fathers. First Series*, vol. 5. of *St. Augustine: Anti-Pelagian Writings*, ed. Philip Schaff (New York: Cosimo, 2007 [1887]), 19.

3. Walter Brueggemann, *Genesis* (Louisville, John Knox Press, 1982), 47–48.

4. Augustine, *Nicene and Post-Nicene Fathers. First Series*, vol. 5. of *St. Augustine: Anti-Pelagian Writings*, ed. Philip Schaff (New York: Cosimo, 2007 [1887]), 176.
5. Chris Jenks, *Transgression* (London: Routledge, 2003), 2.
6. Michael Taussig, "Transgression," in *Critical Terms for Religious Studies*, ed. Mark C. Taylor (Chicago: Chicago University Press,1998), 350.
7. John Jervis, *Transgressing the Modern: Explorations in the Western Experience of Otherness* (Oxford: Blackwell, 1999), 1.
8. Michel Foucault, "A Preface to Transgression," in *Religion and Culture by Michel Foucault*, ed. Jeremy Carrette (London: Routledge, 1999), 60.
9. Jeffrey C. Alexander, *The Meanings of Social Life: A Cultural Sociology* (New York: Oxford University Press, 2003), 110.
10. Jenks, *Transgression*, 15.
11. Durkheim's *The Elementary Forms of Religious Life* was clearly indebted to the work of anthropologists such as E.B. Tylor and James Frazer, both of whom developed an evolutionary theory of religion, which maintained as a scientific principle that to understand a complex phenomenon, such as modern societies, one must begin with its simplest form, "primitive" societies.
12. Gordon Lynch's rereading of Durkheim is a good example of this: *Sacred in the Modern World*.
13. Émile Durkheim, *The Rules of Sociological Method*, trans. Sarah Solovay and John Mueller (New York: The Free Press, 1938), 14.
14. Durkheim, *The Rules of Sociological Method*, 3.
15. Durkheim, *The Rules of Sociological Method*, 13.
16. Durkheim, *The Rules of Sociological Method*, 10.
17. Zygmunt Bauman, "Durkheim's Society Revisited," in *The Cambridge Companion to Durkheim*, eds. Jeffrey C. Alexander and Philip Smith (Cambridge: Cambridge University Press, 2005), 363.
18. Jim Morrison, quoted in Jerry Hopkins and Danny Sugarman, *No One Here Gets Out Alive* (London: Plexus, 1980), 232.
19. Jim Morrison, quoted in James Riordan and Jerry Prochnicky, *Break on Through: The Life and Death of Jim Morrison* (London: Plexus, 1991), 373.
20. See the FBI record reproduced in Riordan and Prochnicky, *Break on Through*, 375
21. Ray Manzarek, quoted in Riordan and Prochnicky, *Break on Through*, 373.
22. Jim Morrison, quoted in Riordan and Prochnicky, *Break on Through*, 373.
23. Mark Cladis, "Introduction," in Durkheim, *Elementary Forms of Religious Life*, xxii.
24. See Durkheim, *Elementary Forms of Religious Life*, 104.
25. Durkheim, *Elementary Forms of Religious Life*, 154.
26. Alexander Riley, " 'Renegade Durkheimianism' and the Transgressive Left Sacred," in Alexander and Smith, *Cambridge Companion to Durkheim*, 274.
27. The ontological theories of the sacred developed by, particularly, Mircea Eliade, have taught scholars of religion to think of the sacred and the profane as modes of being in the world, expressed subjectively and culturally through common structures, such as myth, space, and time. See Mircea Eliade, *The Sacred and the Profane: The Nature of Religion* (Orlando: Harcourt, 1987).
28. William S.F. Pickering, *Durkheim's Sociology of Religion: Themes and Theories* (London: Routledge and Kegan Paul, 1984), 124–125.
29. Lynch, *Sacred in the Modern World*, 19.
30. Durkheim, *Elementary Forms of Religious Life*, 306–307.
31. Paul Hegarty, *Noise/Music: A History* (New York: Continuum, 2007), ix.
32. See Alexander Riley's analysis of this in terms of "impure play": *Impure Play: Sacredness, Transgression, and the Tragic in Popular Culture* (Lanham: Lexington Books, 2010).
33. For a short time, Bataille was closely associated with André Breton, with whom he founded the anti-Fascist group Contre-Attaque (1935–1936).
34. Riley, "Renegade Durkheimianism," 285.

35. Riley, "Renegade Durkheimianism," 285.

36. Pickering, *Durkheim's Sociology of Religion*, 124–125.

37. Georges Bataille, *The Accursed Share*, trans. Robert Hurley, vol. 1 (New York: Zone Books, 1991); *The Accursed Share*, trans. Robert Hurley, vols. 2 & 3 (New York: Zone Books, 1991).

38. Fred Botting and Scott Wilson, "Introduction: From Experience to Economy," in *The Bataille Reader*, eds. Fred Botting and Scott Wilson (Oxford: Blackwell, 1997), 1–2.

39. Georges Bataille, *Inner Experience*, trans. Leslie Anne Boldt (Albany: State University of New York Press, 1988), 3. It should be noted, as Bataille makes clear in this volume, that he has an ambivalent attitude toward mysticism, particularly the way the experience is interpreted within Christianity, in that it is linked to a teleology, to a salvific process.

40. Georges Bataille, *Eroticism: Death and Sensuality*, trans. Mary Dalwood (San Francisco: City Lights Books, 1986), 67.

41. Bataille, *Eroticism*, 67–68.

42. P-Orridge has provided copies of the newspaper articles reporting Fairbairn's comments and illustrating the media outrage at the time in *Painful But Fabulous: The Lives and Art of Genesis P-Orridge* (New York: Soft Skull Shortwave, 2002), 163.

43. P-Orridge, *Painful But Fabulous*, 6.

44. Genesis P-Orridge, "Genesis P-Orridge," in *Modern Pagans: An Investigation of Contemporary Paganism*, ed. V. Vale (San Francisco: RE/Search, 2001), 122.

45. Marc Almond's *Violent Silence* was originally performed at The Bloomsbury Theatre, London, on Wednesday September 26, 1984. It was part of an event celebrating the work of Bataille: "Violent Silence: Celebrating Georges Bataille." See the published program: Paul Buck, ed., *Violent Silence: Celebrating Georges Bataille* (London: The Georges Bataille Event, 1984).

46. Alexander, *The Meanings of Social Life*, 110.

47. Georges Bataille, quoted in Alexander, *The Meanings of Social Life*, 110.

48. See Victor Turner, *The Ritual Process: Structure and Anti-Structure* (Chicago: Aldine, 1969), vii, 201.

49. Turner, *Ritual Process*, 95. See also Victor Turner, "Variations on a Theme of Liminality," in *Secular Ritual*, eds. Sally Moore and Barbara Myerhoff (Amsterdam: Van Gorcum, 1977), 36–52.

50. See Edith Turner, "The Literary Roots of Victor Turner's Anthopology," in *Victor Turner and the Construction of Cultural Criticism: Between Literature and Anthropology*, ed. Kathleen Ashley (Bloomington: Indiana University Press, 1990), 167.

51. Victor Turner, *Dramas, Fields and Metaphors* (Ithaca: Cornell University Press, 1974), 13–14.

52. John Peel and Sheila Ravenscroft, *Margrave of the Marshes* (London: Bantam Press, 2005), 305.

53. See Hugh McLeod, *The Religious Crisis of the 1960s* (Oxford: Oxford University Press, 2007).

54. See Georges Bataille, "The Use Value of D.A.F. de Sade (An Open Letter to My Current Comrades)," in Georges Bataille, *Visions of Excess: Selected Writings 1927–1939*, ed. and trans. Allan Stoekl (Manchester: Manchester University Press, 1985). For an excellent analysis of the concept, see Julian Pefanis, *Heterology and the Postmodern: Bataille, Baudrillard, and Lyotard* (Durham: Duke University Press, 1991). A good collection of representative texts taken from Bataille's work on heterology can be found in Botting and Wilson, *Bataille Reader*, 119–164.

55. Central to this articulation of "the Other," of course, is the theologically oriented work of Emmanuel Levinas, for whom the "infinite other" was key. See Bernhard Waldenfels, "Levinas and the Face of the Other," in *The Cambridge Companion to Levinas*, eds. Simon Critchley and Robert Bernasconi (Cambridge: Cambridge University Press, 2002), 63–81; Edith Wyschogrod, "Language and Alterity in the Thought of Levinas," in *Cambridge Companion to Levinas*, eds. Critchley and Bernasconi, 188–205.

56. For a good discussion of the connections between sound, pain and violence in popular music see Bruce Johnson and Martin Cloonan, *Dark Side of the Tune: Popular Music and Violence* (Aldershot: Ashgate, 2009).

57. Turner, *Dramas, Fields and Metaphors*, 13–14.

58. See Edwin Pouncey's excellent, concise introduction to Merzbow (Masami Akita): "Consumed by Noise," *The Wire* 198 (2000): 26–32.

59. Whitney Bauman, *Theology, Creation and Environmental Ethics: From Creation Ex Nihilo to Terra Nullius* (New York: Routledge, 2009), 16.

60. Bataille references his work in his discussion of the sacred and the profane: Bataille, *Eroticism*, 68.

61. Roger Caillois, *Man and the Sacred*, trans. Meyer Barash (Urbana: University of Illinois Press, 2001), 112.

62. Derek B. Scott, *From the Erotic to the Demonic: On Critical Musicology* (Oxford; Oxford University Press, 2003), 130.

63. See Scott, *From the Erotic to the Demonic*, 128–152.

64. See Christopher Partridge and Eric Christianson, eds., *The Lure of the Dark Side: Satan and Western Demonology in Popular Culture* (London: Equinox, 2009).

65. See, for example, Philip Johnson, "Devil Music," *Circuit: Devil Music* (Spring, 2002): 43–47.

66. Jon Michael Spencer, "The Mythology of the Blues," in *Sacred Music of the Secular City: From Blues To Rap* (special issue *Black Sacred Music: A Journal of Theomusicology*, 6.1), ed. Jon Michael Spencer (Durham: Duke University Press, 1992), 105.

67. Jon Michael Spencer, "The Mythology of the Blues," 106–107.

68. It should be noted that such names, while culturally significant, need to be interpreted cautiously. On the one hand, they were rare and, on the other, they betray significant overtones of the comic and the machismo. Nevertheless, as we have seen, they do point to deep social issues regarding to the reception of the blues. See David Evans, "From Bumble Bee Slim to Black Boy Shine: Nicknames of Blues Singers," in *Ramblin' On My Mind: New Perspectives on the Blues*, ed. David Evans (Urbana: University of Illinois Press, 2008), 201–202.

69. Jon Michael Spencer, *Blues and Evil* (Knoxville: University of Tennessee Press, 1993), 28.

70. Spencer, *Blues and Evil*, 11.

71. Paul Oliver, *Blues Fell This Morning: Meaning in the Blues*, 2nd ed. (Cambridge: Cambridge University Press, 1990), 117.

72. Spencer, *Blues and Evil*, 35.

73. James H. Cone, *The Spirituals and the Blues* (Maryknoll: Orbis Books, 1991), 99.

74. Cone, *Spirituals and the Blues*, 113.

75. Rubin Lacy, quoted in Spencer, *Blues and Evil*, 96.

76. Oliver, *Blues Fell This Morning*, 117.

77. Allan F. Moore, *Song Means: Analysing and Interpreting Recorded Popular Song* (Farnham: Ashgate, 2012), 123.

78. See Luigi Monge, "Preachin' the Blues: A textual Analysis of Son House's 'Dry Spell Blues'," in Evans, *Ramblin' On My Mind*, 226.

79. Cecil Sharp, *English Folk Song: Some Conclusions* (London: Simpkin & Co., 1907), 134–135.

80. Arnold, *Culture and Anarchy*, 46.

81. An excellent overview of music censorship around the world can be found in Marie Korpe, ed., *Shoot the Singer! Music Censorship Today* (London: Zed Books, 2004).

82. See Claude Chastagner, "The Parents' Music Resource Center: From Information to Censorship," *Popular Music* 18 (1999): 179–192.

83. See Eric Nuzum, *Parental Advisory: Music Censorship in America* (New York: HarperCollins, 2001), 13–43.

84. Lynch, *Sacred in the Modern World*, 28.

85. Nuzum, *Parental Advisory*, 6.

86. Jenks, *Transgression*, 183. See also, David Altheide, "The Columbine Shootings and the Discourse of Fear," *American Behavioral Scientist* 52 (2009): 1356–1357.

87. Scott Wilson, *Great Satan's Rage: American Negativity and Rap/Metal in the Age of Supercapitalism* (Manchester: Manchester University Press, 2008), 110.

88. Wilson, *Great Satan's Rage*, 110.

89. Quoted in John Blanchard, *Pop Goes the Gospel* (Welwyn: Evangelical Press, 1983), 56.

90. Mike Adams, quoted in Jeffrey Victor, *Satanic Panic: The Creation of a Contemporary Legend* (Chicago: Open Court, 1993), 168.

91. David Keenan, "Childhood's End," *The Wire* 163 (1997): 35. See also Peter Webb, *Exploring the Networked Worlds of Popular Music* (New York: Routledge, 2007), 60–109.

92. Hegarty, *Noise/Music*, 105.

93. Keenan, "Childhood's End," 35.

94. Hegarty, *Noise/Music*, 105–106.

95. Hegarty, *Noise/Music*, 106.

96. P-Orridge, "Genesis P-Orridge," 122.

97. Hugh Urban, *Magia Sexualis: Sex, Magic, and Liberation in Modern Western Esotericism* (Berkeley: University of California Press, 2006), 11.

98. Hegarty, *Noise/Music*, 107.

99. Don Watson, "Beyond Evil," *The Wire* 182 (1999): 30.

100. Zygmunt Bauman, "Durkheim's Society Revisited," in Alexander and Smith, *Cambridge Companion to Durkheim*, 363.

101. Genesis P-Orridge, quoted in Simon Dwyer, "Throbbing Gristle Biography," in *Re/Search 4/5: William S Burroughs, Throbbing Gristle, Brion Gysin*, ed. V. Vale (San Francisco: RE/Search, 2007), 63.

102. See Simon Ford, *Wreckers of Civilization: The Story of Coum Transmissions and Throbbing Gristle* (London: Black Dog Publishing, 1999), 6.22–6.23.

103. See Ford, *Wreckers of Civilization*, 6.22–6.23.

104. See Hans Peter Broedel, *The Malleus Maleficarum and the Construction of Witchcraft: Theology and Popular Belief* (Manchester: Manchester University Press, 2003).

105. See James Richardson, Joel Best and David Bromley, eds., *The Satanism Scare* (New York: Aldine De Gruyter, 1991); Victor, *Satanic Panic*.

106. See Johnson and Cloonan, *Dark Side of the Tune*; Martin Cloonan, *Banned! Censorship of Popular Music in Britain: 1967–1992* (Aldershot: Ashgate, 1996); Martin Cloonan and Reebee Garofalo, eds., *Policing Pop* (Philadelphia: Temple University Press, 2003); Sarah Thornton, "Moral Panic, the Media and British Rave Culture," in *Microphone Fiends: Youth Music & Youth Culture*, eds. Andrew Ross and Tricia Ross (New York: Routledge, 1994), 176–192.

107. See David Keenan, *England's Hidden Reverse: A Secret History of the Esoteric Underground* (London: SAF Publishing, 2003), 224–227.

108. Stanley Cohen, *Folk Devils and Moral Panics*, 3rd ed. (London: Routledge, 2002), 1: "A condition, episode, person or group of persons emerges to become defined as a threat to societal values and interests; its nature is presented in a stylized and stereotypical fashion by the mass media; the moral barricades are manned by editors, bishops, politicians and other right-thinking people; social accredited experts pronounce their diagnoses and solutions; ways of coping are evolved or (more often) resorted to; the condition then disappears, submerges or deteriorates and becomes more visible."

109. Alexander, *The Meanings of Social Life*, 110.

110. Bernhard Giesen, "Performing the Sacred: A Durkheimian Perspective on the Performative Turn in the Social Sciences," in *Social Performance: Symbolic Action, Cultural Progmatics, and Ritual*, eds. Jeffrey C. Alexander, Bernhard Giesen, and Jason Mast (Cambridge: Cambridge University Press, 2006), 345.

111. Christopher Partridge, "Esoterrorism and the Wrecking of Civilization: Genesis P-Orridge and the Rise of Industrial Paganism," in Bennett and Weston, *Pop Pagans*.

112. The term is taken from Ronald Hutton's "The Roots of Modern Paganism," 45.

113. Recorded in London between 8:10 p.m. and 9:00 p.m. on Saturday, February 16, 1980 at the studios of Industrial Records (their own label).

114. See V. Vale and Andrea Juno, eds., *Re/Search 6/7: Industrial Culture Handbook* (San Francisco: RE/Search, 1983).

115. Georges Bataille, quoted in Alexander, *The Meanings of Social Life*, 110.

116. Genesis P-Orridge, quoted in Ford, *Wreckers of Civilization*, 9.25.

117. Genesis P-Orridge, quoted in Drew Daniel, *20 Jazz Funk Greats* (New York: Continuum, 2008), 32.

118. Omer Bartov, *Murder in Our Midst: The Holocaust, Industrial Killing, and Representation* (New York: Oxford University Press, 1996), 4 (emphasis added).

119. Jean Baudrillard, *Symbolic Exchange and Death*, trans. Iain Hamilton Grant (London: Sage, 1993), 18. See also, Jean Baudrillard, *Simulacra and Simulation*, trans. Sheila Faria Glaser (Ann Arbor: University of Michigan Press, 1992), 75–78.

120. See Keith Kahn-Harris, *Extreme Metal: Music and Culture on the Edge* (Oxford: Berg, 2007); Michael Moynihan and Didrik Søderlind, *Lords of Chaos: The Bloody Rise of the Satanic Metal Underground*, 2nd ed. (Los Angeles, Feral House, 2003).

121. It's also worth noting that David Tibet, a former member of Psychic TV, named his new band Current 93 because this is an important term in Crowleyan thought, 93 being the numerological value of the letters making up the word "Thelema."

122. Genesis P-Orridge, quoted in Ford, *Wreckers of Civilization*, 11. 15–16.

123. The title of the CD is taken from Richard von Krafft-Ebing's *Psychopathia Sexualis: eine Klinisch-Forensische Studie* (Stuttgart: Verlag Von Ferdinand Enke, 1886), the important, early study of sexual practices which popularized the terms "sadism" and "masochism." Similarly, The Velvet Underground took the title of their 1967 song "Venus in Furs" (*Velvet Underground*) from Leopold von Sacher-Masoch's (from whom Krafft-Ebing derived the term "masochism") 1870 novella *Venus in Furs* (London: Penguin, 2000).

124. P-Orridge, quoted in Ford, *Wreckers of Civilization*, 11.15–16.

125. Mick Fish, *Industrial Evolution: Through the Eighties with Cabaret Voltaire* (London: SAF Publishing, 2002), 111.

126. Jenks, *Transgression*, 109.

127. Jenks, *Transgression*, 109.

128. P-Orridge, quoted in Ford, *Wreckers of Civilization*, 6). 10.

129. Bataille, *Eroticism*, 38. See also, Jürgen Habermas, "The French Path to Postmodernity: Bataille between Eroticism and General Economics," in Botting and Wilson, *Bataille*, 167–190.

130. Roland Boer, *Nick Cave: A Study of Love, Death and Apocalypse* (Sheffield: Equinox, 2012), 44.

131. See Jean Baudrillard, "Death in Bataille," in Botting and Wilson, *Bataille*, 139–145.

132. For an engaging, popular overview of the scene, see Albert Mudrian, *Choosing Death: The Improbable History of Death Metal and Grindcore* (Los Angeles: Feral House, 2004).

133. Victor Turner, "Variations on a Theme of Liminality," in Moore and Myerhoff, *Secular Ritual*, 37.

134. Michelle Phillipov, *Death Metal and Music Criticism: Analysis at the Limits* (Plymouth: Lexington Books, 2012), 90.

135. Phillipov, *Death Metal and Music Criticism*, 90.

136. This point has been made by a number of contemporary theorists of Gothic: e.g. Catherine Spooner, "Preface," in *Twenty-First Century Gothic*, eds. Brigid Cherry, Peter Howell and Caroline Ruddell (Newcastle: Cambridge Scholars Publishing, 2010), xi.

137. See David Shumway and Heather Arnet, "Playing Dress Up: David Bowie and the Roots of Goth," in *Goth: Undead Subculture*, eds. Lauren Goodlad and Michael Bibby (New Haven: Yale University Press, 2007), 129–142.

138. Lauren Goodlad and Michael Bibby, "Introduction," in Goodlad and Bibby, *Goth*, 1–2.

139. Significantly, of course, influenced by dub and dance, post punk recording were increasingly lengthy and released on 12" vinyl, thereby allowing for the creation of reflective affective spaces.

140. Catherine Spooner, *Contemporary Gothic* (London: Reaktion Books, 2006), 9.

141. The new romantics, of course, had been heavily influenced by David Bowie and Roxy Music, and influence which flowed through into goth culture. See, for example, Dave Rimmer, *New*

Romantics: The Look (London: Omnibus Press, 2003). This new romantic influence is often ignored, even by those, such as David Shumway and Heather Arnet, who seek to make the connection with Bowie and Roxy Music: "Playing Dress Up: David Bowie and the Roots of Goth," in Goodlad and Bibby, *Goth*, 129–142.

142. Nick Cave, *The Complete Lyrics, 1978–2007* (London: Penguin, 2007), 397.

143. Boer, *Nick Cave*, 47.

144. Rebecca Schraffenberger, "This Modern Goth (Explains Herself)," in Goodlad and Bibby, *Goth*, 124.

145. Nick Cave, quoted in Boer, *Nick Cave*, 44.

146. An "aureola" is a circle of light or depiction of radiance and luminescence surrounding the head or body of a deity or saint, which suggests power and transcendence above the mundane. In using the term "aureolize" here, I want to suggest a process in popular culture whereby the mundane and the profane glow with a particular significance related to the sacred. They have an aura which communicates a particular type of meaning.

147. Schraffenberger, "This Modern Goth (Explains Herself)," 124.

148. Spooner, *Contemporary Gothic*, 63.

149. Eugenia Parry, "The Dark Poetry By Which I Live," in Joel-Peter Witkin, *The Bone House* (San Francisco: Twin Palms Publishers, 2000), 184.

150. Peter Stallybrass and Allon White, *The Politics and Poetics of Transgression* (London: Methuen & Co., 1986), 21.

151. See Stallybrass and White, *Politics and Poetics of Transgression*, 21–22.

152. See Ronald Hutton, *Witches, Druids and King Arthur* (London: Hambledon and London, 2003), 193–214.

153. Mikhail Bakhtin, *Rabelais and His World*, trans. Hélène Iswolsky (Bloomington: Indiana University Press, 1984), 319.

154. Julie Wilson, "As It Is," in P-Orridge, *Painful But Fabulous*, 76–80.

155. Rudolf Otto, *The Idea of the Holy: An Inquiry into the Non-rational Factor in the Idea of the Divine and its Relation to the Rational*, trans. John Harvey (Oxford: Oxford University Press, 1958).

156. Agent Orange and Circle Jerks, quoted in Steven Blush, *American Hardcore: A Tribal History* (Los Angeles: Feral House, 2010), 14–15.

157. Michael Azerrad, *Our Band Could Be Your Life: Scenes from the American Indie Underground, 1981–1991* (Boston: Little Brown and Company, 2001), 32.

158. Blush, *American Hardcore*, 39. See also Azerrad, *Our Band Could Be Your Life*, 30–32; Noah Levine, *Dharma Punx: A Memoir* (New York: HarperCollins, 2003), 43–84.

159. Husker Dü, quoted in Blush, *American Hardcore*, 39.

160. See Bob Mould, *See a Little Light: The Trail of Rage and Melody* (New York: Little Brown and Company, 2011).

161. Mould, *See a Little Light*, 90.

162. "Moshing," a term which emerged out of the hardcore scene in the early 1980s, refers to the violent and frenzied "slam-dancing" that takes place during such gigs. The "mosh pit" is the center of activity, usually in front of the stage, where there are often explicitly ritualized behaviors and ringleaders who control those behaviors. Although this is, effectively, pseudo-violence, the letting of blood is often sought. A useful, although rather too sanguine description of mosh pit violence is provided by Randall Collins in *Violence: A Micro-Sociological Theory* (Princeton: Princeton University Press, 2008), 277–281.

163. Durkheim, *Elementary Forms of Religious Life*, 171.

164. Lynch, *Sacred in the Modern World*, 23–24.

165. Rina Arya, "The Religious Significance of Violence in Football," in *Holy Terror: Understanding Religion and Violence in Popular Culture*, eds. Eric Christianson and Christopher Partridge (London: Equinox, 2010), 130.

166. Arya, "The Religious Significance of Violence in Football," 130.

167. Arya, "The Religious Significance of Violence in Football," 130.

168. Azerrad, *Our Band Could Be Your Life*, 22.
169. René Girard, *Violence and the Sacred*, trans. Patrick Gregory (Maryland: John Hopkins University Press, 1977), 4.
170. Girard, *Violence and the Sacred*, 4.
171. See Paul Brannigan, "Just Say No," *Mojo* 217 (December, 2011): 52–56; and Andrew Earles, *Hüsker Dü: The Story of the Noise-Pop Pioneers Who Launched Modern Rock* (Minneapolis: Voyageur Press, 2010), 103.
172. "Search and Destroy" is the title of a well-known song by The Stooges (*Raw Power*, 1973).
173. Girard, *Violence and the Sacred*, 255, 257.
174. Arya, "The Religious Significance of Violence in Football," 132.
175. Girard, *Violence and the Sacred*, 30.
176. See: Craig O'Hara, *The Philosophy of Punk: More Than Noise!* (London: AK Press, 1999); Noah Levine, *Dharma Punx: A Memoir* (New York: HarperCollins, 2003). A thoughtful and arresting critique of the approaches to punk developed within Cultural Studies and a restatement of its revolutionary potential is provided by Shane Green in "The Problem of Peru's Punk Underground: An Approach to Under-Fuck the System," *Journal of Popular Music Studies* 24 (2012): 578–589.
177. See the interviews with MacKaye and Rollins in Ben Myers, *American Heretics: Rebel Voices in Music* (Hove: Codex Books, 2002), 12–31, 198–219.
178. Francis Elizabeth Stewart has produced an ethnography of contemporary hardcore culture: "'Punk Rock is My Religion': An Exploration of Straight Edge Punk as a Surrogate of Religion" (doctoral dissertation, Stirling University, 2011).
179. See Blush, *American Hardcore*, 159; see also, 28–31.
180. See Ross Haenfler, *Straight Edge: Clean-Living Youth, Hardcore Punk, and Social Change* (New Brunswick: Rutgers University Press, 2006); Robert Wood, *Straightedge Youth: Complexity and Contradictions of a Subculture* (Syracuse: Syracuse University Press, 2006); Kennet Granholm, "Metal, the End of the World, and Radical Environmentalism: Ecological Apocalypse in the Lyrics of Earth Crisis," in Christopher Partridge, *Anthems of Apocalypse: Popular Music and Apocalyptic Thought* (Sheffield: Phoenix Press, 2012), 27–42.
181. Ian MacKaye, quoted in Steven Blush, *American Hardcore: A Tribal History* (Los Angeles: Feral House, 2010), 28.
182. For a useful discussion of issues surrounding the concept the concept of "counterculture," see Andy Bennett, "Pour une réévaluation du concept de contre-culture," *Volume: La revue des musiques des populaires* 9:1 (2012): 19–31.
183. Sarah Thornton, *Club Cultures: Music, Media and Subcultural Capital* (Cambridge: Polity Press, 1995).
184. Jock Young, "The Subterranean World of Play," in *The Subcultures Reader*, eds. Ken Gelder and Sarah Thornton (London: Routledge, 1997), 79.
185. See Howard Parker, Judith Aldridge, and Fiona Measham, *Illegal Leisure: The Normalization of Adolescent Recreational Drug Use* (London: Routledge, 1998); Martin Plant and Moira Plant, *Risk-Takers: Alcohol, Drugs, Sex and Youth* (London: Routledge, 1992); and, more recently, Geoffrey Hunt, Molly Moloney, and Kristin Evans, *Youth, Drugs, and Nightlife* (Abingdon: Routledge, 2010).
186. Gang Green, quoted in Blush, *American Hardcore*, 29.
187. Lynch, *Sacred in the Modern World*, 29.
188. SS Decontrol, quoted in Blush, *American Hardcore*, 31.
189. In order to prevent minors purchasing alcohol at music venues, their hands were marked with a large X. This was then adopted by straight-edgers as a mark of pride signifying their choice to abstain. See Wood, *Straightedge Youth*, 115–118.
190. Randall Collins in *Violence: A Micro-Sociological Theory* (Princeton: Princeton University Press, 2008), 269.

191. Ian MacKaye, quoted in Azerrad, *Our Band Could Be Your Life*, 137. See also, Haenfler, *Straight Edge*, 45.

192. Nathan Strejcek, quoted in Azerrad, *Our Band Could Be Your Life*, 136.

193. Henry Rollins, *Black Coffee Blues* (London: Virgin Books, 2005), 52.

194. Quoted in Haenfler, *Straight Edge*, 39.

195. Ian MacKaye, quoted in Azerrad, *Our Band Could Be Your Life*, 136.

196. Wood, *Straightedge Youth*, 51. See also Granholm, "Metal, the End of the World," 27–42.

197. Cf. Paul Roubiczek's *Thinking in Opposites* (London: Routledge & Kegan Paul, 1952), which has been sadly overlooked almost since its publication, and has much thoughtful and creative analysis of binary thought and boundaries, particularly in relation to issues in the philosophy of religion.

198. Bakhtin, *Rabelais and His World*, 73.

199. Calvin Stapert, *A New Song for an Old World: Musical Thought in the Early Church* (Grand Rapids: Eerdmans, 2007), 131–148.

200. Bakhtin, *Rabelais and His World*, 73.

201. Bakhtin, *Rabelais and His World*, 73.

202. Bakhtin, *Rabelais and His World*, 73.

203. Bakhtin, *Rabelais and His World*, 74.

204. Bakhtin, *Rabelais and His World*, 74.

205. See Chris Humphrey, *The Politics of Carnival: Festive Misrule in Medieval England* (Manchester: Manchester University Press, 2001); Ronald Hutton, *The Rise and Fall of Merry England: The Ritual Year*, 1400–1700 (Oxford: Oxford University Press, 1994).

206. Bakhtin, *Rabelais and His World*, 74. See also, Hutton, *Rise and Fall of Merry England*.

207. Caillois, *Man and the Sacred*, 97–127.

208. Quoted in Bakhtin, *Rabelais and His World*, 75.

209. Claire Sponsler, quoted in Chris Humphrey, *The Politics of Carnival: Festive Misrule in Medieval England* (Manchester: Manchester University Press, 2001), 26.

210. See Ronald Hutton, *The Stations of the Sun: A History of the Ritual Year in Britain* (Oxford: Oxford University Press, 1996), 105–106.

211. See Neil Nehring, *Popular Music, Gender and Postmodernism: Anger Is an Energy* (Thousand Oaks: Sage, 1997), 150–179.

212. Lynch, *Sacred in the Modern World*, 20.

213. Bakhtin, *Rabelais and His World*, 91.

214. Bakhtin, *Rabelais and His World*, 90–91.

215. Lynch, *Sacred in the Modern World*, 42–43.

216. Bakhtin, *Rabelais and His World*, 90.

217. See Katerina Clark and Michael Holquist, *Mikhail Bakhtin* (Cambridge: Harvard University Press, 1984), 301.

218. Mikhail Bakhtin, *Problems of Dostoevsky's Poetics*, trans. Caryl Emerson (Minneapolis: University of Minnesota Press, 1984), 128.

219. Bakhtin, *Problems of Dostoevsky's Poetics*, 128.

220. See Michael Bull, *Sound Moves: iPod Culture and the Urban Experience* (London: Routledge, 2007).

221. Bakhtin, *Rabelais and His World*, 74–75. Cf. Jacques Attali, *Noise: The Political Economy of Music*, trans. Brian Massumi (Manchester: Manchester University Press, 1985), 21–22.

222. For more information about the Valencia Biennial, see: http://www.biennialfoundation.org/

223. David Byrne, quoted in Andrew Monko, "Shame on You: David Byrne Reveals New Paths to Eternal Damnation," *David Byrne*, http://www.davidbyrne.com/art/new_sins/about/new_sins_resonance.php (accessed 21 March, 2012).

224. David Byrne, *The New Sins/Los Nuevos Pecados* (London: Faber and Faber, 2001), 39, 49, 51, 63, 87, 89. See also his interview with Andrew Monko: "Shame on You: David Byrne Reveals New Paths to Eternal Damnation."

225. Bakhtin, *Problems of Dostoevsky's Poetics*, 122, 128.

226. Ann Jefferson, "Bodymatters: Self and Other in Bakhtin, Sartre and Barthes," in *Bakhtin and Cultural Theory*, eds. Ken Hirschkop and David G. Shepherd (Manchester: Manchester University Press, 2001), 215.

227. McClary, *Feminine Endings*, 151.

228. See, for example, Scott, *From the Erotic to the Demonic*, 15–57.

229. McClary, *Feminine Endings*, 152.

230. Holly Kruse, "Gender," in Horner and Swiss, *Key terms in Popular Music and Culture*, 88.

231. Kruse, "Gender," 88.

232. See Helen Reddington, *The Lost Women of Rock Music: Female Musicians of the Punk Era* (Sheffield: Equinox, 2012).

233. Liz Naylor, quoted in Lucy O'Brien, *She Bop II: The Definitive History of Women in Rock, Pop, and Soul* (London: Continuum, 2002), 134.

234. Anna Feigenbaum, "Remapping the Resonances of Riot Grrrl: Feminisms, Postfeminisms, and 'processes' of Punk," in *Interrogating Postfeminism: Gender and the Politics of Popular Culture*, eds. Yvonne Tasker and Diane Negra (Durham: Duke University Press, 2007), 132–152; Gillian Gaar, *She's a Rebel: The History of Women in Rock and Roll* (New York: Seal Press, 1992); Mary Celeste Kearney, "The Missing Links: Riot Grrrl-Feminism-Lesbian Culture," in *Sexing the Groove: Popular Music and Gender*, ed. Sheila Whiteley (London: Routledge, 1997), 207–229; Marion Leonard, *Gender in the Music Industry: Rock, Discourse and Girl Power* (Aldershot: Ashgate, 2007); Marion Leonard, "'Rebel Girl, You Are the Queen of My World': Feminism, 'Subculture' and Grrrl Power," in Whiteley, *Sexing the Groove*, 230–255; Nadine Monem, ed., *Riot Grrrl: Revolution Girl Style Now!* (London: Black Dog Publishing, 2007); Ian Penman, "Matters of Life and Death: Diamanda Galás," *The Wire* 190/191 (2000): 58–65; Jessica Rosenberg and Gitana Garofalo, "Riot Grrrl: Revolutions from Within," *Signs: Journal of Women in Culture and Society* 23 (1998): 809–841; Kristen Schilt, "'Riot Grrrl Is . . . ': The Contestation over Meaning," in *Music Scenes: Local, Translocal, and Virtual*, eds. Andy Bennett and Richard A. Peterson (Nashville: Vanderbilt University Press, 2004), 115–130; Schilt, Kristen and Elke Zobl, "Connecting the Dots: Riot Grrrls, Ladyfests, and the International Grrrl Zine Network," in *Next Wave Cultures: Feminism, Subcultures, Activism*, ed. Anita Harris (New York: Routledge, 2008), 171–192; Chérie Turner, *The Riot Grrrl Movement: The Feminism of a New Generation* (New York: The Rosen Publishing Group, 2001).

235. Clarissa Pinkola Estés, *Women Who Run With Wolves: Contacting the Power of the Wild Woman* (London: Rider, 1992), xiii. See also, Melissa Raphael, "Theology, Redemption, and the Call of the Wild," *Feminist Theology* 5 (1997).

236. Jane Schaberg, *The Resurrection of Mary Magdalene: Legends, Apocrypha and the Christian Testament* (New York: Continuum, 2004), 8.

237. Schaberg, *Resurrection of Mary Magdalene*, 8.

238. Mélisse Lafrance, "Me'Shell Ndegéocello, 'Mary Magdalene,'" in *Disruptive Divas: Feminism, Identity and Popular Music*, eds. Lori Burns and Mélisse Lafrance (New York: Routledge, 2002).

239. Richard Middleton, *Voicing the Popular: On the Subjects of Popular Music* (New York: Routledge, 2006), 99–100.

240. See her liner notes to *Radio Ethiopia*.

241. Victor Bockris, *Patti Smith* (London: Fourth Estate, 1998), 125–126.

242. She has suggested that this is the case. See, for example, Bockris, *Patti Smith*, 250.

243. Gerda Lerner, *The Creation of Patriarchy* (Oxford: Oxford University Press, 1986).

244. Naomi Goldenberg, *Changing of the Gods: Feminism and the End of Traditional Religions* (Boston: Beacon Press, 1979).

245. See Cathy Swichtenberg, ed., *The Madonna Connection: Representational Politics, Subcultural Identities and Cultural Theory* (Boulder: Westview Press, 1993). Although a little dated now, this is an excellent collection of discussions and, at the time, an important contribution to cultural criticism.

246. Although she provides no significant analysis of the intertextual relationship with religious signification, which is odd, Sheila Whiteley's analysis of eroticism and desire in Madonna's work is useful: *Women and Popular Music: Sexuality, Identity and Subjectivity* (London: Routledge, 2000), 136–151.

247. Laurie Schultze, Anne Barton White and Jane Brown, "'A Sacred Monster in Her Prime': Audience Construction of Madonna as the Low-Other," in *The Madonna Connection: Representational Politics, Subcultural Identities and Cultural Theory*, ed. Cathy Swichtenberg (Boulder: Westview Press, 1993), 15.

248. See Rosemary Radford Ruether, *Sexism and God-Talk: Towards a Feminist Theology* (London: SCM, 1983).

249. See, for example, Sheila Whiteley's discussion of her videos in "Seduced by the Sign: An Analysis of the Textual Links Between Sound and Image in Pop Videos." In Whiteley, *Sexing the Groove*, 259–276.

250. Madonna, *Sex* (New York: Warner Books, 1992).

251. Tori Amos, quoted in Lucy O'Brien, *Madonna: Like an Icon* (London: Transworld Publishers, 2007), 14–15.

252. On Madonna and liberation theologies, see Mark D. Hulsether, "Like a Sermon: Popular Religion in Madonna Videos," in *Religion and Popular Culture in America*, eds., Bruce David Forbes, and Jeffrey H. Mahan (Berkeley: University of California Press, 2000), 77–100.

253. Tori Amos, quoted in Burns and Lafrance, *Disruptive Divas*, 63.

254. Mélisse Lafrance, "A Cultural Studies Approach to Women and Popular Music," in Burns and Lafrance, *Disruptive Divas*, 2.

255. Judith Butler, quoted in Burns and Lafrance, *Disruptive Divas*, 67.

256. Burns and Lafrance, *Disruptive Divas*, 67.

257. Tori Amos, quoted in Jake Brown, *Tori Amos: In the Studio* (Toronto: ECW Press, 2011), 27. She has since committed herself to the victims of oppression and sexual violence, particularly through the Rape, Abuse, and Incest National Network, and has explored her own struggles as a result of her ordeal throughout the songs on her second album *Under the Pink*.

258. Tori Amos, quoted in Brown, *Tori Amos*, 27.

259. Zygmunt Bauman, "Durkheim's Society Revisited," 363.

260. See Jenks, *Transgression*, 178–180.

261. Slavoj Žižek, *On Belief* (London: Routledge, 2001), 20; see also 41.

262. Slavoj Žižek, *The Universal Exception: Selected Writings* (London: Continuum, 2006), 28.

263. Žižek, *Universal Exception*, 28–29.

264. Lilian Smith, *Strange Fruit* (Orlando: Harcourt Brace Jovanovich, 1993).

265. Anne Loveland, quoted in Kathy A. Perkins and Judith Louise Stephens, *Strange Fruit: Plays on Lynching by American Women* (Bloomington: Indiana University Press, 1998), 221.

266. Quoted, in Perkins and Stephens, *Strange Fruit*, 222.

267. Žižek, *Universal Exception*, 29.

268. Reinhold Niebuhr, quoted in Robert Moats Miller, "The Protestant Churches and Lynching, 1919–1939," *The Journal of Negro History* 42 (1957): 118–131.

269. John Peel, "Introduction," in Mudrian, *Choosing Death*, 18.

Chapter 4

1. William Blake, *The Complete Illuminated Works* (London: Thames & Hudson/The William Blake Trust, 2000), 86, 410.

2. Søren Kierkegaard, quoted in Bernard Reardon, *Religion in the Age of Romanticism* (Cambridge: Cambridge University Press, 1985), 1.

3. See David Cunningham, "Kraftwerk and the Image of the Modern," in *Kraftwerk: Music Non-Stop*, eds. Sean Albiez and David Pattie (London: Continuum, 2011), 44–62.

4. Robert Pattison, *The Triumph of Vulgarity: Rock Music in the Mirror of Romanticism* (New York: Oxford University Press, 1987), xi.

5. Pattison, *Triumph of Vulgarity*, 4.

6. Pattison, *Triumph of Vulgarity*, 23.

7. Pattison, *Triumph of Vulgarity*, 5.

8. Pattison, *Triumph of Vulgarity*, 102.

9. See for example, Camille Paglia, *Sex, Art and American Culture* (New York: Vintage Books, 1992).

10. Theodore Gracyk, *Rhythm and Noise: An Aesthetic of Rock* (London: I.B. Tauris, 1996), 193.

11. Gracyk, *Rhythm and Noise*, 195.

12. William Wordsworth, quoted in R. Keith Sawyer, *Explaining Creativity: The Science of Human Innovation*, 2nd ed. (New York: Oxford University Press, 2012), 24.

13. Sawyer, *Explaining Creativity*, 24.

14. Paul Marshall, *Mystical Encounters with the Natural World: Experiences and Explanations* (Oxford: Oxford University Press, 2005), 38.

15. Joshua Schmidt, "(En)countering the Beat: Paradox in Israeli Psytrance," in *The Local Scenes and Global Culture of Psytrance*, ed. Graham St. John (London: Routledge, 2010), 138.

16. Iggy Pop, quoted in Dimitri Ehrlich, *Inside the Music: Conversations with Contemporary Musicians about Spirituality, Creativity, and Consciousness* (Boston: Shambhala, 1997), 90.

17. Allan Moore, "The Contradictory Aesthetics of Woodstock," in *Remembering Woodstock*, ed. Andy Bennett (Aldershot: Ashgate, 2004), 76.

18. Rupert Till, *Pop Cult: Religion and Popular Music* (London: Continuum, 2010), 37.

19. Mick Jagger, quoted in Ehrlich, *Inside the Music*, 60–61.

20. Iggy Pop, quoted in Ehrlich, *Inside the Music*, 89.

21. John Zorn, "Preface," in *Arcana V: Music, Magic and Mysticism*, ed. John Zorn, (New York: Hips Road, 2010), v.

22. Zorn, "Preface," v-vi.

23. Zorn, "Preface," vi.

24. Zorn, *Arcana V*.

25. See Erik Davis, *Led Zeppelin IV* (New York: Continuum, 2005).

26. See Nina Antonia, *The One and Only: Peter Perrett—Homme Fatale* (Wembley: SAF Publishing, 1996), 93–94.

27. See Mark Fisher, "'Memorex for the Krakens': The Fall's Pulp Modernism," in *Mark E. Smith and The Fall: Art, Music and Politics*, eds. Michael Goddard and Benjamin Halligan (Farnham: Ashgate, 2010), 95–110.

28. Historically, while it is difficult to avoid the continuities between Romanticism and Gothic, is not unproblematic. See Emma McEvoy, "Gothic and the Romantics," in *The Routledge Companion to Gothic*, eds. Catherine Spooner and Emma McEvoy (Abingdon: Routledge, 2007), 19–28. See also, Michael Gamer, *Romanticism and the Gothic: Genre, Reception, and Canon Formation* (Cambridge: Cambridge University Press, 2000).

29. See Lilian Furst, *Romanticism in Perspective: A Comparative Study of Aspects of the Romantic Movements in England, France and Germany*, 2nd ed. (London: Macmillan, 1979).

30. On the contemporary use of the term "spiritual," see Giselle Vincett and Linda Woodhead, "Spirituality," in *Religions in the Modern World: Traditions and Transformations*, eds. Linda Woodhead, Hiroko Kawanami, and Christopher Partridge, 2nd ed. (London: Routledge, 2009), 319–337.

31. Reardon, *Religion in the Age of Romanticism*, vii.

32. Reardon, *Religion in the Age of Romanticism*, vii.

33. Timothy Miller, *The Hippies and American Values*, 2nd ed. (Knoxville: University of Tennessee Press, 2011), 41–42.

34. Reardon, *Religion in the Age of Romanticism*, vii.

35. Reardon, *Religion in the Age of Romanticism*, viii.

36. See Alan Moore, "Authenticity as Authentication," *Popular Music* 21 (2002): 209–223.

37. David Hesmondhalgh and Georgina Born, "Othering, Hybridity, and Fusion in Transnational Popular Musics," in *Western Music and Its Others: Difference, Representation, and Appropriation*

in Music, eds. Georgina Born and David Hesmondhalgh (Berkeley: University of California Press, 2000), 30.

38. Although one would think he studiously avoids reference to the sacred, Richard Middleton's analysis of "authenticity" is, I think, particularly helpful for the discussion here: *Voicing the Popular: On the Subjects of Popular Music* (New York: Routledge, 2006), 199–146.

39. Nicola Dibben, *Björk* (London: Equinox, 2009), 132.

40. Samuel Taylor Coleridge and William Wordsworth, *Lyrical Ballads 1798 and 1800*, eds. Michael Gamer and Dahlia Porter (Ontario: Broadview Press, 2008), 173–174.

41. Rob Young, *Electric Eden: Unearthing Britain's Visionary Music* (London: Faber & Faber, 2010), 428–429.

42. Richard Thompson, quoted in Clinton Heylin, *Gypsy Love Songs and Sad Refrains: The Recordings of Richard Thompson and Sandy Denny* (Sale: Labour of Love Publications, 1989), 7.

43. William Wordsworth, "Lines written a few miles above Tintern Abbey."

44. William Blake, "Auguries of Innocence."

45. Lynn White, "The Historical Roots of Our Ecologic Crisis," *Science* 155 (1967): 1203–1207. See also, Arnold Toynbee, "The Religious Background of the Present Environmental Crisis," in *Ecology and Religion in History*, eds. David and Eileen Spring (New York: Harper & Row, 1974), 137–149.

46. Bronislaw Szerszynski, *Nature, Technology and the Sacred* (Oxford: Blackwell, 2005), 32.

47. Keith Thomas, *Religion and the Decline of Magic: Studies in Popular Beliefs in Sixteenth and Seventeenth Century England* (Harmondsworth: Penguin, 1973).

48. For a discussion of problems with "the White thesis," see Szerszynski, *Nature, Technology and the Sacred*, 32–37.

49. Miller, *Hippies and American Values*, 92.

50. Theodore Roszak, *The Making of a Counter Culture: Reflections on the Technocratic Society and Its Youthful Opposition* (London: Faber, 1970), xiii.

51. Young, *Electric Eden*, 7.

52. Miller, *Hippies and American Values*, 49.

53. Jeremy Sandford and Ron Reid, *Tomorrow's People* (London: Jerome Publishing, 1974), 62.

54. Sandford and Reid, *Tomorrow's People*, 70.

55. Sandford and Reid, *Tomorrow's People*, 105.

56. Sandford and Reid, *Tomorrow's People*, 70.

57. Sandford and Reid, *Tomorrow's People*, 71. See also George McKay, *Glastonbury: A Very English Fair* (London: Victor Gollancz, 2000).

58. Crispin Aubrey and John Shearlaw, *Glastonbury: An Oral History of the Music, Mud and Magic* (London: Ebury Press, 2005), 22. See also, Andrew Kerr, *Intolerably Hip: A Memoir* (Norwich: Frontier Publishing, 2011).

59. Sandford and Reid, *Tomorrow's People*, 126.

60. See Christopher, Partridge "The Spiritual and the Revolutionary: Alternative Spirituality, British Free Festivals, and the Emergence of Rave Culture," *Culture and Religion* 7: 1 (2006): 41–60.

61. John Street, "'This is Your Woodstock': Popular Memories and Political Myths," in Bennett, *Remembering Woodstock*, 33.

62. On the history of such alternative interpretations of Glastonbury, see Ronald Hutton, *Witches, Druids and King Arthur* (London: Hambledon and London, 2003), 59–87.

63. Miller, *Hippies and American Values*, 46.

64. See Kennet Granholm, "Metal, the End of the World, and Radical Environmentalism: Ecological Apocalypse in the Lyrics of Earth Crisis," in *Anthems of Apocalypse: Popular Music and Apocalyptic Thought* by Christopher Partridge (Sheffield: Phoenix Press, 2012), 27–42.

65. See Granholm, "Metal, the End of the World, and Radical Environmentalism," in Partridge, *Anthems of Apocalypse*, 27–42; Christopher Partridge, "Babylon's Burning: Reggae, Rastafari and Millenarianism," in *The End All Around Us: Apocalyptic Texts and Popular Culture*, eds. John Walliss and Kenneth Newport (London: Equinox, 2009), 43–70; David Janssen and

Edward Whitelock, *Apocalypse Jukebox: The End of the World in American Popular Music* (Brooklyn: Soft Skull Press, 2009).

66. Miller, *Hippies and American Values*, 137.

67. Paul Stump, *Digital Gothic: A Critical Discography of Tangerine Dream* (London: SAF Publishing, 1997), 48.

68. Middleton, *Voicing the Popular*, 214.

69. See Marion Bowman, "The Noble Savage and the Global Village: Cultural Evolution in New Age and Neo-Pagan Thought," *Journal of Contemporary Religion* 10 (1995): 139–149.

70. Reardon, *Religion in the Age of Romanticism*, 3.

71. Reardon, *Religion in the Age of Romanticism*, 3.

72. See Kate McCarthy, "Deliver Me from Nowhere," in *God in the Details: American Religion in Popular Culture*, eds. Eric Mazur and Kate McCarthy (New York: Routledge, 2001), 23–45.

73. Albion is an ancient word for England that tends to evoke its mythologies and core national values. See Peter Ackroyd, *Albion: The Origins of the English Imagination* (London; Vintage, 2004).

74. See Dibben, *Björk*, 24–52; "Nature and Nation: National Identity and Environmentalism in Icelandic Popular Music Video and Music Documentary," *Ethnomusicology Forum* 18:1 (2009): 131–151.

75. For more information about Head Heritage, see: http://www.headheritage.co.uk/

76. A quotation by from the band The Residents, reproduced in the booklet accompanying Julian Cope, *Peggy Suicide* (1991).

77. Julian Cope, from the liner notes to *Jehovahkill* (1992).

78. See Bowman, "The Noble Savage and the Global Village," 139–149.

79. Edward Burnett Tylor, *Primitive Culture: Researches Into the Development of Mythology, Philosophy, Religion, Art, and Custom*, vol. 1 (London: John Murray, 1871), 65.

80. Tylor, *Primitive Culture*, vol. 1, 7.

81. Ursula Vaughan Williams, *R.V.W.: A Biography of Ralph Vaughan Williams* (Oxford: Oxford University Press, 1964), 100.

82. Bob Pegg, *Rites and Riots: Folk Customs of Britain and Europe* (Poole: Blandford Press, 1981), 8.

83. Storey, *Inventing Popular Culture*, 10–11.

84. Storey, *Inventing Popular Culture*, 11.

85. Hubert Parry, quoted in Storey, *Inventing Popular Culture*, 11.

86. Hubert Parry, quoted in Storey, *Inventing Popular Culture*, 11.

87. Philip Abrams and Andrew McCulloch, *Communes, Sociology, and Society* (Cambridge: Cambridge University Press, 1976), 2.

88. Young, *Electric Eden*, 18–19.

89. Donovan, quoted in Young, *Electric Eden*, 19–20.

90. See Tony Dale, "A Conversation with Vashti Bunyan," *The Ptolemaic Terrascope* 30 (2001): http://www.terrascope.co.uk/MyBackPages/Vashti%20Bunyan%20PT30.pdf (accessed: May 2, 2012).

91. Vashti Bunyan, quoted in Young, *Electric Eden*, 34–35.

92. Lesley P. Hartley, *The Go-Between* (Harmondsworth: Penguin, 1958), 1.

93. Lyrically and musically, the single from the album, "Hole in My Shoe," is an excellent example of English pastoral psychedelia.

94. David Dalton, "A Last Look at Traffic: 'Who Knows What Tomorrow May Bring?,'" *Rolling Stone* 32 (May 3, 1969): 14.

95. Dalton, "A Last Look at Traffic," 14–15. As news spread about rural retreat and its influence on creativity, other artists gradually made their way there to draw what inspiration they could from the "numinous" land, "filled with spirits." As Mike Kellie of Spooky Tooth commented, "we were living on a farm just a few miles away, so we drove over quite regularly. It became a real gathering place. Trevor Burton from The Move had grown sick of being a 'pop' star and wanted to make 'serious' music, so he moved up to the cottage and virtually lived there as well."

He continues, "we'd play through the night. . . . The standard of playing at those jams was fantastic. People just seemed to turn up, like Ritchie Furay and Steve Stills from Buffalo Springfield." Mike Kellie, quoted in Johnny Black, "Eyewitness: Traffic Get Their Heads Together in the Country," *Q* 103 (April, 1995): 60.

96. Dalton, "A Last Look at Traffic," 14–15.

97. Dalton, "A Last Look at Traffic," 14–15.

98. Lawrence Levine, *Black Culture and Black Consciousness: Afro-American Folk Thought from Slavery to Freedom* (Oxford: Oxford University Press, 1977), 39.

99. Levine, *Black Culture and Black Consciousness*, 32, 175.

100. Jimmy Page, quoted in Davis, *Led Zeppelin IV*, 28.

101. Linda McCartney, quoted in Young, *Electric Eden*, 37.

102. James E. Perone, *Music of the Counterculture Era* (Westport: Greenwood Press, 2004), 144.

103. Alistair Cooke, quoted in Simon Warner, "Reporting Woodstock: Some Contemporary Press Reflections on the Festival," in Bennett, *Remembering Woodstock*, 69.

104. Joni Mitchell, quoted in Lloyd Whitesell, *The Music of Joni Mitchell* (New York: Oxford University Press, 2008), 33.

105. Michael Lang, *The Road to Woodstock* (New York: HarperCollins, 2009), 118.

106. See: *Deeply Vale Free Festival*, http://www.deeplyvale.com/history.htm (accessed: April 31, 2012) and *Woodstock 69 Festival and Concert*, http://www.woodstock69.com/archive/ (accessed: April 31, 2012).

107. John Street, "'This is Your Woodstock': Popular Memories and Political Myths," in Bennett, *Remembering Woodstock*, 31.

108. Greil Marcus, quoted in Miller, *Hippies and American Values*, 49–50.

109. Michael Marinacci, quoted in Chas S. Clifton, *Her Hidden Children: The Rise of Wicca and Paganism in America* (Lanham: AltaMira Press, 2006), 150.

110. Young, *Electric Eden*, 300.

111. Warren Hinckle, "A Social History of the Hippies," in *The 1960s: A Documentary Reader*, ed. Brian Ward (Oxford: Blackwell, 2010), 101.

112. Graham Harvey, *Listening People, Speaking Earth: Contemporary Paganism* (London: Hurst & Co., 1997), 181–182.

113. See Martin Barker, "On Being a 1960s Tolkien Reader," in *From Hobbits to Hollywood: Essays on Peter Jackson's Lord of the Rings*, eds. Ernest Mathijs and Murray Pomerance (Amsterdam: Rodopi, 2006), 81–100; Bruce Beatie, "The Tolkien Phenomenon: 1954–1968," *Journal of Popular Culture* 3 (1970): 689–703; John Ryan, *Tolkien: Cult or Culture?* (Armidale, New South Wales: University Press of New England, 1969).

114. Mike Oldfield, *Changeling* (London: Virgin Books, 2008), 106. See also, Randall Holm, "'Pulling back the Darkness': Starbound with Jon Anderson," in *Call Me the Seeker: Listening to Religion in Popular Music*, ed. Michael J. Gilmour (London: Continuum, 2005), 158–71.

115. Young, *Electric Eden*, 465–466.

116. See Miller, *Hippies and American Values*, 149–151.

117. Young, *Electric Eden*, 466.

118. Paul Hegarty and Martin Halliwell, *Beyond and Before: Progressive Rock Since the 1960s* (New York: Continuum, 2011), 58.

119. Trevor Dann, *Darker Than the Deepest Sea: The Search for Nick Drake* (London: Piatkus Books, 2006), 161.

120. Ross Grainger, quoted in Dann, *Darker Than the Deepest Sea*, 161.

121. Kenneth Grahame, *Pagan Papers* (Teddington: The Echo Library, 2006 [1904]), 33.

122. Davis, *Led Zeppelin IV*, 7.

123. Jane Ormsby-Gore, quoted in Young, *Electric Eden*, 296. Ormsby-Gore was reputedly the inspiration for The Rolling Stones' song "Lady Jane" (*Aftermath*).

124. See C.J. Stone, *Last of the Hippies* (London: Faber and Faber, 1999), 68–83; Christopher Partridge, "The Spiritual and the Revolutionary: Alternative Spirituality, British Free Festivals, and the Emergence of Rave Culture," *Culture and Religion* 7: 1 (2006): 41–60.

125. Rowan Williams, "Foreword," in Whittaker, *Be Glad*, 6.

126. See Robert Pendleton, "Kindred Spirits," in Whittaker, *Be Glad*, 68–82.

127. Björk, quoted in Dibben, *Björk*, 55.

128. An excellent archive of UK festivals held between 1960 and 1990, including photographs, can be found at: http://www.ukrockfestivals.com/ (accessed: May 01, 2012). See also, George McKay, *Senseless Acts of Beauty: Cultures of Resistance Since the Sixties* (London: Verso, 1996), 15.

129. Kevin Hetherington, *New Age Travellers: Vanloads of Uproarious Humanity* (London: Cassell, 2000), 47.

130. Wally Russell, quoted in Matthew Collin, *Altered States: the Story of Ecstasy Culture and Acid House* (London: Serpent's Tail, 1998), 185.

131. See Young, *Electric Eden*, 503; Andy Worthington, *Stonehenge: Celebration and Subversion* (Loughborough: Alternative Albion, 2004), 41.

132. Michael Clarke, *The Politics of Pop Festivals* (London: Junction Books, 1982), 85.

133. See McKay, *Glastonbury*, 148.

134. Wally Russell, quoted in Matthew Collin, *Altered States: the Story of Ecstasy Culture and Acid House* (London: Serpent's Tail, 1998), 185.

135. Phil Russell/Wally Hope, quoted in Young, *Electric Eden*, 503–504.

136. Björk, quoted in Dibben, *Björk*, 40.

137. Arne Naess, "The Basics of Deep Ecology," in *The Green Fuse: The Schumacher Lectures 1983– 1988*, ed. John Button (London: Quartet Books, 1990), 135.

138. Warwick Fox, "Deep Ecology: A New Philosophy of Our Time?" *The Ecologist* 14 (1984): 196.

139. Fox, "Deep Ecology," 196.

140. J. Baird Callicott, quoted in David Kinsley, *Ecology and Religion: Ecological Spirituality in Cross-Cultural Perspective* (Englewood Cliffs: Prentice Hall, 1995), 187–188 (emphasis added).

141. John Seed, quoted in Simon Hailwood, *How to be a Green Liberal: Nature, Value, and Liberal Philosophy* (Chesham: Acumen, 2004), 38.

142. Simon Reynolds, *Energy Flash: A Journey Through Rave Music and Dance Culture* (London: Picador, 1998), 138.

143. Hegarty and Halliwell, *Beyond and Before*, 56.

144. Hegarty and Halliwell, *Beyond and Before*, 56.

145. Toni Arthur, quoted in Young, *Electric Eden*, 440.

146. Clinton Heylin, *Gypsy Love Songs and Sad Refrains: The Recordings of Richard Thompson and Sandy Denny* (Sale: Labour of Love Publications, 1989), 7.

147. Robin Hardy and Anthony Shaffer also produced a novel five years after the release of the film: *The Wicker Man* (London: Pan Books, 2000 [1978]).

148. James G. Frazer, *The Golden Bough: A Study in Magic and Religion*, abridged edition (London: Macmillan, 1922).

149. See Jon Fitzgerald and Philip Hayward, "Inflamed: Synthetic Folk Music and Paganism in the Island World of *The Wicker Man*," in *Terror Tracks: Music, Sound and Horror Cinema*, ed. Philip Hayward (London: Equinox, 2009), 103.

150. See Fitzgerald and Hayward, "Inflamed," 101–111.

151. Jason Pitzl-Waters, "Musical Influence of The Wicker Man Soundtrack": http://www.adarkershadeofpagan.com/labels/The%20Wicker%20Man.html (accessed: May 01, 2012).

152. See http://www.compulsiononline.com/wickerman5.htm (accessed: May 04, 2012).

153. Quoted by Jason Pitzl-Waters, "Musical Influence of The Wicker Man Soundtrack": http://www.adarkershadeofpagan.com/labels/The%20Wicker%20Man.html (accessed: May 01, 2012).

154. Quoted by Jason Pitzl-Waters, "Musical Influence of The Wicker Man Soundtrack": http://www.adarkershadeofpagan.com/labels/The%20Wicker%20Man.html (accessed: May 01, 2012).

155. For an interesting discussion of the apocalyptic in Tibet's work, see Sérgio Fava, "'When Rome Falls, Falls the World': Current 93 and Apocalyptic Folk," in Partridge, *Anthems of Apocalypse*, 72–89.

156. Julia Kristeva, quoted in Jonathan Culler, *The Pursuit of Signs: Semiotics, Literature, Deconstruction* (London: Routledge, 2001), 116. See also Julia Kristeva, *Desire in Language: A Semiotic Approach to Literature and Art* (New York: Columbia University Press 1980.

157. "Current 93" is itself a Thelemic reference, in that in Crowley's *Book of the Law*, the number references, using the system of isopsephy, two key terms: "Thelema" (9) and "Love" (3).

158. David Tibet, quoted in Keith Moliné, "The Road to Salvation: Current 93," *The Wire* 269 (2006): 32; see also, David Keenan, "Childhood's End," *The Wire* 163 (1997): 34–37.

159. It is difficult to resist making a connection between "Noddy" and Blake's conception of God as "Nobodaddy" in the poem "To Nobodaddy."

160. David Tibet, quoted in Keenan, "Childhood's End," 36.

161. David Tibet, quoted in Keenan, "Childhood's End," 36.

162. David Tibet, quoted in Keenan, "Childhood's End," 37.

163. David Tibet, quoted in Keenan, "Childhood's End," 37.

164. Keenan, *England's Hidden Reverse*, 151.

165. David Tibet, quoted in Keenan, "Childhood's End," 35.

166. Harry Smith, "Liner Notes," *Anthology of American Folk Music* (Folkways, 1952): 18. The Smithsonian Institution has made Harry Smith's liner notes, along with the notes from the 1997 release of the anthology, available for download at: http://www.folkways.si.edu/albumdetails.aspx?itemid=2426 (accessed July 04, 2012).

167. David Keenan, "The Fire Down Below: Welcome to the New Weird America," *The Wire* 234 (August, 2003): 34.

168. Ben Chasny, quoted in Keenan, "The Fire Down Below," 40.

169. Keenan, "The Fire Down Below," 37.

170. Ben Chasny, quoted in Keenan, "The Fire Down Below," 40.

171. Ben Chasny, quoted in Keenan, "The Fire Down Below," 40.

172. Gavin Baddeley, *Lucifer Rising: Sin, Devil Worship & Rock 'n' Roll* (London: Plexus, 1999), 47. See also, Bill Landis, *Anger: The Unauthorised Biography of Kenneth Anger* (San Francisco: HarperCollins, 1995).

173. A busy workload with Led Zeppelin and an escalating drug habit prevented Page from devoting much time to the project. Hence, he took far too long, only finally releasing the 23-minute soundtrack in 1987, which is now available through his website as *Lucifer Rising and Other Soundtracks* (2012). See Christopher Knowles, "Symphony for the Devil," *Classic Rock* 96 (Summer, 2006): 32–43; Peter Makowski, "Jimmy Page on *Lucifer Rising*," *Classic Rock* 96 (Summer, 2006): 44–45; Christopher Knowles, "Bobby Beausoleil on Recording *Lucifer Rising*," *Classic Rock* 96 (Summer, 2006): 41.

174. Quoted in Baddeley, *Lucifer Rising*, 48.

175. Jeffrey Burton Russell, "The Romantic Devil," in *Satan*, ed. Harold Bloom (New York: Chelsea House Publishers, 2005), 160.

176. Russell, "The Romantic Devil," 160.

177. See for example, Jason Bivins' discussion of conservative Evangelical fear and popular music: *Religion of Fear: The Politics of Horror in Conservative Evangelicalism* (New York: Oxford, 2008), 89–128.

178. Russell, "The Romantic Devil," 166.

179. Alexander, *The Meanings of Social Life*, 110.

180. Jann S. Wenner, "The *Rolling Stone* Interview: Jagger Remembers," http://www.jannswenner.com/Archives/Jagger_Remembers.aspx (accessed February 05, 2012).

181. For example, see Michael Hendrick, "Happy Birthday to Mikhail Bulgakov from Patti Smith and Beatdom!" *Beatdom: Beat News* (May 15, 2012). Available at: http://www.beatdom.com/?p=1573 (accessed, July 06, 2012).

182. Mikhail Bulgakov, *The Master And Margarita*, trans. Richard Pevear and Larissa Volokhonsky (London: Penguin, 1997), 360.

183. Georges Bataille, quoted in the following article, which should be consulted: Jeffrey Alexander, "Toward a Sociology of Evil: Getting Beyond Modernist Common Sense About the Alternative to 'the Good,'" in *Rethinking Evil: Contemporary Perspectives*, ed. María Pía Lara (Berkeley: University of California Press, 2001), 153.

184. Russell, "The Romantic Devil," 160.

185. Jesper Aagaard Petersen, "Introduction: Embracing Satan," in *Contemporary Religious Satanism: A Critical Anthology*, ed. Jesper Aagaard Petersen (Farnham: Ashgate, 2009), 2. See also, Per Faxneld and Jesper Aagaard Petersen, eds., *The Devil's Party: Satanism in Modernity* (New York: Oxford University Press, 2012).

186. See Amina Olander Lap, "Categorizing Modern Satanism: An Analysis of LaVey's Early Writings," in *The Devil's Party: Satanism in Modernity*, eds. Per Faxneld and Jesper Aagaard Petersen (New York: Oxford University Press, 2012), 83–102. See also Paul Heelas, *The New Age Movement: The Celebration of the Self and the Sacralization of Modernity* (Oxford: Blackwell, 1996), 23–27.

187. Anton S. LaVey, *The Devil's Notebook* (Portland: Feral House, 1992), 9–10.

188. Anton S. LaVey, quoted in B. H. Wolfe, "Introduction," in Anton S. LaVey, *The Satanic Bible* (New York: Avon Books, 1969), 13.

189. Jean LaFontaine, "Satanism and Satanic Mythology," in *Witchcraft and Magic in Europe: the Twentieth Century*, eds. Bengt Ankarloo and Stuart Clark (Philadelphia: University of Pennsylvania Press, 1999), 97.

190. Petersen, "Introduction," 8–9. See also, Michael Moynihan and Didrik Søderlind, *Lords of Chaos: The Bloody Rise of the Satanic Metal Underground*, 2nd ed. (Los Angeles: Feral House, 2003), 257–265.

191. Asbjørn Dyrendal, "Darkness Within: Satanism as a Self-Religion," in *Contemporary Religious Satanism: A Critical Anthology*, ed. Jesper Aagaard Petersen (Farnham: Ashgate, 2009), 66.

192. Jean LaFontaine, "Satanism and Satanic Mythology," in Ankarloo and Clark, *Witchcraft and Magic in Europe*, 97.

193. Dyrendal, "Satanism and Popular Music," 29–30.

194. As Michael Moynihan and Didrik Søderlind comment, "the type of Satanism preached in the early stages of Black Metal was just an inversion of doctrinal Christianity. Whereas international Satanic groups like the Church of Satan view Satan in an archetypal or symbolic sense, to the Norwegian teenagers he was most certainly real. In a similar manner to fundamentalist Christians, they viewed the world as eternally locked in a struggle between good and evil – the only real difference being which side they chose to fight on." *Lords of Chaos*, 76.

195. Carel Rowe, "Illuminating Lucifer," *Film Quarterly* 27: 4 (1974): 26.

196. Kenneth Anger, quoted in Rowe, "Illuminating Lucifer," 26.

197. Rowe, "Illuminating Lucifer," 26.

198. Richard Henderson, "Anger is an Energy," *The Wire* 247 (September, 2004): 32.

199. Quoted in Edwin Pouncey, "Industrial Light and Magick," *The Wire* 247 (September, 2004): 35.

200. Alexander Scriabin, quoted in Faubian Bowers, *Scriabin: A Biography*, vol. 2, 2nd ed. (New York: Dover Publications, 1996), 244–245.

201. Bowers, *Scriabin*, vol. 2, 244–245.

202. "Many of the devout who feared the future fell into hateful, blackhearted sects. Sadism and cannibalism were practiced by a few. Nikolai Sperling (1880–1815), painter and friend of Scriabin, drank human blood and ate human flesh . . . in an effort to derive mystical experience. But this was scarcely out of tradition. After all, Tolstoi in the Caucasus had relished cocktails made of vodka, gunpowder and congealed blood. Satan was worshipped in blasphemous, perverse and even sexual 'Black Masses.' The Anti-Christ, dreaded by some, sought by others, was admitted by all." Bowers, *Scriabin*, vol. 1, 47–48.

203. A good overview of Scriabin's understanding of music as a "purveyor of the spiritual" can be found in Antony Copley, *Music and the Spiritual: Composers and Politics in the 20th Century* (London: Ziggurat Books International, 2012), 56–76.

204. Yevgeny Sudbin, "Scriabin Liner Notes": http://www.yevgenysudbin.com/artist.php?view=essays&rid=456 (accessed on May 13, 2012).

205. See Kip Trevor's revealingly frank interview with Baddeley in *Lucifer Rising*, 98–99.

206. The text from the talk is available at: http://www.killingjoke.org.uk/aid/courtauld.html (accessed July 06, 2012).

207. P-Orridge, "Genesis P-Orridge," 122.

208. Carl Abrahamsson, "Changing Compositions," in P-Orridge, *Painful But Fabulous*, 29.

209. He was born Geoffrey Burton, but later, following the remarriage of his mother, changed his name to Geoffrey Rushton, and finally to John Balance (also spelt Jhonn and Jhon).

210. P-Orridge, in order to distinguish between him and another David he knew, taking into account his spiritual interests, gave him the name David Tibet.

211. Gavin Semple, quoted in Keenan, *England's Hidden Reverse*, 41.

212. Quoted in Keenan, *England's Hidden Reverse*, 104.

213. See Keenan, *England's Hidden Reverse*, 104.

214. A good interview with Tibet, exploring his beliefs can be found in Charles Neal, *Tape Delay* (Wembley: SAF Publishing, 1987), 205–211.

215. Quoted in Keenan, *England's Hidden Reverse*, 40 (emphasis added).

216. Carl Abrahamsson, "Changing Compositions." In P-Orridge, *Painful But Fabulous*, 29.

217. Ford, *Wreckers of Civilization*, 10.29. See also V. Vale and Andrea Juno, eds., *Re/Search 6/7: Industrial Culture Handbook* (San Francisco: RE/Search, 1983), 62–77; P-Orridge, *Painful But Fabulous*.

218. Of particular interest is *In the Shadow of the Sun*, an occult film by Derek Jarman for which Throbbing Gristle produced a particularly menacing soundtrack—*In the Shadow of the Sun* (1980).

219. Neville Drury, *Echoes From the Void: Writings on Magic, Visionary Art and the New Consciousness* (Bridport: Prism Press, 1994), 86.

220. See Austin Osman Spare, *Ethos: The Magical Writings of Austin Osman Spare* (Thame: I-H-O Books, 2001); Phil Baker, *Austin Osman Spare: The Life and Legend of London's Lost Artist* (London: Strange Attractor, 2010).

221. Drury, *Echoes From the Void*, 86.

222. Zero Kama's "Prayer of Zos" is based on Spare's 1927 occult interpretation of "The Lord's Prayer."

223. Davis, *Led Zeppelin IV*, 42–43.

224. David Tibet was a member Grant's occult order, Typhonian Ordo Templi Orientis.

225. Genesis P-Orridge, "'Sigils'–An Alphabet of Desire," in *Painful But Fabulous*, ed. P-Orridge, 133.

226. Spare's thought has also been very influential within contemporary Chaos Magick. Indeed, if one were to seek a natural home for much of P-Orridge's thought, Chaos Magick would be a good place to begin.

227. V. Vale, ed., *RE/Search 4/5: William S. Burroughs, Brion Gysin and Throbbing Gristle* (San Francisco: RE/Search Publications, 2007), 87; see also 64–65.

228. Kenneth Anger, quoted in Rowe, "Illuminating Lucifer," 26.

229. Genesis P-Orridge, "The Splinter Test," in Zorn, *Arcana V*, 313. This, of course, is similar to the use of "I" words in Rastafari and reggae. See Jack Johnson-Hill, *I-sight: The World of Rastafari: An Interpretative Sociological Account* (Lanham: Scarecrow Press, 1995), 143–199.

230. Erik Davis, *Led Zeppelin IV* (New York: Continuum, 2005), 26.

231. Genesis P-Orridge, "The Lion in a Cage," in Vale, *RE/Search 4/5*, 87 (emphasis added).

232. William S. Burroughs, "Uranium Willie and the Heavy Metal Kid: A Near-Forgotten 1975 Talk with Jimmy Page," in John Bream, *Whole Lotta Led Zeppelin: The Illustrated History of the Heavi-*

est Band of All Time (Minneapolis: Voyageur Press, 2008), 168. The article first appeared in the June 1975 issue of *Crawdaddy*.

233. Jason Louv, "Introduction: On the Way to Thee Garden," in Genesis P-Orridge, *Thee Psychick Bible: Thee Apocryphal Scriptures of Genesis P-Orridge and Thee Third MIND ov Psychic TV*, ed. Jason Louv (Port Townsend: Feral House, 1994), 18.

234. Jason Louv, "Introduction," 18.

235. TOPY, *Thee Grey Book*. http://www.kondole.com/theegreybook/greycover.htm (accessed October 05, 2010).

236. John Balance, quoted in Young, *Electric Eden*, 605.

237. John Everall, "Obscure Mechanics," *The Wire* 134 (April, 1995): 18.

238. Everall, "Obscure Mechanics," 18.

239. Coil, quoted in Neal, *Tape Delay*, 117.

240. John Balance, quoted in Everall, "Obscure Mechanics," 18.

241. John Balance, quoted in Everall, "Obscure Mechanics," 18.

242. Everall, "Obscure Mechanics," 18.

243. The year of his meeting with Gysin isn't entirely clear. In one early interview he couldn't remember when he first met Gysin—Vale, *RE/Search 4/5*, 71—but later, in 2000, he seems to have reached the conclusion that it was 1980—John Geiger, *Nothing is True, Everything is Permitted: The Life of Brion Gysin* (New York: Disinformation Company, 2005), 292.

244. See Genesis P-Orridge, *Esoterrorist: Selected Essays 1980–1988* (London: OV Press, 1988), 34–37. Also available at: http://www.scribd.com/doc/21064820/Genesis-P-Orridge-Esoterrorist (accessed August 11, 2010).

245. The Dream Machine, developed with the British electrical engineer, Ian Sommerville, was essentially a rather basic stroboscope, consisting of a tube with slits cut into it, through which the light from a bulb would shine. Inside the tubes, calligraphic symbols were painted. The construction was then placed on a record turntable and rotated at 78 rpm. By focussing on the flashes of light produced, "visions start with a kaleidoscope of colors on a plane in front of the eyes and gradually become more complex and beautiful, breaking like a surf on a shore until whole patterns of colour are pounding to get in. After a while the visions were permanently behind my eyes and I was in the middle of the whole scene with limitless patterns being generated around me. There was an almost unbearable feeling of spatial movement for a while but it was well worth getting through for I found that when it stopped I was high above the earth in a universal blaze of glory. Afterwards I found that my perception of the world around me had increased very notably." Quoted in Geiger, *Nothing is True*, 161–162.

246. William S. Burroughs and Brion Gysin, *The Third Mind* (New York: Viking Press, 1978), 44.

247. See Genesis P-Orridge, "Eyes Wide Shut," *The Guardian* (November 15, 2003). Available at: http://www.guardian.co.uk/books/2003/nov/15/art.classics (accessed, May 14, 2012).

248. P-Orridge, "Eyes Wide Shut."

249. P-Orridge, "The Splinter Test," 297.

250. He was able to do this when, in 1998, he was awarded $1.5 million when he sued the producer Rick Rubin, following serious injuries, including nearly losing his left arm, when escaping a fire at his Los Angeles home.

251. For a good discussion of the posthuman in relation to Marilyn Manson, see Kim Toffoletti, *Cyborgs and Barbie Dolls: Feminism, Popular Culture and the Posthuman Body* (London: I.B. Tauris, 2007), 81–105.

252. "Third being" is a reference to the "third mind," created by cut-up, as discussed by Gysin and Burroughs in *The Third Mind*.

253. See for example: Fritjof Capra, *The Turning Point: Science, Society and the Rising Culture* (London: Flamingo, 1983); Marilyn Ferguson, *The Aquarian Conspiracy: Personal and Social Transformation in Our Times* (London: Paladin, 1982); Ken Wilber, "The Atman-Project," in *Holistic Revolution: The Essential New Age Reader*, ed. William Bloom (Harmondsworth: Allen Lane, Penguin Press, 2000), 77–83; Wouter Hanegraaff, *New Age Religion and Western Culture:*

Esotericism in the Mirror of Secular Thought (New York: State University of New York Press, 1998).

254. Genesis P-Orridge, *Esoterrorist: Selected Essays 1980-1988* (London: OV Press, 1988), 18.

255. It's interesting to compile list of those musicians and artists that have collaborated with Psychic TV, which includes a range of countercultural icons from Timothy Leary to Derek Jarman. As well as the usual suspects from Coil and Current 93 (and related musicians such as Larry Thrasher, The Hafler Trio and Nurse With Wound), other bands and musicians include The Cult, The Master Musicians of Jajouka, Soft Cell and Andrew Weatherall.

256. On Tibet and Current 93, see Fava, "When Rome Falls, Falls the World," 72–89; Moliné, "The Road to Salvation," 28–33.

257. On The Process Church of the Final Judgment, see William S. Bainbridge, *Satan's Power: A Deviant Psychotherapy Cult* (Berkeley: University of California Press, 1978); Timothy Wyllie, *Love, Sex, Fear, Death: The Inside Story of the Process Church of the Final Judgment*, ed. Adam Parfray (Port Townsend, WA: Feral House, 2009).

258. See Genesis P-Orridge, "The Process is the Product: The Processean Influence on Thee Temple Ov Psychick Youth," in Wyllie, *Love, Sex, Fear, Death*, 173–184.

259. It should be noted that, at the end of January 2008, its US website reported that "Thee Temple Ov Psychick Youth North America will be directing all of its attention at the launch of the new phase in our communal growth, the Autonomous Individuals' Network." See http://www.ain23.com/topy.net/news.html (accessed January 23, 2011).

260. In his appreciative discussion of Psychic TV, Julian Cope concurs with P-Orridge's negative assessment of television: "Our brains experience some waxy build-up, coagulating most unfortunately into a kind of scabby psychic shell around our doors of perception, denying us access to all but the most familiar concepts and thoughts." *Copendium: An Expedition Into the Rock 'n' Roll Underworld* (London: Faber & Faber, 2012), 365.

261. P-Orridge, *Esoterrorist*, 18–19.

262. As is common in occulture, this Western occult understanding of the *Kangling* is a little sensational and misleading. While it's interesting because it tells us something about Psychic TV's interests and motivations, in actual fact, used within tantric Buddhism, in the Chöel ritual, the sound is understood to be "terrifying to evil spirits. Tibetan shamans ... employ the thighbone trumpet in many rituals of exorcism and weather control. Here the instrument's threatening drone is said to unhinge the powers of malignant spirits. . . . In the tantric tradition the left femur of a sixteen-year-old Brahmin girl was considered to be the most effective. . . . The femur of a 'twice-born' brahmin was the next best kind of bone, followed by the thighbone of a murder victim, then a person who died from a sudden accidental death, then one who died from a virulent or contagious disease. The bones of a person who died from old age or 'natural causes' were considered virtually powerless in its efficacy against the powers of evil spirits." Robert Beer, *The Encyclopedia of Tibetan Symbols and Motifs* (Chicago: Serindia Publications, 2004), 259.

263. Interviewed by Neal in *Tape Delay*, 209.

264. Quoted in Keenan, *England's Hidden Reverse*, 104; see also Balance's comments in Neal, *Tape Delay*, 119.

265. Ashley Hutchings, quoted in Leech, *Seasons They Change*, 187.

266. Ashley Hutchings, quoted in Leech, *Seasons They Change*, 187. Hutchings is actually referring to the National Front, not the British National Party, which was formed in 1982 by John Tyndall.

267. See Billy Bragg, *The Progressive Patriot: A Search for Belonging* (London: Bantam Press, 2006).

268. Eliza Carthy, "Traditional English Song Has No Links to the Far Right or Nick Griffin," *The Guardian* (January 26, 2010), http://www.guardian.co.uk/commentisfree/2010/jan/26/nick-griffin-bnp-folk-music (accessed May 30, 2012).

269. Hunter S. Thompson, *The Great Shark Hunt: Strange Tales from a Strange Time* (London: Picador, 2010), 98.

270. Lawrence Grossberg, *We Gotta Get Out of This Place: Popular Conservatism and Postmodern Culture* (London: Routledge, 1992), 80.

271. Grossberg, *We Gotta Get Out of This Place*, 80–81.

272. Grossberg, *We Gotta Get Out of This Place*, 82.

273. Grossberg, *We Gotta Get Out of This Place*, 82.

274. Grossberg, *We Gotta Get Out of This Place*, 83–84.

275. Paul Nelson, quoted in Gerard DeGroot, *The 60s Unplugged: A Kaleidoscopic History of a Disorderly Decade* (London: Macmillan, 2008), 232.

276. Hugh McLeod, *The Religious Crisis of the 1960s* (Oxford: Oxford University Press, 2007), 25.

277. Grossberg, *We Gotta Get Out of This Place*, 84.

278. Einar Selvik, "Sowing New Seeds, Strengthening Old Roots," *Wardruna* (2007): Available at: http://www.wardruna.com/about/ (accessed, July 10, 2012).

279. Gry Mørk, "Why Didn't the Churches Begin to Burn a Thousand Years Earlier?" in *Religion and Popular Music in Europe*, eds. Thomas Bossius, Andreas Häger, and Keith Kahn-Harris (London: IB Tauris, 2011), 135.

280. See http://blackmetaltheory.blogspot.co.uk/ (accessed: July 11, 2012).

281. *The Misanthrope* (Peaceville, 2007). Directed by Ted Skjellum.

282. Tom Howells, "Introduction," in *Black Metal: Beyond the Darkness*, ed. Tom Howells (London: Black Dog Publishing, 2012), 5.

283. See Diarmuid Hester, "'Individualism Above All': Black Metal in American Writing," in *Black Metal: Beyond the Darkness*, ed. Tom Howells (London: Black Dog Publishing, 2012), 78–83.

284. Vindkall, a member of the Swedish black metal band Domgård, quoted in Mørk, "Why Didn't the Churches Begin to Burn A Thousand Years Earlier?" 131.

285. Varg Vikernes, "Kingdoms of the Sun," *Burzum.Org* http://www.burzum.org/eng/library/the_kingdom_of_the_sun.shtml (accessed: April 23, 2012). See also, his *Sorcery and Religion in Ancient Scandinavia* (London: Abstract Sounds Books, 2011).

286. Björk, quoted in Dibben, *Björk*, 62.

287. Björk, quoted in Dibben, *Björk*, 64.

288. Dibben, *Björk*, 66.

289. Björk, quoted in Dibben, *Björk*, 40.

290. Dibben, *Björk*, 40.

291. The name is taken from the title of Georgina Boyes's study of folk song and dance revivals since the nineteenth century, *The Imagined Village: Culture, Ideology and the English Folk Revival* (Manchester: Manchester University Press, 1993).

292. In response to the London bombings of July 2005, as well as everyday violence motivated by cultural differences, Billy Bragg's book *The Progressive Patriot* posits a multicultural patriotism as a positive form of resistance to right-wing, nationalist patriotism; see also, "Does National Pride Matter?" *National Trust Magazine* (Summer 2012): 15; Billy Bragg and the Blokes, *England, Half English* (2002).

293. Available at: *The Imagined Village*, http://imaginedvillage.com/ (accessed April 2, 2012).

294. Robert A. Georges and Michael Owen Jones, *Folkloristics: An Introduction* (Bloomington: ndiana University Press, 1995), 60.

295. See Roszak, *Making of a Counter Culture*; Partridge, *Re-Enchantment of the West*.

296. Paul McCartney, quoted in Timothy Leary, *Politics of Ecstasy* (London: Paladin, 1970), 93.

297. See Nick Bromell, *Tomorrow Never Knows: Rock and Psychedelics in the 1960s* (Chicago: Chicago University Press, 2000).

298. Arthur Marwick, *The Sixties: Cultural Revolution in Britain, France, Italy, and the United States c.1958–c.1974* (Oxford: Oxford University Press, 1998), ch. 3.

299. Ian MacDonald, *The People's Music* (London: Pimlico, 2003), 87.

300. See Max Weber, *From Max Weber: Essays in Sociology*, eds. Hans H. Gerth and C. Wright Mills (London: Routledge & Kegan Paul, 1948), 155.

301. See Richard Dawkins, *The God Delusion* (London: Bantam Press, 2006), 151–152.

302. Peter Berger, *The Sacred Canopy: Elements of a Sociological Theory of Religion* (New York: Anchor Books, 1967), 151.

303. Berger, *Sacred Canopy*, 151.

304. Robert Wuthnow, *After Heaven: Spirituality in America Since the 1950s* (Berkeley: University of California Press, 1998), 53. See also Jane Iwamura's *Virtual Orientalism: Asian Religions and American Popular Culture* (New York: Oxford University Press, 2011), in which she provides a close reading of the depiction of the "oriental monk" in popular magazines, television and film between 1950 and 1975.

305. See McLeod, *Religious Crisis of the 1960s*, 83–92.

306. Berger, *Sacred Canopy*, 127.

307. Steve Bruce, "Pluralism and Religious Vitality," in *Religion and Modernization: Historians Debate the Secularization Thesis*, ed. Steve Bruce (Oxford: Oxford University Press, 1992), 170.

308. Paul Heelas and Linda Woodhead, *The Spiritual Revolution: Why Religion is Giving Way to Spirituality* (Oxford: Blackwell, 2004), 2.

309. On the expressivist significance of "love," see Talcott Parsons, *Action Theory and the Human Condition* (New York: Free Press, 1978), 313.

310. See Russell Reising and Jim LeBlanc, "Within and Without: *Sgt. Peppers Lonely Hearts Club Band* and Psychedelic Insight," in *Sgt. Pepper and The Beatles: It Was Forty Years Ago Today*, ed. Olivier Julien (Aldershot: Ashgate, 2008), 103–121; David Reck, "The Beatles and Indian Music," in Julien, *Sgt. Pepper and The Beatles*, 63–74.

311. Talcott Parsons, *Action Theory and the Human Condition* (New York: Free Press, 1978), 320.

312. See Diamuid Hester, "'Individualism Above All': Black Metal in American Writing," in Howells, *Black Metal*, 78–83.

313. See Graham St. John, ed. *Rave Culture and Religion* (London: Routledge, 2004).

314. See McLeod, *Religious Crisis of the 1960s*.

315. Andrew Rawlinson, *The Book of Enlightened Masters: Western Teachers in Eastern Traditions* (Chicago: Open Court, 1997), 56, 58, 82.

316. Callum Brown, *The Death of Christian Britain: Understanding Secularisation, 1800–2000*, 2nd ed. (London: Routledge, 2009), 1.

317. Brown, *Death of Christian Britain*, 176 (emphasis added).

318. Brown, *Death of Christian Britain*, 179. See also McLeod, *Religious Crisis of the 1960s*, 128.

319. Brown, *Death of Christian Britain*, 179.

320. Colin Campbell, "The Secret Religion of the Educated Classes," *Sociological Analysis* 39 (1978): 146.

321. See the interesting early study of LSD and religious experience by Ray Gordon, "LSD and Mystical Experiences," *Journal of Bible and Religion* 31 (1963): 114–123.

322. Robert Wuthnow, *After Heaven: Spirituality in America Since the 1950s* (Berkeley: University of California Press, 1998), 54.

323. Wade Clark Roof, *Spiritual Marketplace: Baby Boomers and the Remaking of American Religion* (Princeton: Princeton University Press, 1999), ch. 2.

324. See Richard Cole (Radha Mohan Das), "Forty Years of Chanting: A Study of the Hare Krishna Movement from its Foundation to the Present Day," in *The Hare Krishna Movement: Forty Years of Chant and Change*, eds. Graham Dwyer and Richard Cole (London: I.B. Tauris, 2007), 30–32.

325. See Andy Roberts, "Changing Horses," in Whittaker, *Be Glad*, 131–133.

326. See Johnny Rogan, *Van Morrison: No Surrender* (London: Vintage, 2006), 343–352.

327. See Jonathon Bellman, "Indian Resonances in the British Invasion, 1965–1968," in *The Exotic in Western Music*, ed. Jonathon Bellman (Boston: Northeastern University Press, 1998), 293–294.

328. See Jennie Skerl, *Reconstructing the Beats* (New York: Palgrave Macmillan, 2004).

329. Fritjof Capra, *The Tao of Physics: An Exploration of Parallels Between Modern Physics and Eastern Mysticism* (London: Fontana, 1976), 11.

330. Capra, *Tao of Physics*, 12–13.

331. Capra, *Tao of Physics*, 209.

332. John V. Cody, "Gerald Heard: Soul Guide to the Beyond Within," *Gnosis* 26 (1993): 68.

333. Bromell, *Tomorrow Never Knows*, 153–154.

334. Timothy Leary, *High Priest* (Berkeley: Ronin Publishing, 1995 [1968]), 2.

335. Allen Ginsberg, "A Tale of the Tribe (from Preface to 'Jail Notes')," in the liner notes to Timothy Leary, *Beyond Life With Timothy Leary* (Mercury, 1997).

336. Martin A. Lee and Bruce Shlain, *Acid Dreams: The Complete Social History of LSD* (New York: Grove Press, 1992), 98.

337. See Jay Stevens, *Storming Heaven: LSD and the American Dream* (London: Flamingo, 1993).

338. Quoted in, Robin Sylvan, *Traces of the Spirit: The Religious Dimensions of Popular Music* (New York: New York University Press, 2002), 94–95.

339. Paul McCartney, quoted in Bromell, *Tomorrow Never Knows*, 61.

340. George Harrison, quoted in Bromell, *Tomorrow Never Knows*, 72.

341. David Farber, quoted in Bromell, *Tomorrow Never Knows*, 6.

342. Jack Kerouac, *Dharma Bums* (New York: Viking, 1957).

343. Having first appeared as an article in the *Chicago Review* in 1958, Watts expanded "Beat Zen, Square Zen, and Zen" into a pamphlet in 1959. It was later published in Alan Watts, *This Is It and Other Essays on Zen and Spiritual Experience* (New York: Vintage Books, 1973).

344. Although the book does not use the term "psychedelic," it is often cited as one of, if not *the* founding text of psychedelia. See Aldous Huxley, *The Doors of Perception and Heaven and Hell* (London: Flamingo, 1994).

345. David Reck, "The Beatles and Indian Music." In Julien, *Sgt. Pepper and The Beatles*, 63, 65.

346. See Bellman, "Indian Resonances in the British Invasion," 294–297.

347. Steve Marriott, quoted in Gerry Farrell, *Indian Music and the West* (Oxford: Oxford University Press, 1997), 168.

348. Ian MacDonald, *The People's Music* (London: Pimlico, 2003), 87. See also, David Reck, "The Beatles and Indian Music," in Julien, *Sgt. Pepper and The Beatles*, 63–74.

349. Timothy Leary, quoted in Lee and Shlain, *Acid Dreams*, 179.

350. Leary, *Politics of Ecstasy*, 137–138.

351. See Bromell, *Tomorrow Never Knows*, 124–125; Gerry Carlin and Mark Jones, "Cease to Exist: Manson Family Movies and Mysticism," in *Holy Terror: Understanding Religion and Violence in Popular Culture*, eds. Eric Christianson and Christopher Partridge (London: Equinox, 2010), 53–62.

352. Leary, *Politics of Ecstasy*, 185.

353. Warren Hinckle, "A Social History of the Hippies," in Ward, *The 1960s*, 103.

354. Leary, *Politics of Ecstasy*, 182–193.

355. See Gilbert Shelton, *The Fabulous Furry Freak Brothers: Omnibus* (London: Knockabout Comics, 2008).

356. Ronald Reagan, quoted in Bromell, *Tomorrow Never Knows*, 128, 140.

357. See Timothy Leary, *Flashbacks. A Personal and Cultural History of an Era: An Autobiography* (New York: G.P. Putnam's Sons, 1990), 275–286.

358. Lee and Shlain, *Acid Dreams*, 239.

359. Leary, *Flashbacks*, 281.

360. Ian MacDonald's excellent study of The Beatles: *A Revolution in the Head: The Beatles' Records and the Sixties*, 2nd ed. (London: Pimlico, 1998), 316.

361. See Arun Saldanha, *Psychedelic White: Goa Trance and the Viscosity of Race* (Minneapolis: University of Minnesota Press, 2007).

362. In 1997, 87% of those attending raves took recreational drugs, the most popular being ecstasy and cannabis, with LSD being far less widely used. Release, *Release Drugs and Dance Survey: An Insight Into the Culture* (London: Release, 1997).

363. Stuart Metcalfe, "Ecstasy Evangelists and Psychedelic Warriors," in *Psychedelia Britannica: Hallucinogenic Drugs in Britain*, ed. Antonio Melechi (London: Turnaround, 1997), 170.

364. Metcalfe, "Ecstasy Evangelists and Psychedelic Warriors," 171.

365. Sheila Whiteley, "Altered Sounds," in Melechi, *Psychedelia Britannica*, 139.

366. Metcalfe, "Ecstasy Evangelists and Psychedelic Warriors," 170.

367. David G. Dodd and Diana Spaulding (eds), *The Grateful Dead Reader* (New York: Oxford University Press, 2000), 3. See also, Graham St. John, "Introduction," in *Rave Culture and Religion*, ed. Graham St. John (London: Routledge, 2004), 3–4.

368. Mary Anna Wright, "The Great British Ecstasy Revolution," in *DIY Culture: Party and Protest in Nineties Britain*, ed. George McKay (London: Verso, 1998), 228.

369. Simon Reynolds, *Energy Flash: A Journey Through Rave Music and Dance Culture* (London: Picador, 1998), 406.

370. See Luther Elliott, "Goa is a State of Mind: On the Ephemerality of Psychedelic Social Placements," in *The Local Scenes and Global Culture of Psytrance*, ed. Graham St. John (London: Routledge, 2010), 21–39.

371. See Anthony D'Andrea, "Global Nomads: Techno and New Age as Transnational Countercultures in Ibiza and Goa," in St. John, *Rave Culture and Religion*, 242; see also, Anthony D'Andrea, *Global Nomads: Techno and New Age as Transnational Countercultures in Ibiza and Goa* (Abingdon: Routledge, 2007), 175–221; Saldanha, *Psychedelic White*; Nicholas Saunders, *Ecstasy and the Dance Culture* (London: Nicholas Saunders, 1995), 196.

372. Steve Hillage, quoted in Saunders, *Ecstasy and the Dance Culture*, 198.

373. Jane Bussmann, *Once in a Lifetime: the Crazy Days of Acid House and Afterwards* (London: Virgin Books, 1998), 108.

374. James Munro, quoted in, Sarah Champion, "Goa," in *Deep Trance and Ritual Beats*, ed. Tony Marcus—a booklet included with the CD *Deep Trance and Ritual Beats* (London: Return to the Source, 1995), 40–42.

375. James Munro, quoted in Champion, "Goa," 45.

376. James Munro, quoted in Champion, "Goa," 49.

377. See Graham John St., "Total Solar Eclipse Festivals, Cosmic Pilgrims and Planetary Culture." In Andy Bennett and Donna Weston (eds), *Pop Pagans: Paganism and Popular Music* (Durham: Acumen, 2012), 126–144.

378. Simon Reynolds, "Back to Eden: Innocence, Indolence and Pastoralism in Psychedelic Music, 1966–1996," in Melechi, *Psychedelia Britannica*, 159.

379. Des Tramacchi, "Field Tripping: Psychedelic *communitas* and Ritual in the Australian Bush," *Journal of Contemporary Religion* 15 (2000): 203.

380. Chris Deckker, "Introduction," in Marcus, *Deep Trance and Ritual Beats*, 2–3. See also Charles de Ledesma, "Psychedelic Trance Music Making in the UK: Rhizomatic Craftsmanship and the Global Market Place," in St. John, *Local Scenes and Global Culture of Psytrance*, 89–113.

381. Chris Deckker, "Introduction," 3.

382. DJ Chrisbo, quoted in Ian Gittins, "Return to the Source," in Marcus, *Deep Trance and Ritual Beats*, 16.

383. Jules, quoted in Ian Gittins, "Return to the Source," in Marcus, *Deep Trance and Ritual Beats*, 16–17. This type of eclecticism is particularly evident in one of the earliest rave outfits, Eat Static. Formed in 1989 by Merv Pepler and Joie Hinton, who were at the time in the free festival band Ozric Tentacles, they drew heavily on the occultural fascination with extraterrestrial visitation, while also articulating an interest in psychedelic, pagan and Eastern ideas (e.g., *Prepare Your Spirit* (1992); *Abduction* (1993); *Implant* (1994); *Science of the Gods* (1997)).

384. See St. John, *Local Scenes and Global Culture of Psytrance*; Anthony D'Andrea, *Global Nomads: Techno and New Age as Transnational Countercultures in Ibiza and Goa* (Abingdon: Routledge, 2007).

385. Goa Gil, quoted in Anthony D'Andrea, "The Decline of Electronic Dance Scenes: The Case of Psytrance in Goa," in *The Local Scenes and Global Culture of Psytrance*, ed. Graham St. John (London: Routledge, 2010), 45. See also D'Andrea's discussion of the links with Osho: *Global Nomads*.

386. Nicholas Saunders, Anja Saunders and Michelle Pauli, *In Search of the Ultimate High: Spiritual Experience Through Psychoactives* (London: Rider, 2000), 189. See also Saunders, *Ecstasy and the Dance Culture*, 120–123.

387. Robin Sylvan, *Trance Formation: The Spiritual and religious Dimensions of Global Rave Culture* (New York: Routledge, 2005), 182.

388. Charles Taylor, *A Secular Age* (Cambridge: Harvard University Press, 2007), 38.

389. Taylor, *Secular Age*, 38–39.

Chapter 5

1. Guy Beck, "Introduction," in *Sacred Sounds: Experiencing Music in World Religions*, ed. Guy Beck (Waterloo: Wilfred Laurier University Press, 2006), 1.

2. Francesco Pelosi, *Plato on Music, Soul and Body*, trans. Sophie Henderson (Cambridge: Cambridge University Press, 2010), 6.

3. See Fraser Watts, Rebecca Nye, Sara Savage, *Psychology for Christian Ministry* (London: Routledge, 2002); Ralph W. Hood, Jr., Peter C. Hill, and Bernard Spilka, *The Psychology of Religion: An Empirical Approach*, 4th ed. (New York: Guilford Press, 2009).

4. Hood, Hill, and Spilka, *Psychology of Religion*, 74. See also, Karen Brummel-Smith, "Music and the Meditative Mind: Toward a Science of the Ineffable," in Koen, *Oxford Handbook of Medical Ethnomusicology*, 308–330.

5. Benjamin Koen, "Music-Prayer-Meditation Dynamics in Healing," in Koen, *Oxford Handbook of Medical Ethnomusicology*, 99–100.

6. Quoted in Storr, *Music and the Mind*, 17. See Jeremy Begbie's theological analyses of music and the arts: *Theology, Music, and Time* (Cambridge: Cambridge University Press, 2000); *Voicing Creation's Praise: Towards a Theology of the Arts* (London: Continuum, 1991).

7. Nusrat Fateh Ali Khan, quoted in Dimitri Ehrlich, *Inside the Music: Conversations with Contemporary Musicians About Spirituality, Creativity, and Consciousness* (Boston: Shambhala, 1997), 121.

8. See John Corrigan, ed., *Religion and Emotion: Approaches and Interpretations* (Oxford: Oxford University Press, 2004); John Corrigan, ed., *The Oxford Handbook of Religion and Emotion* (Oxford: Oxford University Press, 2008); Douglas J. Davies, *Emotion, Identity and Religion: Hope, Reciprocity, and Otherness* (Oxford: Oxford University Press, 2011); Ole Riis and Linda Woodhead, *A Sociology of Religious Emotion* (Oxford: Oxford University Press, 2010).

9. Graham Hughes, *Worship as Meaning: A Liturgical Theology for Late Modernity* (Cambridge: Cambridge University Press, 2003), 110–111; see also 13; and Brenda Eatman Aghahowa, "Definitions of Praising and a Look at Black Worship," in *Readings in African American Church Music and Worship*, ed. James Abbington (Chicago: GIA Publications, 2001), 370.—there is "less emphasis on printed materials and greater emphasis on creating a prayerful mood, calling forth the learner's deepest needs, and bringing these to prayer."

10. See, for example: Beck, *Sacred Sounds*; Beck, *Sonic Theology*; Judith Becker, *Deep Listeners: Music, Emotion and Trancing* (Bloomington: Indiana University Press, 2004); Mark Evans, *Open Up the Doors: Music in the Modern Church* (London; Equinox, 2006); Rosalind Hackett, "Sound, Music, and the Study of Religion," *Temenos: Nordic Journal of Comparative Religion* 48 (2012): 11–27; David Harnish and Anne Rasmussen eds., *Divine Inspirations: Music and Islam in Indonesia* (Oxford: Oxford University Press, 2011); Annemette Kirkegaard, "Music and Transcendence: Sufi Popular Performances in East Africa," *Temenos: Nordic Journal of Comparative Religion* 48 (2012): 29–48; Bettina E. Schmidt, *Caribbean Diaspora in USA: Diversity of Caribbean Religions in New York City* (Aldershot: Ashgate, 2008), 157; Dale A. Olsen, "Shamanism, Music and Healing in Two Contrasting South American Cultural Areas," in Koen, *Oxford Handbook of Medical Ethnomusicology*, 331–360.

11. Guy Beck, "Introduction," in Beck, *Sacred Sounds*, 1 (emphasis added).

12. Storr, *Music and the Mind*, 22.

13. Henry Herbert Farmer, *Revelation and Religion: Studies in the Theological Interpretation of Religious Types* (London: Nisbet, 1954), 190–191.

14. Farmer, *Revelation and Religion*, 175. See also Jonathan Amos, "Organ Music 'Instils Religious Feelings'." BBC News (September 8, 2003), http://news.bbc.co.uk/1/hi/sci/tech/3087674. stm (accessed November 12, 2005); Storr, *Music and the Mind*, 46–48.

15. Christopher Partridge, *H. H. Farmer's Theological Interpretation of Religion* (Lewiston: Edwin Mellen Press, 1998).

16. Henry Herbert Farmer, *The World and God: A Study of Prayer, Providence and Miracle in Christian Experience*, 2nd ed. (London: Nisbet, 1936), 26.

17. The significance of Farmer's work should not be underestimated, in that an ignorance of the significance of emotion in religion is still evident in much theology, even in the thinking of those wanting to develop a connection between identity and liturgy. A recent example, in which the significance of emotion is effectively dismissed, is Ken Christoph Miyamoto's "Mission, Liturgy and the Transformation of Identity," *Mission Studies* 27(2010): 56–70.

18. H. Richard Niebuhr, *Christ and Culture* (New York: Harper & Row, 2001), xvi.

19. Niebuhr, *Christ and Culture*, 45–82.

20. Of course, similar concerns have been expressed by Christians in relation to other areas of popular culture, such as role-playing games, particularly *Dungeons and Dragons*. For example, see, John Walliss, "The Road to Hell is Paved with D20s: Evangelical Christianity and Role-playing Gaming," in *Handbook of Hyper-Real Religions*, ed. Adam Possamai(Leiden: Brill, 2012), 207–224.

21. Niebuhr, *Christ and Culture*, 83–115.

22. Jeff Keuss, *Your Neighbour's Hymnal: What Popular Music Teaches Us About Faith, Hope and Love* (Eugene: Cascade Books, 2011), 8.

23. Keuss, *Your Neighbour's Hymnal*, 10.

24. Keuss, *Your Neighbour's Hymnal*, 10.

25. Niebuhr, *Christ and Culture*, 190–229.

26. Niebuhr, *Christ and Culture*, 190.

27. Don Cusic, *Encyclopedia of Contemporary Christian Music: Pop, Rock, and Worship* (Santa Barbara: ABC-CLIO, 2010), 64.

28. William Booth, quoted in Pamela J. Walker, *Pulling the Devil's Kingdom Down: The Salvation Army in Victorian Britain* (Berkeley: University of California Press, 2001), 190. See also, Diane Winston, "All the World's a Stage: The Performed Religion of the Salvation Army, 1880–1920," in *Religion in the Age of the Media: Explorations in Media, Religion and Culture*, eds. Stewart M. Hoover and Lynn Schofield Clark (New York: Columbia University Press, 2002), 113–137.

29. Walker, *Pulling the Devil's Kingdom Down*, 194.

30. Walker, *Pulling the Devil's Kingdom Down*, 59.

31. Niebuhr, *Christ and Culture*, 40.

32. The Columbine High School massacre on April 20, 1999, was carried out by two students, Eric Harris and Dylan Klebold, who embarked on a shooting spree, which resulted in the deaths of twelve students and one teacher. See David Altheide, "The Columbine Shootings and the Discourse of Fear," *American Behavioral Scientist* 52 (2009): 1354–1370.

33. Plato, *The Republic*, trans. Desmond Lee (London: Penguin, 1987), 97–98.

34. Walter Brueggemann, "Vulnerable Children, Divine Passion and Human Obligation," in *The Child in the Bible*, eds. Marcia Bunge, Terence Fretheim, and Beverly Gaventa (Grand Rapids: Wm. B. Eerdmans Publishing Co., 2008), 420; see also, Gordon Lynch, *The Sacred in the Modern World: A Cultural Sociological Approach* (Oxford: Oxford University Press, 2012), 54–86.

35. Allison James, Chris Jenks and Alan Prout, *Theorizing Childhood* (Cambridge: Polity Press, 1998), 152.

36. Nicholas Fairbairn, quoted in P-Orridge, *Painful But Fabulous*, 163.

37. Kenneth Thompson, *Moral Panics* (Abingdon: Routledge, 1998), 4.

38. Jason C. Bivins, *Religion of Fear: The Politics of Horror in Conservative Evangelicalism* (New York: Oxford, 2008), 90.

39. Eileen Luhr, *Witnessing Suburbia: Conservatives and Christian Youth Culture* (Berkeley: University of California Press, 2009), 38.

40. See John Birch Society, "Beliefs and Principles of the John Birch Society," in *Extremism in America: A Reader*, ed. Lyman T. Sargent (New York: New York University Press, 1995), 105–110. The particular concerns of the John Birch Society relating to the socialist profanation of children's minds are evident in Gary Allen's article (originally published in *American Opinion*, 1971, "New Education: The Radicals Are After Your Children.") in *Extremism in America: A Reader*, 223–234.

41. Interestingly, an extract attacking Bob Dylan from Noebel's *Rhythm, Riots, and Revolution* has been reproduced by Brian Ward in his *The 1960s: A Documentary Reader* (Oxford: Blackwell, 2010), 65–68.

42. Daniel Wojcik, *The End of the World As We Know It: Faith, Fatalism, and Apocalypse in America* (New York: New York University Press, 1997), 141. See also, Michael Barkun, *A Culture of Conspiracy: Apocalyptic Visions in Contemporary America* (Berkeley: University of California Press, 2003).

43. David Noebel, *Rhythm, Riots, and Revolution: An Analysis of the Communist Use of Music, the Communist Master Music Plan* (Tulsa: Christian Crusade Publications, 1966), 30 (original emphasis).

44. Noebel, *Rhythm, Riots, and Revolution*, 26–27.

45. Noebel, *Rhythm, Riots, and Revolution*, 10.

46. Matthew Arnold, *Culture and Anarchy* (Cambridge: Cambridge University Press, 1971), 34.

47. Noebel, *Rhythm, Riots, and Revolution*, 12.

48. Noebel, *Rhythm, Riots, and Revolution*, 14.

49. See Berndt Ostendorf, "Rhythm, Riots, and Revolution: Political Paranoia, Cultural Fundamentalism, and African American Music," in *Enemy Images in American History*, eds. Ragnhild Fiebig-von Hase and Ursula Lehmkuhl (Providence: Berghahn Book, 1997), 159–179.

50. Timothy Fitzgerald, *Discourse on Civility and Barbarity: A Critical History of Religion and Related Categories* (Oxford: Oxford University Press, 2007).

51. Noebel, Rhythm, Riots, and Revolution, 78.

52. Noebel, *Rhythm, Riots, and Revolution*, 78.

53. Noebel, *Rhythm, Riots, and Revolution*,79.

54. David Noebel, *The Beatles: A Study in Drugs, Sex and Revolution* (Tulsa: Christian Crusade Publications, 1965), 6–7; *The Marxist Minstrels: A Handbook on Communist Subversion of Music* (Tulsa: American Christian College Press, 1974), 69.

55. Noebel, *Rhythm, Riots, and Revolution*, 81; *Communism, Hypnotism and The Beatles* (Tulsa: Christian Crusade Publications, 1969), 14, 25.

56. Noebel, *Communism, Hypnotism and The Beatles*, 14–15.

57. See Noebel, *The Marxist Minstrels*, 45.

58. Noebel, *Rhythm, Riots, and Revolution*, 90–91.

59. Barkun, *Culture of Conspiracy*, 6.

60. Blanchard, *Pop Goes the Gospel*, 40–41.

61. See Barkun, *Culture of Conspiracy*, 3–4.

62. Jeff Godwin, quoted in Bivins, *Religion of Fear*, 97. See also Andreas Häger's discussion of Godwin in "Moral Boundaries in Christian Discourse on Popular Music," in *Research in the Social Scientific Study of Religion*, eds. Joanne Marie Greer and David O. Mober, volume 11 (Stamford: JAI Press, 2000), 155–171.

63. Jeffrey S. Victor, *Satanic Panic: The Creation of a Contemporary Legend* (Chicago: Open Court, 1993), 167–168.

64. Mark LeVine, *Heavy Metal Islam: Rock, Resistance, and the Struggle for the Soul of Islam* (New York: Three Rivers Press, 2008), 67.

65. LeVine, *Heavy Metal Islam,* 67.

66. See LeVine, *Heavy Metal Islam,* 29–30.

67. Hubert Spence, *Confronting Contemporary Christian Music: A Plain Account of Its History, Philosophy and Future* (Dunn: Forwarding the Faith Publications,2011), 222.

68. Bob Larson, *The Day the Music Died* (Carol Stream: Creation House, 1972), 204; *Larson's Book of Spiritual Warfare* (Nashville: Thomas Nelson Publishers, 1999), 23.

69. Blanchard, *Pop Goes the Gospel,* 21, 154. See also, John Blanchard and Dan Lucarini, *Can We Rock the Gospel? Rock Music's Impact on Worship and Evangelism* (Welwyn: Evangelical Press, 2006).

70. Rabbi Ephraim Luft, quoted in Wyre Davies, "Rabbis Black-list Non-kosher Music," *BBC News* (September 12, 2008), http://news.bbc.co.uk/1/hi/world/middle_east/7609859.stm (accessed July 26, 2012).

71. Committee for Jewish Music, "Rules for Playing Kosher Music," *BBC News* http://news.bbc.co.uk/1/shared/bsp/hi/pdfs/11_9_08_kosher_music.pdf (accessed July 26, 2012).

72. Rabbi Efraim Luft, quoted in Davies, "Rabbis Black-list Non-kosher Music."

73. Judaism, of course, has a vibrant popular music culture. See Keith Kahn-Harris, "Jews United and Divided by Music: Contemporary Jewish Music in the UK and America," in Bossius, Häger, and Kahn-Harris, *Religion and Popular Music in Europe,* 71–91.

74. Andy Morgan, in "Mali: No Rhythm or Reason as Militants Declare War on Music," *The Guardian* (October 23,2012), http://www.guardian.co.uk/world/2012/oct/23/mali-militants-declare-war-music (accessed October 28, 2012).

75. Quoted by Andy Morgan, in "Mali: No Rhythm or Reason as Militants Declare War on Music," *The Guardian* (October 23, 2012), http://www.guardian.co.uk/world/2012/oct/23/mali-militants-declare-war-music (accessed October 28, 2012). See also, Rose Skelton, "Can Musical Mali Play On?" *The Independent* (August 18, 2012), http://www.independent.co.uk/news/world/africa/can-musical-mali-play-on-8057347.html (accessed October 28, 2012).

76. Niebuhr, *Christ and Culture,* 40–41.

77. Niebuhr, *Christ and Culture,* 190.

78. Jay R. Howard and John M. Streck, in their book *Apostles of Rock: The Splintered World of Contemporary Christian Music* (Lexington: University Press of Kentucky, 1999), also make use of Niebuhr's work in their identification of three distinct paradigms, each of which articulates a unique rationale for the production of Christian music: "separational CCM"; "integrational CCM"; and "transformative CCM." While this is a helpful typology, it is also problematic, not least because most Christian music is transformational to some extent and little of it is "separational" in Niebuhr's "Christ against culture" sense (discussed above). Hence, while their work is an important and informed contribution to the study of contemporary Christian music, the culture is more nuanced than they allow.

79. Mark Rimmer, *Cross Rhythms,* "Christafari: Mark Mohr Talks About Their New Album and Bob Marley's Conversion", http://www.crossrhythms.co.uk/articles/music/Christafari_Mark_Mohr_talks_about_their_new_album_and_Bob_Marleys_conversion/37845/p1/ (accessed September 25, 2012).

80. Mark Rimmer, *Cross Rhythms,* "Christafari: Mark Mohr Talks About Their New Album and Bob Marley's Conversion," http://www.crossrhythms.co.uk/articles/music/Christafari_Mark_Mohr_talks_about_their_new_album_and_Bob_Marleys_conversion/37845/p1/ (accessed September 25, 2012). See also, Mark Mohr, "Is Haile Selassie God or Christ?," *Gospel/Reggae. com,* http://www.gospelreggae.com/faq/78da334f010000d4009c/display.html (accessed October 5, 2012).

81. See also, Mark Mohr, "Rastas' Beliefs and Marijuana as a Holy Sacrament', *Gospel/Reggae. com,* http://www.gospelreggae.com/faq/78da33310400009b0066/display.html (accessed October 5, 2012).

82. Mark Mohr, "Christafari Biography": http://www.christafari.com/bio.html (accessed September 25, 2012).

83. Harry S. Stout, *The Divine Dramatist: George Whitefield and the Rise of Modern Evangelicalism* (Grand Rapids: Eerdmans, 1991), 79.

84. Stout, *Divine Dramatist*, 79.

85. See Paul Creasman, "Looking Beyond the Radio for Listeners," in *Understanding Evangelical Media: The Changing Face of Christian Communication*, eds. Quentin Schultze and Robert Woods Jr. (Downers Grove: InterVarsity Press, 2008), 33–45; Richard Kyle, *Evangelicalism: An Americanized Christianity* (New Brunswick: Transaction Publishers, 2006), 283.

86. See Robert Ellwood, *One Way: The Jesus Movement and Its Meaning* (Englewood Cliffs: Prentice-Hall, 1973), 64. See also, David W. Stowe, *No Sympathy for the Devil: Christian Pop Music and the Transformation of American Evangelicalism* (Chapel Hill: University of North Carolina Press, 2011), 11–33.

87. Stowe, *No Sympathy for the Devil*, 26.

88. William Romanowski, "Evangelicals and Popular Music: The Contemporary Christian Music Industry," in *Religion and Popular Culture in America*, eds. Bruce David Forbes and Jeffrey H. Mahan, (Berkeley: University of California Press, 2000), 109.

89. Billy Ray Hearn, quoted in Romanowski, "Evangelicals and Popular Music," 110. See also the interview with his son, Bill Hearn, in Andrew Beaujon, *Body Piercing Saved My Life: Inside the Phenomenon of Christian Rock* (New York: Da Capo Press, 2006), 179–186.

90. Romanowski, "Evangelicals and Popular Music," 106.

91. Romanowski, "Evangelicals and Popular Music," 106.

92. For a useful short discussion of the particular economic pressures facing the conservative Christian music industry, see Pete Ward, "The Economies of Charismatic Evangelical Worship," in Religion, Media and Culture: A Reader, eds. Gordon Lynch, Jolyon Mitchell, and Anna Strhan (London: Routledge, 2011), 23–30.

93. Romanowski, "Evangelicals and Popular Music," 108.

94. Amy Grant, quoted in Romanowski, "Evangelicals and Popular Music," 107.

95. Bil Carpenter, *Uncloudy Days: The Gospel Music Encyclopaedia* (San Francisco: Backbeat Books, 2005), 158.

96. See Jeff Keuss's short discussion of Sufjan Stevens in *Your Neighbour's Hymnal: What Popular Music Teaches Us About Faith, Hope and Love* (Eugene: Cascade Books, 2011), 68–70.

97. P.O.D., quoted in Marc Weingarten, "P.O.D.: Who Says God Doesn't Like Metal?," *Rolling Stone* 856/857 (December 14, 2000): 102.

98. Jeremy Allen, "Adz And It Shall Be Given Unto You: Sufjan Stevens Interviewed," *The Quietus* (October 12, 2010), http://thequietus.com/articles/05085-the-age-of-adz-sufjan-stevens-interview (accessed October 5, 2012).

99. Terry Watkins, "What About P.O.D.?," http://www.av1611.org/crock/pod.html (accessed October 5, 2012).

100. See Marcus Moberg, *Faster for the Master: Exploring Issues of Religious Expression and Alternative Christian Identity within the Finnish Christian Metal Music Scene* (Åbo: Åbo Akademi University Press, 2009).

101. Steve Rowe, "Infiltration Squad," http://www.roweproductions.com/store/ (accessed October 3, 2012).

102. Johannes Jonsson, "Frequently Asked Questions About Christian Metal", http://www.metalforjesus.org/faq.html (accessed October 2, 2012).

103. Jonsson, "Frequently Asked Questions About Christian Metal."

104. Moberg, *Faster for the Master*, 139–140.

105. Ian Christie, *Sound of the Beast: The Complete Headbanging History* (New York: HarperCollins, 2003), 239.

106. Moberg, *Faster for the Master*, 40.

107. George Marsden, *Jonathan Edwards: A Life* (New Haven: Yale University Press, 2003), 220.

108. Stephen Williams, quoted in Marsden, *Jonathan Edwards*, 220.

109. The sonic environment, the discourses, the signifying practices, the subcultural style—including the distinctive gothic calligraphy typical of the evocative black metal logos produced

by the designer Christophe Szpajdel—have all been learned from extreme metal. They are then converted within the constraints imposed by that discourse: the inverted crucifix is inverted, a finger is dropped from the horned hand sign, making a "one way" hand sign—indicative of the salvific uniqueness of Christ—and so on. See Christophe Szpajdel, "Band Identity," in Howells, *Black Metal*, 138–145.

110. Partridge, *Re-Enchantment of the West*, 207–278.

111. Georges Bataille, *Visions of Excess: Selected Writings 1927–1939*, ed. and trans. Allan Stoekl (Manchester: Manchester University Press, 1985), 119.

112. Moberg, *Faster for the Master*, 165.

113. Marcus Moberg, personal correspondence with the author (October 11, 2012).

114. Moberg, *Faster for the Master*, 165.

115. See Partridge, *Re-Enchantment of the West*, vol. 2, 6–12. See also, Paul Heelas and Linda Woodhead, *The Spiritual Revolution: Why Religion is Giving Way to Spirituality* (Oxford: Blackwell, 2004).

116. Pilgrim Bestiarius, quoted in Anders Nordström, "The Divine Darkness: At Home with Crimson Moonlight's Frontman," *HM: Special "Best of HM" Issue* (2010): 35.

117. Derek Walmsley, "Chants Encounters," *The Wire* 352 (June, 2013): 29.

118. Steve Barrow and Peter Dalton, *Reggae: The Rough Guide* (London: Rough Guides, 1997), 129.

119. Yasus Afari, *Overstanding Rastafari* (Jamaica: Senya-Cum, 2007), 128.

120. Afari, *Overstanding Rastafari*, 128.

121. Afari, *Overstanding Rastafari*, 89.

122. Afari, *Overstanding Rastafari*, 126.

123. Afari, *Overstanding Rastafari*, 126.

124. Afari, *Overstanding Rastafari*, 125–126.

125. Simon Jones, *Black Culture, White Youth: The Reggae Tradition from JA to UK* (London: Macmillan Education, 1988), 3.

126. Leonard E. Barrett, *The Rastafarians* (Boston: Beacon Press, 1997), 29.

127. Linton Kwesi Johnson, quoted in Angus MacKinnon, "Forces of Reality," *New Musical Express* (21 April, 1979): 52.

128. Richard D. E. Burton, *Afro-Creole: Power, Opposition, and Play in the Caribbean* (Ithaca: Cornell University Press, 1997), 13–46. See also, Michael Craton, *Searching for the Invisible Man: Slaves and Plantation Life in Jamaica* (Cambridge: Harvard University Press, 1978).

129. Dick Hebdige, *Cut 'N' Mix: Culture, Identity, and Caribbean Music* (London: Routledge, 1987), 25.

130. Hebdige, *Cut 'N' Mix*, 22.

131. See, for example, Jones, *Black Culture, White Youth*, 12–15.

132. Dick Hebdige, *Subculture: The Meaning of Style* (London: Methuen, 1979), 32, 33–34.

133. Nathaniel Murrell, "Introduction: The Rastafari Phenomenon," in *Chanting Down Babylon: The Rastafari Reader*, eds. Nathaniel Murrell, William Spencer and Adrian McFarlane (Philadelpia: Temple University Press), 5.

134. Martin Luther, *Three Treatises* (Philadelphia: Fortress Press, 1970).

135. Ennis Edmonds, *Rastafari: From Outcasts to Culture Bearers* (New York: Oxford University Press, 2003), 33. See also, Burton, *Afro-Creole*, 99–101.

136. Patrick Taylor, "Rastafari, the Other, and Exodus Politics: EATUP," *Journal of Religious Thought* 17 (1991): 102–103.

137. Barrett, *Rastafarians*, 115–117.

138. See Hollis R. Lynch, *Edward Wilmott Blyden: Pan Negro Patriot 1832–1912* (Oxford: Oxford University Press, 1967).

139. Pan-Africanism is complex, but at a basic level, it is a political movement dedicated to the establishment of a single African state to which those in the African diaspora can return. More broadly and amorphously, Pan-Africanism seeks culturally to unite Africans in Africa and in the diaspora through literary and artistic projects.

140. Neil Savishinsky, "African Dimensions of the Jamaican Rastafarian Movement," in Murrell, Spencer and McFarlane, *Chanting Down Babylon*, 135.

141. Edmonds, *Rastafari*, 34.

142. Barrett, *Rastafarians*, 75.

143. See Vivien Goldman, *The Book of Exodus: The Making and Meaning of Bob Marley and the Wailers' Album of the Century* (New York: Three Rivers Press, 2006), 289.

144. Edward Wilmott Blyden, quoted in Lynch, *Edward Wilmott Blyden*, 121.

145. Barrett, *Rastafarians*, 76.

146. Peter B. Clarke, *Black Paradise: The Rastafarian Movement*. Black Political Studies No.5 (San Bernardino: Borgo Press, 1994), 37.

147. For analysis of the significance of the Black Star Line in particular, see Ramla Bandele, *Black Star: African American Activism in the International Political Economy* (Urbana: University of Illinois Press, 2008).

148. Marcus Garvey, *The Philosophy and Opinions of Marcus Garvey*, vol.1, edited by Amy J. Garvey (Dover: Majority Press, 1986), 44.

149. For a useful introduction to relevant ideas relating to liberation theology, see Dwight Hopkins, "Black Theology of Liberation," in *The Modern Theologians: An Introduction to Christian Theology Since 1918*, eds. David Ford and Rachel Muers, 3rd ed. (Oxford: Blackwell, 2005), 451–468. See also Robert Beckford's argument that Bob Marley can be understood as a black liberation theologian: *Jesus is Dread: Black Theology and Black Culture in Britain* (London: Darton, Longman & Todd, 1998), 115–129.

150. Afari, *Overstanding Rastafari*, 140.

151. Garvey, *Philosophy and Opinions*, vol. 1, 81.

152. While the Garvey scholar Robert Hill argues that no evidence has so far been found to indicate that Garvey ever made such claims, he does draw attention to a comment made in September, 1924 by James Morris Webb, a black clergyman concerning the advent of a "universal black king" as the fulfilment of biblical prophecy (Robert Hill, "Leonard P. Howell and the Millenarian Visions in Early Rastafari," *Jamaica Journal* 16.1 (1983): 25). Others, however, have argued that, although no documentation has been found, "it is likely that Garvey made some oral declaration . . . and that it was kept alive in the memory of people steeped in oral tradition." Edmonds, *Rastafari*, 147 n.34.

153. Barrett, *Rastafarians*, 81.

154. Clarke, *Black Paradise*, 36.

155. The full text can be found in Rupert Lewis, "Marcus Garvey and the Early Rastafarians: Continuity and Discontinuity," in Murrell, Spencer and McFarlane, *Chanting Down Babylon*, 145–146.

156. Robert Hill, "Leonard P. Howell and the Millenarian Visions in Early Rastafari," *Jamaica Journal* 16.1 (1983): 26–28.

157. L.F.C. Mantle, quoted in Robert Hill, "Leonard P. Howell and the Millenarian Visions in Early Rastafari," *Jamaica Journal* 16.1 (1983): 27.

158. Horace Campbell, *Rasta and Resistance: From Marcus Garvey to Walter Rodney* (St. John's, Antigua: Hansib Caribbean, 1997), 71, 144; Ernest E. Cashmore, *Rastaman: The Rastafarian Movement in England* (London: Unwin Paperbacks, 1983), 22; Barry Chevannes, *Rastafari: Roots and Ideology* (Syracuse: Syracuse University Press, 1994), 121; Robert Hill, "Leonard P. Howell and the Millenarian Visions in Early Rastafari," *Jamaica Journal* 16.1 (1983): 28; Michael G. Smith, Roy Augier, and Rex Nettleford, *The Rastafari Movement in Kingston, Jamaica* (Mona: Institute for Social and Economic Research, University College of the West Indies, 1960), 6; William Spencer, "Chanting Change Around the World Through Rasta Ridim and Art," in Murrell, Spencer and McFarlane, *Chanting Down Babylon*, 361.

159. Robert Hill, "Leonard P. Howell and the Millenarian Visions in Early Rastafari," *Jamaica Journal* 16.1 (1983): 28.

160. Ras Bongo Time, quoted in Eleanor Wint (in consultation with members of the Nyabinghi Order), "Who is Haile Selassie? His Imperial Majesty in Rasta Voices," in Murrell, Spencer and McFarlane, *Chanting Down Babylon*, 161.

161. Chris Morrow, *Stir It Up: Reggae Album Cover Art* (San Francisco: Chronicle Books, 1999), 24.

162. See Clarke, *Black Paradise*, 49; Partridge, *Dub in Babylon*, 30–40.

163. William Spencer, "Chanting Change Around the World Through Rasta Ridim and Art," in Murrell, Spencer and McFarlane, *Chanting Down Babylon*, 266.

164. Caroline Cooper, "Chanting Down Babylon: Bob Marley's Song as Literary Text," *Jamaica Journal* 19.4 (1987): 5.

165. Peter Tosh, quoted in Roger Steffens, "Bob Marley: Rasta Warrior," in Murrell, Spencer and McFarlane, *Chanting Down Babylon*, 255.

166. Tony Rebel, quoted in William Spencer, "Chanting Change Around the World Through Rasta Ridim and Art," in Murrell, Spencer and McFarlane, *Chanting Down Babylon*, 267.

167. Clarke, *Black Paradise*, 51.

168. See Walter Rodney, *The Groundings with My Brothers* (London: Bogle-L'Overture Publications, 1969); Campbell, *Rasta and Resistance*, 128–133.

169. Partridge, *Dub in Babylon*.

170. Cashmore, *Rastaman*, vi.

171. Hebdige, *Subculture*.

172. See Len Garrison, *Black Youth, Rastafarianism, and the Identity Crisis in Britain* (London: Afro-Caribbean Education Resource Project, 1979), 24–25; Velma Pollard, "The Social History of Dread Talk," *Caribbean Quarterly* 28.2 (1982): 29.

173. Caroline Cooper, "Chanting Down Babylon: Bob Marley's Song as Literary Text," *Jamaica Journal* 19.4 (1987): 4. See also, Stephen Davis, "Bob Marley – A Final Interview," in *Reggae International*, eds. Stephen Davis and Peter Simon (London: Thames & Hudson, 1983), 91.

174. Morrow, *Stir It Up*, 86.

175. Neville Garrick, "Foreword." in Morrow, *Stir It Up*, 6.

176. Hal Lindsey, *The Late Great Planet Earth* (Grand Rapids, Michigan: Zondervan, 1970).

177. Stephen Davis, "Bob Marley – A Final Interview," in Davis and Simon, *Reggae International*, 91.

178. Partridge, *Dub in Babylon*.

179. Christopher Partridge, "King Tubby Meets the Upsetter at the Grass Roots of Dub: Some Thoughts on the Early History and Influence of Dub Reggae," *Popular Music History* 2 (2007): 309–331.

180. See, for example, Steve Barrow, "Version Therapy," *The Wire* 132 (1995): 30–31; Steve Barrow and Peter Dalton, *Reggae: The Rough Guide* (London: Rough Guides, 1997), 199; Lloyd Bradley, *This is Reggae Music: The Story of Jamaica's Music* (New York: Grove Press, 2000), 314; Hebdige, *Cut "N" Mix*, 83; Mark Prendergast, *The Ambient Century: From Mahler to Trance—The Evolution of Sound in the Electronic Age* (London: Bloomsbury, 2000), 372; David Toop, *Ocean of Sound: Aether Talk, Ambient Sound and Imaginary Worlds* (London: Serpent's Tail, 1995), 116.

181. Lloyd James was a friend and apprentice of King Tubby who has since become one of Jamaica's most successful producers.

182. Prince Jammy, quoted in Barrow and Dalton, *Reggae*, 205.

183. Steve Barrow, "Dub Gone Crazy." Liner notes to King Tubby, *Dub Gone Crazy* (1994).

184. Prince Jammy, quoted in Barrow and Dalton, *Reggae*, 202.

185. Richard Williams, "The Sound Surprise," in *Reggae, Rasta, Revolution: Jamaican Music from Ska to Dub*, ed. Chris Potash (London: Books With Attitude, 1997), 146. The article was originally published in *Melody Maker* on August 21, 1976.

186. Luke Ehrlich, "X-Ray Music: The Volatile History of Dub," in Davis and Simon, *Reggae International*, 106.

187. Toop, *Ocean of Sound*, 115.

188. See Michael Nyman, *Experimental Music: Cage and Beyond*, 2nd ed. (Cambridge: Cambridge University Press, 1999), 11–12.

189. Simon Frith, *Performing Rites: Evaluating Popular Music* (Oxford: Oxford University Press, 1996), 154.

190. Jonathon Kramer, quoted in Frith, *Performing Rites*, 154–155.

191. Frith, *Performing Rites*, 155.

192. Frith, *Performing Rites*, 88.

193. See Simon Jones, "Rocking the House: Sound System Cultures and the Politics of Space," *Journal of Popular Music Studies* 7 (1995): 1–24.

194. Paul Bradshaw, Vivien Goldman, and Penny Reel, "A Big, Big, Sound System Splashdown," *New Musical Express* (February 21, 1981): 29.

195. The Disciples, "BSL Sound System," http://www.disciplesbslbm.co.uk/bslp6.html (accessed October 25, 2005).

196. Linton Kwesi Johnson, "Jamaican Rebel Music," *Race and Class* 17 (1976): 398–399.

197. See Helen Phillips, "Hearing the Vibrations," *Nature Science Update* (August 13, 1998), http://www.nature.com/news/1998/980813/pf/980813-3_pf.html (accessed October 30, 2005); Erica Klarreich, "Feel the Music," *Nature Science Update* (November 27, 2001), http://www.nature.com/news/2001/011127/full/news011129-10.html (accessed August 14, 2012).

198. Jonathan Amos, "Organ Music 'Instils Religious Feelings'," *BBC News* (September 8, 2003), http://news.bbc.co.uk/1/hi/sci/tech/3087674.stm (accessed August 14, 2012).

199. See Neil P.M. Todd and Frederick W. Cody, "Vestibular Responses to Loud Dance Music: A Physiological Basis of the 'Rock and Roll Threshold'?" *The Journal of the Acoustical Society of America* 107 (2000): 496–500.

200. Fred D'Aguiar, "Introduction: Chanting Down Babylon," in Linton Kwesi Johnson, *Mi Revalueshanary Fren: Selected Poems* (London: Penguin, 2002), x.

201. Greg M. Whitfield, "Bass Cultural Vibrations: Visionaries, Outlaws, Mystics, and Chanters," *3 a.m. Magazine* (2002), http://www.3ammagazine.com/musicarchives/2002_oct/bass_cultural_vibrations.html (accessed October 25, 2005).

202. Hebdige, *Cut "N" Mix*, 90.

203. Lol Bell-Brown, "King of the Zulu Tribe ina Roots and Culture Style," *Boom-Shacka-Lacka* 1 (1988), http://www.disciplesbslbm.co.uk/shak1.html (accessed October 12, 2005).

204. Julian Henriques, "Sonic Dominance and the Reggae Sound System Session," in Bull and Back, *Auditory Culture Reader* (Oxford: Berg, 2003): 451–452. It is perhaps not surprising, therefore, that bass has been linked, very explicitly, to sex: Bass Erotica, *Sexual Bass* (1995), *Bass Ecstasy* (1996) and *Erotic Bass Delight* (1996).

205. Kodwo Eshun, *More Brilliant Than the Sun: Adventures in Sonic Fiction* (London: Quartet, 1998), 63, 65.

206. Mick Sleeper, "Shocks of the Mighty," in Potash, *Reggae, Rasta, Revolution*, 160.

207. Generally speaking, Obeah, understood as sorcery, was used to curse individuals and to manipulate events malevolently, and Myalism was understood to be the remedy, a force of good that was able to resist evil influence. See Alan Richardson, "Romantic Voodoo: Obeah and British Culture, 1797–1807," in *Sacred Possessions: Vodou, Santería, Obeah and the Caribbean*, eds. Margarite Fernandez Olmos and Lizabeth Paravisini-Gebert (New Brunswick: Rutgers University Press, 1997), 171–194; Nathanial S. Murrell, *Afro-Caribbean Religions: An Introduction to Their Historical, Cultural, and Sacred Traditions* (Philadelphia: Temple University Press, 2009), 225–245.

208. David Katz, *People Funny Boy: The Genius of Lee "Scratch" Perry* (Edinburgh: Payback Press, 2000), 182.

209. Lee Perry, quoted in Kodwo Eshun, *More Brilliant Than the Sun: Adventures in Sonic Fiction* (London: Quartet, 1998), 65.

210. See David Toop, "Telematic Nomad: Bill Laswell," *The Wire* 130 (1994): 32–35, 80.

211. William Gibson, *Neuromancer* (London: HarperCollins, 1995), 230.

212. Gibson, *Neuromancer*, 128.

213. Lisa Lewis, "Introduction," in *The Adoring Audience: Fan Culture and Popular Media*, ed. Lisa Lewis (London: Routledge, 1992), 1.

214. Barth, *Wolfgang Amadeus Mozart*, 15.

215. Barth, *Wolfgang Amadeus Mozart*, 16.

216. Lawrence Grossberg, "Is There a Fan in the House? The Affective Sensibility of Fandom," in *The Adoring Audience: Fan Culture and Popular Media*, ed. Lisa Lewis (London: Routledge, 1992), 63.

217. Grossberg, "Is There a Fan in the House?" 63.

218. Mark Simpson, *Saint Morrissey* (London: SAF, 2004).

219. Eoin Devereux, "'Heaven Knows We'll Soon be Dust': Catholicism and Devotion in The Smiths," in *Why Pamper Life's Complexities? Essays on The Smiths*, eds. Sean Campbell and Colin Coulter (Manchester: Manchester University Press, 2010), 73.

220. Dennis McNally, "Meditations on the Grateful Dead," in Dodd and Spaulding, *Grateful Dead Reader*, 169.

221. Tim Olaveson, "'Connectedness' and the Rave Experience: Rave as a New Religious Movement?" in *Rave Culture and Religion*, ed. Graham St. John (London: Routledge, 2004), 92.

222. Quoted in Sarah Champion, "Goa," in *Deep Trance and Ritual Beats*, ed. Tony Marcus—a booklet included with the CD *Deep Trance and Ritual Beats* (London: Return to the Source, 1995), 40–42.

223. James Munro, quoted in Champion, "Goa," 45.

224. See Jane Bussmann, *Once in a Lifetime: the Crazy Days of Acid House and Afterwards* (London: Virgin Books, 1998), 134. See also Christopher Partridge, *The Re-Enchantment of the West: Alternative Spiritualities, Sacralization, Popular Culture and Occulture*, vol. 2 (London: T&T Clark International, 2005), 107–111.

225. See Riis and Woodhead, *A Sociology of Religious Emotion*.

226. Arthur Danto, *The Transfiguration of the Commonplace: A Philosophy of Art* (Cambridge: Harvard University Press, 1981).

227. Christine King, "His Truth Goes Marching On: Elvis Presley and the Pilgrimage to Graceland," in *Pilgrimage in Popular Culture*, eds. Ian Reader and Tony Walter (Houndmills: Palgrave, 1993), 103.

228. See Riis and Woodhead, *Sociology of Religious Emotion*, 135.

229. Quoted in Christine King, "His Truth Goes Marching On: Elvis Presley and the Pilgrimage to Graceland," in *Pilgrimage in Popular Culture*, eds. Ian Reader and Tony Walter (Houndmills: Palgrave, 1993), 103; see also, Bono, "Elvis: American David." in *Elvis + Marilyn: 2 x Immortal*, eds. Geri De Paoli and Wendy McDaris (New York: Rizzoli International Publications, 1994), 18.

230. Kiki Apostolakos, an Elvis fan, quoted in Erika Doss, "Believing in Elvis: Popular Piety in Material Culture," in *Religion in the Age of the Media: Explorations in Media, Religion and Culture*, eds. Stewart M. Hoover and Lynn Schofield Clark (New York: Columbia University Press, 2002), 63–64.

231. Mark Duffett's forthright rejection of analyses of "fandom" in terms of "religion" (some of which are admittedly crude), misunderstands this process, as well as the complex nature of "religion" and the "sacred." Mark Duffett, "False Faith or False Comparison? A Critique of the Religious Interpretation of Elvis Fan Culture," *Popular Music and Society* 26 (2003): 514–522.

232. Gregory Reece, *Elvis Religion: The Cult of the King* (London: I.B. Tauris, 2006), 2.

233. Chris Rojek, *Celebrity* (London: Reaktion Books, 2001), 64.

234. See Xing Lu, *Rhetoric of the Chinese Cultural Revolution: The Impact on Chinese Thought, Culture and Communication* (Columbia: University of South Carolina Press, 2004).

235. Lucinda Ebersole, "The God and Goddess of the Written Word," in De Paoli and McDaris, *Elvis + Marilyn*, 137, 40.

236. Ian Reader, "Conclusions," in Reader and Walter, *Pilgrimage in Popular Culture*, 222.

237. King, "His Truth Goes Marching On," 92.

238. Quoted in, King, "His Truth Goes Marching On," 96.

239. Jerry Hopkins and Danny Sugarman, *No One Here Gets Out Alive* (London: Plexus, 1980), vii.

240. Jim Morrison, quoted in Jerry Hopkins and Danny Sugarman, *No One Here Gets Out Alive* (London: Plexus, 1980), 232.

241. Jim Morrison, quoted in James Riordan and Jerry Prochnicky, *Break on Through: The Life and Death of Jim Morrison* (London: Plexus, 1991), 373.

242. See the FBI record reproduced in Riordan and Prochnicky, *Break on Through*, 375

243. Hopkins and Sugarman, *No One Here Gets Out Alive*, vii, viii, ix.

244. On Oliver Stone's fascination with Jim Morrison, see Stephen Talbot, "Sixties Something," *Mother Jones Magazine* 16:2 (March-April, 1991): 47–49, 69–70.

245. Peter Jan Margry, "The Pilgrimage to Jim Morrison's Grave at Père Lachaise Cemetery: The Social Construction of Sacred Space," in *Shrines and Pilgrimage in the Modern World: New Itineraries Into the Sacred*, ed. Peter Jan Margry (Amsterdam: Amsterdam University Press, 2008), 146.

246. Another compilation album, *The Best of the Doors*, released in 2000 by Elektra, uses another photograph of Brodsky's photographs from the *Young Lion* series. See also The Morrison Hotel Gallery: https://www.morrisonhotelgallery.com/photographer/default.aspx?photographerID = 22 (accessed, October 9, 2012).

247. Margry, "The Pilgrimage to Jim Morrison's Grave," 147.

248. See Émile Durkheim, *The Elementary Forms of Religious Life*, trans. Carol Cosman (Oxford: Oxford University Press, 2001), 46.

249. King, "His Truth Goes Marching On," 103.

250. King, "His Truth Goes Marching On," 103.

251. King, "His Truth Goes Marching On," 103.

252. See De Paoli and McDaris, *Elvis + Marilyn*; for Bar-min-ski's portrait *Elvis Christ*, see the cover of Death Ride '69' s *Elvis Christ* (1988).

253. Durkheim, *Elementary Forms of Religious Life*, 46.

254. Sir John Herschel, quoted in Simon Frith, *Sound Effects: Youth, Leisure, and the Politics of Rock "n" Roll* (New York: Pantheon, 1981), 39.

255. Durkheim, *Elementary Forms of Religious Life*, 46.

256. Keuss, *Your Neighbor's Hymnal.*

257. Keuss, *Your Neighbor's Hymnal*, x.

BIBLIOGRAPHY

Abrahamsson, Carl, "Changing Compositions." In Genesis P-Orridge (ed.), *Painful but Fabulous: The Lives and Art of Genesis P-Orridge* (New York: Soft Skull Shortwave, 2002), 29–39.

Abrams, Philip, and Andrew McCulloch, *Communes, Sociology, and Society* (Cambridge: Cambridge University Press, 1976).

Abbington, James (ed.), *Readings in African American Church Music and Worship* (Chicago: GIA Publications, 2001).

Ackroyd, Peter, *Albion: The Origins of the English Imagination* (London; Vintage, 2004).

Adorno, Theodor W., *Philosophy of New Music*. Translated by Robert Hullot-Kentor (Minneapolis: University of Minnesota Press, 2006).

Adorno, Theodor W., *The Stars Down to Earth and Other Essays on the Irrational in Culture*, edited by Stephen Crook (London: Routledge, 1994).

Adorno, Theodor W., *The Culture Industry* (London: Routledge, 1991).

Adorno, Theodor W., "On Popular Music." In Simon Frith and Andrew Goodwin (eds.), *On Record: Rock, Pop, and the Written Word* (New York: Pantheon Books, 1990), 301–314.

Adorno, Theodor W., *Introduction to the Sociology of Music*. Translated by E.B. Ashby (New York: Seabury, 1976).

Adorno, Theodor W., and Max Horkheimer, "The Culture Industry: Enlightenment as Mass Deception." In Simon During (ed.), *The Cultural Studies Reader* (London: Routledge, 1993), 29–43.

Afari, Yasus, *Overstanding Rastafari* (Jamaica: Senya-Cum, 2007).

Agamben, Giorgio, *Homo Sacer: Sovereign Power and Bare Life*. Translated by Daniel Heller-Roazen (Stanford: Stanford University Press, 1998).

Aghahowa, Brenda Eatman, "Definitions of Praising and a Look at Black Worship." In James Abbington (ed.), *Readings in African American Church Music and Worship* (Chicago: GIA Publications, 2001), 353–378.

Agnew, *Vanessa Enlightenment Orpheus: The Power of Music in Other Worlds* (New York: Oxford University Press, 2008).

Aitken, Don, "20 Years of Free Festivals in Britain," *Festival Eye* (1990): 18–21.

Aldridge, Alan, *The Beatles Illustrated Lyrics* (London: Macdonald Unit 75, 1969).

Aldridge, David, and Jörg Fachner (eds.), *Music and Altered States: Consciousness, Transcendence, Therapy and Addictions* (London: Jessica Kinglsey Publishers, 2006).

Alexander, Jeffrey C., *The Meanings of Social Life: A Cultural Sociology* (New York: Oxford University Press, 2003).

Alexander, Jeffrey C., "Toward a Sociology of Evil: Getting Beyond Modernist Common Sense About the Alternative to 'the Good.'" In María Pía Lara (ed.), *Rethinking Evil: Contemporary Perspectives* (Berkeley: University of California Press, 2001), 153–172.

Allen, Gary, "New Education: The radicals Are After Your Children." In Lyman T. Sargent (ed.), *Extremism in America: A Reader* (New York: New York University Press, 1995), 223–234.

Allen, Jeremy, "Adz And It Shall Be Given Unto You: Sufjan Stevens Interviewed," *The Quietus* (October 12, 2010): http://thequietus.com/articles/05085-the-age-of-adz-sufjan-stevens-interview (accessed October 25, 2012).

Allen, Steve, "Madonna," *Journal of Popular Culture* 27.1 (1993): 1–11.

Almond, Marc, *Tainted Life: The Autobiography* (London: Sidgwick & Jackson, 1999).

Altheide, David, "The Columbine Shootings and the Discourse of Fear," *American Behavioral Scientist* 52 (2009): 1354–1370.

Amos, Jonathan, "Organ Music 'Instils Religious Feelings.'" *BBC News* (September 8, 2003): http://news.bbc.co.uk/1/hi/sci/tech/3087674.stm (accessed August 14, 2012).

Anderson, Don, "A Discography of Goth Rock Artists." In Carol Siegel, *Goth's Dark Empire* (Bloomington: Indiana University Press, 2005), 169–183.

Anderson, Gary, *Sin: A History* (New Haven: Yale University Press, 2009).

Antonia, Nina, *The One and Only: Peter Perrett—Homme Fatale* (Wembley: SAF Publishing, 1996).

Aranza, Jacob, *Backward Masking Unmasked* (Shreveport and Lafayette: Huntington House, 1983).

Armitt, Lucie, *Twentieth-Century Gothic* (Cardiff: University of Wales Press, 2011).

Arnheiter, Carl, "Julian Cope: Enlightenment and Salvation is just a Stamp Away" *The Ptolemaic Terrascope* 20 (1996): http://www.terrascope.co.uk/MyBackPages/Julian_Cope.htm (accessed May 08, 2012).

Arnold, Matthew, *Culture and Anarchy* (Cambridge: Cambridge University Press, 1971).

Arnold, Matthew, *Discourses in America* (London: Macmillan & Co., 1912).

Arya, Rina, "The Religious Significance of Violence in Football." In Eric Christianson and Christopher Partridge (eds.), *Holy Terror: Understanding Religion and Violence in Popular Culture* (London: Equinox, 2010), 122–134.

Atkinson, Paul, Amanda Coffey, Sara Delamont, John Lofland and Lyn Lofland (eds.), *Handbook of Ethnography* (London: Sage, 2001).

Attali, Jacques, *Noise: The Political Economy of Music*. Translated by Brian Massumi (Manchester: Manchester University Press, 1985).

Aubrey, Crispin, and John Shearlaw, *Glastonbury: An Oral History of the Music, Mud and Magic* (London: Ebury Press, 2005).

Augustine, *Nicene and Post-Nicene Fathers. First Series*, Vol. 5. *St. Augustine: Anti-Pelagian Writings*, edited by Philip Schaff (New York: Cosimo, 2007 [1887]).

Avatara, "Avatara." In Chris Deckker (ed.), *The Chakra Journey*, a booklet issued with the following CD: Various Artists, *The Chakra Journey* (Return to the Source, 1996), 26–27.

Azerrad, Michael, *Our Band Could Be Your Life: Scenes from the American Indie Underground, 1981–1991* (Boston: Little Brown and Company, 2001).

Baddeley, Gavin, *Lucifer Rising: Sin, Devil Worship & Rock 'n' Roll* (London: Plexus, 1999).

Bainbridge, William S., *Satan's Power: A Deviant Psychotherapy Cult* (Berkeley: University of California Press, 1978).

Baldini, Chiara, "Dionysus Returns: Contemporary Tuscan Trancers and Euripodes' *The Bacchae*." In Graham St John (ed.), *The Local Scenes and Global Culture of Psytrance* (London: Routledge, 2010), 170–185.

Baker, Phil, *Austin Osman Spare: The Life and Legend of London's Lost Artist* (London: Strange Attractor, 2010).

Bakhtin, Mikhail, *Problems of Dostoevsky's Poetics*. Translated by Caryl Emerson (Minneapolis: University of Minnesota Press, 1984).

Bakhtin, Mikhail, *Rabelais and His World*. Translated by Hélène Iswolsky (Bloomington: Indiana University Press, 1984).

Bandele, Ramla, *Black Star: African American Activism in the International Political Economy* (Urbana: University of Illinois Press, 2008).

Barker, Martin, "On Being a 1960s Tolkien Reader." In Ernest Mathijs and Murray Pomerance (eds.), *From Hobbits to Hollywood: Essays on Peter Jackson's Lord of the Rings* (Amsterdam: Rodopi, 2006), 81–100.

Barkun, Michael, *A Culture of Conspiracy: Apocalyptic Visions in Contemporary America* (Berkeley: University of California Press, 2003).

Barrett, Leonard E., *The Rastafarians* (Boston: Beacon Press, 1997).

Barrow, Steve, "Version Therapy," *The Wire* 132 (1995): 28–32.

Barrow, Steve, "Dub Gone Crazy." Liner notes to King Tubby, *Dub Gone Crazy* (Blood & Fire, 1994).

Barrow, Steve, and Peter Dalton, *Reggae: The Rough Guide* (London: Rough Guides, 1997).

Barth, Karl, *Wolfgang Amadeus Mozart*. Translated by Clarence K. Pott (Grand Rapids: Wm. B. Eerdmans Publishing Co., 1986).

Barthes, Roland, *Image, Music, Text*. Translated by Stephen Heath (London: Fontana Press, 1977).

Bartov, Omer, *Murder in Our Midst: The Holocaust, Industrial Killing, and Representation* (New York: Oxford University Press, 1996).

Bataille, Georges, *The Absence of Myth*. Translated by Michael Richardson (London: Verso, 1994).

Bataille, Georges, *The Accursed Share*, Vol. I. Translated by Robert Hurley (New York: Zone Books, 1991).

Bataille, Georges, *The Accursed Share*, Vols. II & III. Translated by Robert Hurley (New York: Zone Books, 1991).

Bataille, Georges, *Theory of Religion*. Translated by Robert Hurley (New York: Zone Books, 1989).

Bataille, Georges, *Inner Experience*. Translated by Lesley Anne Boldt (Albany, New York: State University of New York Press, 1988).

Bataille, Georges, *Eroticism: Death and Sensuality*. Translated by Mary Dalwood (San Francisco: City Lights Books, 1986).

Bataille, Georges, *Visions of Excess: Selected Writings 1927–1939*, Edited and Translated by Allan Stoekl (Manchester: Manchester University Press, 1985).

Baudrillard, Jean, "Death in Bataille." In Fred Botting and Scott Wilson (eds.), *Bataille: A Critical Reader* (Oxford: Blackwell, 1998), 139–145.

Baudrillard, Jean, *Symbolic Exchange and Death*. Translated by Iain Hamilton Grant (London: Sage, 1993).

Baudrillard, Jean, *Simulacra and Simulation*. Translated by Sheila Faria Glaser (Ann Arbor: University of Michigan Press, 1992).

Bauer, Walter, *Orthodoxy and Heresy in Earliest Christianity*. Translated by Robert Kraft (Philadelphia: Fortress Press, 1971).

Bauman, Whitney, *Theology, Creation and Environmental Ethics: From Creation Ex Nihilo to Terra Nullius* (New York: Routledge, 2009).

Bauman, Zygmunt, "Durkheim's Society Revisited." In Jeffrey C. Alexander and Philip Smith (eds.), *The Cambridge Companion to Durkheim* (Cambridge: Cambridge University Press, 2005), 360–382.

Beard, David, and Kenneth Gloag, *Musicology: The Key Concepts* (Abingdon: Routledge, 2005).

Beatie, Bruce, "The Tolkien Phenomenon: 1954–1968," *Journal of Popular Culture* 3 (1970): 689–703.

Beaujon, Andrew, *Body Piercing Saved My Life: Inside the Phenomenon of Christian Rock* (New York: Da Capo Press, 2006).

Beck, Guy, "Introduction." In Guy Beck (ed.), *Sacred Sounds: Experiencing Music in World Religions* (Waterloo: Wilfred Laurier University Press, 2006), 1–27.

Beck, Guy (ed.), *Sacred Sounds: Experiencing Music in World Religions* (Waterloo: Wilfred Laurier University Press, 2006).

Beck, Guy, *Sonic Theology: Hinduism and Sacred Sound* (Delhi: Motilal Banarsidass Publishers, 1995).

Becker, Judith, *Deep Listeners: Music, Emotion and Trancing* (Bloomington: Indiana University Press, 2004).

Beckerley, Tim, "Glastonbury Entertains," *Festival Eye* 19 (2003), 10.

Beckford, Robert, *Jesus Dub: Theology, Music and Social Change* (London: Routledge, 2006).

Beckford, Robert, *Jesus is Dread: Black Theology and Black Culture in Britain* (London: Darton, Longman & Todd, 1998).

Beckwith, Karl, "'Black Metal is for White People: Constructs of Colour and Identity Within the Extreme Metal Scene," *M/C Journal: A Journal of Media and Culture* 5:3 (July, 2002): http:// journal.media-culture.org.au/0207/blackmetal.php (accessed April 23, 2012).

Beer, Robert, *The Encyclopedia of Tibetan Symbols and Motifs* (Chicago: Serindia Publications, 2004).

Begbie, Jeremy, *Theology, Music, and Time* (Cambridge: Cambridge University Press, 2000).

Begbie, Jeremy, *Voicing Creation's Praise: Towards a Theology of the Arts* (London: T&T Clark, 1991).

Bell-Brown, Lol, "King of the Zulu Tribe ina Roots and Culture Style," *Boom-Shacka-Lacka* 1 (1988): http://www.disciplesbslbm.co.uk/shak1.html (accessed October 12, 2005).

Bellman, Jonathan, "Indian Resonances in the British Invasion, 1965–1968." In Jonathon Bellman (ed.), *The Exotic in Western Music* (Boston: Northeastern University Press, 1998), 292–306.

Bellman, Jonathon (ed.), *The Exotic in Western Music* (Boston: Northeastern University Press, 1998).

Bennett, Andy, "Pour une réévaluation du concept de contre-culture," *Volume: La revue des musiques des populaires* 9: 1 (2012): 19–31.

Bennett, Andy, *Cultures of Popular Music* (Buckingham: Open University Press, 2001).

Bennett, Andy, *Popular Music and Youth Culture: Music, Identity and Place* (Houndmills: Macmillan, 2000).

Bennett, Andy, Barry Shank, and Jason Toynbee (eds.), *The Popular Music Studies Reader* (London: Routledge, 2006).

Bennett, Andy, Barry Shank, and Jason Toynbee, "Introduction." In Andy Bennett, Barry Shank, and Jason Toynbee (eds.), *The Popular Music Studies Reader* (London: Routledge, 2006).

Bennett, Andy, and Donna Weston (eds.), *Pop Pagans: Paganism and Popular Music* (Durham: Acumen, 2012).

Bennett, Gillian, "Geologists and Folklorists: Cultural Evolution and the Science of Folklore," *Folklore* 105 (1994): 25–37.

Bennett, Gillian, "Folklore Studies and English Rural Myth," *Rural History* 4 (1993): 77–91.

Bennett, Tony, *Culture: A Reformer's Science* (London: Sage, 1998).

Berger, Peter, *The Sacred Canopy: Elements of a Sociological Theory of Religion* (New York: Anchor Books, 1967).

Bernstein, Leonard, *The Unanswered Question: Six Talks at Harvard* (Cambridge: Harvard University Press, 1976).

Bhabha, Homi, *The Location of Culture* (London: Routledge, 1994).

Bibby, Michael, "Atrocity Exhibitions: Joy Division, Factory Records, and Goth." In Lauren Goodlad and Michael Bibby (eds.), *Goth: Undead Subculture* (Durham: Yale University Press, 2007), 233–256.

Bicknell, Jeanette, *Why Music Moves Us* (London: Palgrave Macmillan, 2009).

Bilby, Kenneth, and Elliot Leib, "Kumina, the Howellite Church and the Emergence of Rastafarian Traditional Music," *Jamaica Journal* 19: 3 (1986): 22–28.

Bishop, Peter, *Dreams of Power: Tibetan Buddhism and the Western Imagination* (London: Athlone, 1993).

Bivins, Jason C., *Religion of Fear: The Politics of Horror in Conservative Evangelicalism* (New York: Oxford University Press, 2008).

Black, Johnny, "Eyewitness: Traffic Get Their Heads Together in the Country," *Q* 103 (April, 1995): 59–60.

Blake, William, *The Complete Illuminated Works* (London: Thames & Hudson/The William Blake Trust, 2000).

Blanchard, John, *Pop Goes the Gospel* (Welwyn: Evangelical Press, 1983).

Blanchard, John, and Dan Lucarini, *Can We Rock the Gospel? Rock Music's Impact on Worship and Evangelism* (Welwyn: Evangelical Press, 2006).

Bloom, Harold, *William Blake* (New York: Chelsea House Publishers, 2006).

Blush, Steven, *American Hardcore: A Tribal History* (Los Angeles: Feral House, 2010).

Bockris, Victor, *Patti Smith* (London: Fourth Estate, 1998).

Boer, Roland, *Nick Cave: A Study of Love, Death and Apocalypse* (Sheffield: Equinox, 2012).

Bono, "Elvis: American David." In Geri De Paoli and Wendy McDaris (eds.), *Elvis + Marilyn: 2 x Immortal* (New York: Rizzoli International Publications, 1994), 17–18.

Bossius, Thomas, Andreas Häger, and Keith Kahn-Harris (eds.), *Religion and Popular Music in Europe* (London: IB Tauris, 2011).

Botting, Fred, and Scott Wilson, "Introduction: From Experience to Economy." In Fred Botting and Scott Wilson (eds.), *The Bataille Reader* (Oxford: Blackwell, 1997), 1–34.

Botting, Fred, and Scott Wilson (eds.), *The Bataille Reader* (Oxford: Blackwell, 1997).

Bourdieu, Pierre, *Distinction: A Social Critique of the Judgement of Taste* (Cambridge: Harvard University Press, 1984).

Bowers, Faubian, *Scriabin: A Biography*, 2 vols, 2nd edition (New York: Dover Publications, 1996).

Bowman, Rob, "Argh Fuck Kill – Canadian Hardcore Goes on Trial: The Case of the Dayglo Abortions." In Martin Cloonan and Reebee Garofalo (eds.), *Policing Pop* (Philadelphia: Temple University Press, 2003), 113–139.

Bowman, Marion, "Glastonbury as a Site of Consumption." In Gordon Lynch, Jolyon Mitchell, and Anna Strhan (eds.), *Religion, Media and Culture: A Reader* (London: Routledge, 2011), 11–22.

Bowman, Marion, "The Noble Savage and the Global Village: Cultural Evolution in New Age and Neo-Pagan Thought," *Journal of Contemporary Religion* 10 (1995): 139–149.

Boyes, Georgina, *The Imagined Village: Culture, Ideology and the English Folk Revival* (Manchester: Manchester University Press, 1993).

Bragg, Billy, *The Progressive Patriot: A Search for Belonging* (London: Bantam Press, 2006).

Bragg, Billy, "Does National Pride Matter?" *National Trust Magazine* (Summer 2012), 15.

Bright, Kimberley, *Chris Spedding: Reluctant Guitar Hero* (Lincoln: iUniverse, 2007).

Bradley, Lloyd, *This is Reggae Music: The Story of Jamaica's Music* (New York: Grove Press, 2000). Published in the UK as *Bass Culture: When Reggae Was King* (London: Viking, 2000).

Bradshaw, Paul, Vivien Goldman, and Penny Reel, "A Big, Big, Sound System Splashdown," *New Musical Express* (February 21, 1981): 26–29, 53.

Brannigan, Paul, "Just Say No," *Mojo* 217 (December, 2011): 52–56.

Brocken, Michael, *The British Folk Revival, 1944–2002* (Aldershot: Ashgate, 2003).

Broedel, Hans Peter, *The Malleus Maleficarum and the Construction of Witchcraft: Theology and Popular Belief* (Manchester: Manchester University Press, 2003).

Bromell, Nick, *Tomorrow Never Knows: Rock and Psychedelics in the 1960s* (Chicago: Chicago University Press, 2000).

Brown, Callum, *The Death of Christian Britain: Understanding Secularisation, 1800–2000*, 2nd edition (London: Routledge, 2009).

Brown, Frank Burch, "Music." In John Corrigan (ed.), *The Oxford Handbook of Religion and Emotion* (Oxford: Oxford University Press, 2008), 200–222.

Brown, Jake, *Tori Amos: In the Studio* (Toronto: ECW Press, 2011).

Brown, Peter, *The Body and Society: Men, Women, and Sexual Renunciation in Early Christianity* (New York: Columbia University Press, 1988).

Brown, Roger, and James Kulik, "Flashbulb Memories," *Cognition* 5: 1 (1977), 73–99.

Bruce, Steve, *God Is Dead: Secularization in the West* (Oxford: Blackwell, 2002).

Bruce, Steve, "Pluralism and Religious Vitality." In Steve Bruce (ed.), *Religion and Modernization: Historians Debate the Secularization Thesis* (Oxford: Oxford University Press, 1992), 170–194.

Brueggemann, Walter, "Vulnerable Children, Divine Passion and Human Obligation." In Marcia Bunge, Terence Fretheim, and Beverly Gaventa (eds.), *The Child in the Bible* (Grand Rapids: Wm. B. Eerdmans Publishing Co., 2008), 399–422.

Brueggemann, Walter, *Genesis* (Louisville, John Knox Press, 1982).

Brummel-Smith, Karen, "Music and the Meditative Mind: Toward a Science of the Ineffable." In Benjamin D. Koen (ed.), *The Oxford Handbook of Medical Ethnomusicology* (New York: Oxford University Press, 2008), 308–330.

Buck, Paul (ed.), *Violent Silence: Celebrating Georges Bataille* (London: The Georges Bataille Event, 1984).

Bugliosi, Vincent, and Curt Gentry, *Helter Skelter* (London: Arrow Books, 1992 [1974]).

Bulgakov, Mikhail, *The Master And Margarita*. Translated by Richard Pevear and Larissa Volokhonsky (London: Penguin, 1997).

Bull, Michael, *Sound Moves: iPod Culture and the Urban Experience* (London: Routledge, 2007).

Burroughs, William S., "Uranium Willie and the Heavy Metal Kid: A Near-Forgotten 1975 Talk with Jimmy Page." In Jon Bream, *Whole Lotta Led Zeppelin: The Illustrated History of the Heaviest Band of All Time* (Minneapolis: Voyageur Press, 2008), 166–169.

Burroughs, William S., and Brion Gysin, *The Third Mind* (New York: Viking Press, 1978).

Burton, Richard D. E., *Afro-Creole: Power, Opposition, and Play in the Caribbean* (Ithaca: Cornell University Press, 1997).

Bussmann, Jane, *Once in a Lifetime: the Crazy Days of Acid House and Afterwards* (London: Virgin Books, 1998).

Butler, Judith, *Bodies That Matter: On the Discursive Limits of "Sex"* (London: Routledge, 1993).

Byrne, David, *The New Sins/Los Nuevos Pecados* (London: Faber and Faber, 2001).

Caillois, Roger, *Man and the Sacred*. Translated by Meyer Barash (Urbana: University of Illnois Press, 2001 [1939]).

Campbell, Colin, "The Secret Religion of the Educated Classes," *Sociological Analysis* 39 (1978): 146–156.

Campbell, Colin, "The Cult, the Cultic Milieu and Secularization." In Michael Hill (ed.), *Sociological Yearbook of Religion in Britain* 5 (London: SCM Press, 1972), 119–136.

Campbell, Don (ed.), *Music: Physician for the Times to Come*, 2nd edition (Wheaton: Quest Books, 2000).

Campbell, Horace, *Rasta and Resistance: From Marcus Garvey to Walter Rodney* (St John's, Antigua: Hansib Caribbean, 1997).

Campbell, Robert A., "Georges Bataille's Surrealistic Theory of Religion," *Method and Theory in the Study of Religion* 11 (1999): 127–142.

Capra, Fritjof, *The Turning Point: Science, Society and the Rising Culture* (London: Flamingo, 1983).

Capra, Fritjof, *The Tao of Physics: An Exploration of Parallels Between Modern Physics and Eastern Mysticism* (London: Fontana, 1976).

Carlin, Gerry, and Mark Jones, "Cease to Exist: Manson Family Movies and Mysticism." In Eric Christianson and Christopher Partridge (eds.), *Holy Terror: Understanding Religion and Violence in Popular Culture* (London: Equinox, 2010), 53–62.

Carpenter, Bil, *Uncloudy Days: The Gospel Music Encyclopaedia* (San Francisco: Backbeat Books, 2005).

Carrette, Jeremy (ed.), Religion and Culture: Michel Foucault (London: Routledge, 1999).

Carthy, Eliza, "Traditional English Song Has No Links to the Far Right or Nick Griffin," *The Guardian* (January 26, 2010): http://www.guardian.co.uk/commentisfree/2010/jan/26/nick-griffin-bnp-folk-music (accessed May 30, 2012).

Cary, John, *What Good Are the Arts?* (London: Faber & Faber, 2005).

Cashmore, Ernest E., *Rastaman: The Rastafarian Movement in England* (London: Unwin Paperbacks, 1983).

Cavallaro, Dani, *The Gothic Vision: Three Centuries of Horror, Terror and Fear* (London: Continuum, 2002).

Cave, Nick, *The Complete Lyrics, 1978–2007* (London: Penguin, 2007).

Certeau, Michel de, *The Practice of Everyday Life*. Translated by Steven Rendall (Berkeley: University of California Press, 1984).

Champion, Sarah, "Goa." In Tony Marcus (ed.), *Deep Trance and Ritual Beats*—a booklet included with the CD *Deep Trance and Ritual Beats* (London: Return to the Source, 1995), 36–51.

Chastagner, Claude, "The Parents' Music Resource Center: From Information to Censorship," *Popular Music* 18 (1999): 179–192.

Chevannes, Barry, *Rastafari: Roots and Ideology* (Syracuse: Syracuse University Press, 1994).

Chevannes, Barry, *The Social Origins of Rastafari* (Kingston: Institute of Social and Economic Research, University of the West Indies, 1979).

Christie, Ian, *Sound of the Beast: The Complete Headbanging History* (New York: HarperCollins, 2003).

Cladis, Mark, "Introduction." In Émile Durkheim, *The The Elementary Forms of Religious Life.* Translated by Carol Cosman (Oxford: Oxford University Press, 2001), vii–xxxv.

Clark, Katerina, and Michael Holquist, *Mikhail Bakhtin* (Cambridge: Harvard University Press, 1984).

Clarke, Donald, *The Rise and Fall of Popular Music* (Harmondsworth: Penguin, 1995).

Clarke, Michael, *The Politics of Pop Festivals* (London: Junction Books, 1982).

Clarke, Peter B., *Black Paradise: The Rastafarian Movement,* Black Political Studies No.5 (San Bernardino: Borgo Press, 1994).

Clifton, Chas S., *Her Hidden Children: The Rise of Modern Wicca and Paganism in America* (Lanham: Alta Mira Press, 2006).

Cloonan, Martin, *Banned! Censorship of Popular Music in Britain: 1967–1992* (Aldershot: Ashgate, 1996).

Cloonan, Martin, and Reebee Garofalo (eds.), *Policing Pop* (Philadelphia: Temple University Press, 2003).

Cloud, David, *Rock Music Vs. the God of the Bible* (Port Huron: Way Life Literature, 2000).

Clucas, Stephen (ed.), *John Dee: Interdisciplinary Studies in English Renaissance Thought,* International Archives of the History of Ideas 193 (Dordrecht: Springer, 2006).

Cobb, Kelton, *The Blackwell Guide to Theology and Popular Culture* (Oxford: Blackwell, 2005).

Cody, John V., "Gerald Heard: Soul Guide to the Beyond Within," *Gnosis* 26 (1993): 64–70.

Cohen, Sara, "Ethnography and Popular Music Studies," *Popular Music* 12 (1994): 179–190.

Cohen, Stanley, *Folk Devils and Moral Panics,* 3rd edition (London: Routledge, 2002).

Cole, Richard (Radha Mohan Das), "Forty Years of Chanting: A Study of the Hare Krishna Movement from its Foundation to the Present Day." In Graham Dwyer and Richard Cole (eds.), *The Hare Krishna Movement: Forty Years of Chant and Change* (London: I.B. Tauris, 2007), 26–53.

Coleridge, Samuel Taylor, and William Wordsworth, *Lyrical Ballads 1798 and 1800.* Edited by Michael Gamer and Dahlia Porter (Ontario: Broadview Press, 2008).

Collin, Matthew, *Altered States: the Story of Ecstasy Culture and Acid House* (London: Serpent's Tail, 1998).

Collins, Randall, *Violence: A Micro-Sociological Theory* (Princeton: Princeton University Press, 2008).

Committee for Jewish Music, "Rules for Playing Kosher Music": http://news.bbc.co.uk/1/shared/bsp/hi/pdfs/11_9_08_kosher_music.pdf (accessed July 26, 2012).

Cone, James H., *The Spirituals and the Blues* (Maryknoll: Orbis Books, 1991 [1972]).

Cooper, Caroline, "Chanting Down Babylon: Bob Marley's Song as Literary Text," *Jamaica Journal* 19.4 (1987): 2–8.

Cope, Julian, *Copendium: An Expedition Into the Rock 'n' Roll Underworld* (London: Faber & Faber, 2012).

Cope, Julian, *The Megalithic European: The 21st Century Traveller in Prehistoric Europe* (London: Element, 2004).

Cope, Julian, *The Modern Antiquarian: A Pre-Millennial Odyssey Through Megalithic Britain* (London: Thorsons, 1998).

Cope, Julian, "From Punk to Pre-history," *Kindred Spirit* 45 (1998–1999): 25–28.

Corrigan, John (ed.), *The Oxford Handbook of Religion and Emotion* (Oxford: Oxford University Press, 2008).

Corrigan, John (ed.), *Religion and Emotion: Approaches and Interpretations* (Oxford: Oxford University Press, 2004).

Cox, Christopher, and Daniel Warner (eds.), *Audio Culture: Readings in Modern Music* (New York: Continuum, 2004).

Cox, Harvey, *Turning East: The Promise and Peril of the New Orientalism* (New York: Simon and Schuster, 1977).

Craig, Daniel, "Exploring Music Preference: Meaningfulness of Music as a Function of Emotional Reactions," *Nordic Journal of Music Therapy* 18: 1 (2009): 57–69.

Craton, Michael, *Searching for the Invisible Man: Slaves and Plantation Life in Jamaica* (Cambridge: Harvard University Press, 1978).

Creasman, Paul, "Looking Beyond the Radio for Listeners." In Quentin Schultze and Robert Woods Jr. (eds.), *Understanding Evangelical Media: The Changing Face of Christian Communication* (Downers Grove: InterVarsity Press, 2008), 33–45.

Cross, Ian, and Elizabeth Tolbert, "Music and Meaning." In Susan Hallam, Ian Cross, and Michael Thaut (eds.), *The Oxford Handbook of Music Psychology* (Oxford: Oxford University Press, 2009), 24–34.

Crowley, Vivianne, *Wicca: The Old Religion in the New Millennium* (London: Thorsons, 1996).

Crowther, Paul, *Defining Art, Creating a Canon: Artistic Value in an Era of Doubt* (Oxford: Oxford University Press, 2007).

Culler, Jonathan, *The Pursuit of Signs: Semiotics, Literature, Deconstruction* (London: Routledge, 2001).

Cunningham, David, "Kraftwerk and the Image of the Modern." In Sean Albiez and David Pattie (eds.), *Kraftwerk: Music Non-Stop* (London: Continuum, 2011), 44–62.

Cusic, Don, *Encyclopedia of Contemporary Christian Music: Pop, Rock, and Worship* (Santa Barbara: ABC-CLIO, 2010).

D'Aguiar, Fred, "Introduction: Chanting Down Babylon." In Linton Kwesi Johnson, *Mi Revalueshanary Fren: Selected Poems* (London: Penguin, 2002), ix–xiv.

Dale, Tony, "A Conversation with Vashti Bunyan," *The Ptolemaic Terrascope* 30 (2001): http://www.terrascope.co.uk/MyBackPages/Vashti%20Bunyan%20PT30.pdf (accessed May 02, 2012).

Dale, Tony, "Six Organs of Admittance," *The Ptolemaic Terrascope* 28 (2000): http://www.terrascope.co.uk/MyBackPages/Six%20Organs%20of%20Admittance.pdf (accessed May 07, 2012).

Dalton, David, "A Last Look at Traffic: 'Who Knows What Tomorrow May Bring?,'" *Rolling Stone* 32 (May 3, 1969): 14–15.

D'Andrea, Anthony, "The Decline of Electronic Dance Scenes: The Case of Psytrance in Goa." In Graham St. John (ed.), *The Local Scenes and Global Culture of Psytrance* (London: Routledge, 2010), 40–54.

D'Andrea, Anthony, *Global Nomads: Techno and New Age as Transnational Countercultures in Ibiza and Goa* (Abingdon: Routledge, 2007).

D'Andrea, Anthony, "Global Nomads: Techno and New Age as Transnational Countercultures in Ibiza and Goa." In Graham St. John (ed.), *Rave Culture and Religion* (London: Routledge, 2004), 236–255.

Daniel, Drew, *20 Jazz Funk Greats* (New York: Continuum, 2008).

Dann, Trevor, *Darker Than the Deepest Sea: The Search for Nick Drake* (London: Piatkus Books, 2006).

Danto, Arthur, *The Transfiguration of the Commonplace: A Philosophy of Art* (Cambridge: Harvard University Press, 1981).

Davies, Douglas J., *Emotion, Identity and Religion: Hope, Reciprocity, and Otherness* (Oxford: Oxford University Press, 2011).

Davies, Stephen "Philosophical Perspectives on Music's Expressiveness." In Patrik N. Juslin & John Sloboda (eds.), *Music and Emotion: Theory and Research* (Oxford: Oxford University Press, 2001), 23–44.

Davies, Wyre, "Rabbis Black-list Non-kosher Music," *BBC News* (September 12, 2008): http://news.bbc.co.uk/1/hi/world/middle_east/7609859.stm (accessed July 26, 2012).

Davis, Colin, "Hauntology, Spectres and Phantoms." *French Studies* 59 (2005): 373–379.

Davis, Erik, *Led Zeppelin IV* (New York: Continuum, 2005).

Davis, James D., "Children of the Ras." In Chris Potash (ed.), *Reggae, Rasta, Revolution: Jamaican Music from Ska to Dub* (London: Books With Attitude, 1997), 253–254.

Davis, Stephen, and Peter Simon (eds.), *Reggae International* (London: Thames & Hudson, 1983).

Davis, Stephen, "Bob Marley – A Final Interview." In Stephen Davis and Peter Simon (eds.), *Reggae International* (London: Thames & Hudson, 1983), 88–91.

Dawkins, Richard, *The God Delusion* (London: Bantam Press, 2006).

Day, Aidan, *Romanticism* (London: Routledge, 1996).

Day, Timothy, *A Century of Recorded Music: Listening to Musical History* (New Haven: Yale University Press, 2000).

Deckker, Chris, "Introduction." In Tony Marcus (ed.), *Deep Trance and Ritual Beats*—a booklet included with the CD *Deep Trance and Ritual Beats* (London: Return to the Source, 1995), 2–3.

DeGroot, Gerard, *The 60s Unplugged: A Kaleidoscopic History of a Disorderly Decade* (London: Macmillan, 2008).

De Gruchy, John W., *Christianity, Art, and Transformation: Theological Aesthetics in the Struggle for Justice* (Cambridge: Cambridge University Press, 2001).

De Paoli, Geri, and Wendy McDaris (eds.), *Elvis + Marilyn: 2 x Immortal* (New York: Rizzoli International Publications, 1994).

de Ledesma, Charles, "Psychedelic Trance Music Making in the UK: Rhizomatic Craftsmanship and the Global Market Place." In Graham St. John (ed.), *The Local Scenes and Global Culture of Psytrance* (London: Routledge, 2010), 89–113.

DeNora, Tia, "Aesthetic Agency and Musical Practice: New Directions in the Sociology of Music." In Patrik Juslin and John Sloboda (eds.), *Music and Emotion: Theory and Research.* (Oxford: Oxford University Press, 2001), 161–180.

DeNora, Tia, *Music in Everyday Life* (Cambridge: Cambridge University Press, 2000).

Derrida, Jacques, "Marx and Sons." In Michael Sprinker (ed.), *Ghostly Demarcations: A Symposium on Jacques Derrida's Spectres of Marx* (London: Verso, 1999), 213–269.

Derrida, Jacques, *Spectres of Marx: The State of the Debt, the Work of Mourning, and the New International* (New York: Routledge, 1994).

Devereux, Eoin, "'Heaven Knows We'll Soon be Dust': Catholicism and Devotion in The Smiths." In Sean Campbell and Colin Coulter (eds.), *Why Pamper Life's Complexities? Essays on The Smiths* (Manchester: Manchester University Press, 2010), 65–80.

Dibben, Nicola, *Björk* (London: Equinox, 2009).

Dibben, Nicola, "Nature and Nation: National Identity and Environmentalism in Icelandic Popular Music Video and Music Documentary," *Ethnomusicology Forum* 18: 1 (2009): 131–151.

Disciples, The, "BSL Sound System": http://www.disciplesbslbm.co.uk/bslp6.html (accessed October 25, 2005).

Dobbelaere, Karel, "Secularization: A Multi-Dimensional Concept," *Current Sociology* 29 (1981): 3–153.

Dodd, David G., and Diana Spaulding (eds.), *The Grateful Dead Reader* (New York: Oxford University Press, 2000).

Doss, Erika, "Believing in Elvis: Popular Piety in Material Culture." In Stewart M. Hoover and Lynn Schofield Clark (eds.), *Religion in the Age of the Media: Explorations in Media, Religion and Culture* (New York: Columbia University Press, 2002), 63–86.

Douglas, Mary, *Purity and Danger: An Analysis of the Concept of Pollution and Taboo* (London: Routledge, 2002 [1966]).

Drewett, Michael, and Martin Cloonan (eds.), *Popular Music and Censorship in Africa* (Aldershot: Ashgate, 2006).

Drury, Neville, *Echoes From the Void: Writings on Magic, Visionary Art and the New Consciousness* (Bridport: Prism Press, 1994).

Duffett, Mark, "False Faith or False Comparison? A Critique of the Religious Interpretation of Elvis Fan Culture," *Popular Music and Society* 26 (2003): 514–522.

Durham, Martin, *White Rage: The Extreme Right and American Politics* (Abingdon: Routledge, 2007).

During, Jean, "Therapeutic Dimensions of Music in Islamic Culture." In Benjamin D. Koen (ed.), *The Oxford Handbook of Medical Ethnomusicology* (New York: Oxford University Press, 2008), 361–392.

During, Simon (ed.), *The Cultural Studies Reader* (London: Routledge, 1993).

Durkheim, Émile, *The Elementary Forms of Religious Life*. Translated by Carol Cosman (Oxford: Oxford University Press, 2001).

Durkheim, Émile, *The Rules of Sociological Method*. Translated by Sarah Solovay and John Mueller (New York: The Free Press, 1938).

Durkheim, Émile, *The Division of Labour in Society*. Translated by George Simpson (New York: Macmillan, 1933).

Dwyer, Simon, "Throbbing Gristle Biography." In V. Vale (ed.), *Re/Search 4/5: William S Burroughs, Throbbing Gristle, Brion Gysin* (San Francisco: RE/Search, 2007), 62–65.

Dyer, Richard, "In Defense of Disco." In Simon Frith and Andrew Goodwin (eds.), *On Record: Rock, Pop, and the Written Word* (New York: Pantheon Books, 1990), 410–418.

Dyrendal, Asbjørn, "Satanism and Popular Music." In Christopher Partridge and Eric Christianson (eds.), *The Lure of the Dark Side: Satan and Western Demonology in Popular Culture* (London: Equinox, 2009), 25–38.

Dyrendal, Asbjørn, "Darkness Within: Satanism as a Self-Religion." In Jesper Aagaard Petersen (ed.), *Contemporary Religious Satanism: A Critical Anthology* (Farnham: Ashgate, 2009), 59–73.

Earles, Andrew, *Hüsker Dü: The Story of the Noise-Pop Pioneers Who Launched Modern Rock* (Minneapolis: Voyageur Press, 2010).

Ebersole, Lucinda, "The God and Goddess of the Written Word." In Geri De Paoli and Wendy McDaris (eds.), *Elvis + Marilyn: 2 x Immortal* (New York: Rizzoli International Publications, 1994), 136–145.

Eco, Umberto, *The Name of the Rose* (Orlando: Harcourt Brace Jovanovich, 1983).

Edmonds, Ennis, *Rastafari: From Outcasts to Culture Bearers* (New York: Oxford University Press, 2003).

Eno, Brian, "Ambient Music." In Christopher Cox and Daniel Warner (eds.), *Audio Culture: Readings in Modern Music* (New York: Continuum, 2004), 94–97.

Ehrlich, Dimitri, *Inside the Music: Conversations with Contemporary Musicians About Spirituality, Creativity, and Consciousness* (Boston: Shambhala, 1997).

Ehrlich, Luke, "X-Ray Music: The Volatile History of Dub." In Stephen Davis and Peter Simon (eds.), *Reggae International* (London: Thames & Hudson, 1983), 105–109.

Eliade, Mircea, *The Sacred and the Profane: The Nature of Religion* (Orlando: Harcourt Brace Jovanovich, 1987).

Elliott, Luther, "Goa is a State of Mind: On the Ephemerality of Psychedelic Social Placements." In Graham St. John (ed.), *The Local Scenes and Global Culture of Psytrance* (London: Routledge, 2010), 21–39.

Ellwood, Robert S., *One Way: The Jesus Movement and Its Meaning* (Englewood Cliffs: Prentice-Hall, 1973).

Emerson, Ralph Waldo, *Selected Essays, Lectures and Poems*, edited by Robert D. Richardson Jr. (New York: Bantam, 1990).

Eshun, Kodwo, *More Brilliant Than the Sun: Adventures in Sonic Fiction* (London: Quartet, 1998).

Estés, Clarissa Pinkola, *Women Who Run With Wolves: Contacting the Power of the Wild Woman* (London: Rider, 1992).

Evans, David, "From Bumble Bee Slim to Black Boy Shine: Nicknames of Blues Singers." In David Evans (ed.), *Ramblin' On My Mind: New Perspectives on the Blues* (Urbana: University of Illinois Press, 2008), 179–221.

Evans, Mark, *Open Up the Doors: Music in the Modern Church* (London; Equinox, 2006).

Everall, John, "Obscure Mechanics," *The Wire* 134 (April, 1995): 18.

Farmer, Henry Herbert, *Reconciliation and Religion: Some Aspects of the Uniqueness of Christianity as a Reconciling Faith*. Edited by Christopher Partridge (Lewiston, New York: Edwin Mellen Press, 1998).

Farmer, Henry Herbert, *Revelation and Religion: Studies in the Theological Interpretation of Religious Types* (London: Nisbet, 1954).

Farmer, Henry Herbert, *The World and God: A Study of Prayer, Providence and Miracle in Christian Experience*, 2nd edition (London: Nisbet, 1936).

Farrell, Gerry, *Indian Music and the West* (Oxford: Oxford University Press, 1997).

Fast, Susan, *In the Houses of the Holy: Led Zeppelin and the Power of Rock Music* (New York: Oxford University Press, 2001).

Fava, Sérgio, "'When Rome Falls, Falls the World': Current 93 and Apocalyptic Folk." In Christopher Partridge, *Anthems of Apocalypse: Popular Music and Apocalyptic Thought* (Sheffield: Phoenix Press, 2012), 72–89.

Faxneld, Per, and Jesper Aagaard Petersen (eds.), *The Devil's Party: Satanism in Modernity* (New York: Oxford University Press, 2012).

Feigenbaum, Anna, "Remapping the Resonances of Riot Grrrl: Feminisms, Postfeminisms, and 'processes' of Punk." In Yvonne Tasker and Diane Negra (eds.), *Interrogating Postfeminism: Gender and the Politics of Popular Culture* (Durham: Duke University Press, 2007), 132–152.

Fenimore, Ross J., "Voices That Lie Within: The Heard and the Unheard in *Psycho*." In Neil Lerner (ed.), *Music in the Horror Film* (New York: Routledge, 2010), 80–97.

Ferguson, Marilyn, *The Aquarian Conspiracy: Personal and Social Transformation in Our Times* (London: Paladin, 1982).

Fish, Mick, *Industrial Evolution: Through the Eighties with Cabaret Voltaire* (London: SAF Publishing, 2002).

Fish, Stanley, *Is There a Text in This Class? The Authority of Interpretive Communities* (Cambridge: Harvard University Press, 1980).

Fish, Stanley, "Literature in the Reader: Affective Stylistics," *New Literary History* 2.1 (1970), 123–162.

Fisher, Mark, "'Memorex for the Krakens': The Fall's Pulp Modernism." In Michael Goddard and Benjamin Halligan (eds.), *Mark E. Smith and The Fall: Art, Music and Politics* (Farnham: Ashgate, 2010), 95–110.

Fiske, John, *Understanding Popular Culture* (London: Routledge, 1989).

Fitzgerald, Jon, and Philip Hayward, "Inflamed: Synthetic Folk Music and Paganism in the Island World of *The Wicker Man*." In Philip Hayward (ed.), *Terror Tracks: Music, Sound and Horror Cinema* (London: Equinox, 2009), 101–111.

Fitzgerald, Timothy, *Discourse on Civility and Barbarity: A Critical History of Religion and Related Categories* (Oxford: Oxford University Press, 2007).

Floyd, Jr., Samuel A. *The Power of Black Music: Interpreting its History from Africa to the United States* (New York: Oxford University Press, 1995).

Forbes, Bruce David, and Jeffrey H. Mahan, "Introduction: Finding Religion in Unexpected Places." In Bruce David Forbes and Jeffrey H. Mahan (eds.), *Religion and Popular Culture in America* (Berkeley: University of California Press, 2000), 1–20.

Forbes, Bruce David, and Jeffrey H. Mahan (eds.), *Religion and Popular Culture in America* (Berkeley: University of California Press, 2000).

Ford, Simon, *Wreckers of Civilization: The Story of Coum Transmissions and Throbbing Gristle* (London: Black Dog Publishing, 1999).

Forsyth, Peter Taylor, *Christ on Parnassus: Lectures on Art, Ethic and Theology* (London: Hodder and Stoughton, 1911).

Forte, Charles, *The Complete Books of Charles Forte* (Toronto: Dover Publications, 1974).

Foucault, Michel, "A Preface to Transgression." In Jeremy Carrette (ed.), *Religion and Culture: Michel Foucault* (London: Routledge, 1999), 57–71.

Fox, George, *Journal of George Fox* (Cambridge: Cambridge University Press, 1952).

Fox, Warwick, "Deep Ecology: A New Philosophy of Our Time?," *The Ecologist* 14 (1984): 194–200.

Francmanis, John, "National Music to National Redeemer: The Consolidation of a 'Folk-song' construct in Edwardian England," *Popular Music* 21 (2002): 1–25.

Frazer, James G., *The Golden Bough: A Study in Magic and Religion*, Abridged Edition (London: Macmillan, 1922).

Frith, Simon, *Taking Popular Music Seriously: Selected Essays* (Aldershot: Ashgate, 2007).

Frith, Simon, "The Industrialization of Music." In Andy Bennett, Barry Shank and Jason Toynbee (eds.), *The Popular Music Reader* (London: Routledge, 2006), 231–38.

Frith, Simon, "The Popular Music Industry." In Simon Frith, Will Straw and John Street (eds.), *The Cambridge Companion to Pop and Rock* (Cambridge: Cambridge University Press, 2001), 26–52.

Frith, Simon, *Performing Rites: Evaluating Popular Music* (Oxford: Oxford University Press, 1996).

Frith, Simon, *Sound Effects: Youth, Leisure, and the Politics of Rock 'n' Roll* (New York: Pantheon, 1981).

Frith, Simon, Will Straw and John Street (eds.), *The Cambridge Companion to Pop and Rock* (Cambridge: Cambridge University Press, 2001).

Frith, Simon, and Angela McRobbie, "Rock and Sexuality." In Simon Frith and Andrew Goodwin (eds.), *On Record: Rock, Pop, and the Written Word* (New York: Pantheon Books, 1990), 371–389.

Frontani, Michael, *The Beatles: Image and the Media* (Jackson: University Press of Mississippi, 2007).

Furst, Lilian, *Romanticism in Perspective: A Comparative Study of Aspects of the Romantic Movements in England, France and Germany*, 2nd edition (London: Macmillan, 1979).

Fyfe, Andy, *When the Levee Breaks: The Making of Led Zeppelin IV* (London: Unanimous, 2003).

Gaar, Gillian, *She's a Rebel: The History of Women in Rock and Roll* (New York: Seal Press, 1992).

Gamer, Michael, *Romanticism and the Gothic: Genre, Reception, and Canon Formation* (Cambridge: Cambridge University Press, 2000).

Gardner, Gerald, *Witchcraft Today* (London: Rider, 1954).

Garnett, Robert, "Too Low to be Low: Art Pop and the Sex Pistols." In Roger Sabin (ed.), *Punk Rock: So What?* (London: Routledge, 1999), 17–30.

Garrick, Neville, "Foreword." In Chris Morrow, *Stir It Up: Reggae Album Cover Art* (San Francisco: Chronicle Books, 1999), 6–7.

Garrison, Len, *Black Youth, Rastafarianism, and the Identity Crisis in Britain* (London: Afro-Caribbean Education Resource Project, 1979).

Garvey, Marcus, *The Philosophy and Opinions of Marcus Garvey*, Vol. 1, edited by A. J. Garvey (Dover: Majority Press, 1986).

Geiger, John, *Nothing is True, Everything is Permitted: The Life of Brion Gysin* (New York: Disinformation Company, 2005).

Georges, Robert A., and Michael Owen Jones, *Folkloristics: An Introduction* (Bloomington: Indiana University Press, 1995).

Gibbons, Brian J., *Spirituality and the Occult: From the Renaissance to the Modern Age* (London: Routledge, 2001).

Gibson, William, *Neuromancer* (London: HarperCollins, 1995).

Giddens, Anthony, *The Transformation of Intimacy* (Stanford: Stanford University Press, 1993).

Giddens, Anthony, *Modernity and Self-Identity: Self and Society in the Late Modern Age* (Stanford: Stanford University Press, 1991).

Giesen, Bernhard, "Performing the Sacred: A Durkheimian Perspective on the Performative Turn in the Social Sciences." In Jeffrey C. Alexander, Bernhard Giesen, and Jason Mast (eds.), *Social Performance: Symbolic Action, Cultural Progmatics, and Ritual* (Cambridge: Cambridge University Press, 2006), 325–367.

Gilbert, Alan, D., *The Making of Post-Christian Britain: A History of the Secularization of Modern Society* (London: Longman, 1980).

Gilmore, Lee, *Theater in a Crowded Fire: Ritual and Spirituality at Burning Man* (Berkeley: University of California Press, 2010).

Gilmour, Michael J., (ed.), *Call Me the Seeker: Listening to Religion in Popular Music* (London: Continuum, 2005).

Gilroy, Paul, "Between the Blues and the Blues Dance: Some Soundscapes of the Black Atlantic." In Michael Bull and Les Back (eds.), *The Auditory Culture Reader* (Oxford: Berg, 2003): 381–395.

Ginsberg, Allen, "A Tale of the Tribe (from Preface to "Jail Notes")." Liner notes to Timothy Leary, *Beyond Life With Timothy Leary* (Mercury, 1997).

Girard, René, *Violence and the Sacred*. Translated by Patrick Gregory (Maryland: John Hopkins University Press, 1977).

Gittins, Ian, "Return to the Source." In Tony Marcus (ed.), *Deep Trance and Ritual Beats*—a booklet included with the CD *Deep Trance and Ritual Beats* (London: Return to the Source, 1995), 4–17.

Godwin, Jeff, *Rock and Roll Religion: A War Against God* (Bloomington: Rock Ministries, 1995).

Godwin, Jeff, *Dancing With Demons: The Music's Real Master* (Chino: Chick, 1988).

Godwin, Jeff, *The Devil's Disciples: The Truth About Rock* (Chino: Chick, 1985).

Godwin, Jocelyn (ed.), *Music, Mysticism and Magic: A Sourcebook* (London: Penguin, Arkana, 1986).

Goldenberg, Naomi, *Changing of the Gods: Feminism and the End of Traditional Religions* (Boston: Beacon Press, 1979).

Goldman, Vivien, *The Book of Exodus: The Making and Meaning of Bob Marley and the Wailers' Album of the Century* (New York: Three Rivers Press, 2006).

Goodlad, Lauren, and Michael Bibby, "Introduction." In Lauren Goodlad and Michael Bibby (eds.), *Goth: Undead Subculture* (Durham: Yale University Press, 2007), 1–37.

Goodrick-Clarke, Nicholas, *Black Sun: Aryan Cults, Esoteric Nazism, and the Politics of Identity* (New York: New York University Press, 2002).

Goodrick-Clarke, Nicholas, *The Occult Roots of Nazism* (New York: New York University Press, 1992).

Gordon, Ray, "LSD and Mystical Experiences," *Journal of Bible and Religion* 31 (1963): 114–123.

Gracyk, Theodore, *Listening to Popular Music: Or, How I Learned to Stop Worrying and Love Led Zeppelin* (Ann Arbor: University of Michigan Press, 2007).

Gracyk, Theodore, *Rhythm and Noise: An Aesthetics of Rock* (London: I.B. Tauris, 1996).

Graf, Fritz, and Sarah Johnston, *Ritual Texts for the Afterlife: Orpheus and the Bacchic Gold Tablets* (Abingdon: Routledge, 2007).

Grahame, Kenneth, *Pagan Papers* (Teddington: The Echo Library, 2006 [1904]).

Gramsci, Antonio, *Selections from Cultural Writings*. Translated by W. Boelhower (Cambridge MA: Harvard University Press, 1985).

Granholm, Kennet, "Metal, the End of the World, and Radical Environmentalism: Ecological Apocalypse in the Lyrics of Earth Crisis." In Christopher Partridge, *Anthems of Apocalypse: Popular Music and Apocalyptic Thought* (Sheffield: Phoenix Press, 2012), 27–42.

Grant, Kenneth, *Images and Oracles of Austin Osman Spare* (London: Frederick Muller, 1975).

Graves, Robert, *The While Goddess: A Historical Grammar of Poetic Myth* (London: Faber & Faber, 1948).

Green, Shane, "The Problem of Peru's Punk Underground: An Approach to Under-Fuck the System," *Journal of Popular Music Studies* 24 (2012): 578–589.

Greenberg, Clement, *The Collected Essays and Criticism. Volume 1: Perceptions and Judgments 1939–1944*. Edited by John O'Brien (Chicago: University of Chicago Press, 1986).

Grier, Chris, "Salt of the Earth: Alan Lomax," *The Wire* 224 (2002): 24–25.

Grossberg, Lawrence, *We Gotta Get Out of This Place: Popular Conservatism and Postmodern Culture* (London: Routledge, 1992).

Grossberg, Lawrence, "Is There a Fan in the House? The Affective Sensibility of Fandom." In Lisa Lewis (ed.), *The Adoring Audience: Fan Culture and Popular Media* (London: Routledge, 1992), 50–65.

Grossberg, Lawrence, "Another Boring Day in Paradise: Rock and Roll and the Empowerment of Everyday Life." In Ken Gelder and Sarah Thornton (eds.), *The Subcultures Reader* (London: Routledge, 1997), 477–493.

Guilbert, Georges-Claude, *Madonna As Postmodern Myth: How One Star's Self-Construction Rewrites Sex, Gender, Hollywood and the American Dream* (Jefferson: McFarland & Company, 2002).

Guzy, Lydia (ed.), *Religion and Music: Proceedings of the Interdisciplinary Workshop at the Institute for Scientific Studies of Religions, Freie Universität Berlin, May 2006* (Berlin: Weißensee Verlag, 2008).

Habermas, Jürgen, *The Theory of Communicative Action: A Critique of Functionalist Reason*, Vol. 2. Translated by Thomas McCarthy (London: Polity Press, 1987).

Hackett, Rosalind, "Sound, Music, and the Study of Religion," *Temenos: Nordic Journal of Comparative Religion* 48 (2012): 11–27.

Haenfler, Ross, *Straight Edge: Clean-Living Youth, Hardcore Punk, and Social Change* (New Brunswick: Rutgers University Press, 2006).

Häger, Andreas, "Moral Boundaries in Christian Discourse on Popular Music." In Joanne Marie Greer and David O. Mober (eds.), *Research in the Social Scientific Study of Religion*, Volume 11 (Stamford: JAI Press, 2000), 155–171.

Hailwood, Simon, *How to be a Green Liberal: Nature, Value, and Liberal Philosophy* (Chesham: Acumen, 2004).

Hainsworth, Paul, *The Extreme Right in Western Europe* (Abingdon: Routledge, 2008).

Hall, John R., and Philip Schuyler, "The Mystical Apocalypse of the Solar Temple." In James R. Lewis (ed.), *The Order of the Solar Temple: The Temple of Death* (Aldershot: Ashgate, 2006), 55–90.

Hall, Stuart, "Recent Developments in Theories of Language and Ideology: A Critical Note." In Stuart Hall, Dorothy Hobson, Andrew Lowe and Paul Willis (eds.), *Culture, Media, Language: Working Papers in Cultural Studies 1972–1979* (London: Hutchinson, 1980), 157–162.

Hallam, Susan, Ian Cross, and Michael Thaut (eds.), *The Oxford Handbook of Music Psychology* (Oxford: Oxford University Press, 2009).

Hanegraaff, Wouter, *New Age Religion and Western Culture: Esotericism in the Mirror of Secular Thought* (New York: State University of New York Press, 1998).

Hanser, Suzanne, "Music, Health and Well-Being," in Patrik N. Juslin and John Sloboda (eds.), *Handbook of Music and Emotion: Theory, Research, Applications* (Oxford: Oxford University Press, 2010), 849–878.

Hardy, Robin, and Anthony Shaffer, *The Wicker Man* (London: Pan Books, 2000).

Hargreaves, David J., Dorothy Miell, and Raymond A.R. MacDonald, "What Are Musical Identities, and Why Are They Important?" In Raymond A.R. MacDonald, David J. Hargreaves, and Dorothy Miell (eds.), *Musical Identities* (Oxford: Oxford University Press, 2002), 1–20.

Harnish, David, and Anne Rasmussen (eds.), *Divine Inspirations: Music and Islam in Indonesia* (Oxford: Oxford University Press, 2011).

Hart, Lowell, *Satan's Music Exposed* (Chattanooga: AMG, 1981).

Hartley, Lesley P., *The Go-Between* (Harmondsworth: Penguin, 1958).

Harvey, Graham, *Listening People, Speaking Earth: Contemporary Paganism* (London: Hurst & Co., 1997).

Hebdige, Dick, *Cut 'N' Mix: Culture, Identity, and Caribbean Music* (London: Routledge, 1987).

Hebdige, Dick, *Subculture: The Meaning of Style* (London: Methuen & Co., 1979).

Hebdige, Dick, "Reggae, Rastas, and Rudies: Style and the Subversion of Form." CCCS Occasional Paper, Birmingham: Centre for Contemporary Cultural Studies, University of Birmingham, 1974.

Heelas, Paul, *The New Age Movement: The Celebration of the Self and the Sacralization of Modernity* (Oxford: Blackwell, 1996).

Heelas, Paul, and Linda Woodhead, *The Spiritual Revolution: Why Religion is Giving Way to Spirituality* (Oxford: Blackwell, 2004).

Hegarty, Paul, *Noise/Music: A History* (New York: Continuum, 2007).

Hegarty, Paul, *Georges Bataille: Core Cultural Theorist* (London, Sage, 2000).

Hegarty, Paul, and Martin Halliwell, *Beyond and Before: Progressive Rock Since the 1960s* (New York: Continuum, 2011).

Heinlein, Robert, *Stranger in a Strange Land* (New York: G. P. Putnam's Sons, 1961).

Hendershot, Heather, *Shaking the World for Jesus: Media and Conservative Evangelical Culture* (Chicago: University of Chicago Press, 2004).

Henderson, Richard, "Anger is an Energy," *The Wire* 247 (September, 2004): 32–33.

Hendrick, Michael, "Happy Birthday to Mikhail Bulgakov from Patti Smith and Beatdom!" *Beatdom: Beat News* (May 15, 2012): http://www.beatdom.com/?p=1573 (accessed, July 06, 2012).

Henriques, Julian, "Sonic Dominance and the Reggae Sound System Session." In Michael Bull and Les Back (eds.), *The Auditory Culture Reader* (Oxford: Berg, 2003), 451–480.

Hester, Diamuid, " 'Individualism Above All': Black Metal in American Writing." In Tom Howells (ed.), *Black Metal: Beyond the Darkness* (London: Black Dog Publishing, 2012), 78–83.

Hetherington, Kevin, *New Age Travellers: Vanloads of Uproarious Humanity* (London: Cassell, 2000).

Heylin, Clinton, *Gypsy Love Songs and Sad Refrains: The Recordings of Richard Thompson and Sandy Denny* (Sale: Labour of Love Publications, 1989).

Hiley, David, *Gregorian Chant* (Cambridge: Cambridge University Press, 2009).

Hill, Robert, "Leonard P. Howell and the Millenarian Visions in Early Rastafari," *Jamaica Journal* 16 (1983): 24–39.

Hinckle, Warren, "A Social History of the Hippies." In Brian Ward (ed.), *The 1960s: A Documentary Reader* (Oxford: Blackwell, 2010), 101–104.

Hobsbawm, Eric, *Age of Extremes* (London: Abacus, 1995).

Hoffmann, Ernst T.A., *Kreisleriana*. In David Charlton (ed.), *E.T.A. Hoffmann's Musical Writings: Kreisleriana, The Poet and the Composer, Music Criticism* (Cambridge: Cambridge University Press, 1989), 21–165.

Hoggart, Richard, *The Uses of Literacy* (New Brunswick: Transaction Publishers, 1998 [1957]).

Hollier, Denis, "The Dualistic Materialism of Georges Bataille." In Fred Botting and Scott Wilson (eds.), *Bataille: A Critical Reader* (Oxford: Blackwell, 1998), 59–73.

Holm, Randall, " 'Pulling back the Darkness': Starbound with Jon Anderson." In Michael J. Gilmour (ed.), *Call Me the Seeker: Listening to Religion in Popular Music* (London: Continuum, 2005), 158–171.

Hood, Jr., Ralph W., Peter C. Hill, and Bernard Spilka, *The Psychology of Religion: An Empirical Approach*, 4th edition (New York: Guilford Press, 2009).

Hoover, Stewart M., *Religion in the Media Age* (London: Routledge, 2006).

Hopkins, Dwight, "Black Theology of Liberation. In David Ford and Rachel Muers (eds.), *The Modern Theologians: An Introduction to Christian Theology Since 1918*, 3rd edition (Oxford: Blackwell, 2005), 451–468.

Hopkins, Jerry, *The Jimi Hendrix Experience* (New York: Arcade Publishing, 1996).

Hopkins, Jerry, and Danny Sugarman, *No One Here Gets Out Alive* (London: Plexus, 1980).

Hopps, Gavin, *Morrissey: The Pageant of his Bleeding Heart* (London: Continuum, 2009).

Horner, Bruce, and Thomas Swiss (eds.), *Key Terms in Popular Music and Culture* (Oxford: Blackwell, 1999).

Howard, Jay R., and John M. Streck, *Apostles of Rock: The Splintered World of Contemporary Christian Music* (Lexington: University Press of Kentucky, 1999).

Howells, Tom (ed.), *Black Metal: Beyond the Darkness* (London: Black Dog Publishing, 2012).

Hughes, Graham, *Worship as Meaning: A Liturgical Theology for Late Modernity* (Cambridge: Cambridge University Press, 2003).

Hulsether, Mark D., "Like a Sermon: Popular Religion in Madonna Videos." In Forbes, Bruce David, and Jeffrey H. Mahan (eds.), *Religion and Popular Culture in America* (Berkeley: University of California Press, 2000), 77–100.

Humphrey, Chris, *The Politics of Carnival: Festive Misrule in Medieval England* (Manchester: Manchester University Press, 2001).

Hunt, Geoffrey, Molly Moloney, and Kristin Evans, *Youth, Drugs, and Nightlife* (Abingdon: Routledge, 2010).

Huron, David, *Sweet Anticipation: Music and the Psychology of Expectation* (Cambridge, MA: MIT Press, 2006).

Hutnyk, John, *Critique of Exotica: Music, Politics, and the Culture Industry* (London: Pluto Press, 2000), 87–113.

Hutton, Ronald, *Witches, Druids and King Arthur* (London: Hambledon and London, 2003).

Hutton, Ronald, *The Triumph of the Moon: A History of Modern Pagan Witchcraft* (Oxford: Oxford University, Press, 1999).

Hutton, Ronald, *The Stations of the Sun: A History of the Ritual Year in Britain* (Oxford: Oxford University Press, 1996).

Hutton, Ronald, *The Rise and Fall of Merry England: The Ritual Year, 1400–1700* (Oxford: Oxford University Press, 1994).

Huxley, Aldous, *The Doors of Perception and Heaven and Hell* (London: Flamingo, 1994).

Ingle, H. Larry, *First Among Friends: George Fox and the Creation of Quakerism* (New York: Oxford University Press, 1994).

Inglis, Ian, "Cover Story: Magic, Myth and Music." In Olivier Julien (ed.), *Sgt. Pepper and The Beatles: It was Forty Years ago Today* (Aldershot: Ashgate, 2008), 91–102.

Irwin, Alexander, "Ecstasy, Sacrifice and Communication: Bataille on Religion and Inner Experience," *Soundings* 76 (1993), 105–128.

Iwamura, Jane, *Virtual Orientalism: Asian Religions and American Popular Culture* (New York: Oxford University Press, 2011).

jagodzinski, jan, *Music in Youth Culture: A Lacanian Approach* (New York: Palgrave Macmillan, 2005).

James, Allison, Chris Jenks and Alan Prout, *Theorizing Childhood* (Cambridge: Polity Press, 1998).

Jameson, Frederic, "Marx's Purloined Letter." In Michael Sprinker (ed.), *Ghostly Demarcations: A Symposium on Jacques Derrida's Spectres of Marx* (London: Verso, 1999), 26–67.

Janssen, David, and Edward Whitelock, *Apocalypse Jukebox: The End of the World in American Popular Music* (Brooklyn: Soft Skull Press, 2009).

Jefferson, Ann, "Bodymatters: Self and Other in Bakhtin, Sartre and Barthes." In Ken Hirschkop and David G. Shepherd (eds.), *Bakhtin and Cultural Theory* (Manchester: Manchester University Press, 2001), 201–228.

Jenks, Chris, *Childhood*, 2nd edition (London: Routledge, 2005).

Jenks, Chris, *Transgression* (London: Routledge, 2003).

Jervis, John, *Transgressing the Modern: Explorations in the Western Experience of Otherness* (Oxford: Blackwell, 1999).

John Birch Society, "Beliefs and Principles of the John Birch Society." In Lyman T. Sargent (ed.), *Extremism in America: A Reader* (New York: New York University Press, 1995), 105–110.

Johnson, Bruce, and Martin Cloonan, *Dark Side of the Tune: Popular Music and Violence* (Aldershot: Ashgate, 2009).

Johnson, Julian, *Who Needs Classical Music? Cultural Choice and Musical Value* (New York: Oxford University Press, 2002).

Johnson, Linton Kwesi, *Mi Revalueshanary Fren: Selected Poems* (London: Penguin, 2002).

Johnson, Linton Kwesi, "Jamaican Rebel Music," *Race and Class* 17(1976): 397–412.

Johnson, Philip, "Devil Music," *Circuit: Devil Music* (Spring, 2002), 43–47.

Johnson-Hill, Jack, *I-sight: The World of Rastafari: An Interpretative Sociological Account* (Lanham: Scarecrow Press, 1995).

Jolly, Karen L., *Popular Religion in Late Saxon England: Elf Charms in Context* (Chapel Hill: University of North Carolina Press, 1996).

Jones, Simon, "Rocking the House: Sound System Cultures and the Politics of Space," *Journal of Popular Music Studies* 7 (1995): 1–24.

Jones, Simon, *Black Culture, White Youth: The Reggae Tradition from JA to UK* (London: Macmillan Education, 1988).

Jonsson, Johannes, "Frequently Asked Questions About Christian Metal": http://www.metalforjesus.org/faq.html (accessed October 2, 2012).

Jury, Louise, "Pavarotti Makes His First Pop Album After Agonising Year of Bereavements," *The Independent* (October 7, 2003): http://www.independent.co.uk/arts-entertainment/music/news/pavarotti-makes-his-first-pop-album-after-agonising-year-of-bereavements-582533.html (accessed August 22, 2011).

Juslin, Patrik N., and John Sloboda (eds.), *Handbook of Music and Emotion: Theory, Research, Applications* (Oxford: Oxford University Press, 2010).

Juslin, Patrik N., and Daniel Västfjäll, "Emotional Responses to Music: The Need to Consider Underlying Mechanisms," *Behavioral and Brain Sciences* 31 (2008): 559–621.

Juslin, Patrik N., and John Sloboda (eds.), *Music and Emotion: Theory and Research* (Oxford: Oxford University Press, 2001).

Kahn-Harris, Keith, "Jews United and Divided by Music: Contemporary Jewish Music in the UK and America." In Thomas Bossius, Andreas Häger, and Keith Kahn-Harris (eds.), *Religion and Popular Music in Europe* (London: IB Tauris, 2011), 71–91.

Kahn-Harris, Keith, *Extreme Metal: Music and Culture on the Edge* (Oxford: Berg, 2007).

Kant, Immanuel, *Critique of Judgement*. Translated by J.H. Bernard (New York: Hafner Press, 1951).

Karpeles, Maud, *Cecil Sharp: His Life and Work* (London: Routledge & Kegan Paul, 1967).

Kassabian, Anahid, "Popular." In Bruce Horner and Thomas Swiss (eds.), *Key Terms in Popular Music and Culture* (Oxford: Blackwell, 1999), 113–123.

Katz, David, *Solid Foundation: An Oral History of Reggae* (London: Bloomsbury, 2004).

Katz, David, *People Funny Boy: The Genius of Lee 'Scratch' Perry* (Edinburgh: Payback Press, 2000).

Kearney, Mary Celeste, "The Missing Links: Riot Grrrl-Feminism-Lesbian Culture." In Sheila Whiteley (ed.), *Sexing the Groove: Popular Music and Gender* (London: Routledge, 1997), 207–229.

Keenan, David, "The Fire Down Below: Welcome to the New Weird America," *The Wire* 234 (2003): 32–41.

Keenan, David, *England's Hidden Reverse: A Secret History of the Esoteric Underground* (London: SAF Publishing, 2003).

Keenan, David, "Childhood's End," *The Wire* 163 (1997): 34–37.

Keightley, Keir, "Taking Popular Music (and Tin Pan Alley and Jazz) Seriously," *Journal of Popular Music Studies* 22 (2010): 90–97.

Kerman, Joseph, *Contemplating Music: Challenges to Musicology* (Cambridge: Harvard University Press, 1985).

Kerouac, Jack, *Dharma Bums* (New York: Viking, 1957).

Kerr, Andrew, *Intolerably Hip: A Memoir* (Norwich: Frontier Publishing, 2011).

Keuss, Jeff, *Your Neighbor's Hymnal: What Popular Music Teaches Us About Faith, Hope, and Love* (Eugene: Cascade Books, 2011).

King, Christine, "His Truth Goes Marching On: Elvis Presley and the Pilgrimage to Graceland." In Ian Reader and Tony Walter (eds.), *Pilgrimage in Popular Culture* (Houndmills: Pagrave, 1993), 92–104.

Kinsley, David, *Ecology and Religion: Ecological Spirituality in Cross-Cultural Perspective* (Englewood Cliffs: Prentice Hall, 1995).

Kirkegaard, Annemette, "Music and Transcendence: Sufi Popular Performances in East Africa," *Temenos: Nordic Journal of Comparative Religion* 48 (2012): 29–48.

Klarreich, Erica, "Feel the Music," *Nature Science Update* (November 27, 2001): http://www.nature.com/news/2001/011127/full/news011129-10.html (accessed August 14, 2012).

Knight, Wendy E.J., and Nikki S. Rickard, "Relaxing Music Prevents Stress-Induced Increases in Subjective Anxiety, Systolic Blood Pressure, and Heart rate in Healthy Males and Females," *Journal of Music Therapy* 38: 4 (2001): 254–272.

Knott, Kim, *The Location of Religion: A Spatial Analysis* (London: Equinox, 2005).

Knowles, Christopher, "Symphony for the Devil," *Classic Rock* 96 (Summer, 2006): 32–43.

Knowles, Christopher, "Bobby Beausoleil on Recording *Lucifer Rising*," *Classic Rock* 96 (Summer, 2006): 41.

Koen, Benjamin (ed.), *The Oxford Handbook of Medical Ethnomusicology* (New York: Oxford University Press, 2008).

Koen, Benjamin, "Music-Prayer-Meditation Dynamics in Healing." In Benjamin Koen (ed.), *The Oxford Handbook of Medical Ethnomusicology* (New York: Oxford University Press, 2008), 93–120.

Koenig, Harold, "Religion, Spirituality, and Healing: Research, Dialogue, and Directions." In Benjamin D. Koen (ed.), *The Oxford Handbook of Medical Ethnomusicology* (New York: Oxford University Press, 2008), 46–71.

Kopf, Biba, "Unnatural Highs," *The Wire* 140 (October, 1995): 26–30.

Kopf, Biba, "Bacillus Culture." In Charles Neal, *Tape Delay* (London: SAF Publishing, 1987), 10–15.

Korpe, Marie (ed.), *Shoot the Singer! Music Censorship Today* (London: Zed Books, 2004).

Krafft-Ebing, Richard von, *Psychopathia Sexualis: eine Klinisch-Forensische Studie* (Stuttgart: Verlag Von Ferdinand Enke, 1886).

Kramer, Lawrence, *Classical Music and Postmodern Knowledge* (Berkeley: University of California Press, 1995).

Krims, Adam, "The Hip-hop Sublime as a Form of Commodification." In Regula B. Qureshi (ed.), *Music and Marx: Ideas, Practice, Politics* (New York: Routledge, 2002), 63–78.

Krims, Adam, *Rap Music and the Poetics of Identity* (Cambridge: Cambridge University Press, 2000).

Kripal, Jeffrey, *Authors of the Impossible: The Paranormal and the Sacred* (Chicago: Chicago University Press, 2010).

Kristeva, Julia, *Desire in Language: A Semiotic Approach to Literature and Art* (New York: Columbia University Press 1980).

Kruse, Holly, "Gender." In Bruce Horner and Thomas Swiss (eds.), *Key Terms in Popular Music and Culture* (Oxford: Blackwell, 1999), 85–100.

Kyle, Richard, *Evangelicalism: An Americanized Christianity* (New Brunswick: Transaction Publishers, 2006).

Lady Gaga, "Amen Fashion": http://amenfashion.tumblr.com/ (accessed December 02, 2012).

LaFontaine, Jean, "Satanism and Satanic Mythology." In Bengt Ankarloo and Stuart Clark (eds.), *Witchcraft and Magic in Europe: the Twentieth Century* (Philadelphia: University of Pennsylvania Press, 1999), 81–140.

Lafrance, Mélisse, "A Cultural Studies Approach to Women and Popular Music." In Lori Burns and Mélisse Lafrance, *Disruptive Divas: Feminism, Identity and Popular Music* (New York: Routledge, 2002), 1–30.

Laing, Dave, "Scrutiny to Subcultures: Notes on Literary Criticism and Popular Music," *Popular Music* 13: 2 (1994), 179–190.

Laing, Dave, "'Sadeness,' Scorpions and Single Markets: National and Transnational Trends in European Popular Music," *Popular Music* 11 (1992): 127–140.

Landis, Bill, *Anger: The Unauthorised Biography of Kenneth Anger* (San Francisco: HarperCollins, 1995).

Lang, Michael, *The Road to Woodstock* (New York: HarperCollins, 2009).

Lanza, Joseph, *Elevator Music: A Surreal History of Muzak, Easy-Listening, and Other Moodsong* (Ann Arbor: University of Michigan Press, 2004).

Lap, Amina Olander, "Categorizing Modern Satanism: An Analysis of LaVey's Early Writings." In Per Faxneld and Jesper Aagaard Petersen (eds.), *The Devil's Party: Satanism in Modernity* (New York: Oxford University Press, 2012), 83–102.

Laqueur, Walter, *Fascism: Past, Present, Future* (Oxford: Oxford University Press, 1996).

Larson, Bob, *Larson's Book of Spiritual Warfare* (Nashville: Thomas Nelson Publishers, 1999).

Larson, Bob, *Larson's Book of Rock* (Wheaton: Tyndale House, 1987).

Larson, Bob, *Hippies, Hindus and Rock 'n' Roll* (Carol Stream: Creation House, 1972).

Larson, Bob, *The Day the Music Died* (Carol Stream: Creation House, 1972).

Larson, Bob, *Rock 'n' Roll: the Devil's Diversion* (McCook: Bob Larson Ministries, 1971).

LaVey, Anton S., *The Devil's Notebook* (Portland: Feral House, 1992).

Leary, Timothy, *Flashbacks. A Personal and Cultural History of an Era: An Autobiography* (New York: G.P. Putnam's Sons, 1990).

Leary, Timothy, *Politics of Ecstasy* (London: Paladin, 1970).

Leary, Timothy, *High Priest* (Berkeley: Ronin Publishing, 1995 [1968]).

Leavis, Frank R., "Mass Civilization and Minority Culture." In John Storey (ed.), *Cultural Theory and Popular Culture: A Reader* (Harlow: Pearson Education, 2006), 12–20.

Leavis, Frank R., and Denys Thompson, *Culture and Environment* (Westport: Greenwood Press, 1977).

Lee, Martin. A., and Bruce Shlain, *Acid Dreams: The Complete Social History of LSD* (New York: Grove Press, 1992).

Leech, Jeanette, *Seasons They Change: The Story of Acid and Psychedelic Folk* (London: Jawbone Press, 2010).

Lefèvre, Jérôme, "Pure. Fucking. Armageddon. Black Metal in *CS (Conservative Shithead) Journal.*" In Tom Howells (ed.), *Black Metal: Beyond the Darkness* (London: Black Dog Publishing, 2012), 116–129.

Leonard, Marion, *Gender in the Music Industry: Rock, Discourse and Girl Power* (Aldershot: Ashgate, 2007).

Leonard, Marion, "'Rebel Girl, You Are the Queen of My World': Feminism, 'Subculture' and Grrrl Power." In Sheila Whiteley (ed.), *Sexing the Groove: Popular Music and Gender* (London: Routledge, 1997), 230–255.

Leonard, Neil, *Jazz: Myth and Religion* (New York: Oxford University Press, 1987).

Lerner, Gerda, *The Creation of Patriarchy* (Oxford: Oxford University Press, 1986).

Lerner, Neil (ed.), *Music in the Horror Film* (New York: Routledge, 2010).

Lesiuk, Teresa, "The Effect of Music Listening on Work Performance," *Psychology of Music* 33 (2005): 173–191.

Levine, Lawrence, *Black Culture and Black Consciousness: Afro-American Folk Thought from Slavery to Freedom* (Oxford: Oxford University Press, 1977).

LeVine, Mark, *Heavy Metal Islam: Rock, Resistance, and the Struggle for the Soul of Islam* (New York: Three Rivers Press, 2008).

Levine, Noah, *Dharma Punx: A Memoir* (New York: HarperCollins, 2003).

Levi-Strauss, Claude, *Structural Anthropology*. Translated by Claire Jacobson and Brooke Schoepf (New York: Basic Books).

Levitin, Daniel, *This Is Your Brain on Music: Understanding a Human Obsession* (London: Atlantic Books, 2007).

Lewis, Ioan M., *Ecstatic Religion: A Study of Shamanism and Spirit Possession*, 3rd edition (London: Routledge, 2003).

Lewis, James R. (ed.), *The Order of the Solar Temple: The Temple of Death* (Aldershot: Ashgate, 2006).

Lewis, Lisa, "Introduction." In Lisa Lewis (ed.), *The Adoring Audience: Fan Culture and Popular Media* (London: Routledge, 1992), 1–6.

Lewis, Rupert, "Marcus Garvey and the Early Rastafarians: Continuity and Discontinuity." In Nathaniel Murrell, William Spencer and Adrian McFarlane (eds.), *Chanting Down Babylon: The Rastafari Reader* (Philadelpia: Temple University Press, 1998), 145–158.

Lindsey, Hal, *The Late Great Planet Earth* (Grand Rapids, Michigan: Zondervan, 1970).

Locke, Ralph, "On Music and Orientalism." In Derek B. Scott (ed.), *Music, Culture, and Society: A Reader* (Oxford: Oxford University Press, 2000), 103–109.

Lockwood, Dean, "Dead Souls: Post-Punk Music as Hauntological Trigger." In Brigid Cherry, Peter Howell and Caroline Ruddell (eds.), *Twenty-First Century Gothic* (Newcastle: Cambridge Scholars Publishing, 2010), 99–111.

Lomax, Alan, *Folk Song Style and Culture* (Washington, DC: American Association for the Advancement of Science, 1968).

Louv, Jason, "Introduction: On the Way to Thee Garden." In Genesis P-Orridge, *Thee Psychick Bible: Thee Apocryphal Scriptures of Genesis P-Orridge and Thee Third MIND ov Psychic TV*. Edited by Jason Louv (Port Townsend: Feral House, 1994), 17–28.

Lu, Xing, *Rhetoric of the Chinese Cultural Revolution: The Impact on Chinese Thought, Culture and Communication* (Columbia: University of South Carolina Press, 2004).

Luckmann, Thomas, *The Invisible Religion* (London: Macmillan, 1967).

Luhr, Eileen, *Witnessing Suburbia: Conservatives and Christian Youth Culture* (Berkeley: California University Press, 2009).

Lurie, Robert, *No Certainly Attached: Steve Kilbey and The Church* (Portland: Verse Chorus Press, 2009).

Luther, Martin, *Three Treatises* (Philadelphia: Fortress Press, 1970).

Lynch, Gordon, *On the Sacred* (Durham: Acumen, 2012).

Lynch, Gordon, *The Sacred in the Modern World: A Cultural Sociological Approach* (Oxford: Oxford University Press, 2012).

Lynch, Gordon, *Understanding Theology and Popular Culture* (Oxford: Blackwell, 2005).

Lynch, Gordon (ed.), *Between Sacred and Profane: Researching Religion and Popular Culture* (London: I.B. Tauris, 2007).

Lynch, Gordon, Jolyon Mitchell, and Anna Strhan (eds.), *Religion, Media and Culture: A Reader* (London: Routledge, 2011).

Lynch, Hollis R., *Edward Wilmott Blyden: Pan Negro Patriot 1832–1912* (Oxford: Oxford University Press, 1967).

Edward Macan, *Rocking the Classics: English Progressive Rock and the Counterculture* (New York: Oxford University Press, 1997).

MacDonald, Ian, *The People's Music* (London: Pimlico, 2003).

MacDonald, Ian, *Revolution in the Head: The Beatles' Records and the Sixties*, 2nd edition (London: Pimlico, 1998).

Machin, David, and John Richardson, "Discourses of Unity and Purpose in the Sounds of fascist Music: A Multimodal Approach," *Critical Discourse Studies* 9 (2012): 329–345.

MacKinnon, Angus, "Forces of Reality," *New Musical Express* (21 April, 1979): 7–8, 52.

Madonna, *Sex* (New York: Warner Books, 1992).

Makowski, Peter, "Jimmy Page on *Lucifer Rising*," *Classic Rock* 96 (Summer, 2006): 44–45.

Margry, Peter Jan, "The Pilgrimage to Jim Morrison's Grave at Père Lachaise Cemetery: The Social Construction of Sacred Space." In Peter Jan Margry (ed.), *Shrines and Pilgrimage in the Modern World: New Itineraries Into the Sacred* (Amsterdam: Amsterdam University Press, 2008), 143–172.

Marr, Johnny, "Christ, Communists and Rock 'n' Roll: Anti-Rock 'n' Roll Books, 1966–1987." In Dave the Spazz (ed.), *The Best of LCD: The Art and Writing of WFMU-FM 91.1 FM* (New York: Princeton Architectural Press, 2008), 92–98.

Marsden, George, *Jonathan Edwards: A Life* (New Haven: Yale University Press, 2003).

Marshall, Paul, *Mystical Encounters with the Natural World: Experiences and Explanations* (Oxford: Oxford University Press, 2005).

Martin, Peter J., *Music and the Sociological Gaze: Art Worlds and Cultural Production* (Manchester: Manchester University Press, 2006).

Martin, Peter J., *Sounds and Society: Themes in the Sociology of Music* (Manchester: Manchester University Press, 1995).

Marwick, Arthur, *The Sixties: Cultural Revolution in Britain, France, Italy, and the United States c.1958–c.1974* (Oxford: Oxford University Press, 1998).

Masuzawa, Tomoko, "Culture." In Mark C. Taylor (ed.), *Critical Terms for Religious Studies* (Chicago: University of Chicago Press, 1998), 70–93.

McCarthy, Kate, "Deliver Me from Nowhere." In Eric Mazur and Kate McCarthy (eds.), *God in the Details: American Religion in Popular Culture* (New York: Routledge, 2001), 23–45.

McClary, Susan, *Feminine Endings: Music, Gender and Sexuality* (Minneapolis: University of Minnesota Press, 1991).

McEvoy, Emma, "Gothic and the Romantics." In Catherine Spooner and Emma McEvoy (eds.), *The Routledge Companion to Gothic* (Abingdon: Routledge, 2007), 19–28.

McKay, George, *Glastonbury: A Very English Fair* (London: Victor Gollancz, 2000).

McKay, George, *Senseless Acts of Beauty: Cultures of Resistance Since the Sixties* (London: Verso, 1996).

McKerrell, Simon, "Hearing Sectarianism: Understanding Scottish Sectarianism as Song," *Critical Discourse Studies* 9 (2012): 363–374.

McKinnon, Andrew M., "Reading 'Opium of the People': Expression, Protest and the Dialectics of Religion," *Critical Sociology* 31 (2005): 15–38.

McKinnon, James, *Music in Early Christian Literature* Cambridge: Cambridge University Press, 1987).

McLeod, Hugh, *The Religious Crisis of the 1960s* (Oxford: Oxford University Press, 2007).

McNally, Dennis, "Meditations on the Grateful Dead." In David G. Dodd and Diana Spaulding (eds.), *The Grateful Dead Reader* (New York: Oxford University Press, 2000), 163–174.

McNeil, Legs, and Gillian McCain, *Please Kill Me: The Uncensored Oral History of Punk* (New York: Grove Press, 1996).

Mellers, Wilfred, *Twilight of the Gods: The Beatles in Retrospect* (London: Faber & Faber, 1973).

Mercer-Taylor, Peter, "Between Hymn and Horror Film: How do we Listen to the Cradle of Filth?" In Christopher Partridge and Eric Christianson (eds.), *The Lure of the Dark Side: Satan and Western Demonology in Popular Culture* (London: Equinox, 2009), 39–59.

Metcalfe, Stuart, "Ecstasy Evangelists and Psychedelic Warriors." In Antonio Melechi (ed.), *Psychedelia Britannica: Hallucinogenic Drugs in Britain* (London: Turnaround, 1997), 166–184.

Meyer, Leonard B, *Emotion and Meaning in Music* (Chicago: University of Chicago Press, 1956).

Miller, Robert Moats, "The Protestant Churches and Lynching, 1919–1939," *The Journal of Negro History* 42 (1957): 118–131.

Miklitsch, Robert, *Roll Over Adorno: Critical Theory, Popular Culture, Audiovisual Media* (Albany: State University of New York Press, 2006).

Middleton, Richard, *Voicing the Popular: On the Subjects of Popular Music* (New York: Routledge, 2006).

Middleton, Richard, *Studying Popular Music* (Milton Keynes: Open University Press, 1990).

Miller, Paul, *Sound Unbound: Sampling, Digital Music and Culture* (Cambridge, MA: MIT Press, 2000).

Miller, Timothy, *The Hippies and American Values*, 2nd edition (Knoxville: University of Tennessee Press, 2011).

Miller, Timothy, *The 60s Communes: Hippies and Beyond* (Syracuse: Syracuse University Press, 1999).

Miyamoto, Ken Christoph, "Mission, Liturgy and the Transformation of Identity," *Mission Studies* 27 (2010): 56–70.

Moberg, Marcus, *Faster for the Master: Exploring Issues of Religious Expression and Alternative Christian Identity within the Finnish Metal Scene* (Åbo: Åbo Akademi University Press, 2009).

Mohr, Mark, "Is Haile Selassie God or Christ?" *Gospel/Reggae.Com*: http://www.gospelreggae.com/faq/78da334f010000d4009c/display.html (accessed October 5, 2012).

Mohr, Mark, "Rastas' Beliefs and Marijuana as a Holy Sacrament" *Gospel/Reggae.com*: http://www.gospelreggae.com/faq/78da33310400009b0066/display.html (accessed October 5, 2012).

Mohr, Mark, "Christafari Biography," *Christafari*: http://www.christafari.com/bio.html (accessed September 25, 2012).

Moliné, Keith, "The Road to Salvation: Current 93," *The Wire* 269 (2006): 28–33.

Monem, Nadine (ed.), *Riot Grrrl: Revolution Girl Style Now!* (London: Black Dog Publishing, 2007).

Monge, Luigi, "Preachin' the Blues: A textual Analysis of Son House's 'Dry Spell Blues.'" In David Evans (ed.), *Ramblin' On My Mind: New Perspectives on the Blues* (Urbana: University of Illinois Press, 2008), 222–257.

Monko, Andrew, "Shame on You: David Byrne Reveals New Paths to Eternal Damnation," *David-Byrne.Com*: http://www.davidbyrne.com/art/new_sins/about/new_sins_resonance.php (accessed March 21, 2012).

Moore, Allan F., *Song Means: Analysing and Interpreting Recorded Popular Song* (Farnham: Ashgate, 2012).

Moore, Allan F., "The Contradictory Aesthetics of Woodstock." In Andy Bennett (ed.), *Remembering Woodstock* (Aldershot: Ashgate, 2004), 75–89.

Moore, Allan F., "Authenticity as Authentication," *Popular Music* 21 (2002), 209–223.

Moore, Karenza, "Exploring Symbolic, Emotional and Spiritual Expression Among 'Crash Clubbers.' " In Sylvia Collins-Mayo and Pink Dandelion (eds.), *Religion and Youth* (Farnham: Ashgate, 2010), 89–96.

Morgan, David (ed.), *Key Words in Religion, Media and Culture* (New York: Routledge, 2008).

Mørk, Gry, "Why Didn't the Churches begin to Burn a Thousand Years Earlier?" In Thomas Bossius, Andreas Häger, and Keith Kahn-Harris (eds.), *Religion and Popular Music in Europe* (London: IB Tauris, 2011), 124–144.

Mørk, Gry, " 'With my art I am the fist in the face of God': On Old-School Black Metal." In Jesper Aagaard Petersen (ed.), *Contemporary Religious Satanism: A Critical Anthology* (Farnham: Ashgate, 2009), 171–198.

Morrow, Chris, *Stir It Up: Reggae Album Cover Art* (San Francisco: Chronicle Books, 1999).

Motherwell, William, *Minstrelsy, Ancient and Modern*, Vol. 1 (Boston: William D. Tcknor & Co., 1846).

Mould, Bob, *See a Little Light: The Trail of Rage and Melody* (New York: Little Brown and Company, 2011).

Moynihan, Michael, and Didrik Søderlind, *Lords of Chaos: The Bloody Rise of the Satanic Metal Underground*, 2nd edition (Los Angeles, Feral House, 2003).

Mudrian, Albert, *Choosing Death: The Improbably History of Death Metal and Grindcore* (Los Angeles: Feral House, 2004).

Murray, Penelope, and Peter Wilson (ed.), *Music and the Muses: The Culture of Mousike in the Classical Athenian City* (Oxford: Oxford University Press, 2004).

Murrell, Nathaniel S., *Afro-Caribbean Religions: An Introduction to Their Historical, Cultural, and Sacred Traditions* (Philadelphia: Temple University Press, 2009).

Murrell, Nathaniel S., "Introduction: The Rastafari Phenomenon." In Nathaniel Murrell, William Spencer and Adrian McFarlane (eds.), *Chanting Down Babylon: The Rastafari Reader* (Philadelpia: Temple University Press, 1998), 1–19.

Myers, Ben, *American Heretics: Rebel Voices in Music* (Hove: Codex Books, 2002).

Naess, Arne, "The Basics of Deep Ecology," in John Button (ed.), *The Green Fuse: The Schumacher Lectures 1983–1988* (London: Quartet Books, 1990), 130–137.

Nagashima, Yoshiko, *Rastafarian Music in Contemporary Jamaica: A Study of Socio-religious Music of the Rastafarian Movement in Jamaica* (Tokyo: Institute for the Study of Languages and Cultures of Asia and Africa, 1984).

Neal, Charles, *Tape Delay* (Wembley: SAF Publishing, 1987).

Nehring, Neil, *Popular Music, Gender and Postmodernism: Anger Is an Energy* (Thousand Oaks: Sage, 1997).

Niebuhr, H. Richard, *Christ and Culture* (New York: Harper & Row, 1951).

Nietzsche, Friedrich W., *The Birth of Tragedy and Other Writings*. Translated by Ronald Speirs (Cambridge: Cambridge University Press, 1999).

Noebel, David, *The Marxist Minstrels: A Handbook on Communist Subversion of Music* (Tulsa: American Christian College Press, 1974).

Noebel, David, *Communism, Hypnotism and The Beatles* (Tulsa: Christian Crusade Publications, 1969).

Noebel, David, *Rhythm, Riots, and Revolution: An Analysis of the Communist Use of Music, the Communist Master Music Plan* (Tulsa: Christian Crusade Publications, 1966).

Noebel, David, *The Beatles: A Study in Drugs, Sex and Revolution* (Tulsa: Christian Crusade Publications, 1965).

Nordström, Anders, "The Divine Darkness: At Home with Crimson Moonlight's Frontman," *HM: Special 'Best of HM' Issue* (2010): 32–35.

North, Adrian C., David J. Hargreaves, and Jennifer McKendrick, "The Influence of In-Store Music on Wine Selections," *Journal of Applied Psychology* 84 (1999): 271–276.

NSBM (*National Socialist Black Metal*): http://www.nsbm.org/ (accessed May 29, 2012).

NSBM, "About NSBM.ORG and National Socialist Black Metal (NSBM)": http://www.nsbm.org/white_power_music/ (accessed May 29, 2012).

Nuzum, Eric, *Parental Advisory: Music Censorship in America* (New York: HarperCollins, 2001).

Nyman, Michael, *Experimental Music: Cage and Beyond*, 2nd edition (Cambridge: Cambridge University Press, 1999).

Oakley, Giles, *The Devil's Music: A History of the Blues*, 2nd edition (New York: Da Capo Press, 1997).

O'Brien, Lucy, *She Bop II: The Definitive History of Women in Rock, Pop, and Soul* (London: Continuum, 2002).

O'Brien, Lucy, *Madonna: Like an Icon* (London: Transworld Publishers, 2007).

O'Driscoll, Dennis, *Stepping Stones: Interviews with Seamus Heaney* (London: Faber and Faber, 2008).

O'Hara, Craig, *The Philosophy of Punk: More Than Noise!* (London: AK Press, 1999).

Olaveson, Tim, "'Connectedness' and the Rave Experience: Rave as a New Religious Movement?" In Graham St. John (ed.), *Rave Culture and Religion* (London: Routledge, 2004), 83–106.

Oldfield, Mike, *Changeling* (London: Virgin Books, 2008).

Oliver, Paul, *Blues Fell This Morning: Meaning in the Blues*, 2nd edition (Cambridge: Cambridge University Press, 1990).

Olsen, Dale A., "Shamanism, Music and Healing in Two Contrasting South American Cultural Areas." In Benjamin D. Koen (ed.), *The Oxford Handbook of Medical Ethnomusicology* (New York: Oxford University Press, 2008), 331–360.

Ostendorf, Berndt, "Rhythm, Riots, and Revolution: Political Paranoia, Cultural Fundamentalism, and African American Music." In Ragnhild Fiebig-von Hase and Ursula Lehmkuhl (eds.), *Enemy Images in American History* (Providence: Berghahn Book, 1997), 159–179.

Otto, Rudolf, *The Idea of the Holy: An Inquiry into the Non-Rational Factor in the Idea of the Divine and its Relation to the Rational*. Translated by John Harvey (Oxford: Oxford University Press, 1958).

Owens, Joseph, *Dread: The Rastafarians of Jamaica* (London: Heinemann, 1976).

Paglia, Camille, *Sex, Art and American Culture* (New York: Vintage Books, 1992).

Palmer, Susan, "Purity and Danger in the Solar Temple." In James R. Lewis (ed.), *The Order of the Solar Temple: The Temple of Death* (Aldershot: Ashgate, 2006), 39–54.

Parett, Herman, "Kant on Music and the Hierarchy of the Arts," *Journal of Aesthetics and Art Criticism* 56 (1998): 251–264.

Parker, Howard, Judith Aldridge, and Fiona Measham, *Illegal Leisure: The Normalization of Adolescent Recreational Drug Use* (London: Routledge, 1998).

Parry, Eugia, "The Dark Poetry By Which I Live." In Joel-Peter Witkin, *The Bone House* (San Francisco: Twin Palms Publishers, 2000), 182–187.

Parsons, Talcott, *Action Theory and the Human Condition* (New York: Free Press, 1978).

Partridge, Christopher, "Esoterrorism and the Wrecking of Civilization: Genesis P-Orridge and the Rise of Industrial Paganism." In A. Bennett and D. Weston (eds.), *Pop Pagans: Paganism and Popular Music* (Durham: Acumen, 2013), 189–212.

Partridge, Christopher, "Haunted Culture: The Persistence of Belief in the Paranormal." In O. Jenzen and S. Munt (eds.), *Research Companion to Paranormal Cultures* (Farnham: Ashgate, forthcoming).

Partridge, Christopher, "Occulture is Ordinary." In Kennet Granholm and Egil Asprem (eds.), *Contemporary Esotericism* (Sheffield: Equinox, 2013), 113–133.

Partridge, Christopher (ed.), *Anthems of Apocalypse: Popular Music and Apocalyptic Thought* (Sheffield: Phoenix Press, 2012).

Partridge, Christopher, "Popular Music, Affective Space, and Meaning," in Gordon Lynch, Jolyon Mitchell and Anna Strhan (eds.), *Religion, Media and Culture: A Reader* (London: Routledge, 2011), 182–193.

Partridge, Christopher, *Dub in Babylon: Understanding the Evolution and Significance of Dub Reggae in Jamaica and Britain from King Tubby to Post-punk* (London: Equinox, 2010).

Partridge, Christopher, "Babylon's Burning: Reggae, Rastafari and Millenarianism." In John Walliss and Kenneth Newport (eds.), *The End All Around Us: Apocalyptic Texts and Popular Culture* (London: Equinox, 2009), 43–70.

Partridge, Christopher, "Religion and Popular Culture." In Linda Woodhead, Hiroko Kawanami, and Christopher Partridge (eds.), *Religions in the Modern World: Traditions and Transformations*, 2nd edition (London: Routledge, 2009), 489–522.

Partridge, Christopher, "King Tubby Meets the Upsetter at the Grass Roots of Dub: Some Thoughts on the Early History and Influence of Dub Reggae," *Popular Music History* 2 (2007): 309–331.

Partridge, Christopher, "The Spiritual and the Revolutionary: Alternative Spirituality, British Free Festivals, and the Emergence of Rave Culture," *Culture and Religion* 7: 1 (2006): 41–60.

Partridge, Christopher, *The Re-Enchantment of the West: Alternative Spiritualities, Sacralization, Popular Culture and Occulture*, 2 vols. (London: T&T Clark International, 2004, 2005).

Partridge, Christopher, *H. H. Farmer's Theological Interpretation of Religion* (Lewiston: Edwin Mellen Press, 1998).

Patel, Anniruddh D., *Music, Language and the Brain* (New York: Oxford University Press, 2008).

Pattison, Robert, *The Triumph of Vulgarity: Rock Music in the Mirror of Romanticism* (New York: Oxford University Press, 1987).

Pearson, Joanne, Richard Roberts, and Geoffrey Samuel, "Introduction." In Joanne Pearson, Richard Roberts, and Geoffrey Samuel (eds.), *Nature Religion Today: Paganism in the Modern World* (Edinburgh: Edinburgh University Press, 1998), 1–7.

Peel, John, and Sheila Ravenscroft, *Margrave of the Marshes* (London: Bantam Press, 2005).

Peel, John, "Introduction." In Albert Mudrian, *Choosing Death: The Improbable History of Death Metal and Grindcore* (Los Angeles: Feral House, 2004), 16–18.

Pefanis, Julian, *Heterology and the Postmodern: Bataille, Baudrillard, and Lyotard* (Durham: Duke University Press, 1991).

Pegg, Bob, *Rites and Riots: Folk Customs of Britain and Europe* (Poole: Blandford Press, 1981).

Pelosi, Francesco, *Plato on Music, Soul and Body*. Translated by Sophie Henderson (Cambridge: Cambridge University Press, 2010).

Pendleton, Robert, "Kindred Spirits." In Adrian Whittaker (ed.), *Be Glad: An Incredible String Band Compendium* (London: Helter Skelter, 2003), 68–82.

Penman, Ian, "Matters of Life and Death: Diamanda Galas," *The Wire* 190/191 (2000): 58–65.

Penn, Lea, "Music is my Religion," *Haaretz.com* (January 07, 2011): http://www.haaretz.com/weekend/week-s-end/music-is-my-religion-1.370696 (accessed July 16, 2011).

Perkins, Kathy A., and Judith Louise Stephens, *Strange Fruit: Plays on Lynching by American Women* (Bloomington: Indiana University Press, 1998).

Perlmutter, Dawn, "The Art of Idolatry: Violent Expressions of the Spiritual in Contemporary Performance Art." In Eric Mazur (ed.), *Bucknell Review: Art and the Religious Impulse* 46: 1 (2002): 125–140.

Perone, James E., *Music of the Counterculture Era* (Westport: Greenwood Press, 2004).

Peters, Dan, and Steve Peters, *Why Knock Rock?* (Minneapolis: Bethany House, 1984).

Peters, Dan, and Steve Peters, *Rock's Hidden Persuader: The Truth About Backmasking* (Minneapolis: Bethany House, 1985).

Petersen, Jesper Aagaard, "Introduction: Embracing Satan." In Jesper Aagaard Petersen (ed.), *Contemporary Religious Satanism: A Critical Anthology* (Farnham: Ashgate, 2009), 1–24.

Phillipov, Michelle, *Death Metal and Music Criticism: Analysis at the Limits* (Plymouth: Lexington Books, 2012).

Phillips, Helen, "Hearing the Vibrations," *Nature Science Update* (August 13, 1998): http://www.nature.com/news/1998/980813/pf/980813-3_pf.html (accessed October 30, 2005).

Pickering, William S.F., *Durkheim's Sociology of Religion: Themes and Theories* (London: Routledge and Kegan Paul, 1984).

Pitzl-Waters, Jason, "Musical Influence of The Wicker Man Soundtrack," *A Darker Shade of Pagan*: http://www.adarkershadeofpagan.com/labels/The%20Wicker%20Man.html (accessed May 01, 2012).

Plant, Martin, and Moira Plant, *Risk-Takers: Alcohol, Drugs, Sex and Youth* (London: Routledge, 1992).

Plant, Sadie, *Writing on Drugs* (New York: Farrar, Straus & Giroux, 1999).

Plato, *The Republic*. Translated by Desmond Lee (London: Penguin, 1987).

Pollard, Velma, "The Social History of Dread Talk," *Caribbean Quarterly* 28.2 (1982): 17–40.

P-Orridge, Genesis, "The Splinter Test." In John Zorn (ed.), *Arcana V: Music, Magic and Mysticism* (New York: Hips Road, 2010), 297–313.

P-Orridge, Genesis, "The Process is the Product: The Processean Influence on Thee Temple Ov Psychick Youth." In Timothy Wyllie, *Love, Sex, Fear, Death: The Inside Story of the Process Church of the Final Judgment*. Edited by Adam Parfray (Port Townsend, WA: Feral House, 2009), 173–184.

P-Orridge, Genesis, "The Lion in a Cage." In V. Vale (ed.), *RE/Search 4/5: William S. Burroughs, Brion Gysin and Throbbing Gristle* (San Francisco: RE/Search Publications, 2007), 87.

P-Orridge, Genesis, "Eyes Wide Shut," *The Guardian* (November 15, 2003): http://www.guardian.co.uk/books/2003/nov/15/art.classics (accessed, May 14, 2012).

P-Orridge, Genesis (ed.), *Painful But Fabulous: The Lives and Art of Genesis P-Orridge* (New York: Soft Skull Shortwave, 2002).

P-Orridge, Genesis, "Genesis P-Orridge." In V. Vale (ed.), *Modern Pagans: An Investigation of Contemporary Paganism* (San Francisco: RE/Search, 2001), 122–127.

P-Orridge, Genesis, *Esoterrorist: Selected Essays 1980–1988* (London: OV Press, 1988). Also available at: http://www.scribd.com/doc/21064820/Genesis-P-Orridge-Esoterrorist (accessed August 11, 2010).

Porter, Roy, "Witchcraft and Magic in Enlightenment, Romantic and Liberal Thought." In Bengt Ankarloo and Stuart Clark (eds.), *Witchcraft and Magic in Europe: The Eighteenth and Nineteenth Centuries* (Philadelphia: University of Pennsylvania Press 1999), 193–274.

Pouncey, Edwin, "Consumed by Noise," *The Wire* 198 (2000): 26–32.

Pouncey, Edwin, "Industrial Light and Magick," *The Wire* 247 (September, 2004): 34–35.

Powell, Anna, "God's Own Medicine: Religion and Parareligion in UK Goth Culture." In Lauren Goodlad and Michael Bibby (eds.), *Goth: Undead Subculture* (Durham: Yale University Press, 2007), 357–374.

Powell, Erin, "Death in June Interview: 2005-Heathen Harvest": http://www.deathinjune.org/modules/mediawiki/index.php/Interview:2005-Heathen_Harvest (accessed February 13, 2011).

Prendergast, Mark, *The Ambient Century: From Mahler to Trance—The Evolution of Sound in the Electronic Age* (London: Bloomsbury, 2000).

Qureshi, Regula B. (ed.), *Music and Marx: Ideas, Practice, Politics* (New York: Routledge, 2002).

Raphael, Melissa, "Thealogy, Redemption, and the Call of the Wild," *Feminist Theology* 5 (1997): 55–72.

Rawlinson, Andrew, *The Book of Enlightened Masters: Western Teachers in Eastern Traditions* (Chicago: Open Court, 1997).

Reader, Ian, "Conclusions." In Ian Reader and Tony Walter (eds.), *Pilgrimage in Popular Culture* (Houndmills: Pagrave, 1993), 220–246.

Reardon, Bernard M.G., *Religion in the Age of Romanticism* (Cambridge: Cambridge University Press, 1985).

Reck, David, "The Beatles and Indian Music." In Olivier Julien (ed.), *Sgt. Pepper and The Beatles: It was Forty Years ago Today* (Aldershot: Ashgate, 2008), 63–74.

Reckford, Verena, "From Burru Drums to Reggae Ridims: The Evolution of Rasta Music." In Nathaniel Murrell, William Spencer and Adrian McFarlane (eds.), *Chanting Down Babylon: The Rastafari Reader* (Philadelpia: Temple University Press, 1998), 231–252.

Reckford, Verena, "Rastafarian Music: An Introductory Study," *Jamaica Journal* 11 (1977): 1–13.

Reddington, Helen, *The Lost Women of Rock Music: Female Musicians of the Punk Era* (Sheffield: Equinox, 2012).

Reece, Gregory, *Elvis Religion: The Cult of the King* (London: I.B. Tauris, 2006).

Reilly, Edward J., *American Popular Culture Through History: The 1960s* (Westport: Greenwood Press, 2003).

Reimar, Bennett, *A Philosophy of Music Education*, 3rd edition (Englewood Cliffs: Prentice-Hall, 2003).

Reinach, Salomon, *Orpheus: A History of Religions*, trans. Florence Simmonds (London: George Routledge & Sons, 1931).

Reising, Russell, and Jim LeBlanc, "Within and Without: *Sgt. Pepper's Lonely Hearts Club Band* and Psychedelic Insight." In Olivier Julien (ed.), *Sgt. Pepper and The Beatles: It was Forty Years ago Today* (Aldershot: Ashgate, 2008), 103–121.

Release, *Release Drugs and Dance Survey: An Insight Into the Culture* (London: Release, 1997).

Reynolds, Simon, *Energy Flash: A Journey Through Rave Music and Dance Culture* (London: Picador, 1998).

Reynolds, Simon, "Back to Eden: Innocence, Indolence and Pastoralism in Psychedelic Music, 1966–1996." In Antonio Melechi (ed.), *Psychedelia Britannica: Hallucinogenic Drugs in Britain* (London: Turnaround, 1997), 143–165.

Richardson, Alan, "Romantic Voodoo: Obeah and British Culture, 1797–1807." In Margarite Fernandez Olmos and Lizabeth Paravisini-Gebert (eds.), *Sacred Possessions: Vodou, Santería, Obeah and the Caribbean* (New Brunswick: Rutgers University Press, 1997), 171–194.

Richardson, James, Joel Best and David Bromley (eds.), *The Satanism Scare* (New York: Aldine De Gruyter, 1991).

Richardson, Nick, "In-between Worlds: Grouper," *The Wire* 334 (December, 2011): 26–29.

Richman, Michèle H., *Sacred Revolutions: Durkheim and the Collège de Sociologie* (Minneapolis: University of Minnesota Press, 2002).

Rickard, Nikki S., and Katrina McFerran (eds.), *Lifelong Engagement with Music: Benefits for Mental Health and Well-Being* (New York: Nova Publishers, 2012).

Riis, Ole, and Linda Woodhead, *A Sociology of Religious Emotion* (Oxford: Oxford University Press, 2010).

Riley, Alexander, *Impure Play: Sacredness, Transgression, and the Tragic in Popular Culture* (Lanham: Lexington Books, 2010).

Riley, Alexander, "'Renegade Durkheimianism' and the Transgressive Left Sacred." In Jeffrey C. Alexander and Philip Smith (eds.), *The Cambridge Companion to Durkheim* (Cambridge: Cambridge University Press, 2005), 274–301.

Rimmer, Dave, *New Romantics: The Look* (London: Omnibus Press, 2003).

Rimmer, Mark, "Christafari: Mark Mohr Talks About Their New Album and Bob Marley's Conversion," *Christafari*: http://www.crossrhythms.co.uk/articles/music/Christafari_Mark_Mohr_talks_about_their_new_album_and_Bob_Marleys_conversion/37845/p1/ (accessed September 25, 2012).

Riordan, James, and Jerry Prochnicky, *Break on Through: The Life and Death of Jim Morrison* (London: Plexus, 1991).

Ritz, David, *Blues All Around Me: The Autobiography of B. B. King* (New York: Avon Books, 1996).

Roberts, Andy, "Changing Horses." In Adrian Whittaker (ed.), *Be Glad: An Incredible String Band Compendium* (London: Helter Skelter, 2003), 131–133.

Roberts, Richard H., "Body." In Robert A. Segal (ed.), *The Blackwell Companion to the Study of Religion* (Oxford: Blackwell, 2006), 213–228.

Rodney, Walter, *The Groundings with My Brothers* (London: Bogle-L'Overture Publications, 1969).

Rogan, Johnny, *Van Morrison: No Surrender* (London: Vintage, 2006).

Rojek, Chris, *Celebrity* (London: Reaktion Books, 2001).

Rollins, Henry, *Black Coffee Blues* (London: Virgin Books, 2005).

Romanowski, William, "Evangelicals and Popular Music: The Contemporary Christian Music Industry." In Bruce David Forbes and Jeffrey H. Mahan (eds.), *Religion and Popular Culture in America* (Berkeley: University of California Press, 2000), 105–124.

Romanowski, William, "Move Over Madonna: The Crossover Career of Gospel Artist Amy Grant," *Popular Music and Society* 17: 2 (1993): 47–68.

Roof, Wade Clark, *Spiritual Marketplace: Baby Boomers and the Remaking of American Religion* (Princeton: Princeton University Press, 1999).

Rosenberg, Jessica, and Gitana Garofalo, "Riot Grrrl: Revolutions from Within," *Signs: Journal of Women in Culture and Society* 23 (1998): 809–841.

Rosenblatt, Louise, *The Reader, The Text, The Poem: The Transactional Theory of the Literary Work* (Carbondale: Southern Illinois University Press, 1978).

Roszak, Theodore, *The Making of a Counter Culture: Reflections on the Technocratic Society and Its Youthful Opposition* (London: Faber, 1970).

Roubiczek, Paul, *Thinking in Opposites* (London: Routledge & Kegan Paul, 1952).

Rowe, Carel, "Illuminating Lucifer," *Film Quarterly* 27: 4 (1974): 24–33.

Rowe, Sharon, "Liminal Sports: Liminal Ritual or Liminoid Leisure? In Graham St. John (ed.), *Victor Turner and Contemporary Cultural Performance* (Oxford: Bergahn Books, 2008), 94–108.

Rowe, Steve, "Infiltration Squad," *Rowe Productions*: http://www.roweproductions.com/store/ (accessed October 3, 2012).

Ruether, Rosemary Radford, *Sexism and God-Talk: Towards a Feminist Theology* (London: SCM, 1983).

Rushkoff, Douglas, *Cyberia: Life in the Trenches of Hyperspace*, 2nd edition (Manchester: Clinamen Press, 2002).

Russell, Jeffrey Burton, "The Romantic Devil." In Harold Bloom (ed.), *Satan* (New York: Chelsea House Publishers, 2005), 155–192.

Ryan, John, *Tolkien: Cult or Culture?* (Armidale, New South Wales: University Press of New England, 1969).

Ryman, Cheryl, "Kumina – Stability and Change," *African Caribbean Institute of Jamaica Research Review* 1 (1984): 81–128.

Sabin, Roger (ed.), *Punk Rock: So What?* (London: Routledge, 1999).

Sacher-Masoch, Leopold von, *Venus in Furs*. Translated by Joachim Neugroschel (London: Penguin, 2000).

Sacks, Oliver, *Musicophilia: Tales of Music and the Brain* (London: Picador, 2008).

Saldanha, Arun, *Psychedelic White: Goa Trance and the Viscosity of Race* (Minneapolis: University of Minnesota Press, 2007).

Sandford, Christopher, *Bowie: Loving the Alien* (New York: De Capo, 1998).

Sandford, Jeremy, and Ron Reid, *Tomorrow's People* (London: Jerome Publishing, 1974).

Saunders, Nicholas, Anja Saunders and Michelle Pauli, *In Search of the Ultimate High: Spiritual Experience Through Psychoactives* (London: Rider, 2000).

Saunders, Nicholas, *Ecstasy and the Dance Culture* (London: Nicholas Saunders, 1995).

Saunders, Nicholas, *Alternative London* (London: Saunders, 1970).

Savishinsky, Neil, "African Dimensions of the Jamaican Rastafarian Movement." In Nathaniel Murrell, William Spencer and Adrian McFarlane (eds.), *Chanting Down Babylon: The Rastafari Reader* (Philadelpia: Temple University Press, 1998), 125–144.

Sawyer, R. Keith, *Explaining Creativity: The Science of Human Innovation*, 2nd edition (New York: Oxford University Press, 2012).

Schaberg, Jane, *The Resurrection of Mary Magdalene: Legends, Apocrypha and the Christian Testament* (New York: Continuum, 2004).

Schilt, Kristen, "'Riot Grrrl Is . . .': The Contestation over Meaning in a Music Scene." In Andy Bennett and Richard A. Peterson (eds.), *Music Scenes: Local, Translocal, and Virtual* (Nashville: Vanderbilt University Press, 2004), 115–130.

Schilt, Kristen, and Elke Zobl, "Connecting the Dots: Riot Grrrls, Ladyfests, and the International Grrrl Zine Network." In Anita Harris (ed.), *Next Wave Cultures: Feminism, Subcultures, Activism* (New York: Routledge, 2008), 171–192.

Schmidt, Bettina E., *Caribbean Diaspora in USA: Diversity of Caribbean Religions in New York City* (Aldershot: Ashgate, 2008).

Schmidt, Joshua, "(En)countering the Beat: Paradox in Israeli Psytrance." In Graham St John (ed.), *The Local Scenes and Global Culture of Psytrance* (London: Routledge, 2010), 131–148.

Schraffenberger, Rebecca, "This Modern Goth (Explains Herself)." In Lauren Goodlad and Michael Bibby (eds.), *Goth: Undead Subculture* (Durham: Yale University Press, 2007), 121–128.

Schultze, Laurie, Anne Barton White and Jane Brown, "'A Sacred Monster in Her Prime': Audience Construction of Madonna as the Low-Other." In Cathy Swichtenberg (ed.), *The Madonna Connection: Representational Politics, Subcultural Identities and Cultural Theory* (Boulder: Westview Press, 1993), 15–37.

Scott, Derek B., *Musical Style and Social Meaning: Selected Essays* (Farnham: Ashgate, 2010).

Scott, Derek B., *From the Erotic to the Demonic: On Critical Musicology* (Oxford: Oxford University Press, 2003).

Scott, Derek B., "Music, Culture, and Society: Changes in Perspective." In Derek B. Scott (ed.), *Music, Culture, and Society: A Reader* (Oxford: Oxford University Press, 2000), 1–19.

Scruton, Roger, *Understanding Music: Philosophy and Interpretation* (London: Continuum, 2009).

Selvik, Einar, "Sowing New Seeds, Strengthening Old Roots," *Wardruna* (2007): http://www.wardruna.com/about/ (accessed, July 10, 2012).

Shapiro, Peter, "Bass Invader: Jah Wobble," *The Wire* 140 (October, 1995): 32–35.

Sharp, Cecil, *English Folk Song: Some Conclusions* (London: Simpkin & Co., 1907).

Shelton, Gilbert, *The Fabulous Furry Freak Brothers: Omnibus* (London: Knockabout Comics, 2008).

Shuker, Roy, *Understanding Popular Music*, 2nd edition (London: Routledge, 2001).

Shumway, David, and Heather Arnet, "Playing Dress Up: David Bowie and the Roots of Goth." In Lauren Goodlad and Michael Bibby (eds.), *Goth: Undead Subculture* (Durham: Yale University Press, 2007), 129–142.

Shusterman, Richard, *Pragmatist Aesthetics: Living Beauty, Rethinking Art* (Oxford: Blackwell, 1992).

Siegal, Carol, "That Obscure Object of Desire Revisited: Poppy Z. Brite and the Goth Hero as Masochist." In Lauren Goodlad and Michael Bibby (eds.), *Goth: Undead Subculture* (Durham: Yale University Press, 2007), 335–356.

Siegel, Carol, *Goth's Dark Empire* (Bloomington: Indiana University Press, 2005).

Simpson, Mark, *Saint Morrissey* (London: SAF, 2004).

Skelton, Rose, "Can Musical Mali Play On?," *The Independent* (August 18, 2012): http://www.independent.co.uk/news/world/africa/can-musical-mali-play-on-8057347.html (accessed October 28, 2012).

Sleeper, Mick, "Shocks of the Mighty." In Chris Potash (ed.), *Reggae, Rasta, Revolution: Jamaican Music from Ska to Dub* (London: Books With Attitude, 1997), 157–162.

Sloboda, John, *Exploring the Musical Mind: Cognition, Emotion, Ability, Function* (Oxford: Oxford University Press, 2005).

Smajić, Srdjan, *Ghost-Seers, Detectives, and Spiritualists: Theories of Vision in Victorian Literature and Science* (New York: Oxford University Press, 2010).

Smith, Christian (ed.), *The Secular Revolution: Power Interests and Conflict in the Secularization of American Public Life* (Berkeley: University of California Press, 2003).

Smith, Harry, "Liner Notes," *Anthology of American Folk Music* (1952), 1–18.

Smith, Lilian, *Strange Fruit* (Orlando: Harcourt Brace Jovanovich, 1993).

Smith, Michael G., Roy Augier, and Rex Nettleford, *The Rastafari Movement in Kingston, Jamaica* (Mona: Institute for Social and Economic Research, University College of the West Indies, 1960).

Spare, Austin Osman, *Ethos: The Magical Writings of Austin Osman Spare* (Thame: I-H-O Books, 2001).

Spence, Hubert, *Confronting Contemporary Christian Music: A Plain Account of Its History, Philosophy and Future* (Dunn: Forwarding the Faith Publications, 2011).

Spencer, Jon Michael, *Blues and Evil* (Knoxville: University of Tennessee Press, 1993).

Spencer, Jon Michael, "The Mythology of the Blues." In Jon Michael Spencer (ed.), *Sacred Music of the Secular City: From Blues Rap*. A Special Issue *Black Sacred Music: A Journal of Theomusicology* 6.1 (Durham: Duke University Press, 1992): 98–140.

Spencer, William, "Chanting Change Around the World Through Rasta Ridim and Art." In Nathaniel Murrell, William Spencer and Adrian McFarlane (eds.), *Chanting Down Babylon: The Rastafari Reader* (Philadelpia: Temple University Press, 1998), 267–283.

Spooner, Catherine, "Preface." In Brigid Cherry, Peter Howell and Caroline Ruddell (eds.), *Twenty-First Century Gothic* (Newcastle: Cambridge Scholars Publishing, 2010), ix–xii.

Spooner, Catherine, *Contemporary Gothic* (London: Reaktion Books, 2006).

Stallybrass, Peter, and Allon White, *The Politics and Poetics of Transgression* (London: Methuen & Co., 1986).

Stannard, Joseph, "The Gathering Storm," *The Wire* 302 (April, 2009): 42–47.

Stapert, Calvin, *A New Song for an Old World: Musical Thought in the Early Church* (Grand Rapids: Eerdmans, 2007).

Star Children, "Sacred Reunion." In Chris Deckker (ed.), *Sacred Sites*, a booklet issued with the following CD: Various Artists, *Sacred Sites* (Return to the Source, 1997), 44–45.

Steffens, Roger, "Bob Marley: Rasta Warrior." In Nathaniel Murrell, William Spencer and Adrian McFarlane (eds.), *Chanting Down Babylon: The Rastafari Reader* (Philadelpia: Temple University Press, 1998), 253–265.

Stevens, Jay, *Storming Heaven: LSD and the American Dream* (London: Flamingo, 1993).

Stewart, Francis Elizabeth, "'Punk Rock is My Religion': An Exploration of Straight Edge Punk as a Surrogate of Religion" (doctoral dissertation, Stirling University, 2011).

St. John, Graham, "Total Solar Eclipse Festivals, Cosmic Pilgrims and Planetary Culture." In Andy Bennett and Donna Weston (eds.), *Pop Pagans: Paganism and Popular Music* (Durham: Acumen, 2012), 126–144.

St. John, Graham, "Liminal Culture and Global Movement: The Transitional World of Psytrance." In Graham St. John (ed.), *The Local Scenes and Global Culture of Psytrance* (London: Routledge, 2010), 220–246.

St. John, Graham (ed.), *The Local Scenes and Global Culture of Psytrance* (London: Routledge, 2010).

St. John, Graham, *Technomad: Global Raving Countercultures* (London: Equinox, 2009).

St. John, Graham (ed.), *Rave Culture and Religion* (London: Routledge, 2004).

St. John, Graham, "Introduction." In Graham St. John (ed.), *Rave Culture and Religion* (London: Routledge, 2004), 1–15.

Stone, C.J., *Fierce Dancing: Adventures in the Underground* (London: Faber and Faber, 1996).

Stone, C.J., *Last of the Hippies* (London: Faber and Faber, 1999).

Storey, John, *Inventing Popular Culture: From Folklore to Globalization* (Oxford: Blackwell, 2003).

Storey, John (ed.), *Cultural Theory and Popular Culture: A Reader* (Harlow: Pearson Education, 2006).

Storey, John, *An Introduction to Cultural Theory and Popular Culture*, 2nd edition (London: Prentice Hall, 1997).

Storr, Anthony, *Music and the Mind* (London: HarperCollins, 1992).

Stout, Harry S., *The Divine Dramatist: George Whitefield and the Rise of Modern Evangelicalism* (Grand Rapids: Eerdmans, 1991).

Stowe, David W., *No Sympathy for the Devil: Christian Pop Music and the Transformation of American Evangelicalism* (Chapel Hill: University of North Carolina Press, 2011).

Strachan, Guy, "Eastern Europe: Around the Bloc," *Terrorizer* 128 (February, 2005): 39.

Straw, Will, "Consumption." In Simon Frith, Will Straw and John Street (eds.), *The Cambridge Companion to Pop and Rock* (Cambridge: Cambridge University Press, 2001), 53–73.

Street, John, "'This is Your Woodstock': Popular Memories and Political Myths." In Andy Bennett (ed.), *Remembering Woodstock* (Aldershot: Ashgate, 2004), 29–42.

Strinati, Dominic, *An Introduction to Theories of Popular Culture*, 2nd edition (London: Routledge, 2004).

Stump, Paul, *Digital Gothic: A Critical Discography of Tangerine Dream* (London: SAF Publishing, 1997).

Sudbin, Yevgeny, "Scriabin Liner Notes": http://www.yevgenysudbin.com/artist.php?view= essays&rid=456 (accessed on May 13, 2012).

Sullivan, Mark, "'More Popular Than Jesus': The Beatles and the Religious Far Right," *Popular Music* 6 (1987): 313–326.

Sutherland, Steve, "The Pyramid," *Glastonbury: A Celebration of the World's Greatest Festival. NME Special* (2003): 10.

Swichtenberg, Cathy (ed.), *The Madonna Connection: Representational Politics, Subcultural Identities and Cultural Theory* (Boulder: Westview Press, 1993).

Sylvan, Robin, *Trance Formation: The Spiritual and Religious Dimensions of Global Rave Culture* (New York: Routledge, 2005).

Sylvan, Robin, *Traces of the Spirit: The Religious Dimensions of Popular Music* (New York: New York University Press, 2002).

Szerszynski, Bronislaw, *Nature, Technology and the Sacred* (Oxford: Blackwell, 2005).

Szpajdel, Christophe, "Band Identity." In Tom Howells (ed.), *Black Metal: Beyond the Darkness* (London: Black Dog Publishing, 2012), 138–145.

Szwed, John, *Alan Lomax: The Man Who Recorded the World* (London: Arrow Books, 2011).

Tagg, Philip, "Analysing Popular Music: Theory, Method and Practice," *Popular Music* 2 (1982): 37–65.

Talbot, Stephen, "Sixties Something," *Mother Jones Magazine* 16:2 (March–April, 1991), 47–49, 69–70.

Taussig, Michael, "Transgression." In Mark C. Taylor (ed.), *Critical Terms for Religious Studies* (Chicago: University of Chicago Press, 1998), 349–364.

Taylor, Charles, *A Secular Age* (Cambridge: Harvard University Press, 2007).

Taylor, Charles, *The Ethics of Authenticity* (Cambridge: Harvard University Press, 1991).

Taylor, Mark C. (ed.), *Critical Terms for Religious Studies* (Chicago: University of Chicago Press, 1998).

Taylor, Patrick, "Rastafari, the Other, and Exodus Politics: EATUP," *Journal of Religious Thought* 17 (1991): 95–107.

Taylor, Patrick, "Perspectives on History in Rastafari Thought," *Studies in Religion* 19 (1990): 191–205.

Thomas, Keith, *Religion and the Decline of Magic: Studies in Popular Beliefs in Sixteenth and Seventeenth Century England* (Harmondsworth: Penguin, 1973).

Thompson, Kenneth, *Moral Panics* (Abingdon: Routledge, 1998).

Thompson, Hunter S., *The Great Shark Hunt: Strange Tales from a Strange Time* (London: Picador, 2010).

Thompson, William Forde, *Music, Thought and Feeling: Understanding the Psychology of Music* (New York: Oxford University Press, 2009).

Thornton, Sarah, *Club Cultures: Music, Media and Subcultural Capital* (Cambridge: Polity Press, 1995).

Thornton, Sarah, "Moral Panic, the Media and British Rave Culture." In Andrew Ross and Tricia Ross (eds.), *Microphone Fiends: Youth Music & Youth Culture* (New York: Routledge, 1994), 176–192.

Till, Rupert, *Pop Cult: Religion and Popular Music* (London: Continuum, 2010).

Todd, Neil P.M., and Frederick W. Cody, "Vestibular Responses to Loud Dance Music: A Physiological Basis of the 'Rock and Roll Threshold'?" *The Journal of the Acoustical Society of America* 107 (2000): 496–500.

Toffoletti, Kim, *Cyborgs and Barbie Dolls: Feminism, Popular Culture and the Posthuman Body* (London: I.B. Tauris, 2007).

Toop, David, *Haunted Weather: Music, Silence and Memory* (London: Serpent's Tail, 2004).

Toop, David, *Ocean of Sound: Aether Talk, Ambient Sound and Imaginary Worlds* (London: Serpent's Tail, 1995).

Toop, David, "Telematic Nomad: Bill Laswell," *The Wire* 130 (1994): 32–35, 80.

TOPY, *Thee Grey Book*: http://www.kondole.com/theegreybook/greycover.htm (accessed October 05, 2010).

TOPY, "TOPY London Interviewed by AntiClockwise Magazine 1991": http://www.uncarved.org/23texts/clockwise.html (accessed August 31, 2003).

Toynbee, Arnold, "The Religious Background of the Present Environmental Crisis." In David and Eileen Spring (eds.), *Ecology and Religion in History* (New York: Harper & Row, 1974), 137–149.

Tramacchi, Des, "Field Tripping: Psychedelic *Communitas* and Ritual in the Australian Bush," *Journal of Contemporary Religion* 15 (2000): 201–213.

Turner, Chérie, *The Riot Grrrl Movement: The Feminism of a New Generation* (New York: The Rosen Publishing Group, 2001).

Turner, Edith, "The Literary Roots of Victor Turner's Anthopology." In Kathleen Ashley (ed.), *Victor Turner and the Construction of Cultural Criticism: Between Literature and Anthropology* (Bloomington: Indiana University Press, 1990), 163–169.

Turner, Victor, *Dramas, Fields and Metaphors* (Ithaca: Cornell University Press, 1974).

Turner, Victor, *The Ritual Process: Structure and Anti-Structure* (Chicago: Aldine, 1969).

Turner, Victor, "Variations on a Theme of Liminality." In Sally Moore and Barabara Myerhoff (eds.), *Secular Ritual* (Amsterdam: Van Gorcum, 1977), 36–52.

Tylor, Edward Burnett, *Primitive Culture*, Vol. 1 (London: John Murray, 1871).

Urban, Hugh, *Magia Sexualis: Sex, Magic, and Liberation in Modern Western Esotericism* (Berkeley: University of California Press, 2006).

Vale, V., and Andrea Juno (eds.), *Re/Search 6/7: Industrial Culture Handbook* (San Francisco: RE/Search, 1983).

Vale, V. (ed.), *RE/Search 4/5: William S. Burroughs, Brion Gysin and Throbbing Gristle* (San Francisco: RE/Search Publications, 2007).

Vaughan Williams, Ursula, *R.V.W.: A Biography of Ralph Vaughan Williams* (Oxford: Oxford University Press, 1964).

Veal, Michael E., *Dub: Soundscapes and Shattered Songs in Jamaican Reggae* (Middletown: Wesleyan University Press, 2005).

Victor, Jeffrey S., *Satanic Panic: The Creation of a Contemporary Legend* (Chicago: Open Court, 1993).

Vikernes, Varg, *Sorcery and Religion in Ancient Scandinavia* (London: Abstract Sounds Books, 2011).

Vikernes, Varg, "Kingdoms of the Sun," *Burzum.Org*: http://www.burzum.org/eng/library/the_kingdom_of_the_sun.shtml (accessed April 23, 2012).

Vincett, Giselle, and Linda Woodhead, "Spirituality." In Linda Woodhead, Hiroko Kawanami, and Christopher Partridge (eds.), *Religions in the Modern World: Traditions and Transformations*, 2nd edition (London: Routledge, 2009), 319–337.

Wach, Joachim, *The Comparative Study of Religions* (New York: Columbia University Press, 1958).

Waldenfels, Bernhard, "Levinas and the Face of the Other." In Simon Critchley and Robert Bernasconi (eds.), *The Cambridge Companion to Levinas* (Cambridge: Cambridge University Press, 2002), 63–81.

Walker, Daniel P., "Orpheus the Theologian and Renaissance Platonists," *Journal of the Warburg and Courtauld Institutes* 16 (1953): 100–120.

Walker, Pamela J., *Pulling the Devil's Kingdom Down: The Salvation Army in Victorian Britain* (Berkeley: University of California Press, 2001).

Walliss, John, "The Road to Hell is Paved with D20s: Evangelical Christianity and Role-playing Gaming." In Adam Possamai (ed.), *Handbook of Hyper-real Religions* (Leiden: Brill, 2012), 207–224.

Walmsley, Derek, "Chants Encounters," *The Wire* 352 (June, 2013): 29.

Walser, Robert, "The Rock 'n' Roll Era." In David Nicholls (ed.), *The Cambridge History of American Music* (Cambridge: Cambridge University Press, 1998), 345–387.

Ward, Brian (ed.), *The 1960s: A Documentary Reader* (Oxford: Blackwell, 2010).

Ward, Pete, "The Economies of Charismatic Evangelical Worship." In Gordon Lynch, Jolyon Mitchell, and Anna Strhan (eds.), *Religion, Media and Culture: A Reader* (Abingdon: Routledge, 2011), 23–30.

Warner, Simon, "Reporting Woodstock: Some Contemporary Press Reflections on the Festival." In Andy Bennett (ed.), *Remembering Woodstock* (Aldershot: Ashgate, 2004), 55–74.

Watkins, Terry, "What About P.O.D.?": http://www.av1611.org/crock/pod.html (accessed October 5, 2012).

Watson, Don, "Beyond Evil," *The Wire* 182 (1999): 30–35.

Watts, Alan, *This Is It and Other Essays on Zen and Spiritual Experience* (New York: Vintage Books, 1973).

Watts, Alan, *The Joyous Cosmology: Adventures in the Chemistry of Consciousness* (New York: Vintage Books, 1962).

Watts, Alan, *Beat Zen, Square Zen, and Zen* (San Francisco: City Lights Books, 1959).

Watts, Fraser, Rebecca Nye, Sara Savage, *Psychology for Christian Ministry* (London: Routledge, 2002).

Webb, Peter, *Exploring the Networked Worlds of Popular Music* (New York: Routledge, 2007).

Weber, Max, *From Max Weber: Essays in Sociology*. Edited by Hans H. Gerth and C. Wright Mills (London: Routledge & Kegan Paul, 1948).

Weingarten, Marc, "P.O.D.: Who Says God Doesn't Like Metal?," *Rolling Stone* 856/857 (14–December 21, 2000): 102.

Welch, David, *The Third Reich: Politics and Propaganda*, 2nd edition (London: Routledge, 2002).

Welsh, Graham F., & D. M. Howard, "Gendered Voice in the Cathedral Choir," *Psychology of Music* 30 (2002): 102–120.

Wenner, Jann S., "The *Rolling Stone* Interview: Jagger Remembers": http://www.jannswenner.com/Archives/Jagger_Remembers.aspx (accessed February 05, 2012).

West, Therese, and Gail Ironson, "Effects of Music on Human Health and Wellness: Physiological Measurements and Research Design." In Benjamin D. Koen (ed.), *The Oxford Handbook of Medical Ethnomusicology* (New York: Oxford University Press, 2008), 410–443.

White, Garth, "The Development of Jamaican Popular Music: Part 2," *African Caribbean Institute of Jamaica Research Review* 1 (1984): 47–80.

White, Lynn, "The Historical Roots of Our Ecologic Crisis," *Science* 155 (1967): 1203–1207.

Whiteley, Sheila, " '1, 2, 3 What Are We Fighting 4?' Music, Meaning and 'The Star Spangled Banner.' " In Andy Bennett (ed.), *Remembering Woodstock* (Aldershot: Ashgate, 2004), 18–28.

Whiteley, Sheila, *Women and Popular Music: Sexuality, Identity and Subjectivity* (London: Routledge, 2000).

Whiteley, Sheila, *Sexing the Groove: Popular Music and Gender* (London: Routledge, 1997).

Whiteley, Sheila, "Altered Sounds." In Antonio Melechi (ed.), *Psychedelia Britannica: Hallucinogenic Drugs in Britain* (London: Turnaround, 1997), 120–142.

Whiteley, Sheila, "Seduced by the Sign: An Analysis of the Textual Links Between Sound and Image in Pop Videos." In Sheila Whiteley (ed.), *Sexing the Groove: Popular Music and Gender* (London: Routledge, 1997), 259–276.

Whiteley, Sheila, *The Space Between the Notes: Rock and the Counter-Culture* (London: Routledge, 1992).

Whitesell, Lloyd, *The Music of Joni Mitchell* (New York: Oxford University Press, 2008).

Whitfield, Greg M., "Bass Cultural Vibrations: Visionaries, Outlaws, Mystics, and Chanters," *3 AM Magazine* (2002): http://www.3ammagazine.com/musicarchives/2002_oct/bass_cultural_vibrations.html (accessed October 25, 2005).

Whittaker, Adrian (ed.) *beGlad: An Incredible String band Compendium* (London: Helter Skelter Publishing, 2003).

Wierzbicki, James, "Psycho-Analysis: Form and Function in Bernard Hermann's Music for Hitch-cock's Masterpiece." In Philip Hayward (ed.), *Terror Tracks: Music, Sound and Horror Cinema* (London: Equinox, 2009), 14–46.

Wilber, Ken, "The Atman-Project." In William Bloom (ed.), *Holistic Revolution: The Essential New Age Reader* (Harmondsworth: Allen Lane, Penguin Press, 2000), 77–83.

Williams, Raymond, "Culture is Ordinary." In Ann Gray and Jim McGuigan (eds.), *Studying Culture: An Introductory Reader* (London: Arnold, 1993), 5–14.

Williams, Raymond, *Television: Technology and Cultural Form* (London: Routledge, 1990).

Williams, Raymond, *Keywords: A Vocabulary of Culture and Society* (London: Fontana, 1988).

Williams, Raymond, *The Long Revolution* (London: Penguin, 1965).

Williams, Raymond, *Culture and Society: 1780–1950* (New York: Anchor Books, 1960).

Williams, Rowan, "Foreword." In Adrian Whittaker (ed.), *beGlad: An Incredible String Band Com-pendium* (London: Helter Skelter, 2003), 5–6.

Williams, Richard, "The Sound Surprise." In Chris Potash (ed.), *Reggae, Rasta, Revolution: Jamaican Music from Ska to Dub* (London: Books With Attitude, 1997), 145–148.

Williams, Simon, *Wagner and the Romantic Hero* (Cambridge: Cambridge University Press, 2004).

Willis, Paul, *Profane Culture* (London: Routledge, 1978).

Wilson, Julie, "As It Is." In Genesis P-Orridge (ed.), *Painful but Fabulous: The Lives and Art of Genesis P-Orridge* (New York: Soft Skull Shortwave, 2002), 51–110.

Wilson, Robert Anton, "The 23 Phenomenon," *Fortean Times* 23 (1977): http://www.forteantimes.com/features/commentary/396/the_23_phenomenon.html (accessed May 23, 2010).

Wilson, Robert Anton, and Robert Shea, *The Illuminatus! Trilogy; The Eye in the Pyramid, The Golden Apple, Leviathan* (New York: Dell Publishing, 1975).

Wilson, Scott, *Great Satan's Rage: American Negativity and Rap/Metal in the Age of Supercapitalism* (Manchester: Manchester University Press, 2008).

Winston, Diane, "All the World's a Stage: The Performed Religion of the Salvation Army, 1880–1920." In Stewart M. Hoover and Lynn Schofield Clark (eds.), *Religion in the Age of the Media: Explorations in Media, Religion and Culture* (New York: Columbia University Press, 2002), 113–137.

Wint, Eleanor (in consultation with members of the Nyabinghi Order), "Who is Haile Selassie? His Imperial Majesty in Rasta Voices." In Nathaniel Murrell, William Spencer and Adrian McFarlane (eds.), *Chanting Down Babylon: The Rastafari Reader* (Philadelpia: Temple Univer-sity Press, 1998), 159–165.

Wise, Sue, "Sexing Elvis." In Simon Frith and Andrew Goodwin (eds.), *On Record: Rock, Pop, and the Written Word* (New York: Pantheon Books, 1990), 390–398.

Witkin, Joel-Peter, *The Bone House* (San Francisco: Twin Palms Publishers, 2000).

Witkin, Robert W., *Adorno on Music* (London: Routledge, 1998).

Wobble, Jah (2010) "Welcome to My World," *30 Hertz Records*: http://www.30hertzrecords.com/ (accessed June 26, 2010).

Wojcik, Daniel, *The End of the World As We Know It: Faith, Fatalism, and Apocalypse in America* (New York: New York University Press, 1997).

Wolfe, Burton H., "Introduction." In Anton S. LaVey, *The Satanic Bible* (New York: Avon Books, 1969), 9–18.

Wood, Robert, *Straightedge Youth: Complexity and Contradictions of a Subculture* (Syracuse: Syracuse University Press, 2006).

Worthington, Andy, *Stonehenge: Celebration and Subversion* (Loughborough: Alternative Albion, 2004).

Wright, Mary Anna, "The Great British Ecstasy Revolution." In George McKay (ed.), *DIY Culture: Party and Protest in Nineties Britain* (London: Verso, 1998), 228–242.

Wuthnow, Robert, *After Heaven: Spirituality in America Since the 1950s* (Berkeley: University of California Press, 1998).

Wylie, Donovan, *Losing Ground* (London: Fourth Estate, 1998).

Wyllie, Timothy, *Love, Sex, Fear, Death: The Inside Story of the Process Church of the Final Judgment.* Edited by Adam Parfray (Port Townsend, WA: Feral House, 2009).

Wyschogrod, Edith, "Language and Alterity in the Thought of Levinas." In Simon Critchley and Robert Bernasconi (eds.), *The Cambridge Companion to Levinas* (Cambridge: Cambridge University Press, 2002), 188–205.

Yates, Francis, *The Occult Philosophy in the Elizabethan Age* (London: Ark 1983).

Young, Jock, "The Subterranean World of Play." In Ken Gelder and Sarah Thornton (eds.), *The Subcultures Reader* (London: Routledge, 1997), 71–80.

Young, Rob, *Electric Eden: Unearthing Britain's Visionary Music* (London: Faber & Faber, 2010).

Young, Robert, *Colonial Desire: Hybridity in Theory, Culture and Race* (London: Routledge, 1995).

Žižek, Slavoj, *In Defence of Lost Causes* (London: Verso, 2008).

Žižek, Slavoj, *The Universal Exception: Selected Writings* (London: Continuum, 2006).

Žižek, Slavoj, *On Belief* (London: Routledge, 2001).

Zorn, John (ed.), *Arcana V: Music, Magic and Mysticism* (New York: Hips Road, 2010).

Zorn, John, "Preface." In John Zorn (ed.), *Arcana V: Music, Magic and Mysticism* (New York: Hips Road, 2010), v–vii.

DISCOGRAPHY

ALBUMS

2 Live Crew, *As Nasty As They Wanna Be* (Atlantic Records, 1989).

Eivind Aarset, *Sonic Codex* (Jazzland Records, 2007).

Aborted, *The Purity of Perversion* (Uxicon Records, 1999)

Ryan Adams, *Demolition* (Lost Highway, 2002).

African Head Charge, *Songs of Praise* (On-U Sound, 1990).

African Head Charge, *In Pursuit Of Shashamane Land* (On-U Sound, 1993).

Agalloch, *Whitedivisiongrey* (Licht von Dämmerung Arthouse, 2012).

Agathocles/Lunatic Invasion, *Agathocles/Luncatic Invasion* (Morbid Records, 1991).

Agent Orange, *Living in Darkness* (Posh Boy, 1981).

Laurel Aitken, *Pioneer of Jamaican Music, Vol. 1* (Reggae Retro, 2000).

Aksak Maboul, *Onze Danses Pour Combattre la Migraine* (Crammed Discs, 1977).

Alabama 3, *Coldharbour Lane* (One Little Indian, 1997).

Alabama 3, *La Peste* (Elemental Records, 2000).

Alabama 3, *Power in the Blood* (One Little Indian, 2002).

Alabama 3, *There will be Peace in the Valley . . . When We Get the Keys to the Mansion on the Hill* (Hostage Music, 2011).

Alabama 3, *Shoplifting for Jesus* (Hostage Music, 2011).

Damon Albarn, *Dr Dee* (Parlophone, 2012).

Damon Albarn, *Mali Music* (Honest Jon's/EMI, 2002).

Marc Almond, *Violent Silence* (Virgin, 1986).

Alpha and Omega, *The Sacred Art of Dub* (A&O Records, 1998).

Alpha Blondy, *Jerusalem* (Shanachie, 1986).

Altorių Šešėliai, *Margi Sakalai* (Todestrieb Records, 2008).

Tori Amos, *Little Earthquakes* (Atlantic, 1992).

Tori Amos, *Under the Pink* (Atlantic, 1994).

Tori Amos, *Abnormally Attracted to Sin* (Island Records, 2009).

Tori Amos, *Midwinter Graces* (Universal Republic, 2009).

Aphex Twin, *Come to Daddy* (Warp Records, 1997).

Dave and Toni Arthur, *Hearken to the Witches Rune* (Trailer, 1970).

Baka Beyond, *Spirit of the Forest* (Hannibal Records, 1993).

Baka Beyond, *The Meeting Pool* (Hannibal Records, 1995).

Bass Erotica, *Sexual Bass* (Neurodisc, 1995).

Bass Erotica, *Bass Ecstasy* (Neurodisc, 1996).

Bass Erotica, *Erotic Bass Delight* (Neurodisc, 1996).

Bass Lo-Ryders, *Ryder Style* (Neurodisc 2004).

Bat for Lashes, *Two Suns* (Parlophone, 2009).

Beastie Boys, *Licensed to Ill* (Def Jam/Columbia, 1986).

The Beatles, *Rubber Soul* (Parlophone, 1965).

The Beatles, *Revolver* (Parlophone, 1966).

The Beatles, *Yesterday and Today* (Capitol, 1966).

The Beatles, *Sgt. Pepper's Lonely Hearts Club Band* (Parlophone, 1967).

The Beatles, *The Beatles* (Apple Records, 1968).

The Beatles, *Abbey Road* (Apple Records, 1969).

The Beatles, *Let It Be* (Apple Records, 1970).

Behemoth, *Zos Kia Cultus (Here And Beyond)* (Olympic Recordings, 2002).

Belenos, *Spicilège* (Sacral Productions, 2002).

Peter Bellamy, *Merlin's Isle of Gramarye* (Argo Records, 1972).

Jane Birkin and Serge Gainsbourg, *Jane Birkin*, Serge Gainsbourg (Fontana Records, 1968).

Björk, *Homogenic* (One Little Indian, 1997).

Björk, *Vespertine* (One Little Indian, 2001).

Björk, *Medúlla* (One Little Indian, 2004).

Björk, *Volta* (One Little Indian, 2007).

Black Flag, *Damaged* (SST Records, 1981).

Black Sabbath, *Black Sabbath* (Vertigo, 1970).

Black Sabbath, *Paranoid* (Vertigo, 1970).

Black Widow, *Sacrifice* (CBS, 1970).

Tim Blake, *Blake's New Jerusalem* (Barclay, 1978).

Graham Bond, *Holy Magick* (Vertigo, 1970).

Graham Bond, *We Put Our Magick on You* (Vertigo, 1971).

The Bonzo Dog Doo-Dah Band, *The Doughnut in Granny's Greenhouse* (Liberty Records, 1968).

Billy Bragg and the Blokes, *England, Half English* (Elektra, 2002).

Mike Brooks, *Book of Revelation* (I-Sound, 2001).

Barry Brown, *Cool Pon Your Corner* (Trojan, 1979).

Dennis Brown, *The Promised Land* (Blood and Fire, 2002).

Dennis Brown, *Dennis Brown in Dub* (Heartbeat, 2002).

Vashti Bunyan, *Just Another Diamond Day* (Philips, 1970).

Burning Spear, *Marcus Garvey* (Island Records, 1975).

Burning Spear, *Hail H.I.M.* (EMI, 1980).

Burzum, *Aske* (Deathlike Silence Productions, 1993).

Burzum, *Hvis Lyset Tar Oss* (Misanthropy Records, 1994).

Burzum, *Filosofem* (Misanthropy Records, 1996).

Burzum, *Hliðskjálf* (Misanthropy Records, 1999).

Burzum, *Belus* (Byelobog Productions, 2010).

Junior Byles, *Beat Down Babylon* (Trojan, 1972).

David Byrne, *Uh-Oh* (Luaka Bop, 1992).

David Byrne, *Look Into the Eyeball* (Virgin Records, 2001).

Canned Heat, *Living the Blues* (Liberty, 1969).

Cannibal Corpse, *Butchered at Birth* (Metal Blade, 1991).

Cannibal Corpse, *Tomb of the Mutilated* (Metal Blade, 1992).

Carcass, *Reek of Putrifaction* (Earache Records, 1988).

Carcass, *Symphonies of Sickness* (Earache Records, 1989).

Don Carlos, *Plantation* (CSA, 1984).

Wendy Carlos, *Sonic Seasonings* (Columbia, 1972).

Carpathian Forest, *Strange Old Brew* (Avantgarde Music, 2000).

Johnny Cash, *American IV: The Man Comes Around* (American Recordings, 2002).

Caustic Window, *Caustic Window* (Rephlex, 1995).

Nick Cave and the Bad Seeds, *Abattoir Blues/The Lyre Of Orpheus* (Mute, 2004).

Nick Cave and the Bad Seeds, *Murder Ballads* (Mute, 1996).

Christafari, *No Compromise* (Lion of Zion Entertainment, 2009).

The Church, *Starfish* (Arista, 1987).

Circle Jerks, *Group Sex* (Frontier Records, 1980).

The Clash, *London Calling* (CBS, 1979).

Coil, *Scatology* (Force and Form, 1985).

Coil, *Love's Secret Domain* (Torso, 1991).

Coil, *Musick to Play in the Dark* (Chalice, 1999).

Cold Fairyland, *Seeds on the Ground* (Cold Fairyland, 2008).

Shirley Collins, *Fountain of Snow* (Durtro, 1992).

Comus, *First Utterance* (Dawn Records, 1971).

Julian Cope, *Peggy Suicide* (Island Records, 1991).

Julian Cope, *Jehovahkill* (Island Records, 1992).

Julian Cope and Donald Ross Skinner, *Rite* (Ma-Gog Records, 1992).

Julian Cope, *Breath of Odin* (Head Heritage, 1999).

Count Ossie and the Mystic Revelation of Rastafari, *Grounation* (MRR, 1973).

Count Ossie and the Rasta Family, *Man From Higher Heights* (Vista, 1983).

Coven, *Witchcraft Destroys Minds and Reaps Souls* (Mercury, 1969).

The Cramps, *Songs the Lord Taught Us* (Illegal, 1980).

The Cramps, *Bad Music for Bad People* (IRS, 1984).

Crosby, Stills, Nash and Young, *Déjà Vu* (Atlantic, 1970).

Culture, *Two Sevens Clash* (Joe Gibbs, 1977).

Culture, *International Herb* (High Note, 1977).

The Cure, *Pornography* (Fiction, 1982).

Current 93, *Nature Unveiled* (L.A.Y.L.A.H Antirecords, 1984).

Current 93, *Swastikas for Noddy* (L.A.Y.L.A.H Antirecords, 1988)

Current 93, *Earth Covers Earth* (United Dairies, 1988).

Darkthrone, *Transilvanian Hunger* (Peaceville, 1994).

Darkthrone, *Panzerfaust* (Moonfog Productions, 1995; Peaceville, 2010).

Dead Can Dance, *Aion* (4AD, 1990).

The Dead Kennedys, *Fresh Fruit for Rotting Vegetables* (Faulty Products/Alternative Tentacles, 1980).

Death, *Scream Bloody Gore* (Under One Flag, 1987).

Death in Vegas, *Scorpio Rising* (Concrete, 2002).

Death in Vegas, *Satan's Circus* (Drone Records, 2004).

Death Ride '69, *Elvis Christ* (Little Sister, 1988).

Deep Forest, *Deep Forest* (Columbia, 1992).

Deep Forest, *Boheme* (550 Music, Epic, Columbia, 1995).

Deep Forest, *Pacifique* (Saint George, 2000).

Deep Forest, *Deep Brasil* (Vox Terrae, 2008).

Deep Purple, *Concerto for Group and Orchestra* (Tetragrammaton, 1969; Harvest Records, 1970).

Deep Purple, *Deep Purple in Rock* (Warner Brothers, 1970; Harvest Records, 1970).

Deerhoof, *Friend Opportunity* (Kill Rock Stars, 2007).

Deicide, *Deicide* (Roadrunner Records, 1990).

Deicide, *Once Upon the Cross* (Roadrunner Records, 1995).

Demdike Stare, *Forest of Evil* (Modern Love, 2010).

Sandy Denny, *The North Star Grassman and the Ravens* (Island Records, 1971).

Sandy Denny, *Who Knows Where the Time Goes?* (Island Records, 1985).

Depeche Mode, *Violator* (Mute, 1990).

The Disciples Meet the Rootsman, *Rebirth* (Third Eye Music, 1997).

Donovan, *Fairytale* (Hickory Records, 1965).

Donovan, *A Gift From A Flower To A Garden* (Epic, 1967).

The Doors, *The Best of the Doors* (Elektra, 1985).

Dornenreich, *Hexen Wind* (Prophecy Productions, 2005).

Dornenreich, *Durch Den Traum* (Prophecy Productions, 2006).

Doves, *Lost Sides* (Heavenly Records, 2003).

Nick Drake, *Five Leaves Left* (Island Records, 1969).

Nick Drake, *Time of No Reply* (Hannibal, 1986).

Mikey Dread, *World War III* (Dread at the Controls, 1980).

Dredd Foole, *In Quest of Tense* (Forced Exposure, 1994).

Dr. Strangely Strange, *Kip if the Serenes* (Island Records, 1969).

Dub Syndicate, *Research and Development: A Selection of Dub Syndicate Remixes* (On-U Sound, 1996).

Bob Dylan, *The Times They Are a Changing* (Columbia, 1964).

Bob Dylan, *Bringing It All Back Home* (Columbia, 1965).

Bob Dylan, *John Wesley Harding* (Columbia, 1967).

Steve Earle, *Washington Square Serenade* (New West Records, 2007).

Earth, *Angels of Darkness*, Demons of Light I (Southern Lord, 2011).

Earth, *Angels of Darkness*, Demons of Light II (Southern Lord, 2012).

Earth Crisis, *Destroy All Machines* (Victory Records, 1995).

Earth Crisis, *Gomorah's Season Ends* (Victory Records, 1996).

Eat Static, *Prepare Your Spirit* (Alien Records, 1992).

Eat Static, *Abduction* (Planet Dog, 1993).

Eat Static, *Implant* (Planet Dog, 1994).

Eat Static, *Science of the Gods* (Planet Dog, 1997).

Eluveitie, *Evocation I: The Arcane Dominion* (Nuclear Blast, 2009).

Emerson, Lake and Palmer, *Brain Salad Surgery* (Manticore Records, 1973).

Eminem, *The Slim Shady LP* (Interscope, 1999).

Emperor, *Anthems to the Welkin at Dusk* (Candlelight Records, 1997).

Enigma, *MCMXC a.D.* (Virgin, 1990).

Brian Eno, *Music for Airports* (Editions EG, 1978).

Brian Eno, *On Land* (Editions EG, 1982).

Brian Eno, *The Shutov Assembly* (Opal, 1992).

Brian Eno and David Byrne, *My Life in the Bush of Ghosts* (Sire, 1981).

Enthroned, *Prophecies of a Pagan Fire* (Evil Omen Records, 1995).

Exhumed, *Goregasm* (self-released cassette, 1992).

Fairport Convention, *Liege and Lief* (Island Records, 1969).

Faith and the Muse, *The Burning Season* (Metropolis Records, 2003).

The Fall, *Dragnet* (Step Forward, 1979).

The Fall, *Hex Enduction Hour* (Kamera, 1982).

The Fall, *I Am Kurious Oranj* (Beggar's Banquet, 1988).

Bill Fay Group, *Tomorrow*, Tomorrow and Tomorrow (Durtro, 2005).

The Focus Group, *We Are All Pan's People* (Ghost Box, 2007).

The Focus Group, *Sketches and Spells* (Ghost Box, 2011).

Forest, *Forest* (Harvest, 1969).

Forest, *Forest* (Stellar Winter Records, 2000).

Fotheringay, *Fotheringay* (Island Records, 1970).

Fourth World, *Encounters with the Fourth World* (B&W Music, 1996).

Fourth World, *Last Journey* (MELT, 2000).

Front 242, *Official Version* (Wax Trax! Records, 1987).

Future Sound of London, *Accelerator* (Jumpin' and Pumpin', 1991).

Fun-da-mental, *All Is War: The Benefits of G-Had* (5 Uncivilised Tribes, 2006).

Gang Green, *Another Wasted Night* (Taang! Records, 1986).

David Garret, *Free* (Decca, 2007).

Genesis, *Foxtrot* (Charisma, 1972).

Genesis, *Genesis Archive 1967–75* (Virgin/Atlantic, 1998).

The Gladiators, *Babylon Street* (Jam Rock, 1977).

The Go! Team, *Proof of Youth* (Tearbridge International (Japan), 2007).

Amy Grant, *Heart in Motion* (A&M Records, 1991).

Grant Lee Buffalo, *Storm Hymnal: Gems from the Vault of Grant Lee Buffalo* (Slash Records, 2001).

The Grateful Dead, *Live/Dead* (Warner Brothers, 1969).

Graveland, *Thousand Swords* (Isengard Distribution, 1995).

The Green Man, *From Irem to Summerisle* (Hau Ruck! SPQR, 2009).

Greyhound, *Black and White* (Trojan, 1971).

Grouper, *Wide* (Free Porcupine Society, 2006).

Grouper, *Dragging a Dead Deer Up a Hill* (Type, 2008).

Gryphon, *Glastonbury Song* (Hux Records, 2003).

Peter Hammill, *In Camera* (Charisma, 1974).

The Handsome Family, *Twilight* (Carrot Top Records, 2001).

The Handsome Family, *Singing Bones* (Carrot Top Records, 2003).

Bo Hansson, *Music Inspired by Lord of the Rings* (Silence, 1970)

Bo Hansson, *Magician's Hat* (Charisma, 1972).

George Harrison, *All Things Must Pass* (Apple Records, 1970).

George Harrison, *Living in a Material World* (Apple Records, 1973).

George Harrison, *Dark Horse* (Apple Records, 1974).

Hawkwind, *Warrior on the Edge of Time* (United Artists, 1975).

Hazardous Dub Company, *Dangerous Dubs, Vol. 2* (Acid Jazz, 1993).

Jimi Hendrix, *Are You Experienced?* (Reprise Records, 1967).

Jimi Hendrix, *Rainbow Bridge: Original Motion Picture Soundtrack* (Reprise Records, 1971).

Jimi Hendrix, *Jimi Plays Monterey* (Reprise Records, 1986).

Jimi Hendrix, *Live at Woodstock* (MCA Records, 1999).

Heron, *Twice as Nice and Half the Price* (Dawn Records, 1971).

Steve Hillage, *Rainbow Dome Musick* (Virgin, 1979).

The Hobbits, *Down to Middle Earth* (Decca, 1967).

John Lee Hooker, *The Healer* (Virgin, 1989).

Husker Dü, *Zen Arcade* (SST Records, 1984).

The Imagined Village, *The Imagined Village* (Real World Records, 2007).

Immortal, *Diabolical Fullmoon Mysticism* (Osmose Productions, 2007).

Incredible String Band, *5000 Spirits or the Layers of the Onion* (Elektra, 1967).

The Incredible String Band, *The Hangman's Beautiful Daughter* (Elektra, 1968).

The Incredible String Band, *Changing Horses* (Elektra, 1969).

Inquisicion, *Steel Vengeance* (Deifer Records, 1996).

In the Woods, *Heart of the Ages* (Misanthropy Records, 1995).

Iron Maiden, *The X Factor* (EMI, 1995).

Iron Maiden, *Brave New World* (EMI, 2000).

Jah Shaka, *Revelation Songs* (Jah Shaka Music, 1983).

Jah Shaka, *Dub Symphony* (Island Records, 1990).

Jethro Tull, *Living in the Past* (Chrysalis, 1972).

Jethro Tull, *Minstrel in the Gallery* (Chrysalis, 1975).

Jethro Tull, *Songs from the Wood* (Chrysalis, 1977).

Elton John, *Goodbye Yellow Brick Road* (MCA Records, 1973).

Bob Johnson and Peter Knight, *The King of Elfland's Daughter* (Chrysalis, 1977).

Jóhann Jóhannsson, *And In The Endless Pause There Came The Sound Of Bees* (Type, 2009).

Linton Kwesi Johnson, *Forces of Victory* (Island Records, 1979).

Linton Kwesi Johnson, *Bass Culture* (Island Records, 1980).

Robert Johnson, *The Complete Recordings* (CBS, 1990).

Killing Joke, *The Courtauld Talks* (Invisible Records, 1989).

King Tubby, *Dub Gone Crazy* (Blood and Fire, 1994).

Knights of the Occasional Table, *Knees Up Mother Earth* (Fairy Cake Universe, 1993).

Knowledge, *Straight Outta Trenchtown* (Makasound, 2002).

Kraftwerk, *Autobahn* (Philips, 1974).

Kraftwerk, *Radioactivity* (Capital Records, 1975).

Kraftwerk, *Trans-Europe Express* (Capital Records, 1977).

Kraftwerk, *The Man-Machine* (Capital Records, 1978).

Kraftwerk, *Computer World* (EMI, 1981).

Bill Laswell, *Silent Recoil: Dub System One* (Low, 1995).

Bill Laswell, *Sacred System: Chapter 1—Book of Entrance* (ROIR, 1996).

Bill Laswell, *Sacred System: Chapter 2* (ROIR, 1997).

Bill Laswell, *Dub Chamber 3* (ROIR, 2000).

Bill Laswell, *Sacred System: Dub Chamber 4—Book of Exit* (ROIR, 2002).

Bill Laswell, *ROIR Dub Sessions* (ROIR, 2003).

Bill Laswell, *Sacred System: Nagual Site* (Wicklow/BMG, 1998).

Bill Laswell, *Axiom Dub: Mysteries of Creation* (Axiom, 1996).

Bill Laswell (Divination), *Divination: Ambient Dub, Vol. I* (Subharmonic, 1993).

Bill Laswell (Divination), *Divination: Dead Slow—Ambient Dub, Vol. II* (Subharmonic, 1993).

Bill Laswell (Divination), *Divination: Akasha* (Subharmonic, 1995).

Bill Laswell (Divination), *Divination: Distill* (Submeta, 1996).

Bill Laswell (Divination), *Divination: Sacrifice* (Meta Records, 1998).

Bill Laswell and Nicholas James Bullen, *Bass Terror* (Sub Rosa, 1995).

Bill Laswell and Jah Wobble, *Radioaxiom: A Dub Transmission* (Palm Pictures, 2001).

LA Vampires meets Zola Jesus, *LA Vampires meets Zola Jesus* (Not Not Fun Records, 2010).

Timothy Leary, *Beyond Life With Timothy Leary* (Mercury, 1997).

Led Zeppelin *IV* (Atlantic, 1971)—officially, the title of the album is *Four Symbols*.

Led Zeppelin, *Aleister Crowley Magician's Club Band* (Ars Magica Industria, 2011).

Limbo, *Zos Kia Kaos* (Discordia, 1994).

Fred Locks, *Black Star Liner* (Vulcan, 1976).

Fred Locks, *Glorify the Lord* (Cou$ins Records, 2008).

Love, *Love* (Elektra, 1966).

Lurker of Chalice, *Lurker of Chalice* (Southern Lord, 2005).

Ewan MacColl and Peggy Seeger, *Cold Snap* (Folkways Records, 1978).

Madonna, *Madonna* (Sire, 1983).

Madonna, *Like a Virgin* (Sire, 1984).

Madonna, *Like a Prayer* (Sire, 1989).

Madonna, *The Immaculate Collection* (Sire, 1990).

Madonna, *Erotica* (Sire, 1992).

Mahavishnu Orchestra, *The Inner Mounting Flame* (Columbia, 1971).

Mahavishnu Orchestra, *Between Nothingness and Eternity* (Columbia, 1973).

Marilyn Manson, *Antichrist Superstar* (Nothing Records, 1996).

Marilyn Manson, *Mechanical Animals* (Nothing Records, 1998).

Marilyn Manson, *Lest We Forget: The Best Of* (Interscope Records, 2004).

Marillion, *Script for a Jester's Tear* (Capiton Records, 1983).

Bob Marley and the Wailers, *Catch a Fire* (Island Records, 1973).

Bob Marley and the Wailers, *Burnin'* (Island Records, 1973).

Bob Marley and the Wailers, *Exodus* (Island Records, 1976).

Bob Marley and the Wailers, *Survival* (Island Records, 1979).

Bob Marley and the Wailers, *Uprising* (Tuff Gong/Island Records, 1980).

Bob Marley and the Wailers, *Confrontation* (Tuff Gong/Island Records, 1983).

Bob Marley and the Wailers, *Rebel Music* (Tuff Gong/Island Records, 1986).

Malcolm McLaren, *Duck Rock* (Island Records, 1990).

John Martyn, *Bless the Weather* (Island Records, 1971).

John Martyn, *One World* (Island Records, 1977).

Matthews Southern Comfort, *Later That Same Year* (MCA Records, 1970).

Paul and Linda McCartney, *Ram* (Apple Records, 1971).

John McLaughlin, *My Goal's Beyond* (Douglas, 1971).

The Mediaeval Baebes, *Mirabilis* (EMI, 2005).

Mellow Candle, *Swaddling Songs* (Deram, 1972).

The Memory of Justice Band, *Mash Down Babylon* (Platinum Press, 1983).

Merger, *Exiles in Babylon* (Ultra, 1977).

Merzbow, *Merzbient* (Soleilmoon, 2010).

Mighty Diamonds, *Right Time* (Well Charge, 1976).

Mighty Maytones, *Madness* (Burning Sounds, 1976).

Minor Threat, *Minor Threat* (Dischord Records, 1981).

Misty in Roots, *Wise and Foolish* (People Unite, 1981).

Joni Mitchell, *Ladies of the Canyon* (Reprise, 1970).

Momus and Anne Laplantine, *Summerisle* (Analog Baroque, 2004).

The Moody Blues, *In Search of the Lost Chord* (Deram Records, 1968).

Morrissey, Ringleader of the Tormentors (Sanctuary Records, 2005).

Van Morrison, *No Guru, No Method, No Teacher* (Mercury Records, 1986).

Mortification, *Mortification* (Intense Records, 1991).

Mortification, *Scrolls Of The Megilloth* (Intense Records, 1992).

Mortification, *Blood World* (Intense Records, 1994).

Mr. Fox, *The Gipsy* (Transatlantic, 1971).

Mr. Scruff, *Mr. Scruff* (Pleasure Music, 1997; Ninja Tune, 2005).

Mr. Scruff, *Keep It Unreal* (Ninja Tune, 1999).

Mr. Scruff, *Ninja Tuna* (Ninja Tune, 2008).

Mutabaruka, *Outcry* (Shanachie, 1984).

Mysticum, *In the Streams of Inferno* (Full Moon Productions, 1996).

Nadja, *Radiance of Shadows* (Alien8 Recordings, 2007).

Naked City, *Torture Garden* (Shimmy Disc, 1992).

Naked City, *Grand Guignol* (Avant, 1992).

Naked City, *Heretic: Jeux Des Dames Cruelles* (Avant, 1992).

Naked City, *Leng Tch'e* (Toys Factory, 1992).

Nature and Organization, *Beauty Reaps The Blood of Solitude* (Durtro, 1994).

Me'Shell Ndegéocello, *Peace Beyond Passion* (Maverick, 1996).

Drew Nelson, *Immigrant Son* (Mackinaw Harvest, 2005).

Tom Newman, *Faerie Symphony* (Decca, 1977).

Nine Inch Nails, *Downward Spiral* (Nothing/Interscope, 1994).

Nirvana, *Nevermind* (DGC Records, 1991).

Nirvana, *In Utero* (DGC Records, 1993).

NWA, *Straight Outta Compton* (EMI, 1988).

Mike Oldfield, *Hergest Ridge* (Virgin, 1974).

Mike Oldfield, *Ommadawn* (Virgin, 1975).

Sally Oldfield, *Water Bearer* (Bronze Records, 1978).

Ozzy Osbourne, *Blizzard of Ozz* (Jet, 1980).

The Overnight Players, *Babylon Destruction* (Cha Cha, 1981).

Jimmy Page, *Lucifer Rising and Other Soundtracks* (Jimmypage.com, 2012).

Passengers, *Original Soundtracks 1* (Island Records, 1995).

Luciano Pavarotti, *Essential Pavarotti 1* (Decca, 1990).

Luciano Pavarotti, *Essential Pavarotti 2* (Decca, 1991).

Luciano Pavarotti, *Ti Adoro* (Universal/Deutsche Grammophon, 2003).

Pink Floyd, *Piper at the Gates of Dawn* (Columbia/EMI, 1967).

Pink Floyd, *A Saucerful of Secrets* (EMI, 1968).

Pink Floyd, *Ummagumma* (Harvest Records/EMI, 1969).

Plague Lounge, *The Wicker Image* (New World Of Sound/Holy Mountain, 1996).

P.O.D., *Fundamental Elements Of Southtown* (Atlantic, 1999).
P.O.D., *Satellite* (Atlantic, 2001).
Jocelyn Pook, *Flood* (Virgin, 1999).
The Power Steppers, *Bass Enforcement* (Universal Egg, 1995).
The Power Steppers, *Bass Re-Enforcement* (Universal Egg, 1996).
Primordial, *The Gathering Wilderness* (Metal Blade Records, 2005).
Prince, *Purple Rain* (Warner Brothers, 1984).
Prince, *Sign 'o' the Times* (Paisley Park/Warner Brothers 1987).
Prince Far I, *Long Life* (Virgin Records, 1978).
Maddy Prior and The Carnival Band, *Hang Up Sorrow and Care* (Park Records, 1995).
Michael Prophet, *Righteous are the Conqueror* (Greensleeves, 1980).
The Prodigy, *The Fat of the Land* (XL Recordings, 1997).
Psychic TV, *Force the Hand of Chance* (Some Bizzare Records, 1982).
Psychic TV, *First Transmission* (Self-released, 1982).
Psychic TV, *Cold Blue Torch* (Cleopatra, 1996).
Psychic TV, *Trip Reset* (Cleopatra, 1996).
Pungent Stench, *Been Caught Buttering* (Nuclear Blast, 1991).
Pyewackett, *The Man in the Moon Drinks Claret* (Familiar Records, 1982).
Quintessence, *In Blissful Company* (Island Records, 1969).
Quintessence, *Quintessence* (Island Records, 1970).
Rahowa, *The Cult of Holy War* (Resistance Records, 1995).
Ranking Ann, *Something Fishy Going On* (Ariwa, 1984).
Ranking Joe, *Armageddon* (Kingdom, 1982).
Ranking Trevor and Trinity, *Three Piece Chicken and Chips* (Cha Cha, 1978).
Ras Michael and the Sons of Negus, *Nyabinghi* (Trojan, 1974).
The Red Krayola, *The Parable of Arable Land* (International Artists, 1967).
Revelation, *Book of Revelation* (Burning Sounds, 1979).
Winston Riley, *Meditation Dub* (Techniques, 1976).
The Rolling Stones, *Aftermath* (Decca, 1966)
The Rolling Stones, *Their Satanic Majesties Request* (Decca, 1967).
The Rolling Stones, *Beggars Banquet* (Decca, 1968).
Junior Ross, *Babylon Fall* (Stars, 1976).
The Ruts, *The Crack* (Virgin, 1979).
Santana, *Lotus* (CBS, 1975).
Carlos Santana and Alice Coltrane, *Illuminations* (CBS, 1974).
The Sex Pistols, *Never Mind the Bollocks, Here's The Sex Pistols* (Virgin, 1977).
The Sex Pistols, *God Save the Queen* (Virgin, 1977).
Shaggy, *Intoxication* (VP Records, 2007).
Singers and Players, *Staggering Heights* (On-U Sound, 1983).
Singers and Players featuring Bim Sherman, *War of Words* (On-U Sound, 1982).
Siouxsie and the Banshees, *Join Hands* (Polydor, 1979).
Sism-X, *Dub Assault* (Assault Dub, 2003).
Sism-X, *Dub Strike* (Sounds Around, 2004).
Earl Sixteen, *Songs of Love and Hardship* (Kingdom, 1984).
Slayer, *Reign in Blood* (Def Jam, 1986).
Slayer, *South of Heaven* (Def Jam, 1988).
Slayer, *Diabolus in Musica* (American Recordings, 1998).
Slayer, *God Hates Us All* (American Recordings, 2001).
Patti Smith, *Horses* (Arista, 1975).
Patti Smith, *Radio Ethiopia* (Arista, 1976).
Patti Smith Group, *Easter* (Arista, 1978).
Patti Smith Group, *Wave* (Arista, 1979).
Smith and Mighty, *Bass is Maternal* (More Rockers/STUD!O K7, 1995).

The Smiths, *Meat is Murder* (Rough Trade, 1985).

Sneaker Pimps, *Becoming X* (Clean Up Records, 1996).

Spacemen 3, *The Perfect Prescription* (Glass Records, 1987).

Spacemen 3, *Taking Drugs to Make Music to Take Drugs To* (BOMP!, 1994).

Chris Spedding, *Chris Spedding* (Rak Records, 1976).

Spinal Tap, *Spinal Tap* (Polydor, 1984).

Spirit, *Twelve Dreams of Dr. Sardonicus* (Epic, 1970).

Splinter Test, *Spatial Memory* (Dossier, 1996).

Splinter Test, *Thee Fractured Garden* (Invisible, 1996).

SS Decontrol, *Get It Away* EP (Xclaim! 1982).

Steeleye Span, *Time* (Park Records, 1996).

Steel Pulse, *Earth Crisis* (Elektra, 1984).

Steppenwolf, *Steppenwolf* (ABC Dunhill, 1968).

The Stooges, *Raw Power* (Columbia, 1973).

The Story, *Arcane Rising* (Sunbeam, 2007).

Sun God, *Sun God* (Fifth Colvmn Records, 1995).

System of a Down, *Steal This Album!* (Columbia, 2002).

The Talking Heads, *Speaking in Tongues* (Sire, 1983).

The Talking Heads, *Little Creatures* (EMI, 1985).

The Talking Heads, *True Stories* (Sire, 1986).

Talk Talk, *The Colour of Spring* (EMI, 1986).

Talk Talk, *Spirit of Eden* (Parlophone, 1988).

Tangerine Dream, *Electronic Meditation* (Ohr, 1967).

Tangerine Dream, *Atem* (Ohr, 1973).

Tangerine Dream, *Phaedra* (Virgin, 1974).

Tengkorak, *Civil Emergency* (Bloodbath Records, 2005).

Tengkorak, *Agenda Suram* (Sabelas April, 2007).

Thee Majesty, *Thee Fractured Garden* (Temple Records, 2004).

This Mortal Coil, *It'll End in Tears* (4AD, 1984).

Thor's Hammer, *A Fate Worse Than Death* (No Colours Records, 2002).

Throbbing Gristle, *20 Jazz Funk Greats* (Industrial Records, 1979).

Throbbing Gristle, *Heathen Earth* (Industrial Records, 1980).

Throbbing Gristle, *In the Shadow of the Sun* (Illuminated, 1984; Mute, 1993).

Peter Tosh, *No Nuclear War* (CBS, 1987).

Traffic, *Mr. Fantasy* (Island Records, 1967).

Traffic, *Traffic* (Island Records, 1968).

Traffic, *John Barleycorn Must Die* (Island Records, 1970).

Trees, *On the Shore* (CBS, 1970).

T. Rex, *Futuristic Dragon* (EMI/T.Rex Wax Co., 1976).

T. Rex, *Dandy in the Underworld* (EMI/T.Rex Wax Co., 1977).

Trinity, *Showcase* (Burning Sounds, 1978).

Twinkle Brothers, *Dub Massacre (In a Murder Style)* (Twinkle, 1983).

Tyrannosaurus Rex, *My People Were Fair and Had Sky in Their Hair . . . But Now They're Content to Wear Stars on Their Brows* (Regal Zonophone, 1968).

Tyrannosaurus Rex, *Prophets Seers and Sages: The Angels of the Ages* (Regal Zonophone, 1968).

Tyrannosaurus Rex, *Unicorn* (Regal Zonophone, 1969).

Tyrannosaurus Rex, *A Beard of Stars* (Regal Zonophone, 1970).

Ulver, *Bergtatt* (Head Not Found, 1994).

Ulver, *Nattens Madrigal—Aatte Hymne Til Ulven I Manden* (Century Media, 1997).

Uriah Heep, *Demons and Wizards* (Bronze, 1972).

Uriah Heep, *The Magician's Birthday* (Bronze, 1972).

U Roy, *Dread in a Babylon* (TR International, 1975).

U Roy, *Babylon Burning* (Burning Bush, 2002).

Us and Them, *Summerisle* (Fruits De Mer, 2011).
Various Artists, *Anthology of American Folk Music*, edited by Harry Smith (Smithsonian Folkways, 1952).
Various Artists, *Woodstock* (Cotillion, 1970).
Various Artists, *Drums of Defiance: Maroon Music from the Earliest Free Black Communities of Jamaica* (Smithsonian Folkways, 1992).
Various Artists, *Apollo* (R & S Records, 1993).
Various Artists, *Apollo 2: The Divine Compilation* (R & S Records, 1995).
Various Artists, *Deep Trance and Ritual Beats* (Return to the Source, 1995).
Various Artists, *The Chakra Journey* (Return to the Source, 1996).
Various Artists, *The Black Ark Presents Rastafari Liveth Itinually* (Justice League, 1996).
Various Artists, *Sacred Sites* (Return to the Source, 1997).
Various Artists, *Churchical Chants of the Nyabingi* (Heartbeat, 1997).
Various Artists, *12 Voice Showcase* (Twelve Tribes of Israel, 1998).
Various Artists, *Dub Solidarity* (Dubhead, 2003).
Various Artists, *Trojan Nyahbinghi Box Set* (Trojan, 2003).
Various Artists, *Shake the Nations! A New Breed of Dub 4* (Dubhead, 2004).
Various Artists, *Looking for Europe: A Neofolk Compendium* (Auerbach Tonträger, 2005).
Martha Velez, *Escape from Babylon* (Sire, 1976).
The Velvet Underground, *Velvet Underground* (Verve Records, 1967).
Venetian Snares, *Rossz Csillag Alatt Született* (Planet Mu, 2005).
Venetian Snares, *Detrimentalist* (Planet Mu, 2008).
Venetian Snares, *Filth* (Planet Mu, 2009).
Venom, *Welcome to Hell* (Neat, 1981).
Venom, *Black Metal* (Neat, 1982).
Bunny Wailer, *Black Heart Man* (Island, 1976).
Wardruna, *Runaljod—Gap Var Ginnunga* (Indie Recordings, 2009).
The Waterboys, *A Pagan Place* (Ensign Records, 1984).
The Waterboys, *Dream Harder* (Geffen Records, 1993).
The Watersons, *Frost and Fire: A Calendar of Ritual and Magical Songs* (Topic Records, 1965).
Whitehouse, *Psychopathia Sexualis* (Come Organisation, 1982).
The Who, *Tommy* (Polydor, 1969).
The Who, *Quadrophenia* (Polydor, 1973).
Wicked Messenger, *Vision Rites and Techniques of Ecstasy* (Plague Recordings, 2009).
Wingless Angels, *Wingless Angels* (Island Jamaica, 1996).
Woods of Infinity, *F&L* (Total Holocaust Records, 2004).
:Wumpscut:, *Blutkind* (Beton Kopf Media, 2000).
Tammy Wynette, *Stand By Your Man* (Epic, 1969).
XTC, *English Settlement* (Virgin, 1982).
Yabby You, *Chant Down Babylon Kingdom* (Nationwide, 1976).
Peter Yellow, *Hot* (Black Music, 1982).
Yes, *Tales From Topographic Oceans* (Atlantic, 1963).
Neil Young, *After the Gold Rush* (Reprise, 1970).
Neil Young, *Harvest* (Reprise, 1972).
Earl Zero, *Visions of Love* (Epiphany, 1979).
Zero Kama, *The Goatherd And The Beast* (Athanor, 2001).
Zos Kia/Coil, *Transparent* (Nekrophile Records, 1984).

SINGLES AND EPS

GG Allin, "The Troubled Troubadour EP" (Mountain Records, 1990).
Bauhaus, "Bela Lugosi's Dead" (Small Wonder Records, 1979).
The Beatles, "All You Need is Love" (Parlophone, 1967).

Black Widow, "Come to the Sabbat" (CBS, 1970).

James Brown, "Sex Machine" (Polydor, 1975).

The Dead Kennedys, "Too Drunk To Fuck" (IRS Records, 1981).

Ian Dury, "Sex and Drugs and Rock and Roll" (Stiff Records, 1977).

Folks Brothers, "O Carolina" (Prince Buster, 1959).

Screamin' Jay Hawkins, "I Put a Spell on You" (Okeh, 1957).

Billie Holiday, "Strange Fruit" (Commodore, 1939).

Michael Jackson, "Earth Song" (Epic, 1995).

Killing Joke, "Turn to Red" (Malicious Damage, 1979).

The Kinks, "See My Friends" (Pye Records, 1965).

Elton John, "Blue Eyes" (Rocket, 1982).

Lady Gaga, "Born This Way" (Streamline Records, 2011).

Nine Inch Nails, "Closer" (Nothing/Interscope, 1994).

Northside, "Shall we Take a Trip" (Factory Records, 1990).

Ministry, "(Everyday is) Halloween" (Wax Trax! Records, 1985).

Gary Numan, "Cars" (Beggar's Banquet, 1979).

Public Image Ltd, "Death Disco" (Virgin, 1979).

Sister Sledge, "Lost in Music" (Cotillon Records/Atlantic, 1979).

Linval Thompson, "I Love Marijuana" (Attack, 1978).

Throbbing Gristle, "Zyklon B Zombie" (Industrial Records, 1978).

Wings, "Mull of Kintyre" (Capitol Records, 1977).

X-Ray Spex, "Oh Bondage Up Yours!" (Virgin Records, 1977).

The Yardbirds, "Heart Full of Soul" (EMI, 1965).

FILMOGRAPHY

Cracked Actor (1974). Directed by Alan Yentob.
The Dam Busters (1955). Directed by Michael Anderson.
Das Cabinet des Dr. Caligari (1920). Directed by Robert Wiene.
The Devil Rides Out (1968). Directed by Terence Fisher.
The Doors (1991). Directed by Oliver Stone.
Eyes Wide Shut (1999). Directed by Stanley Kubrick.
Ich für dich, du für mich (1934). Directed by Carl Froelich.
In the Shadow of the Sun (1980). Directed by Derek Jarman.
Journey of a Misanthrope (2008). Directed by Russell Menzies (Striborg/Sin Nanna).
Jubilee (1978). Directed by Derek Jarman.
The Misanthrope (2007). Directed by Ted Skjellum (Nocturno Culto).
The Ninth Gate (1999). Directed by Roman Polanski.
The Wicker Man (1973). Directed by Robert Hardy.

INDEX